D0709608

QuickBooks®
Complete
2018

For QuickBooks Pro, Premier and Accountant 2018

Copyright © 2018

Product Name   QuickBooks Complete - Version 2018
                      ISBN: 978-1-942417-21-7

Trademarks   Intuit, the Intuit logo, QuickBooks, QuickBooks Pro, QuickBase, Quicken,
                      TurboTax, ProSeries, Lacerte, EasyStep, and QuickZoom, among others, are
                      registered trademarks and/or registered service marks of Intuit Inc. in the
                      United States and other countries. QuickBooks ProAdvisor is a trademark
                      and/or service mark of Intuit Inc. in the United States and other countries.
                      Other parties' trademarks or service marks are the property of their
                      respective owners and should be treated as such.

Copyright   © 2018 Questiva Consultants
                      All rights reserved

                      Published by Questiva Consultants

Disclaimer   This material is intended as a learning aid for QuickBooks software users.
                      Under no circumstances shall the author or publisher be liable for any
                      damages, including any lost profits, lost data or other indirect damages
                      arising out of anything written in this document or expressed directly or
                      indirectly by the author or publisher.

Developed and   Douglas Sleeter
Written By   Deborah Pembrook

Contributing   Pat Carson
Authors, Testers,   Tricia Lippincott
and Reviewers   Ellen Orr

Questiva Consultants
1501 Dry Creek Road, San Jose, CA 95125
Phone: 408 440 4182
Fax : 408 351 0473
www.questivaconsultants.com

*Questiva Consultants is the publisher
and supplier of QuickBooks Accounting Textbooks
to students, community colleges and business/trade schools.
These textbooks were originally developed by the Sleeter Group.*

Table of Contents

Preface

This guide introduces you to QuickBooks – Intuit's easy-to-use, powerful accounting system for small businesses.

This guide is designed to teach you how to use many of the features available in QuickBooks Software for Windows Desktop. The main focus of this guide is on how to use the features in QuickBooks Premier and Accountant, but most exercises can be completed using QuickBooks Pro. This guide does not cover how to use the features in QuickBooks Online or QuickBooks Pro for Mac.

While this guide does not specifically address how to use QuickBooks Enterprise Solutions, many of the procedures described in the guide will work with Enterprise Solutions editions. If you restore the exercise file using a QuickBooks Enterprise Solutions product, QuickBooks walks you through the file update process that is necessary for Enterprise Solutions to be able to read the file.

QuickBooks 2018 Versions

This textbook will guide you through learning the QuickBooks 2018 and comes with a Student Trial.

Using QuickBooks 2018 Student Trial

QuickBooks Accountant 2018 Student Trial is a full-featured version of QuickBooks that is included with this guide. You can install it on your computer and use it to complete the exercises in this guide and to practice using QuickBooks.

QuickBooks Accountant can "toggle" to other versions of QuickBooks, including QuickBooks Premier, Pro, and Industry editions. The trial software can be used to explore any of these versions of QuickBooks.

To install QuickBooks Accountant 2018, follow the directions on the card at the back of this book.

You can use this product for 5 months after installation.

Using This Book

Throughout this book, you will find tips on how to set up and use QuickBooks so that you and your company have the information you need to make business decisions.

Each chapter covers how to manage a general part of your business. To allow you to learn the chapters in any order, each chapter uses a separate QuickBooks data file that you can use with QuickBooks to complete the practice lessons.

Academy Photography, Inc. is the model company used throughout the chapters. By performing the in-chapter practices, students gain hands-on experience with the topics discussed in the chapter, which are based on the day-to-day operations of this small corporation.

Each chapter is designed to aid understanding by providing an overview of topics, numerous hands-on tutorial practices, key terms, the "accounting behind the scenes," and many extra notes. The illustrated text includes step-by-step instructions with hands-on computer exercises to provide you with practical experience.

The end-of-chapter applications include comprehension questions, multiple choice questions, completion sentences, and real-world problems that require the student to perform tasks with the software.

The final two chapters of this book are business simulations. They consist of summary problems covering topics culled from all the chapters in this book.

From using this book, you will gain confidence in every aspect of QuickBooks by trying out each feature as you complete problems and simulations of a "real" business. You will want to keep this book for reference for years to come.

Integrating QuickBooks with other products

If you plan to use the Microsoft Office integration features available in QuickBooks, such as exporting to Excel, you will need to have Microsoft® Office installed on your system.

About the exercise files

Exercise files are used with the chapters and problems throughout this book. For each chapter and problem in this guide, you'll restore a copy of the exercise file named in the beginning of the section and use that file to complete the chapter and chapter problem. This means that at the start of each lesson, you will be restoring a new file. It is very important to be in the correct file to ensure that your screen will match the book's screenshots.

Installing the exercise files

The exercise files for the chapters and problems are available at the following address:

www.questivaconsultants.com/downloads/

To install the files on your hard drive, follow these steps:

Step 1.   Go to www.questivaconsultants.com/downloads/

Step 2.   Find this book's title and click the link. You will be taken to the support page for this book.

Step 3.   Click the *Product Support Download* tab and click the link to download *QuickBooks_2018_Classroom_Files.zip*. Save the files to the desired location on your local system. If you are using a computer in a classroom or lab environment, ask your instructor for the proper location to store your exercise files.

Step 4.   Once you have saved the file to the proper location, you will need to "unzip" it. Select the zip file in Windows Explorer. You should see an option at the top of the window to *Extract*. Click the **Extract** option and choose **Extract All**.

> **Important:**
> The Classroom Files are in QuickBooks Portable File Format. You cannot open these files by double clicking them. For more on how to begin using these files, see page 9.

Instructor Resources

Instructor resources, including the Instructor's Manual, test banks, solution files, and PowerPoints are available at www.questivaconsultants.com/downloads. You must be a verified instructor with an accredited school to access these files. If you do not already have an instructor login, please contact info@questivaconsultants.com.

Restoring exercise files

Each chapter uses a separate practice file (e.g., Intro-18.QBW) for performing the in-chapter practices. In order to open this file, you must "restore" it as described in the first chapter (see page 9).

In the beginning of each chapter, the *Restore This File* instruction (see example below) instructs you to restore the practice file for that chapter to use with the computer practice lessons.

Example *Restore this file* instruction:

> **Restore this File:**
> This chapter uses XXXXX-18.QBW. See page 9 for more information.

The lessons are identified throughout the book with the words **COMPUTER PRACTICE**.

In some cases, concepts are presented in step form, but are not intended to be performed in your data file. In this case, you'll see a note at the top of the section that says:

> **DO NOT PERFORM THESE STEPS NOW. THEY ARE FOR REFERENCE ONLY.**

For these sections, you should look through and understand the material, but you should not enter any of the data in your practice file.

Certification

This book is excellent preparation for the QuickBooks User Certification Exam. This certification validates your QuickBooks knowledge. After successfully completing the exam, you will become an **Intuit QuickBooks Certified User**. For more information and for locations of testing centers, visit http://www.certiport.com/quickbooks.

Acknowledgements

We would like to extend our heartfelt thanks to the co-authors, consultants, copy editors, and contributors who have worked on all of our college textbooks over the years. Many people have put their head and their heart into each edition. All of you have improved and enhanced this textbook and we offer our gratitude.

We hope you enjoy this book.

Chapter 1
Introducing QuickBooks

Topics

In this chapter, you will learn about the following topics:

- The QuickBooks Product Line (page 1)
- Accounting 101 (page 2)
- QuickBooks Files (page 5)
- Opening Portable Company Files (page 9)
- Restoring Backup Files (page 13)
- QuickBooks User Interface Features (page 17)
- Entering Transactions in QuickBooks (page 21)
- QuickBooks Help (page 26)

QuickBooks is one of the most powerful tools you will use in managing your business. QuickBooks isn't just a robust bookkeeping program, QuickBooks is a *management tool*. When set up and used properly, QuickBooks allows you to track and manage income, expenses, bank accounts, receivables, inventory, job costs, fixed assets, payables, loans, payroll, billable time, and equity in your company. It also provides you with detailed reports that are essential to making good business decisions.

QuickBooks helps small business owners run their businesses efficiently without worrying about the debits and credits of accounting entries. However, to use QuickBooks effectively, you still need to understand how QuickBooks is structured, how its files work, how to navigate in the system to do tasks, and how to retrieve information about your business. In this chapter you'll learn some of the basics of the QuickBooks program and then you will explore the world of accounting.

The QuickBooks Product Line

The QuickBooks family of products is designed to be easy to use, while providing a comprehensive set of accounting tools including: general ledger, inventory, accounts receivable, accounts payable, sales tax, and financial reporting. In addition, a variety of optional, fee-based payroll services, merchant account services, and other add-on products integrate with the QuickBooks software.

QuickBooks Desktop vs. QuickBooks Online

Intuit offers two distinctly different ways to use QuickBooks. One version is installed on your local computer and is referred to as *QuickBooks Desktop*. The other is a cloud-based application that isn't installed on your individual computer but is available online through a web browser or app on a smartphone or tablet. This version is called *QuickBooks Online*. The online edition has different, yet similar, features to *QuickBooks Desktop*. This textbook covers *QuickBooks Desktop*.

QuickBooks Editions

The QuickBooks Desktop product line includes several separate product editions: *QuickBooks Pro, QuickBooks Premier, QuickBooks Accountant* and *QuickBooks Enterprise*. The *Premier* and *Enterprise* editions are further broken down into six industry-specific editions for *General Business, General*

Contractor, Manufacturing & Wholesale, Nonprofit, Professional Services, and *Retail.* All editions of QuickBooks support multiple users, however, each user must have the same version of QuickBooks to access the file.

This book covers the features and usage of *QuickBooks Pro, Premier (non-industry specific),* and *Accountant,* since most small businesses will use one of these editions. Also, once you learn how to use one of these editions, you'll be prepared to use *any* of the other editions. For a comparison of all editions and options, see www.quickbooks.com.

QuickBooks Releases

Occasionally, errors are found in the QuickBooks software after the product is released for sale. As errors are discovered, Intuit fixes the problem and provides program "patches" via the Internet. Each patch increases the **Release Level** of the QuickBooks application. To see what release level of the software you have, press **Ctrl+1** (or **F2**) while QuickBooks is running. At the top of the window, you will see the QuickBooks product information including the release level.

Product Information	✖
Product QuickBooks Accountant Desktop 2018 Release R4P	

Figure 1-1 Product information window showing version and release

This book is based on QuickBooks Accountant 2018 release R4P. If you have a different release, you may see some slight differences compared to the screens in this book, but most likely you won't see any differences.

To patch your software with the latest maintenance release, download this release by selecting the *Help* menu and then selecting **Update QuickBooks**. Follow the instructions on these screens to download and install maintenance releases in QuickBooks via the Internet.

Accounting 101

Having a basic background in the accounting process will help you learn QuickBooks and run your business. In this section, we look at some basic accounting concepts and how they relate to QuickBooks.

Accounting's Focus

Accounting's primary concern is the accurate recording and categorizing of transactions so that you can produce reports that accurately portray the financial health of your organization. Put another way, accounting's focus is on whether your organization is succeeding and how well it is succeeding.

The purpose of accounting is to serve management, investors, creditors, and government agencies. Accounting reports allow any of these groups to assess the financial position of the organization relative to its debts (liabilities), its capabilities to satisfy those debts and continue operations (assets), and the difference between them (net worth or equity).

The fundamental equation (called the *Accounting Equation*) that governs all accounting is:

Assets = Liabilities + Equity, or Equity = Assets - Liabilities.

Accounts, Accounts, Everywhere Accounts

Many factors go into making an organization work. Money and value are attached to everything that is associated with operating a company — cash, equipment, rent, utilities, wages, raw materials, merchandise, and so on. For an organization to understand its financial position, business transactions need to be recorded, summarized, balanced, and presented in reports according to the rules of accounting.

Business transactions (e.g., sales, purchases, operating expense payments) are recorded in several types of *ledgers*, called accounts. The summary of all transactions in all ledgers for a company is called the *General Ledger*. A listing of every account in the General Ledger is called the *Chart of Accounts*.

Each account summarizes transactions that increase or decrease the equity in your organization. The figure below shows a general picture of the effect your accounts have on the equity of your organization. Some accounts (those on the left) increase equity when they are increased, while others (those on the right) decrease equity when they are increased.

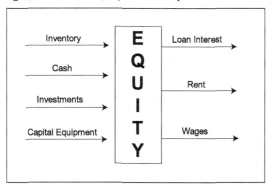

So, let's return to the Accounting Equation. To understand the accounting equation, consider the following statement. **Everything a company owns was purchased by funds from creditors or by the owner's stake in the company.**

Account Types and Financial Reports

Each account in the general ledger has a type, which describes what kind of business transaction is stored in that account. There are primarily five types of accounts: asset, liability, equity, income, and expense. Assets, liabilities, and equity accounts are associated with the **Balance Sheet** report which is used to analyze the net worth of a business. The income and expense accounts are associated with the **Profit and Loss** report (also called Income Statement) which is used to analyze the operating profit or loss for a business over a specific time range (month, quarter, year, etc.).

The Balance Sheet report preserves the fundamental accounting equation - **Total assets always equal the total liabilities plus equity**, between the accounts. This means that the total of the assets (which represent what the company "owns") is always equal to the sum of the liabilities (representing what the company owes) plus the equity (representing the owner's interest in the company). Although income and expense accounts are not directly shown in the accounting equation, they do affect this equation via the equity account as shown below.

The income and expenses are tracked throughout the year, as business transactions occur, and are totaled at the end of the year to calculate Net Income (or Loss). **Net income (total revenues minus total expenses) increases the owner's equity in the business, and net loss (when expenses exceed revenues) decreases the owner's equity in the business.** Thus, the Income and Expense accounts indirectly affect the Equity component of the Accounting Equation of Assets = Liabilities + Equity, where **Equity increases or decreases each year depending on whether the year's income exceeds expenses or not.**

At the end of the year, the balance of each income and expense account is reset to zero so these accounts can track the next year's transactions.

Double-Entry Accounting

Double-entry accounting is the technique that makes the Accounting Equation work. It divides each account into two sides. One side is a record of transactions that increase the account and the other side is a record of all transactions that decrease the account. One side (the left side) is for debits, and the other (the right side) is for credits. Depending on the type of account, a debit might increase the account or decrease it. The same is true of credits. Therefore, debits are not always bad and credits are not always good. They are just part of the system of accounting. However, the rule of double-entry accounting is that **total debits must always equal total credits.** Every transaction creates a debit in one or more accounts and a credit in one or more accounts. If the debits and credits for any transaction are not equal, the transaction has an error or is incomplete.

Accounting Behind the Scenes

Recording and categorizing all of your business transactions into the proper accounts, summarizing and adjusting them, and then preparing financial statements *can be an enormous, labor-intensive task* without the help of a computer and software. This is where QuickBooks comes in. **QuickBooks focuses on ease of use and hiding accounting details.** To make all this possible, QuickBooks uses components like accounts, items, forms, registers, and lists, which are discussed later in the chapter. Familiar-looking forms such as invoices, checks, and bills are used for data entry. As you enter data in forms, QuickBooks handles the accounting entries for you. Thus, business owners can use QuickBooks to efficiently run a business without getting bogged down with the debits and credits of accounting entries.

QuickBooks also handles double-entry for you. Every transaction you enter in the program automatically becomes a debit to one or more accounts and a credit to one or more other accounts, and QuickBooks won't let you record the transaction until the total of the debits equals the total of the credits. This means you can create reports that show the transactions in the full double-entry accounting format whenever you need them, allowing you to focus on the business transaction rather than the debits and credits in the General Ledger.

Cash or accrual method, as discussed in the next section, is handled in QuickBooks as a simple reporting option. You can create reports for either cash or accrual basis regardless of the method you use for taxes.

As the book introduces new transaction types (e.g., Invoices, Bills, or Checks), the text will include a section called "The accounting behind the scenes." For example, when you first learn about invoices you will see the following message:

> **The accounting behind the scenes:**
> When you create an **Invoice**, QuickBooks increases (with a debit) **Accounts Receivable** and increases (with a credit) the appropriate **income** account. If applicable, **Invoices** and **Sales Receipts** also increase (with a credit) the sales tax liability account.

Letting QuickBooks handle the accounting behind the scenes means you can focus on your organization and identify the important factors that will help you succeed. Once you identify these factors, you can use QuickBooks to monitor them and provide information that will guide you in managing your operations.

Accounting for the Future: Cash or Accrual?

Another critical aspect of accounting is managing for the future. Many times, your organization will have assets and liabilities that represent money owed to the company, or owed to others by the company, but are not yet due. For example, you may have sold something to a customer and sent an invoice, but the payment has not been received. In this case, you have an outstanding *receivable*. Similarly, you may have a bill for insurance that is not yet due. In this case, you have an outstanding *payable*.

An accounting system that uses the *accrual basis* method of accounting tracks these receivables and payables and uses them to evaluate a company's financial position. The *accrual basis* method specifies that revenues and expenses are *recognized* in the period in which the transactions occur, rather than in the period in which cash changes hands. This helps you more accurately understand the true profitability of the business in each period. Assets, liabilities, income, and expenses are entered when you know about them, and they are used to identify what you need on hand to meet both current, and known, future obligations.

In the *cash basis* method, revenues and expenses are not *recognized* until cash changes hands. So, revenue is recognized when the customer pays, and an expense is recognized when you pay the bill for the expense. In most cash basis systems, you must use an outside system to track open invoices and unpaid bills, which means you cannot view both cash and accrual reports without going to several places to find information. However, in QuickBooks, you can record transactions such as invoices and bills to facilitate *accrual basis* reporting, and you can create *cash basis* reports that remove the receivables and payables with the same system.

Although certain types of organizations can use the cash basis method of accounting (many are not allowed to do so under IRS regulations), the accrual method provides the most accurate picture for managing your organization. You should check with your tax accountant to determine which accounting method — cash or accrual — is best for you.

Academy Photography

Throughout this book, you will see references to a fictitious company called Academy Photography. Academy Photography is a photography studio that also sells camera equipment. This company uses QuickBooks for its accounting and business management. Academy Photography may not be exactly like your business; however, the examples in this text that focus on Academy Photography are generic enough to guide you on your own use of QuickBooks.

Academy Photography has two locations, one in San Jose and another in Walnut Creek. In order for management to separately track revenue and expenses for each store, Academy Photography uses **Classes** in QuickBooks. As you proceed through the book, you'll see how each transaction (bill, check, invoice, etc.) is tagged with what *Class* it belongs to, so that later you can create reports like Profit & Loss by Class. Classes can be used to separately track departments, profit centers, store locations, or funds in any business.

Academy Photography also needs to separately track revenue and expenses for each job it performs. When a customer orders a photo shoot, Academy Photography needs to track all of the revenue and expenses specifically related to that job so it can look back and see how profitable the job was. This concept is called *job costing*, and many different businesses need to track jobs in similar ways.

As you think through the examples with Academy Photography, ask yourself what parallels you see to your own organization. Certainly, areas such as salaries, supplies, equipment, and others will be appropriate for your setup, but the names and specifics of the accounts, items, lists, and forms will probably be different.

QuickBooks Files

Before using QuickBooks, it is important for you to understand how QuickBooks files are structured and used. QuickBooks has three primary types of files described below. All file types can be opened using the *Open or Restore Company* option from the *File* menu.

1. *Working Data Files* – These files are used to enter transactions and create reports. These can also be called the Company Files. *(File Extension .QBW)*
2. *Portable Company Files* –These files are a compact version of the company data files and are used to transport the file between computers. These files should never be used to back up your QuickBooks data. These files must be "Restored" to a working data file to be used. *(File Extension .QBM)*
3. *Backup Files* –These files are a compressed version of the company data files and are used as backup to safeguard the information. These files cannot be used directly within QuickBooks and must be "Restored" to working data file format. *(File Extension .QBB)*

This means, if you name your company file ABC, QuickBooks will store the working data file as "ABC.QBW." When you back up your company file using the QuickBooks Backup function, QuickBooks will store your backup file with the name "ABC.QBB." If you create a portable data file using the QuickBooks Portable file creation function, the portable file "ABC.QBM" will be created.

In addition to the Backup and Restore process, which moves the complete QuickBooks file between computers, QuickBooks also has a feature called the Accountant's Copy. This feature enables an accounting professional to review and make corrections to a special copy of the client's company file while the client continues to work. Then the client can *merge* the accountant's changes back into the original file. See the QuickBooks Help Index for information on this feature.

Important:
Each file type has a specific purpose and should be used accordingly. Working data files are used to enter data and run reports, backup files are used to safeguard the data, and portable files are compressed files used to transport data via the Internet where smaller files transfer faster.

Creating a New File

There are four ways to create a new QuickBooks file, *Express Start, Detailed Start, Company Based on an Existing Company,* and *Conversion from Other Accounting Software.* Although it is possible to create a QuickBooks file relatively quickly using *Express Start,* we recommend utilizing a 12-Step process for creating a file to properly set up accounts and account balances. We have placed the chapter that explains file setup later in the book so you will be able to utilize knowledge gained in earlier chapters. You can learn more about file setup in our File Setup chapter starting on page 437.

Opening a QuickBooks Sample File

For learning purposes, QuickBooks provides sample data files that allow you to explore the program. To open a sample data file, follow these steps:

COMPUTER PRACTICE

Step 1.   Launch the QuickBooks program by double clicking the icon on your desktop or selecting it from the Windows Start menu.

Step 2.   When QuickBooks opens, you will either see the **No Company Open** window (Figure 1-2) or you will be prompted to enter the password for the last working data file used.

              No Company Open window is displayed if you are opening QuickBooks for the first time or if you closed the working data file *before* exiting in your last session. By default, the last working data file used will open, if you closed the QuickBooks *program* before closing the file.

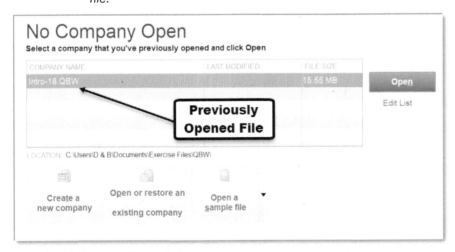

Figure 1-2 No Company Open window

Step 3. If you don't see the **No Company Open** window (Figure 1-2), but instead see a prompt to enter a password to the last working data file used (Figure 1-3). Click **Cancel**.

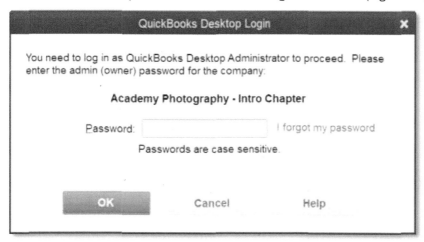

Figure 1-3 QuickBooks Desktop Login window

Step 4. Click **Open a Sample file** button and select *Sample product-based business* from the list. The selected sample file will open with the *QuickBooks Information* screen (see Figure 1-4).

Step 5. Click **OK** to continue.

Figure 1-4 Sample File Information Screen

Step 6. The sample file you selected will open. If you see the *Accountant Center* or the *External Accountant* message, close the window by clicking the X in the top right corner. You can uncheck the box that says **Show window when opening a company file** and close the window of the *Accountant Center,* or check **Don't show this again** in the *External Accountant* window.

Opening Other QuickBooks Data Files

If you want to open a QuickBooks company file, other than the sample data files, follow the steps below. We will not complete these steps now, but will use a restored portable file in the next section.

> DO NOT PERFORM THESE STEPS. THEY ARE FOR REFERENCE ONLY.

1. Launch the QuickBooks program by double clicking the icon on your desktop or selecting it from the Windows Start menu. When QuickBooks opens, it launches the data file you previously had open when you last exited the program, unless you specifically closed the data file before exiting.

2. To open a different file, select the **File** menu and then select **Open or Restore Company** (see Figure 1-5).

Figure 1-5 File menu

3.   In the *Open or Restore Company* window, select **Open a company file** and click **Next**.

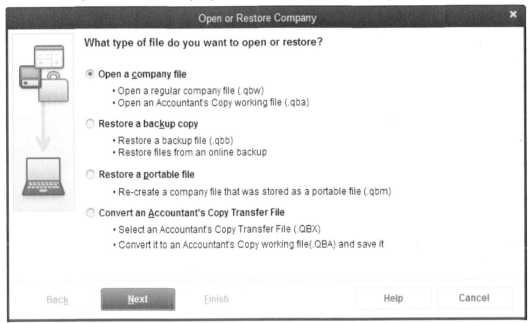

Figure 1-6 Open or Restore Company

4.   Set the *Look in* field to the folder on your hard disk where you store your QuickBooks file (see Figure 1-7).

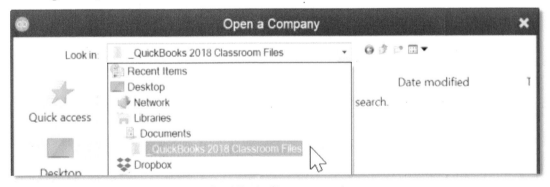

Figure 1-7 Selecting the folder where the QuickBooks files are stored

5.   Select the file from the list of QuickBooks files. Then click **Open**.

> **Note:** When you open a data file, depending on today's date, you may see one or more "Alerts" for learning to process credit cards, pay taxes, or similar activities. Click Mark as Done when you see these alerts.

Your company file will open, and you'll be ready to work with QuickBooks.

Closing QuickBooks Files

Step 1.   Close the company data file by selecting **Close Company** from the *File* menu (see Figure 1-8). If you skip this step, this data file will open automatically the next time you start the QuickBooks program.

Figure 1-8 Close Company File option

Opening Multiple Files

It is possible to open two company files at the same time if you are using QuickBooks Accountant or Enterprise, however, the activities that can be performed in the second file are very limited. We recommend that you use one file at a time by closing a file before opening or restoring a different file.

Closing the QuickBooks Program

Just as with any other Windows program, you can close the QuickBooks program by clicking the close button, which looks like an *X*, at the upper right hand corner of the QuickBooks window, or by selecting **Exit** from the *File* menu. The *Exiting QuickBooks* window will appear to confirm that you want to exit the QuickBooks program, as opposed to closing a window in QuickBooks. You can disable this message by checking the box next to Do *not display this message in the future* (see Figure 1-9).

Figure 1-9 Exiting QuickBooks window

Opening Portable Company Files

Portable Company Files are compact company data files that can be easily transported. The exercise files that accompany this book are Portable Company Files. You will need to open these exercise files at the start of each chapter and each problem.

> **Note:**
> When you move a data file from one computer (computer A) to another (computer B), any data you enter on computer B will cause the file on the computer A to become "obsolete." Take care to make sure you are always working in the true, active data file.

COMPUTER PRACTICE

To open portable files follow the steps below.

Step 1.   Select the **Open or Restore Company** option from the *File* menu

Step 2.   QuickBooks displays the *Open or Restore Company* window (see Figure 1-10). Select **Restore a portable file (.QBM)** and click **Next**.

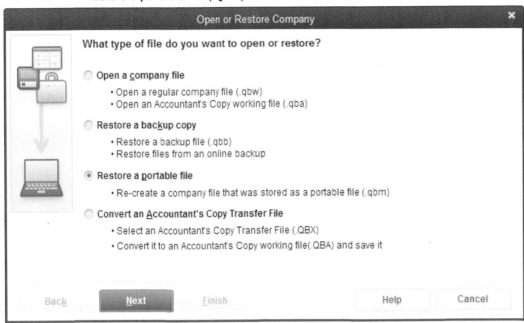

Figure 1-10 Open or Restore Company window

Step 3.   QuickBooks displays the *Open Portable Company File* window (see Figure 1-11). Navigate to the location of your exercise files. You may need to ask your instructor if you do not know this location. Once you are viewing the contents of the correct folder, select Intro-18.QBM and click **Open**.

Figure 1-11 Open Portable Company File window

Step 4.   Next you will need to tell QuickBooks where to save the working file that will be created from the portable file (see Figure 1-12). Click **Next** in the *Open or Restore Company* window to continue.

Figure 1-12 Open or Restore Company Location

Step 5.   The *Save Company File as* window displays (see Figure 1-13): Ask your instructor or choose a location to save the file. When you have navigated to the appropriate folder, click **Save**.

Figure 1-13 Save Company File as window

Step 6.   The QuickBooks Desktop Login window opens (see Figure 1-3). The password to this and every exercise file in this book is *Sleeter18*. The password is case sensitive so make sure you capitalize the first letter S in *Sleeter18*. Enter ***Sleeter18*** in the *Password* field and click **OK**.

> **Note:**
> Every QuickBooks file that uses the QuickBooks 2018 edition is required to have a
> complex password. The complex password is required to be 7 characters long and
> contain at least one uppercase letter and at least one numerical digit. Although we use
> the same password for all the exercise files in this textbook, we recommend that you use
> a different password for your own or your employer's QuickBooks file. For more on file
> passwords see page 474.

Step 7.   If asked to update your company file, click **Yes**.

Step 8.   If you see the *QuickBooks Desktop Information* window saying that the Portable company
               file has been successfully opened, click **OK** to continue.

Step 9.   Once the Intro-18.QBW company file finishes opening, you will see the Home page.

Creating Portable Company Files

Although we will not create one now, you can also create a Portable file using the following steps.

> **DO NOT PERFORM THESE STEPS. THEY ARE FOR REFERENCE ONLY.**

1.   Select the **Create Copy** option from the *File* menu (see Figure 1-14).

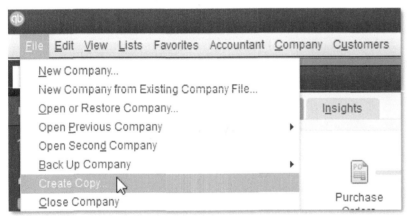

Figure 1-14 Create Copy

2.   The *Save Copy or Backup* window displays. Select the **Portable company file** option and click **Next**.

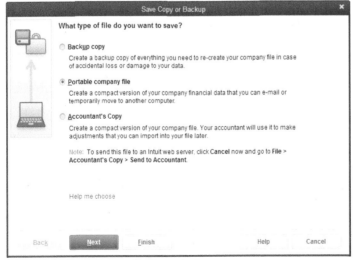

Figure 1-15 Save Copy or Backup window

3. The *Save Portable Company File* window appears. The default file name in the *File name* field is the same as the working file name with "(Portable)" added to the end. Navigate to the student file location and click **Save**.

4. The message shown in Figure 1-16 will appear before the portable file is created. Click **OK** to continue.

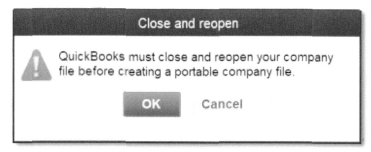

Figure 1-16 Message for creating portable company file

5. QuickBooks displays the *QuickBooks Desktop Information* dialog box (see Figure 1-17). Click **OK** to return to the working data file.

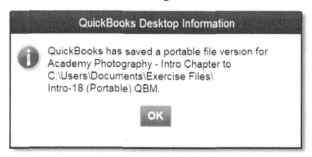

Figure 1-17 Message that the Portable File has been successfully created

Restoring Backup Files

When working with important financial information, creating backup files is a crucial safeguard against data loss. Every business should conduct regular backups of company information. QuickBooks has useful tools to automate this process.

In the event of an emergency, you may need to restore lost or damaged data. For example, if your computer's hard drive fails, you can restore your backup onto another computer and continue to work.

> **Note:**
> Portable files should never be used as a substitute for backup files. Backup files are larger than portable files and hold more information about the company.

Backing up Your Data File

Backing up your data is one of the most important safeguards you have to ensure the safety of your data.

> **DO NOT PERFORM THESE STEPS. THEY ARE FOR REFERENCE ONLY.**

1. To back up your company file, select **Create Copy** from the *File* menu.

2. Choose **Backup copy** from the *Save Copy or Backup* window (see Figure 1-18). Click **Next**.

3.   You are given the option to save the backup to a local area, such as a removable hard disk, or an
      online backup using a fee-based service available from Intuit. Online backup is a good option for
      many companies.

      Choose **Local backup** and click **Next**.

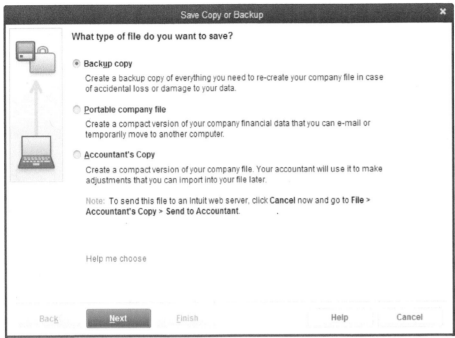

Figure 1-18 Save Copy or Backup window

4.   The *Backup Options* window is displayed (see Figure 1-19). Under the *Local backup only* section,
      click the Browse button.

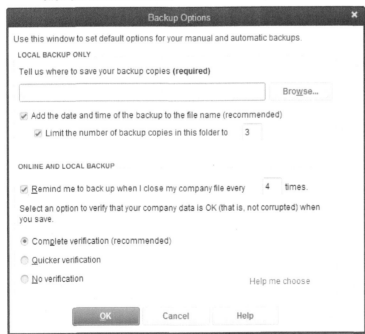

Figure 1-19 Backup Options window

5.   Select the folder where you want to store your backup file (see Figure 1-20). You should store the
      backup files in a safe location, preferably on a different drive than your working data file. That
      way, if the drive with the working file is damaged, the backup will still be available.

Figure 1-20 Backup options Browse for Folder window

6. When finished, click OK.

7. The *Save Copy or Backup* window is displayed (see Figure 1-21). You can save a backup now, schedule future backups, or both. Select **Only schedule future backups** and click **Next**.

Figure 1-21 Save Copy or Backup window

8. In the *Save Copy or Backup* window, select **New** under the *Back up on a schedule* area.

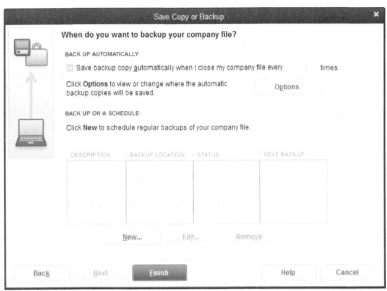

Figure 1-22 Save Copy or Backup window

9. The *Schedule Backup* window appears (see Figure 1-23). Enter a descriptive name for the backup, the location of the folder to contain the backups, and the time when the backup file will be created.

Figure 1-23 Schedule Backup window

10. When finished, click **OK** to close the *Schedule Backup* window.

11. The *Store Windows Password* window opens. Enter your Windows username and password and click **OK**.

12. Click **Finish** to close the *Schedule Backup* window.

13. If necessary, click **OK** to close the *QuickBooks: Backups have been scheduled as specified.* Window.

14. If necessary, click **No, Thanks** for the offer to try Online Backup.

Restoring a Backup File

To restore a QuickBooks backup file, follow these steps.

DO NOT PERFORM THESE STEPS. THEY ARE FOR REFERENCE ONLY.

1. Select the **File** menu and then select **Open or Restore Company**.
2. Choose **Restore a backup copy** from the *Open or Restore Company* window and click **Next**.
3. In the *Open or Restore Company* window you can specify whether the file is stored locally or through Intuit's fee-based *Online Backup* service. Choose **Local backup** and click **Next**.
4. The *Open Backup Copy* window allows you to specify where the backup file is located. Navigate to the folder that contains the file, select it and click **Open**.
5. The *Open or Restore Company* window displays. Click **Next**.
6. The *Save Company File as* window allows you to specify where to restore the working files. Navigate to the appropriate folder and click **Save**. QuickBooks will then restore your backup file in the folder you specified. You may be prompted to enter a password. When QuickBooks restores the file, it creates a **.QBW** file.
7. After completion, a window displays that the new file has been successfully restored (see Figure 1-24).

Figure 1-24 After restoring backup file

Note: When you restore a data file, depending on today's date, you may see one or more "Alerts" for learning to process credit cards, pay taxes, or similar activities. Click *Mark as Done* when you see these alerts.

QuickBooks User Interface Features

QuickBooks provides a number of shortcuts and aids that assist the user in entering information and transactions. You should become familiar with these features so you can get to a task quickly. There are various methods of accessing the data entry windows: the **Home** page, **Snapshots**, **Menus**, **QuickBooks Centers**, **Icon Bar**, and **Shortcut Keys**.

Home Page

As soon as you open a company file, QuickBooks displays the *Home* page (Figure 1-25). The *Home* page is broken into five sections – each dealing with a separate functional area of a business. These areas are: Vendors, Customers, Employees, Company, and Banking. Each area has icons to facilitate easy access to QuickBooks tasks. The *Home* page also displays a flow diagram showing the interdependency between tasks.

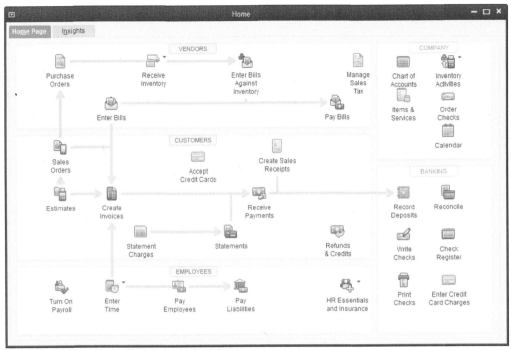

Figure 1-25 QuickBooks Accountant 2018 Home page

To start a task, just click on its related icon on the *Home* page. If you close the *Home* page, it can be opened by clicking on the **Home** icon on the Icon bar, or by selecting *Home Page* from the <u>Company</u> <u>menu</u>.

Centers

QuickBooks *Centers* are organized to give pertinent information in one place. There are several Centers for specific relationships and tasks.

Customer, Vendor, and Employee Centers are very important since they provide the only way to access a list of all your customers, vendors, and employees. These three lists are referred to as the *Center-based Lists*. These Centers summarize general information and transactions in the same area. For example, the Customer Center shows the customer balance, their general information, and all transactions for each customer (see Figure 1-26).

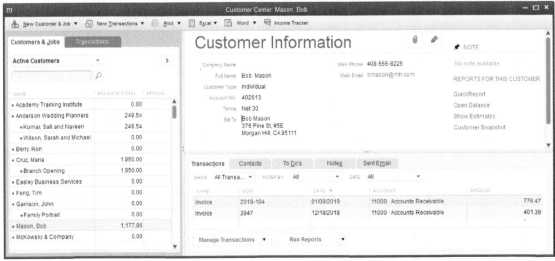

Figure 1-26 Customer Center

Other Centers include the *App Center, Bank Feeds Center, Report Center,* and *Doc Center.* These Centers will be addressed later in this book. *Centers* can be opened from the *Menus, Home Page* and *Iconbar.*

Snapshots

The *Snapshots* is a single screen summary of different aspects of a company. Charts such as *Income and Expense Trends, Previous Year Income Comparison,* and *Expense Breakdown* are displayed along with important lists such as *Account Balances* and *Customers Who Owe Money.* The Snapshots can be easily customized to show the information that is of most interest to you and your company.

Figure 1-27 Snapshots - *your screen may vary*

Income Tracker

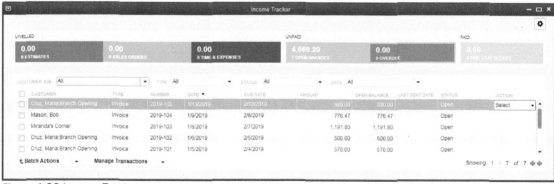

Figure 1-28 Income Tracker – *your screen may vary*

The Income Tracker provides a fast way to see the status of your unbilled and unpaid transactions as well as features for billing and collections.

Icon Bar

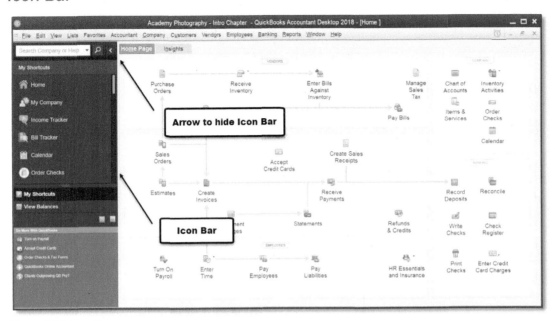

Figure 1-29 Icon Bar

The QuickBooks *Icon Bar* allows you to select activities and available services by clicking icons on the bar (see Figure 1-29). For example, you can open the Home page by clicking **Home** on the Icon Bar.

Calendar

You can view transactions on a *Calendar*. The calendar displays transactions on the *Entered* date and the *Due* date.

> **Note:**
> The *Entered* date is not literally the date when the transaction is entered into QuickBooks. It is the transaction date that is input on the transaction form. If you create an invoice on January 5th, 2019 and enter the date 1/6/2019 in the date field, the invoice will show on January 6th, 2019 on the Calendar.

Figure 1-30 QuickBooks Calendar- your screen may vary

COMPUTER PRACTICE

Step 1.   Click the Calendar icon on the Company section of the Home page.

Step 2.   The Calendar window opens (see Figure 1-30). When finished, close the Calendar window.

Entering Transactions in QuickBooks

Whenever you buy or sell products or services, pay a bill, make a deposit at the bank, or transfer money, you need to enter a transaction into QuickBooks.

Forms

In QuickBooks, transactions are created by filling out familiar-looking forms such as invoices, bills, and checks. When you finish filling out a form, QuickBooks automatically records the accounting entries behind the scenes. Most forms in QuickBooks have drop-down lists to allow you to pick from a list instead of spelling the name of a customer, vendor, item, or account.

COMPUTER PRACTICE

Step 1.   Click the **Enter Bills** icon on the *Home page* Vendors section (see Figure 1-31).

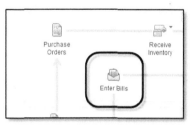

Figure 1-31 Enter Bills on the Home page

Step 2.   Click the **Previous** button in the upper left corner of the *Enter Bills* window until you see the previously entered bill in Figure 1-32.

Step 3.   Click the down arrow next to the vendor field to see the drop-down list for vendors.

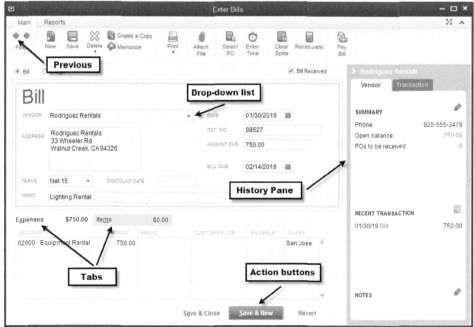

Figure 1-32 Bill form

Step 4.   Click the calendar icon next to the date to see the calendar drop-down menu.

Step 5.   When finished exploring, click the **Revert** button which will return the transaction to the last saved state.

Step 6.   Close the Enter Bills window.

By using forms to enter transactions, you provide QuickBooks with *all of the details* of each transaction. For example, by using the Enter Bills form in Figure 1-32, QuickBooks will track the vendor balance, the due date of the bill, the discount terms, and the debits and credits in the General Ledger. This is a good example of how QuickBooks handles the accounting behind the scenes, and also provides management information beyond just the accounting entries.

Lists

Lists are one of the most important building blocks of QuickBooks. Lists store information that is used again and again to fill out forms. For example, when you set up a customer, including their name, address and other details, QuickBooks can use the information to automatically fill out an invoice. Similarly, when an Item is set up, QuickBooks can automatically fill in the Item's description, price, and associated account information. This helps speed up data entry and reduce errors.

> **Note:**
> There are two kinds of lists — **menu-based** and **center-based**. Menu-based lists are accessible through the *Lists* menu and include the *Item* list and *Terms* list. Center-based lists include the *Customer Center* and *Vendor Center*, discussed on page 18.

Lists can be viewed by selecting an icon from the *Home* page (for example, the *Items & Services* button), choosing a menu option from the *Lists* menu, or viewing a list through one of the various QuickBooks Centers.

Accounts

QuickBooks provides the means to efficiently track all of your business transactions by categorizing them into *accounts*. The **Chart of Accounts** is the list of these accounts.

COMPUTER PRACTICE

Step 1.   To display the Chart of Accounts, click the *Chart of Accounts* icon on the *Home* page. Alternatively, you could select **Chart of Accounts** from the *List* menu, or press **Ctrl+A**.

Step 2.   Scroll through the list. Leave the *Chart of Accounts* open for the next exercise.

By default, the Chart of Accounts is sorted *by account number* within each account type (see Figure 1-33). The *Name* column shows the account names that you assign; the *Type* column shows their account type; the *Balance Total* column shows the balance for asset, liability, and equity accounts (except Retained Earnings), and the **Attach** column shows if there are attached documents.

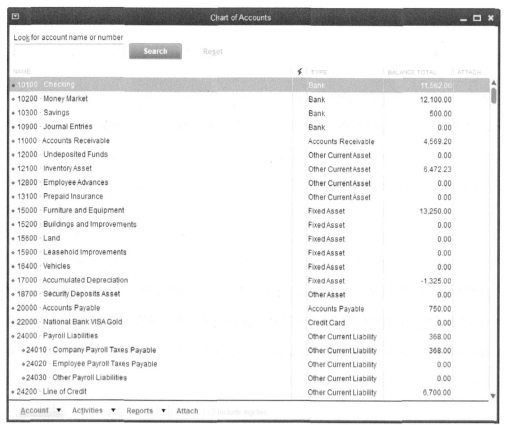

Figure 1-33 Chart of Accounts List

> **Note:**
> New with QuickBooks 2018, you can now search for accounts in the *Chart of Accounts*.

Registers

Each asset, liability, and equity account (except Retained Earnings) has a *register* (see page 2 for more information on these account types). Registers allow you to view and edit transactions in a single window. Income and expense accounts do not have registers; rather, their transactions must be viewed in a report.

COMPUTER PRACTICE

Step 1.   To open the *Checking* account register, double click on **10100 Checking** in the *Chart of Accounts* list.

Step 2.   The **Checking** register opens (see Figure 1-34). Scroll through the register.

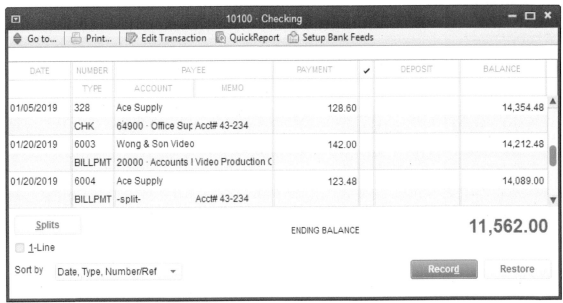

Figure 1-34 Checking account register

Step 3.   Close the Checking account register by clicking the close button in the upper right corner.

Step 4.   Double click the **40000 Services** account. You may need to scroll down. This is an *Income* account.

Step 5.   Instead of opening a register, QuickBooks opens a report (see Figure 1-35).

Step 6.   If necessary, change the *Dates* field to **All**.

Step 7.   Close the report.

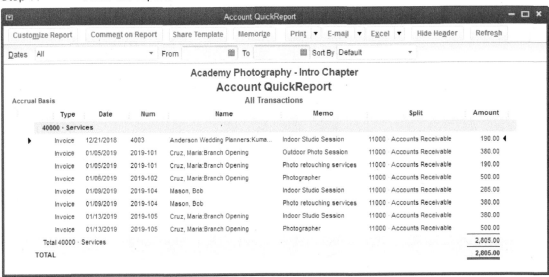

Figure 1-35 Services Account QuickReport – your screen may vary

Step 8.   Close the Chart of Accounts.

Items

Items are used to track products and services. Since every business has its own unique set of products and services, QuickBooks can be customized by creating Items for each service or product your company buys or sells. For more detail on Items and the different Item Types, see page 253.

When you define Items, you associate Item names with Accounts in the Chart of Accounts. This association between Item names and Accounts is the "magic" that allows QuickBooks to automatically create the accounting entries behind each transaction.

For example, Figure 1-37 displays the *Item* list. The Item, **Camera SR32**, is associated, or linked, to the **Sales** account in the Chart of Accounts. Every time the **Camera SR32** Item is entered on an invoice, the dollar amount actually affects the **Sales** account in the Chart of Accounts.

Items are necessary because to use a sales form in QuickBooks (e.g., invoices and sales receipts), you must use Items. On an invoice, for example, every line item will have a QuickBooks Item which may represent products, services, discounts, or sales tax.

COMPUTER PRACTICE

Step 1.   To see what Items are available in the file, click the **Items & Services** icon on the *Home page in the Company* section (see Figure 1-36). Alternatively, you could select **Item List** from the *Lists* menu.

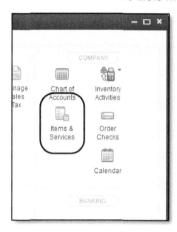

Figure 1-36 Items & Services button on Home page

Step 2.   Figure 1-37 shows the *Item* list. Double click the **Camera SR32** item.

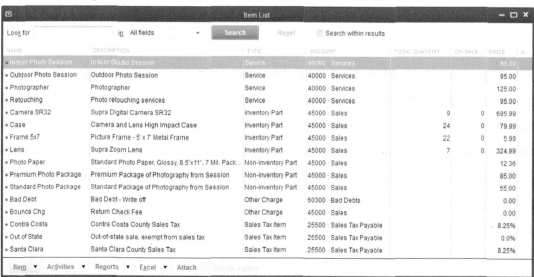

Figure 1-37 Item List

Step 3.   If the New Feature window opens, click **OK**.

Step 4.   The *Edit Item* window opens (see Figure 1-38). Notice this item is linked to the Sales account. Every time this item is entered on an invoice, it changes the **Sales** account.

Step 5.   Close the *Edit Item* and *Item List* windows.

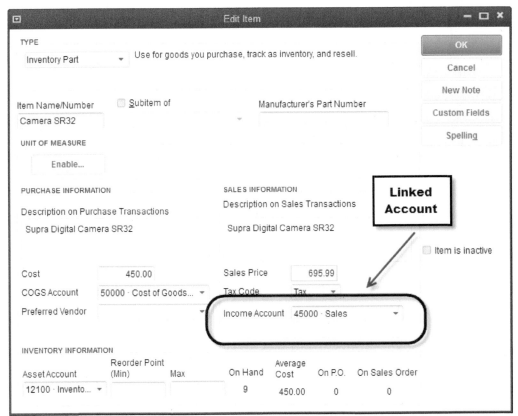

Figure 1-38 Camera SR32 Edit Item window – your screen may vary

QuickBooks Help

Support Resources

QuickBooks provides a variety of support resources that assist in using the program. Some of these resources are on the Internet and others are stored in help files locally along with the QuickBooks software on your computer. To access the support resources, select the *Help* menu and then select **QuickBooks Desktop Help**. QuickBooks will display answers to problems you might be having based on your recent activity. You can also enter a question and QuickBooks will search its Help Content and the Online Community for related answers.

Certified QuickBooks ProAdvisors

Certified QuickBooks ProAdvisors are independent consultants, accountants, bookkeepers, and educators who are proficient in QuickBooks and who can offer guidance to small businesses in various areas of business accounting. To find a Certified ProAdvisor, select **Find a Local QuickBooks Desktop Expert** from the *Help* menu.

Review Questions

Comprehension Questions

1. Explain the difference between a QuickBooks working data file, a QuickBooks backup file and a QuickBooks portable file. How can you differentiate between the three types of files on your hard disk?

2. What is the main reason for creating portable files?

3. Explain the importance of the QuickBooks *Home* page.

4. Explain why it is important to enter transactions in QuickBooks using Forms rather than accounting entries.

5. Describe the primary purpose of accounting in business.

Multiple Choice

Select the best answer(s) for each of the following:

1. The fundamental accounting equation that governs all accounting is:
   a) Net income = Revenue - expenses.
   b) Assets + Liabilities = Equity.
   c) Assets = Liabilities + Equity.
   d) Assets = Liabilities - Equity.

2. Which of the following statements is true?
   a) Debits are bad because they reduce income.
   b) Equity is increased by a net loss.
   c) Debits - credits = 0.
   d) Assets are increased with a credit entry.

3. Under accrual accounting:
   a) A sale is not recorded until the customer pays the bill.
   b) Income and expenses are recognized when transactions occur.
   c) An expense is not recorded until you write the check.
   d) You must maintain two separate accounting systems.

4. QuickBooks is:
   a) A job costing system.
   b) A payroll system.
   c) A double-entry accounting system.
   d) All of the above.

5. Which is not a method of accessing the data entry screens?
   a) Menus
   b) Home page
   c) Icon bar
   d) Data entry button

Completion Statements

1. As you enter data in familiar-looking _____, QuickBooks handles the _____ entries for you.

2. You should _____ your data file regularly because it is one of the most important safeguards you can do to ensure the safety of your data.

3. When you open your working data file, QuickBooks displays the _____ _____. This page is broken into five sections – each dealing with a separate functional area of a business.

4. _____ are used in QuickBooks Sales forms and represent what the company buys and sells.

5. A list which shows all the accounts in your working data file is called the _____ ___ _____.

Introduction Problem 1

> Restore the Intro-18Problem1.QBM file. The password to access this file is *Sleeter18*.

1. Select **Customers** from the QuickBooks *Icon* Bar. This will display the *Customer Center*.
    a)   What is the first customer listed on the left of the Customer Center?

> **Note:**
> The answer to this first question is **AAA Services**. If you don't see AAA Services in the *Customer Center*, make sure to restore *Intro-18Problem1.QBM* as directed in the box above. *This book uses specific files for each chapter and each problem. If you don't restore the correct file, you will have trouble completing the exercises.*

    b)   In the Customers & Jobs Center, single click on **Mason, Bob**. What is Bob Mason's balance?
    c)   Click the *Date* drop down list above the transaction listing in the right-hand panel and scroll up to the top of the list to select **All**. How many transactions do you see and of what type?
    d)   Close the Customer Center.

2. From the *Home Page*, click the **Enter Bills** icon. The *Enter Bills* window opens.
    a)   Click the previous button in the upper left corner. What is the name of the Vendor displayed on this Bill?
    b)   What is the *Bill Due* date on this bill?

3. From the *Home* page, click the **Chart of Accounts** icon to display the Chart of Accounts.
    a)   What type of account is the **Checking** Account?
    b)   How many total accounts are there of this same type?
    c)   What is the Balance Total for the **Money Market** account?

Introduction Problem 2 (Advanced)

> Restore the Intro-18Problem2.QBM file. The password to access this file is *Sleeter18*.

1. Select **Customers** from the QuickBooks *Icon* Bar. This will display the *Customer Center*.

a) What is the first customer listed on the left of the Customer Center?

> **Note:**
> The answer to this first question is **ABC International**. If you don't see ABC International in the *Customer Center*, make sure to restore *Intro-18Problem2.QBM* as directed in the box above. *This book uses specific files for each chapter and each problem. If you don't restore the correct file, you will have trouble completing the exercises.*

b) In the Customers & Jobs Center, single click on **Cruz, Maria**. What is Maria Cruz's balance?

c) Click the *Date* drop down list above the transaction listing in the right-hand panel and scroll up to the top of the list to select **All**. How many transactions do you see and of what type?

d) Close the Customer Center.

2. Select **Vendors** from the QuickBooks *Icon* Bar. This displays the *Vendor Center*.

a) Double click *Boswell Consulting* . This opens the *Edit Vendor* window. What is the Address? Close the *Edit Vendor* window.

b) Single click on *Sinclair Insurance*. What is the amount of Bill number 5055 to *Sinclair Insurance*? (You may need to set the *Date* to **All** as in Step 1.)

c) Close the Vendor Center.

3. From the *Home* page, click the **Chart of Accounts** icon to display the Chart of Accounts.

a) What type of account is the **Payroll Liabilities** Account?

b) How many accounts of type **Fixed Asset** are in the Chart of Accounts?

c) How many accounts of type **Other Current Asset** are in the Chart of Accounts?

4. While still in the **Chart of Accounts**, Double click the **Checking** account on the Chart of Accounts list. This will open the register for the Checking account.

a) Who was the payee for the check on 2/10/2019?

b) What was the amount of the check?

c) Close the checking account register and Chart of Accounts list.

5. Click the **Create Invoices** icon on the *Home page*, and then click on the **Previous** arrow (top left).

a) What is the Invoice Number?

b) Who is the Customer listed on this invoice?

c) What is the first *Item* listed on this invoice?

d) Close the invoice.

6. Select the **Chart of Accounts** option from the *Lists* menu. Double click on the **Checking** account.

a) Which vendor was paid by the last bill payment (BILLPMT) in the register?

b) What is the Bill Payment Number?

c) What is the amount of the last bill payment in the register?

d) Close the **Checking** register and close the **Chart of Accounts** list.

7. Click the **Write Checks** icon on the *Home* page and follow these steps:

  a) Click on the *Calendar* icon immediately to the right of the *Date* field. Select **tomorrow's date** in the *Date* field and press **Tab**.

  b) In the Pay to the Order of field, enter *Ace Supply*. Press **Tab**.

  c) Enter *80.00* in the *Amount* field and press **Tab**.

  d) Check the **Print Later** check box at the top of the window.

  e) What is the city displayed in the Address field on the check for *Ace Supply*?

  f) Click **Clear** and then close the check window.

8. Select the **Chart of Accounts** option from the *Lists* menu and double click on **Accounts Receivable**.

  a) What is the ending balance in the account?

  b) Who was the customer on the last transaction in the register?

  c) Close the register and the Chart of Accounts.

9. Click the **Check Register** icon on the Home page.

  a) Select **10100 – Checking** from the *Use Register* dialog box.

  b) What is the ending balance in the checking register?

  c) Close the Checking Register.

10. Close the working data file Intro-18Problem2.QBW.

Chapter 2
The Sales Process

Topics

In this chapter, you will learn about the following topics:

- Tracking Company Sales (page 31)
- Setting Up Customers (page 34)
- Job Costing (page 40)
- Recording Sales (page 41)
- Receiving Payments from Customers (page 54)
- Making Bank Deposits (page 62)
- Income Tracker (page 70)

> **Restore this File:**
> This chapter uses Sales-18.QBW. See page 9 for more information. The password to access this file is *Sleeter18*.

In this chapter, you will learn how QuickBooks can help you record and track revenues in your business.

Each time you sell products or services, you will record the transaction using one of QuickBooks' forms. When you fill out a QuickBooks **Invoice** or **Sales Receipt**, QuickBooks tracks the detail of each sale, allowing you to create reports about your sales.

Tracking Company Sales

Sales are recorded two different ways, either with a *Sales Receipt* when the customer pays at the time of sale or service (called *cash customers*), or an *Invoice* when the customer pays after the sale or service (*credit customers*). Transactions with cash customers follow a specific process. At the time of sale, a Sales Receipt is issued, and then a deposit is recorded. This process is displayed graphically on the Home Page (Figure 2-1). A Sales Receipt records both the items sold and the amount received. Then the funds are deposited.

> **Note:**
> Payment with a credit card is received immediately, therefore a customer who pays at the time of sale with a credit card is a cash customer.

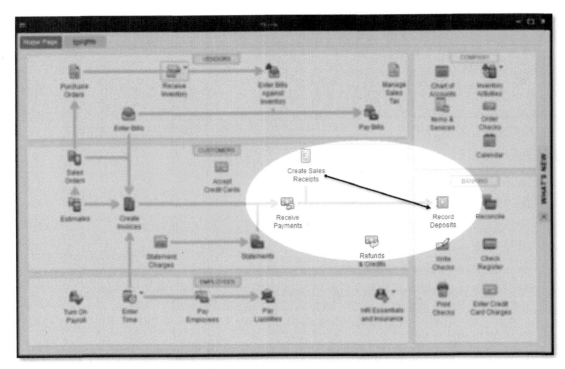

Figure 2-1 Payment with Cash Sale Workflow

When working with a credit customer, the sales process has a different workflow. Often, the first step is to create an Invoice. The payment is received and the amount is applied to the Invoice. Then a deposit is recorded. This process is displayed in Figure 2-2.

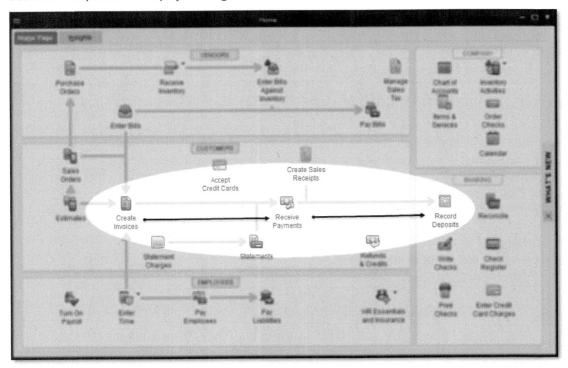

Figure 2-2 Invoicing Workflow

Table 2-1 provides more details about the cash and credit customer sales processes. In this table, you can see how to record business transactions for cash and credit customers. In addition, the table shows the *accounting behind the scenes* of each transaction. As discussed on page 4, the accounting behind the scenes is critical to your understanding of how QuickBooks converts the information on forms (Invoices, Sales Receipts, etc.) into accounting entries.

Each row in the table represents a business transaction you might enter as you proceed through the sales process.

Business Transaction	Cash Customers (Pay at time of sale)		Credit Customers (Pay after the sale date)	
	QuickBooks Transaction	Accounting Entry	QuickBooks Transaction	Accounting Entry
Estimate (Optional)	Not Usually Used		Estimates	Non-posting entry used to record estimates (bids) for Customers or Jobs
Sales Order (Optional)	Not Usually Used		Sales Orders	Non-posting entry used to record customer orders
Recording a Sale	Create Sales Receipts	Increase (debit) **Undeposited Funds**, increase (credit) *income* account	Create Invoices	Increase (debit) **Accounts Receivable**, increase (credit) *income* account
Receiving Money in Payment of an Invoice	No additional action is required on the sales form.		Receive Payments	Increase (debit) **Undeposited Funds**, decrease (credit) **Accounts Receivable**
Depositing Money in the Bank	Record Deposits	Decrease (credit) **Undeposited Funds**, increase (debit) *bank* account	Record Deposits	Decrease (credit) **Undeposited Funds**, increase (debit) *bank* account

Table 2-1 Steps in the sales process

The *Sales Receipt* form records the details of who you sold to and what you sold and then uses, by default, a special account called **Undeposited Funds**. This account is an *Other Current Asset* account, and it can be thought of as a drawer where you keep your checks and other deposits before depositing in the bank. See page 45 for more information on **Undeposited Funds**.

The accounting behind the scenes:
When you create a **Sales Receipt**, QuickBooks increases (with a debit) **a bank account or Undeposited Funds,** and increases (with a credit) the appropriate *income* account. If applicable, **Sales Receipts** also increase (with a credit) the *sales tax liability* account. If the sale includes an Inventory Item, it also decreases (credits) the *Inventory asset* and increases (debits) the *Cost of Goods Sold account*.

For credit customers, the sales process usually starts with creating an **Invoice**. The **Invoice** form records the details of who you sold to and what you sold.

> **The accounting behind the scenes:**
> When you create an **Invoice**, QuickBooks increases (with a debit) **Accounts Receivable** and increases (with a credit) the appropriate *income* account. If applicable, **Invoices** also increase (with a credit) the *sales tax liability account*. If the sale includes an Inventory Item, it also decreases (credits) the *Inventory asset* and increases (debits) the *Cost of Goods Sold account.*

When you receive money from your credit customers, use the **Receive Payments** function to record the receipt. If you have created an *Invoice*, you must accept payment through this process to close the *Invoice*.

> **The accounting behind the scenes:**
> When you record a received **Payment**, QuickBooks increases (with a debit) **Undeposited Funds** or a bank account, and decreases (with a credit) **Accounts Receivable**.

Whether you posted to Undeposited Funds through a **Sales Receipt** or a **Payment**, the last step in the process is to make a **Deposit** to your bank account. This step is the same for both cash and credit customers. Use the **Make Deposits** function to record the deposit to your bank account.

If you prepare estimates (sometimes called bids) for Customers or Jobs, you can create an **Estimate** to track the details of what the sale will include. Estimates are provided to customers to help them decide on their purchases, products or services. QuickBooks does not post **Estimates** to the **General Ledger**, but it helps you track the estimate until the job is complete. QuickBooks also provides reports that help you compare estimated vs. actual revenues and costs.

> **The accounting behind the scenes:**
> When you create an **Estimate**, QuickBooks records the estimate, but there is no accounting entry made. **Estimates** are "non-posting" entries.

If you use sales orders in your business, you can use a **Sales Order** form to track the details of what the sale will include. For example, if you order goods you currently have out of stock for a specific customer, you could create a **Sales Order** to track the Customer's order. **Sales Orders** are very similar to **Estimates** because they are both non-posting entries, and they both help you track future sales. QuickBooks does not post **Sales Orders** to the **General Ledger**, but it helps you track your orders until they are shipped to the customer. **Sales Orders** are only available in QuickBooks Premier, Accountant and Enterprise Solutions.

> **The accounting behind the scenes:**
> When you create a **Sales Order**, QuickBooks records the sales order, but there is no accounting entry made. **Sales Orders** are "non-posting" entries.

In the following sections, you will learn about each step of the payment at the time of sale and invoicing workflows.

Setting Up Customers

For each of your customers, create a record in the **Customers & Jobs** list of the *Customer Center*. Academy Photography has a new credit customer – Dr. Tim Feng. To add this new customer, follow these steps:

COMPUTER PRACTICE

Step 1.   Select the **Customers** button from the *Icon bar.*

Step 2.   To add a new customer, select **New Customer** from the **New Customer & Job** drop-down
               menu (see Figure 2-3).

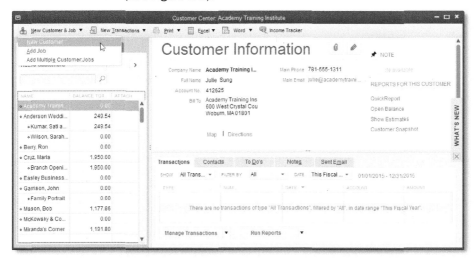

Figure 2-3 Adding a new customer record

Step 3.   Enter **Feng, Tim** in the *Customer Name* field (see Figure 2-4) and then press **Tab**.

Step 4.   Press **Tab** twice to skip the *Opening Balance* and *as of* fields. Since you will not enter an
               amount in the *Opening Balance* field, there is no need to change the *as of* date.

Figure 2-4 New Customer window

> **Important Tip:**
> It is best NOT to use the *Opening Balance* field in the customer record. When you enter
> an opening balance for a customer in the *Opening Balance* field, QuickBooks creates a
> new account in your Chart of Accounts called Uncategorized Income. Then, it creates an
> **Invoice** that increases (debits) **Accounts Receivable** and increases (credits) **Uncategorized
> Income.**

It is preferable to enter the actual open *Invoices* for each customer when you set up your company file. That way, you will have all of the details of which Invoice is open, and what Items were sold on the open Invoices. When you use Invoices, the actual income accounts will be used instead of **Uncategorized Income**.

Step 5.   Because this customer is an individual (i.e., not a company), press **Tab** to skip the *Company Name* field.

Step 6.   Continue entering information in the rest of the fields using the data in Table 2-2. You do not need to enter anything in the fields not included below.

Field	Data
Mr./Mrs.	Dr.
First Name	Tim
M.I.	S.
Last Name	Feng
Job Title	Owner
Main Phone	408-555-8298
Main Email	drf@df.biz
Invoice/Bill To Address Hint: Press **Enter** to move to a new line in this field.	Tim S. Feng 300 N. First St. San Jose, CA 95136
Ship To	Click **Copy>>**. This displays the *Add Shipping Address Information* window (see Figure 2-5). Type **Office** in the Address Name field and click **OK**. In QuickBooks, you can select multiple Ship To addresses for your customers.

Table 2-2 Data to complete the Address Info tab

Figure 2-5 Add Ship To Address Information window

Figure 2-6 shows the finished Address Info section of the customer record. Verify that your screen matches Figure 2-6.

> **Note:**
> In QuickBooks, you can use multiple *Ship-To Addresses*. This is useful when one customer requests that products be sent to more than one address.

Figure 2-6 Completed Address Info tab

> **Tip:**
> There are four name lists in QuickBooks: **Vendor**, **Customer:Job**, **Employee**, and **Other Names**. After you enter a name in the *Customer Name* field of the *New Customer* window, you cannot use that name in any of the other three lists in QuickBooks.
>
> **When Customers are Vendors:**
> When you sell to and purchase from the same company, you'll need to create two records – one in the Vendor List and one in the Customer:Job list. Make the two names slightly different. For example, you could enter Feng, Tim-C in the *New Customer* window and Feng, Tim-V in the *New Vendor* window. The vendor and customer records for Tim Feng can contain the same contact information.

Step 7. Click the **Payment Settings** tab on the left of the *New Customer* window to continue entering information about this customer as shown in Figure 2-7.

Step 8. Enter *3546* in the *Account No.* field to assign a customer number by which you can sort or filter reports. Press **Tab**.

Step 9. Enter *8,000.00* in the *Credit Limit* field and press **Tab**.

QuickBooks will warn you if you record an Invoice to this customer when the balance due (plus the current sale) exceeds the credit limit. Even though QuickBooks warns you, you'll still be able to record the Invoice.

Step 10. Select **Net 30** from the *Payment Terms* drop-down list as the terms for this customer and then press **Tab**.

QuickBooks is *terms smart*. For example, if you enter terms of 2% 10 Net 30 and a customer pays within 10 days, QuickBooks will automatically calculate a 2% discount. For more information about setting up your Terms list, see page 259.

Figure 2-7 Completed Payment Settings tab

Step 11.   Select **Commercial** from the *Price Level* drop-down list. See page 261 for information on
                setting up and using price levels. Press **Tab** twice.

Step 12.   Leave the default setting of **Email** in the *Preferred Delivery Method* field.

                You can use the *Preferred Delivery Method* field if you plan to email Invoices to a
                customer on a regular basis or if you plan to use QuickBooks' Invoice printing and mailing
                service.

> **Note:**
> For more information on the QuickBooks invoice payment and mailing service, select the **Help**
> menu and then select **Add QuickBooks Services**. You will then be directed online to the Intuit
> website. Click on the **Learn More** button under the *Get Paid Faster* section. Additional
> transaction fees apply for this service.

Step 13.   Select **Visa** from the *Preferred Payment Method* drop-down list and then press **Tab**.
                When you set the fields on this window, you won't have to enter the credit card
                information each time you receive money from the customer.

> **Tip:**
> If more than one person accesses your QuickBooks file, set up a separate user name and
> password for each additional user. When you set up a user, you can restrict him or her
> from accessing *Sensitive Accounting Activities*. This will prevent the additional user from
> seeing the customer's credit card number. See page 474 for more information about
> setting up user names and passwords.

Step 14.   Enter the remaining data as shown in Figure 2-7 in the *Credit Card Information* section.
                Some of the fields will auto-populate as you tab into those fields. You may overwrite the
                auto-populated values if needed.

                If you use the QuickBooks merchant account service, enter the default credit card
                number in the *Preferred Payment Method* area. This sets defaults on sales transactions
                for this customer.

> **Note:**
> If you track multiple jobs for each customer, it is best NOT to enter job information on the *Job Info* tab of the main customer record. If you want to track jobs for this customer, you can create separate job records in the **Customers & Jobs** list.

Step 15. Click the **Sales Tax Settings** tab in the *New Customer* window (see Figure 2-8).

Step 16. Press **Tab** twice to accept the **Tax** default **Sales Tax Code** in the *Tax Code* field.

Sales Tax Codes serve two purposes. First, they determine the default taxable status of a customer, item, or sale. Second, they are used to identify the type of tax exemption. For complete information on sales tax codes, see page 95.

Step 17. Set the *Tax Item* field to **Santa Clara**. This indicates which sales tax rate to charge and which agency collects the tax. Press **Tab** when finished.

> **Tip:**
> In most states, you charge sales tax based on the delivery point of the shipment. Therefore, the **Sales Tax Item** should be chosen to match the tax charged in the county (or tax location) of the *Ship To* address on the *Address Info* tab.

Step 18. Leave the *Resale No.* field blank.

If the customer is a reseller, you would enter his or her reseller number.

Figure 2-8 Completed Sales Tax Settings tab

Step 19. Select the **Additional Info** tab in the *New Customer* window (see Figure 2-9).

Step 20. Select **Business** from the *Customer Type* drop-down list and then press **Tab**.

QuickBooks allows you to group your customers into common types. By grouping your customers into types, you'll be able to create reports that focus on one or more types. For example, if you create two types of customers, Residential and Business, you are able to tag each customer with a type. Then you can create reports, statements, or mailing labels for all customers of a certain type.

Step 21. Select **MM** or Mike Mazuki in the *Rep* drop-down list and then press **Tab**.

The *Rep* field can contain the initials of one of your employees or vendors. Use this field to assign a sales rep to this customer. If you use the *Rep* field, you can create reports (e.g., Sales by Rep report) that provide the sales information you need to pay commissions. Each sales form (**Invoice** or **Sales Receipt**) can have a different name in the *Rep* field.

Step 22. Enter *Santa Clara* in the *County* field.

The **Define Fields** button on the **Additional Info** tab allows you to define **Custom Fields** to track more information about your customers. For more information on setting up and using custom fields, see page 263.

Figure 2-9 Completed Additional Info tab

Step 23.   Click **OK** to save and close the *New Customer* window.

> **Note:**
> If you see an error message when saving the Feng, Tim customer (see Figure 2-10), you may not be in the correct exercise file. Make sure you restore the correct file at the start of each chapter and problem, otherwise your exercises may not match the activities in this book. For this chapter, you should be using Sales-18.QBW. For instructions on restoring portable files, please see page 9.

Figure 2-10 Error Message when saving a Name that already exists

Step 24.   Close the Customer Center by clicking the close button on the *Customer Center* window or by pressing the **Esc** key.

Job Costing

Each customer listed in the *Customer Center* can have one or more jobs. Setting up *Jobs* for *Customers* helps you track income and expenses by job and therefore create reports showing detailed or summarized information about each job. This is particularly important for some industries, such as construction.

To create a job for an existing customer record, open the *Customer Center*, then select the customer, and then select **Add Job** from the **New Customer & Job** drop down menu. You don't need to do this now, because the sample data file already has Jobs set up.

Figure 2-11 Adding a Job to an existing customer record

> **Key Term:**
> Tracking income and expenses separately for each Job is known as *Job Costing*. If your company needs to track job costs, make sure you include the Job name on each income and expense transaction as these transactions are entered.

In the **Name** column of the *Customers & Jobs* list, Jobs are slightly indented under the Customer name.

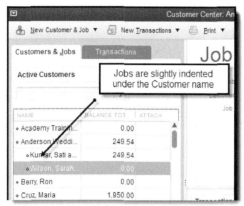

Figure 2-12 Customers & Jobs list

> **Did You Know?**
> To *Quick Add* a **Job** for a **Customer** on an Invoice or Sales Receipt, enter the Customer's name followed by a colon (the Customer name must already exist in the Customer list first). After the colon, enter the name of the job. QuickBooks will then prompt you to either *Quick Add* or *Set Up* the Job. If the *Customer* record already includes job information on its Job Info tab, you won't be able to use *Quick Add* to create a Job for the customer. In this case, you will need to create the job in the **Customers & Jobs** list before you begin entering sales.

Recording Sales

Now that you've set up your *Customers*, you're ready to begin entering sales. We will look at the *Sales Receipts* form first. Use this form when you receive a cash, check, or credit card payment at the time of the sale. We will also look at the *Invoice*, the other way to enter sales. Use this form when you record credit sales to customers.

Entering Sales Receipts

When customers pay at the time of the sale by cash, check, or credit card, create a **Sales Receipt** transaction.

COMPUTER PRACTICE

Step 1.　　Click the **Create Sales Receipts** icon in the *Customers* section on the *Home* page (see Figure 2-13). This opens the *Enter Sales Receipts* window (see Figure 2-14).

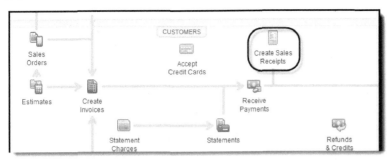

Figure 2-13 Selecting Create Sales Receipts icon on the Home page

Step 2.   Enter **Perez, Jerry** in the *Customer:Job* field (Figure 2-14) and press **Tab**.

> **Note:**
> Many forms display Customer Summary information in the *History Pane* on the right side
> of the form, which includes two tabs – one for *Customer* (also called *Name*) information
> and the other for *Transaction* information. Jerry Perez is a new Customer and therefore
> does not have any information or history to display.

Step 3.   When the *Customer:Job Not Found* warning window appears (see Figure 2-15), click
                Quick Add to add this new customer to the *Customer:Job* list. If you choose this option,
                you can edit the customer record later to add more details.

Figure 2-14 Sales Receipt form

> **Note:**
> **Quick Add** works on all your lists. Whenever you type a new name into any field on any
> form, QuickBooks prompts you to **Quick Add**, **Set Up**, or **Cancel** the name.
>
> **Tip:**
> If your customer is an individual (i.e., not a business), it's a good idea to enter the
> customer's last name first. This way, your **Customer:Job** list sorts by last name so it will be
> easier to find names in the list.

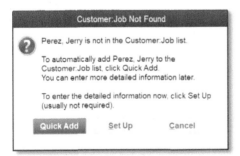

Figure 2-15 Use Quick Add to add new customers

Step 4.   Enter *San Jose* in the *Class* field and then press **Tab**.

QuickBooks uses Classes to separately track income and expenses for departments, functions, activities, locations, or profit centers. For more information on classes, see page 117. Note that if the Class has already been set up, it will appear in that field as you type it or in the drop-down menu.

Step 5.   In the *Template* field, **Custom Sales Receipt** is already selected. Press **Tab**.

You can create your own custom forms, as you'll learn in the section beginning on page 265.

Step 6.   Click on **Check** for payment method, then press **Tab**.

If you wanted to add a new payment method, you would click on the *More* button.

Step 7.   Enter *1/27/2019* in the *Date* field and then press **Tab** (see Figure 2-16).

Did You Know?

Whenever you enter a date in QuickBooks, you can use any of several shortcut keys to quickly change the date. For example, if you want to change the date to the first day of the year, press **y**. "Y" is the first letter of the word "year," so it's easy to remember this shortcut. The same works for the end of the year. Press **r** since that's the last letter of the word "year." The same works for "month" (**m** and **h**) and "week" (**w** and **k**). You can also use the **+** and **-** keys to move the date one day forward or back. All of these shortcuts will be relative to the date already entered in the date field. Finally, press **t** for "today" or the system date.

Step 8.   Enter *2019-1* in the *Sale No.* field.

The first time you enter a *Sales Receipt*, enter any number you want in the *Sale No.* field. QuickBooks will automatically number future Sales Receipts incrementally. You can change or reset the numbering at any time by overriding the *Sale No.* on a Sales Receipt.

Step 9.   Press **Tab** to skip the *Sold To* field.

QuickBooks automatically fills in this field, using the information in the *Invoice/Bill To* field of the customer record. Since you used *Quick Add* to add this customer, there is no address information. You could enter an address in the *Sold To* field by entering it directly on the sales form. When you record the Sales Receipt, QuickBooks will give you the option of adding the address in the *Invoice/Bill To* field of the customer record.

Step 10.   Enter *3459* in the *Check No.* field and then press **Tab**.

The number you enter here shows up on your printed deposit slips. If you were receiving a cash or credit card payment, you would leave this field blank.

Step 11.   Select **Outdoor Photo Session** from the *Item* drop-down list and then press **Tab**.

Step 12.   Press **Tab** to accept the default description *Outdoor Photo Session* in the *Description* column.

As soon as you enter an Item, QuickBooks enters the description, rate, and sales tax code using data from the Item that has already been set up.

Step 13.   In the *Tax* column, the *SRV* sales tax code is already selected. Press **Tab**.

Step 14.   Enter *3* in the *Qty.* (quantity) column and then press **Tab**.

Step 15.   Leave the default rate at *95.00* in the *Rate* column and then press **Tab**.

Step 16.   Press **Tab** to accept the calculated amount in the *Amount* column.

                After you enter the rate and press **Tab**, QuickBooks calculates the amount by multiplying
                the quantity by the rate. If you override the *Amount* field, QuickBooks calculates a new
                rate by dividing the amount by the quantity.

Step 17.   Select **Premium Photo Package** from the *Item* drop-down list and then press **Tab** three
                times.

Step 18.   Enter *2* in the *Qty.* column and press **Tab**.

Step 19.   Press **Tab** to accept the default rate of *85.00*.

                You can override this amount directly on the Sales Receipt if necessary. As with the line
                above, QuickBooks calculates the total in the *Amount* column and QuickBooks uses the
                default sales tax code *Tax,* which is set up for the *Premium Photo Package* Item.

Step 20.   Select **Thank you for your business.** from the *Customer Message* drop-down list.

                You can enter a message in the *Customer Message* field that will show on the printed
                Sales Receipt. This is typically a thank you message, but it can be whatever you want. If
                you type in a new message, *Quick Add* will prompt you to add your new message to the
                Customer Message list. If you want to edit an existing Customer Message, or if you want
                to remove a Customer Message from the list, select the *Lists* menu, then select *Customer
                & Vendor Profile Lists,* and then select *Customer Message List*.

Step 21.   Press **Tab** and enter *Santa Clara* in the *Tax* field, then **Tab** again to advance to the *Memo*
                field.

                The Sales Tax item shown in the *Tax* field determines the rate of tax to be charged on all
                Taxable Items shown on the form. Each line in the body of the Invoice is marked with a
                Sales Tax Code that determines the taxability or non-taxability of the item on that line
                (see Figure 2-16).

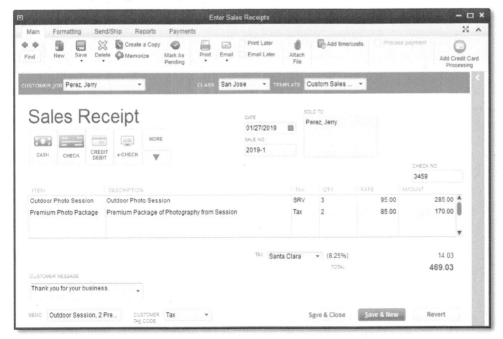

Figure 2-16 Completed Sales Receipt

Step 22.   Enter **Outdoor Session, 2 Premium Packages** in the Memo field.

Step 23.   Click **Save & Close** to record the sale.

QuickBooks does not record any of the information on any form until you save the transaction by clicking *Save, Save & Close, Save & New, Previous,* or *Next.*

> **Note:**
> If you prefer to use your keyboard over the mouse, you can use the *Alt* key in combination with other keys to execute commands. QuickBooks will tell you which key can be used in connection with the *Alt* key by underlining the letter in the command. For example, in the Sales Receipt window, the S is underlined on the *Save & New* button. You can save the receipt and move to a new Sales Receipt window by pressing the **Alt** key with the **S.**

Step 24.   QuickBooks displays the *Information Changed* dialog box (see Figure 2-17). This dialog box appears because you added the *Class* and *Tax Item* fields after creating the Customer using *Quick Add*. Click the **Yes** button.

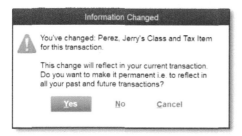

Figure 2-17 Information Changed dialog box

Undeposited Funds

The **Undeposited Funds** account is a special account that is automatically created by QuickBooks. The account works as a temporary holding account where QuickBooks tracks monies received from customers before the money is deposited in a bank account.

As illustrated in Figure 2-18, as you record Payments and Sales Receipts, QuickBooks gives you a choice between (Option 1) grouping all receipts into the **Undeposited Funds** account or (Option 2) immediately depositing the funds to one of your bank accounts.

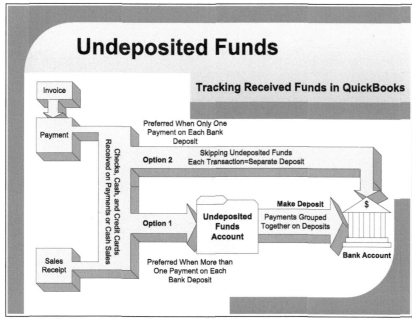

*Figure 2-18 All funds from sales transactions go through **Undeposited Funds** or directly to a bank account.*

There is a tradeoff here. When you use the **Undeposited Funds** account, you have to create a separate transaction (an additional step) to actually deposit money into a bank account. At first that might seem like extra work. However, when you skip the **Undeposited Funds** account, each sales transaction creates a separate deposit in your bank account.

Since it is most common to have multiple sales transactions per bank deposit, QuickBooks has a default preference setting that makes all Payments and Sales Receipts affect the balance in the **Undeposited Funds** account. Then when you actually make a deposit at the bank, you record a single deposit transaction in QuickBooks that empties the **Undeposited Funds** account into the bank account. This method makes it much easier to reconcile the bank account at the end of each month because the deposits on the bank statement will match the deposits in your QuickBooks bank account. Unless you only make one sale each day and your deposits include only the funds from that single sale, you will want to keep this default preference.

COMPUTER PRACTICE

You can modify the **Undeposited Funds** preference by following these steps:

Step 1.   Select the *Edit* menu and then select **Preferences**.

Step 2.   Select **Payments** on the left side of the *Preferences* window.

Step 3.   In the **Company Preferences** tab, the box next to **Use Undeposited Funds as a default deposit to account** is checked (see Figure 2-19).

> **Note:**
> Entering the spacebar on the keyboard when a checkbox is selected will either check or uncheck that checkbox.

Step 4.   If you prefer to deposit payments individually, uncheck the box next to **Use Undeposited Funds as a default deposit to account**. You will then have the option to select an account to deposit to in the *Sales Receipt* and *Receive Payment* windows.

Step 5.   Click **Cancel** to leave default setting for the use of **Undeposited Funds**.

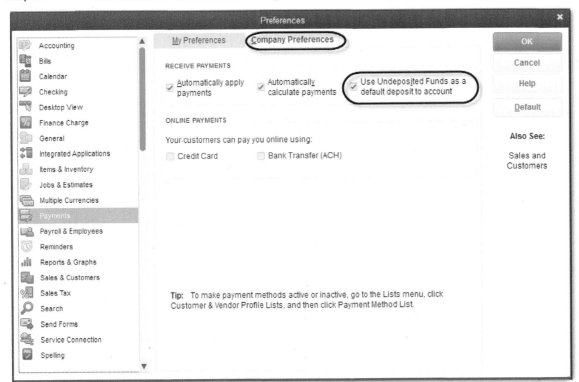

*Figure 2-19 Preference for Payments to go to **Undeposited Funds** or another account*

When this preference is off (see Figure 2-20), QuickBooks displays the **Deposit To** field on the **Receive Payments** and **Enter Sales Receipt** windows (see Figure 2-21).

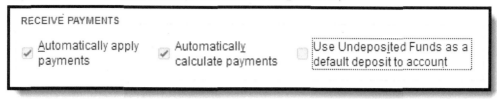

*Figure 2-20 Setting for **Undeposited Funds** on Company Preferences for Payments*

You must choose a destination account for the transaction from the *Deposit to* drop-down list.

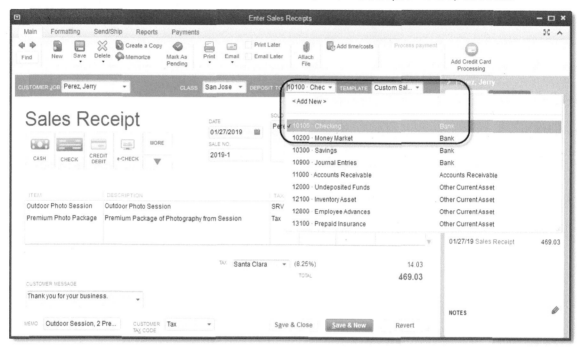

*Figure 2-21 The **Deposit To** field shows on Sales Receipts when the Undeposited Funds preference is off.*

Creating Invoices

Invoices are very similar to **Sales Receipts**. The only difference is that **Invoices** increase **Accounts Receivable** while **Sales Receipts** increase **Undeposited Funds** (or the specified bank account). You should use **Invoices** to record sales to your credit customers.

COMPUTER PRACTICE

To create an Invoice, follow these steps:

Step 1.   From the *Customer Center* select **Mason, Bob** from the *Customers & Jobs* list. Then select **Invoices** from the *New Transactions* drop-down list.

Alternatively, click the **Create Invoices** icon on the *Home page* and select **Mason, Bob** from the *Customer:Job* drop-down list. Press **Tab** (see Figure 2-22).

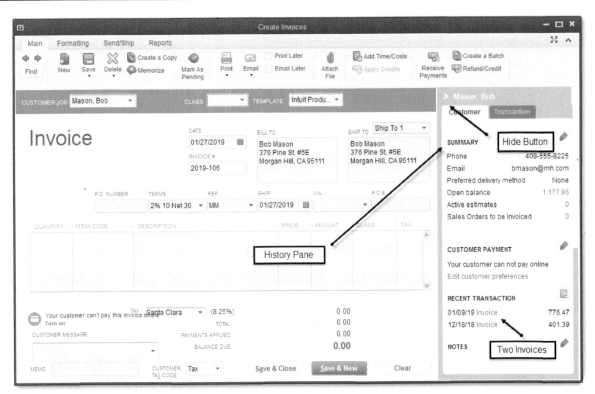

Figure 2-22 Invoice after Customer:Job field selected, before remaining data entered.

> **Did You Know?**
> When you type the first few characters of any field that has a list behind it, QuickBooks completes the field using a feature called *QuickFill*. QuickFill uses the first few characters you type to find the name in the list. If the name does not come up right away, keep typing until the correct name appears.

Step 2.   Notice that Bob Mason has two open invoices listed in the *History Pane*.

              The *History Pane* displays recent transactions and notes about a customer or a transaction on *Invoices* and *Sales Receipts*.

Step 3.   Click the **Hide** button to hide the *History Pane*. The Hide button is a right facing triangle on the top left edge of the *History Pane* (see Figure 2-22).

Step 4.   Click in the **Class** field. Enter an **s** in the *Class* field. QuickBooks will QuickFill the field with the full name *San Jose*. Then press **Tab**.

Step 5.   In the *Template* field, select **Academy Photo Service Invoice**. Press **Tab**.

Step 6.   Enter *1/28/2019* in the *Date* field and then press **Tab**.

Step 7.   Leave *2019-106* in the *Invoice* # field and then press **Tab**.

              The first time you enter an Invoice, enter any number you want in the *Invoice* # field. QuickBooks will automatically number future Invoices incrementally. You can change or reset the numbering at any time by overriding the number on a future Invoice.

Step 8.   Press **Tab** to accept the default information in the *Bill To* field.

QuickBooks automatically enters the address in this field, using the information in the *Invoice/Bill To* field of the customer record. If necessary, change the *Bill To* address by typing over the existing data.

Step 9.   Leave the *P.O. Number* field blank and then press **Tab**.

The P.O. (purchase order) number helps the customer identify your Invoice. When your customers use purchase orders, make sure you enter their P.O. numbers on Invoices you create for them.

> **Warning:**
> Make sure you enter the P.O. number if your customer uses purchase orders. Some customers may reject Invoices that do not reference a P.O. number.

Step 10.   In the *Terms* field, *2% 10 Net 30* is already selected. Press **Tab** to proceed to the next field.

The *Terms* field on the *Invoice* indicates the due date for the *Invoice* and how long your customer can take to pay you. The entry in this field determines how this Invoice is reported on Customers & Receivables reports such as the *A/R Aging Summary* and the *Collections Report*. To learn more about the *Terms List*, and how to set up terms, see page 259.

Step 11.   Enter the sale of 1 Hour for an **Indoor Photo Session** and 1 **Standard Photo Package** into the body of the *Invoice* as shown in Figure 2-23.

Step 12.   Select **Thank you for your business** from the *Customer Message* drop-down list and then press **Tab**.

Step 13.   **Santa Clara** in the *Tax* field is already selected. Press **Tab**.

As with Sales Receipts, QuickBooks selects the *Sales Tax Item* based on the defaults in *Sales Tax Preferences* or in the Customer's record.

Step 14.   Enter *1 Hr Indoor Session, 1 Standard Package* in the *Memo* field at the bottom of the form.

> **Tip:**
> If you intend to send statements to your customers, the *Memo* field is extremely important. QuickBooks allows you to show line item detail from your customer's Invoices. However, if you want your statements to be more concise, you can choose not to show the line item detail and show the text from the *Memo* field instead. The text from the *Memo* field will show along with the information in the *Invoice #,* and *Date* fields. The customer's statement will also show a three-letter code "INV" representing the Invoice transaction. Therefore, it is best to include information about the products or services you sold to the customer in the *Memo* field.

Step 15.   Compare your screen with the Invoice shown in Figure 2-23. If you see any errors, correct them. Otherwise, click **Save & Close** to record the Invoice.

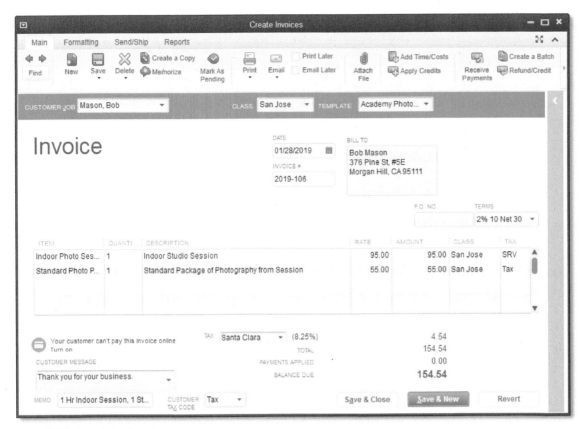

Figure 2-23 Completed Invoice

QuickBooks automatically tracks all of the accounting details behind this transaction so that all of your reports will immediately reflect the sale. For example, the Open Invoices report, the Profit & Loss Standard report, and the Balance Sheet Standard report will all change when you record this Invoice.

Adding Calculating Items to an Invoice

On the next Invoice, you'll learn how to include discounts and subtotals on an **Invoice**. Discounts and subtotals are called *Calculating Items*.

> **Key Term:**
> *Calculating Items* use the amount of the preceding line to calculate their amount. For example, if you enter 10% in the Discount item setup window and then enter the Discount item on an Invoice, QuickBooks will multiply the line just above the Discount item by 10% and enter that number, as a negative, in the **Amount** column for the discount line.

COMPUTER PRACTICE

To create an Invoice with a calculating item, follow these steps:

Step 1.   From the *Customer Center* select the **Wilson, Sarah and Michael** job for Anderson Wedding Planners from the *Customers & Jobs* list.

Step 2.   Select **Invoices** from the *New Transactions* drop-down list; or, press Ctrl+ I.

Step 3.   The *Wilson, Sarah and Michael* job for *Anderson Wedding Planners* is already selected. Press **Tab**.

Step 4.   Enter *San Jose* in the *Class* field and then press **Tab**.

Step 5.   The Academy Photo Service Invoice template in the *Template* drop-down list is already selected. Press **Tab**.

Step 6.   *1/28/2019* is already entered in the *Date* field. Press **Tab**.

Step 7.   Notice the *Invoice #* is automatically entered for you with the next Invoice number (i.e., **2019-107**). Press **Tab** to skip to the next field.

Step 8.   Press **Tab** to skip the *Bill To* field.

Step 9.   Press Tab twice to skip the *P.O. No. and the Terms* fields.

Step 10.   Enter the two items shown in Table 2-3 in the body of the **Invoice**.

Item	Description	Qty	Rate	Amount
Camera SR32	Supra Digital Camera SR32	3	695.99	2,087.97
Lens	Supra Zoom Lens	1	324.99	324.99

Table 2-3 Data for use in the Invoice

Step 11.   On the third line of the body of the Invoice, in the **Item** column, enter **Subtotal** to sum the previous two item lines, and press **Tab** twice.

               Notice that QuickBooks automatically calculates the sum of the first two lines on the Invoice.

Step 12.   Enter *Disc 10%* in the **Item** column and press **Tab**.

               The *Disc 10%* Item is a special Calculating Item that calculates a percentage of the preceding line on sales forms. Since it is a **Discount Item**, QuickBooks performs the calculation and enters a negative amount for your discount. This subtracts the discount from the total of the Invoice and adjusts sales tax accordingly.

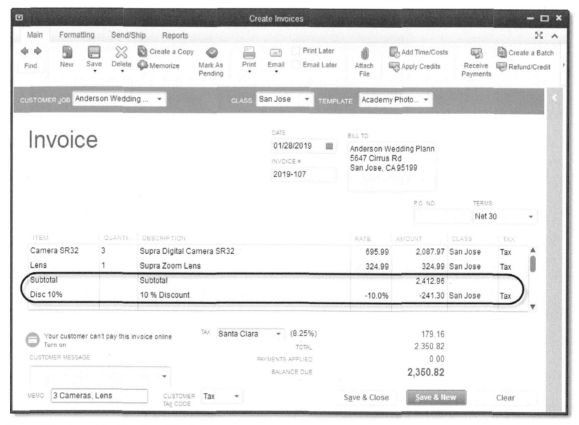

Figure 2-24 Completed Invoice with discount

Did You Know?

Shortcuts can help you save time when entering items on forms. You can copy, paste, insert or delete lines on an Invoice (or any other form). To copy a line, put your cursor in the line you wish to copy and press **Ctrl+Alt+Y** (or select the **Edit** menu, and then select **Copy Line**). To Paste, put your cursor in the line you wish to paste and press **Ctrl+Alt+V** (or select the **Edit** menu, and then select **Paste Line**). To insert a line between two existing lines, click on the line that you want to move down and press Ctrl+Insert (or select the **Edit** menu, and then select **Insert Line**). To delete a line, click on the line you want to delete and press Ctrl+Delete (or select the **Edit** menu, and then select **Delete Line**).

Step 13.   Leave the *Customer Message* field blank.

Step 14.   Leave **Santa Clara** in the *Tax* field. Also leave **Tax** in the *Customer Tax Code* field.

Step 15.   Enter *3 Cameras, Lens* in the *Memo* field.

Step 16.   Verify that your screen matches Figure 2-24. To save the Invoice, click **Save** in the *Main* tab at the top of the *Invoice.* Leave this window open for the next Computer Exercise.

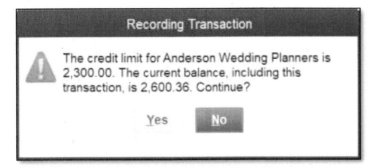

Figure 2-25 Recording Transaction window warns you about the customer's credit limit

Step 17.   If you see the *Recording Transaction* warning about Anderson Wedding Planners exceeding their credit limit (Figure 2-25), click **Yes**.

Open Invoices Report

Now that you've entered Invoices for your customers, QuickBooks' reports reflect the Invoices that are "open" and the "age" of each Invoice. The Open Invoices report is shown in Figure 2-27.

COMPUTER PRACTICE

Step 1.   Select the **Reports** tab at the top of the invoice, and click on **View Open Invoices** icon, as shown in Figure 2-26. Or, alternatively, select the **Reports** menu, select **Customers & Receivables**, and then select **Open Invoices**.

Step 2.   Set the *Dates* field at the top of the report to *1/31/2019* and then press **Tab**.

Step 3.   Verify that your Open Invoices report matches Figure 2-27.

Step 4.   Close the report by clicking the X in the upper right corner of the window.

Figure 2-26 View Reports Tab

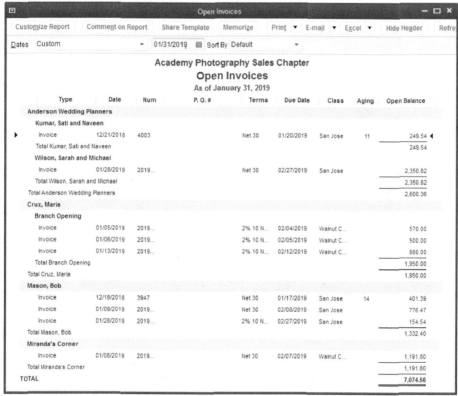

Figure 2-27 Open Invoices report

Step 5.   If you see a Memorize Report dialog box, click the No button (see Figure 2-28).

Step 6.   Click Save & Close to close the Invoice.

Step 7.   Close the *Customer Center*.

Figure 2-28 Memorize Reports window

> **Did You Know?**
> You can adjust the width of any column on the report by dragging the three small dots at the right of the column title to the left (narrowing the columns) or to the right (widening the columns).

Receiving Payments from Customers

Receiving Payments by Check

To record payments received from your customers and apply the payments to specific Invoices, follow these steps:

COMPUTER PRACTICE

Step 1.   Click **Receive Payments** on the *Home* page.

Step 2.   Select **Mason, Bob** in the *Received From* field of the *Receive Payments* window (see Figure 2-29). Once a customer is selected, the *Customer Payment* window shows the open Invoices for that specific customer. This section shows the dates of the Invoices, along with the Invoice number, original amount, the last date for the prompt payment discount, and the amount due.

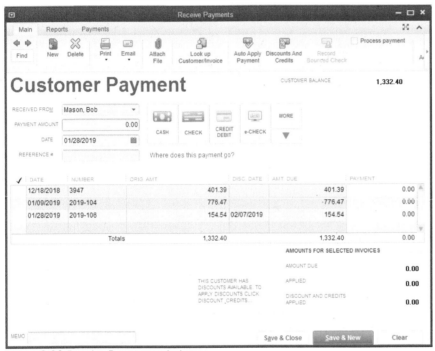

Figure 2-29 Receive Payments window

Step 3.   Enter 401.39 in the *Payment Amount* field and then press **Tab**.

Step 4.   Enter *1/28/2019* in the *Date* field and then press **Tab** (see Figure 2-30).

Step 5.   Select **Check** as *Pmt. Method* and then press **Tab**.

Step 6.   Enter *5256* in the *Check #* field and then press **Tab**.

Step 7.   Confirm that **Invoice #3947** is already checked.

> **Note:**
> **When One Payment Applies to More than One Invoice**
> You can apply one check from a customer to multiple Invoices. When you receive payments, you can override the amounts in the **Payment** column to apply the payment to Invoices in whatever combination is necessary.

When You Don't Want to Apply the Entire Amount of the Payment

If you don't want to apply the entire amount of the customer's check to the Invoice, reduce the amount in the **Payment** column. You can apply the remaining balance of the customer's check to additional Invoices. If you do not, QuickBooks will give you a choice to either hold the remaining balance as a credit for the customer or refund the amount to the customer.

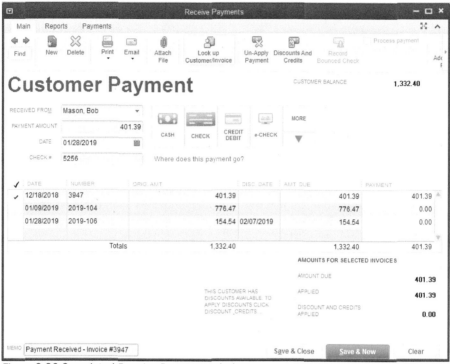

Figure 2-30 Completed Receive Payments window

Step 8.   Verify that the **Amount Due** and **Payment** columns for the selected invoice both show *$401.39*.

The checkmark to the left of the **Date** column indicates the Invoice to which QuickBooks will apply the payment. QuickBooks automatically selected this Invoice because the amount of the customer's check is the same as the unpaid amount of the Invoice (see page 57). If applicable, you can deselect the Invoice by clicking on the checkmark. You can then select another Invoice from the list.

Step 9.   Enter *Payment Received - Invoice #3947* in the *Memo* field and then press **Tab**.

When entering a memo, type **Payment Received** followed by the Invoice number. Memos do not affect the application of payments to specific Invoices, but they are helpful in two very important ways. First, if you send your customers statements, only the information in the *Check #, Date,* and *Memo* fields will show on statements, along with a three-letter code (PMT), representing the Payment transaction. Also, if you ever have to go back to the transaction and verify that you've applied the payment to the correct Invoice(s), you'll be able to look at the *Memo* field to see the Invoice(s) to which you *should* have applied the payments.

Step 10.   Verify that your screen matches Figure 2-30. If you see errors, correct them.

Step 11.   Click **Save & Close** to record the Payment transaction.

Handling Partial Payments

In the last example, Bob Mason paid Invoice #3947 in full. However, if a customer pays only a portion of an Invoice, you should record the payment just as you did in the last example except that the amount would be less than the full amount due on any of the open Invoices. Apply the payment to the appropriate Invoice. QuickBooks will give the option to either leave the Invoice open or write off the unpaid amount. By clicking the *View Customer Contact Information* button, QuickBooks displays the *Edit Customer* window that allows you to see the customer's contact information. This is helpful if you need to contact the customer to ask a question about the partial payment (see Figure 2-31).

Figure 2-31 Partial Payment of Invoice

If you chose to leave the underpayment, the next time you use the **Receive Payments** function for that customer, the Invoice will show the remaining amount due. You can record additional payments to the Invoice in the same way as before.

Receiving Payments by Credit Card

The next example shows that Maria Cruz paid off the amount owing on the Branch Opening job. Maria Cruz used a credit card to pay her invoices, so this example shows how to receive credit card payments.

COMPUTER PRACTICE

Step 1.   From the *Customer Center* select the **Cruz, Maria:Branch Opening** job from the *Customers & Jobs* list. Select **Receive Payments** from the *New Transactions* drop-down list.

Step 2.   Enter data into the *Amount,* and *Date* fields as shown in Figure 2-33.

Step 3.   Select the **Credit Debit** button as payment method. The *Enter Card Information* window opens (see Figure 2-32).

Step 4.   Enter **Visa** in the *Payment* field.

Step 5.   Enter **1234-1234-1234-1234** in the Card Number field. QuickBooks shows the credit card number with some x's for security purposes.

Step 6.   Enter *10/2020* as *Exp Date* as shown in (See Figure 2-32). Click **Done** when finished.

Figure 2-32 Credit Card Information

Step 7.   Leave the *Reference#* field blank. Press **Tab**.

Step 8.   Enter *Payment Received - 3 Invoices* in the *Memo* field.

Step 9.   Verify that your screen matches Figure 2-33 and click **Save & Close**. If the Merchant Account Service Message appears, click the **Not Now** button.

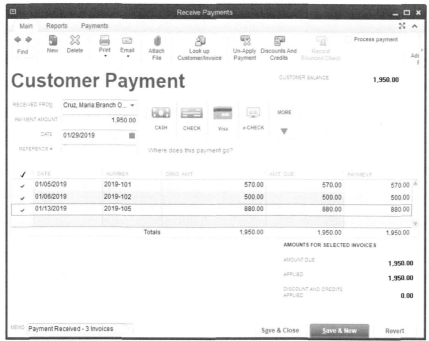

Figure 2-33 Customer Payment by Credit Card

> **Note:**
> If you want to keep a record of the customer's credit card information, including card
> number, expiration date, billing address and billing zip code, enter credit card information
> into the *Payment Settings* tab of the Customer or Job record before you process the
> payment through the Receive Payments window. When you enter the customer or job
> name, QuickBooks will enter the credit card information automatically.

Where Do the Payments Go?

Recall the earlier discussion about **Undeposited Funds** beginning on page 45. Unless you turned off
"Use **Undeposited Funds** as a default deposit to account" preference, QuickBooks does not increase
your bank balance when you receive payments. Instead, when you record a payment transaction as
shown above, QuickBooks reduces the balance in **Accounts Receivable** and increases the balance in
Undeposited Funds. In order to have your payments show up in your bank account (and reduce
Undeposited Funds), you must **Make Deposits.** See the section called *Making Bank Deposits* beginning
on page 62.

> **The accounting behind the scenes:**
> Payments increase (debit) **Undeposited Funds** (or a bank/other current asset account)
> and decrease (credit) **Accounts Receivable.**

Preferences for Applying Payments

As soon as you enter the customer name at the top of the *Receive Payments* window and press **Tab**,
QuickBooks displays all of the open Invoices for that customer in the lower section of the window. See
Figure 2-34.

✓	DATE	NUMBER	ORIG. AMT.	AMT. DUE	PAYMENT
✓	01/05/2019	2019-101	570.00	570.00	570.00
	01/06/2019	2019-102	500.00	500.00	0.00
	01/13/2019	2019-105	880.00	880.00	0.00
		Totals	1,950.00	1,950.00	570.00

Figure 2-34 Payment automatically applied to the oldest Invoice

Then, when you enter the payment amount, QuickBooks looks at all of the open Invoices for that customer. If it finds an amount due on an open Invoice that is the exact amount of the payment, it matches the payment with that Invoice. If there is no such match, it applies the payment to the *oldest* Invoice first and continues applying to the next oldest until the payment is completely applied. If this auto application of payments results in a partially paid Invoice, QuickBooks holds the balance on that Invoice open for the unpaid amount. This is a feature called *Automatically Apply Payments*.

If you select an *Invoice* in the *Receive Payments* form before entering an *Amount*, QuickBooks calculates the sum of the selected Invoice(s) and enters that sum into the *Payment Amount* field. This feature is called *Automatically Calculate Payments*.

COMPUTER PRACTICE

To modify the Automatically Apply Payments and Automatically Calculate Payments settings, change the Company Preferences for Payments.

Follow these steps:

Step 1.   Select the *Edit* menu and then select **Preferences**.

Step 2.   Select the **Payments** icon from the preference category in the list on the left. Then click the **Company Preferences** tab (see Figure 2-35).

Step 3.   Check or uncheck the *Automatically apply payments* box to change it. For now, leave it checked.

With this feature disabled, in the Receive Payments window you will have to click Auto Apply Payment for each payment you process, or you will have to manually apply payments to Invoices by clicking in the column to the left of the Invoice and modifying the amount in the Payment column as necessary.

Step 4.   You can change the *Automatically calculate payments* box by checking or unchecking it. For now, leave it checked.

When this preference is on, QuickBooks will automatically calculate the payment received from the customer in the Amount field of the Receive Payments window as you select the Invoices. When this preference is off, QuickBooks does not automatically calculate payments.

Step 5.   Click OK.

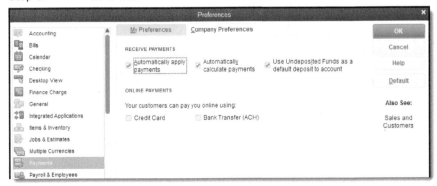

Figure 2-35 Payments Company Preferences

Recording Customer Discounts

What if your customer takes advantage of the discount you offer on your Invoice? In the next example, the payment you receive is less than the face amount of the Invoice because the customer took advantage of the 2% 10 Net 30 discount terms that Academy Photography offers.

COMPUTER PRACTICE

Follow these steps to record a payment on which the customer took a discount:

Step 1.   From the *Customer Center* select **Mason, Bob** from the *Customers & Jobs* list. Then select **Receive Payments** from the *New Transactions* drop-down list.

Step 2.   Enter all the customer payment information as shown in Figure 2-36. The customer is paying for Invoice #2019-106 after taking the discount allowed by the terms.

Figure 2-36 Top portion of the Receive Payments window

Step 3.   The bottom portion of the *Receive Payments* window (see Figure 2-37) displays the open Invoices for this customer. If the customer is eligible for discounts, a message will appear as shown just below the open Invoices. The **Disc. Date** column shows the date through which the customer is eligible to take a discount.

If the amount paid is not an exact match with any Invoice balance, QuickBooks will automatically apply the payment to the oldest Invoices. Here, Invoice #2019-104 is automatically selected since the amount $151.45 does not match any open invoices. The underpayment is also displayed. We'll fix this in the next step.

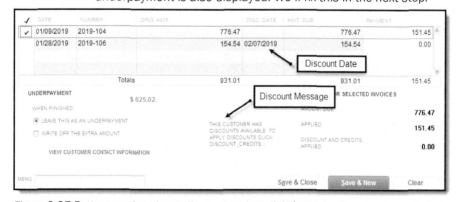

Figure 2-37 Bottom portion shows discount and credit information box, Invoice selected and Underpayment

> **Note:**
> In the *Receive Payments* window the Underpayment amount is displayed with options to **Leave this as an underpayment** or **Write off the extra amount**. These options are displayed when the payment is less than the amount due on the selected Invoices. Similarly, Overpayment amounts are displayed with options to **Leave the credit to be used later** or **Refund the amount to the customer** when the payment is more than the amount due on the selected Invoices.
>
> **Tip:**
> If the payment amount doesn't add up exactly to the discounted amount, you'll need to make a choice. If the payment is too high, you could reduce the amount of the discount by lowering the amount in the *Discounts and Credits* window. If the payment is too low, you could raise the amount in the *Discounts and Credits* window. If the payment amount is significantly different, you can apply the amount of the payment and then send a Statement to the customer showing the balance due (if the payment is too low) or send a refund to the customer (if the payment is too high).

Step 4.   Click in the column to the left of Invoice **#2019-104** to uncheck it and then click to check Invoice **#2019-106** (see Figure 2-38). This moves the payment so that it now applies to Invoice #2019-106. Make sure to uncheck #2019-104 before checking #2019-106, or you will see a Warning message.

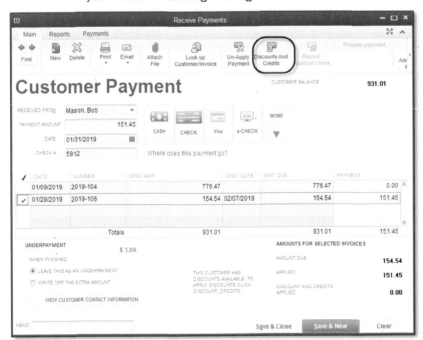

Figure 2-38 Payment is now applied to the correct Invoice

Step 5.   Since the customer took advantage of the 2% 10 Net 30 terms that Academy Photography offered him, you'll need to reduce the amount due by 2%. To apply the discount to this Invoice, click **Discount and Credits** button at the top of the *Receive Payments* window.

Step 6.   QuickBooks calculates and enters a suggested discount based on the terms on the customer's Invoice as shown in Figure 2-39. You can override this amount if necessary. Press **Tab**.

Figure 2-39 Discounts and Credits window

Step 7.   Select **46000 Sales Discounts** in *the Discount Account* field. Press **Tab**.

The *Discount Account* field is where you assign an account that tracks the discounts you give to your customers.

Step 8.   Enter *San Jose* in the *Discount Class* field and then click **Done**.

Since Academy Photography uses class tracking, you will need to enter the appropriate class in this field. If you do not classify this transaction, QuickBooks will display the amount in an *Unclassified* column on the **Profit & Loss by Class** report. Refer to the Invoice you are discounting to determine the Class. Academy Photography used the *San Jose* Class when recording Invoice 2019-106.

After recording the discount, the *Receive Payments* window reflects Total Discount and Credits Applied at the bottom of the Receive Payments window.

Figure 2-40 Receive Payments window after (recording the discount)

Step 9.   Verify that your screen matches Figure 2-40.

Step 10.   Click **Save & Close** to record the transaction.

Step 11.   Close the Customer Center.

Making Bank Deposits

As you record payments from customers using the **Enter Sales Receipts** and **Receive Payments** windows, by default these payments are posted to a special QuickBooks account called **Undeposited Funds**. To deposit these payments into your bank account, you will need to record a *Deposit* transaction. Deposit transactions move money from the **Undeposited Funds** account to the appropriate bank account. As you will see in this section, QuickBooks provides a special window (the *Payments to Deposit* window) to help you identify which payments are included on each deposit.

Since you will probably receive payments from your customers in several different ways (checks, cash, and credit cards), record deposits of each payment type separately. This way, your deposits in QuickBooks will match how your bank posts these transaction. This will make bank reconciliations much easier. Start with the checks and cash, followed by the VISA, MasterCard and Discover receipts and then the American Express receipts.

Depositing Checks and Cash

COMPUTER PRACTICE

To enter a deposit, follow these steps:

Step 1.   The Record Deposits Icon on the Home page shows you that you have payments stored in Undepostied Funds. (see Figure 2-41). From the *Home* page select **Record Deposits**.

Figure 2-41 Record Deposits Icon on the Home page showing the number of deposits

Step 2.   Since you have payments stored in the **Undeposited Funds** account, QuickBooks displays the *Payments to Deposit* window (see Figure 2-42).

Figure 2-42 Select the payments to deposit

Step 3.   Select **Cash and Check** from the *View payment method type* drop-down list (see Figure 2-43).

Since the checks and cash you deposit in your bank account will post to your account separately from credit card receipts, it is best to filter the report by payment type and then create a separate deposit for each payment type. Depending on your merchant service, you will probably need to create a single deposit for your VISA, MasterCard and Discover receipts. Most merchant services combine MasterCard, VISA and Discover receipts when they credit your bank account.

> **Tip:**
> Since you can filter the *Payments to Deposit* window by only one payment method at a time, using a single *Payment Method* for *Checks* and *Cash* will allow you to filter for both payment methods on this window. Depending on your merchant service, you may want to create a single *Payment Method* for MasterCard, VISA and Discover as well. To edit *Payment Methods* select the *Lists* menu, then select *Customer & Vendor Profile Lists*, and then select *Payment Method List*. Once the *Payment Method List* window opens, select the Payment Method and select *Edit Payment Method* from the *Payment Method* menu.

Figure 2-43 Cash and Check payments

Step 4. The Payments to Deposit window now only shows payments received through Cash and Check (see Figure 2-44). Click **Select All** to select all of the cash and check deposits Click **OK**.

A checkmark in the column on the left indicates that QuickBooks will include the payment in the deposit.

Figure 2-44 Select the payments to deposit

Step 5.   In the *Make Deposits* window, the **Checking** account is already selected in the *Deposit To* field (see Figure 2-45). The payments will be deposited to this bank account. Press **Tab**.

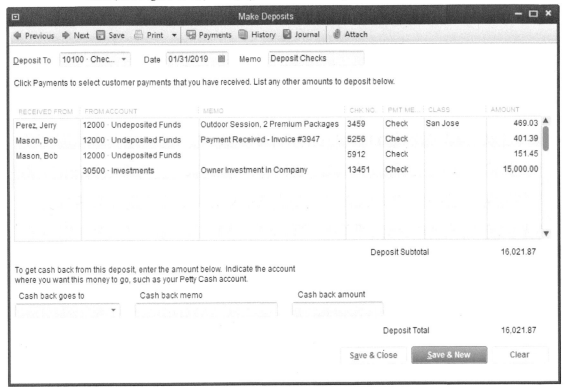

Figure 2-45 Make Deposits window

Step 6.   Enter *1/31/2019* if it does not already display in the *Date* field and press **Tab**.

Step 7.   Enter **Deposit Checks** in the *Memo* field and press **Tab**.

Step 8.   On this deposit, we will add a non-sales-related item. Occasionally, you will have deposits that are not linked to other transactions in QuickBooks, which can be entered directly in the *Make Deposits* window. Complete the following steps:

    a)   On the first blank line, enter **Investments** in the *From Account* column and press **Tab**. The *From Account* column on the *Make Deposits* window shows the account that the deposit is coming "from".

    b)   Enter **Owner Investment in Company** in the *Memo* column and press **Tab**.

    c)   Enter *13451* in the *Chk No.* column and press **Tab**.

    d)   Enter **Check** in the *Pmt Meth.* column and press **Tab**.

    e)   Press **Tab** to skip the *Class* column.

    f)   Enter *15,000.00* in the *Amount* column.

Step 9.   If you wish to print the deposit slip, click **Print** on the *Make Deposits* window. Click **Save & Close** to record the deposit.

> **The accounting behind the scenes:**
> In the deposit transaction (Figure 2-45) the checking account will increase (with a debit) by the total deposit ($16,021.87). All of the customer checks are coming from the **Undeposited Funds** account, and the owner investment is coming from the **Investments** account. The customer checks will decrease (credit) the balance in **Undeposited Funds** and the loan from the owner will increase (credit) the balance in the **Investments** account.

Holding Cash Back from Deposits

If you hold cash back when you make your deposits to the bank, fill in the bottom part of the deposit slip indicating the account to which you want to post the cash (see Figure 2-46).

Figure 2-46 The bottom of the deposit slip deals with cash back

There are two ways you might use the cash back section of the deposit:

1. If you're splitting the deposit between two different bank accounts, you could enter the other bank account and amount here. For example, if you send part of the funds from the deposit to the Money Market account, you could enter **Money Market** in the *Cash back goes to* field and the amount in the *Cash back amount* field.

2. If you routinely hold back funds from your deposits and use them for several different purchases, you may want to set up a new QuickBooks bank account called **Petty Cash** and enter that account in the *Cash back goes to* field. The Petty Cash account is not really a bank account, but it's an account where you can track all your cash expenditures.

> **Tip:**
> It's not a good idea to hold cash back from deposits as "pocket money". If your business is a Sole Proprietorship, it's better to write a separate check (or ATM withdrawal) and then code it to **Owner's Draw**. This is a much cleaner way to track the money you take out for personal use. Discuss this with your QuickBooks ProAdvisor, or with your accountant.

Printing Deposit Slips

QuickBooks can print deposit slips on preprinted deposit slips.

> **DO NOT PERFORM THESE STEPS. THEY ARE FOR REFERENCE ONLY.**

To print on preprinted deposit slips, follow these steps:

1. Display the most recent deposit transaction by selecting the *Banking* menu and then selecting **Make Deposits.**

    Click **Cancel** if you see the *Payments to Deposit* window. Then click the **Previous** button on the *Make Deposits* window. Alternatively, you could double click the deposit transaction from the checking account register window.

2. Click **Print** on the *Make Deposits* window (see Figure 2-47).

3. Select **Deposit slip and deposit summary** on the window shown in Figure 2-48 and click **OK**.

    Normally, you would load the preprinted deposit slips into the printer before printing. However, if you do not have a deposit slip print the deposit on blank paper.

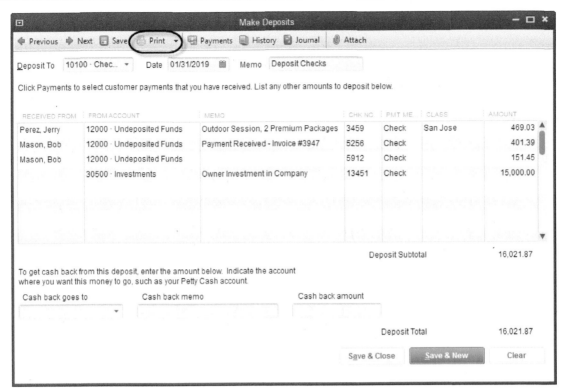

Figure 2-47 Printing a deposit

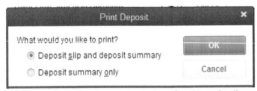

Figure 2-48 Print Deposit window for deposit slips

4.   Check the settings on the Print Deposit Slips window shown in Figure 2-49.

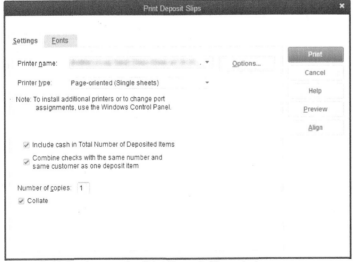

Figure 2-49 Settings on the Print Deposit Slips window

5.   Select your printer in the *Printer name* field.

6.   Click **Print** to print the deposit slip (see Figure 2-50).

7.   Click **Save & Close** to save the Deposit.

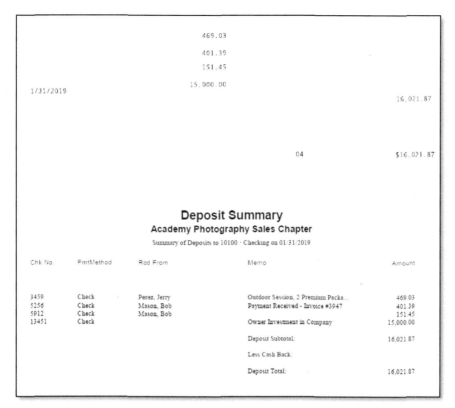

Figure 2-50 Deposit slip and deposit summary

Depositing Credit Card Payments

As mentioned previously, to ensure that your bank reconciliations go smoothly, you should always deposit your checks and cash separately from your credit card payments.

COMPUTER PRACTICE

Step 1.   Select the **Banking** menu, and then select **Make Deposits**. The *Payments to Deposit* window opens.

Step 2.   Select **MasterCard, Visa, Discover** from the *View payment method type* drop-down list (see Figure 2-51).

Step 3.   Click in the left column on the line to select the payment to deposit. Then click **OK**. The *Make Deposits* window opens.

Figure 2-51 Payments to Deposit window

Step 4.   The **Checking** account is already selected in the *Deposit To* field. Press **Tab**.

Step 5.   Enter *1/31/2019* if it is not already entered in the *Date* field. Press **Tab**.

Step 6.   Enter *Deposit Visa* in the *Memo* field.

As stated earlier, make sure you group together receipts in a way that agrees with the actual deposits made to your bank. This is a critical step in making your bank reconciliation process go smoothly.

Step 7.   On the first blank line of the deposit slip, enter **Bankcard Fees** in the **From Account** column and then press **Tab**.

You only need to create this line if your credit card processing company (or your bank) charges a discount fee on each credit card deposit rather than monthly.

Step 8.   Enter *Discount Fee* in the **Memo** column and then press **Tab**.

Step 9.   Press **Tab** to skip the **Chk No.** column.

Step 10.   Enter *Visa* in the **Pmt Meth.** column and then press **Tab**.

Step 11.   Enter *Walnut Creek* in the *Class* column and then press **Tab**.

Step 12.   You can use the QuickMath feature to enter the discount fee directly on the **Make Deposits** window. Enter *1950.00 * -.02* in the *Amount* column and press **Enter**.

QuickMath is a feature that helps you add, subtract, multiply, or divide in any QuickBooks Amount field. When you enter the first number (1950.00), it shows normally in the *Amount* column. Then when you enter the * (asterisk key or Shift+8), QuickMath shows a small adding machine tape on your screen (see Figure 2-52). Continue typing your formula for recording the discount fee. If the discount is 2%, enter *-.02* (minus point zero two) and press *Enter*. The result of the calculation shows in the *Amount* column (-39.00). **The minus sign makes the result a negative number and reduces the amount of your deposit.** This also increases (debits) your **Bankcard Fees** expense account.

Step 13.   Press **Tab** to have the total of the deposit updated automatically.

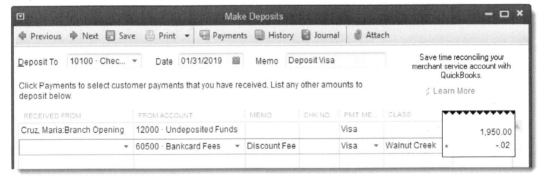

Figure 2-52 QuickMath makes an adding machine tape appear

Step 14.   Verify that your screen matches Figure 2-53. Click **Save & Close**.

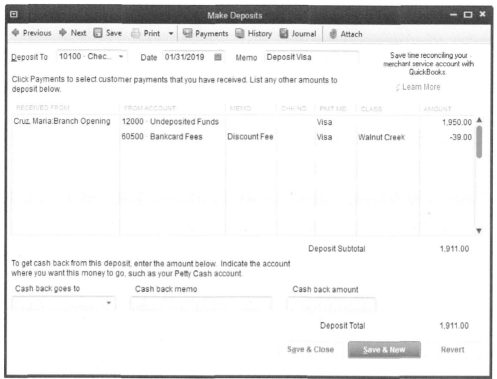

Figure 2-53 Make Deposits window after a credit card deposit

Now that you have entered your deposits, the checking account register shows each deposit and the updated balance in the account.

COMPUTER PRACTICE

To see the detail of a deposit, follow these steps:

Step 1.   Click the **Chart of Accounts** icon on the *Home* page.

Step 2.   Double click on the **Checking** account in the *Chart of Accounts* window.

Step 3.   Scroll up until you see the two deposit transactions shown in Figure 2-54.

Step 4.   Close the *Checking* register and *Chart of Accounts*.

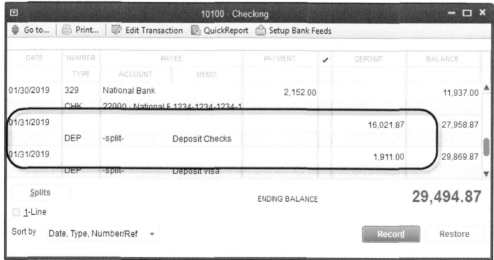

Figure 2-54 Checking register after entering deposits

Income Tracker

The **Income Tracker** provides you with a fast way to see the status of your unbilled and unpaid sales transactions all from one location. It also provides features to improve billing/collections as well as create new sales transactions. You can access the **Income Tracker** from the icon in the *Customer Center* (see Figure 2-55). Alternatively, use the *Customer Menu* or the Icon Bar.

Figure 2-55 Income Tracker icon in Customer Center

From the **Income Tracker** you can:

- See all of your unbilled and unpaid sales transactions
- Select just one category by clicking on the colored bar or using filters
- Right click on any sales transaction for options to view or edit that transaction, *Customer*, or *Job*
- Print or send a copy of a sales transaction by email
- Convert an *Estimate* or *Sales Order* into an *Invoice*
- Sort the list by clicking on any column heading
- Print a group of sales transactions in a batch
- Create new *Customer* transactions

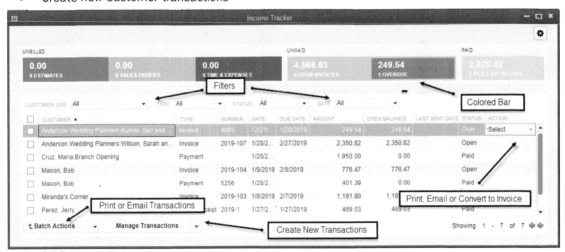

Figure 2-56 Income Tracker. Your screen may vary.

COMPUTER PRACTICE

To use the **Income Tracker** to process a transaction:

Step 1.   Click the **Income Tracker** icon on the *Icon Bar* (Figure 2-57).

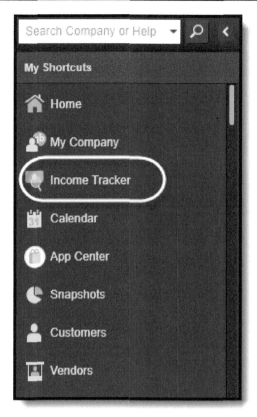

Figure 2-57 Income Tracker on Icon Bar

Step 2.   Check **Miranda's Corner,** on the left side of the **Income Tracker.**

Step 3.   Click on the drop-down arrow in the *Action* column for **Miranda's** Corner, and choose **Receive Payment.**

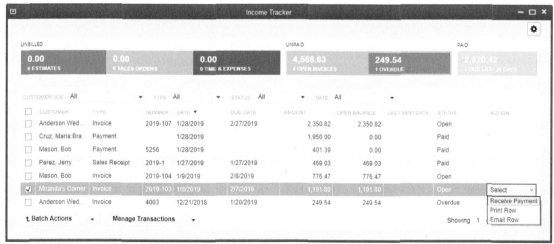

Figure 2-58 Receive Payment in Income Tracker. Your screen may vary.

Step 4.   **Receive Payment** for $1,191.80.

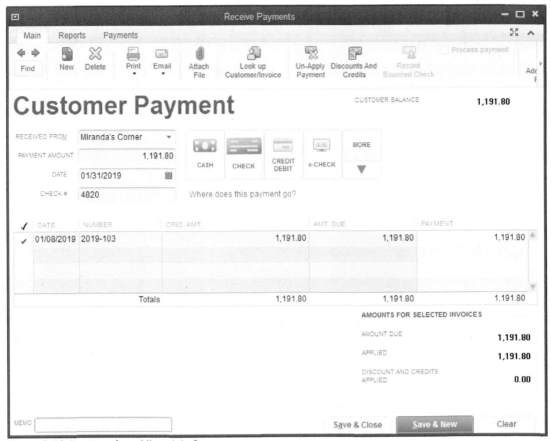

Figure 2-59 Payment from Miranda's Corner

Step 5.   Verify that your screen matches Figure 2-59.

Step 6.   Click **Save & Close** to record the transaction.

Step 7.   Close **Income Tracker.**

Review Questions

Comprehension Questions

1. When you make a sale to a customer who pays at the time of the sale, either by check or by credit card, which type of form should you use in QuickBooks to record the transaction?

2. Explain how the **Undeposited Funds** account works and why it is best to use the option, **Use Undeposited Funds as a default deposit to account**, as a *Payments* preference.

3. How does the *Automatically Apply Payments* feature work?

4. How does the *Automatically Calculate Payments* feature work?

Multiple Choice

Select the best answer(s) for each of the following:

1. In the *New Customer* window, you find everything except:
   a) Customer Name.
   b) Customer Invoice/Bill To and Ship To address.
   c) Customer active/inactive status.
   d) Year-to-date sales information.

2. You should record a Sales Receipt when the customer pays:
   a) By cash, check, or credit card at the time of sale.
   b) By cash, check, or credit card at the end of the month.
   c) Sales tax on the purchase.
   d) For the order upon receipt of Invoice.

3. Which statement is false?
   a) Invoices are very similar to the Sales Receipt form.
   b) Invoices decrease Accounts Receivable.
   c) Sales Receipts have no effect on Accounts Receivables.
   d) Invoices should be created when customers are going to pay after the date of the initial sale.

4. You may specify payment Terms on the *New Customer* window; however:
   a) The payment Terms will only show on Sales Receipt transactions.
   b) The Terms can only be changed once a year.
   c) The sales representative must be informed.
   d) You are also permitted to override the Terms on each sale.

5. Your company has just accepted a payment for an Invoice. What should you do in QuickBooks to record this payment?
   a) Open the Invoice by clicking the *Invoices* icon on the *Home* page.
   b) Create a Sales Receipt by clicking the *Sales Receipt* icon on the *Home* page.
   c) Make a deposit by clicking the *Record Deposits* icon on the *Home* page.
   d) Receive the payment by clicking the *Receive Payments* icon on the *Home* page.

6. Which statement is false?
   a) Many customers reject Invoices that do not reference a P.O. (purchase order) number.
   b) The P.O. number helps the customer identify your Invoice.
   c) The P.O. number is required on all Invoices.
   d) The P.O. number is generated by the customer's accounting system.

7. To record a deposit in QuickBooks:
   a) Make a separate deposit that includes both Checks and Cash receipts.
   b) Make a separate deposit that includes both VISA and MasterCard receipts.
   c) Make a separate deposit that includes American Express receipts.
   d) All of the above.

8. Your company has just received an order from a customer who will pay within 30 days. How should you record this transaction in QuickBooks?
   a) Create an invoice by clicking the *Create Invoices* button on the *Home* page.
   b) Create a sales receipt by clicking the *Sales Receipt* button on the *Home* page.
   c) Make a deposit by clicking the *Record Deposits* button on the *Home* page.
   d) Receive the payment by clicking the *Receive Payment* button on the *Home* page.

9. When you make a deposit, all of the following are true except:

    a)   You must print a deposit slip in order to process a deposit.

    b)   A "Make Deposit" transaction typically transfers money from **Undeposited Funds** into your bank account.

    c)   You should separate your deposits by payment type.

    d)   You should create deposits so that they match exactly with the deposits on your bank statement.

10. Which statement is true regarding *Calculating Items* ?

    a)   *Calculating Items* cannot be used on *Invoices* because the total is calculated automatically.

    b)   A *Calculating Item* always calculates the amount of all the lines above it.

    c)   It is best to avoid using *Calculating Items* to apply a discount.

    d)   A *Calculating Item* uses the amount of the preceding line to calculate its amount.

11. When creating a customer record, which statement is false?

    a)   After you enter a name in the *Customer Name* field of the *New Customer* window, you cannot use that name in any of the other name lists in QuickBooks.

    b)   The credit limit can be added in the new customer window.

    c)   A sales rep must be selected when creating a new customer.

    d)   When you sell to and purchase from the same company, you should create two records, one in the Vendor List, and one in the Customer: Job List.

12. When receiving payments from customers to whom you have sent invoices, you must:

    a)   Receive the payment in full. Partial payments cannot be accepted in QuickBooks.

    b)   Enter them directly into the checking account register.

    c)   Enter the payment into the receive payments window and check off the appropriate invoice(s) to which the payment applies.

    d)   Delete the invoice so it does not show on the customer's open records.

13. You need to calculate the amount of a bankcard fee by multiplying the amount of the received payments by -1%. What useful QuickBooks feature could you use?

    a)   Calculating Items

    b)   QuickMath

    c)   Quick Add

    d)   The *Fees* button on the bottom of the *Make Deposit* window

14. The Undeposited Funds account tracks:

    a)   Bad debts.

    b)   Funds that have been received but not deposited.

    c)   Funds that have not been received or deposited.

    d)   All company sales from the point an invoice is created until it is deposited in the bank.

15. After entering an existing customer in the *Customer:Job* field of an invoice, a *Customer:Job Not Found* dialog box opens to say the customer is not on the *Customer List*. What should you do?

    a)   Click the *Quick Add* button to add the customer to the *Customer List*.

    b)   Click the *Set Up* button to enter the customer's information in a *New Customer* window.

    c)   Click *Cancel* to check the name you entered in the *Customer:Job* field for typos or other errors.

    d)   None of the above.

Completion Statements

1. A new customer can be added to the customer list without opening the *New Customer* window by clicking _____ _____ after entering a new customer name on a sales form.

2. When you create a Sales Receipt, QuickBooks increases (with a debit) a(n) _____ account or the _____ _____ account.

3. Discounts and subtotals are called _____ Items.

4. Receiving payments reduces the balance in _____ _____ and increases the balance in the **Undeposited Funds** or a bank account.

5. _____ helps you add, subtract, multiply or divide numbers in an *Amount* field.

Sales Problem 1

Restore the Sales-18Problem1.QBM file. The password to access this file is **Sleeter18**.

1. Enter your own name and address information into the *Customer Center*. Then print the Customer List by selecting the *Reports* menu, **List**, and then **Customer Contact List**.

2. Enter a Sales Receipt using the data in Table 2-4. The payment will be automatically grouped with other payments in **Undeposited Funds** account. You'll need to create the customer record using Quick Add, or by setting it up in the list before adding the sale. Print the sale on blank paper.

Field	Data
Customer Name	Pavlovich, Anna
Class	Walnut Creek
Date	1/24/2019
Sale No.	2019-1
Sold To	Anna Pavlovich 512 SW Chestnut St. Walnut Creek, CA 94599
Check No	211
Payment Method	Check
Item	Camera SR32, Qty 4
Sales Tax	Contra Costa (8.25%) – Auto Calculates
Customer Tax Code	Tax
Memo	4 Cameras

Table 2-4 Use this data for a Sales Receipt in Step 2

3. Enter an Invoice using the data in Table 2-5. Print the Invoice on blank paper.

Field	Data
Customer Name	Berry, Ron
Class	Walnut Creek
Custom Template	Academy Photo Service Invoice
Date	1/26/2019
Invoice #	2019-106
Bill To	Ron Berry 345 Cherry Lane Walnut Creek, CA 94599
PO No.	842-5028
Terms	Net 30
Item	Indoor Photo Session, Qty 3, $95/hour (SRV tax code)
Item	Retouching, Qty 4 (hrs), $95/hour (SRV tax code)
Sales Tax	Contra Costa (8.25%) – Auto Calculates
Memo	3 Hour Session, 4 Hours Retouching

Table 2-5 Use this data for an Invoice in Step 3

4. Record a payment dated *2/5/2019* for the full amount from Ron Berry (check #9951123) and apply it to Invoice **2019-106**.

5. Deposit everything from the **Undeposited Funds** account into the **Checking** account on **2/8/2019**. Print **Deposit Slip and Deposit Summary** onto blank paper.

Sales Problem 2 (Advanced)

APPLYING YOUR KNOWLEDGE

Restore the Sales-18Problem2.QBM file. The password to access this file is *Sleeter18*.

1. Enter a Sales Receipt using the data in Table 2-6. The payment will be automatically grouped with other payments in **Undeposited Funds** account. You'll need to create the customer record using *Quick Add*, or by setting it up in the *Customer Center* before adding the sale. Print the sale on blank paper.

Field	Data
Customer Name	Pinto, Felix
Class	Walnut Creek
Date	1/29/2019
Sale No.	2019-1
Sold To	Felix Pinto 877 N. Judge St. Walnut Creek, CA 94599
Check No	642
Payment Method	Check
Item	Camera SR32, Qty 3, $695.99
Item	Lens, Qty 3, $324.99
Sales Tax	Contra Costa (8.25%) – Auto Calculates
Customer Tax Code	Tax
Memo	Cameras, Lenses

Table 2-6 Use this data for a Sales Receipt in Step 1

2. Enter an Invoice using the data in Table 2-7. Print the Invoice on blank paper.

Field	Data
Customer Name	Pelligrini, George: 1254 Wilkes Rd.
Class	San Jose
Custom Template	Academy Photo Service Invoice
Date	1/30/2019
Invoice #	2019-106
Bill To	Pelligrini Builders 222 Santana Ave. Los Gatos, CA 94482
PO No.	8324
Terms	Net 30
Item	Indoor Photo Session, Qty 4, $95/hour (SRV tax code)
Item	Retouching, Qty 4(hrs), $95/hour (SRV tax code)
Sales Tax	Santa Clara (8.25%) – Auto Calculates
Memo	4 Hour Session, 4 Hours Retouching

Table 2-7 Use this data for an Invoice in Step 2

3. Enter a second Invoice using the data in Table 2-8. Print the Invoice on blank paper. You will need to add this customer either through *Quick Add* or entering the customer information in the *Customer Center*.

Field	Data
Customer Name	Masood, Jameel
Class	San Jose
Custom Template	Academy Photo Service Invoice
Date	1/31/2019
Invoice #	2019-107
Bill To	Jameel Masood
	339 Walnut St.
	Santa Clara, CA 95111
PO Number	75224
Terms	2% 10 Net 30
Item	Indoor Photo Session, Qty 3, $95/hour (SRV tax code)
Sales Tax	Santa Clara (8.25%) – Auto Calculates
Memo	3 Hour Session

Table 2-8 Use this data for an Invoice in Step 3

4. Record a payment dated **2/15/2019** for the full amount from Jameel Masood (check #5342) and apply it to Invoice **2019-107**.

5. On **2/15/2019,** you received a partial payment from George Pelligrini for the *1254 Wilkes Rd.* Job for $350. Visa payment on card #4321-4321-4321-4321, expires in 5/2020.

6. On **2/15/2019**, deposit everything from the **Undeposited Funds** account using the following:

    a) Deposit Cash and Check payments together (Memo: Deposit Checks). Print **Deposit Slip and Deposit Summary** onto blank paper.

    b) Deposit Visa payments separately (Memo: Deposit Visa). Record a 2% bankcard discount fee (use QuickMath to calculate) on the credit card deposit. Use the following data: Account - Bankcard Fee, Payment Method - Visa, Memo-2% Discount Fee. This amount should be a negative number. Print **Deposit Summary Only** onto blank paper.

Chapter 3
Additional Customer
Transactions

Topics

In this chapter, you will learn about the following topics:

> **Restore this File:**
> This chapter uses Customers-18.QBW. See page 9 for more information. The password to access this file is *Sleeter18*.

In the last chapter, you learned about sales forms and the accounts receivable process. In this chapter, you will learn how QuickBooks records customer returns and refunds, creates customer *Statements*, and processes sales reports.

Recording Customer Returns and Credits

To record customer returns or credits, use QuickBooks *Credit Memos*. *Credit Memos* can be used in the following situations:

- To record the cancellation of an order that has already been invoiced.
- To record a return of merchandise from a customer.
- To record a credit-on-account for a customer.
- To record the first step of making a refund to a customer.

> **Key Term:**
> *Credit Memos* are sales forms that reduce the amount owed to your company by a customer.
>
> **The accounting behind the scenes:**
> *Credit Memos* reduce (credit) Accounts Receivable and reduce (debit) Income and, in some cases, Sales Tax Payable.

When you create a *Credit Memo* in QuickBooks, you must apply the credit to one or more *Invoices*, or use it to give a refund to the customer.

Refunding Customers

There are several situations when you may need to issue a refund to a customer:

1.   When a customer pays for merchandise and then returns the merchandise.

2.   When a customer requests a discount or refund on merchandise or services for which she or he has already paid.

3.   When a customer overpays an *Invoice* and requests a refund.

If the customer paid with cash or check, you should issue a refund check. If the customer paid with a credit card, you should credit the customer's credit card.

COMPUTER PRACTICE

The first step in issuing a customer refund is to create a *Credit Memo* showing the detail of what is being refunded. Typically, the detail will include the products and/or services returned or discounted.

Bob Mason paid for but returned 10 packs of *Standard Photo Paper*. In this exercise, you will create a *Credit Memo* directly from an *Invoice*. This has the advantage of including the details of the *Invoice* in the *Credit Memo*. Later, you will see other ways to create a *Credit Memo*, such as directly from the *Home* page.

Step 1.   Click **Customers** in the *Icon* bar to open the *Customer Center*.

Step 2.   Select **Mason, Bob** from the *Customer Center* list.

Step 3.   If necessary, choose **All** from the *Date* field in the list of transactions in the *Customer Center*. From the list of transactions displayed, double click on Invoice #3947. This will open the *Invoice*.

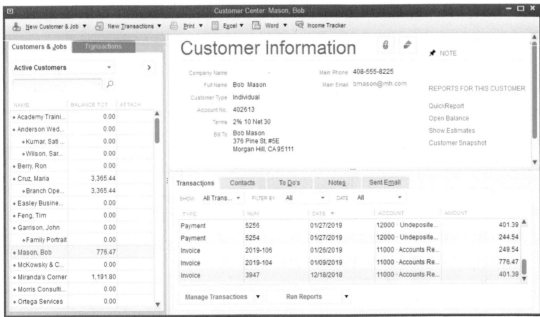

Figure 3-1 Opening Invoice from Customer Center

Step 4.   Click the **Refund/Credit** button at the top of the *Create Invoices* window (see Figure 3-2).

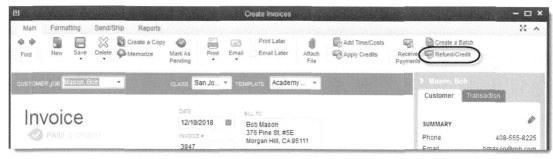

Figure 3-2 Refund/Credit button in Create Invoices window

Step 5.   A *Credit Memo* opens with the information from the previous *Invoice* (see Figure 3-3).

Credit Memos look similar to *Invoices*, but they perform the opposite function. That is, a *Credit Memo* reduces (debits) Sales, reduces (credits) Accounts Receivable, and in some cases reduces Sales Tax Payable. If Inventory is involved, a *Credit Memo* increases (debits) the Inventory asset and reduces (credits) the Cost of Goods Sold account.

Step 6.   Press **Tab** to move to the *Date* field and enter *2/15/2019*. Press **Tab**.

Step 7.   Enter *3947C* in the *Credit No.* field. Press **Tab** three times.

This credit transaction is included on statements and customer reports, so using the *Invoice* number followed by a "C" in the *Credit No.* field helps identify which *Invoice* this *Credit Memo* should apply to.

Step 8.   Leave *Photo Paper* in the *Item* field and tab to the *Qty* field. Change the *Qty* to *10*.

Step 9.   Enter **Refunded 10 Packs Standard Photo Paper** to the *Memo* field.

Step 10.   Make sure your screen matches Figure 3-3. When done press **Save & Close**.

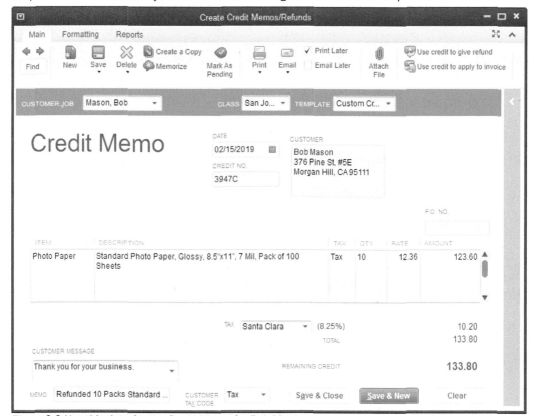

Figure 3-3 Use this data for the Credit Memo for Bob Mason

Step 11.   After you save the *Credit Memo*, QuickBooks displays the *Available Credits* window (see Figure 3-4). Select **Give a Refund** and click **OK**.

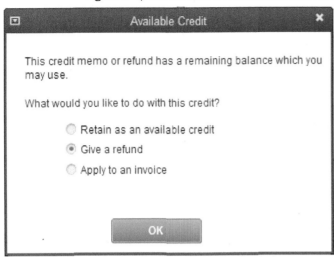

Figure 3-4 *Give a refund option in Available Credit window*

Step 12.   QuickBooks opens the *Issue a Refund* window (see Figure 3-5). Most of the information is already filled in. Enter **Refunded 10 Packs Standard Photo Paper** in the *Memo* field. Click **OK** to record the refund check.

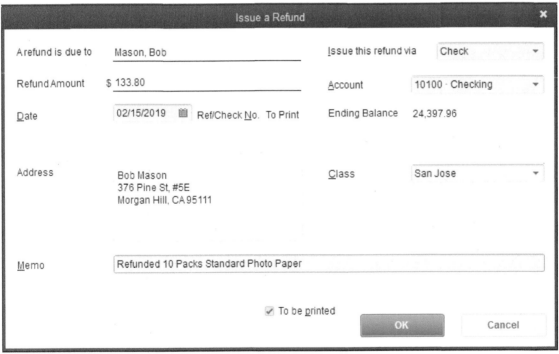

Figure 3-5 *Issue a Refund for Photo Paper*

Step 13.   When you click **OK**, QuickBooks creates the refund check in the checking account and records the *Credit Memo*.

Step 14.   To redisplay the *Credit Memo*, double click it in the *Customer Center* (see Figure 3-6).

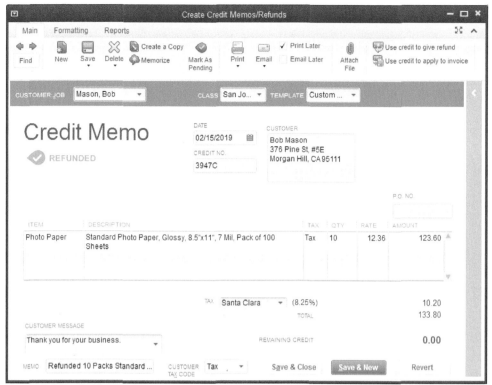

Figure 3-6 Credit Memo after the refund

Step 15.   Close the *Credit Memo* window. Close the *Invoice* window.

Step 16.   Although you will not do it now, this is when you would print the refund check.

Refunding Credit Cards

> **Note:**
> To process a credit card refund using QuickBooks Merchant Account Services, click the **Process credit card refund when saving** field that will display at the bottom of the *Issue a Refund* window. See the onscreen help for more information.

The process for refunding a customer's credit card is similar to the last example on refunding by check, except while check refunds allow you to write a physical check to refund the customer, credit card refunds are held in the Undeposited Funds account and processed in a "batch" each day.

> **DO NOT PERFORM THESE STEPS. THEY ARE FOR REFERENCE ONLY.**

1.   To give a customer a credit card refund, begin by creating a Credit Memo. In this example, Maria Cruz: Branch Opening has been given a $250.00 refund for 2 Hours Photographer Session.

2.   Select **Refunds & Credits** from the *Home* page.

3.   Fill in the *Credit Memo*, such as the one displayed in Figure 3-7.

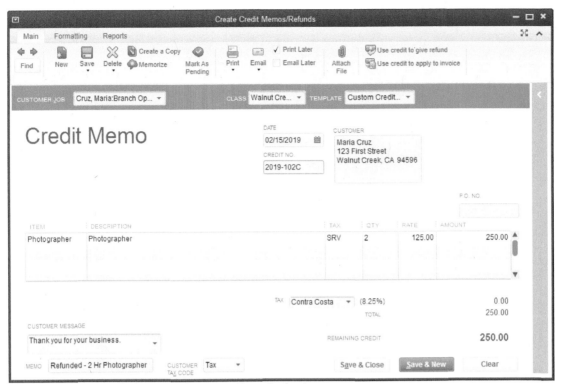

Figure 3-7 Maria Cruz Credit Memo for the credit card refund

4.   Click **Save & Close** to save the *Credit Memo*.

5.   Select **Give a refund** in the *Available Credit* window and click **OK** (see Figure 3-8).

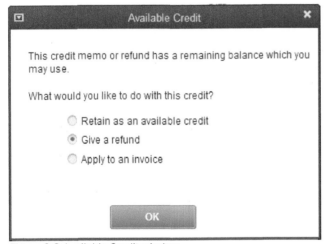

Figure 3-8 Available Credit window

6.   In the *Issue a Refund* window, fill in the needed information as shown in Figure 3-9. Then click **OK**.

Figure 3-9 Issue a Refund window

> **The Accounting Behind the Scenes**
> Creating a Credit Memo and issuing a refund in this example decreases (or debits) the income account associated with the item on the Credit Memo (i.e. Services) and decreases (or credits) the Undeposited Funds account.

7. To record the credit card refund into the bank account, select **Make Deposits** from the *Banking* menu. Click on the credit card refund in the *Select Payments to Deposit* section and click **OK**.

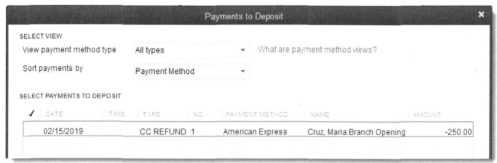

Figure 3-10 Payments to Deposit window with credit card refund

8. In the *Make Deposits* window, check to make sure your screen matches Figure 3-11.
9. Click **Save & Close**.

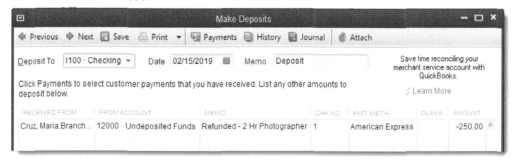

Figure 3-11 Make Deposits window

This example assumes that your merchant account service does not deduct a discount fee from each transaction. If your credit card company processes merchant discount fees with each transaction, you will need to calculate the discount in the **Checking** account line and add a **Bankcard fees** account line recorded as a negative amount.

1. Re-display the original *Credit Memo*. Notice that the REFUNDED stamp along the form confirms that the refund has been processed in QuickBooks.

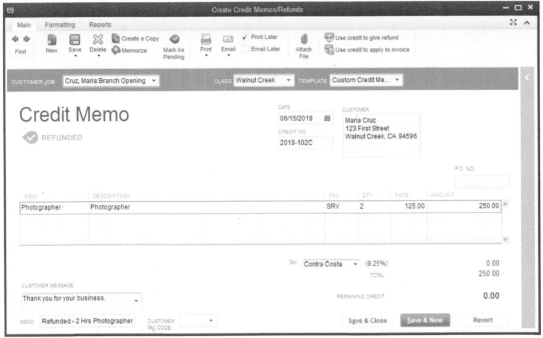

Figure 3-12 Credit Memo showing completed refund process

Did You Know?

Merchant services companies normally charge two types of fees for processing credit cards: a *transaction* fee and a *discount* fee. A **transaction** fee is a standard fee for each credit card transaction, regardless of if it is a sale or refund. A **discount** fee is a percentage charge based on the transaction amount. Some merchant services companies only charge a discount fee for credit card sales. Other companies, however, charge a discount fee for both credit card sales and refunds. Intuit's QuickBooks Merchant Account Services for credit card processing currently charges a discount fee for both sales and refunds.

Writing Off a Bad Debt

If an *Invoice* becomes uncollectible, you'll need to write off the debt. If you use the cash basis of accounting, the uncollectible *Invoice* has not yet been recognized as income on your *Profit & Loss* report, and therefore, you *could* simply delete the *Invoice* to remove it from your records. However, good accounting practice dictates that you enter a new entry to credit the customer balance and reverse the sale (and the sales tax if appropriate).

To properly write off the bad debt, use a *Credit Memo* and a *Bad Debt* Item as shown in the following practice. In the "Customizing QuickBooks" chapter, you'll learn more about Items, but for now, we'll set up a *Bad Debt* Item in the sample file.

COMPUTER PRACTICE

Step 1.   From the *Lists* menu select **Item List.**

Step 2.   Press **Ctrl+N** to display the *New Item* window.

Step 3.   Create an *Other Charge* Item called **Bad Debt** as shown in Figure 3-13. Link the *Bad Debt* Item to the Bad Debts expense account. Click **OK.**

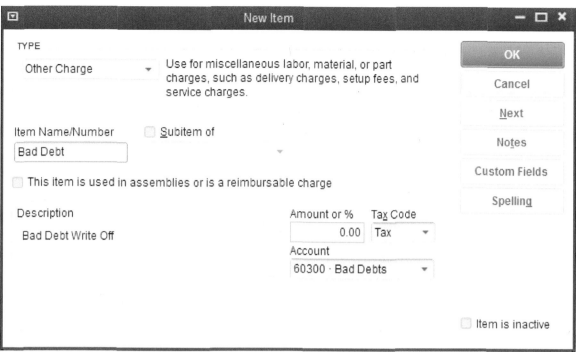

Figure 3-13 Bad Debt Other Charge Item

Step 4.   Close the *Item List*.

Step 5.   From the *Home* page select **Refunds & Credits**. This opens a *Credit Memo*. Alternatively, you could open the *Invoice* and create a *Credit Memo* from the *Refund/Credit* button.

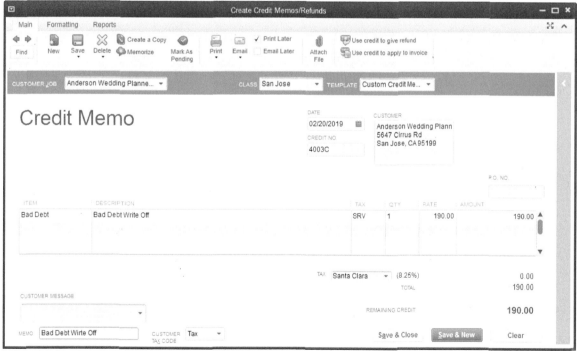

Figure 3-14 Write off a bad debt with a Credit Memo

Step 6.   Fill out the **Credit Memo** as shown in Figure 3-14. Choose *Anderson Wedding Planners: Kumar, Sati and Naveen* in the *Customer:Job* field. Because you are writing off a non-taxed item, set the *Tax* column to **SRV**.

Step 7.   QuickBooks displays a warning message because *Invoices* and *Credit Memos* normally increase or decrease Income accounts, rather than Expense accounts (see Figure 3-15). Click **OK**.

Figure 3-15 Warning about the Bad Debt Item pointing to an expense account

> **Note:**
> Under many circumstances, your Bad Debt write-off should not affect sales tax. However, if the sale you are writing off does need to affect your sales tax liability, you'll need to use separate lines to record all taxable and all non-taxable items on the credit memo.
>
> On the first line of the *Credit Memo*, use the **Bad Debt** Item and enter the total of all taxable items in the sale (not including the sales tax) in the *Amount* column. Select **Tax** (or the appropriate Code) in the *Tax Code* column. QuickBooks will calculate the sales tax and reduce your liability by that amount.
>
> On the second line, use the same **Bad Debt** Item and enter the total of the non-taxable items from the original *Invoice*, including any shipping or miscellaneous charges (excluding sales tax). Select a non-taxable *Tax Code* for this line.

Step 8.   Click **Save & Close** to record the *Credit Memo*. The *Available Credit* window (see Figure 3-16) will be displayed. Select **Apply to an Invoice** option and click **OK**.

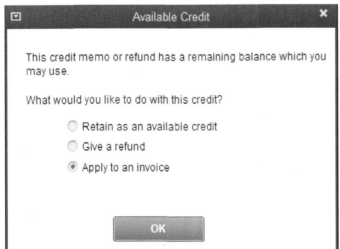

Figure 3-16 Apply to an Invoice option on Available Credit window

> **The accounting behind the scenes:**
> When you use the Bad Debt Item on a *Credit Memo*, the *Credit Memo* decreases (credit) Accounts Receivable and increases (debit) Bad Debts expense.

Applying the Bad Debt Credit Memo to an Open Invoice

COMPUTER PRACTICE

Step 1.   The *Apply Credit to Invoices* window is automatically displayed with Invoice #4003 **Check** (✓) column checked (see Figure 3-17).

Figure 3-17 *Apply Credit to Invoices window*

Step 2.   Click **Done** to apply the bad debt to the selected *Invoice*.

Create Batch Invoices

Batch Invoices allow you to quickly create invoices for multiple customers, however, the invoices all need to be for the same item at the same price. Companies and nonprofit organizations that offer subscription services or monthly dues or fees can use this feature to invoice all designated customers at one time.

> **DO NOT PERFORM THESE STEPS. THEY ARE FOR REFERENCE ONLY.**

In this example, Academy Photography will create a *Batch Group* for their Photo Club Members and then create invoices for their monthly dues.

1.   Open the **Customers** menu and select **Create Batch Invoices.** The *Batch Invoice* window opens (see Figure 3-18).

   If the *Is your customer info set up correctly?* window displays, click **OK**. QuickBooks uses the terms, sales tax rate and send method set up for each customer to create the invoices so you will need to verify that your settings are correct before you start.

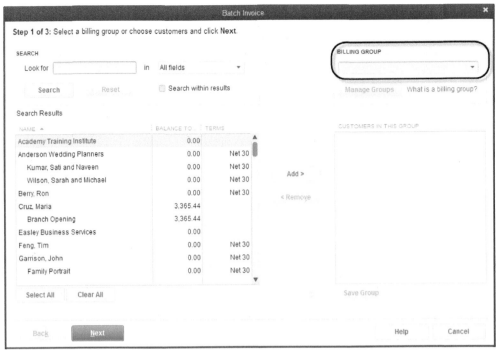

Figure 3-18 Batch Invoice Window

2.   Click on the drop down arrow in the *Billing Group* section and select **Add New**.

3.   Type *Photo Club* in the name field (see Figure 3-19) and click **Save**.

Figure 3-19 Batch Invoice Group

4.   ***Double click*** on **Berry, Ron; Feng, Tim;** and **Mason, Bob** to move them to the column on the right –
      Customers in This Group (see Figure 3-20). This adds these three customers to the Billing Group.

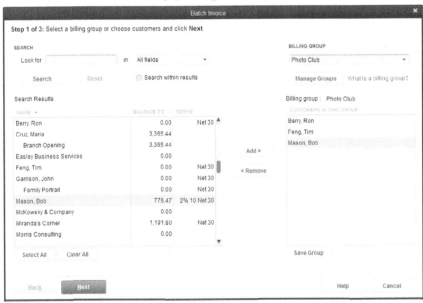

Figure 3-20 Select Customers for Batch Invoice

5.   Click **Next**. Click **Yes** if asked to save.

6.   Enter the information for the invoice as seen in Figure 3-21. Click **Next.**

Figure 3-21 Select Items for Batch Invoice

7.   QuickBooks shows you a review of the invoices to be created (see Figure 3-22).

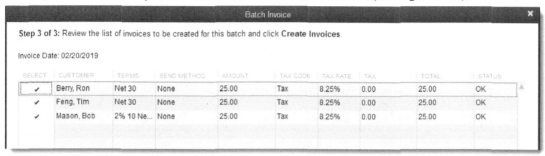

Figure 3-22 Create Batch Invoice

8.   You can uncheck the checkmark on the left to skip invoicing a specific customer. When finished reviewing, click **Create Invoices.**

9.   You can Print and/or email your invoices or click Close to print/email in a batch later (see Figure 3-23).

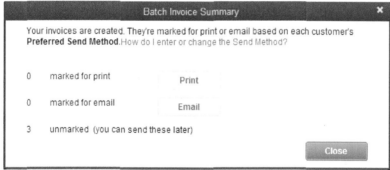

Figure 3-23 Batch Invoice Summary

Creating Customer Statements

QuickBooks Customer *Statements* provide a summary of the activity for a credit Customer during the period you specify. When you create *Statements*, you can show either all of the Customer's activity or just the transactions that are currently open.

COMPUTER PRACTICE

Step 1.   From the *Home* page click the **Statements** icon to open the *Create Statements* window (see Figure 3-24). Alternatively, click **Create Statements** from the *Customers* menu.

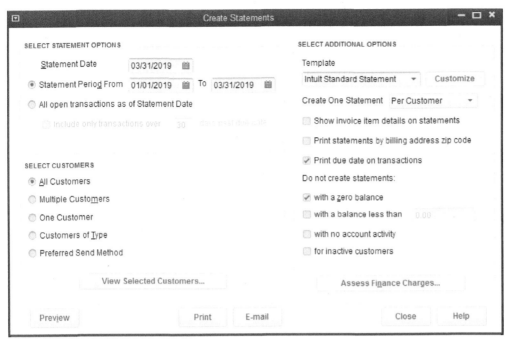

Figure 3-24 Create Statements window

Step 2.   Enter **3/31/2019** in the *Statement Date* field.

Step 3.   Set the *Statement Period From* and *To* fields to **1/1/2019** and **3/31/2019** respectively.

                       You need to include a *Statement Date* and a *Statement Period* because the *Statement Date* is the "current" date that will appear on the *Statement*, while *Statement Period* dates include the period for which accounts receivable transactions will show on the *Statement*.

Step 4.   Leave **All Customers** selected in the *Select Customers* section. The options available under *Select Customers* allow you to choose which Statement or Statements to print.

> **Note:**
> If you want to print only the open *Invoices* for each Customer, select **All open transactions as of Statement Date** at the top left of the *Create Statements* window. If you want to show the detail from the *Invoice*, make sure the *Show invoice item details on statements* option is selected.

Step 5.   Leave **Per Customer** selected in the *Create One Statement* drop-down list.

Step 6.   Check the **with a zero balance** box in the *Do not create statements* section.

Step 7.   Click **Preview**.

Step 8.   After previewing the three pages of statements in the *Print Preview* window (see Figure 3-25), click the **Close** button.

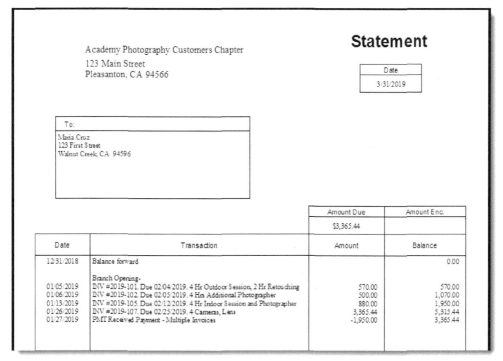

Figure 3-25 Preview of statement

Assessing Finance Charges

When a customer is late in paying an invoice, you can assess finance charges. To set up your finance charge settings, follow these steps:

DO NOT PERFORM THESE STEPS. THEY ARE FOR REFERENCE ONLY.

1. Click **Assess Finance Charges** button on the *Create Statements* window (see Figure 3-24).
2. Click **Yes** in the *Set up Finance Charges* window (see Figure 3-26).

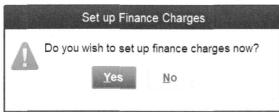

Figure 3-26 Set up Finance Charges window

Another Way:
You can also access the Finance Charge settings by selecting **Preferences** from the *Edit* menu. Select **Finance Charge** from the *Preferences* list and select the **Company Preferences** tab.

3. The Finance Charges Company Preferences window is displayed. Enter the information in Figure 3-27.

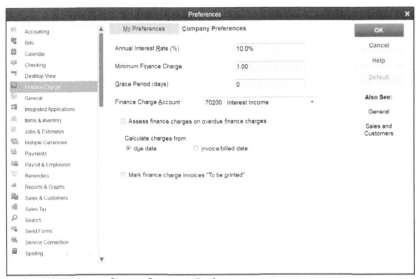

Figure 3-27 Finance Charge Company Preferences

4. When finished entering, click **OK** to set the Finance Charge Company Preferences.

5. The *Assess Finance Charges* window displays. Enter *3/31/2019* in the *Assessment Date* field and press **Tab**.

6. All customers with overdue balances appear (see Figure 3-28). Review the finance charge amounts in the **Finance Charge** column. QuickBooks automatically calculated these amounts based on the amount in the *Annual Interest Rate (%)* field of the Finance Charge Company Preferences. You can override the amount of the finance charge for each customer by editing the amount in the **Finance Charge** column.

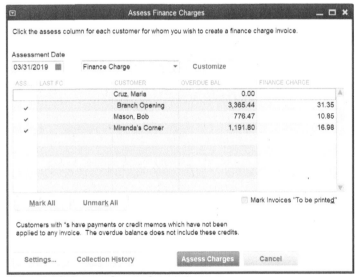

Figure 3-28 Finance Charge Calculation

7. The **Assess** column for each customer is already selected. You can deselect each customer separately by clicking on the appropriate checkmarks in the **Assess** column or you can deselect all customers by clicking **Unmark All**. Leave these customers selected.

8. Click the **Assess Charges** button to record the finance charges.

> **Note:**
> Finance Charges increase with time and are reset each time Finance Charges are applied. If you apply Finance Charges twice on the same *Assessment Date*, the second Finance Charge will be the minimum amount. In this exercise the minimum is $1. If your window looks different from Figure 3-28, it may be because you have already assessed Finance Charges. Finance Charges create invoices, so if you need to edit previously assessed charges, you can edit their invoices.

9. Click **Preview** again to view your statements on the *Print Preview* window as shown in Figure 3-29. Note that the statements now include assessed finance charges.

10. Close all open windows.

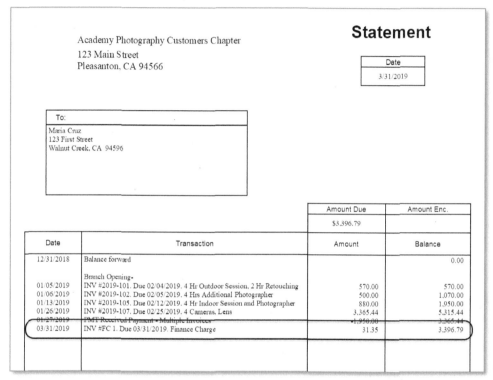

Figure 3-29 Customer after adding finance charges

Collecting Sales Tax

If you sell products and certain types of services, chances are you will need to collect and remit sales tax. In many states, aside from the state tax, each county or city may impose an additional tax that businesses are required to track and report.

If you sell non-taxable goods and services, or if you sell to customers that are exempt from paying sales tax, your state will probably require a breakdown of non-taxable sales and the reason sales tax was not imposed.

These differing conditions may not apply in all jurisdictions, but QuickBooks allows you to track sales tax for all of these different situations. If you are not familiar with the sales tax rates or reporting requirements in your area, consult your state agency, your local QuickBooks ProAdvisor, or an accountant for guidance.

Setting up Sales Tax

You must set up your **Sales Tax Preferences** before using the Sales Tax feature in QuickBooks.

COMPUTER PRACTICE

Step 1.   Click the **Manage Sales Tax** button on the *Home Page*. Or you can choose **Manage Sales Tax** from the *Sales Tax* option on the *Vendors* menu.

Step 2.   The *Manage Sales Tax* dialog box will appear (see Figure 3-30).

Step 3.   Click the **Sales Tax Preferences** button in the *Set Up Sales Tax* section. Alternatively, you could select **Preferences** from the *Edit* menu, then select the *Sales Tax Company* Preferences.

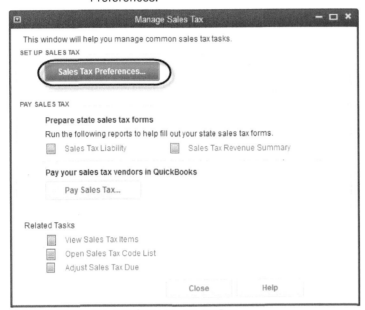

Figure 3-30 The Manage Sales Tax Dialog Box

Step 4.   The Sales Tax Company Preferences dialog box appears.

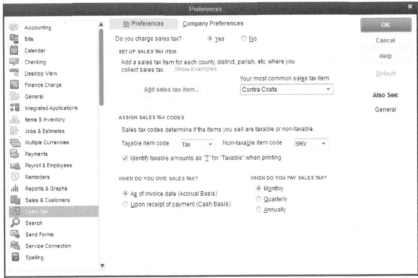

Figure 3-31 Sales Tax Company Preferences

Step 5.   Leave **Yes** selected in the *Do you charge sales tax?* section.

Step 6.   In the *Set Up Sales Tax Item* section, notice *Out of State* is selected in the *Your most common sales tax item* field. Change this field to **Contra Costa** (see Figure 3-31).

> **Note:**
> The sales tax item listed in the *Your most common sales tax item* field becomes the default sales tax item on new customer records, as well as on *Sales Receipts* and *Invoices*.

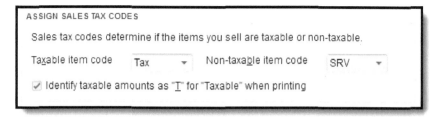

Figure 3-32 Assign Sales Tax Codes area of Sales Tax Company Preferences Window

Step 7.   In the *Assign Sales Tax Codes* section, **Tax** is the default code in the *Taxable item code* field and **SRV** is the default for the *Non-taxable item code* field. For more information about *Sales Tax Codes,* see page 99.

Step 8.   Review the remaining Preferences. When finished, click **OK** to save your changes and then **Close** to close the *Manage Sales Tax* window.

Sales Tax Items

Sales Tax Items are used on sales forms to calculate the amount of sales tax due on each sale. You can view the *Sales Tax Item* on the bottom of the form, separately from the rest of the *Items* (see Figure 3-33).

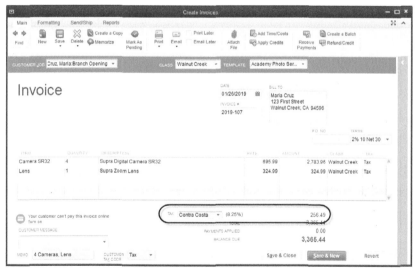

Figure 3-33 Invoice using the Contra Costa Sales Tax Item

To set up your Sales Tax Items, follow these steps:

COMPUTER PRACTICE

Step 1.   Select the *Lists* menu and then select **Item List**. Alternatively, click the **Items & Services** icon on the *Home* page.

Step 2.   To add a new Item, select the **Item** button at the bottom of the *Item List* and then select **New**.

Step 3.   Select **Sales Tax Item** in the *Type* drop-down list and press **Tab**.

Step 4.   Enter the *Sales Tax Name, Description, Tax Rate,* and *Tax Agency,* as shown in Figure 3-34.

This item will track all sales activity (taxable and nontaxable) for Alameda County and will charge each customer 8.75% in sales tax. The sales taxes collected using the *Alameda Sales Tax Item* will increase the amount due to the *State Board of Equalization.*

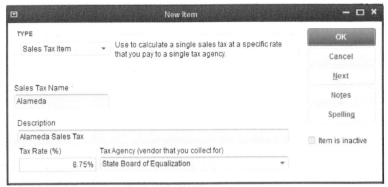

Figure 3-34 Setting up a Sales Tax item

Step 5.   Click **OK** to save the Item.

The accounting behind the scenes:
Sales Tax Items automatically calculate the sales tax on each sales form by applying the sales tax rate to all taxable items on that sale. QuickBooks increases (credits) Sales Tax Payable for the amount of sales tax on the sale. Also, QuickBooks tracks the amount due (debits) by *Tax Agency* in the *Sales Tax Liability* report and in the *Pay Sales Tax* window.

Your sample file includes three additional *Sales Tax Items* for tracking sales in *Contra Costa* and *Santa Clara* counties, as well as *Out of State* sales. After you add the *Alameda Sales Tax Item*, your Item list will look like Figure 3-35.

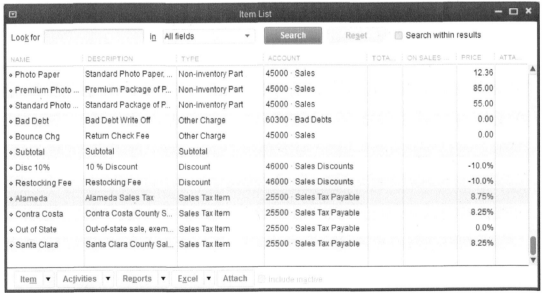

Figure 3-35 Item list scrolled down to Sales Tax Items

Note:
If you remit sales tax to **only one agency** (e.g., California's State Board of Equalization) but you collect sales tax in several different counties or cities, create a separate *Sales Tax Item* for each taxable location in which you sell products. This allows you to track different sales tax rates for each locale.

> **Note:**
> If you pay sales tax to **more than one agency**, you should use *Sales Tax Groups* to combine several different Sales Tax Items into a group tax rate.

Sales Tax Codes

Sales Tax Codes are an additional classification for calculating and reporting sales tax. A Sales Tax Code is assigned to each product or service Item, as well as to each Customer.

Sales Tax Codes serve two purposes. First, Sales Tax Codes indicate whether a specific product or service is taxable or non-taxable. Secondly, Sales Tax Codes categorize revenue based on the reason you charged or did not charge sales tax.

Using Sales Tax Codes on Sales Forms

If you use a taxable *Sales Tax Code* in the *Customer Tax Code* field on sales forms, QuickBooks will apply sales tax (see Figure 3-36). If you use a non-taxable *Sales Tax Code*, QuickBooks will not apply sales tax unless you override the sales tax code (to a taxable code) on one of the lines in the body of the form.

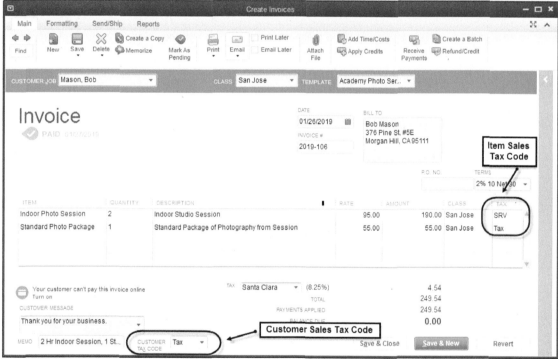

Figure 3-36 Invoice with taxable items

When you set up a Customer record, the *Sales Tax Code* you enter in the Customer record becomes the default in the *Customer Tax Code* field on sales forms.

Similarly, when you set up Items, the *Sales Tax Code* you enter in the *Item* record becomes the default *Tax Code* in the body of sales forms.

You can override the *Sales Tax Code* at the bottom of sales forms by using the *Customer Tax Code* drop-down list, or on each line in the body of the Invoice.

Setting up Sales Tax Codes

COMPUTER PRACTICE

One of your customers, Miranda's Corner, purchases various frames from Academy Photography to resell to her customers, and therefore does not pay sales tax.

Step 1.   From the *Lists* menu select **Sales Tax Code List**. QuickBooks displays the *Sales Tax Code List* window (see Figure 3-37).

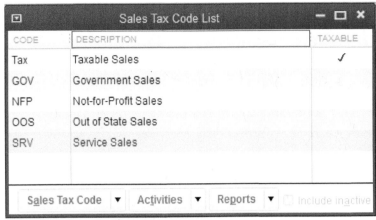

Figure 3-37 Sales Tax Code List

Step 2.   This file already has five *Sales Tax Codes*. To create a new *Sales Tax Code*, select **New** from the *Sales Tax Code* button at the bottom of the window.

Step 3.   Enter the information shown in Figure 3-38. This creates a *Sales Tax Code* for tracking customers who do not pay sales tax because they are resellers.

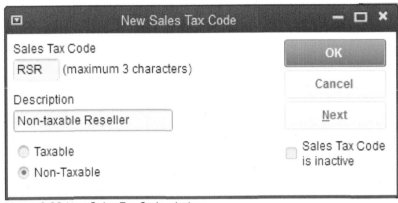

Figure 3-38 New Sales Tax Code window

Step 4.   Click OK to save this Sales Tax Code.

Step 5.   Close the Sales Tax Code List window.

Step 6.   Open the *Customer Center*. Double click **Miranda's Corner** in the *Customer Center*.

Step 7.   In the *Edit Customer* window, click on the **Sales Tax Settings** tab.

Step 8.   Enter **RSR** from the *Tax Code* field in the *Sales Tax Information* section (see Figure 3-39).

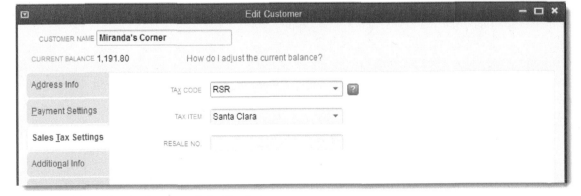

Figure 3-39 Changing the Customer Sales Tax Code

Step 9.   Click **OK** to close the *Edit Customer* window. Close the *Customer Center*.

Calculating Sales Tax on Sales Forms

When you properly set up your QuickBooks *Items, Customers, Sales Tax Codes,* and *Preferences,* QuickBooks automatically calculates and tracks sales tax on each sale.

As illustrated in Figure 3-40 and detailed in the steps above, each line on a sale shows a separate *Item* that is taxed according to the combination of how the *Item, Tax Code,* and *Customer* are set up. Only taxable customers will be charged sales tax. If the customer is taxable, then the sum of the *Taxable Items* is multiplied by the Sales Tax Rate. In the example below, the customer is taxable. The only taxable *Item* on the *Invoice* is the *Standard Photo Package,* so the *Amount* of the *Standard Photo Package* ($55.00) is multiplied by the rate for Santa Clara County (8.25%) for a resulting sales tax of $4.54.

If necessary, you can override the *Tax Code* on each line of the sales form or at the bottom of the form. The *Tax Item,* which can also be overridden, determines the rate to charge on the sum of all taxable line items on the sale.

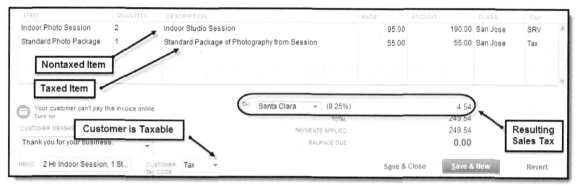

Figure 3-40 Calculating Sales Tax in QuickBooks

For more on paying the collected sales tax, see page 151.

Creating Sales Reports

In this section, you'll learn how to create reports that will help you analyze your company's sales.

Customer Open Balance Report

You can create a *Customer Open Balance* report to view the open *Invoices* and the *Credit Memo* for this customer.

Step 1.   If necessary, display the **Customer Center** and then select **Cruz, Maria: Branch Opening** as shown in Figure 3-41.

Step 2.   Under the *Reports for this Job* section, select the **Open Balance** link (see Figure 3-41). You may need to expand the window to see the Reports section.

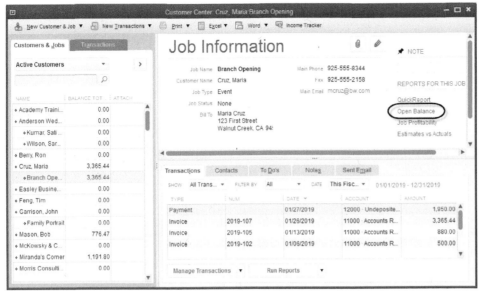

Figure 3-41 Select the job and click the needed report in the Customer Center

Step 3.   The *Customer Open Balance* report opens (see Figure 3-42).

Step 4.   Click the Close Window button at the top right of the window to close the report or press **Esc** to close the window.

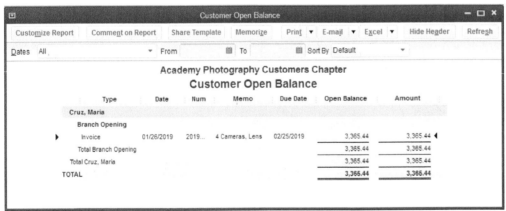

Figure 3-42 Customer Open Balance report

Sales by Customer Summary Report

The *Sales by Customer Summary* report shows how much you have sold to each of your customers over a given date range.

COMPUTER PRACTICE

To create this report, follow these steps:

Step 1.   From the *Report Center* select **Sales** from the category list and then double click the **Sales by Customer Summary** report in the *Sales by Customer* section.

Step 2.   Enter *1/1/2019* in the *From* date field and then press **Tab**.

Step 3.   Enter *2/28/2019* in the *To* date field and then press **Tab**.

                         Figure 3-43 shows the *Sales by Customer Summary* report for the first two months of 2019.

Step 4.   To print the report, click **Print** at the top of the report.

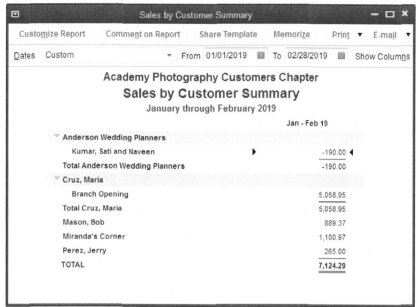

Figure 3-43 Sales by Customer Summary report

Step 5.   Close the *Sales by Customer Summary* report. If the *Memorize Report* dialog box opens, click **No** (see Figure 3-44).

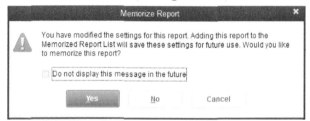

Figure 3-44 Memorize Report dialog box

Sales by Item Report

The *Sales by Item* report shows how much you have sold of each Item over a given date range. To create this report, follow these steps:

COMPUTER PRACTICE

Step 1.   From the *Report Center* select **Sales** from the category list and then double click the **Sales by Item Summary** report in the *Sales by Item* section. You may need to scroll down.

Step 2.   Enter *1/1/2019* in the *From* date field and then press **Tab**.

Step 3.   Enter *2/28/2019* in the *To* date field and then press **Tab**.

Figure 3-45 shows the *Sales by Item Summary* report for the first two months of 2019.

Step 4.   To print the report, click **Print** at the top of the report.

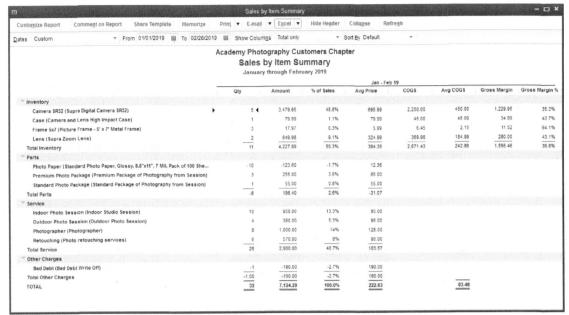

Figure 3-45 Sales by Item Summary report

Step 5.   Close the *Sales by Item Summary* report. If the *Memorize Report* window opens, click **No**.

Review Questions

Comprehension Questions

1. When would you choose to give a refund after creating a *Credit Memo*?

2. How can *Credit Memos* be used?

Multiple Choice

Select the best answer(s) for each of the following:

1. Customer *Statements*:

    a)   Provide a summary of all accounts receivable activity for a Customer during the period you specify.

    b)   Are not available in QuickBooks.

    c)   Automatically assess and calculate finance charges for overdue accounts without any user action.

    d)   Should only be created and mailed if the Customer's balance is over $500.

2. Which of the following options is not available on the *Available Credit* window?

    a)   Give a refund.

    b)   Retain as an available credit.

    c)   Apply to an *Invoice*.

    d)   Use with *Receive Payments*.

3. What is the best way to write off a bad debt?

    a) Delete the original *Invoice*.

    b) Create a *Credit Memo* using a *Bad Debt* Item and apply the credit to the past due *Invoice*.

    c) Create a *Credit Memo* for the amount of the past due *Invoice* and retain the available credit.

    d) Any of the above.

4. In which of the following situations would you create a *Credit Memo*?

    a) You need to record a cancelled order that has already been invoiced but not paid.

    b) A customer returns merchandise and wants the return credited to a future *Invoice*.

    c) A customer requests a refund.

    d) Any of the above.

5. The *Credit Memo Number* should be

    a) The next number after the *Credit Memo Number* on the last *Credit Memo*.

    b) The next number after the *Invoice Number* on the last *Invoice*, followed by a "C."

    c) Any unique number.

    d) The same number as the *Invoice* to which the *Credit Memo* is linked, followed by a "C."

6. You need to issue a refund to a customer. The customer originally paid with a Visa card. How do you issue the credit?

    a) Pay the refund with your company's credit card.

    b) Pay the refund using any method of payment.

    c) Pay the refund by issuing a refund check.

    d) Pay the refund through the customer's credit card.

7. Your company policy is that each Finance Charge should be at least $5. Where is the best place to set this value in QuickBooks?

    a) Enter a value of at least $5 in the *Finance Charge* field in the *Assess Finance Charges* window.

    b) Enter $5 in the *Minimum Finance Charge* field in the *Finance Charge Company Preferences* window.

    c) Enter $5 on the last line of each statement.

    d) Enter $5 in the *Minimum Finance Charge* field in the *Create Statements* window.

8. Which report would you run to see a summary of income by products and services?

    a) The Sales by Item Summary Report

    b) The Sales by Customer Summary Report

    c) The Customer Open Balance Report

    d) The Revenue by Item Summary Report

9. Which of the following is a way to issue a credit?

    a) Delete an open invoice.

    b) Deposit a check from a customer without receiving a payment.

    c) Create a *Credit Memo*.

    d) Apply for a credit card.

10. Which type of business would most likely use Batch Invoices?

    a) Gym Club which charges monthly dues

    b) Home Builder

    c) Accounting & Tax business

    d) Retail Store

11. A past due invoice contains items that were taxed and items that were not taxed. How would you write off this invoice as a bad debt?

    a) Delete the original invoice.

    b) Delete the taxed items from the original invoice and then delete the entire invoice.

    c) Create a *Credit Memo* with two *Bad Debt* items, the first set to non-taxable with the total of non-taxable items, the second set to taxable with the total of taxable items. Apply this *Credit Memo* to the original invoice.

    d) Create a *Credit Memo* for the taxable amount from the original invoice. Apply the *Credit Memo* to the invoice, and then delete the invoice.

12. Which statement is true?

    a) If you assess Finance Charges for one past due customer, you have to assess them for all past due customers.

    b) You must preview statements before printing them.

    c) Finance Charges are assessed automatically when you create a statement.

    d) You can create a statement for a single customer.

13. After issuing a refund check,

    a) The *Credit Memo* is marked *Refunded* and the *Remaining Credit* field is 0.00.

    b) The *Credit Memo* is removed.

    c) The original *Invoice* is marked *Refunded* and the *Remaining Credit* field is 0.00.

    d) The *Total* field on the original invoice is 0.00.

14. Which of the following is true?

    a) You can only apply a *Credit Memo* to an *Invoice* if the *Remaining Credit* amount is equal to the *Amount Due*.

    b) *Credit Memos* are automatically applied to open invoices.

    c) *Credit Memos* look similar to invoices but perform the opposite function, reducing (debiting) Sales accounts and reducing (crediting) Accounts Receivable.

    d) You should not use a *Credit Memo* to write off a bad debt.

15. In which of the following situations would you assess a Finance Charge?

    a) A customer returns merchandise and you want to charge a restocking fee.

    b) You want to write off a bad debt.

    c) A customer's invoice is 60 days past due.

    d) Any of the above.

Completion Statements

1. Regarding Refunds: If the customer paid by _____ or _____, you will need to issue a refund check. If the customer paid with a(n) _____ _____, you will need to credit the customer's credit card account.

2. _____ _____ are used to issue refunds or apply credits to existing invoices.

3. You can _____ _____ an uncollectible invoice as a bad debt.

4. When a customer is late paying an invoice, you can assess _____ _____.

5. A customer _____ is a summary of all activity on an account in a specified period.

Customers Problem 1

> Restore the Customers-18Problem1.QBM file. The password to access this file is
> *Sleeter18*.

1. On Feb. 1, 2019, create Invoice #2019-108 to *Feng, Tim*. *Class* is *San Jose*. The customer purchased a 5 hour Indoor Photo Session. Use the *Santa Clara* Tax Item. Print the *Invoice*.

2. Tim Feng only needed a two hour Indoor Photo Session. On Feb 5, 2019, create a Credit Memo #2019-108C to write off the 3 additional hours of Indoor Photo Session for Tim Feng. Apply the credit to the open invoice. Print the *Credit Memo*.

3. Print Sales by Customer Summary report for February 2019.

4. Print Sales by Item Summary report for February 2019.

5. Create and print customer *Statements* for the period of February 1, 2019 through February 28, 2019. Print *Statements* for all customers who have a balance due.

Customers Problem 2 (Advanced)

> Restore the Customers-18Problem2.QBM file. The password to access this file is
> *Sleeter18*.

1. On Feb 7, 2019, create Invoice #2019-108 to Morris Consulting. Use the Walnut Creek class, terms 2% 10, Net 30. (Note: Special terms apply to this *Invoice* only.) The customer purchased a 5 hour Indoor Photo Session ($95 per hour) and 6 hours with a Photographer ($125 per hour). Use the Out of State Sales Tax Item. Print the *Invoice*.

2. On Feb 9, 2019, create Invoice #2019-109 to Easley Business Services. Use the class San Jose. Terms are Net 30. The customer purchased 4 Cameras ($695.99), 4 Lenses ($324.99), and 4 Cases ($79.99). Use the Out of State Sales Tax Item. Print the *Invoice*.

3. On Feb 10, 2019, receive check #58621 in the amount of $1,200.50 from Morris Consulting in full payment of Invoice #2019-108. He took a 2% discount of $24.50. Use the Sales Discount account and the Walnut Creek class.

4. On Feb 15, 2019, Donald Easley of Easley Business Services called and gave his VISA credit card number to pay off the balance on his open Invoices. The payment amount was $4,403.88 VISA #4444-3333-2222-1111; Exp. 05/2022.

5. On Feb 23, 2019, Morris Consulting requested a refund for one hour of Photographer services. Create Credit Memo #2019-108C and use the Walnut Creek class. Issue Morris Consulting a refund check.

6. On Feb 26, 2019, create a Credit Memo to write off Invoice 3696 to Ortega Services. You will need to create a Bad Debt item. Since Invoice 3696 included a taxable item, you will need to use the Bad Debt item on the *Credit Memo* for the amount $695.99 and mark it as taxable. Use the Walnut Creek class and Credit No. 3696C. The entire amount of the write-off is $753.41. Apply the *Credit Memo* to the open *Invoice*.

7. On Feb 26, 2019, receive payment for $1,191.80 from Miranda's Corner in payment of Invoice #2019-103. She uses her VISA card number 7777-8888-9999-0000 expiration date 12/2021, to pay this *Invoice*.

8. On Feb 28, 2019, issue Credit Memo #2019-103C to Miranda's Corner for Invoice #2019-103. The customer returned 1 Camera ($695.99). A 10% restocking fee applies. Use the San Jose class and the Santa Clara County sales tax. Issue a refund to Miranda's Corner's VISA card on Credit Memo #2019-103C. Total refund: $683.81. Print the *Credit Memo* after the refund.

9. Deposit the check in the Undeposited Funds account on 2/28/2019. Print the Deposit Slip.

10. Deposit all VISA receipts on 2/28/2019. Record a 2% bankcard discount fee (use QuickMath to calculate) on the credit card deposit. Total deposit amount is $4,813.63. Print the Deposit Summary.

11. Print Sales by Customer Summary report for January through February 2019.

12. Print Sales by Item Summary report for January through February 2019.

13. Create and print customer *Statements* for the period of February 1, 2019 through February 28, 2019. Print *Statements* for all customers who have a balance due: one for Anderson Weddings and one for Bob Mason.

Chapter 4
Managing Expenses

Topics

In this chapter, you will learn about the following topics:

- Entering Expenses in QuickBooks (page 109)
- Setting Up Vendors (page 112)
- Activating Class Tracking (page 117)
- Tracking Job Costs (page 119)
- Paying Vendors (page 119)
- Printing Checks (page 133)
- Voiding Checks (page 136)
- Applying Vendor Credits (page 139)
- Tracking Company Credit Cards (page 142)
- Paying Sales Tax (page 151)
- Accounts Payable Reports (page 152)

> **Restore this File:**
> This chapter uses Expenses-18.QBW. See page 9 for more information. The password to access this file is **Sleeter18**.

In this chapter, we will discuss several ways to track your company's expenditures and vendors. We will start by adding vendors to your file, and then discuss several methods of paying them. In addition, this chapter shows you how to track expenses by job.

Entering Expenses in QuickBooks

QuickBooks provides several tools to help you track and manage the expenses in your business. These tools allow you to track your expenses in detail so that you can create extensive reports that help you manage your vendor relationships and control the costs in your business.

The Process of Entering Expenses in QuickBooks

The *Vendors* section of the *Home* page window provides you with a graphical flow of the steps involved in managing vendors, purchases, and payments (see Figure 4-1).

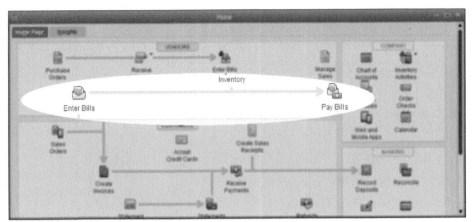

Figure 4-1 QuickBooks Home page

Clicking the Vendors icon on the Home page or on the Icon Bar displays the Vendor Center (see Figure 4-2). The *Vendor Center* displays information about all of your vendors and their transactions in a single place. You can add a new vendor, add a transaction to an existing vendor, or print the *Vendor List* or *Transaction List*.

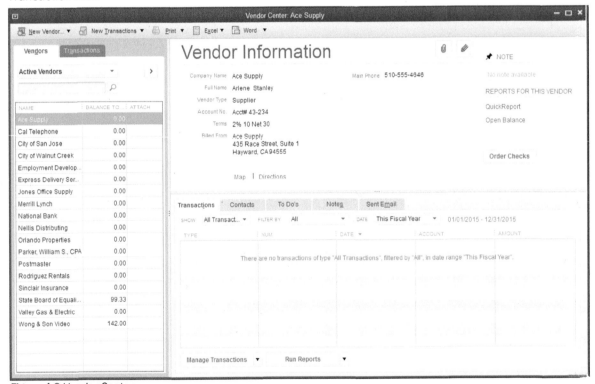

Figure 4-2 Vendor Center

In addition to the *Vendor Center*, the *Banking* section of the *Home* page contains options to help you navigate making deposits, writing checks, opening a check register, and reconciling with the bank statement. Figure 4-3 displays the *Banking* section of the *Home* page.

Figure 4-3 Banking section of the Home page

Table 4-1 shows many of the business transactions that might occur in dealing with vendors to process expenses in QuickBooks.

For illustrative purposes, we have defined two major groups of vendors – cash vendors and credit vendors. Table 4-1 shows how to enter transactions for each of these two groups of Vendors. The table also shows what QuickBooks does "behind the scenes" to record these transactions.

For some vendors, you will decide to track *Bills* and *Bill Payments*. This means the Accounts Payable account will be used to track how much you owe these vendors. We will refer to these as your credit vendors.

With other vendors, you will skip the Accounts Payable account and just write checks or otherwise pay them directly, coding the transactions to the appropriate expense accounts. We will refer to these as your cash vendors. Although you probably will not pay these vendors with actual cash, but with checks or credit cards, we will use the term cash vendor to distinguish them from credit vendors described previously.

Business Transaction	Cash Vendors		Credit Vendors	
	QuickBooks Transaction	Accounting Entry	QuickBooks Transaction	Accounting Entry
Recording a Purchase Order	Not usually used		Purchase Orders	Non-posting entry used to track *Purchase Orders*
Recording a Bill from a Vendor	Not usually used		Enter Bills	Increase (debit) **Expenses,** Increase (credit) **Accounts Payable**
Paying Bills	Write Checks	Increase (debit) **Expenses,** Decrease (credit) **Checking**	Pay Bills	Decrease (debit) **Accounts Payable,** Decrease (credit) the **Checking Account**

Table 4-1 Steps for entering expenses

Recording Transactions

The first row in Table 4-1 references *Recording a Purchase Order*. Some vendors require *Purchase Orders* so they can properly process orders. When a *Purchase Order* is recorded, no accounting transaction is entered into QuickBooks; rather, a "memo" entry is made to track the *Purchase Order*. For details on using *Purchase Orders*, refer to the **Inventory** chapter beginning on page 275.

The second row references *Recording a Bill from a Vendor*. When you receive a bill from a vendor, you will record it using the *Enter Bills* window. Then, when it is time to pay your *Bills*, you will use the *Pay Bills* window in QuickBooks to select the *Bills* you want to pay. As shown below in Figure 4-4, both of these commands are available from the *New Transactions* drop-down menu in the Vendor Center.

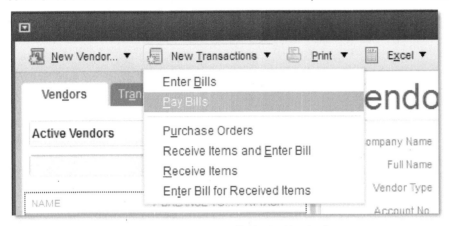

Figure 4-4 New Transactions Menu drop-down list in the Vendor Center

The third row references *Paying Bills*. Sometimes you will need to write a check that is not for the payment of a *Bill*. In that case, you will use the *Write Checks* window. *Write Checks* is accessible by clicking the **Write Checks** icon from the *Home* page, the **Write Checks** option from the *Banking* menu, or by pressing **Ctrl+W**.

Setting Up Vendors

Vendors include every person or company from whom you purchase products or services, including trade vendors, service vendors, and 1099 contract workers. Before you record any transactions to a Vendor in QuickBooks, you must set them up in the *Vendor Center*.

> **Tip:**
> When a vendor is also a customer, you will need to set up two separate records: a vendor record in the *Vendor Center* and a customer record in the *Customer Center*. The customer name must be slightly different from the vendor name. For example, you could enter Boswell Consulting as "Boswell Consulting-V" for the vendor name in the *New Vendor* window, and "Boswell Consulting-C" for the customer name in the *New Customer* window. The contact information for both customer and vendor record can be identical.

To set up a vendor, follow these steps:

COMPUTER PRACTICE

Step 1.   To display the *Vendor Center*, select the **Vendors** icon in the Vendors section of the *Home* page (see Figure 4-5). Alternately, click on the **Vendors** icon on the *Icon Bar*.

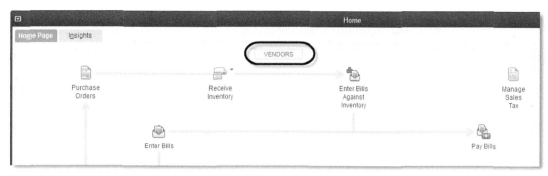

Figure 4-5 Vendors section of the Home page

Step 2.   Click the **New Vendor** button in the *Vendor Center* (see Figure 4-6) and choose **New Vendor** from the drop-down menu.

Figure 4-6 Add New Vendor to the Vendor list

Step 3.   The New Vendor window displays (see Figure 4-7). Notice there are tabs labeled *Address Info, Payment Settings, Tax Settings, Account Settings* and *Additional Info*.

Figure 4-7 The New Vendor window

Step 4.   Enter ***Boswell Consulting*** in the *Vendor Name* field and press **Tab**.

> **Tip:**
> The *Vendor List* sorts alphabetically, just like the *Customer List*. Therefore, if your vendor
> is an individual person, enter the last name first, followed by the first name.

Step 5.   Press **Tab** twice to skip the *Opening Balance* and *as of* fields (see Figure 4-8).

                 The *Opening Balance* field shows only when you create a new *Vendor* record. You will not
                 see this field when you edit an existing vendor. The date in the *as of* field defaults to the
                 current date. Since you will not enter an amount in the *Opening Balance* field, there is no
                 need to change this date.

> **Important:**
> It is best *not* to use the *Opening Balance* field in the *New Vendor* window. If you *do* enter
> an opening balance for a vendor in the *Opening Balance* field, QuickBooks creates a *Bill*
> that increases (credits) Accounts Payable and increases (debits) Uncategorized Expense.
> Instead, enter each unpaid *Bill* separately after you create the vendor record.

Step 6.   Enter **Boswell Consulting** in the *Company Name* field and press **Tab**.

Step 7.   Continue entering data in the rest of the fields on the Vendor record, as shown in Figure
                 4-8. Press **Tab** after each entry.

Figure 4-8 New Vendor window after it has been completed

Step 8.   Click the **Payment Settings** tab to continue entering information about this vendor (see
                 Figure 4-9).

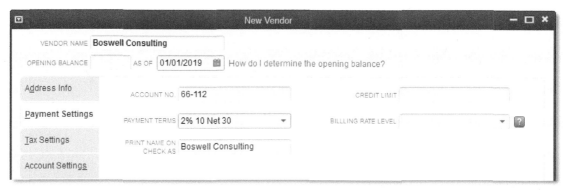

Figure 4-9 The Payment Settings tab of the New Vendor window

Step 9.   Enter **66-112** in the *Account No.* field and press **Tab**.

In this field, you enter the number that your vendor uses to track you as a customer. If your vendor requires you to enter your account number on the checks you send, this is where you enter it. QuickBooks prints the contents of this field on the memo of the check when you pay this vendor's bill.

Step 10.   Press **Tab** to leave the *Credit Limit* field blank.

Step 11.   Select **2% 10 Net 30** from the *Payment Terms* drop-down list and press **Tab**.

QuickBooks allows you to establish different types of default payment terms, including payment terms to accommodate discounts for early payment. In this example, the terms of 2% 10 Net 30 means that if you pay this vendor within 10 days of the invoice date, you are eligible for a 2% discount. In this field, you can set the payment terms default for this vendor. QuickBooks uses these default terms on all new *Bills* for this vendor. You can override the default terms on each *Bill* as necessary. When you create reports for accounts payable (A/P), QuickBooks takes into account the terms on each *Bill*. To learn more about the *Terms List*, and how to set up terms, see page 259.

Step 12.   Choose the **Tax Settings** tab (see Figure 4-10).

Step 13.   Enter **123-12-1234** in the *Vendor Tax ID* field.

The *Vendor Tax ID* field is where you enter the social security or taxpayer identification number of your Form 1099-MISC recipients. QuickBooks prints this number on the Form 1099-MISC at the end of the year.

Step 14.   Check the box next to *Vendor eligible for 1099*.

Select this box for all vendors for whom you expect to file a Form 1099-MISC.

Figure 4-10 The Boswell Consulting Tax Settings tab

Step 15.   Click the **Account Settings** tab.

Step 16.   Select **Professional Fees** from the first *Tell us which expense accounts to prefill when you enter bills for this vendor* field (see Figure 4-11). The *Account Settings* tab allows you to set a default expense account for future transactions with this vendor. This account may be changed as needed whenever you **Enter Bills**.

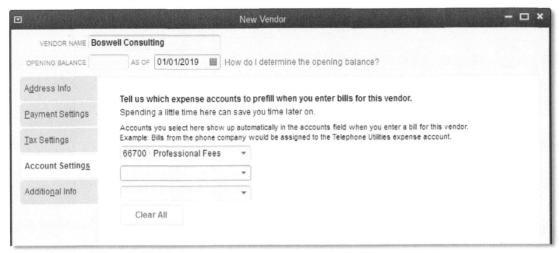

Figure 4-11 The completed Boswell Consulting Account Settings tab

Step 17.   Select the **Additional Info** Tab.

Step 18.   Select **Consultant** from the *Vendor Type* drop-down list and press **Tab**.

QuickBooks allows you to group your vendors into common types. For example, if you create a *Vendor Type* called Consultant and you tag each of your consultants' vendor records with this type, you could later create a report specific to this *Vendor Type*.

Step 19.   Enter *Alameda* in the *County* field and press **Tab**.

The *County* field is a *Custom Field*. The *Define Fields* button in the *New Vendor* window, *Additional Info* tab allows you to define *Custom Fields* to track more information about your vendors. For more information on setting up and using *Custom Fields*, see page 263.

Figure 4-12 Additional Info tab in the New Vendor window

Step 20.   Click **OK** to save and close the New Vendor window.

Activating Class Tracking

In QuickBooks, the *Class* field gives you a way to segregate your transactions other than by account name. You can use QuickBooks *Classes* to separate your income and expenses by line of business, department, location, profit center, or any other meaningful breakdown of your business. Alternatively, if your business is a not-for-profit organization, you could use *Classes* to separately track transactions for each program or activity within the organization.

For example, a dentist might classify all income and expenses as relating to either the dentistry or hygiene department. A law firm formed as a partnership might classify all income and expenses according to which partner generated the business. If you use *Classes*, you'll be able to create separate reports for each *Class* of the business. Therefore, the dentist could create separate Profit & Loss reports for the dentistry and hygiene departments, and the law firm could create separate reports for each partner.

In our sample company, Academy Photography uses *Classes* to track income and expenses for each of its stores - San Jose and Walnut Creek.

COMPUTER PRACTICE

Step 1.   Select the **Edit** menu, and then select **Preferences**.

Step 2.   Select the **Accounting** preference.

Step 3.   Select the **Company Preferences** tab, and make sure the box next to *Use class tracking for transactions* is checked (see Figure 4-13). When you use *Classes* on each transaction (*Checks, Bills, Invoices,* etc.), the *Profit & Loss by Class* report shows the income and expenses for each class.

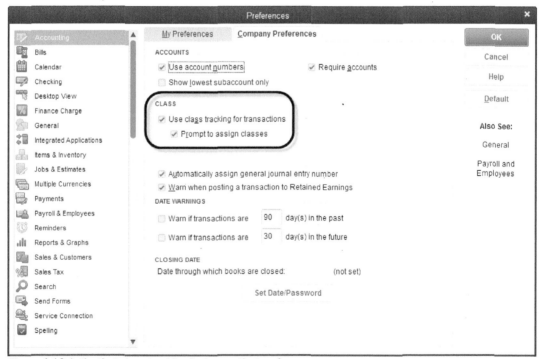

Figure 4-13 Activating class tracking in Accounting preferences

Step 4.   The *Prompt to assign classes* field is already checked. Leave the checkmark in this box.

With this setting, QuickBooks prompts you if you fail to assign a *Class* on any line of the transaction.

Step 5.   Click **OK**.

Figure 4-14 displays a *Bill* from Wong & Son Video. The San Jose Class is selected in the *Class* column. This tracks the Subcontracted Services Expense to the San Jose Class (i.e., the San Jose store) so that the *Profit & Loss by Class* report shows the expense under the column for the San Jose Class.

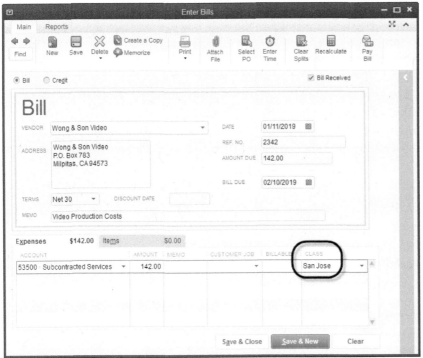

Figure 4-14 The Class field shows on many windows in QuickBooks, including Enter Bills

The *Profit & Loss by Class* report displays the income and expenses for each *Class*. Income and expenses for each Academy Photography store are displayed as separate columns. Note that the *San Jose* column includes the *Subcontracted Services*. For more information about the *Profit & Loss by Class* report, see page 203.

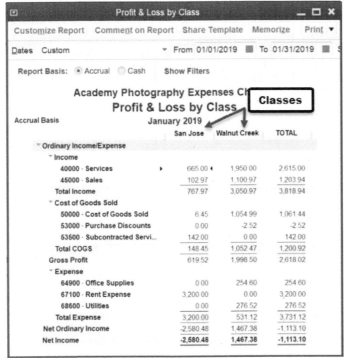

Figure 4-15 Profit & Loss by Class report

Tracking Job Costs

If you want to track the expenses for each *Customer* or *Job* (i.e., track job costs), link each expense with the *Customer* or *Job* to which it applies. In the following sections, you will learn about recording expense transactions in several different situations.

When you record an expense transaction, use the *Customer:Job* column to link each expense account or *Item* with a *Customer* or *Job* (see Figure 4-16).

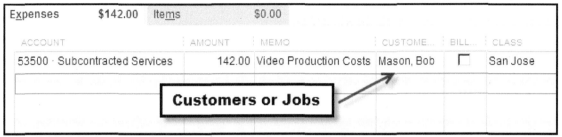

Figure 4-16 Linking expenses to Customers and Jobs (i.e., job costing)

When you track job costs, you can create reports such as the *Profit & Loss by Job* report that shows income and expenses separately for each *Job* (see Figure 4-17). For more information about the *Profit & Loss by Job* report, see page 206.

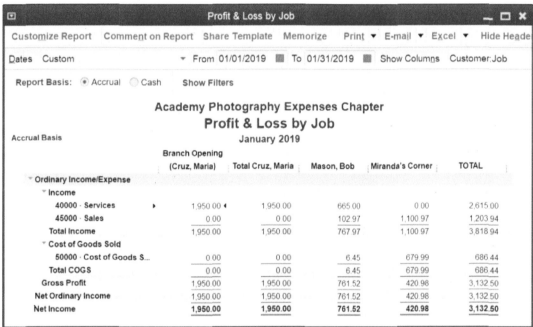

Figure 4-17 Profit & Loss by Job report

Paying Vendors

With QuickBooks, you can pay your vendors in several ways. You can pay by check, credit card, electronic funds transfer, or, though not recommended, cash.

Most of the time, you'll pay your vendors from a checking account, so this section covers three different situations for recording payments out of your checking account. The three situations are:

- Manually writing a check or initiating an electronic funds transfer and recording the transaction in a QuickBooks account register.
- Using the *Write Checks* function to record and print checks.

- Recording accounts payable bills through the *Enter Bills* window and using the *Pay Bills* function to pay these *Bills*.

Using Registers

In this example, you will manually write a check and then record the transaction in the QuickBooks checking account register.

COMPUTER PRACTICE

After you have written a manual check, or made a payment by electronic funds transfer, you will record the transaction in QuickBooks.

Step 1.   Select the **Check Register** icon from the *Home* page. Alternatively, key **Ctrl+R** on your keyboard.

Step 2.   In the *Use Register* dialog box, make sure **Checking** displays in the *Select Account* field and click **OK** (see Figure 4-18).

Figure 4-18 Use Register dialog box

Step 3.   Enter *2/8/2019* in the first empty line of the *Date* column and press Tab (see Figure 4-19).

DATE	NUMBER	PAYEE		PAYMENT	✔	DEPOSIT	BALANCE
	TYPE	ACCOUNT	MEMO				
01/30/2019	329	National Bank		2,152.00			11,939.34
	CHK	22000 · National Bank VIS	1234-1234-1234-1234				
02/07/2019	330	Nellis Distributing		375.00			11,564.34
	BILLPMT	20000 · Accounts Payable					
02/08/2... 🗓		Payee		0.00		Deposit	
		Account	Memo				

ENDING BALANCE   **11,564.34**

Splits   1-Line   Sort by Date, Type, Number/Ref   Record   Restore

Figure 4-19 Entering in manual check information

Step 4.   Enter *331* in the *Number* column and press **Tab**.

If you are entering a previously handwritten check, make sure this number matches the number on the physical check. If you are entering an electronic funds transfer or an ATM withdrawal, enter *EFT* in the check number field. Alternatively, if you are entering a Debit Card transaction, enter *Debit* in the *Number* column.

Step 5.   Enter *Bay Office Supply* in the *Payee* column and press **Tab**.

Since *Bay Office Supply* is not in the *Vendor List*, QuickBooks prompts you to *Quick Add* or *Set Up* the vendor (see Figure 4-20).

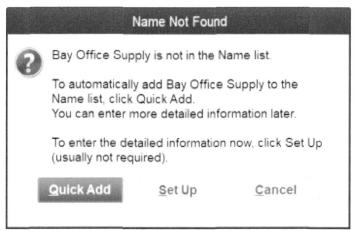

Figure 4-20 Name Not Found dialog box

Step 6.   Click **Quick Add** on the *Name Not Found* dialog box. This adds this vendor without entering the address and other information to completely set up the vendor. You can always go back later and add the other information by editing the vendor record. In the *Select Name Type* dialog box, the *Vendor* Name Type is selected. Click **OK** to add Bay Office Supply to the *Vendor Center* (see Figure 4-21).

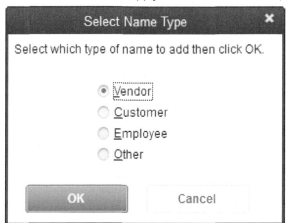

Figure 4-21 Select Name Type options - choose Vendor

Step 7.   Enter *128.60* in the *Payment* column and press **Tab**.

Step 8.   Enter **Office Supplies** in the *Account* column and press **Tab**.

               After you enter the first few characters of the word "**Office**" in the *Account* field, notice that QuickBooks automatically fills in the rest of the field with "Office Supplies." This QuickFill feature helps you to enter data faster.

Step 9.   Enter **Printer Paper** in the *Memo* column.

Step 10.   Verify that you've entered all of the fields in the transaction correctly and click **Record** to save the transaction (see Figure 4-22). If the *Set Check Reminder* dialog box opens, click **Cancel**.

Figure 4-22 Bay Office Supply entry in the Checking register

Notice that QuickBooks automatically updates your account balance after you record the transaction.

Splitting Transactions

Sometimes you will need to split your purchase to more than one account. Let's say that the check you just wrote to Bay Office Supply was actually for the following expenses:

- $100.00 for printer paper, to be used in the San Jose store (*Class*).
- $28.60 for computer cables for the Walnut Creek store (*Class*).

In order to track your printing costs separately from your office supplies, you must *split* the expenses and assign each expense to a separate account.

COMPUTER PRACTICE

Step 1.   With the *Checking* register open, click on check **331** to select it.

Step 2.   Click the **Splits** button as highlighted in Figure 4-23.

QuickBooks displays an area below the check where you can add several lines, memos, and amounts for *splitting* the expenses among multiple accounts.

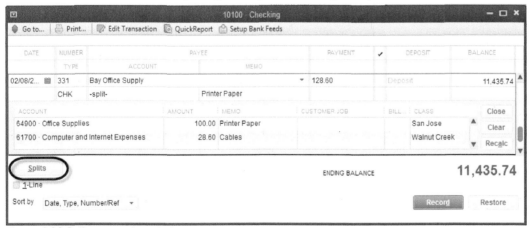

Figure 4-23 Split transaction window

Step 3.   Change the amount on the first line from *128.60* to *100.00*. Then press **Tab**.

Step 4.   Enter *Printer Paper* in the *Memo* column and press **Tab**.

Step 5.   Skip the *Customer:Job* column by pressing **Tab**.

This is the column where you can optionally enter the Customer or Job name where this expense would apply.

Step 6.   Enter *San Jose* in the *Class* column and press **Tab**.

Step 7.   On the second line, enter *Computer and Internet Expenses* in the *Account* column and press **Tab**.

Step 8.   QuickBooks calculates the amount **28.60** in the *Amount* column. This is correct so press **Tab** to leave it and move to the next field.

Step 9.   Enter *Cables* in the *Memo* column and press **Tab**.

Step 10.   Press **Tab** to skip to the **Class** column and enter *Walnut Creek*.

Step 11.   Verify that your screen matches Figure 4-23, and then press **Record**.

Step 12.   QuickBooks displays a dialog box asking if you want to record the changes to the previously recorded transaction. Click **Yes**.

Step 13.   Close the *Checking* register.

Using Write Checks Without Using Accounts Payable

If you are tracking Job costs or *Classes* and are not using the accounts payable feature, it may be best to use the *Write Checks* window instead of the *Register* to record your expenses. If you use *Items* to track purchases and you are not using the accounts payable feature, you *must* use either *Write Checks* or the *Enter Credit Card Charges* window. See page 142 for more information about tracking credit cards.

COMPUTER PRACTICE

Step 1.   To display the *Write Checks* window, click on the **Write Checks** icon on the *Home* page. Alternatively, press **Ctrl+W**.

Step 2.   Make sure *Checking* is already selected in the *Bank Account* field. Press **Tab**.

Step 3.   Check the *Print Later* checkbox next to the *Print* Icon at the top of the window.

This indicates that you want QuickBooks to print this check on your printer. When you print the check, QuickBooks will assign the next check number in the sequence of your checks. To enter a manual check, Debit Card or EFT transaction that does not need to be printed, enter *the manual check number or Debit* in the numbers field.

Step 4.   Enter *2/8/2019* in the *Date* field. Press **Tab**.

Step 5.   Select **Orlando Properties** from the *Pay to the Order of* drop-down list and press **Tab**.

Notice that QuickBooks enters the name and address from the Vendor record as soon as you choose the Vendor name from the list.

Step 6.   Enter *3,200.00* in the *$* field and press **Tab**.

Step 7.   Press **Tab** to skip the *Address* field.

Step 8.   Enter *Rent Expense* in the *Memo* field. Press **Tab**.

Step 9.   Enter *Rent Expense* in the *Account* column of the *Expenses* tab if not already selected and press **Tab**.

If necessary, when you enter your own expenses, use the bottom part of the check to split the payment between several different accounts, *Jobs*, and *Classes*.

Step 10.   Leave the *Amount* column set to *3,200.00* and press **Tab**.

Step 11.   Enter *San Jose Rent* in the *Memo* column, and press **Tab** twice.

Step 12.   Enter *San Jose* in the *Class* column and press **Tab**.

Step 13.   Verify that your screen matches Figure 4-24. Do not print the check now; we will print it later.

Step 14.   Click **Save & Close** to record the transaction.

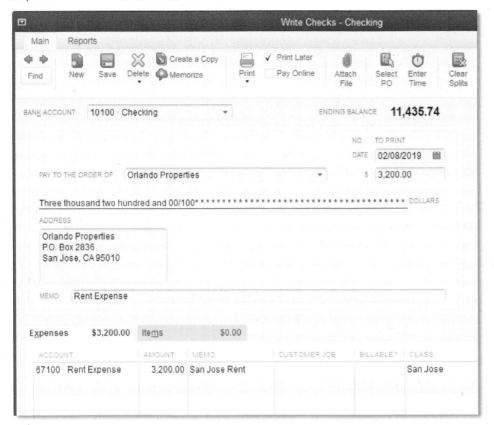

Figure 4-24 Write Checks window for Orlando Properties rent payment

> **Note:**
> In the example above, you recorded the check with a **To Print** status, so that you can print
> it later, perhaps in a batch with other checks. If you wanted to print the check
> immediately after you entered it, you would have clicked **Print** at the top of the *Write
> Checks* window and selected *Check*. QuickBooks would ask you to enter the check
> number.

Managing Accounts Payable

You can also use QuickBooks to track Accounts Payable (A/P). When you receive a bill from a vendor,
enter it into QuickBooks using the *Enter Bills* window. Recording a *Bill* allows QuickBooks to track the
amount you owe to the vendor along with the detail of what you purchased. For a *Bill* to be considered
paid by QuickBooks, you must pay it using the *Pay Bills* window (see page 127).

Entering Bills

When a bill arrives from your vendor, enter it into QuickBooks using the *Enter Bills* window.
COMPUTER PRACTICE

Step 1.   Select the **Vendors** icon from the *Home* page to display the *Vendor Center*. Select the
                 vendor **Ace Supply**, and then select **Enter Bills** from the *New Transactions* drop-down list
                 (see Figure 4-25). Alternatively, you can click the **Enter Bills** icon on the *Home* page and
                 select **Ace Supply** from the Vendor drop-down field.

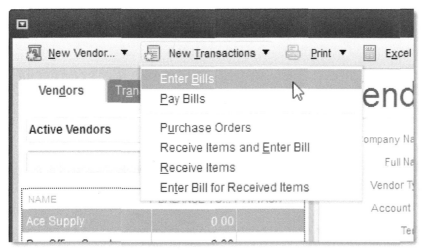

Figure 4-25 Selecting Enter Bills from the New Transactions drop-down list

Step 2.   In the *Enter Bills* window, verify that **Ace Supply** is displayed in the *Vendor* field and press **Tab**.

Notice that QuickBooks completes the *Bill Due*, *Terms*, and *Discount Date* fields automatically when you enter the *Vendor* name. QuickBooks uses information from the *Vendor* record to complete these fields. You can override this information if necessary. QuickBooks calculates the *Discount Date* and the *Bill Due* fields by adding the *Terms* information to the date entered in the *Date* field. If the terms do not include a discount, the *Discount Date* will not appear.

Step 3.   Enter *2/8/2019* in the *Date* field and press **Tab**.

Step 4.   Enter **2085** in the *Ref. No.* field and press **Tab**.

> **Tip:**
> When an A/P transaction increases what is owed, it is called a "bill." However, vendors call them "invoices." Therefore, the *Ref. No.* field on the *Bill* form should match the number on the *Invoice* you received from the vendor. The *Ref. No.* field is important for two reasons. First, it is the number used to identify this *Bill* in the *Pay Bills* window, and second, it is the number that shows on the voucher of the *Bill Payment* check.

Step 5.   Enter **360.00** in the *Amount Due* field and press **Tab**.

Step 6.   Press **Tab** to skip the *Bill Due* field and to accept the due date that QuickBooks has calculated.

Step 7.   Press **Tab** to accept the **2% 10 Net 30** terms already selected.

> **Note:**
> "The default *Terms* were setup in this *Vendor*'s record. You can override them on individual *Bills*. If you do, when you save the *Bill*, QuickBooks will ask if you want to make the change in *Terms* permanent. You should answer **No** unless you want the new *Terms* to be the new default terms to all future *Bills* for this *Vendor*.

Step 8.   Enter **Photo Materials for Jerry Perez Job** in the Memo field and press **Tab**.

> **Important:**
> If your vendor requires you to enter your account number on the checks you send, enter it in the *Account No.* field in the *Vendor* record. QuickBooks will print the contents of that field in the *Memo* field on *Bill Payments* to the vendor.

Step 9.   Enter *Cost of Goods Sold* in the *Account* column of the *Expenses* tab and press **Tab**.

Step 10.   Press **Tab** to accept *360.00* already entered in the *Amount* column.

Step 11.   Enter *Photo Materials* in the *Memo* column and press **Tab**.

Step 12.   To job cost this purchase, enter *Perez, Jerry* in the *Customer:Job* column and press **Tab**.

Step 13.   Leave the *Billable?* field checked. Press **Tab** again and enter *Walnut Creek* in the *Class* column.

Step 14.   Verify that your screen matches that shown in Figure 4-26. Click **Save & Close** to record the **Bill**. Close the **Vendor Center** window.

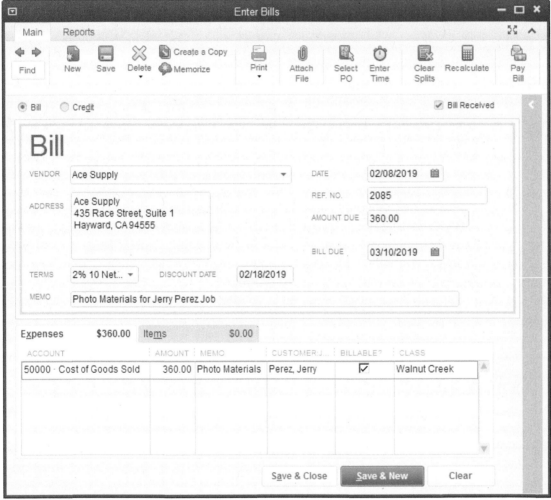

Figure 4-26 Recording Ace Supply bill

Attaching Documents

There are many advantages to storing documents electronically. Going "paperless" increases efficiency and eliminates costly storage.

QuickBooks allows you to attach electronic documents to QuickBooks transactions, such as *Bills*, *Invoices*, and other QuickBooks forms. The attached documents can either be stored on your system for free, or on a secure server managed by Intuit using QuickBooks Document Management for a fee. To attach electronic documentation to a QuickBooks transaction, look for the *Attach File* button in the upper section of the transaction window.

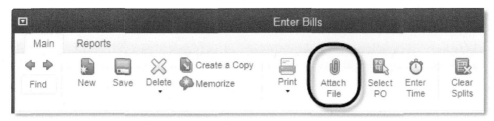

Figure 4-27 Attach File button in Enter Bills window

The Unpaid Bills Detail Report

To view a list of your unpaid *Bills*, use the *Unpaid Bills Detail* report.

COMPUTER PRACTICE

Step 1.   From the *Reports* menu, select **Vendors & Payables** and then select **Unpaid Bills Detail**.

Step 2.   Enter *2/10/2019* in the *Date* field and press **Tab**.

Step 3.   Verify that your screen matches Figure 4-28. Close the report window. Click **No**, if the *Memorize Report* message appears.

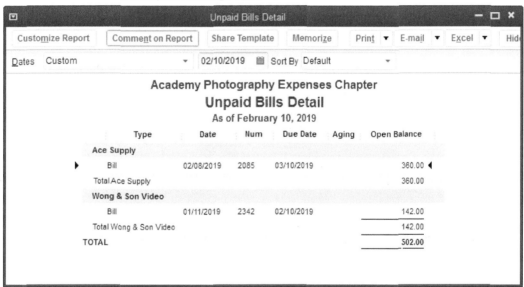

Figure 4-28 Unpaid Bills Detail report

Paying Bills

QuickBooks keeps track of all your bills in the Accounts Payable account. When you pay your bills, you will reduce the balance in Accounts Payable by creating *Bill Payment* checks.

COMPUTER PRACTICE

Step 1.   Select the **Vendors** icon from the *Icon Bar* to display the **Vendor Center**. Select **Pay Bills** from the *New Transactions* drop-down list (see Figure 4-29). You *do not* need to select a vendor first. Alternatively, you can click the **Pay Bills** icon on the *Home* page.

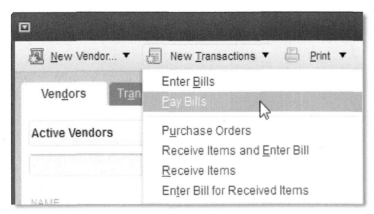

Figure 4-29 Selecting Pay Bills from the New Transactions drop-down list

Step 2.   QuickBooks displays the *Pay Bills* window.

Step 3.   Click on the radio button *Due on or before* and enter **3/10/2019** in the *Due on or before* date field (see Figure 4-30). QuickBooks allows you to filter the *Pay Bills* window so only the *Bills* due on or before a given date are shown.

> **Note:**
> The *Due on or before* field applies only to the *Bill* due date. There is no way to show only the *Bills* whose *discounts* expire on or before a certain date. However, you can sort the list of bills by the discount dates in the *Pay Bills* window by selecting **Discount Date** from the *Sort Bills by* drop-down list.

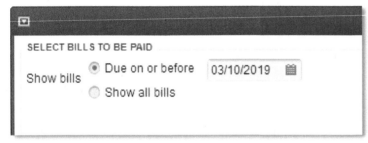

Figure 4-30 Entering the date in the Due on or before field

Step 4.   As shown in Figure 4-31, *Filter By* can be set to **All vendors** or you can select to only show a specific vendor. Also, *Due Date* is already selected from the *Sort By* drop-down list. If you have several *Bills* from the same vendor, it is sometimes easier to see all of the *Bills* sorted by *Vendor*. You can also sort the bills by *Discount Date* or *Amount Due*.

> **Note:**
> If QuickBooks displays a warning, that *This field may not be blank*, select **All Vendors** in the *Filter By* field.

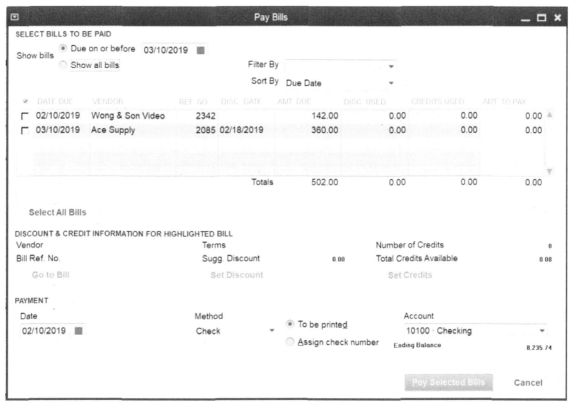

Figure 4-31 Pay Bills window

Step 5.   Leave **Check** in the *Method* field selected. Ensure that the *To be printed* radio button is selected.

Step 6.   Leave **Checking** in the *Account* field.

> **Note:**
> The *Payment Method* field allows you to choose to pay the bills by check or credit card. If you pay by check, QuickBooks automatically creates a check in your checking account for each bill selected for payment. To pay by credit card, select **Credit Card** and select the name of the credit card you want to use for the *Bill Payments*. QuickBooks will then create a separate credit card charge for each *Bill Payment*.

Step 7.   Enter **2/10/2019** in the *Payment Date* field.

Step 8.   Click the **Select All Bills** button in the middle to select both *Bills* that are displayed. Alternately, place a checkmark in front of the *Bills* you want to pay.

> **Tip:**
> If you want to display the original *Bill*, select the *Bill* on the *Pay Bills* window and click **Go to Bill**. This displays the original *Bill* so you can edit it if necessary.
>
> If you want to make a partial payment on a *Bill*, enter only the amount you want to pay in the *Amt. To Pay* column. If you pay less than the full amount due, QuickBooks will track the remaining amount due for that *Bill* in Accounts Payable. The next time you go to the *Pay Bills* window, the partially paid *Bills* will show with the remaining amount due.

Step 9.   To record a discount on the Ace Supply *Bill*, click on the line containing the Ace Supply Bill to select it. The *Discount & Credit Information for Highlighted Bill* section displays the terms and a suggested discount for the *Bill* (see Figure 4-32).

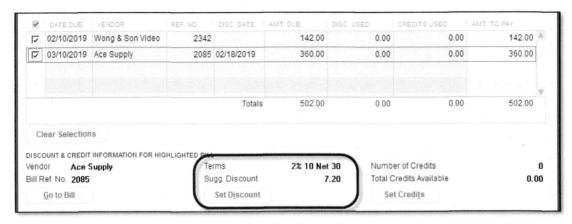

Figure 4-32 Discount section for Ace Supply bill

Step 10.   Click **Set Discount**.

In the *Discount and Credits* window, notice that QuickBooks calculates the discount according to the terms set on the *Bill* (see Figure 4-33). In this case, the terms are *2% 10 Net 30*.

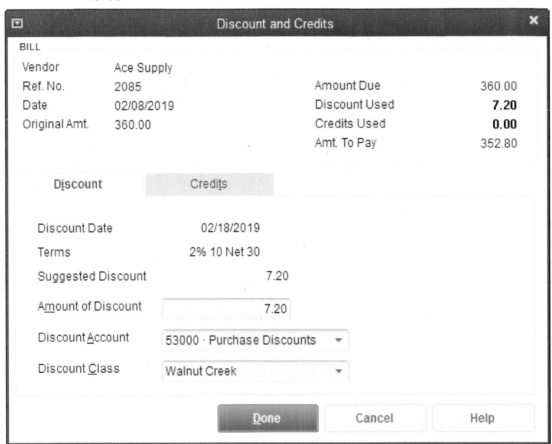

Figure 4-33 Discount and Credits window

Step 11.   Select **Purchase Discounts** in the *Discount Account* field to assign this discount to the proper account.

Step 12.   Enter ***Walnut Creek*** in the *Discount Class* field to assign this discount to the proper *Class*.

Refer to the *Bill* to determine the *Class*. The *Bill* being discounted was originally assigned to the *Walnut Creek Class* so the discount should use that class as well.

Step 13.   Click **Done**. This returns you to the *Pay Bills* window.

> **Note:**
>
> In some cases, it is better to use a *Bill Credit* instead of a discount. For example, when you want to associate the discount with a *Job*, or if you want to track discount items, use *Bill Credits* instead of using discounts in the *Pay Bills* process. You can record items, accounts, classes, and job information on the *Bill Credit*, just as you do on *Bills*. Then, in the *Pay Bills* window, click **Set Credits** to apply the *Bill Credit* to the *Bill*. To see how this would work, see the section on *Applying Vendor Credits* beginning on page 139.

Step 14.   Verify that your *Pay Bills* window matches that shown in Figure 4-34. Click **Pay Selected Bills** to record the *Bill Payments*.

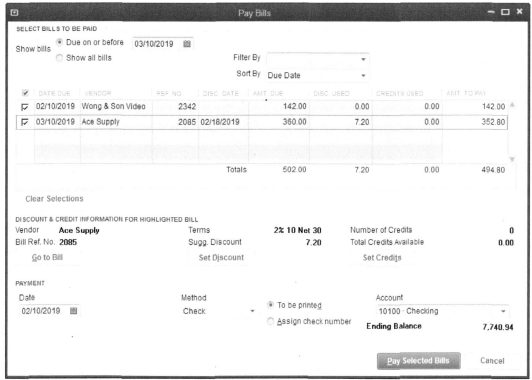

Figure 4-34 Pay Bills window after setting the discount

Step 15.   QuickBooks displays a *Payment Summary* dialog box as shown in Figure 4-35. Review the payments and click **Done**.

Step 16.   Close all windows except for the *Home* page.

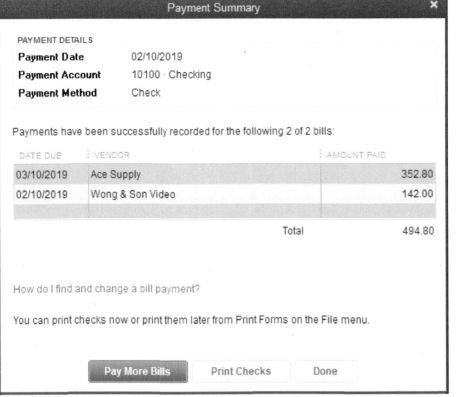

Figure 4-35 Payment Summary dialog box

> **Note:**
> If you select more than one *Bill* for the same vendor, QuickBooks combines all of the amounts onto a single *Bill Payment*.

When you use a check to pay *Bills*, QuickBooks records each *Bill Payment* in the *Checking* account register and in the Accounts Payable account register (see Figure 4-36 and Figure 4-37). *Bill Payments* reduce the balance in both the Checking account (credit) and the Accounts Payable account (debit).

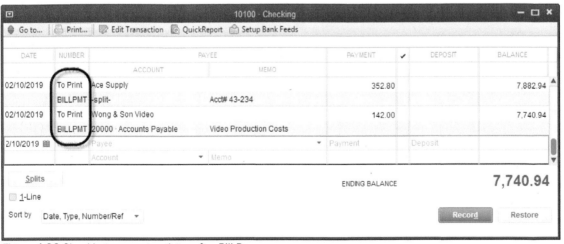

Figure 4-36 Checking account register after Bill Pay

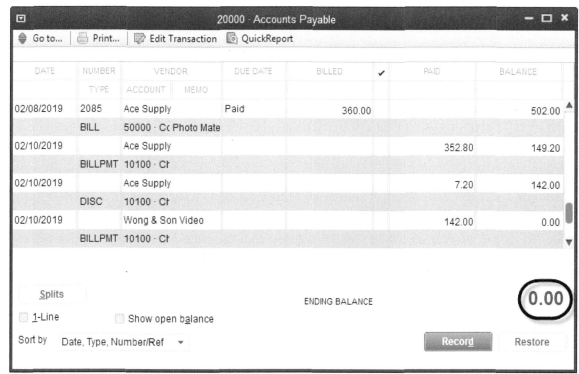

Figure 4-37 Accounts Payable register after Bill Pay

Printing Checks

COMPUTER PRACTICE

You do not need to print each check or *Bill Payment* separately. As you write checks and pay *Bills*, you have the option to record each check with a *Print Later* status. Follow these steps to print checks and *Bill Payments* that you have previously recorded with a *Print Later* status:

Step 1.   From the *File* menu, select **Print Forms** and then select **Checks**.

Step 2.   **Checking** in the *Bank Account* field is already selected (see Figure 4-38). This is the bank account on which the checks are written. Press **Tab**.

Step 3.   Enter **6001** in the *First Check Number* field, if necessary.

The *First Check Number* field is where you set the number of the first check you put in the printer.

> **Note:**
> QuickBooks assigns check numbers when it prints checks. You have the opportunity to set the check number just before you print the checks and after you assign a check number. QuickBooks keeps track of each check it prints and tracks the check number.

Step 4.   QuickBooks automatically selects all of the checks for printing. Click **OK**.

To prevent one or more checks from printing, you can click in the left column to remove the checkmark for each check you don't want to print. Since we did not print the rent check, it shows in Figure 4-38 along with the two *Bill Payments*. We will include it here so we can "batch print" all checks together.

Figure 4-38 Select Checks to Print window

Step 5.   When the *Print Checks* window displays, click **Signature** on the right side of the window
               (see Figure 4-39).

               You can automatically print signed checks by uploading a graphic file of a signature
               during the printing process.

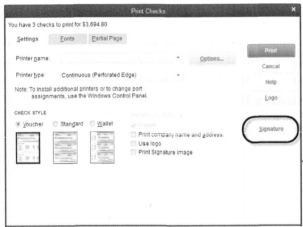

Figure 4-39 Signature Button in Print Checks window

Step 6.   In the *Signature* window, click the **File** button to upload the graphic file (see Figure 4-40).

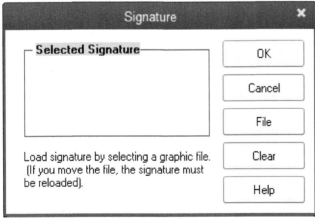

Figure 4-40 Signature window

Step 7.   In the *Open Logo File* window, navigate to where you store your exercise files and open
               Sig.png. This file was included with the portable exercise files.

Step 8.   If QuickBooks displays a warning window, click **OK**. QuickBooks will copy the image file to
               a new folder called *Expenses-15 – Images*.

Step 9.   The *Signature* window now displays an image of the uploaded signature file (see Figure 4-41). Click **OK**.

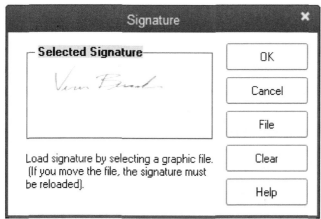

Figure 4-41 Signature window with file uploaded

> **Note:**
> Once you select the signature, QuickBooks will leave the box checked to always print the signature unless you uncheck the *Print Signature Image* shown in Figure 4-42.

Step 10.   Confirm your printer settings on the *Print Checks* window and click **Print** when you are ready to print (see Figure 4-42).

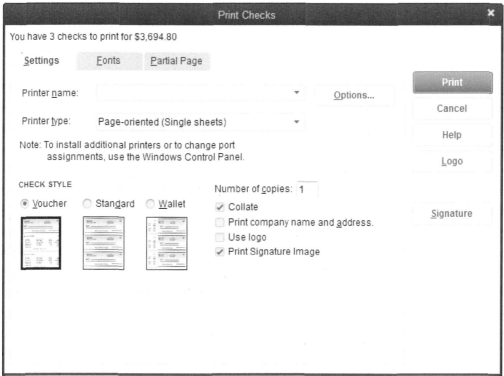

Figure 4-42 Print Checks window

> **Tip:**
> Make sure your checks are oriented correctly in the printer. With some printers, you feed the top of the page in first, and some you feed in bottom first. With some printers, you must insert the check face up, and with others, face down.

Step 11.   When QuickBooks has finished printing the checks, you will see the *Print Checks –*
            Confirmation dialog box in Figure 4-43.

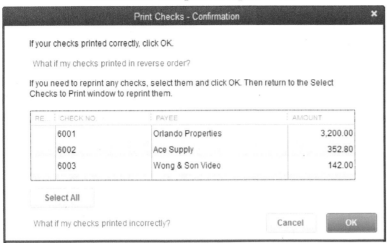

Figure 4-43 Print Checks - Confirmation dialog box

Step 12.   If the *Set Check Reminder* dialog box opens, click **Cancel**.

Step 13.   When the *Print Checks – Confirmation* window displays, click **OK**.

> **Note:**
> If your printer damages your checks and you select checks for reprinting, it is best
> accounting practice to void each damaged check and re-enter a new check in the bank
> account register or on the *Write Checks* window.

> **Tip:**
> If you are paying multiple bills on a single check and you want the vendor to be able to
> identify these bills, you can print a *Bill Payment Stub* by choosing **Bill Payment Stubs** from
> the *Print Forms* submenu on the *File* menu.

Voiding Checks

QuickBooks allows you to keep the information about voided checks so that you retain a record of these
checks. It is important to enter each check into your register even if the check is voided. This will prevent
gaps in your check number sequence.

> **Did You Know?**
> QuickBooks has a special report called *Missing Checks* that allows you to view all of your
> checks sorted by check number. The report highlights any gaps in the check number
> sequence. To view this report, select the **Reports** menu, then select **Banking,** and then
> select **Missing Checks.**

COMPUTER PRACTICE

Step 1.   Open the **Checking** account register and then select check **6003** by clicking anywhere on
            that record. You will be able to tell that the record has been selected as it will be outlined
            in the register.

Step 2.   From the *Edit* menu select **Void Bill Pmt-Check** (see Figure 4-44*).*

When you void a check, QuickBooks changes the amount to zero, marks the check cleared, and adds VOID to the *Memo* field.

Step 3.   Click **Record** to save your changes.

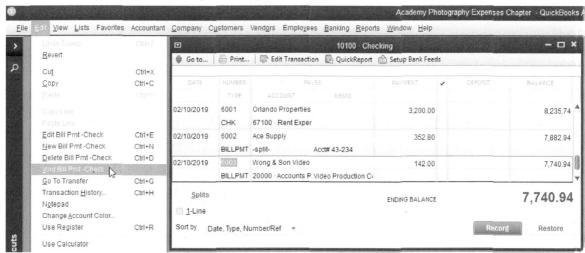

Figure 4-44 Voiding a check from the Edit menu

Since you are voiding a *Bill Payment*, QuickBooks warns you that this change will affect the application of this check to the *Bills* (see Figure 4-45). In other words, voiding a *Bill Payment* will make the *Bill* payable again.

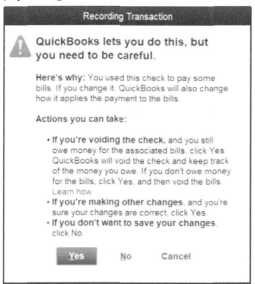

Figure 4-45 Recording Transaction dialog box about voiding BILLPMT check 6003

Step 4.   Click **Yes**.

Notice that the transaction shows as cleared in the register, and that QuickBooks set the amount of the check to zero (see Figure 4-46).

Step 5.   Close all open windows except the *Home* page.

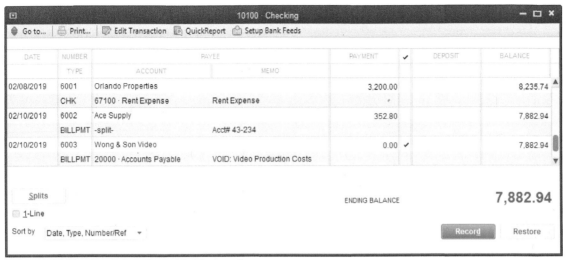

Figure 4-46 Check register after voided transaction

To repay the *Bill*, repeat the bill paying and printing process by following the steps below.

COMPUTER PRACTICE

Step 1.   Select the **Pay Bills** icon on the *Home* page.

Step 2.   Complete the *Pay Bills* window for the **Wong & Son Video** *Bill* per the instructions given in the *Paying Bills* section beginning on page 127. Verify that your screen matches Figure 4-47. Set the Payment Date to *2/16/2019*.

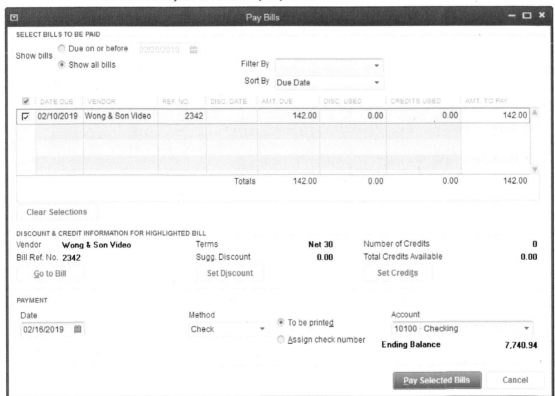

Figure 4-47 Completed Pay Bills window

Step 3.   Click **Pay Selected Bills** on the *Pay Bills* window to record the *Bill* payment.

Step 4.   Click **Done** on the *Payment Summary* dialog box.

Applying Vendor Credits

When a vendor credits your account, you should record the transaction in the *Enter Bills* window as a *Credit* and apply it to one of your unpaid *Bills*. In some situations, it is best to use a *Bill Credit* instead of the *Discount* window to record certain vendor credits, because the *Discount* window does not allow you to record any of the following information:

- Reference numbers or memos – These may be important for reference later.
- Allocation of the credit to multiple accounts.
- Allocation to *Customers* or *Jobs* – This may be critical in many situations.
- Information using *Items*.

COMPUTER PRACTICE

First, create a *Bill* from Nellis Distributing for Custom Framing Material.

Step 1.   Click on the **Enter Bills** icon on the *Home* page.

Step 2.   Enter the *Bill* shown in Figure 4-48.

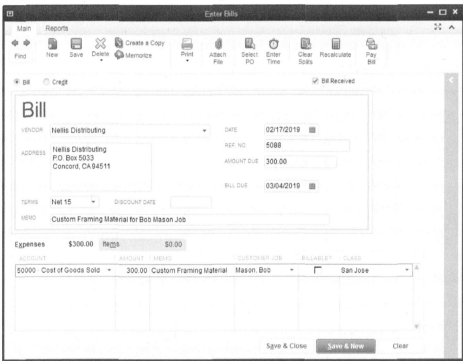

Figure 4-48 Bill from Nellis Distributing for Bob Mason job

Step 3.   When you're finished entering the data in Figure 4-48, click **Save & New**.

COMPUTER PRACTICE

Now, enter a Bill Credit.

Step 1.   On the next (blank) *Bill* form, select the **Credit** radio button at the top left of the window.

Step 2.   Fill in the *Bill Credit* information as shown in Figure 4-49. Click **Save & Close** to record the credit.

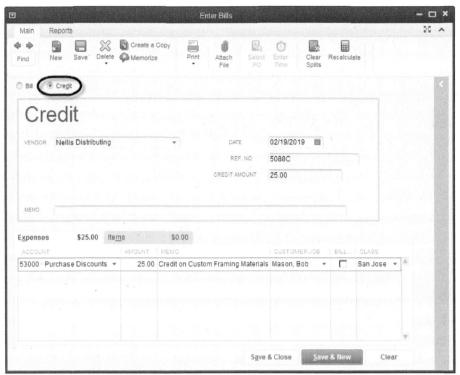

Figure 4-49 Creating a Bill Credit

> **The accounting behind the scenes:**
> When you record the **Bill Credit** shown in Figure 4-49, QuickBooks reduces (debits)
> Accounts Payable and reduces (credits) Purchase Discounts, a Cost of Goods Sold
> account.

COMPUTER PRACTICE

Step 1.   To apply the *Bill Credit* to a *Bill* for that vendor, select **Pay Bills** from the *Home* page (See
                 Figure 4-50).

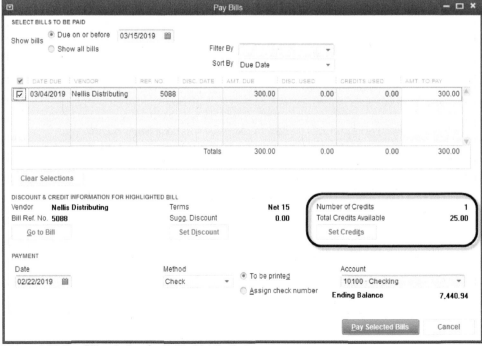

Figure 4-50 Pay Bills window for Nellis Distributing

Step 2.   Enter *3/15/2019* in the *Due on or before* field and press **Tab**. If needed, set Filter By to **All Vendors** .

Step 3.   Leave **Check** in the *Method* field and **Checking** in the *Account* field. Enter **2/22/2019** in the *Date* field.

Important:
In order to apply a *Bill Credit*, the vendor name must be the same on both the *Bill* and the *Bill Credit*.

Step 4.   Select the unpaid Bill for **Nellis Distributing** as shown in Figure 4-50.

When you select a *Bill* from a vendor for whom one or more unapplied credits exist, QuickBooks displays the total amount of all credits for the vendor in the *Total Credits Available* section. Notice the credit of $25.00 in Figure 4-50 for Nellis Distributing which we created above.

Step 5.   Click **Set Credits**.

Figure 4-51 Discount and Credits window to set Bill Credit

In the *Discount and Credits* window, QuickBooks automatically selected the credits to be applied to the *Bill*. You can override what is shown by deselecting the credit (removing the checkmark), or by entering a different amount in the *Amt. To Use* column.

Step 6.   Leave the credit selected as shown in Figure 4-51 and click **Done**.

QuickBooks has applied the $25.00 credit to Bill #5088 and reduced the amount in the *Amt. To Pay* column to $275.00 (see Figure 4-52).

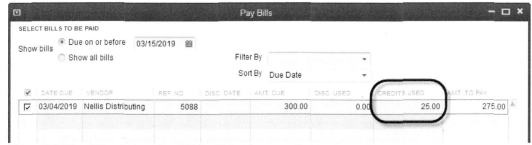

Figure 4-52 Pay Bills window after Bill Credit has been applied

Step 7.   Click **Pay Selected Bills** to pay the bill.

Step 8.   Click **Done** on the *Payment Summary* dialog box.

> **Note:**
> If you want to apply the credit without paying the *Bill*, reduce the *Amt. To Pay* column to zero.

Handling Deposits and Refunds from Vendors

This section covers how to handle more complicated transactions between you and your vendors. These transactions include deposits paid to vendors in advance of receiving the bill, refunds received from vendors for overpayment of a bill, and refunds received from vendors when Accounts Payable is not involved.

Vendor Deposits — When You Use Accounts Payable

Sometimes vendors require you to give them a deposit before they will provide you with services or products. To do this, create a check for the vendor and code it to Accounts Payable. This creates a credit in QuickBooks for the vendor that you can apply to the bill when it arrives.

> **DO NOT PERFORM THESE STEPS. THEY ARE FOR REFERENCE ONLY.**

1. Click on the **Write Checks** icon on the *Home* page.
2. Enter the data as shown in Figure 4-53. Notice that this check is coded to Accounts Payable. You only code checks to A/P when you are sending deposits to a vendor prior to receiving the bill.
3. Click **Save & Close**.

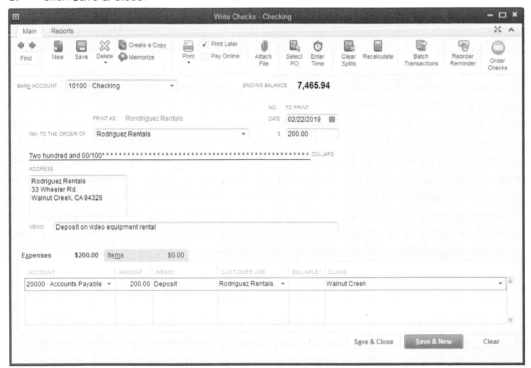

Figure 4-53 Coding check to Accounts Payable

Later, when the Bill is received from the vendor, enter it as you would any other Bill. Then apply the credit resulting from the check created above to the Bill by using the procedures outlined in the **Applying Vendor Credits** section of this chapter, beginning on page 139.

Vendor Refunds — When You Use Accounts Payable

When you receive a refund from a vendor, the kind of transaction you enter in QuickBooks will depend on how you originally paid the vendor.

If you prepaid the vendor using the method above and the amount of your prepayment was more than the bill, your Accounts Payable account will have a negative (debit) balance for that vendor. In this case, you will apply the refund check from the vendor to this credit balance in Accounts Payable.

On the other hand, if you simply wrote a check to the vendor and coded the check to an expense account, you will need to reduce the expense by the amount of the refund. The following tutorials address each of these situations.

To record a refund from a vendor that you prepaid using the deposit check in Figure 4-53, follow the steps below. In this example, you paid Rodriguez Rentals $200.00 in advance of receiving the bill. On a later date, Rodriguez Rentals sent a bill for $185.00. Since your deposit was more than the bill, the vendor also sent you a refund check for $15.00.

Start by entering the bill from the vendor just like any other bill. Then use the *Make Deposits* window to record your refund from the vendor.

> DO NOT PERFORM THESE STEPS. THEY ARE FOR REFERENCE ONLY.

1. Open the *Enter Bills* window and enter the bill from Rodriguez Rentals as shown in Figure 4-54. Click **Save & Close** to record the bill.

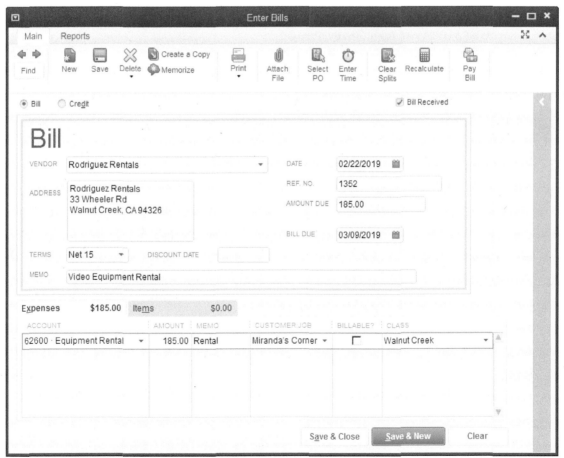

Figure 4-54 Enter Bill received from Rodriguez Rentals

2. Select the **Record Deposits** icon in the *Banking* section of the *Home* page.

3. Press **Tab** to leave *Checking* selected in the *Deposit To* field (see Figure 4-55).

4. Press **Tab** to leave the default date in the *Date* field.

5. Enter *Refund from Rodriguez* in the *Memo* field and press **Tab**.

6. Enter in the remaining data as shown in Figure 4-55. Enter the vendor's name in the Received From column so that QuickBooks will apply this refund to Rodriguez Rentals in A/P reports.

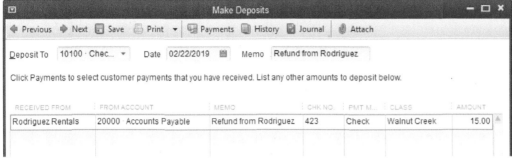

Figure 4-55 Make Deposits window to deposit refund check

7. Click **Save & Close** at the bottom of the window.

After you have recorded the deposit in Figure 4-55, apply the $200.00 prepayment check to both the bill and the refund check you just received (i.e. use the $200.00 prepayment check to *pay* the bill and the refund). Your Accounts Payable reports will not be correct until you make this application.

> **DO NOT PERFORM THESE STEPS. THEY ARE FOR REFERENCE ONLY.**

1. Select the **Pay Bills** icon from the *Home* page.

2. Click *Show all bills* in the *Show bills* field.

3. Leave **Check** in the *Payment Method* field and **Checking** in the *Account* field.

4. Enter *2/24/2019* in the *Payment Date* field.

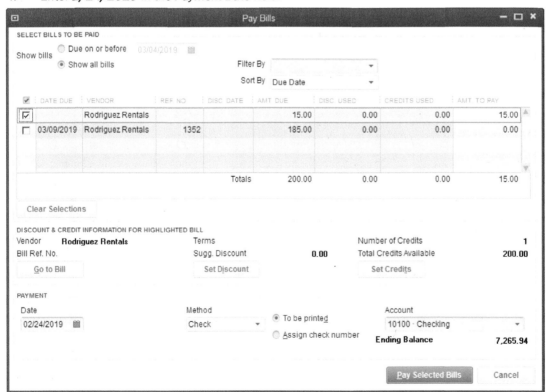

Figure 4-56 Pay Bill window; applying $200 deposit check to $15.00 refund received

5. Place a checkmark on the first line in the *Pay Bills* window ($15.00 deposit) and click **Set Credits** as shown in Figure 4-56.

    Though this window seems to show two bills for Rodriguez Rentals, the first line is actually the refund check you recorded using the *Make Deposits* window as shown in Figure 4-55.

6. In the *Apply Credits* window, QuickBooks automatically applies $15.00 of the $200.00 credit to the refund check (see Figure 4-57).

7. Click **Done**.

Figure 4-57 Apply Credits window

8. The second line in the *Pay Bills* window is the actual Bill from Rodriguez Rentals. Select this Bill and click **Set Credits** (Figure 4-58).

Figure 4-58 Pay Bills window; applying the $200.00 deposit check to the $185.00 bill

9.   In the *Discounts and Credits* window, QuickBooks automatically applies $185.00 of the $200.00 credit to Bill #1352 (see Figure 4-59).

10.   Click **Done**.

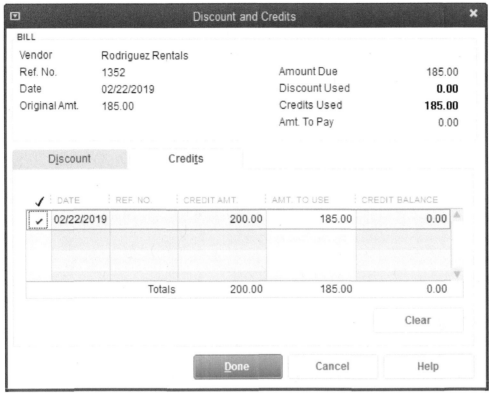

Figure 4-59 Discounts and Credits window

11.   Since the amount of the prepayment ($200.00) is the same as the bill ($185.00) plus the refund check ($15.00), the total in the *Amt. To Pay* field is zero (see Figure 4-60).

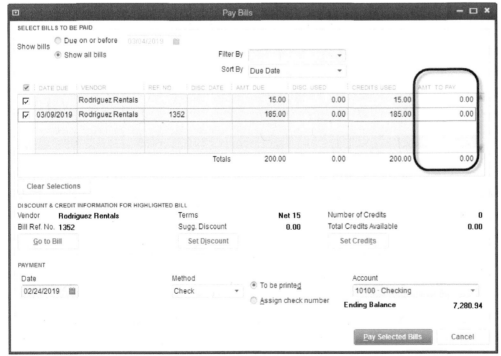

Figure 4-60 Pay Bills window with the deposit applied

12. Click **Pay Selected Bills**. QuickBooks will link these transactions together, clearing them from the Unpaid Bills and Accounts Payable Aging reports. A Bill Payment for zero will appear in the Check Register. This entry can be used to print a bill payment stub to send the vendor if needed.

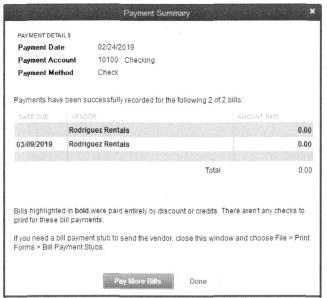

Figure 4-61 Payment Summary for $0 to link and clear transactions

13. Click **Done** on the Payment Summary dialog box.

Vendor Refunds – When You Directly Expensed Payment

If you did not use the Accounts Payable features, but instead wrote a check to the vendor and coded the check to an expense account, record the refund using a deposit transaction. Use the same expense account you used on the original payment to the vendor (see Figure 4-62).

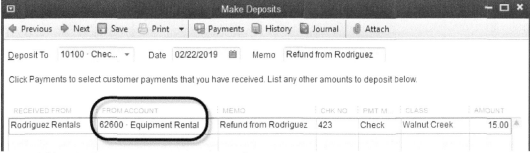

Figure 4-62 Make Deposits window coding the refund to an expense account

Tracking Petty Cash

It is sometimes necessary to use cash for minor expenditures, such as office supplies, postage, parking, or other small items. In order to track these expenditures, you can set up a separate bank account in QuickBooks called *Petty Cash*.

To track a deposit to your Petty Cash account (and the withdrawal of cash from your Checking account), simply write a check to a designated person, the *custodian*, who will cash the check at a local bank and place the money into Petty Cash. Code the check to the Petty Cash account.

When you use Petty Cash for a company expense, enter the expenditure in the *Payment* column of the Petty Cash account register. This reduces the balance in the Petty Cash account so that it always agrees with the actual amount of cash you have on hand. Code each cash expenditure to the appropriate *payee, account, class* and *job*. Click the **Splits** button to split the expenditure among multiple accounts or to assign customer names or classes to the transaction.

Tracking Company Credit Cards

To track charges and payments on your company credit card, set up a separate credit card account in QuickBooks for each card. Then enter each charge individually using the *Enter Credit Card Charges* window. To pay the credit card bill, use *Write Checks* and code the check to the credit card account.

Another Way:
You can also pay your credit card bill by using *Pay Bills* after recording a *Bill* for the balance due, coded to the credit card liability account.

Did You Know?
Many credit cards allow you to download your credit card charges into QuickBooks through the Internet, eliminating the need to enter each charge manually. For more information about the QuickBooks Credit Card download, select the *Banking* menu, select *Bank Feeds*, and then select *Set Up Bank Feed for an Account*.

Entering Credit Card Charges

Each time you use a company credit card, use the *Enter Credit Card Charges* window to record the transaction.

The accounting behind the scenes:
When you record credit card charges, QuickBooks increases (credits) your Credit Card Payable liability account and increases (debits) the expense account shown at the bottom of the window.

Note:
You will need to create an account on your *Chart of Accounts* for each company credit card. Use the *Credit Card* type when creating the account.

COMPUTER PRACTICE

Step 1.	Click the **Enter Credit Card Charges** icon on the *Home Page*. Alternatively, from the *Banking* menu, select **Enter Credit Card Charges**.
Step 2.	Press **Tab** to accept **National Bank VISA Gold** in the *Credit Card* field.
Step 3.	**Purchase/Charge** is already selected. Press **Tab** twice.
	If you used your card when receiving a refund or credit from a vendor, you would select **Refund/Credit** instead of **Purchase/Charge** on this step. QuickBooks will then reduce the balance on your credit card when you record a Credit transaction.
Step 4.	Enter *Bay Office Supply* in the *Purchased From* field and press **Tab**.
Step 5.	Enter *2/24/2019* in the *Date* field. Press **Tab**.
Step 6.	Enter *65432* in the *Ref No.* field and press **Tab**.
	The *Ref No.* field is optional. Its purpose is to tag each charge with the number on the charge slip.
Step 7.	Enter *86.48* in the *Amount* field and press **Tab**.
Step 8.	Enter *Purchase Office Supplies* in *Memo* field and press **Tab**.

Step 9.   Enter the *Account, Amount, Memo,* and *Class* fields as displayed in Figure 4-63.

Step 10.   Verify that your screen matches Figure 4-63. Click **Save & New** to record the credit card charge.

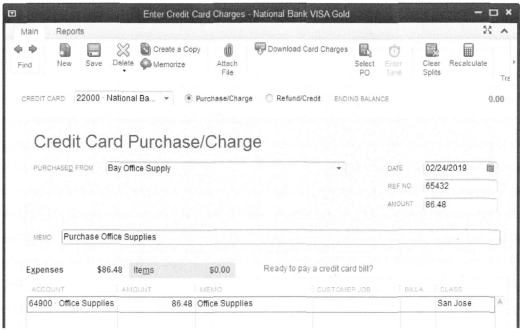

Figure 4-63 Enter Credit Card Charges window for Bay Office Supplies purchase

Step 11.   Enter another credit card charge that matches Figure 4-64. Click **Save & Close**.

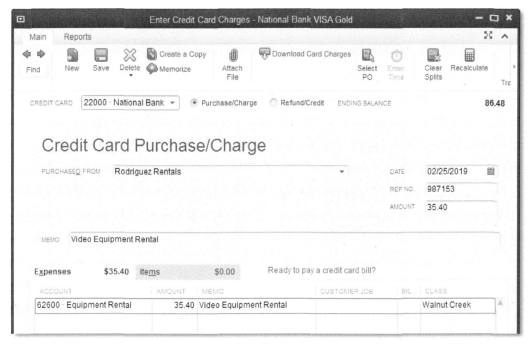

Figure 4-64 Enter Credit Card Charges window for equipment rental

Paying the Credit Card Bill

Follow the steps below to write a check to pay your credit card bill.

> **The accounting behind the scenes:**
> When you record a credit card payment, QuickBooks reduces (credits) the Checking account and reduces (debits) the Credit Card liability account.
> **Note:** There is another method of paying the credit card bill that is part of the reconciliation process. In the reconciliation chapter, you'll learn more about reconciling the credit card account, and then creating a *Bill* for the balance due.

COMPUTER PRACTICE

Step 1.   Click the **Write Checks** icon on the *Home* page.

Step 2.   Enter the check as shown in Figure 4-65. Notice that you will enter the credit card account name in the *Account* column of the *Expenses* Tab.

Step 3.   Click **Save & Close** to record the transaction.

Step 4.   Click **Save Anyway** to bypass *Items not assigned classes* window.

You do not need to enter a class when posting to a credit card account or to any other Balance Sheet account.

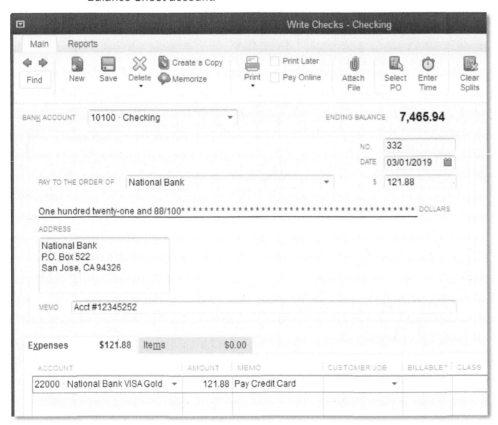

Figure 4-65 Write Checks window to pay credit card bill

To see the detail of your credit card charges and payments, look in the *National Bank VISA Gold* account register (see Figure 4-66). This register can be accessed by pressing **Ctrl+A** to open the Chart of Accounts, and then double clicking on the *National Bank VISA Gold* credit card account. You can also pay credit cards as part of the reconciliation process. For more information, see 185.

Figure 4-66 National Bank VISA Gold account register

Paying Sales Tax

Many QuickBooks users need to collect sales tax each time they sell products and certain types of services. This sales tax needs to be paid to the appropriate state or local agency. Academy Photography files its sales tax return to a single vendor called the State Board of Equalization. In this example, we will run reports for the first quarter of 2019. For more on collecting sales tax, see page 95.

Paying Sales Tax

After you prepare your sales tax return and make necessary adjustments for discounts, interest, penalties or rounding, create a sales tax payment for the amount you owe.

When you pay your sales tax, do not use the *Write Checks* window because the payment will not affect the *Sales Tax Items*. It also will not show properly on the *Sales Tax Liability* reports. To correctly pay your sales tax liability, use the *Pay Sales Tax* window.

COMPUTER PRACTICE

Step 1.   From the *Home* page, select the **Manage Sales Tax** icon.

Step 2.   Click the **Pay Sales Tax** button in the *Manage Sales Tax* window. Alternatively, from the *Vendors* menu, select **Sales Tax** and then select **Pay Sales Tax**.

Step 3.   The *Pay Sales Tax* window displays. In the *Pay From Account* field, **Checking** already displays so press **Tab**. This field allows you to select the account from which you wish to pay your sales tax.

Step 4.   Enter *4/15/2019* in the *Check Date* field and press **Tab**. This field is the date of *when* you are paying the sales tax.

Step 5.   Enter *3/31/2019* in the *Show sales tax due through* field and press **Tab**. In this field, enter the last day of the sales tax reporting period. For example, if you are filing your sales tax return for the first quarter, enter the last day of March in this field.

QuickBooks shows the total tax you owe for each county as well as any adjustments. To pay all the tax and the adjustments for all rows, click the **Pay All Tax** button. You can create a Sales Tax Adjustment by clicking Adjust on this screen.

Step 6.   Leave **333** in the *Starting Check No.* field and press **Tab**. QuickBooks automatically enters the next check number sequentially.

Step 7.   Click in the **Pay** column (see Figure 4-67) on the line with a balance.

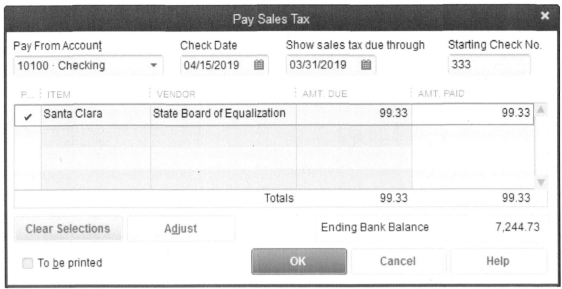

Figure 4-67 Pay Sales Tax window

Step 8.   Click **OK** to record the Sales Tax Payment.

Step 9.   Close the *Manage Sales Tax* window.

After you record the sales tax payment, QuickBooks will create a special type of check called a *Sales Tax Payment* (TAXPMT) in your checking account for the total tax due to each sales tax agency (Vendor).

> **Important:**
> QuickBooks allows you to adjust the amounts in the *Amt. Paid* column. However, if you do you will retain an incorrect (overstated) balance *in Sales Tax Payable* for the period. If you need to change the amount of sales tax due, use a *Sales Tax Adjustment*. To quickly access *the Sales Tax Adjustment* window, click **Adjust** on the *Pay Sales Tax* window.

Accounts Payable Reports

QuickBooks has several reports that you can use to analyze and track your purchases and vendors. Following are two sample reports for you to create. See the Reports chapter for more information on creating reports.

Vendor Balance Detail

The *Vendor Balance Detail* report shows the detail of each *Bill* and *Bill Payment* to each vendor. However, this report only includes transactions that "go through" Accounts Payable. That is, it only shows transactions such as *Bills* and *Bill Payments*. If you write checks to your vendors directly, without first entering a *Bill*, those transactions will not show in this report.

COMPUTER PRACTICE

Step 1.   From the *Reports* menu, select **Vendors & Payables** and then select **Vendor Balance Detail** (see Figure 4-68).

Step 2.   To print the report, click **Print** and click **Report** at the top of the report window. Close the report, and click **No** if the *Memorize Report* message appears.

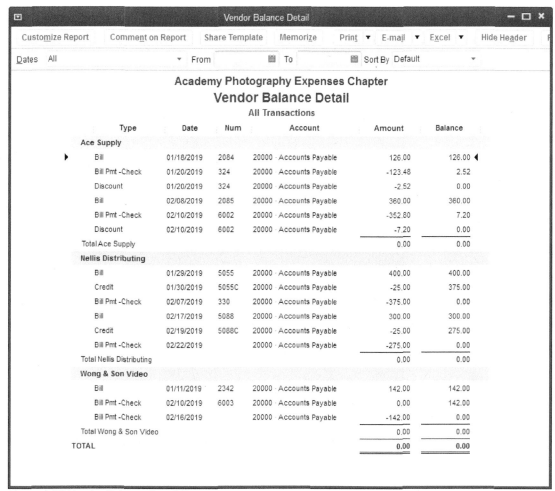

Figure 4-68 Vendor Balance Detail Report

Transaction List by Vendor

The *Transaction List by Vendor* report shows all transactions associated with your vendors, even if the transactions did not "go through" Accounts Payable (e.g., checks and credit card charges).

COMPUTER PRACTICE

Step 1.   From the *Reports* menu, select **Vendors & Payables** and then select **Transaction List by Vendor** (see Figure 4-69).

Step 2.   Set the date fields on the report to *1/1/2019* through *3/31/2019*.

Step 3.   Close all open windows and click **No** if the *Memorize Report* message appears.

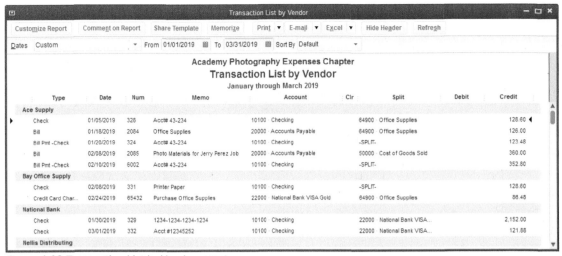

Figure 4-69 Transaction List by Vendor report

Sales Tax Liability

The *Sales Tax Liability* report shows the details of Total Sales broken down into Non-Taxable and Taxable groups along with the Tax Rate and Tax Collected. This report is useful for verifying the amount of sales tax collected for a specific period of time.

COMPUTER PRACTICE

Step 1.   From the *Reports* menu, select **Vendors & Payables** and then select **Sales Tax Liability**. (See Figure 4-70)

Step 2.   Set the date fields on the report to *1/1/2019* through *3/31/2019*.

Step 3.   Close all open windows and click **No** if the *Memorize Report* message appears.

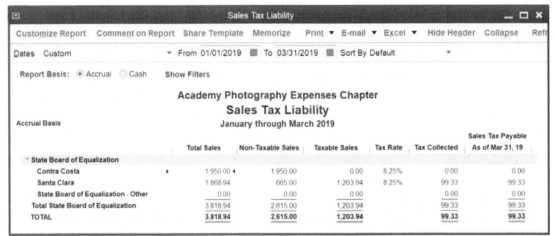

Figure 4-70 Sales Tax Liability report

Tracking Loans using the Loan Manager

You can track detailed information about your loans. You can individually track and amortize each of your loans so that QuickBooks will automatically allocate the principal and interest on each payment.

Setting up a Loan in the Loan Manager

The details of each loan can be set up in the **QuickBooks Loan Manager** to automatically amortize and track each loan. If you plan to have QuickBooks track loan details using the Loan Manager, you'll need to gather the details on each loan so that you have all of the information shown in Table 4-2.

Truck Loan Detail	
Account Name	Truck Loan
Lender	National Bank
Origination Date	12/31/2018
Original Amount	$ 24,000.00
Term	60 Months
Due Date of Next Payment	1/31/2019
Payment Amount	$ 452.16
Next Payment Number	1
Payment Period	Monthly
Does loan have escrow payment?	No
Alert me 10 days before a payment is due	Leave unchecked
Interest Rate	5%
Compounding period	Monthly
Payment Account	Checking
Interest Expense Account	Interest Expense
Fees/Charges Expense Account	Bank Service Charges

Table 4-2 Truck Loan Detail

> **DO NOT PERFORM THESE STEPS. THEY ARE FOR REFERENCE ONLY.**

For this example, Academy Photography owns a Delivery Truck that they purchased on 12/31/2018. When they purchased the truck, they took out a loan with National Bank for $24,000.00 that carries an interest rate of 5% per year, for 5 years.

1. From the *Banking Menu*, select **Loan Manager**.

2. In the *Loan Manager* setup window, click **Add a Loan**.

> **Note:**
> The liability account and the balance for this loan were set up in the data file for this chapter. It is necessary to set up the account and the beginning balance first to ensure correct linking of the loan detail to the General Ledger. For more information click **What you need to do before you add a loan** on the *Loan Manager* setup window (see Figure 4-71).

Figure 4-71 Loan Manager setup window

3.   Complete the loan information in the *Add Loan* window using the data from Table 4-2. Complete the *Enter account information for this* loan section. When completed your screen should look similar to Figure 4-72.

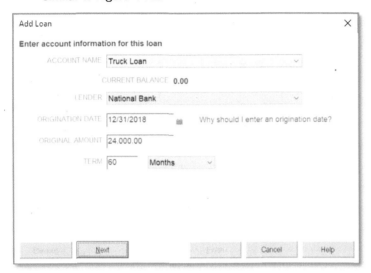

Figure 4-72 Truck loan information – your screen may vary

4.   Click **Next**.

5.   Complete the *Enter payment information for this loan* section using data from Table 4-2. When completed, your screen should look like Figure 4-73.

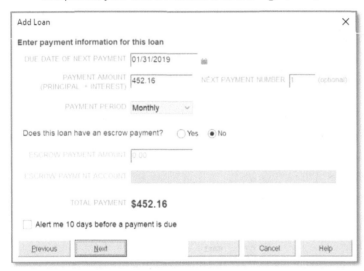

Figure 4-73 Payment information for Truck loan

> **Note:**
> QuickBooks allows you to track escrow amounts separately from principal and interest so you can automatically record these expenditures with each payment. For example, taxes added to your mortgage payment automatically could be posted each month, rather than by a separate manual entry.

6.   Click **Next**.

7.   Complete the *Enter interest information for this loan* section using data from Table 4-2. When completed, your screen should look like Figure 4-74.

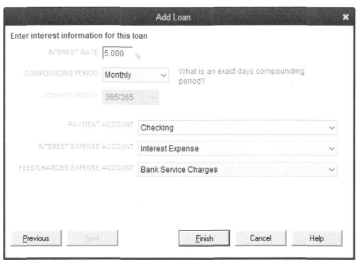

Figure 4-74 Interest information for Truck loan

8. Click **Finish** to save the Truck Loan.

Making Loan Payments using the Loan Manager

In our example, Academy Photography purchased a truck and took out a loan with National Bank for $24,000.00. The loan has been set up in Loan Manager; therefore, all payments on the loan should originate in Loan Manager.

> **Note:**
> The loan manager will only display the Payment Schedule after the origination date of the loan.

> **DO NOT PERFORM THESE STEPS. THEY ARE FOR REFERENCE ONLY.**

1. If Loan Manager is not already open, from the *Banking* menu select **Loan Manager**. QuickBooks displays the *Loan Manager* window as shown in Figure 4-75. Click the *Payment Schedule* tab to see a list of all the payments.

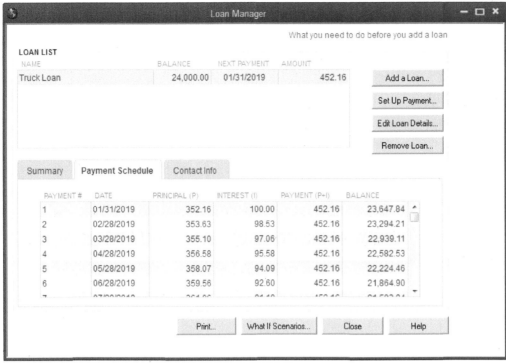

Figure 4-75 Loan Manager window – your screen may vary

2. **Truck Loan** in the *Loan List* is already selected. Click **Set Up Payment** to make a payment for the Truck Loan. QuickBooks displays the window shown in Figure 4-76.

3. Confirm that **A regular payment** is selected in the *This payment is* drop-down list as shown in Figure 4-76.

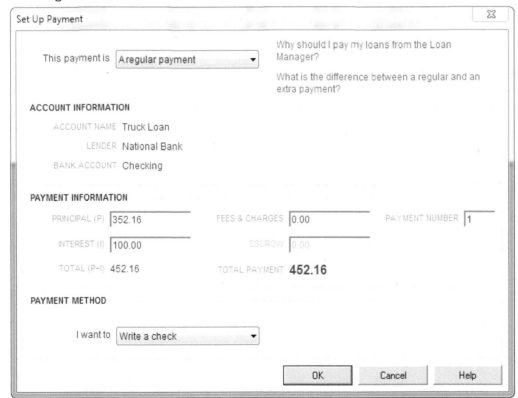

Figure 4-76 Set Up Payment window

> **Note:**
> Select **An extra payment** when you are making a payment in addition to your regular monthly amount.
>
> QuickBooks automatically calculates the amounts for the *Principal* and *Interest* fields based on the information you entered when you set up the loan. Confirm that these amounts agree to your loan statement and enter any fees or charges for the month in the *Fees & Charges* field.

4. In the *I want to* field, leave **Write a check** selected.

5. Click **OK** to create a check to make a payment for this loan. QuickBooks displays the *Write Checks* window and populates each field with the correct information as shown in Figure 4-77. If a manual check number displays in the **No.** field, check the *Print Later* box so that a voucher check can be used.

> **Note:**
> If you want to enter a Bill instead of a Check, select **Enter a bill** in the *I want to* drop-down list in the *Set Up Payment* window in the *Loan Manager*.

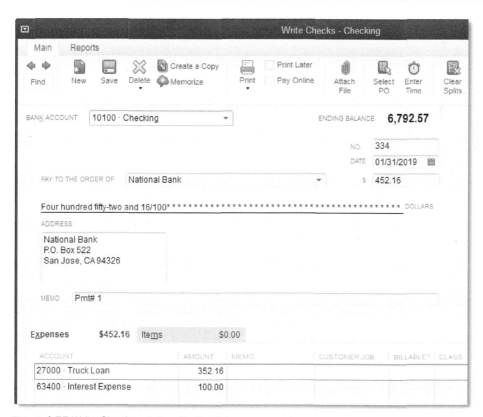

Figure 4-77 Write Checks window for Truck loan payment

6. Enter *1/31/2019* in the *Date* field. QuickBooks uses the current date when creating a **Check** or **Bill** through the *Loan Manager*. Edit the date field as necessary so the **Check** or **Bill** has the correct date.

7. Confirm that your screen matches Figure 4-77.

8. Click **Save & Close.**

Bill Tracker

You can also track bills using the *Bill Tracker*. You can open *Bill Tracker* through a variety of points of access: the *Bill Tracker* icon in the *Icon Bar*, an icon in the *Vendor Center*, or by selecting *Vendors* in the main menu and then *Bill Tracker*.

Managing a large number of purchase orders and bills can be a hassle in QuickBooks. Sometimes, bills are received (and entered) from your vendors before you receive the items ordered. However, it is important to wait to pay those bills so that they are not paid before the items are received. Also, sometimes it is a good idea to prioritize which bills to pay by vendor. In earlier versions of QuickBooks, you have to look at a number of different reports to see all of this information, and that makes it difficult to manage when there are a lot of transactions.

Bill Tracker makes this task simpler. It presents all of the information you need to manage your bills in one screen, presented in the familiar "dashboard"-like visual layout used with the *Income Tracker*. It includes purchase orders as well as unbilled, unpaid, and paid transactions summarized in one screen. Also, clicking on the colored bars at the top filters for one category.

Figure 4-78 Bill Tracker default view – Your screen may vary

The default view in Figure 4-78 displays all unbilled purchase orders, unpaid bills, and unreceived item receipts, as well as any bill payments made in the last 30 days.

There are a number of simple filters that can be applied to this list to make the information more accessible and easy to understand. For example, click on the yellow bar at the top and you will see just the "open bills."

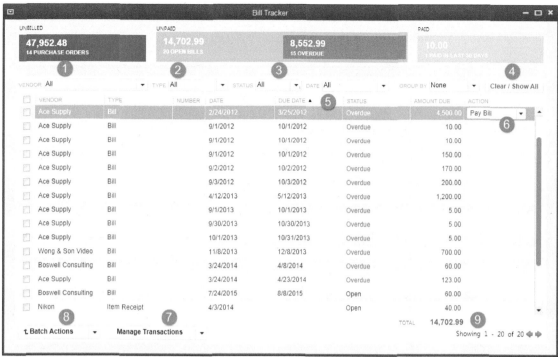

Figure 4-79 Bill Tracker filtered view – Your screen may vary

The numbered items in Figure 4-79 are additional filters and items of interest explained here.

1. The *Vendor* drop down filters for a single vendor, which is useful for seeing what is owed to a particular vendor.

2. The *Type* drop down lets you filter by transaction type. For instance, in the screen shot above, you see both *Bills* and *Item Receipts*, but you can use the type filter to only see the bills.

3. *Status* lets you choose all, open, or overdue transactions.

4. *Clear/Show All* will reset all of the filters to return you to the original state.

5. You can sort the display by clicking on any column heading. You cannot change which columns show.

6. The *Action* column button lets you perform an action on the selected transaction. The actions that are available depends on the type of transaction. As an example, for a *Bill*, you can pay the bill, make a copy, or print it. For a *Purchase Order* your options are to print, close, email, copy, or convert to a bill. For some transactions, no actions are possible.

7. *Manage Transactions* provides shortcuts to create new transactions (*Purchase Order, Bill,* or *Check*), or to edit the highlighted row.

8. *Batch Actions* can be applied to a number of transactions at the same time, if you check the box by the ones to process. The options available are to batch print purchase orders, batch pay bills, or batch close purchase orders.

9. Note that at the bottom, if you apply a filter, the amount due column is totaled.

Another interesting feature is the *Group By* box – it defaults to *None* as shown above, or you can select *Vendor* as shown in Figure 4-80.

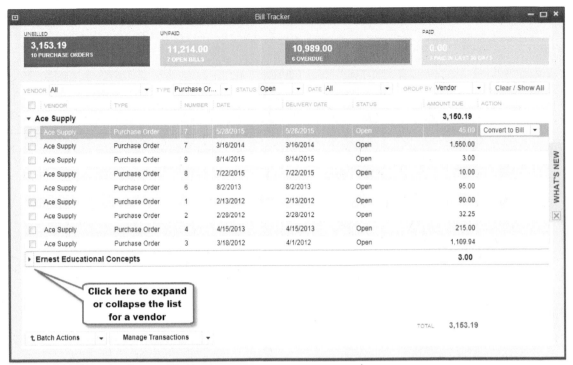

Figure 4-80 Bill Tracker Grouped By Vendor

This is different than sorting by vendor – it also gives you a subtotal by vendor, as well as letting you expand or collapse the list for any given vendor. If you have a large number of transactions, then this can be a useful tool.

Review Questions

Comprehension Questions

1. Describe how classes are used in QuickBooks.

2. Describe how to track expenses by job in QuickBooks.

3. Describe the different types of Accounts Payable transactions you can perform in QuickBooks, and how to use the Forms to perform them.

4. Under what circumstances is it important to use Bill Credits to record discounts?

5. If you want to track credit card charges and payments in a separate liability account, describe the steps you must use to record charges and payments on the credit card.

Multiple Choice

Select the best answer(s) for each of the following:

1. You may record payments to your vendors by:

    a)   Recording a manual entry directly into the check register.

    b)   Using *Write Checks* to write and print a check without using Accounts Payable.

    c)   Using *Enter Bills* to record Accounts Payable and then using *Pay Bills* to pay open Bills.

    d)   All of the above.

2. To display the *Vendor Center:*

   a)   Click *Vendors* on the QuickBooks *Home* page.

   b)   Click the *Vendors* icon on the *Icon Bar.*

   c)   Select the *Vendor* menu and then select *Vendor Center.*

   d)   a, b, or c.

3. You can add a vendor:

   a)   Only at the beginning of the fiscal year.

   b)   Only if you will purchase over $600 from that particular vendor and a Form 1099 will be issued.

   c)   Only at the beginning of the month.

   d)   At any time by selecting *New Vendor* in the *Vendor Center.*

4. Which statement is true?

   a)   QuickBooks records each *Bill Payment* in a bank account register (or credit card account register) and the Accounts Payable register.

   b)   *Bill Payments* increase the balance in both the Checking account and the Accounts Payable account.

   c)   You should assign *Jobs* to all discounts taken.

   d)   You cannot make partial payments on a *Bill.*

5. Which QuickBooks feature allows you to separate your income and expenses by line of business, department, location, profit center, or any other meaningful breakdown of your business?

   a)   Job costing.

   b)   Class tracking.

   c)   Customer types.

   d)   Vendor types.

6. If you void a Bill Payment check, all of the following occur, except:

   a)   QuickBooks retains a trail of the check number, but the amount becomes zero.

   b)   The Bill becomes unpaid.

   c)   The Checking account balance increases.

   d)   The Accounts Payable account decreases.

7. If you want to track the expenses for each customer or job:

   a)   Enter each expense in the job-cost section.

   b)   Use the pay liabilities function.

   c)   Link each expense with the customer or job to which it applies.

   d)   Create a separate expense account for each job.

8. To make a loan payment, you can:

   a)   Select the loan liability account in the Chart of Accounts and choose Make Deposit from the Activities Menu.

   b)   Choose Pay Loan from the Banking Menu.

   c)   Use the *Loan Manager* to calculate the interest and principal amounts. Select the *Loan Manager*, then select the Loan to pay, and then select *Set Up Payment.*

   d)   All of the above.

9. When a vendor credits your account, you record it in:
    a) The *Write Checks* window.
    b) The *Enter Bills* window.
    c) The *Pay Bills* window.
    d) The *Accounts Payable* Register.

10. Which Account-type should you use to track Petty Cash:
    a) Credit Card.
    b) Equity.
    c) Bank.
    d) Checking.

11. The Vendor Balance Detail Report:
    a) Shows the detail of each Bill, Bill Credit, Discount, and Bill Payment to each vendor.
    b) Shows the detail of each payment created using the *Write Checks* window.
    c) Can be created by selecting *Vendor Balance Detail* report from the *Vendor Center*.
    d) None of the above.

12. What is the accounting behind the scenes for the *Pay Bills* window:
    a) Increase (debit) Accounts Payable, Decrease (credit) the Checking Account.
    b) Decrease (debit) Accounts Payable, Decrease (credit) the Checking Account.
    c) Decrease (debit) Accounts Payable, Increase (credit) the Checking Account.
    d) Decrease (debit) Accounts Payable, Decrease (debit) the Checking Account.

13. It's best not to use which field in the new vendor setup window:
    a) Opening Balance.
    b) Vendor Name.
    c) Address.
    d) Terms.

14. In the *Pay Bills* window, you can sort the Bills by:
    a) Due Date.
    b) Vendor.
    c) Discount Date.
    d) All of the above.

15. Which statement is true regarding bill payments:
    a) Bill Payments *increase* the balance in the Accounts Payable account.
    b) When you pay bills by issuing a check using the *Pay Bills* window, QuickBooks records each Bill Payment in the Checking account register and in the Accounts Payable account register.
    c) If you select more than one Bill for the same vendor, QuickBooks creates a separate Bill Payment for each Bill.
    d) Bill Credits that are created from a vendor are automatically applied to Bills that are due for that same vendor.

Completion Statements

1. The _____ _____ shows a graphical representation of the steps involved in recording your expenses.

2. Terms of 2% 10 Net 30 on a bill means that if you pay the bill within _____ days, you are eligible for a(n) _____ discount.

3. To separately track income and expenses for multiple departments, locations, or profit centers, use _____ tracking.

4. To track job costs in QuickBooks, link each expense with the _____ or _____ to which it applies.

5. For a Bill to be considered paid by QuickBooks, you must pay the Bill using the _____ _____ window.

Expenses Problem 1

Restore the Expenses-18Problem1.QBM file. The password to access this file is *Sleeter18*.

1. Activate *Class* tracking in the data file.

2. Add a new vendor to the Vendor list using the data in the table below. Fields that are not provided below can be left blank.

Field Name	Data
Vendor Name	Virtual Video Services
Company Name	Virtual Video Services
Mr./Ms./...	Ms.
First Name	Heather
Last Name	Miller
Main Phone	510-555-8682
Main Email	miller@virtualvideo4u.us
Name and Address	Virtual Video Services
	Heather Miller
	3599 Redwood Way
	Dublin, CA 94508
Account #	576-225
Terms	Net 30
Print on Check as	Virtual Video Services
Tax ID	888-77-9999
Check Box	Vendor eligible for 1099
Account Prefill	Professional Fees
Vendor Type	Consultant
County	Alameda

Table 4-3 Use this data to enter a new vendor

3. Print the **Vendor Contact List**. (From the *Reports* menu, select **Vendors & Payables** and then select **Vendor Contact List**.)

4. Enter *Check* number *331* directly in the *Checking* register on **1/8/2019** to **Oswald Office Supply** for **$725.00**. Use *Quick Add* to add the Vendor. Split the expense to **$435.00** for **Office Supplies** for the **San Jose** store and **$290.00** for **Office Supplies** for the **Walnut Creek** store.

5. Enter *Bill* number *84-6542* from **Sinclair Insurance** on **1/17/2019** for **$1,210.00** with *Terms* of **Net 30**. Code the *Bill* to **Insurance Expense**. Allocate 100% of the cost to the **San Jose** store.

6. Create and print an **Unpaid Bills Detail** report dated **1/20/2019**.

7. Pay all of the *Bills* due on or before **2/20/2019**. Pay the *Bills* from the *Checking* account on **2/20/2019**. Starting check number is **332**.

Expenses Problem 2 (Advanced)

APPLYING YOUR KNOWLEDGE

> Restore the Expenses-18Problem2.QBM file. The password to access this file is *Sleeter18*.

1. Activate *Class* tracking in the data file.

2. Add a new vendor to the Vendor list using the data in the table below. Fields that are not provided below can be left blank.

Field Name	Data
Vendor Name	East Bay Photography Services
Company Name	East Bay Photography Services
Mr./Ms./...	Mr.
First Name	Frank
Last Name	Schwartz
Main Phone	510-555-1414
Main Email	frank@ebphoto.biz
Name and Address	East Bay Photography Services Frank Schwartz 4950 Alma Ave. Castro Valley, CA 94500
Account #	528-963
Terms	Net 30
Print on Check as	East Bay Photography Services
Tax ID	111-22-3333
Check Box	Vendor eligible for 1099
Account Prefill	Professional Fees
Vendor Type	Consultant
County	Alameda

Table 4-4 Use this data to enter a new vendor

3. Print the **Vendor Contact List**. (From the *Reports* menu, select **Vendors & Payables** and then select **Vendor Contact List**.)

4. Enter *Check* number *331* directly in the *Checking* register on **1/12/2019** to **Castro Valley Hardware** for **$677.00**. Use *Quick Add* to add the *Vendor*. Split the expense to **$300.00** for **Office**

Supplies for the San Jose store and $377.00 for Repairs and Maintenance for the Walnut Creek store.

5. Using *Write Checks*, enter a *Check (Print Later)* to **Orlando Properties** dated **1/12/2019** for **$1,500.00** for **Rent** at the **San Jose** store. Make the check printable but don't print the check.

6. Enter *Bill* number *38-9904* from **Nellis Distributing** on **1/18/2019** for **$520.00** with *Terms* of **Net 15**. The *Bill* is for the purchase of supplies for the Bob Mason job, so code the *Bill* to **Cost of Goods Sold**. Bob Mason is a customer in the San Jose store, so link the cost with the appropriate *Job* and *Class*.

7. Enter *Bill* number *4274* from **Sinclair Insurance** on **1/19/2019** for **$1,200.00** with Terms of **Net 30**. Code the *Bill* to **Insurance Expense**. Allocate 50% of the cost to the **San Jose** store and 50% of the cost to the **Walnut Creek** store.

8. Create and print an **Unpaid Bills Detail** report dated **1/20/2019**.

9. Pay all of the *Bills* due on or before **2/28/2019**. *Pay Bills* from the *Checking* account on **1/20/2019**. Make the *Bill Payments* "printable" checks.

10. Print all of the checks that you recorded with a *Print Later* status. Print them on blank paper and start the check numbers at **6001**.

11. Enter a *Credit Card Charge* on the **National Bank VISA** card from **Lakeside Office Supply** (Use *Quick Add* to add the vendor), reference number **1234**, dated **1/25/2019**. The purchase was for **$109.98** for **Office Supplies** for the **Walnut Creek** store.

12. Enter *Bill* number *4635* from **Ace Supply** on **1/25/2019** for **$229.00** with *Terms* of **Net 30**. Code the *Bill* to **Cost of Goods Sold** since it was for supplies for the Ron Berry job. Ron Berry is a customer at the San Jose store. Keep the default *Terms* for *Ace Supply*.

13. Enter a *Bill Credit* from *Ace Supply* on **1/30/2019** for **$50.00**. Use reference number **4635C** on the credit. Code the credit to **Cost of Goods Sold** and link the credit with the *Job* for Ron Berry and the **San Jose** *Class*.

14. Apply the credit to *Bill* number **4635** and pay the remainder of the *Bill* on **1/30/2019** using a printable check.

15. Print the check using number **6005** on blank paper.

16. Print a **Vendor Balance Detail** report for **All** transactions.

Chapter 5
Bank Reconciliation and Bank Transactions

Topics

In this chapter, you will learn about the following topics:

- Reconciling Bank Accounts (page 169)
- Bank Reconciliation Reports (page 175)
- Finding Errors During Bank Reconciliation (page 176)
- Handling Bounced Checks (page 182)
- Reconciling Credit Card Accounts and Paying the Bill (page 185)
- Bank Feeds (page 188)

Restore this File:

This chapter uses BankRec-18.QBW. See page 9 for more information. The password to access this file is *Sleeter18*.

At the end of each month, you must compare the transactions you have entered into QuickBooks with your bank statement to ensure that QuickBooks matches the bank's records. This process is called *reconciling.* It is a very important step in the overall accounting process and ensures the accuracy of your accounting records.

In addition to reconciling bank accounts, you can also reconcile other accounts, such as credit card accounts, using the same process. In fact, you can reconcile almost any Other Current Asset, Fixed Asset, Credit Card, Other Current Liability, Long Term Liability, or Equity account using the same process presented in this chapter. However, even though QuickBooks *allows* you to reconcile many accounts, the primary accounts you'll reconcile are bank and credit card accounts since these types of accounts always have monthly statements.

Reconciling Bank Accounts

Figure 5-1 shows Academy Photography's bank statement for the checking account as of January 31, 2019. Before reconciling the account in QuickBooks, make sure you've entered all of the transactions for that account. For example, if you have automatic payments from your checking account (EFTs) or automatic charges on your credit card, it is best to enter those transactions before you start the reconciliation.

Business Checking Account		
Statement Date:	**January 31, 2019**	*Page 1 of 1*

Summary:

Previous Balance as of 12/31/18:	$	14,384.50
Total Deposits and Credits:	+ $	3,386.02
Total Checks and Debits:	- $	12,345.60
Statement Balance as of 1/31/19	= $	**5,424.92**

Deposits and Other Credits:

DEPOSITS

Date	Description		Amount
30-Jan	Customer Deposit	$	249.54
30-Jan	Customer Deposit	$	1,950.00
31-Jan	Customer Deposit	$	1,177.86
	Deposits:	$	**3,377.40**

INTEREST

Date	Description		Amount
31-Jan	Interest Earned	$	8.62
	Interest:	$	**8.62**

Checks and Other Withdrawals:

CHECKS PAID:

Check No.	Date Paid		Amount
325	2-Jan	$	465.00
326	7-Jan	$	276.52
327	10-Jan	$	128.60
6001**	10-Jan	$	3,200.00
6003**	25-Jan	$	142.00
6004	26-Jan	$	123.48
	Checks Paid:	$	**4,335.60**

OTHER WITHDRAWALS/PAYMENTS

Date	Description	Amount
31-Jan	Transfer	$ 8,000.00
	Other Withdrawals/Payments:	$ **8,000.00**

SERVICE CHARGES

Date	Description		Amount
31-Jan	Service Charge	$	10.00
	Service Charge:	$	**10.00**

Figure 5-1 Sample bank statement

COMPUTER PRACTICE

Using the sample data file for this chapter, follow these steps to reconcile the QuickBooks Checking account with the bank statement shown in Figure 5-1.

Step 1.   Before you begin the reconciliation process, first review the account register to verify that all of the transactions for the statement period have been entered (e.g., deposits, checks, other withdrawals, and payments.) The Academy Photography sample data file for this section already has the deposits, checks, other withdrawals, and payments entered into the register.

Step 2.   If the *Home* page is not already open, select the **Company** menu and then select **Home Page**.

Step 3.   Click the **Reconcile** Icon on the *Banking* section of the *Home* page.

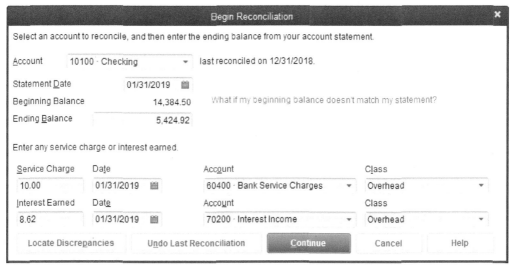

Figure 5-2 Begin Reconciliation window

Step 4.   In the *Begin Reconciliation* window (see Figure 5-2), the *Account* field already shows *Checking*. The account drop-down list allows you to select other accounts to reconcile, however since *Checking* is the account you're reconciling, you don't need to change it now. Press **Tab**.

Step 5.   Leave **1/31/2019** in the *Statement Date* field and press **Tab**.

The default statement date is one month after your last reconciliation date. Since this exercise file was last reconciled on 12/31/2018, QuickBooks entered *1/31/2019*.

> **Tip:**
> If your bank does not date statements at the end of the month, ask the bank to change your statement date to the end of the month. This makes it easier to match the bank statement with your month-end reports in QuickBooks.

Step 6.   Look for the *Previous Balance as of 12/31/2018* on the bank statement (see Figure 5-1). Compare this amount with the *Beginning Balance* amount in the *Begin Reconciliation* window (see Figure 5-2). Notice that they are the same.

> **Note:**
> QuickBooks calculates the *Beginning Balance* field in the *Begin Reconciliation* window by adding and subtracting all previously reconciled transactions. If the beginning balance does not match the bank statement, you probably made changes to previously cleared transactions. See *Finding Errors During Bank Reconciliation* on page 176 for more information.

Step 7.   Enter **5,424.92** in the *Ending Balance* field. This amount is the *Statement Balance as of 1/31/2019* shown on the bank statement in Figure 5-1. Press **Tab**.

> **Note:**
> If you already recorded bank charges in the check register, skip Step 8 through Step 11 to avoid duplicate entry of the charges.

Step 8.   Enter **10.00** in the *Service Charge* field and press **Tab**.

If you have any bank service charges or interest earned in the bank account, enter those amounts in the appropriate fields in the *Begin Reconciliation* window. When you enter these amounts, QuickBooks adds the corresponding transactions to your bank account register.

Step 9.   Leave **1/31/2019** in the *Date* field and press **Tab**.

Step 10.   Select **Bank Service Charges** from the *Account* drop-down list and press **Tab**.

               Each time you reconcile, this field will default to the account you used on the last bank reconciliation. Confirm that this is the correct expense account before proceeding to the next field.

Step 11.   Select **Overhead** from the *Class* drop-down list and press **Tab**.

> **Note:**
> If you already recorded interest income in the check register, skip Step 12 through Step 15 to avoid duplicate entry of the interest income.

Step 12.   Enter **8.62** in the *Interest Earned* field and press **Tab**.

Step 13.   Leave **1/31/2019** in the *Date* field and press **Tab**.

Step 14.   Select **Interest Income** from the *Account* drop-down list and press **Tab**.

Step 15.   Select **Overhead** from the *Class* drop-down list and click **Continue**.

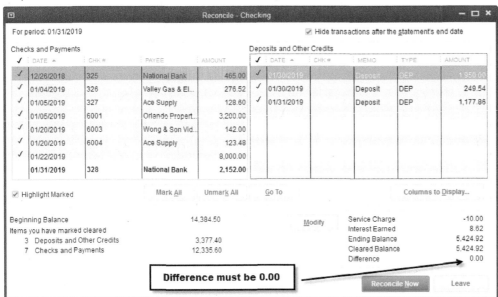

Figure 5-3 Reconcile – Checking window

Step 16.   At the top of the *Reconcile – Checking* window (see Figure 5-3), check the box labeled *Hide transactions after the statement's end date*.

               ☑ Hide transactions after the statement's end date

               This removes transactions dated after the statement date from being displayed on the screen. Since they could not possibly have cleared yet, this simplifies your life so you only have to look at transactions that *could* have cleared the bank as of the statement date.

Step 17.   In the *Deposits and Other Credits* section of the *Reconcile – Checking* window, match the deposits and other credits on the bank statement (see Figure 5-1 on page 170) with the associated QuickBooks transactions. Click anywhere on a line to mark it cleared. The checkmark (✓) indicates which transactions have cleared.

Step 18.   In the *Checks and Payments* section of the *Reconcile – Checking* window, match the checks and other withdrawals on the bank statement with the associated QuickBooks transactions.

> **Tip:**
> Notice that QuickBooks calculates the sum of your marked items at the bottom of the window in the *Items you have marked cleared* section. This section also shows the number of deposits and checks you have marked cleared. Compare the figures to your bank statement. If you find a discrepancy with these totals, you most likely have an error. Search for an item you forgot to mark or one that you marked in error.
>
> **Tip:**
> You can sort the columns in the *Reconcile - Checking* window by clicking the column heading. If you would like to change the columns displayed in the *Reconcile – Checking* window, click the *Columns to Display* button. This will allow you to select which columns you would like to see when you are reconciling (see Figure 5-4).

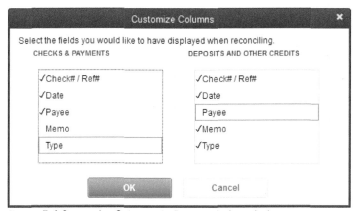

Figure 5-4 Customize Columns in Reconciliation window

Step 19.   After you've marked all the cleared checks and deposits, look at the *Difference* field. It should be **0.00**, indicating that your bank account is reconciled.

After you've marked all the cleared checks and deposits, look at the *Difference* field. It should be **0.00**, indicating that your bank account is reconciled.

If the *Difference* field is not zero, check for errors. For help in troubleshooting your bank reconciliation, see *Finding Errors During Bank Reconciliation* on page 176.

> **Tip:**
> If you need to wait until another time to complete the bank reconciliation, you can click **Leave**. When you click **Leave**, QuickBooks will save your progress so you can complete the reconciliation later.

Step 20.   If the *Difference* field is zero, you've successfully reconciled. Click **Reconcile Now**. If you see a window offering online banking, click **OK** to close.

> **Note:**
> It is very important that you do not click **Reconcile Now** unless the *Difference* field shows **0.00**. Doing so will cause discrepancies in your accounting records. See page 179 for more information.

Step 21.   The *Select Reconciliation Report* dialog box displays. The **Both** option is already selected, so click **Display** to view your reports on the screen (see Figure 5-5).

Figure 5-5 Select Reconciliation Report window

Step 22.   If the *Reconciliation Report* window appears, click **OK**.

Step 23.   QuickBooks creates both a *Reconciliation Summary* report (Figure 5-6) and a *Reconciliation Detail* report (Figure 5-7). The length of the detail report will depend upon how many transactions you cleared on this reconciliation and how many uncleared transactions remain in the account.

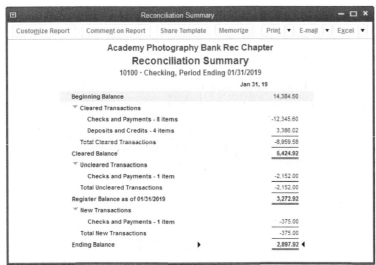

Figure 5-6 Reconciliation Summary report

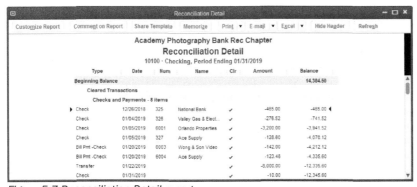

Figure 5-7 Reconciliation Detail report

Step 24.   Close all open report windows.

Bank Reconciliation Reports

Each time you complete a bank reconciliation, QuickBooks walks you through creating a bank reconciliation report for that reconciliation. You can recreate your bank reconciliation reports at any time by following the steps below.

> **Note:**
> If you are using QuickBooks Pro you can create Bank Reconciliation reports for the most recently reconciled month only.

COMPUTER PRACTICE

Step 1.   From the *Reports* menu select **Banking** and then select **Previous Reconciliation**. The *Select Previous Reconciliation Report* window displays (see Figure 5-8).

Step 2.   Confirm that **Checking** is selected in the *Account* field.

If you have more than one bank account, you can select another bank account using the *Account* drop-down list.

Step 3.   Confirm that **1/31/2019** is selected in the *Statement Ending Date* field.

QuickBooks automatically selects the report for your most recent bank reconciliation. You can select another report by highlighting the statement date in this section.

Step 4.   Confirm that **Detail** is selected in the *Type of Report* section.

Step 5.   Confirm that **Transactions cleared at the time of reconciliation** in the *In this report, include* section is selected (see Figure 5-8). When you select this option, QuickBooks displays an Adobe Acrobat PDF file with the contents of the reconciliation report. The Acrobat (PDF) report does not include any changes you may have made to reconciled transactions.

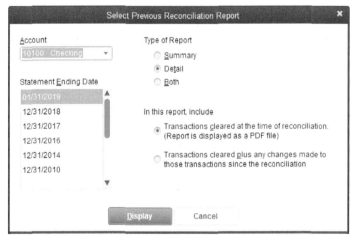

Figure 5-8 Select Previous Bank Reconciliation Report window

Step 6.   Click **Display** to view your bank reconciliation reports on screen.

> **Note:**
> If your screen does not show the Balance column in the window shown in Figure 5-9, you need to set your Printer Setup settings to fit the report to 1 page wide before you perform the bank reconciliation. This is because Acrobat creates the report when you finish the reconciliation and uses the settings in your Printer Setup to determine how to lay out the page.
>
> If you have already created the report, you can undo the reconciliation (see page 177) and then select *Printer Setup* from the *File* menu. When the *Printer setup* window displays, select *Report* from the *Form Name* drop-down list. At the bottom of the window you can check the *Fit report to* option and enter *1* for the number of pages wide you want reports to display, as illustrated below.
>
> ☑ Fit report to   1   page(s) wide

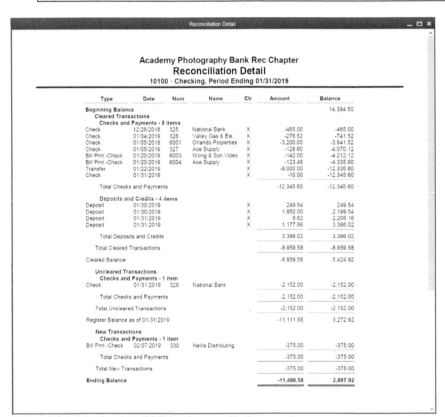

Figure 5-9 Adobe Acrobat (PDF) bank reconciliation report – your screen may vary

Step 7.   Close the Reconciliation Detail report.

> **Note:**
> If you prefer to create a normal QuickBooks reconciliation report (as opposed to an Acrobat PDF report), select the option, *Transactions cleared plus any changes made to those transactions since the reconciliation* in Step 5 above.

Finding Errors During Bank Reconciliation

If you have finished checking off all of the deposits and checks but the *Difference* field at the bottom of the window does not equal zero, there is an error (or discrepancy) that must be found and corrected. To find errors in your bank reconciliation, try the following steps:

Step 1: Review the Beginning Balance Field

Verify that the amount in the *Beginning Balance* field matches the beginning balance on your bank statement. If it does not, you are not ready to reconcile. There are two possibilities for why the beginning balance will no longer match the bank statement:

1. One or more reconciled transactions were voided, deleted, or changed since the last reconciliation; and/or,
2. The checkmark on one or more reconciled transactions in the account register was removed since the last reconciliation.

To correct the problem you have two options:

Option 1: Use the Previous Reconciliation Discrepancy Report to Troubleshoot

In the *Reconcile – Checking* window, click **Modify** to return to the *Begin Reconciliation* window, then click **Locate Discrepancies**. In the *Locate Discrepancies* window, click **Discrepancy Report**. (Alternately, from the *Reports* menu, select **Banking,** and then select **Reconciliation Discrepancy.**)

Review the report for any changes or deletions to cleared transactions. The *Type of Change* column shows the nature of the change to the transaction. Notice that a user deleted a cleared check.

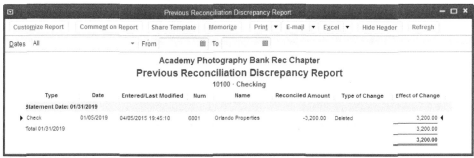

Figure 5-10 Previous Reconciliation Discrepancy report – your screen may vary

1. For each line of the report with "Deleted" in the *Type of Change* column, re-enter the deleted transaction. Then, use the Bank Reconciliation window to re-reconcile the transaction that had been deleted.
2. For each line of the report with "Amount" in the *Type of Change* column, double click the transaction in the *Reconciliation Discrepancy* report to open it (i.e., QuickZoom). Then, change the amount back to the reconciled amount.

After returning all transactions to their original state (as they were at the time of the last reconciliation), you can then proceed to investigate whether the changes were necessary, and if so, enter adjustment transactions.

Option 2: Undo the Bank Reconciliation

The *Previous Reconciliation Discrepancy* report only shows changes to cleared transactions since your most recent bank reconciliation. If the beginning balance was incorrect when you performed previous bank reconciliations, the *Previous Reconciliation Discrepancy* report will not fully explain the problem.

If this is the case, the best way to find and correct the problem is to undo the previous reconciliation(s). Click **Undo Last Reconciliation,** as shown in Figure 5-11.

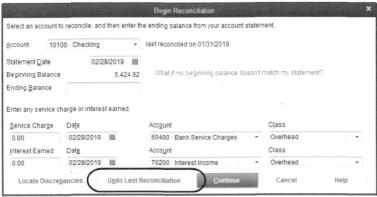

Figure 5-11 Undo Last Reconciliation button in Begin Reconciliation window

> **Note:**
> When you undo a reconciliation, QuickBooks resets your beginning balance to the previous period. However, the bank service charges and interest income that you entered in the prior reconciliation(s) will remain in the check register and will not be deleted.
>
> Therefore, do not enter bank service charges and interest income when repeating the bank reconciliation. Instead, clear those transactions along with the other checks and deposits when you re-reconcile the account.

Step 2: Locate and Edit Incorrectly Recorded Transactions

When you find a discrepancy between a transaction in QuickBooks and a transaction on the bank statement, you need to correct it. You will use different methods to correct the error, depending upon the date of the transaction.

Correcting or Voiding Transactions in the Current Accounting Period

If you find that you need to correct a transaction in QuickBooks and the transaction is dated in the **current accounting period** (i.e., a period for which financial statements and/or tax returns have not yet been issued), correct the error as described in the following paragraphs.

If You Made the Error

If you made an error in your records, you must make a correction in QuickBooks so that your records will agree with the bank. For example, if you wrote a check for $400.00, but you recorded it in QuickBooks as $40.00, you will need to change the check in QuickBooks. Double click the transaction in the **Reconcile** window, or highlight the transaction and click **Go To**. Make the correction, and then click **Save & Close**. This will return you to the *Reconcile* window and you will see the updated amount.

If the Bank Made the Error

If the bank made an error, enter a transaction in the bank account register to adjust your balance for the error and continue reconciling the account. Then, contact the bank and ask them to post an adjustment to your account. When you receive the bank statement showing the correction, enter a subsequent entry in the bank account register to record the bank's adjustment. This register entry will show on your next bank reconciliation, and you can clear it like any other transaction.

For example, Figure 5-12 displays a check register with an adjusting entry of $90.00 on 1/31/2019 where the bank made a deposit error during the month. The $90.00 shortage is recorded on the *Payment* side of the check register so that the register will reconcile with the bank statement. Subsequently, another adjusting entry is made on the *Deposit* side of the check register to record the bank's correction of the previous month's deposit. The $90.00 deposit will show on February's bank statement and can be cleared during the reconciliation process. Notice that *both* adjusting entries in the register are recorded to the same account, *Reconciliation Discrepancies.*

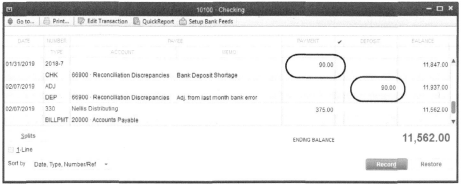

Figure 5-12 Adjusting entries for bank deposit error

Voiding Checks and Stop Payments

When you find a check dated in the **current accounting period** that you know will not clear the bank (e.g., if you stop payment on a check), you will need to void the check. Double click the check from the *Reconcile* window. Select the **Edit** menu and then select **Void Check**. Click **Save & Close** to return to the *Reconcile* window.

Correcting or Voiding Transactions in Closed Accounting Periods

A *closed accounting period* is the period prior to and including the date on which a company officially "closes" its books (for example, 12/31/2018), creates its final financial reports, and presents its finalized reports to external stakeholders such as the IRS and investors. You do not want to change transactions dated in a closed accounting period because doing so will change financial reports during a period for which you have already issued financial statements or filed tax returns.

In QuickBooks, for the closing date protection to work, you must use the *closing date* to indicate the date on which you last closed the accounting period. For example, if you issued financial statements on 12/31/2018, you can set the closing date in QuickBooks to 12/31/2018. This will essentially "lock" your QuickBooks file so that only the administrator (or other authorized users) will be able to modify transactions before 12/31/2018. For more information on setting the closing date, see page 533.

To correct or void a check that is dated in a **closed accounting period**, follow the procedure described below.

> **DO NOT PERFORM THESE STEPS NOW. THEY ARE FOR REFERENCE ONLY.**

1. Display the check in the register as shown in Figure 5-13 and click on the transaction that needs to be voided to select it.

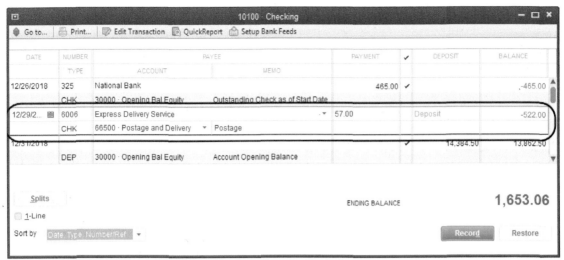

Figure 5-13 Uncleared Check #6006 from Previous Reporting Period

2. From the **Edit** menu, select **Void Check**. QuickBooks zeroes all dollar amounts and adds a "VOID" note in the Memo field as shown in Figure 5-14. Click **Record**.

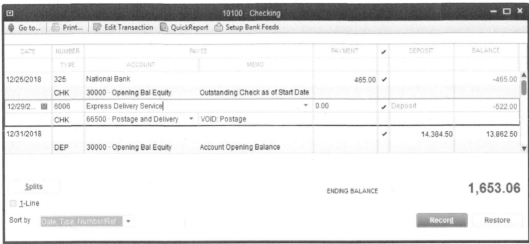

Figure 5-14 Voided Check - #6006

3. QuickBooks prompts you that the transaction you are voiding is cleared and that it is dated in a closed accounting period (Figure 5-15). Click **Yes**.

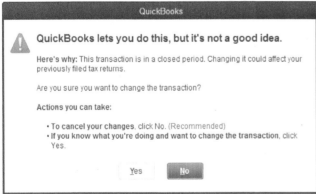

Figure 5-15 Voided Check in Closed Period Prompt

4. QuickBooks then displays the window shown in Figure 5-16. Click **Yes (Recommended).** This is the default response.

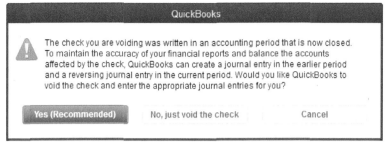

Figure 5-16 Voided Check Adjustment Prompt

5. QuickBooks performs three actions when you click **Yes (Recommended)** on the window shown in Figure 5-16 above.

   1. QuickBooks adds wording to the Memo field of the check showing that the program reversed the impact of the void on the General Ledger.

12/29/2018	6006	Express Delivery Service		0.00	✔	-408.00
	CHK	66500 · Postage and Delivery	VOID: Postage GJE, RGJE created on 04			

Figure 5-17 Voided Check - Additional Memo Text

   2. QuickBooks posts a General Journal Entry (GJE) dated the same date that reverses the impact on the General Ledger caused by the voided check.

12/29/2018	2018-6	Express Delivery Service		57.00	✔	-465.00
	GENJRN	66500 · Postage and Delivery	For CHK 6006 voided on 04/05/2015			

Figure 5-18 Journal Entry - Reverses GL Changes from Voiding the Check

   3. QuickBooks then enters a Reversing General Journal Entry (RGJE) in the current period. The default date for the reversing entry is "today."

01/08/2019	2018-6R	Express Delivery Service			✔	57.00	10,314.38
	GENJRN	66500 · Postage and Delivery	Reverse of GJE 2018-6 -- For CHK 6006				

Figure 5-19 Journal Entry that "moves" the GL Change to the Current Reporting Period

> **Note**
> QuickBooks clears all entries. However, the entries will appear in the Bank Reconciliation window until the client reconciles them using the Bank Reconciliation feature.
>
> **Important:**
> The *Void Checks* option should only be used to void a *Check* during a closed accounting period when it is coded to one or more *Expense* and/or *Other Expense* accounts. The transactions that are generated, as shown above, will not be correct under the following conditions:
> 1. Check is coded to accounts other than *Expense/Other Expense*
> 2. Check includes Items
> 3. Check is not *Check(CHK)* transaction type (e.g., *Bill Payment, Payroll Liability Payment, Sales Tax Payment, Paycheck*)

6. Next, enter the correct amount in a new transaction. Use the date of the current bank statement for the new transaction.

When QuickBooks Automatically Adjusts your Balance

If the difference is not zero when you click **Reconcile Now** in the *Reconcile* window, QuickBooks creates a transaction in the bank account for the difference. The transaction is coded to the *Reconciliation*

Discrepancies expense account. You should not leave this transaction in the register, but research why the discrepancy exists and properly account for it. A balance in this account usually indicates an over- or under-statement in net income.

Handling Bounced Checks

Banks and accountants often refer to bounced checks as NSF (non-sufficient funds) transactions. This means there are insufficient funds in the account to cover the check.

When Your Customer's Check Bounces

If your bank returns a check from one of your customers, enter an NSF transaction in the banking account register.

For example, Bob Mason bounced the check #2526 for $1,177.86 and the bank charged the Company $10.00. Complete the steps below to complete the NSF transaction.

COMPUTER PRACTICE

Step 1.   Open the *Receive Payments* window and click **Previous.** The Customer Payment window for *Bob Mason* opens (see Figure 5-20).

Step 2.   Click the **Record Bounced Check** button at the top of the window.

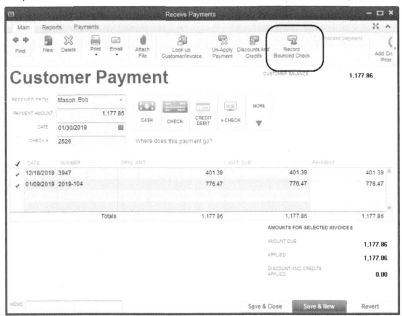

Figure 5-20 Record Bounced Check button in Receive Payments window

Step 3.   The *Manage Bounced Check* window opens. Enter the information in Figure 5-21. When finished click **Next**.

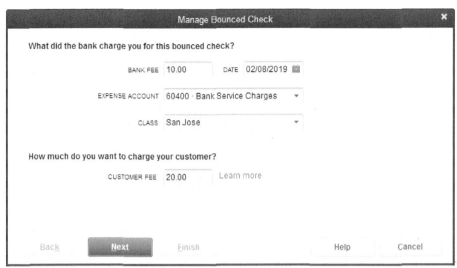

Figure 5-21 Manage Bounced Check window

Step 4. The *Bounced Check Summary* window opens (see Figure 5-22). Review and click **Finish**.

The *Bounced Check Summary* window explains the three changes that will take place once you record this bounced check. First, all the invoices connected with this check will be marked *Unpaid*, so the aging for these invoices will be correct. Second, fees for the check amount and for the service fee will be deducted from the bank account. Third, an invoice for the fee you are charging your customer will be created.

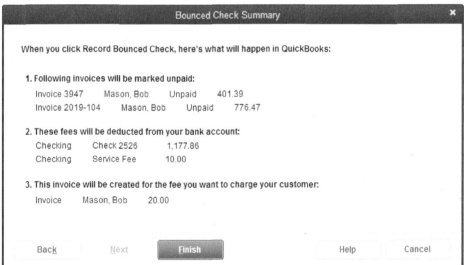

Figure 5-22 Bounced Check Summary window

Step 5. The Receive Payments window is now marked with a Bounced Check alert (see Figure 5-23). Select **Save & Close**.

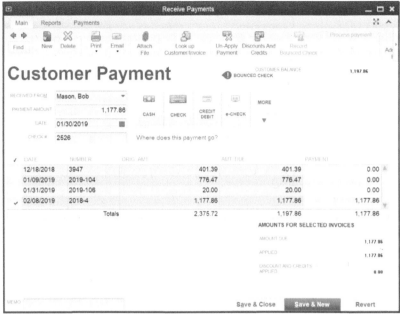

Figure 5-23 Receive Payments window after recording Bounced Check

Receiving and Depositing the Replacement Check

COMPUTER PRACTICE

To record the transactions for receiving and depositing a replacement check, follow these steps:

Step 1.   Select the **Customers** menu, and then select **Receive Payments**.

Step 2.   In this example, Bob Mason sent a replacement check #2538 on 2/10/2019 for $1,197.86 that includes the amount of the check plus the NSF service charge of $20.00. Fill in the customer payment information as shown in Figure 5-24.

           Make sure you apply the payment against the original *Invoices* and the service charge *Invoice* you created earlier.

Step 3.   Click Save & Close.

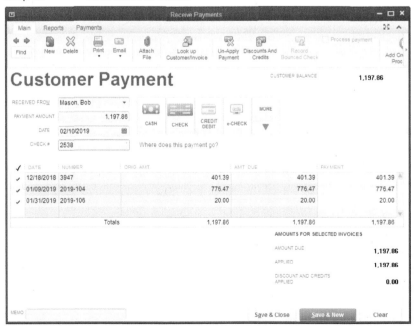

Figure 5-24 The Receive Payments window showing the replacement check

If Your Check Bounces

If you write a check that overdraws your account and your bank returns the check, follow these steps:

1. Decide with your vendor how you will handle the NSF Check (e.g., send a new check, redeposit the same check, or pay by credit card).

2. When the bank sends you the notice that your check was returned, there will be a charge from your bank. Enter a transaction in the bank account register. Code the transaction to Bank Service Charges and use the actual date that the bank charged your account.

3. If your balance is sufficient for the check to clear, tell the vendor to redeposit the check.

4. If your balance is not sufficient, consider other ways of paying the vendor, such as paying with a credit card. Alternatively, negotiate delayed payment terms with your vendor.

5. If your vendor charges an extra fee for bouncing a check, enter a *Bill* (or use *Write Checks*) and code the charge to the Bank Service Charge account.

6. If you bounce a payroll check, use the same process as described. It is good practice, and may be required by law, to reimburse your employee for any bank fees incurred as a result of your mistake.

Reconciling Credit Card Accounts and Paying the Bill

If you use a credit card liability account to track all of your credit card charges and payments, you should reconcile the account every month just as you do with your bank account. The credit card reconciliation process is very similar to the bank account reconciliation, except that when you finish the reconciliation, QuickBooks asks you if you want to pay the credit card immediately, or if you want to enter a bill to pay the credit card, or if you want to leave the credit card liability unpaid.

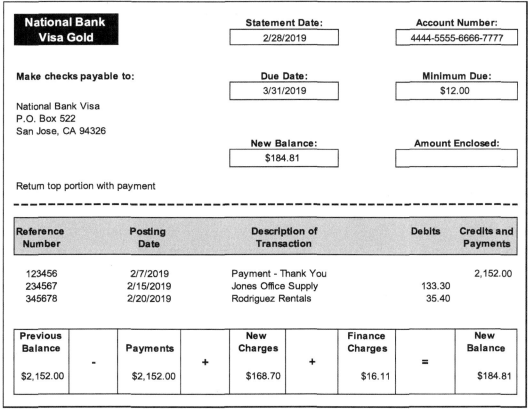

Figure 5-25 National Bank Visa credit card statement

Use the National Bank Visa Gold credit card statement shown in Figure 5-25 to reconcile your account.

COMPUTER PRACTICE

Step 1.   Select the **Banking** menu and then select **Reconcile**.

Step 2.   On the *Begin Reconciliation* window, enter the information from the Credit Card statement as shown in Figure 5-26. Click **Continue**.

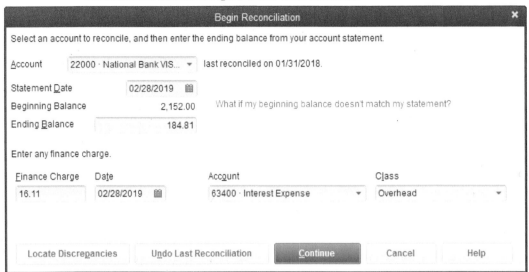

Figure 5-26 Completed Begin Reconciliation window for Credit Card account

Step 3.   Click each cleared transaction in the *Reconcile Credit Card* window as you match it with the credit card statement.

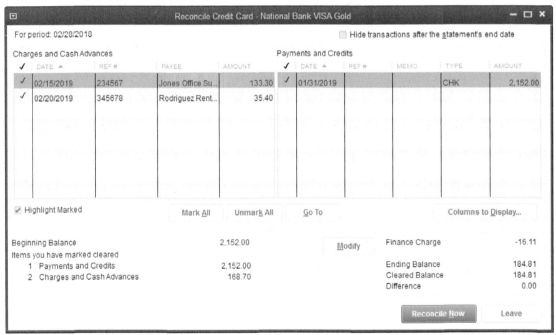

Figure 5-27 Reconcile Credit Card window

Step 4.   Verify that the *Difference* field shows **0.00** (see Figure 5-27). If it doesn't, look for discrepancies between your records and the credit card statement.

Step 5.   Verify that your screen looks like Figure 5-27 and click **Reconcile Now**.

Step 6.   On the *Make Payment* dialog box, click to select **Enter a bill for payment later** and click **OK** (see Figure 5-28).

Figure 5-28 Make Payment window

Step 7.   On the *Select Reconciliation Report* window, click **Close.** Normally you would select **Both** and then click **Print.** However, for this exercise, skip this step. See page 175 for more information about Bank Reconciliation reports.

Step 8.   Enter the information to complete the **Bill** for the VISA payment as shown in Figure 5-29.

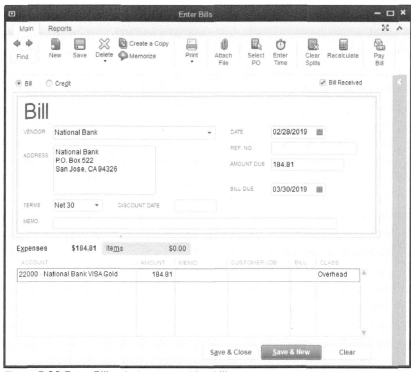

Figure 5-29 Enter Bills window to pay Visa bill

The accounting behind the scenes:

QuickBooks selects the **National Bank VISA Gold** account on the Expenses tab. This reduces the Credit Card liability account (debit) and increases Accounts Payable (credit).

Note:

Although the bill in Figure 5-29 includes the Overhead class, the transaction will not affect the **Profit & Loss by Class** report because the bill does not post to any income or expense accounts.

Step 9.   Click **Save & Close** to record the Bill.

This bill for $184.81 will display in the *Pay Bills* window the next time you select **Pay Bills** from the *Vendor* menu.

> **Important tip for partial payments of credit card bills:**
> If you don't want to pay the whole amount due on a credit card, don't just change the amount in the *Pay Bills* window. Instead, edit the original *Bill* to match the amount you actually intend to pay. By changing the *Bill*, you reduce the amount that is transferred out of the Credit Card account (and into A/P) to the exact amount that is paid. This way, the amount you don't pay remains in the balance of the Credit Card liability account and will match the account balance on your next credit card statement.

Bank Feeds

The QuickBooks Bank Feeds feature allows you to process online transactions, such as payments and transfers, and download bank transactions into your QuickBooks file. Downloaded transactions save you time by decreasing manual entry and increasing accuracy. It is important to review each downloaded transaction to avoid bringing errors into your company file.

Online banking is secure. QuickBooks uses a secure Internet connection and a high level of encryption when transferring information from your financial institution. Bank fees may apply.

Bank Feed Setup

To begin to use Bank Feeds, you will need to set up the appropriate accounts to communicate with the bank. Steps vary by institution. To complete this process, refer to the QuickBooks help files or the video tutorial.

Processing Online Transactions

You may have the option to enter online transactions, such as online payments, bill payments, or transfers (depending on your financial institution). Figure 5-30 displays an example of an online payment. You can create an online payment by opening the **Write Checks** window and checking **Pay Online**. Notice that there are several differences between a standard check form and an online payment form. For example, the check number field displays the word *SEND*.

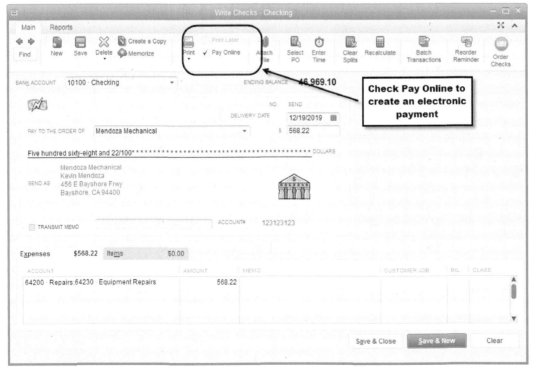

Figure 5-30 Online Payment example

After saving an online payment, the transaction is queued up in the *Bank Feed Center*. By clicking the *Send Items* button in the *Bank Feed Center*, you can send the online payments and other online transactions to, as well as download transactions from, your financial institution.

Your financial institution may require additional steps. Follow any guidelines given after clicking the *Send Items* button. Do not click the *Send Items* button now.

Figure 5-31 Bank Feeds Center – your screen may vary

Opening the Sample File

With Bank Feeds, transactions are processed and downloaded directly from your financial institution through your internet connection. For this section, we will open a sample QuickBooks file for *Sample Rock Castle Construction*. This file contains downloaded transactions pre-loaded in the file.

We will not be able to use this file to set up an online banking connection or to send or receive transactions, since this would require a live account at a financial institution and cannot be simulated in an educational environment. We will use this sample file to process downloaded transactions that have already been loaded into the sample file.

> **Restore this File**
> This section uses BankFeeds-18.QBW. See page 9 for instructions on restoring files. Click *OK* in the QuickBooks Information window notifying you that the file will use 12/15/2019 as the date. For more on sample files see page 6.

Downloaded Transactions

When you click the *Download Transactions* button in the *Bank Feeds Center*, you download all the new transactions from your financial institution. After downloading, the transactions are ready for review. (Do not click the *Download Transactions* button now.)

As the transactions are downloaded, QuickBooks searches for similar transactions that have previously been entered. If an existing transaction is similar to the downloaded transaction, such as by having the same date and amount, QuickBooks **matches** the downloaded transaction with this entry. Any downloaded transaction that is unpaired with an existing entry is **unmatched**.

> **Note:**
> Some transactions will be downloaded with payee names that do not match the names in the *Vendor Center*. Downloaded transactions often include names appended with a numerical code. It is important to avoid creating duplicate vendors. QuickBooks allows you to create **renaming rules** so that these downloaded transactions are linked to the appropriate existing vendor. You can access the renaming rules by clicking the Rules button in the upper left of the *Bank Feeds Center*; however, the renaming rules window is not accessible in the sample file.

COMPUTER PRACTICE

Step 1.   Select **Bank Feeds Center** from the *Bank Feeds* option under the *Banking* menu.

Step 2.   The *Bank Feeds* window opens (see Figure 5-32).

A list of your Bank and Credit Card accounts that have been set up to receive downloaded transactions appears on the left. Information about the selected account appears on the right.

Step 3.   Click on **ANYTIME Financial account** ending in *1235* (the second bank account from the top). This account has 7 transactions downloaded and waiting to be added to QuickBooks.

Figure 5-32 Bank Feeds window

Step 4.   Click the **Transaction List** button on the right side of the window.

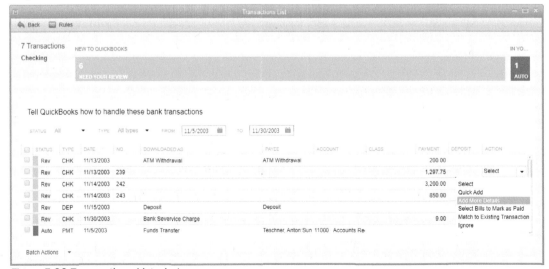

Figure 5-33 Transactions List window

Step 5.   The *Transactions List* window opens (see Figure 5-33). Select the line for **Check 239** dated 11/13/2003.

Of the 7 Transactions that have been downloaded from the bank, 1 transaction has already been entered and 6 transactions need review. The matched transaction is at the bottom of the list and has a status of *Auto*. After reviewing each transaction, you can either select individual transactions for approval or for adding further detail, or approve all transactions in one batch action.

> **Note:**
> Observant students may notice that the downloaded transactions are dated 2003, while most of the transactions in the sample file are dated 2019. Please disregard this discrepancy in the sample file.

Step 1.   An action menu appears on the right end of the row for Check 239. Select **Add More Details** in this action menu.

The bank has not downloaded details about check 239, so this information needs to be added manually to properly link this transaction with the right *Customer* and *Account*. If you need to enter information (such as *Items*) that is not available in the *Transaction Details – Add More Details* window, you can always enter the transaction using *Enter Bill* and *Pay Bill* forms, or using the *Check* form, and match the entered transaction with the downloaded transaction.

Step 2.   The *Transaction Details – Add More Details* window opens. Enter the information in Figure 5-34. Make sure that account *60130 Repairs and Maintenance* is entered in the *Account* field. This account should automatically populate when *Dianne's Auto Shop* is selected.

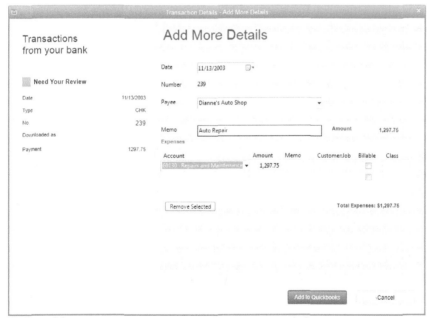

Figure 5-34 The Transaction Details – Add More Details window

Step 3.   Click the **Add to QuickBooks** button to accept the downloaded transaction into your QuickBooks file.

Step 4.   Close the *Transactions List*.

Step 5.   Close the *Bank Feeds* window

Review Questions

Comprehension Questions

1. Explain how QuickBooks calculates the *Beginning Balance* field in the *Begin Reconciliation* window. Why might the beginning balance calculated by QuickBooks differ from the beginning balance on your bank statement?

2. Explain why it's important not to change transactions in closed accounting periods.

3. How is the credit card reconciliation process different from the bank account reconciliation?

Multiple Choice

Select the best answer(s) for each of the following:

1. When the *Beginning Balance* field on the *Begin Reconciliation* window doesn't match the beginning balance on the bank statement, you should:

    a) Call the bank.

    b) Change the amount in QuickBooks to match the bank's amount.

    c) Click **Locate Discrepancies** in the *Begin Reconciliation* window. Click **Discrepancy Report** and/or **Previous Reports** to research what has been changed since the last reconciliation. Then fix the problem before reconciling.

    d) Select the **Banking** menu and then select *Enter Statement Charges*.

2. Which statement is false?

    a) You can enter bank service charges using *Enter Statement Charges*.

    b) You can enter bank service charges on the *Begin Reconciliation* window.

    c) You can enter bank service charges using a register transaction.

    d) You can enter bank service charges using *Write Checks* before you start your reconciliation.

3. When you find an erroneous amount on a transaction while reconciling, correct the amount by:

    a) Selecting the **Banking** menu and then selecting **Correct Error**.

    b) Double clicking on the entry and changing the amount on the transaction.

    c) Selecting the entry in the **Reconcile** window, then clicking **Go To** and changing the amount on the transaction.

    d) Performing either b or c.

4. To properly record a voided check from a closed accounting period:

    a) Delete the check in the register.

    b) Make a deposit in the current period and code it to the same account as the original check you want to void. Then delete both transactions in the **Reconciliation** window.

    c) Find the check in the register, select the **Edit** Menu, and then select **Void Check**.

    d) Change the amount of the check to zero.

5. Which of the following columns cannot be displayed in the *Checks and Payments* section of the *Reconcile* window?

    a) Check #

    b) Class

    c) Date

    d) Payee

6. You know you have reconciled your bank account correctly when:
   a) You make a *Balance Adjustment* entry.
   b) The *Difference* field shows **0.00.**
   c) There are no more register entries to select in the *Reconcile* window.
   d) All of the above.

7. The Reconciliation Summary report shows:
   a) The Beginning Balance shown on the Bank Statement.
   b) Detail of all the entries for the month in the register.
   c) The Ending Balance shown in the register in QuickBooks.
   d) Both a and c.

8. What accounts should be reconciled?
   a) Any account that receives regular statements.
   b) Any bank, income or expense account.
   c) Only bank accounts can be reconciled.
   d) Reconciling is optional for all account types.

9. When you "undo" a bank reconciliation, which statement is true?
   a) Undoing a bank reconciliation does not affect the Beginning Balance.
   b) Balance Adjustments are deleted from the check register.
   c) Interest Income amounts that are entered during the prior bank reconciliation are deleted.
   d) Undoing a bank reconciliation does not delete the Bank Service Charges recorded on the "undone" bank reconciliation.

10. When a customer bounces a check, you should:
    a) Delete the *Deposit* that contained the bounced check.
    b) Mark the customer's invoice as *Unpaid*.
    c) Create an *Invoice* to the customer for NSF charges.
    d) Click the **Record Bounced Check** button in the *Receive Payments* window.

11. When you finish reconciling a credit card account, you:
    a) Can only create a check for the total amount due.
    b) Can create a check for an amount equal to or less than the total amount due.
    c) Cannot choose to bypass making a payment.
    d) Cannot choose to enter a bill for later payment.

12. What is the accounting behind the scenes for a Bill coded to a Credit Card liability account?
    a) Decrease (debit) Accounts Payable, Increase (credit) Credit Card liability.
    b) Decrease (debit) Accounts Payable, Decrease (credit) Credit Card liability.
    c) Increase (credit) Accounts Payable, Decrease (debit) Credit Card liability.
    d) Increase (credit) Accounts Payable, Increase (credit) Credit Card liability.

13. In what account is a transaction created if you complete a reconciliation and your difference is not 0.00?
    a) Opening Balance Equity.
    b) Uncategorized Income.
    c) Reconciliation Discrepancies.
    d) Other Expense.

14. When you void a check written in a closed accounting period, QuickBooks gives you an option to create:

     a)   An adjustment in the *Reconciliation Discrepancies* account.

     b)   A new check to be dated to the current date.

     c)   Two journal entries in the closed accounting period.

     d)   A journal entry in the closed accounting period and a journal entry during the open accounting period.

15. You are notified that you have bounced a check. What should you do?

     a)   Contact the vendor to apologize and arrange payment, such as sending a new check or paying by credit card.

     b)   Contact the bank to arrange payment.

     c)   Wait for the physical check to be returned marked NSF (Not Sufficient Funds) before recording it in QuickBooks using the *NSF* feature.

     d)   You do not need to make any changes in QuickBooks because the bounced check is automatically recorded.

Completion Statements

1. QuickBooks calculates the *Beginning Balance* field in the *Begin Reconciliation* window by adding and subtracting all previously _____ transactions.

2. Voiding, deleting or changing the amount of a transaction you previously cleared in a bank reconciliation causes the _____ _____ field on the *Begin Reconciliation* window to disagree with your bank statement.

3. The *Previous Reconciliation Discrepancy* report shows changes to cleared transactions since your most recent bank _____.

4. You don't want to change transactions dated in a(n) _____ accounting period because doing so would change net income in a period for which you have already issued _____ statements and/or filed the tax returns.

5. Banks and accountants often refer to bounced checks as _____ transactions.

Bank Reconciliation Problem 1

> Restore the BankRec-18Problem1.QBM file. The password to access this file is Sleeter18.

1. Using the sample bank statement shown below, reconcile the checking account for 1/31/2019.

Business Checking Account					
Statement Date:	**January 31, 2019**			*Page 1 of 1*	

Summary:

Previous Balance as of 12/31/18:	$	12,572.80
Total Deposits and Credits:	+ $	4,685.50
Total Checks and Debits:	- $	12,503.50
Statement Balance as of 1/31/19	**= $**	**4,754.80**

Deposits and Other Credits:

DEPOSITS

Date	Description		Amount
12-Jan	Customer Deposit	$	1,709.53
30-Jan	Customer Deposit	$	2,848.27
31-Jan	Customer Deposit	$	119.08
	Deposits:	**$**	**4,676.88**

INTEREST

Date	Description		Amount
31-Jan	Interest Earned	$	8.62
	Interest:	**$**	**8.62**

Checks and Other Withdrawals:

CHECKS PAID:

Check No.	Date Paid		Amount
325	2-Jan	$	324.00
326	7-Jan	$	276.52
327	10-Jan	$	427.50
6001	10-Jan	$	3,200.00
6003	25-Jan	$	142.00
6004	26-Jan	$	123.48
	Checks Paid:	**$**	**4,493.50**

OTHER WITHDRAWALS/PAYMENTS

Date	Description		Amount
31-Jan	Transfer	$	8,000.00
	Other Withdrawals/Payments:	**$**	**8,000.00**

SERVICE CHARGES

Date	Description		Amount
31-Jan	Service Charge	$	10.00
	Service Charge:	**$**	**10.00**

Figure 5-35 Bank statement for January 31, 2019

2. Print a *Reconciliation Summary* and *Reconciliation Detail* report dated 1/31/2019.

Bank Reconciliation Problem 2 (Advanced)

Restore the BankRec-18Problem2.QBM file. The password to access this file is Sleeter18.

1. Receive and deposit check #6021 for $1,506.82 from Tim Feng against invoice 2019-108 on 2/20/2019. Use the **San Jose** class.

2. On 2/21/2019, you learned that check #6021 from Tim Feng bounced. Record the bounced check (San Jose class). The bank charged you an NSF Fee of $10.00. Your company's NSF Customer Fee is $20.00.

3. Enter the transactions necessary to record the receipt and redeposit of Tim Feng's replacement check for $1,506.82 (Check #6027) that did not include the bounce charge. Date the payment *2/27/2019* and apply it to invoice #*2019-108*. Date the deposit on *2/28/2019*.

4. Using the sample bank statement shown below, reconcile the checking account for 2/28/2019.

Business Checking Account

Statement Date:		**February 28, 2019**		Page 1 of 1

Summary:

Previous Balance as of 1/31/19:		$	14,070.26
Total Deposits and Credits	+	$	7,993.78
Total Checks and Debits	-	$	5,164.65
Statement Balance as of 2/28/19:	=	**$**	**16,899.39**

Deposits and Other Credits:

DEPOSITS

Date	Description		Amount
3-Feb	Customer Deposit	$	178.61
4-Feb	Customer Deposit	$	2,460.13
10-Feb	Customer Deposit	$	809.03
11-Feb	Customer Deposit	$	753.41
13-Feb	Customer Deposit	$	775.98
20-Feb	Customer Deposit	$	1,506.82
28-Feb	Customer Deposit	$	1,506.82
	Deposits:	**$**	**7,990.80**

INTEREST

Date	Description		Amount
28-Feb	Interest Earned	$	2.98
	Interest:	**$**	**2.98**

Checks and Other Withdrawals:

CHECKS PAID:

Check No.	Date Paid		Amount
6004	2-Feb	$	123.48
329	14-Feb	$	2,152.00
330	15-Feb	$	342.35
331	24-Feb	$	375.00
332	28-Feb	$	645.00
	Checks Paid:	**$**	**3,637.83**

OTHER WITHDRAWALS/PAYMENTS

Date	Description		Amount
20-Feb	Returned Item	$	1,506.82
20-Feb	NSF Charge	$	10.00
	Other Withdrawals/Payments:	**$**	**1,516.82**

SERVICE CHARGES

Date	Description		Amount
28-Feb	Service Charge	$	10.00
	Service Charge:	**$**	**10.00**

Figure 5-36 Bank statement for February 28, 2019

5. Print a *Reconciliation Summary* and *Reconciliation Detail* report dated 2/28/2019.

6. Print a customer *Statement* for Tim Feng for the period 1/1/2019 through 2/28/2019.

Chapter 6
Reports

Topics

In this chapter, you will learn about the following topics:

- Types of Reports (page 197)
- Cash Versus Accrual Reports (page 198)
- Accounting Reports (page 200)
- Business Management Reports (page 211)
- QuickBooks Graphs (page 216)
- Building Custom Reports (page 218)
- Memorizing Reports (page 226)
- Processing Multiple Reports (page 228)
- Finding Transactions (page 230)
- Exporting Reports to Spreadsheets (page 237)

> **Restore this File:**
> This chapter uses Reports-18.QBW. See page 9 for more information. The password to access this file is *Sleeter18*.

QuickBooks reports allow you to get the information you need to make critical business decisions. In this chapter, you'll learn how to create a variety of reports to help you manage your business. Every report in QuickBooks gives you immediate, up-to-date information about your company's performance.

There are literally hundreds of reports available in QuickBooks. In addition to the built-in reports, you can *modify* reports to include or exclude whatever data you want. To control the look of your reports, you can customize the formatting of headers, footers, fonts, or columns. When you get a report looking just the way you want, you can *memorize* it so that you can quickly create it again later. Or you can export it into a spreadsheet program for more customization.

This chapter also looks at the different search features to allow you to find transactions.

Types of Reports

There are two major types of reports in QuickBooks – accounting reports and business management reports. In addition, most reports have both "detail" and "summary" styles. Detail reports show individual transactions and summary reports show totals for a group of transactions.

Accounting reports contain information about transactions and accounts. For example, the *Profit & Loss* report is a summary report of all transactions coded to income and expense accounts for a specified period of time. Your accountant or tax preparer will need several accounting reports from QuickBooks in order to provide accounting and tax services for your company.

Business management reports are used to monitor different activities of a business to help plan workflow and review transactions that have already occurred. These reports provide critical information that you need to operate your business. For example, the *Customer Contact List* report shows addresses, phone numbers, and other information about Customers.

Report Type	Example Reports
Accounting	Profit & Loss, Balance Sheet, Trial Balance, Cash Flow Forecast, General Ledger, Trial Balance
Business Management	Open Invoices, Unpaid Bills Detail, Check Detail, Sales by Item Detail, Item Profitability, Customer Contact List, Item Price List, Time by Name, Stock Status by Item

Table 6-1 Types of QuickBooks reports

Cash Versus Accrual Reports

QuickBooks can automatically convert reports from the accrual basis to the cash basis, depending on how you set your Preferences or how you customize reports.

If you use cash basis accounting, you regard income or expenses as occurring at the time you actually receive a payment from a customer or pay a bill from a vendor. The cash basis records (or recognizes) income or expense only when cash is received or paid, no matter when the original transaction occurred. If you use accrual basis accounting, you regard income or expenses as occurring at the time you ship a product, render a service, or receive a bill from your vendors. Under this method, the date that you enter a transaction and the date that you actually pay or receive cash may be two separate dates, but income (or expense) is recognized on the day of the original transaction.

You can set the default for all QuickBooks summary reports to the cash or accrual basis by selecting *Cash* or *Accrual* in the *Summary Reports Basis* section of the *Reports & Graphs Preferences* window. Follow these steps:

COMPUTER PRACTICE

Step 1.   Select the **Edit** menu and then select **Preferences**.

Step 2.   Click on the **Reports & Graphs** preference.

Step 3.   Click the **Company Preferences** tab.

> **Note:**
> If you are in multi-user mode you will need to first switch to single-user mode to change company preferences.

Step 4.   To set the basis to match your company's finances, click **Cash** or **Accrual** in the *Summary Reports Basis* section (see Figure 6-1). For this chapter, leave the basis set to **Accrual**.

> **Note:**
> You can also change the default font size and font color on your reports using the *Reports & Graphs Company Preferences*. Click the **Format** button in the *Preferences* window.

Step 5.   Click **OK** to save your changes (if any) and close the *Preferences* window.

> **Did You Know?**
> In QuickBooks, you can leave the *Reporting Preferences* set to the accrual basis for internal management reporting purposes and then create cash-basis reports for tax purposes.

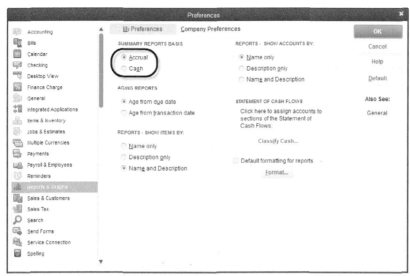

Figure 6-1 Preferences for Reports & Graphs

Irrespective of the default setting in your *Preferences*, you can always switch between cash and accrual reports by modifying reports. To convert the report basis from accrual to cash on any report, follow these steps:

COMPUTER PRACTICE

Step 1.   Click the **Reports** icon on the *Icon Bar*. There are three different views for previewing the reports, *Carousel, List,* and *Grid.*

Step 2.   Click on **Carousel View** in the upper right corner of the *Report Center.*

Step 3.   Select **Company & Financial** from the list on the left of the window, if it is not already selected. *Profit & Loss Standard* is the first report (see Figure 6-2).

You can choose other reports by moving the slider at the bottom of the window. You can also choose a date range from the *Dates* fields at the bottom of the window.

Step 4.   Double click the **Profit & Loss Standard** report image in the *Report Center.*

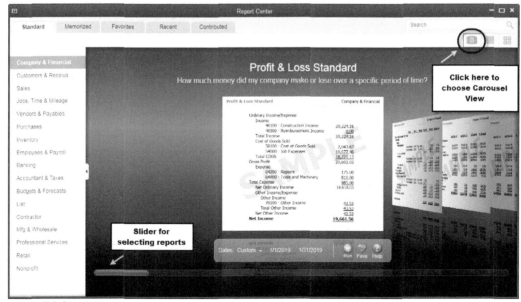

Figure 6-2 Carousel View in the Report Center

Step 5.   Set the *Dates* fields *From 1/1/2019* and *To 1/31/2019*. Press **Tab**.

Step 6.   Click **Cash** in the *Report Basis* section (see Figure 6-3). The information in the report changes from Accrual Basis to Cash Basis. You can click back and forth between these two options to see how it impacts the report.

Step 7.   Close the *Profit & Loss* report window.

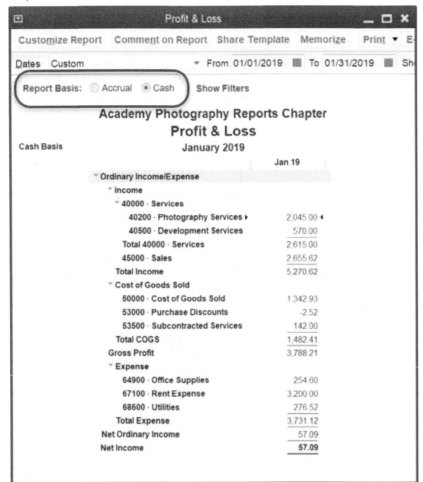

Figure 6-3 Select the Cash report basis in the Report window

Accounting Reports

There are several built-in reports that summarize a group of transactions. These reports help you analyze the performance of your business.

Profit & Loss

The *Profit & Loss* report (also referred to as the *Income Statement*) shows all your income and expenses for a given period. As discussed earlier, the goal of accounting is to provide the financial information you need to measure the success (or failure) of your organization, as well as to file proper tax returns. The *Profit & Loss* report is one of the most valuable sources of this financial information.

COMPUTER PRACTICE

Step 1.   From the *Report Center*, click **Grid View** to choose a report from a different view (see Figure 6-4).

Step 2.   Select **Company & Financial** from the list on the left of the window if it is not already selected, and then double click the **Profit & Loss Standard** report in the upper left of the Grid View.

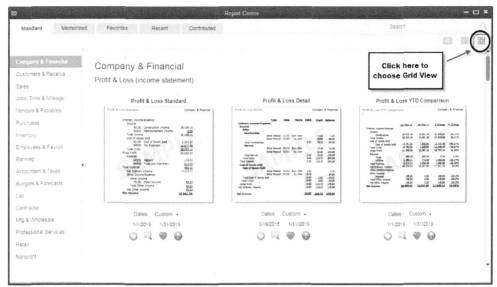

Figure 6-4 Grid View of the Report Center

Step 3.   Set the *Dates* fields *From 1/1/2019* and *To 1/31/2019*. Press **Tab**.

Step 4.   The *Profit & Loss* report (see Figure 6-5) summarizes the totals of all your *Income* accounts, followed by *Cost of Goods Sold* accounts, then *Expenses*, then *Other Income*, and finally *Other Expenses*. The total at the bottom of the report is your *Net Income* (or loss) for the period you specified in the *Dates* fields. The *Profit & Loss* report is a company's operating results, normally for a period of 12 months or less.

Do not close this report.

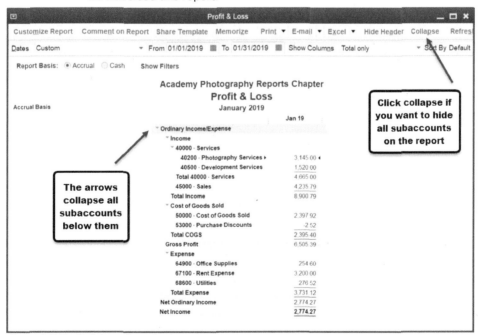

Figure 6-5 Profit & Loss Standard report

Analyzing the Profit & Loss Report

The first section of the *Profit & Loss* report shows the total of each of your income accounts for the period specified on the report. If you have subaccounts, QuickBooks indents those accounts on the report and subtotals them. Notice on Figure 6-5 that the *Services* income category has two subaccounts:

Photography Services and *Development Services*. To hide subaccounts on this report (or any summary report), click the **Collapse** arrow next to any group of accounts or click the **Collapse** button at the top of the report to collapse all accounts.

The next section of the report shows your *Cost of Goods Sold* accounts. You use these accounts to record the costs of the products and services you sell in your business (e.g., inventory, cost of labor, etc.). If you use *Inventory Items*, QuickBooks calculates *Cost of Goods Sold* as each *Inventory Item* is sold, using the *average cost method.* (See the Inventory chapter beginning on page 275 for more information on how QuickBooks calculates average cost.)

The next section of the report shows your expenses for the business. Use these accounts to record costs associated with operating your business (e.g., rent, salaries, supplies, etc.). Expenses are generally recorded in QuickBooks as you write checks or enter bills, but can also be recorded directly into a register or as a journal entry.

The next section of the report shows your *Other Income/Expenses* accounts. Use these accounts to record income and expenses that are generated outside the normal operation of your business. For example, if you provide accounting services but sold an old business computer, the income generated from the sale would be classified as *Other Income* because it was generated outside the normal operation of your business.

At the bottom of the report, QuickBooks calculates your *Net Income* – the amount of your revenue less your Cost of Goods Sold and your operating expenses. You may want to view your expenses (such as rent, office supplies, employee salaries, etc.) as a percentage of total income to help you locate excessive expenses in your business.

COMPUTER PRACTICE

Step 1.   Click the **Customize Report** button at the top left of the *Profit & Loss* report.

Step 2.   Click the **% of Income** box (see Figure 6-6).

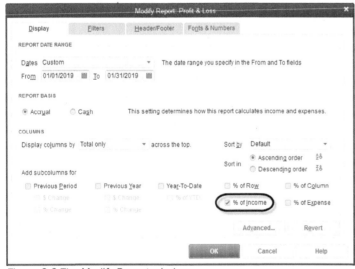

Figure 6-6 The Modify Report window

Step 3.   Click **OK**.

The *Profit & Loss* report now has a *% of Income* column (see Figure 6-7), allowing you to quickly identify numbers that deviate from the norm. Familiarize yourself with the percentages of expenses in your business and review this report periodically to make sure you stay in control of your expenses.

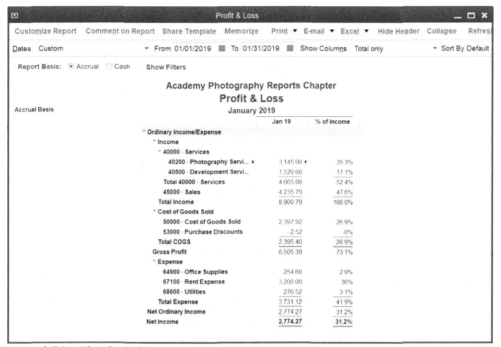

Figure 6-7 Modified Profit & Loss report

Step 4.   To find the details behind any of these numbers, you can use *QuickZoom* (explained on page 236). Double click the *Cost of Goods Sold* line item amount of **2,397.92** in the report (see Figure 6-7).

The report shown in Figure 6-8 shows each transaction coded to the *Cost of Goods Sold* account. Double click on any of these numbers to see the actual transaction.

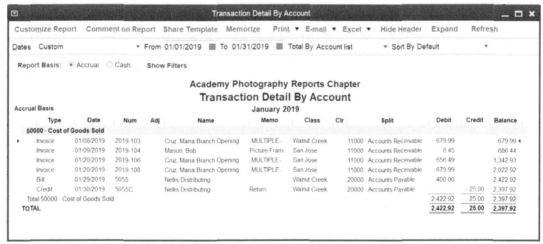

Figure 6-8 Transaction Detail by Account report for the Cost of Goods Sold account

Step 5.   Close both open reports.

Profit & Loss by Class Report

To divide your *Profit & Loss* report into departments (or Classes), use the *Profit & Loss by Class* report.

COMPUTER PRACTICE

Step 1.   From the *Report Center*, click the **List** view (see Figure 6-9)

Step 2. Select **Company & Financial** from the menu on the left if it is not already selected, then double click the **Profit & Loss by Class** report in the *Profit & Loss (income statement)* section.

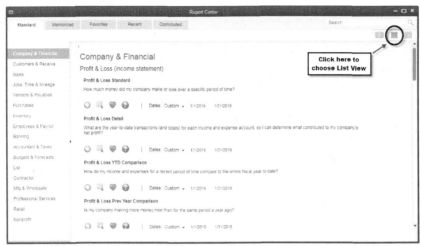

Figure 6-9 List View in the Report Center

Step 3. Enter *1/1/2019* in the *From* field, enter *1/31/2019* in the *To* field at the top of the report, and press **Tab**.

Step 4. Your report should look like the one shown in Figure 6-10. Notice that totals for each Class are displayed in a separate column.

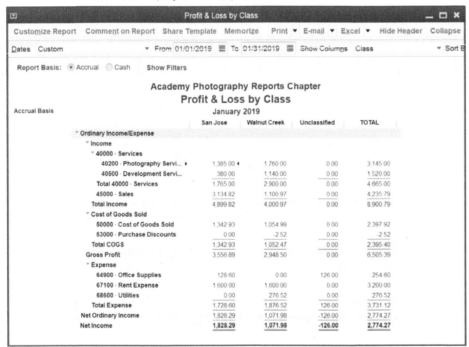

Figure 6-10 Profit and Loss by Class report

This report includes an *Unclassified* column, as shown in Figure 6-10, which means that some of the transactions were not assigned a Class. To classify the unclassified transactions, follow these steps:

Step 5. Double click to QuickZoom on the 126.00 amount in the *Unclassified* column under Office Supplies. This will bring up the *Transaction Detail by Account* report.

Step 6. Double click to QuickZoom on the 126.00 amount again. This opens the *Bill* from Ace Supply.

Step 7. Assign the *Class* **San Jose** to the *Bill* as shown in Figure 6-11.

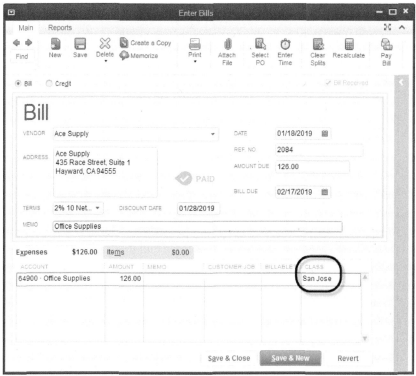

Figure 6-11 Bill from Ace Supply with Class

Step 8. **Save and Close** the *Bill*. Click **Yes** to record your changes.

Step 9. The *Report needs to be refreshed* window appears. If necessary, check the *Do not ask again (apply to all reports and graphs)* box and click **Yes** to refresh the open reports.

Step 10. Close the *Transaction Detail by Account* report. Notice the *Profit & Loss by Class* report no longer has an *Unclassified* column (see Figure 6-12).

Step 11. Close the *Profit & Loss by Class* report.

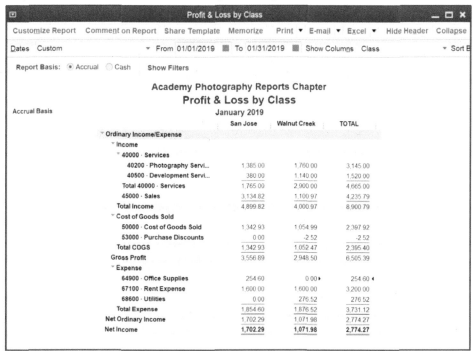

Figure 6-12 Profit & Loss by Class without Unclassified Column

> **Note:**
> When using Classes, be sure to always enter the Class as you are recording each
> transaction. This prevents any transaction from being recorded as *Unclassified*. For
> transactions that do not fall within the normal operating activities of one of the classes in
> your company file, use a general Class such as *Overhead*.

To ensure that transactions are always assigned to Classes, set *Preferences* so that QuickBooks will
prompt you to assign a Class before completing the transaction. To learn more about these *Preferences*,
see page 243.

Profit & Loss by Job Report

To divide your *Profit & Loss* report into *Customers* or *Jobs*, use the *Profit & Loss by Job* report. This
report, sometimes called the Job Cost report, allows you to see your profitability for each *Customer* or
Job. This information helps you to spot pricing problems, as well as costs that are out of the ordinary. For
example, if this report showed that you lost money on all the Jobs where you did an outdoor session, you
would probably want to adjust your prices for outdoor photo shoots. Similarly, if the cost on one Job is
significantly higher or lower than other Jobs of similar size, you might look closer at that Job to see if
adjustments are needed to control costs.

COMPUTER PRACTICE

To create a *Profit & Loss by Job* report, follow these steps:

Step 1.   From the *Report Center*, select **Company & Financial** and then double click the **Profit &**
               Loss By Job link in the *Profit & Loss (income statement)* section.

Step 2.   Enter *1/1/2019* in the *From* field, enter *1/31/2019* in the *To* field, and press **Tab** (see
               Figure 6-13).

Step 3.   After you view the *Profit & Loss by Job* report, close all open report windows.

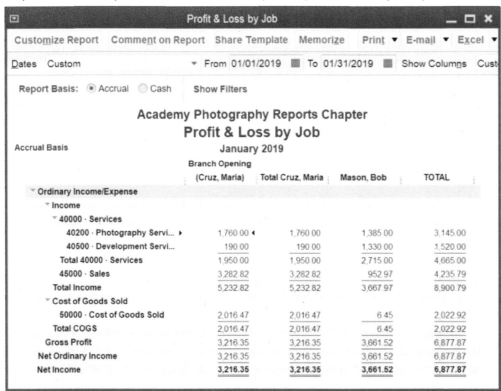

Figure 6-13 Profit & Loss by Job report

Balance Sheet

Another important report for analyzing your business is the *Balance Sheet*. The Balance Sheet shows your financial position, as defined by the balances in each of your assets, liabilities, and equity accounts on a given date.

COMPUTER PRACTICE

1. From the *Report Center*, select **Company & Financial** and then double click the **Balance Sheet Standard** report in the *Balance Sheet & Net Worth* section. You may need to scroll down.

Step 1. Enter *1/31/2019* in the *As of* field and press **Tab**. In Figure 6-14, you can see a portion of the *Balance Sheet* for Academy Photography on 1/31/2019.

> **Tip:**
> Familiarize yourself with how your Balance Sheet changes throughout the year. Banks examine this report very closely before approving loans. Often, the bank will calculate the ratio of your current assets divided by your current liabilities. This ratio, known as the current ratio, measures your ability to satisfy your debts.

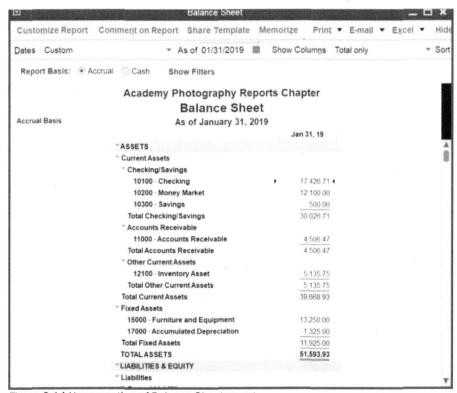

Figure 6-14 Upper portion of Balance Sheet report

Statement of Cash Flows

The *Statement of Cash Flows* provides information about the cash receipts and cash payments of your business during a given period. In addition, it provides information about investing and financing activities, such as purchasing equipment or borrowing. The *Statement of Cash Flows* shows the detail of how you spent the cash shown on the company's *Balance Sheet*.

COMPUTER PRACTICE

Step 1. From the *Report Center*, select **Company & Financial** and then double click the **Statement of Cash Flows** report in the *Cash Flow* section.

Step 2.   Enter *1/1/2019* in the *From* field, enter *1/31/2019* in the *To* field, and press **Tab**.

On the report shown in Figure 6-15, you can see that although there was a net income of $2,774.27, there was a net decrease in cash of $532.89 during the first month of the year. Bankers look closely at this report to determine if your business is able to generate a positive cash flow, or if your business requires additional capital to satisfy its cash needs.

Step 3.   After you view the *Statement of Cash Flows* report, close all open report windows.

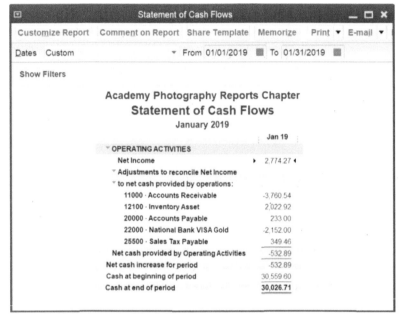

Figure 6-15 Statement of Cash Flows report

General Ledger

The *General Ledger* shows you all of the activity in all of your accounts for a specific period.

COMPUTER PRACTICE

Step 1.   From the *Report Center*, select **Accountant & Taxes** from the list of report categories on the left of the window and then double click the **General Ledger** report in the *Account Activity* section. If the *Collapsing and Expanding Transactions* window appears, read it and click **OK**.

Step 2.   Enter *1/1/2019* in the *From* field, enter *1/31/2019* in the *To* field, and press **Tab** (see Figure 6-16).

Step 3.   Close the *General Ledger* report.

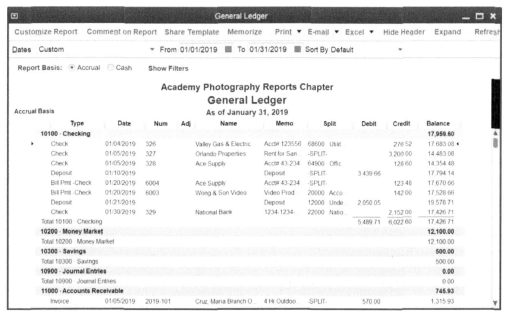

Figure 6-16 Upper portion of General Ledger report

> **Note:**
> The *General Ledger* is a very long report. Every account, even accounts that have a zero balance or that have never been used, are included by default. You can condense the report to only show accounts with a balance by selecting the *In Use* option in the *Advanced Options* window (see Figure 6-17). You can open the *Advanced Options* window from the **Advanced** button in the *Modify Report* window.

Figure 6-17 Advanced Options window

Trial Balance

The *Trial Balance* report shows the balance of each of the accounts as of a certain date. The report shows these balances in a Debit and Credit format. Your accountant will usually prepare this report at the end of each fiscal year.

COMPUTER PRACTICE

Step 1.   From the *Report Center*, select **Accountant & Taxes** and then double click the **Trial Balance** report in the *Account Activity* section.

Step 2.   Enter *1/1/2019* in the *From* field, enter *1/31/2019* in the *To,* field and press **Tab** (see Figure 6-18).

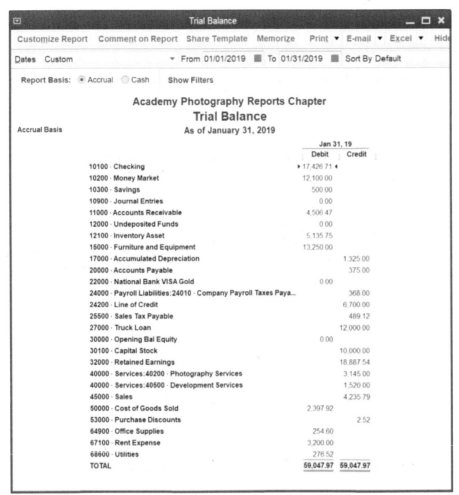

Figure 6-18 Trial Balance - Balance of each account as of a specific date

Step 3.   Close all open reports.

Voided/Deleted Transactions Reports

The *Voided/Deleted Transactions Summary* report shows transactions that have been voided or deleted in the data file. This report assists accountants in detecting errors or fraud and is available under the *Accountant & Taxes* submenu of the *Reports* menu. This feature is very useful when you have a number of users in a file and transactions seem to "disappear" or change without explanation. The standard version of this report presents the transactions in a summary format (see Figure 6-19).

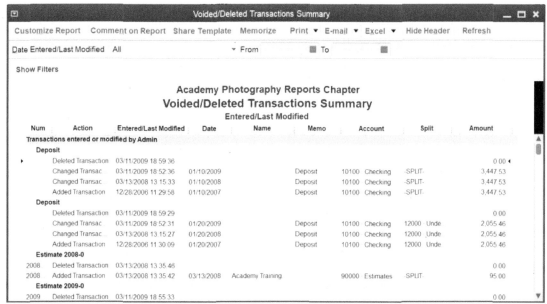

Figure 6-19 Upper portion of Voided/Deleted Transactions Summary Report

The *Voided/Deleted Transactions Detail* report shows all of the line items associated with each affected transaction. This feature makes the original transaction information available so that it can be recreated if necessary (see Figure 6-20).

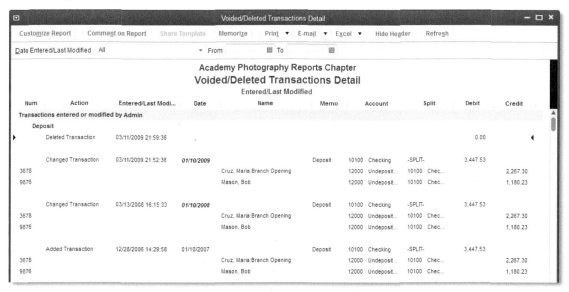

Figure 6-20 Upper portion of Voided/Deleted Transactions Detail Report

Business Management Reports

In the following Computer Practice exercises, you will use QuickBooks to create several different reports that help you manage your business.

Customer Phone List

The *Customer Phone List* shown in Figure 6-21 is a listing of each of your customers and their phone numbers. To create this report, follow these steps:

COMPUTER PRACTICE

Step 1.   From the *Report Center*, select **List** and then double click the **Customer Phone List** report
               in the *Customer* section to display the report (see Figure 6-21).

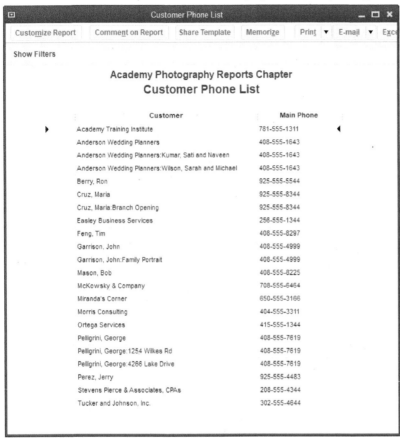

Figure 6-21 Customer Phone List report

Vendor Contact List

The *Vendor Contact List* shown in Figure 6-22 is a listing of your vendors along with each vendor's
contact information. To create this report, follow these steps:

COMPUTER PRACTICE

Step 1.   From the *Report Center*, select **List** and then double click the **Vendor Contact List** report
               in the *Vendor* section to display the report (see Figure 6-22).

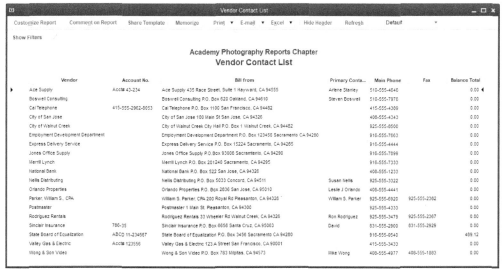

Figure 6-22 Vendor Contact List report

Item Price List

The *Item Price List* shown in Figure 6-23 is a listing of your *Items*. To create this report, follow these steps:

COMPUTER PRACTICE

Step 1.   From the *Report Center*, select **List** and then double click the **Item Price List** report in the *Listing* section to display the report (see Figure 6-23).

Step 2.   After viewing the *Item Price List* report, close all open report windows. Click **No** if QuickBooks prompts you to memorize the reports.

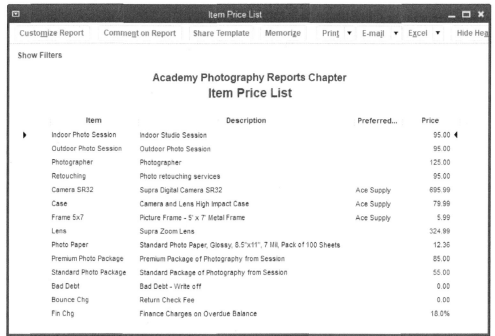

Figure 6-23 Item Price List report

Check Detail Report

The *Check Detail* report is quite valuable if you use accounts payable or payroll. It is frequently necessary to see what expense account(s) are associated with a bill payment. However, the *Register* report only shows that bill payments are associated with accounts payable. That's because a bill payment only involves the checking account and accounts payable. Similarly, paychecks only show in the register report as "Split" transactions because several accounts are associated with each paycheck. The *Check Detail* report shows the detailed expense account information about these types of transactions.

COMPUTER PRACTICE

Step 1.   From the *Report Center*, select **Banking** and then double click the **Check Detail** report in the *Banking* section.

Step 2.   Enter *1/1/2019* in the *From* field and enter *1/31/2019* in the *To* field. Then, press **Tab**.

Step 3.   Scroll down until you see Bill Pmt -Check 6004 (near the bottom of the report).

In Figure 6-24, notice bill payment number 6004. The report shows that QuickBooks split the total amount due of $126.00 between the accounts payable account ($2.52) and the checking account ($123.48).

The amount for $-2.52 is the discount that you took when you paid the *Bill*. Although this report does not show it, you coded this amount to the Purchase Discounts account.

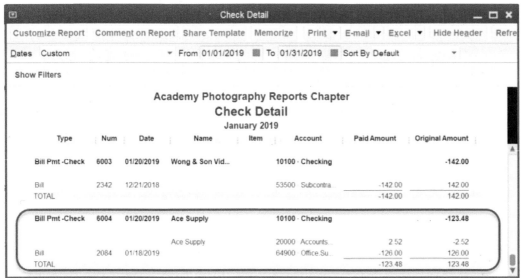

Figure 6-24 Check Detail report

Step 4.   Close all open report windows. Click **No** if QuickBooks prompts you to memorize the reports.

> **Tip:**
> In order to make your *Check Detail* reports easier to read and understand, consider recording your purchase discounts differently. Instead of taking the discount on the *Pay Bills* window (as you did in the example on page 129), consider recording your purchase discounts using *Bill Credits*.

Accounts Receivable and Accounts Payable Reports

There are several reports that you can use to keep track of the money that your Customers owe you (*accounts receivable*) and the money that you owe to your vendors (*accounts payable*).

Collections Report

The *Collections Report* is a report that shows each Customer's outstanding *Invoices* along with the Customer's telephone number.

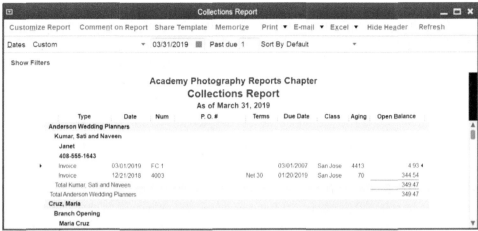

Figure 6-25 Upper portion of Collections Report for Accounts Receivable

COMPUTER PRACTICE

Step 1.   From the *Report Center*, select **Customers & Receivables** and then double click the **Collections Report** in the *A/R Aging* section.

Step 2.   Enter *3/31/2019* in the *Dates* field and press **Tab** (see Figure 6-25).

Customer Balance Detail Report

Use the *Customer Balance Detail* report to see the details of each Customer's transactions and payments. This report shows all transactions that use the accounts receivable account, including *Invoices*, *Payments*, *Discounts*, and *Finance Charges*.

COMPUTER PRACTICE

Step 1.   From the *Report Center*, select **Customers & Receivables** and then double click the **Customer Balance Detail** report in the *Customer Balance* section (see Figure 6-26). The *Dates* field on this report defaults to *All*.

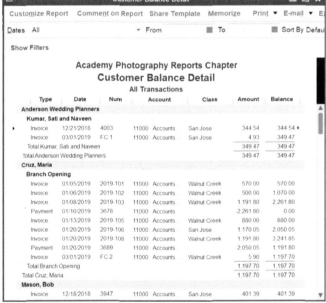

Figure 6-26 Customer Balance Detail report

Vendor Balance Detail Report

The *Vendor Balance Detail* report is similar to the *Customer Balance Detail* report, but it shows transactions that use *Accounts Payable*, including *Bills*, *Bill Credits*, *Bill Payments*, and *Discounts*.

COMPUTER PRACTICE

Step 1.   From the *Report Center*, select **Vendors & Payables** and then double click the **Vendor Balance Detail** report in the *Vendor Balances* section (see Figure 6-27). The *Dates* field on this report defaults to *All*.

Step 2.   Close all open report windows.

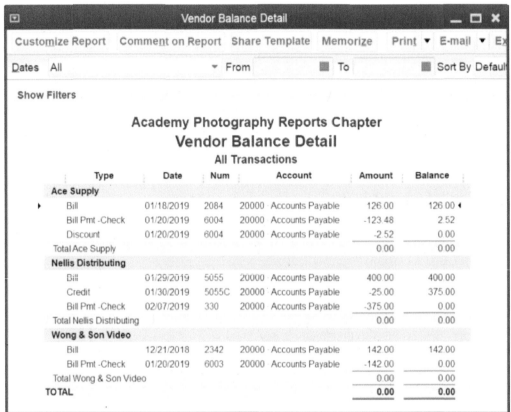

Figure 6-27 Vendor Balance Detail report

QuickBooks Graphs

One of the best ways to quickly get information from QuickBooks is to create a graph.

The *Income and Expense Graph* shows your income and expenses by month, and displays a pie chart showing a summary of your expenses.

COMPUTER PRACTICE

Step 1.   From the *Report Center*, select **Company & Financial** and then double click **Income & Expense Graph** in the *Income & Expenses* section.

Step 2.   Click **Dates** at the top left of the graph.

QuickBooks will display the *Change Graph Dates* window (see Figure 6-28).

Figure 6-28 Enter the dates for your graph in the window.

Step 3.   Enter *1/1/2019* in the *From* field and enter *1/31/2019* in the *To* field. Then, click **OK**.

Step 4.   QuickBooks displays the graph shown in Figure 6-29.

Step 5.   After viewing the graph, close the graph window.

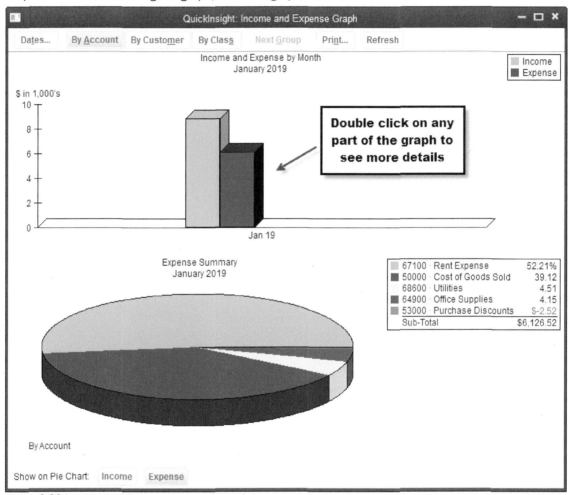

Figure 6-29 Income and Expense by Month graph

QuickBooks graphs highlight interesting facts about your company that are not easy to see from normal reports. For example, you can create a graph that shows your largest Customers or your biggest selling Items, and then you can visually inspect the relative sizes of each section of the graph.

COMPUTER PRACTICE

Step 1.   From the *Report Center*, select **Sales** and then double click **Sales Graph** in the *Sales by Customer* section (see Figure 6-30).

Step 2.   Click **Dates** at the top left of the graph. QuickBooks will display the *Change Graph Dates* window. Press **Tab**.

Step 3.   Enter *1/1/2019* in the *From* field, enter *2/28/2019* in the *To* field, and click **OK**.

Step 4.   Click the **By Customer** button on the top of the *QuickInsight: Sales Graph* window. This redraws the graph to show sales by Customer.

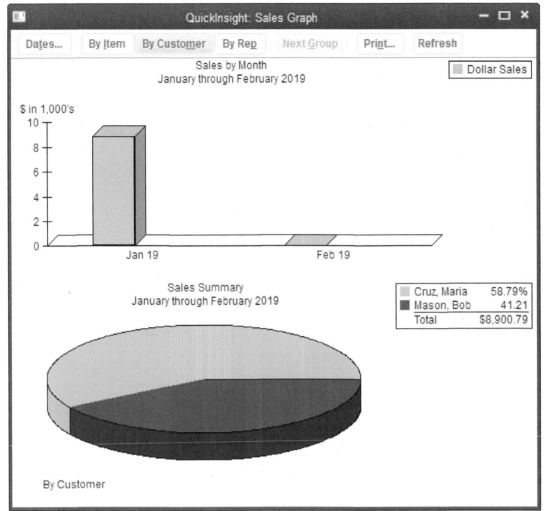

Figure 6-30 Sales Graph by Customer

Step 5.   After viewing the graph, close the window.

Building Custom Reports

To make reports that show only the information you want, you can modify (i.e., customize) an existing report. All reports include at least some modification and filtering options, so familiarize yourself with the tabs in the *Modify Report* window as they are described below.

The *Modify Report* window displays when you click the **Customize Report** button on any report. Four tabs make up the *Modify Report* window. Use the *Display* tab to change the date range, select a report basis, add or delete columns, change how columns are displayed, or add subcolumns on a report. The *Display* tab will show different sections depending upon the report being modified. For example, the *Display* tab for a *Profit and Loss* report does not allow you to select or deselect columns for the report (see Figure 6-31), while the *Display* tab for an *Item Price List* only allows you to select or deselect columns for the report (see Figure 6-32). The *Display* tab shows those sections particular to the report being modified.

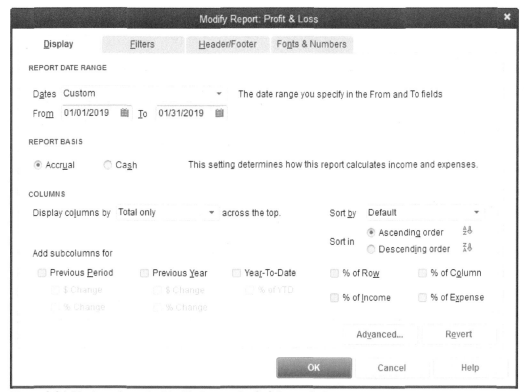

Figure 6-31 Display tab on the Modify Report: Profit & Loss window

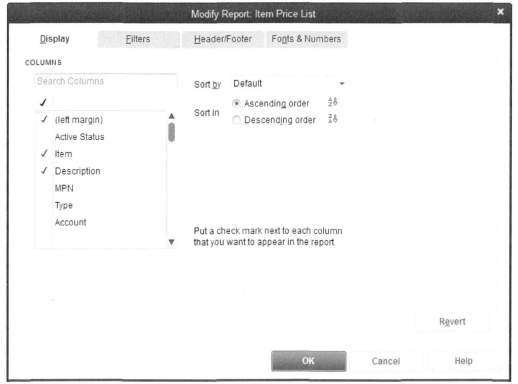

Figure 6-32 Display tab on the Modify Report: Item Price List window

Use the *Filters* tab to narrow the contents of the report so that you can analyze specific areas of your business. On the *Filters* tab, you can filter or choose specific accounts, dates, names, or Items to include in the report (see Figure 6-33).

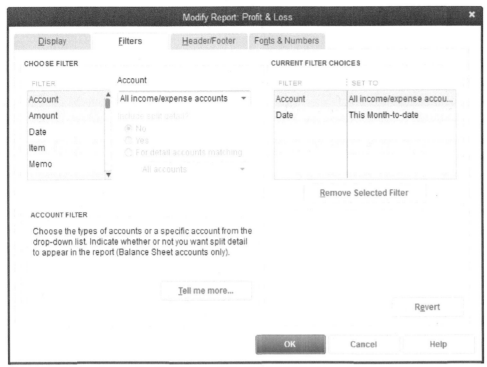

Figure 6-33 Filters tab on the Modify Report: Profit & Loss window

Use the *Header/Footer* tab to select which headers and footers will display on the report. In addition, the *Header/Footer* tab allows you to modify the *Company Name*, *Report Title*, *Subtitle*, *Date Prepared*, *Page Number*, and *Extra Footer Line* (see Figure 6-34).

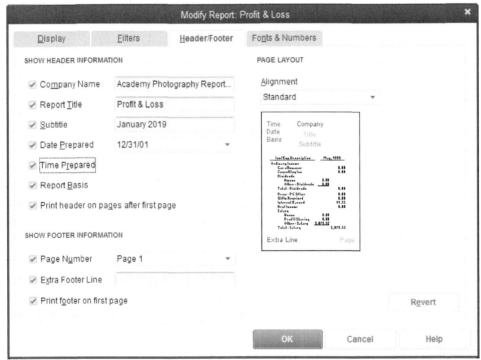

Figure 6-34 Header/Footer tab on the Modify Report: Profit & Loss window

Use the *Fonts & Numbers* tab to change the font and how numbers are displayed on the report. In addition, the *Fonts & Numbers* tab allows you to reduce numbers to multiples of 1000, hide amounts of 0.00, and show dollar amounts without cents (see Figure 6-35).

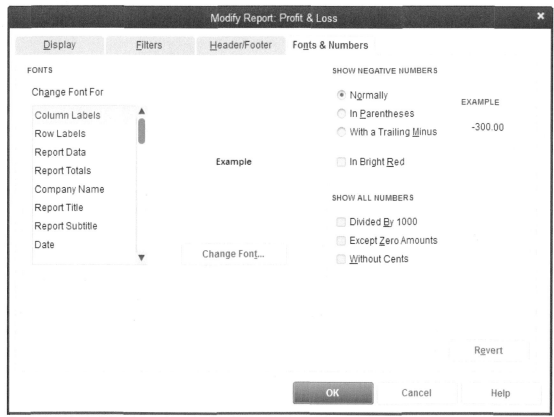

Figure 6-35 Fonts & Numbers tab on the Modify Report: Profit & Loss window

To practice modifying reports, suppose you want to get a report of all transactions that include all *Service Items* (*Photography Service* and *Development Services*) that you sold to Customers who live in *Walnut Creek* during January 2019. In addition, you want QuickBooks to sort and total the report by Customer. The report should only display the type of transaction, the date, transaction number, customer name, city, Item, account, credit and debit. Finally, the report should be titled S*ales of Services to Walnut Creek Customers.*

> **Note:**
> Although Academy Photography uses Classes to track which store their Customers buy from, we want a report about where customers *live.* Specifically, we want the *City* from the Customer's address. This information comes from the field called "Name City" that is used as part of the Customer's billing address.

COMPUTER PRACTICE

Begin by creating a *Custom Transaction Detail* report and then modify the report so that it provides the information you need.

Step 1.   From the *Reports* menu, select **Transaction Detail** from the *Custom Reports* submenu. The *Modify Report: Custom Transaction Detail Report* window displays.

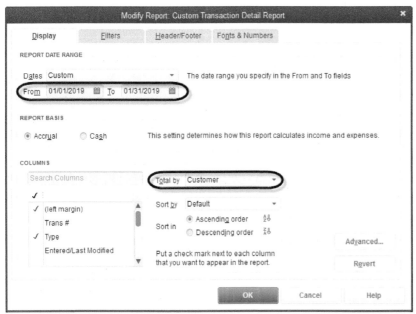

Figure 6-36 Modify Report: Custom Transaction Detail Report window

Step 2.   Enter *1/1/2019* in the *From* field and enter *1/31/2019* in the *To* field.

Step 3.   Select **Customer** from the *Total by* drop-down list and click **OK**.

This report will now show all transactions during January, totaled by Customer (see Figure 6-37).

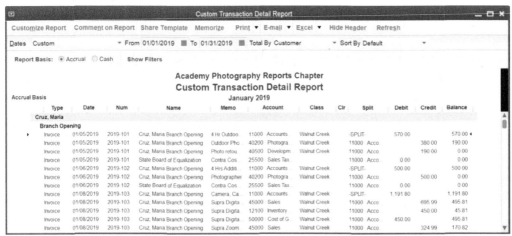

Figure 6-37 Upper portion of Transaction Detail by Account report totaled by Customer

For our purposes there are four problems with this report:

- The report shows more columns than we want to display.

- The report shows all transactions, not just the Service Items sold to Customers.

- The report is not filtered to only show Customers who live in Walnut Creek.

- The report title is not descriptive.

We will modify the report to correct the four problems listed above.

Step 4.   Click **Customize Report**.

Step 5.   In the **Columns** section of the *Display* tab, notice that several fields have check marks (see Figure 6-38). The check marks indicate which columns show on the report. Select **Name City** to turn this column on. Then deselect **Memo, Class, Clr, Split,** and **Balance**. You will need to scroll up and down in the list to find each field, or search in the *Search Columns* box.

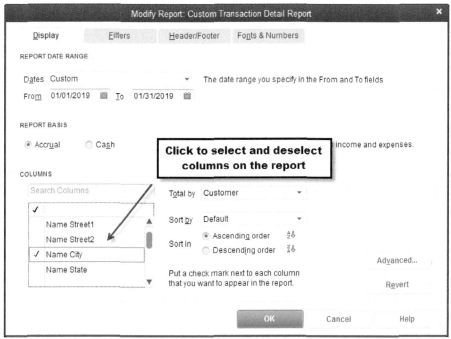

Figure 6-38 Modify columns by checking and unchecking fields in the Columns list

> **Note:**
> There are several other settings on the *Display* tab that you can choose if you want to modify the report further. For example, you could change the basis of the report from Accrual to Cash, or you could set the sorting preferences. Click the **Advanced** button for even more settings. Explore these settings to learn how they affect your reports. For descriptions of each selection, use the QuickBooks **Help** menu.

Step 6.   Click the **Filters** tab.

Step 7.   To filter the report so that it includes only Service Items, select the **Item** filter in the *Choose Filter* section and select **All services** from the *Item* drop-down list (see Figure 6-39) to show only the transactions that involve *Service Items*.

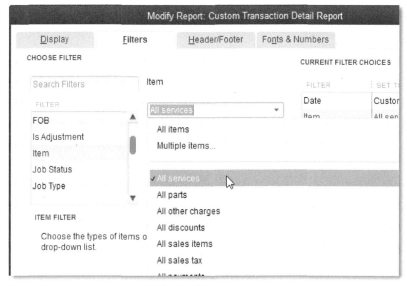

Figure 6-39 Item drop-down list in the Filters window

Step 8.   To filter the report so that it includes only those Customers who live in Walnut Creek, scroll down the *Choose Filter* section and select the **Name City** filter. This displays a **Name City** field to the right of the *Choose Filter* section. Enter **Walnut Creek** in the **Name City** field (see Figure 6-40). Press the **Tab** key.

> **Did You Know?**
> Many fields on the Filter tab act like wildcards. If you enter a portion of the text in a field for a particular filter, QuickBooks will display all records containing that text. For example, if you only type in *nut* or *eek* in the *City* field, all customer records in the city of Walnut Creek will still display, but other cities that contain *nut* or *eek* in their names will also appear. Therefore, be careful when using a wildcard in a field because it can produce an unintended result.

Figure 6-40 Entering a filter for a report

Step 9.   Click the **Header/Footer** tab on the *Modify Report* window.

Step 10.   To modify the title of the report so that it accurately describes the content of the report, enter **Sales of Services to Walnut Creek Customers** in the *Report Title* field as shown in Figure 6-41.

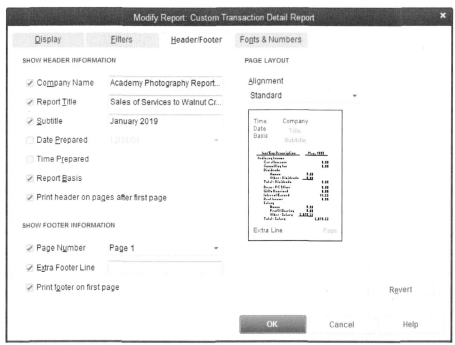

Figure 6-41 Change the report title on the Header/Footer tab

Step 11.   Click **OK** on the *Modify Report* window. You will now see the *Sales of Services to Walnut Creek Customers* report with the settings you just selected.

Step 12.   Click the **Show Filters** text next to the *Report Basis* buttons in the *Sales of Services to Walnut Creek Customers* report window. You can see a display of all the *Filters* you applied to the report (see Figure 6-42).

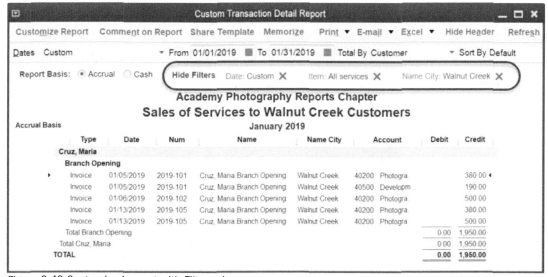

Figure 6-42 Customized report with Filters shown

DO NOT CLOSE THE REPORT. YOU WILL USE IT IN THE NEXT PRACTICE.

In Figure 6-43 you can see your modified report. Notice that its heading reflects its new content. You can modify the width of columns by dragging the column marker on the top right of the column to reduce or expand the width. Also, if you want to move a column left or right, move your cursor over the column header until you see the hand icon. Then, hold your left mouse button down as you drag the column to the left or right.

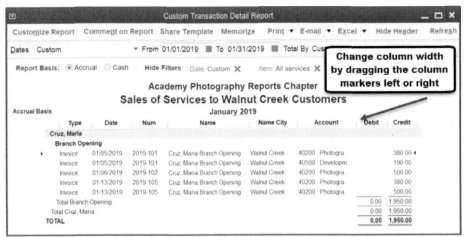

Figure 6-43 The customized report

Memorizing Reports

After you have modified a report, you can *memorize* the format and filtering so that you don't have to perform all of the modification steps the next time you want to view the report.

> **Note:**
> Memorizing a report does not memorize the data on the report, only the format, dates, and filtering.

If you enter specific dates, QuickBooks will use those dates the next time you bring up the report. However, if you select a *relative* date range in the *Dates* field (e.g., Last Fiscal Quarter, Last Fiscal Year, or This Fiscal Year-to-Date) before memorizing a report, QuickBooks will use the relative dates the next time you create the report.

For example, if you memorize a report with the *Dates* field set to *This Fiscal Quarter*, that report will always use dates for the current fiscal quarter as of the date you run the memorized report (see Figure 6-44).

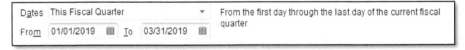

Figure 6-44 The Dates field showing a relative date range

COMPUTER PRACTICE

Step 1.   With the *Sales of Services to Walnut Creek Customers* report displayed, click **Memorize** at the top of the report.

Step 2.   In the *Memorize Report* window, the name for the report is automatically filled in. QuickBooks uses the report title as the default name for the memorized report (see Figure 6-45). The name can be modified if desired.

Figure 6-45 Memorize Report window

Step 3.   Click the Checkbox next to **Save in Memorized Report Group:** and select **Customers** from the drop-down list as shown in Figure 6-45.

You can group your reports into similar types when you memorize them. This allows you to run several reports in a group by selecting them in the *Process Multiple Reports* window.

Step 4.   Leave *Share this report template with others* unchecked.

If checked, this feature would allow you to share your report template with the greater QuickBooks user community. For more on *Contributed Reports*, see page 227.

Step 5.   Click **OK** and close the report.

Viewing Memorized Reports

The next time you want to see this report follow these steps:

COMPUTER PRACTICE

Step 1.   From the *Report Center*, click on the *Memorized* tab at the top of the window.

Notice that QuickBooks displays the reports in groups according to how you memorized them.

Step 2.   Select the report you just memorized by selecting **Customers** on the menu on the left of the window and double click **Sales of Services to Walnut Creek Customers** (see Figure 6-46).

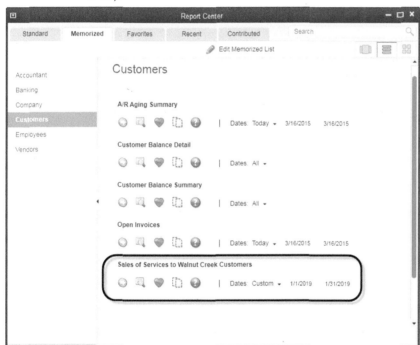

Figure 6-46 Memorized Report in the Report Center

Step 3.   Close all open report windows.

Contributed Reports

When you memorize a report, you are given the option of sharing the report template with others. You can access contributed reports from the Reports Center. Be aware that you may not be able to use certain reports if they utilize features that you do not use, such as multi-currency.

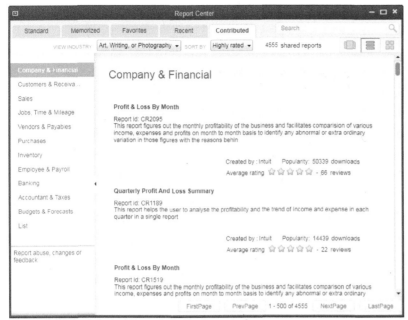

Figure 6-47 Contributed Reports in the Reports Center

Processing Multiple Reports

QuickBooks allows you to combine several memorized reports into a group, so that you can later display and/or print the reports in the group as a batch.

You may want to use this feature to print a series of monthly reports for your files (e.g., monthly *Profit and Loss* and *Balance Sheet* reports).

> **Note:**
> You can also set up QuickBooks so reports are generated and emailed in password protected PDFs on a regular schedule. You can access this features by going to Scheduled Reports from the Reports menu.

COMPUTER PRACTICE

Step 1.   From the *Reports* menu select **Process Multiple Reports** (see Figure 6-48).

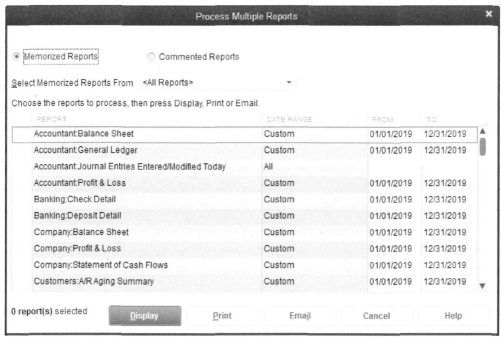

Figure 6-48 Process Multiple Reports window

> **Note:**
> Click in the column to the left of the report you want to include when you print or display your reports. Select the *From* and *To* date ranges of the report you wish to print in the columns on the right. Your date ranges will not match the ones displayed in Figure 6-48 and Figure 6-49. If you print the same group of reports on a régular basis, create a new Report Group in the *Memorized Report List* window to combine the reports under a single group. Then you can select the group name in the *Select Memorized Reports From* field.

Step 2.   Select **Customers** from the *Select Memorized Reports From* drop-down list (see Figure 6-49).

Figure 6-49 Customers Report Group

Step 3.   If you do not want to display or print all the reports in the group, uncheck (√) the left
               column to deselect the reports you want to omit. Click **Display** to show the reports on the
               window (see Figure 6-50) or click **Print** to print all the reports.

> If your *Home* page is maximized, make sure to **Restore Down** the window and choose
> **Cascade** from the *Window* menu to see all reports as shown in Figure 6-50.

Step 4.   Close all open report windows. Click **No** if QuickBooks prompts you to memorize the
               reports.

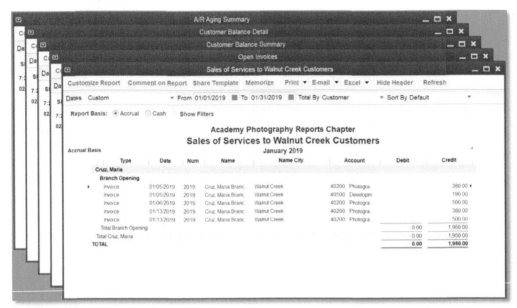

Figure 6-50 All of the reports in the Customer report group

Printing Reports

Every report in QuickBooks is printable. When you print reports, QuickBooks allows you to specify the
orientation (landscape or portrait) and page-count characteristics for the reports.

COMPUTER PRACTICE

Step 1.   Create a *Profit & Loss by Job* report dated *1/1/2019* to *1/31/2019* (see page 206).

Step 2.   To print the report, click **Print** at the top of the window and select **Report**.

> **Another Way:**
> To print a report, press **Ctrl+P** or select the **File** menu and then select **Print Report**.

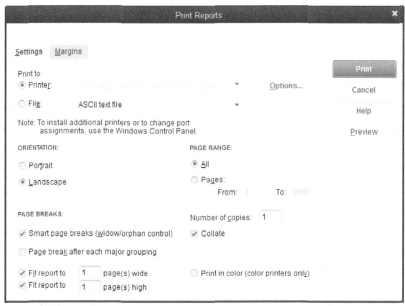

Figure 6-51 Print Report window – your screen may vary

Step 3. The **Print Reports** window displays. Your settings will be different than the settings shown in Figure 6-51.

Step 4. QuickBooks normally selects your default printer, but you can select another printer from the *Printer* drop-down list.

Step 5. Select **Landscape** in the *Orientation* section.

The Portrait setting makes the print appear from left to right across the 8½-inch dimension of the page ("straight up"), while the Landscape setting makes the print appear across the 11-inch dimension of the page ("sideways").

Step 6. Confirm that the **Smart page breaks (widow/orphan control)** setting is selected (see Figure 6-52). This setting keeps related data from splitting across two pages.

PAGE BREAKS:

☑ Smart page breaks (widow/orphan control)

☐ Page break after each major grouping

Figure 6-52 Page Breaks setting

Using **Smart page breaks**, you can control (to some extent) where page breaks occur on reports so that your pages don't break in inappropriate places. Using **Page break after each major grouping**, you can have QuickBooks break the pages after each major grouping of accounts. For example, in the *Profit & Loss* report, all Income and Cost of Goods Sold accounts will be on the first page (or pages), and all the Expense accounts will begin on a new page. In other reports, like the Customer Balance Detail and Vendor Balance Detail reports, this setting will cause each Customer and Vendor to begin on a new page, respectively.

Step 7. Select **Fit report to 1 page(s) wide** and **Fit report to 1 page(s) high** (see Figure 6-53). When you select these options, QuickBooks reduces the font size of the report so that it fits into the desired number of page(s).

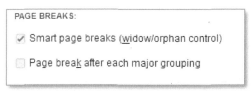

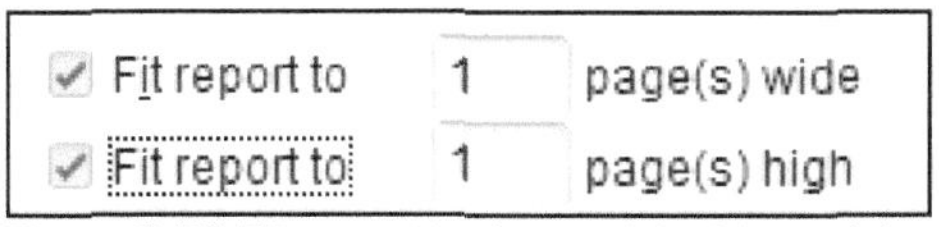

Figure 6-53 Fit report to 1 page(s) wide and 1 page(s) high

Before you print any report, it's a good idea to preview the report to make sure it will print the way you want.

Step 8.   Click the **Preview** button on the *Print Reports* window.

Step 9.   If everything looks right, click **Print** to print the report.

Step 10.   Close all open report windows.

> **Note:**
> QuickBooks saves the setting on the *Print Reports* window when a report is memorized.

Finding Transactions

There are several ways to find transactions in QuickBooks depending on what you are trying to find. Sometimes you only know the date of a transaction and other times you know only the Customer, Item, or amount. Some of the ways you can search for a transaction include finding it in the register, using the **Search** command, using **QuickReports**, or using **QuickZoom**.

Using the Find Button

Unless you just completed a transaction, finding it by clicking the **Previous** button on the transaction form can be impractical. Clicking the **Find** button on the form, such as on the Invoice form on Figure 6-54, allows you to search for a transaction by *Name, Date, Transaction Number,* or *Amount*.

Figure 6-54 Find button

Using the Search Command

If you are looking for a transaction and you do not know which register to look in, or if you want to find more than just a single transaction, you can use the **Search** command.

COMPUTER PRACTICE

You want to find a recent payment by Maria Cruz.

Step 1.   Enter **Cruz** in the *Search* field on the top of the *Icon Bar* and select **Search company file** from the drop-down menu (see Figure 6-55). Click the **Search** icon (see Figure 6-56)

Figure 6-55 The Search field

Figure 6-56 Search icon

Step 2.   The *Search* window opens. QuickBooks returns a keyword search including any transaction or *Name* record that contains the word, or string, "Cruz" (see Figure 6-57). If the *Search* returns no transactions, click the **Update search information** link in the Search window.

You will notice that the search results include both the customer Maria Cruz, as well as Sinclair Insurance which is located in Santa Cruz, CA. Notice that different forms and name entries are included, such as *Customers*, *Vendors*, and *Invoices*.

> **Note:**
> QuickBooks includes an auto suggestion feature in the *Search* window. As you enter characters in the *Search* field in the *Search* window, suggested words will appear in a drop down box below the field. Auto suggestion is not available in the *Search* field in the *Icon Bar*.

Step 3.   Close the *Search* window.

Figure 6-57 Upper portion of results in the Search Window

QuickReports

A *QuickReport* can quickly give you detailed transactions about an *Account*, *Item*, *Customer*, *Vendor*, or other payee. You can generate *QuickReports* from the *Chart of Accounts*, *Centers*, *Lists*, *Account Registers*, or forms. Table 6-2 shows different types of *QuickReports*.

When you are in...	The QuickReport shows you...
Chart of Accounts	All transactions involving that account
Centers and *Lists* (with an *Item* or *Name* selected)	All transactions for that *Item* or *Name*
Registers (with a transaction selected)	All transactions in that register for the same *Name*
Forms (*Invoice*, *Bill*, or *Check*)	All transactions for that particular customer, vendor, or payee within the same *Name* as the current transaction

Table 6-2 Types of QuickReports

COMPUTER PRACTICE

Step 1.   Click the **Chart of Accounts** icon in the *Company* section of the **Home** page.

Step 2.   Select the **Inventory Asset** account.

Step 3.   Click the **Reports** button and select **QuickReport: Inventory Asset**. Alternatively, press **Ctrl+Q** (see Figure 6-58).

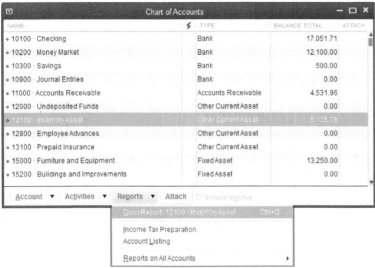

Figure 6-58 QuickReport of the Inventory Asset account

Step 4.   QuickBooks displays all transactions involving the **Inventory Asset** account (see Figure 6-59).

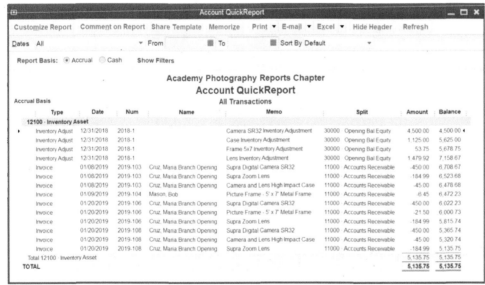

Figure 6-59 All transactions involving the Inventory Asset account

Step 5.   Close the Account *QuickReport* and Chart of Accounts window.

Step 6.   From the *Lists* menu select **Item List**.

Step 7.   Select **Camera SR32** from the *Item list*.

Step 8.   Click the **Reports** button and select **QuickReport: Camera SR32**. Alternatively, press **Ctrl+Q**.

Step 9.   Change the *Dates* range to **All** by typing *A* in the Dates field. QuickBooks displays all transactions involving the **Camera SR32** Item (see Figure 6-60).

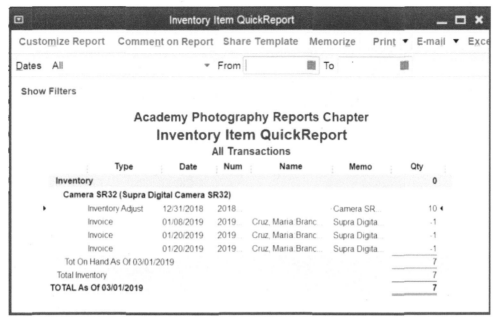

Figure 6-60 All transactions involving the Camera SR32 Item

Step 10.   Close the Item *QuickReport* and Item List window.

Step 11.   Click the **Check Register** icon in the *Banking* section of the *Home* page.

Step 12.   Confirm that *Checking* displays in the *Select Account* field of the *Use Register* dialog box. Click **OK**.

Step 13.   Scroll up and select **BILLPMT #6004**.

Step 14.   Click the **QuickReport** icon at the top of the register (see Figure 6-61) or press **Ctrl+Q**.

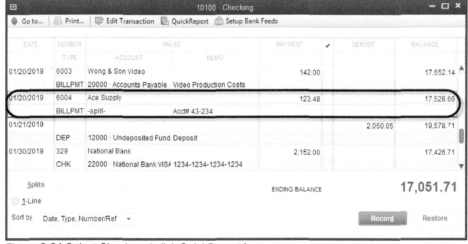

Figure 6-61 Select Check and click QuickReport icon

Step 15.   QuickBooks displays a report of all transactions in the Checking register using the same name as the selected transaction (see Figure 6-62).

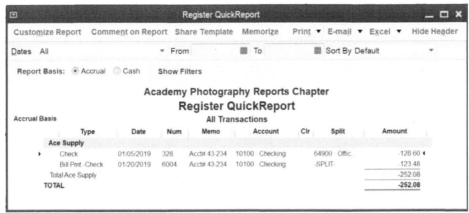

Figure 6-62 QuickReport for Vendor

Step 16.   Close the Register *QuickReport* and Checking register.

> **Did You Know?**
> You can also generate *QuickReports* from the Customer Center, Vendor Center, or Employee Center by selecting the Customer, Vendor, or Employee and clicking on the **QuickReport** link in the upper right-hand corner of the window.

Using QuickZoom

QuickBooks provides a convenient feature called *QuickZoom*, which allows you to see the details behind numbers on reports. For example, the *Profit & Loss* report in Figure 6-63 shows $3,145.00 of *Photography Services* income. Double click on the amount to see the details behind the number.

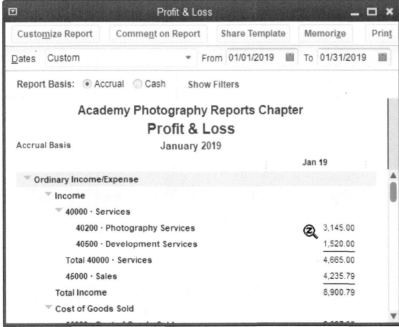

Figure 6-63 QuickZoom allows you to see the details behind a number

As your cursor moves over numbers on the report, it will turn into a magnifying glass with a "z" in the middle. The magnifying icon indicates that you can double click to see the details behind the number on the report. After you double click the number, *QuickZoom* displays a *Transaction Detail By Account* report (see Figure 6-64) that shows the details of each transaction in the account that you zoomed in on.

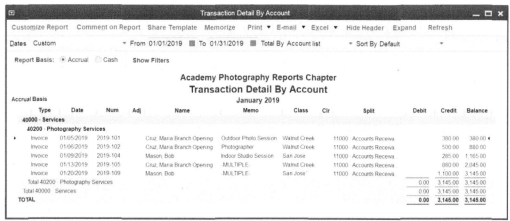

Figure 6-64 Transaction Detail by Account report

Exporting Reports to Spreadsheets

When you need to modify reports in ways that QuickBooks does not allow (e.g., changing the name of a column heading), you will need to export the report to a spreadsheet program.

> **Note:**
> *QuickBooks Statement Writer* is a utility for creating reports in Excel using live QuickBooks data. It is included in QuickBooks Accountant and QuickBooks Enterprise Solutions.

Exporting a Report to Microsoft Excel

COMPUTER PRACTICE

Step 1. From the *Report Center*, select **Sales** and then double click the **Sales by Customer Detail** report in the *Sales by Customer* section to display the report.

Step 2. Enter *1/1/2019* in the *From* field and enter *1/31/2019* in the *To* field. Press **Tab** twice (see Figure 6-65).

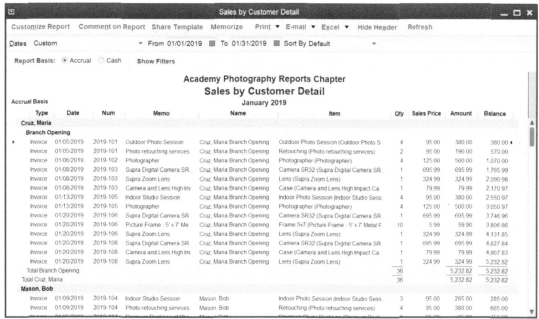

Figure 6-65 Sales by Customer Detail report

Step 3.   Click **Excel** at the top of the report and choose **Create New Worksheet** from the drop down menu.

Step 4.   In the *Send Report to Excel* window, make sure *Create new worksheet* and *in new workbook* are selected. This will export your report to a new Excel worksheet (see Figure 6-66).

> **Note:**
> The **Advanced** button of the *Send Report to Excel* window has many useful features for working with your QuickBooks data in Excel, including Auto Outline, which allows you to collapse and expand detail.

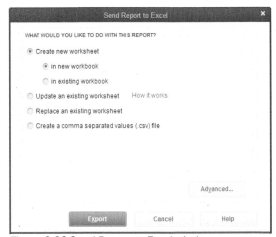

Figure 6-66 Send Report to Excel window

Step 5.   Click **Export** in the *Send Report to Excel* window. QuickBooks will export your report directly to an Excel spreadsheet (see Figure 6-67).

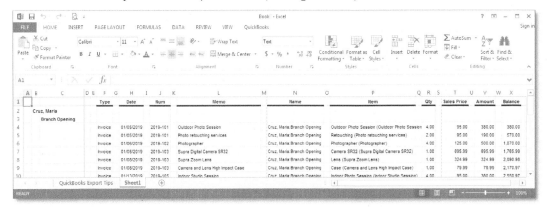

Figure 6-67 The report is now in an Excel spreadsheet. Your screen may vary.

> **Note:**
> After opening a QuickBooks exported report, Excel will display a QuickBooks Tips tab on the Excel ribbon. Once you save the file, you will be able to use the *Update Report* feature to refresh the report with updated information from QuickBooks. Although you can bring in new information to your Excel report from QuickBooks, it is not possible to import changes from this Excel report back into QuickBooks.

Review Questions

Comprehension Questions

1. Explain how the *QuickZoom* feature helps you see more detail about a report.

2. Name an example of how the *Check Detail* report is valuable.

3. How can you hide the subaccounts on the *Profit & Loss* report?

4. Explain how using *Filters* helps you get the reports you want.

5. Explain how memorized reports help you save time.

Multiple Choice

Choose the best answer(s) for each of the following:

1. What are the two major types of reports in QuickBooks?
   a) Register and List.
   b) Monthly and Annual.
   c) Accounting and Business Management.
   d) Balance Sheet and Profit & Loss.

2. Use the **Customize Report** button on any report to:
   a) Add or delete columns or change the accounting basis of the report.
   b) Change the width of columns on the report.
   c) Print the report on blank paper.
   d) Memorize the report for future use.

3. You cannot create a *QuickReport* for:
   a) Customers.
   b) Vendors.
   c) Items.
   d) Incorrectly posted entries.

4. To create a report that lists each of your vendors along with their address and telephone information:
   a) Display the *Vendor Contact List*.
   b) Open the *Search* window and do a search for Vendors and the corresponding Address and Phone Numbers.
   c) Customize the Vendor database.
   d) You must create a *Modified Report* to see this information.

5. In order to analyze the profitability of your company, you should:
   a) Only do an analysis if the company is profitable.
   b) Create a *Profit & Loss* report.
   c) Review all detailed transaction reports.
   d) Review the financial exceptions report.

6. Which statement is false? You may analyze your income and expenses for a given period:

a)   By class.

b)   By job.

c)   By vendor.

d)   For the whole business.

7. Which report shows monies owed to your company by customers?

a)   The Balance Sheet report.

b)   The *Collections* Report.

c)   The Accounts Payable Aging report.

d)   The Daily Charges report.

8. In order to modify the header and footer of your report:

a)   Click the **Customize Report** button and then click the **Filters** tab.

b)   Click the **Titles** button and then click the **Customization** tab.

c)   Click the **Header/Footer** button.

d)   Click the **Customize Report** button and then click the **Header/Footer** tab.

9. *Processing Multiple Reports* allow you to:

a)   Rearrange the report center.

b)   Organize the memorized report list into groups of related reports.

c)   Create groups of filters for your reports.

d)   Group reports by date.

10. The Profit & Loss report shows which of the following:

a)   Assets, Liabilities, and Equity accounts.

b)   Checks written for the period.

c)   Income, Cost of Goods Sold, Expenses, Other Income, and Other Expenses.

d)   Accounts Receivable increases for the period.

11. If the Profit & Loss by Class report has an *Unclassified* column:

a)   There is an error in the filters on the report.

b)   You must refresh the report.

c)   You should eliminate the column using the *Modify Report* window.

d)   Some of the transactions for the period were not assigned to a class.

12. You can export *Reports* to:

a)   Microsoft Excel.

b)   Microsoft Word.

c)   Other Accounting Software.

d)   You cannot export reports.

13. Which is a feature of the **Filters** tab on the *Modify Report* window?

a)   Filters allow you select the columns on a report so that you can analyze specific areas of your business.

b)   Filters allow you to change how reports total and subtotal.

c)   Filters allow you to choose specific accounts, dates, names, or items to include on a report.

d)   Filters allow you to modify the date range on most reports.

14. To modify which columns are displayed on a report, click **Customize Report** and then check the names of columns to be displayed on the:

    a)   Header/Footer tab.

    b)   Display tab.

    c)   Filters tab.

    d)   Fonts & Numbers tab.

15. The **Fit report to 1 page(s) wide** feature does which one of the following:

    a)   Fits the report into a single page for each column.

    b)   Eliminates columns from the report until it fits on a single page.

    c)   Reduces the font size of the report so the width of all columns does not exceed 8½" (in portrait mode) or 11" (in landscape mode).

    d)   Increases the margins on reports to make sure everything fits on one page.

Completion Statements

1.   The _____ _____ _____ is a listing of your vendors along with each vendor's address and telephone information.

2.   To modify the contents of a report, you can _____ it to include certain accounts, names, columns, or transaction types.

3.   QuickBooks provides a convenient feature called _____, which allows you to see the detail behind numbers on reports.

4.   If you're looking for a transaction and you don't know which register to look in, or if you want to find more than just a single transaction, you can use the _____ command.

5.   The _____ _____ is a report that shows your financial position, as defined by the balances in each of your asset, liabilities, and equity accounts on a given date.

Reports Problem 1

> Restore the Reports-18Problem1.QBM file. The password to access this file is *Sleeter18*.

1.   Print the Profit & Loss Standard Report for January 2019.

2.   Print the Balance Sheet Standard Report as of 1/31/2019.

3.   Print the Statement of Cash Flows Report for January 2019.

4.   Print the Customer QuickReport for Bob Mason for January 2019.

5.   Print the Vendor Contact List Report.

6.   Open the Sales by Customer Detail Report for January 2019.

7.   Filter the Sales by Customer Detail Report to only display Sales amounts between $100.00 and $500.00.

8.   Print the customized Sales by Customer Detail Report for January 2019.

Reports Problem 2 (Advanced)

> Restore the Reports-18Problem2.QBM file. The password to access this file is *Sleeter18*.

1. Print the reports listed below for Academy Photography.

    a)   Customer Phone List.

    b)   Check Detail Report for January and February of 2019.

    c)   Customer QuickReport for Maria Cruz for January and February 2019.

    d)   Profit & Loss Standard Report for January and February 2019.

    e)   Profit & Loss by Job Report for January and February 2019.

    f)   Trial Balance Report for January 2019.

    g)   Balance Sheet Standard Report as of January 31, 2019.

2. Create a custom report showing all payments received from customers in January 2019. Modify the report so that it totals by Customer and includes the title and columns displayed in Figure 6-68.

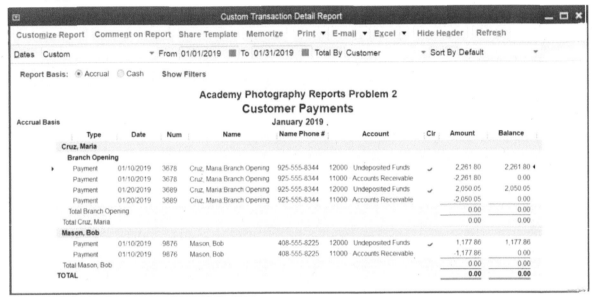

Figure 6-68 Customize your report to look like this.

> **Important:**
> When you complete #2, do not close the report. You will use the modified report in the next step.

3. Print the report you created in Step 2 and then memorize it in the Customers report group. Name the memorized report *Customer Payments*.

4. Create and print a graph of your Income and Expenses (by Class and Show Expense on Pie Chart) for January and February 2019.

Chapter 7
Customizing QuickBooks

Topics

In this chapter, you will learn about the following topics:

- QuickBooks Preferences (page 243)
- Customizing QuickBooks Menus and Windows (page 246)
- QuickBooks Items and Other Lists (page 250)
- Custom Fields (page 263)
- Modifying Sales Form Templates (page 265)

> **Restore this File:**
> This chapter uses the Customizing-18.QBW. See page 9 for more information. The password to access this file is *Sleeter18*.

QuickBooks has many customizable options that allow you to configure the program to meet your own needs and preferences. This chapter introduces you to many of the ways you can make these configurations in QuickBooks using *Preferences*, customizing the *Home* page, menus, and toolbars, and creating templates for forms. This chapter also introduces some new lists, including the *Item List*, the *Terms List*, and the *Template List*.

QuickBooks Preferences

There are two types of *Preferences* in QuickBooks:

1. **User Preferences**. In QuickBooks, User Preferences are specific to the user who is currently logged on to the file. A user can make changes to his or her User Preferences as desired.

2. **Company Preferences**. Use Company Preferences to make global changes to the features and functionality of a company's data file. Only the *Administrator* of the data file can make changes to Company Preferences.

In this section, you will learn about a few of these *Preferences* and how they affect QuickBooks. Clicking the *Help* button in the *Preferences* window will launch QuickBooks Help with specific topics relevant to the *Preference* in the open window.

> **Note:**
> Many of the *Preferences* are discussed in detail in other chapters. For example, the payroll preferences are discussed in the "Payroll Setup" chapter, beginning on page 359.

Setting User Preferences

COMPUTER PRACTICE

To access QuickBooks Preferences, follow these steps:

Step 1.   Select the **Edit** menu, and then select **Preferences**.

User Preferences – Desktop View

Use the *Desktop View* User Preferences ("*My Preferences*" tab) to customize the view of the current user.

COMPUTER PRACTICE

Step 1.　　　　Click the **Desktop View** Preference. See Figure 7-1. Confirm that **Multiple Windows** is selected in the *View* section. In the *Desktop* section, check the **Show Home page when opening a company file**, if needed.

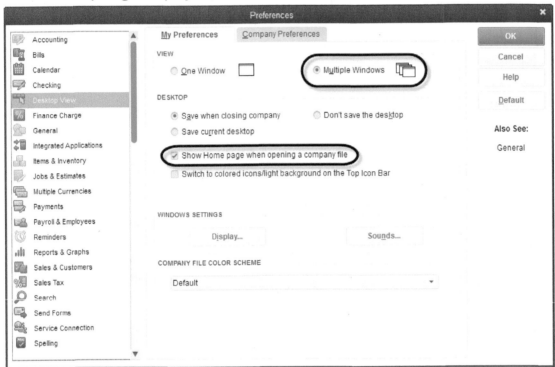

Figure 7-1 User Preferences - Desktop View

The user preferences for *Desktop View* allow you to customize the default windows that show when you open QuickBooks, as well as the company file color scheme. We recommend selecting *Multiple Windows* as shown on Figure 7-1. If you select the *One Widow* preference, you will not be able to display more than one QuickBooks window at a time, and you will not be able to change the size of QuickBooks windows. From the *View* menu, you can also choose between these two *Desktop View* options.

There is also the *Show Home page when opening a company file* option. Activating this Preference causes the *Home* page window to be displayed whenever the company file is opened.

> **Tip:**
> If you use QuickBooks in a multi-user environment, it may be best to select the *Don't save the desktop* radio button on the window shown in Figure 7-1. If you save the desktop, each time you open QuickBooks it will re-open all of the windows and reports you were viewing when you last used the program. If you save the desktop, this may negatively impact performance for other users when they open the data file. If each user has a unique username, each time a new user logs in, he or she will see the saved desktop unique to their username for that *Company* file.

Company Preferences – Desktop View

Administrators may use the *Company Preferences* tab in the *Desktop View* Preferences to control which icons display on the *Home* page. These settings will affect every user who uses this company file.

Step 1. With the *Desktop View Preference* still selected, click the **Company Preferences** tab (see Figure 7-2).

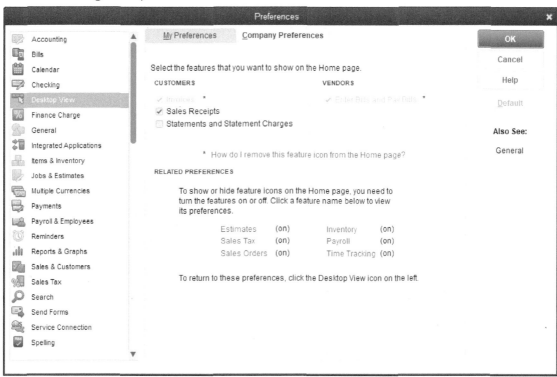

Figure 7-2 The Desktop View—Company Preferences window

Step 2. Click the **Statements and Statement Charges** checkbox to deselect.

In this window, you can remove some icons from displaying on the *Home* page. However, turning off the icon on the *Home* page does not disable the feature, since you can still access the command using the menus. Some features, such as *Estimates, Sales Tax,* and *Sales Orders* listed in the lower portion of the *Desktop View Company Preference* window can only be removed from the *Home* page by disabling the feature using the appropriate *Preferences*. You can access the appropriate *Preference* through the links in the *Desktop View Company Preferences* window.

> **Note:**
> You cannot remove the icons for *Invoices, Enter Bills,* or *Pay Bills* from the *Home* page if certain other features are enabled. For example, the *Invoices* icon must be turned on if your company uses *Estimates* or *Sales Orders*. For a complete list of *Preferences*, see QuickBooks Help.

Step 3. Click **OK** to close the *Preferences* window. Click **OK** in the dialog box that appears about closing open windows.

Step 4. Click the **Home** button on the *Icon Bar*. Notice that the *Statements* branch of the *Customers* section of the *Home* page no longer displays (see Figure 7-3).

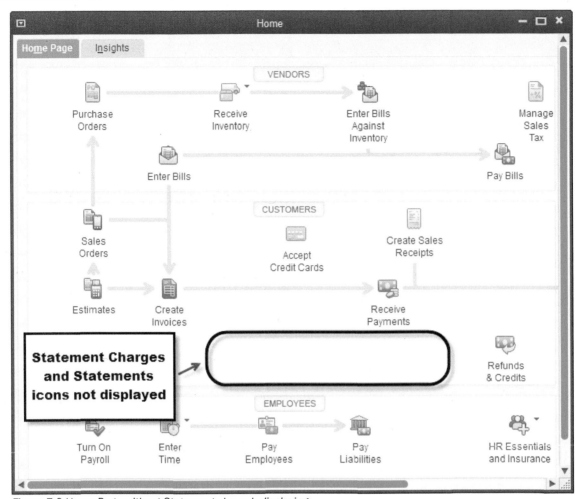

Figure 7-3 Home Page without Statements branch displaying

Customizing QuickBooks Menus and Windows

QuickBooks gives you the ability to set up some special customized features. You can create a *Favorites Menu* for your regular activities. You can also customize the *Icon Bar*, which gives you easy access to various commands.

Favorites Menu

The *Favorites* menu is a customizable menu where you can place any QuickBooks commands that you use frequently. You can also add items that are usually only available through submenus so that the options are more easily accessible.

COMPUTER PRACTICE

Step 1.   Locate the *Favorites* menu between the *Lists* and *Company* menus on the menu bar. (Those using QuickBooks Accountant will see it between the *Lists* and *Accountant* menus).

> **Note:**
> If you do not see the *Favorites* menu, you can turn it on by selecting *Favorites Menu* from the *View* menu.

Step 2.   Select the **Customize Favorites** option from the *Favorites* menu (see Figure 7-4).

Figure 7-4 Customize Favorites option in the Favorites menu

Step 3.   The *Customize Your Menus* window includes all available menu items. You can select a
            menu item to be easily accessed through the *Favorites* Menu. Click **Chart of Accounts** and
            then click **Add** (see Figure 7-5).

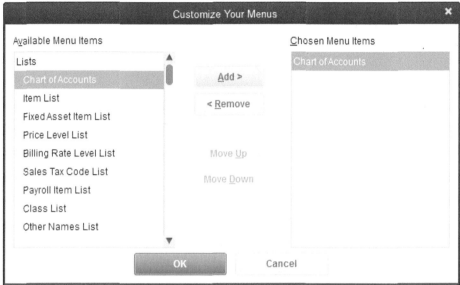

Figure 7-5 Chart of Accounts added to Favorites menu in the Customize Your Menus window

Step 4.   Click **OK** to close the *Customize Your Menus* window.

Step 5.   Select the **Favorites** menu and chose **Chart of Accounts** (see Figure 7-6).

Figure 7-6 Chart of Accounts in the Favorites menu

Step 6.   Close the Chart of Accounts.

QuickBooks Icon Bar

The *Icon Bar* appears at the left of the screen by default (see Figure 7-7). The buttons on the *Icon Bar*
are shortcuts to QuickBooks windows. The *Icon Bar* allows you to create an icon shortcut to almost any
window in QuickBooks.

You can customize the *Icon Bar* through several options under the *View Menu*. You can set the *Icon Bar*
to display at the top of your screen just below the *Menu* by choosing *Top Icon Bar* from the *View Menu*.
When *Top Icon Bar* is displayed, there are slight differences in available shortcuts and the look of the
Home page. You can also *Hide the Icon Bar* from the *View* menu.

Figure 7-7 Default Location for the Icon Bar

Customizing the Icon Bar

You can customize the *Icon Bar* to include icons to commonly used transactions and reports.

Using the Customize Icon Bar Window

Use the *Customize Icon Bar* window to add icons to the *Icon Bar* or to edit or delete existing icons. You can also use this window to add separators between icons and to reposition icons.

COMPUTER PRACTICE

Step 1.   Select **Customize Icon Bar** from the *View* menu. QuickBooks displays the *Customize Icon Bar* window shown in Figure 7-8.

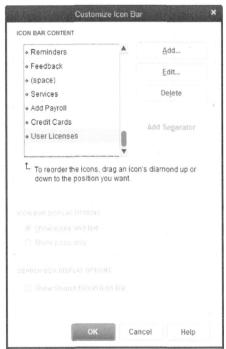

Figure 7-8 Customize Icon Bar window – your screen may vary

Step 2.   To add an Icon to the *Icon Bar* click **Add**. QuickBooks opens the *Add Icon Bar Item* window.

Step 3.   Select **Calculator** from the list of options as shown in Figure 7-9. Scroll down to *Calculator*, if necessary. Notice that QuickBooks automatically selects the preferred icon for the calculator and recommends the label name and description.

Figure 7-9 Add Icon Bar Item window with Calculator selected – your screen may vary

Step 4.   Click **OK** to create the Calculator icon.

Step 5.   The order of the icons on this list dictates the order of the icons on the *Icon Bar*. To move the *Calc* icon, click the diamond next to **Calc** and then drag and drop *Calc* to move it below the **Add Payroll** icon as shown in Figure 7-10.

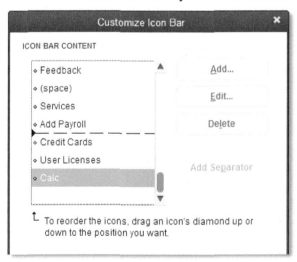

Figure 7-10 Use your mouse to move icons up or down in the list.

Step 6.   Click **OK** to save your changes. Figure 7-11 displays the customized *Icon Bar*. (You may have to scroll down to see it.)

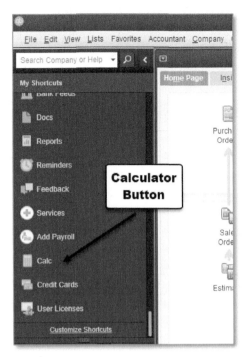

Figure 7-11 Customized Icon Bar

Customizing the Icon Bar – Using Add "window-name" to Icon Bar

You can add Icons to the Icon Bar using the **Add "window-name" to Icon Bar** option from the *View* menu. For example, Academy Photography wants an icon for the **Customer Phone List** report, customized to include the customers' phone numbers and total balances. Follow these steps to add this report to your Icon bar:

> **DO NOT PERFORM THESE STEPS. THEY ARE FOR REFERENCE ONLY.**

1. From the *Reports* menu select **List**, and then select **Customer Phone List**. See Figure 7-12.

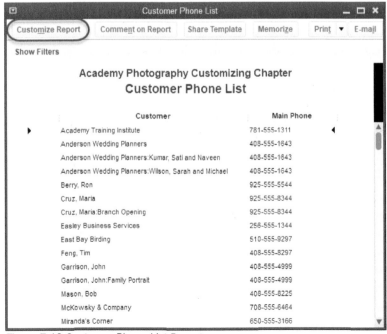

Figure 7-12 Customer Phone List Report

2. Click **Customize Report** and select the **Balance Total** field in the *Columns* list (see Figure 7-13). Click **OK** to save your changes.

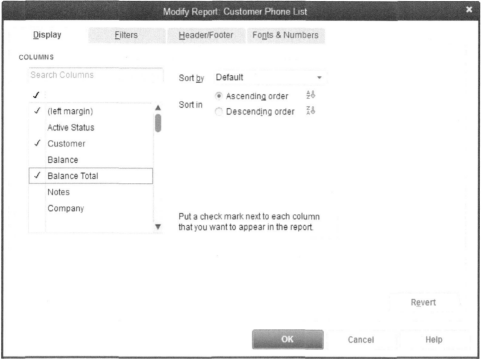

Figure 7-13 Select Balance Total on the Columns List

3. With the modified report displayed, select the *View* menu and then select **Add "Customer Phone List" to Icon Bar**. QuickBooks displays the *Add Window to Icon Bar* window shown in Figure 7-14.

Figure 7-14 Add Window to Icon Bar window

4. Enter **Customer Report** in the Label field as shown in Figure 7-15. Leave the *Description* as Customer Phone List. Click **OK** to save your changes. By default, QuickBooks enters the title of your report in the Label and Description fields. It is usually best to condense the Label so the icon does not use as much space on the Icon Bar.

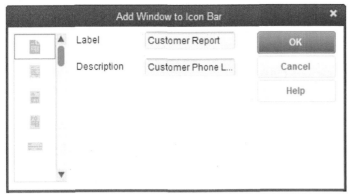

Figure 7-15 Select an icon from the list and edit the Label field.

5.   You may need to scroll down in the Icon Bar to see the **Customer Report** icon. Figure 7-16 displays a portion of the Icon Bar.

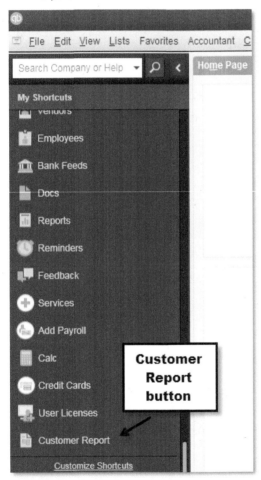

Figure 7-16 Icon Bar with Customer Report added

6.   Close the Customer Phone List. Click **No** if QuickBooks prompts you to memorize the report.

Open Windows List

The QuickBooks *Open Windows List* displays a selection box containing the titles of all open windows in the Icon Bar. To display the window, select **Open Windows List** from the *View* menu or select the Open Windows icon in the Icon Bar (see Figure 7-17).

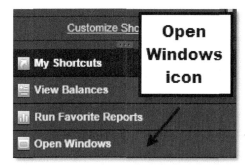

Figure 7-17 Open Windows List button on the Icon Bar

The *Open Windows List* includes window titles that are currently open, allowing you to quickly toggle between reports, forms, lists, or registers. This window is very helpful if you set your *Desktop* User Preferences to view *One Window* at a time or if you typically maximize all windows. You cannot customize the *Open Windows List*. To return the *Icon Bar* to the list of Shortcuts, click the *My Shortcuts* bar below the *Open Windows list* on the *Icon Bar*.

Figure 7-18 Open Windows List

QuickBooks Items and Other Lists

QuickBooks provides several *Lists* that allow you to add more information to each transaction and help you track more details. In this section, you will learn how to create items in the *Item List*, *Terms List* and *Price Level List*.

QuickBooks Items

In this section, you will learn more about QuickBooks *Items* and how they affect the "accounting behind the scenes" as you create transactions. Every time you use an item, the value of the item or items flow into the linked accounts. In this way, items affect the financial statements for a company. You will establish this link to the accounts with each Item created below.

The *Item List* is used to identify the products and services your business purchases and/or sells. *Items* in the *Item List* are also used as part of the sales tax tracking process, as a means of generating subtotals and as a method of calculating discounts.

The *Item List* shows all *Items* already created (see Figure 7-19).

Figure 7-19 The Item List

Item Types

There are several different types of *Items* in QuickBooks (see Figure 7-20). When you create an *Item*, you indicate the *Item Type* along with the name of the *Item* and the *Account* with which the *Item* is associated.

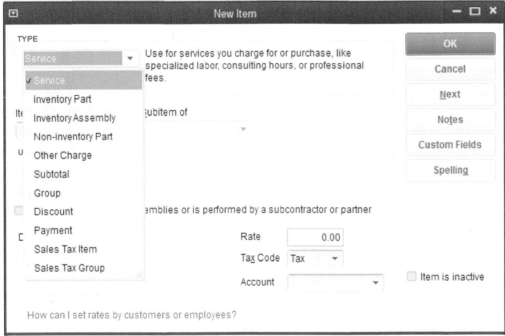

Figure 7-20 The Type menu in the New Item window

- *Service Items* track services you buy and/or sell.
- *Inventory Part Items* track your purchases and sales of inventory.
- *Inventory Assembly Items* track *Items* that contain assemblies of other *Items*. *Inventory Assembly Items* are not available in QuickBooks Pro.
- *Non-inventory Part Items* track products you buy and/or sell but don't keep in inventory.
- *Other Charge Items* track miscellaneous charges such as shipping and finance charges.
- *Subtotal Items* calculate and display subtotals on sales forms.

- *Group Items* allow you to use one *Item* to "bundle" several *Items* together. *Group Items* are similar to *Inventory Assembly Items*, but Group items do not track quantity on hand (or sold) of the Group. Rather, each *Item* within the Group is tracked separately.

- *Discount Items* calculate and display discounts on sales forms.

- *Payment Items* show *Payment Methods* available on *Invoices, Sales Receipts* and *Deposits.*

- *Sales Tax Items* track sales taxes in each location where you sell taxable goods and services.

- *Sales Tax Group Items* are used when you pay sales tax to more than one tax agency.

Service Items

Academy Photography sells photo sessions by the hour. To track the sales of a *Service Item*, create an *Item* called **Photo Session**, and associate the *Item* with the Services income account.

COMPUTER PRACTICE

Step 1.   Select the **Lists** menu and then select **Item List**.

Step 2.   Select the **Item** button and then select **New**.

Step 3.   Select **Service** from the *Type* drop-down list as shown in Figure 7-20 if it is not already selected, and fill in the detail of the *Item* as shown in Figure 7-21.

Step 4.   Click **OK** to save the Item.

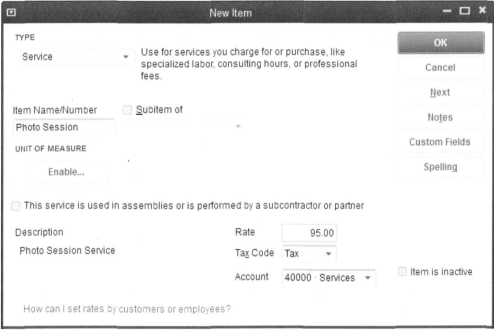

Figure 7-21 New Service Item

If the price for this service fluctuates, you can override this amount when you use it on a sales form. Therefore, when you set up the *Item*, enter the rate you normally charge.

Subcontracted Services

To track your subcontracted services, you can set up a special "two-sided" *Service Item* to track both the income and the expense of the subcontractor. By using a single *Item* to track both the income and expense for the subcontracted service, you can automatically track the profitability of your subcontractors. You might want to have a separate *Item* for each subcontractor.

COMPUTER PRACTICE

Step 1.   With the *Item List* displayed, press **Ctrl+N**. This is another way to set up a new *Item*.

Step 2.   Select **Service** from the *Type* drop-down list if it is not already selected and press **Tab**.

Step 3.   Enter **Video Photographer** in the *Item Name/Number* field and check the *Subitem of* box.

Step 4.   Check the box *Subitem of,* and then select **Photographer** from the drop-down list.

Step 5.   Check the box *This service is used in assemblies or is performed by a subcontractor or partner*.

Selecting this box allows you to use the same *Item* on purchase transactions and sales transactions, but have the *Item* affect different accounts depending on the transaction.

Step 6.   Enter the *Description on Purchase Transactions*, *Cost* (purchase price), *Expense Account*, and *Preferred Vendor* for this *Item* as shown in Figure 7-22.

Step 7.   Enter the *Description on Sales Transactions*, *Sales Price*, *Tax Code* and *Income Account* for this Item as shown in Figure 7-22.

Step 8.   Click **Next** to save the *Item* and open another *New Item* window.

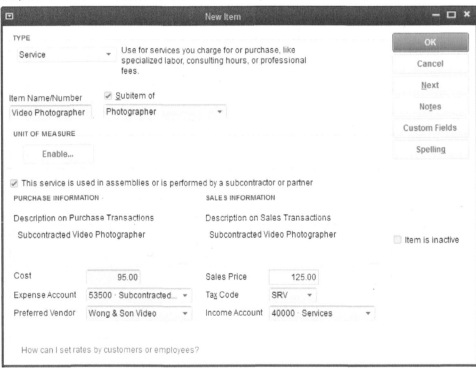

Figure 7-22 Subcontracted Service Item

Non-Inventory Parts

To track products that you buy and/or sell but don't monitor as inventory, set up *Non-Inventory Part Items*. Academy Photography doesn't track custom photo packages in inventory, so they use one generic *Item* called Custom Photo Package.

COMPUTER PRACTICE

Step 1.   Select **Non-inventory Part** from the *Type* drop-down list.

Step 2.   Enter **Custom Photo Package** in the Item Name/Number field.

Step 3.   Fill in the detail of the *Item* as shown in Figure 7-23.

Step 4.   Click **Next** to save the item.

Figure 7-23 Non-inventory Part Item

Non-Inventory Parts - Passed Through

You can also specifically track the income and expenses for each *Non-Inventory Part*. In this case, you should create a "two-sided" *Non-inventory Part Item* to track the purchase costs in a Cost of Goods Sold (or Expense) account, and the sales amounts in an income account. This is particularly useful when you pass the costs on to your customers for special-ordered parts. For example, Academy Photography tracks video camera orders with one *Non-inventory Part Item*.

COMPUTER PRACTICE

Step 1.   If necessary, select **Non-inventory Part** from the *Type* drop-down list. Fill in the detail of the *Item* as shown in Figure 7-24.

Step 2.   Click **Next** to save the item.

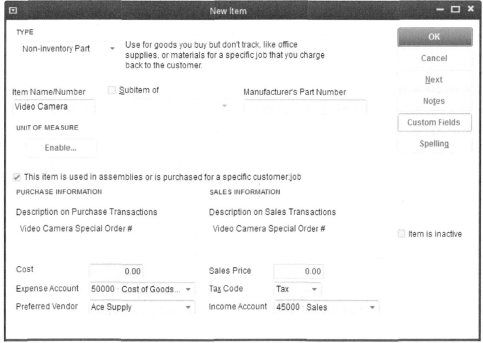

Figure 7-24 Non-inventory Part Item – Two-Sided

Other Charge Items

To track charges like freight, finance charges, or expense reimbursements on your *Invoices*, use *Other Charge Items*.

COMPUTER PRACTICE

Step 1.   Select **Other Charge** from the *Type* drop-down list and fill in the detail of the *Item* as shown in Figure 7-25.

Step 2.   Click **Next** to save the Item.

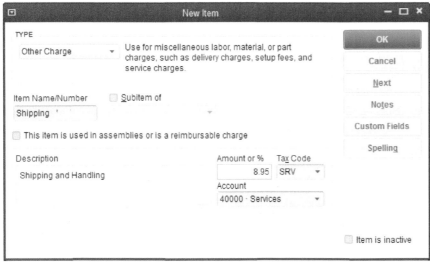

Figure 7-25 Track shipping charges with an Other Charge Item

Sales Tax Items

The *Sales Tax Items* are used to track sales tax.

COMPUTER PRACTICE

Step 1.   Select **Sales Tax Item** from the *Type* drop-down list and fill in the detail of the *Item* as shown in Figure 7-26.

In this example, the *Tax Agency* is the *State Board of Equalization*. Make sure you enter the name of your state's tax collector in the Tax Agency field. QuickBooks needs this name for sales tax reports and sales tax payments.

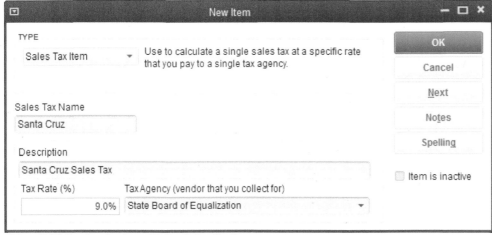

Figure 7-26 Track sales tax with the Sales Tax Item.

Step 2.   Click **OK** to save this *Item* and close the *New Item* window.

You should create a separate *Sales Tax Item* for each tax imposed by each taxing jurisdiction. For example, if you have both state and county sales taxes, then create *Sales Tax Items* for the state taxes and each of the county taxes.

If multiple *Sales Tax Items* are to be billed on a particular sales transaction, then create a *Sales Tax Group Item* to join the individual *Sales Tax Items* together for billing purposes. This allows QuickBooks to correctly track sales taxes by type of tax and by taxing jurisdiction. In most states, you don't need to use *Sales Tax Groups*. Use *Sales Tax Group Items* only if you pay more than one kind of sales tax or you pay tax to more than one agency.

> **Note:**
> If you need to import a large number of *Items* (or other list entries) you can paste data from a spreadsheet using the *Add/Edit Multiple List Entries* option, located in the *Lists* menu.

Printing the Item List

COMPUTER PRACTICE

To print the Item List, follow these steps:

Step 1.   Select the *Reports* menu, select **List**, and then select **Item Listing** (see Figure 7-27).

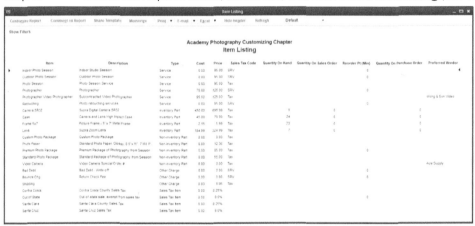

Figure 7-27 Item Listing report

Step 2.   Click **Print** at the top of the report (or select **Print Report** from the *File* menu).

Step 3.   Close the *Item Listing* Report.

Step 4.   Close the *Item List* window.

The Terms List

The *Terms List* is the place where you define the payment terms for *Invoices* and *Bills*. QuickBooks uses terms to calculate when an *Invoice* or *Bill* is due. If the terms specified on the transaction include a discount for early payment, QuickBooks also calculates the date on which the discount expires.

QuickBooks allows you to define two types of terms:

- *Standard Terms* calculate based on how many days from the *Invoice* or *Bill* date the payment is due or a discount is earned.

- *Date-Driven Terms* calculate based on the day of the month that an *Invoice* or *Bill* is due or a discount is earned.

You can override the default terms on each sale or purchase as necessary. When you create reports for *Accounts Receivable* or *Accounts Payable*, QuickBooks takes into account the terms on each *Invoice* or *Bill*.

COMPUTER PRACTICE

Step 1.   Select the *Lists* menu, select **Customers & Vendor Profile Lists**, and then select **Terms List** (see Figure 7-28).

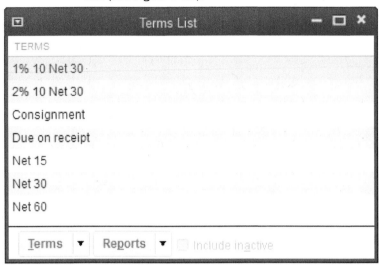

Figure 7-28 Terms List window

Step 2.   The practice file already includes several terms (see Figure 7-28). To set up additional terms, select the **Terms** button from the *Terms List* window, and then select **New**, or press **Ctrl+N**.

Step 3.   To set up a standard term, complete the *New Terms* window as shown in Figure 7-29, and click **Next**.

The window in Figure 7-29 shows how the 2% 7 Net 30 terms are defined. It is a *Standard Terms Item* indicating that full payment is due in 30 days. If the customers pay within 7 days of the *Invoice* date, however, they are eligible for a 2% discount.

Figure 7-29 The New Terms window with standard terms

Step 4.   To set up a date-driven term, enter **1% 5th Net 10th** in the *Terms* field. Be sure to include the ᵗʰ in the term name as 5ᵗʰ (5ᵗʰ day of month) has a very different meaning from 5 (5 days).

Step 5.   Select the **Date Driven** radio button. Fill in the fields as shown in Figure 7-30. Then click **OK**.

The terms in Figure 7-30 are an example of *Date-Driven Terms*, where payment is due on the 5th of the month (e.g. February 5th). If the customer pays by the 5th of the month, they are eligible for a 1% discount. If the *Invoice* is dated less than 10 days before the due date, the *Invoice* (or *Bill*) is due on the 10th of the following month.

Date-driven terms are not applicable in all businesses. They are typically used when *Invoices* are generated at the same time each month, such as invoicing for monthly dues or services. Businesses will often prorate the first month's charges in order to get the customer into the regular billing cycle.

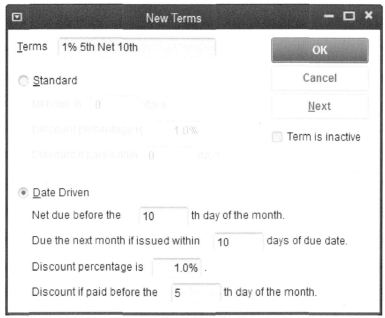

Figure 7-30 The New Terms window with date-driven terms

Step 6.   Close the *Terms List* window.

Price Levels

> **Note:**
> *Per Item Price Levels* are available only in QuickBooks Premier and above.

Price Levels allow you to define custom pricing for different customers. Use *Price Levels* on *Invoices* or *Sales Receipts* to adjust the sales amount of particular items. There are several ways to use *Price Levels* on sales forms:

- You can adjust each item individually by selecting the applicable *Price Level* in the *Rate* column drop-down list (see Figure 7-31).

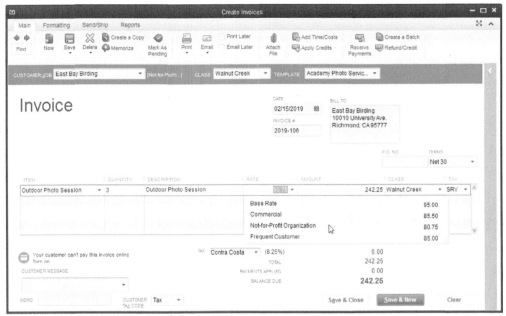

Figure 7-31 Selecting a Price Level on an Invoice

- You can assign a *Price Level* to a Customer's record so that when you use the customer's name in a sales form, QuickBooks will change the default sales price for each *Sales Item* on the form (see Figure 7-32).

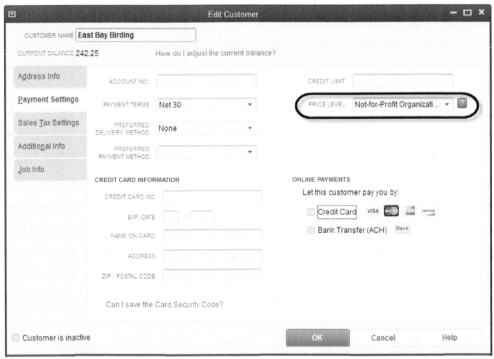

Figure 7-32 Setting a Price Level on a Customer's Record

Price Level Types

There are two types of *Price Levels*, *Fixed Percentage* and *Per Item*. You can create both types of *Price Levels* by opening the *Price Levels List* and selecting **New** from the *Price Levels Menu*. Select the **Lists** menu and then select **Price Level List.**

Fixed Percentage Price Levels allow you to increase or decrease prices of *Items* for a *Customer* or *Job* by a fixed percentage (see Figure 7-33). This price level is recommended for customers who always receive a discount, since the discount will be generated automatically.

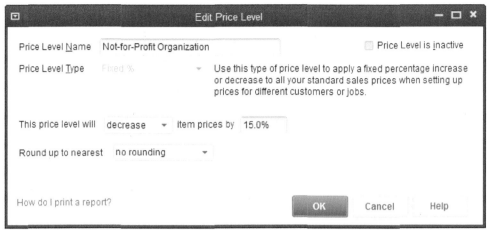

Figure 7-33 Price Level window – Fixed Percentage Price Level Type

Per Item Price Levels let you set specific prices for *Items* (see Figure 7-34).

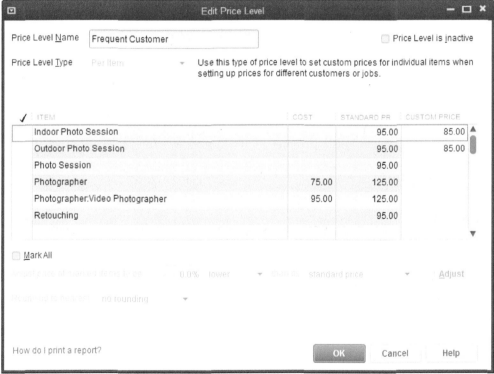

Figure 7-34 Price Level window - Per Item Price Level Type

Custom Fields

When you set up a new *Customer, Vendor* or *Employee* record, you can define *Custom Fields* for tracking additional information specific to your *Customers, Vendors,* and *Employees*.

Academy Photography tracks each *Customer* and *Vendor* by county in order to create reports of total purchases and sales in a city or county. This information allows them to determine the best area to expand business operations.

You can access the *Define Fields* button on the *Additional Info* tab of a *Customer, Vendor* or *Employee* record (see Figure 7-35).

Figure 7-35 Define Fields button in the Additional Info Tab

In the window shown in Figure 7-36, you can define up to fifteen total *Custom Fields* in the QuickBooks data file, and any one name type, i.e., *Customer*, *Vendor*, or *Employee*, can have up to seven *Custom Fields*.

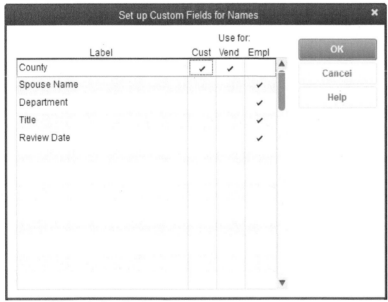

Figure 7-36 The Define Fields window

Adding Custom Field Data to Customer Records

After you have defined a *Custom Field* and checked the box in the *Customer:Job* column, the field appears on the *Customer* record (see Figure 7-37). Fill in the data for *Custom Fields* just as you do for other fields.

Figure 7-37 Fill in the Custom Field for each customer.

Modifying Sales Form Templates

QuickBooks provides templates so that you can customize your sales forms. You can select from the standard forms that QuickBooks provides, or you can customize the way your forms appear on both the screen and the printed page. The first step in modifying your forms is to create a template for the form you want to modify. The templates for all forms are in the *Templates List.*

COMPUTER PRACTICE

Step 1.   Select the *Lists* menu, and then select **Templates** (see Figure 7-38). This list shows the standard templates that come with QuickBooks, as well as any form templates the user may have created.

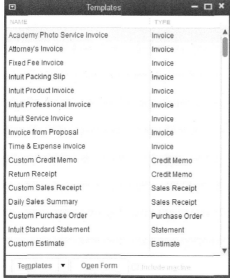

Figure 7-38 Templates List

Step 2.   Select **Intuit Service Invoice**. Then select the **Templates** menu button and select **Duplicate**. The *Intuit Service Invoice* is the template you are using as the basis for your custom template.

Step 3.   Select **Invoice** on the *Select Template Type* window and click **OK** (see Figure 7-39).

Figure 7-39 Select Template Type window

> **Tip:**
> When duplicating a template, you can create the copy as the same template type, or choose any other type from the *Select Template Type* window. This allows you to transfer many of the customizations (e.g., columns, fields, colors, fonts, etc.) between different types of forms.

Step 4.   In the Templates List, *Copy of: Intuit Service Invoice* should already be selected. Select the **Templates** menu and select **Edit Template**.

Step 5.   Click the **Manage Templates** button in the *Basic Customization* window (see Figure 7-40).

Step 6.   In the **Manage Templates** window, enter *My Invoice Template* in the *Template Name* field (see Figure 7-41).

You must enter a unique template name. You must give your template a descriptive name so that you will easily recognize it when selecting it from a form list.

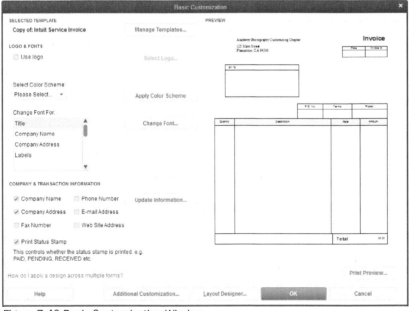

Figure 7-40 Basic Customization Window

> **Note:**
> You can download templates from the Intuit website. Browse through the selection of pre-designed templates by clicking the *Download Templates* button on the *Manage Templates* window.

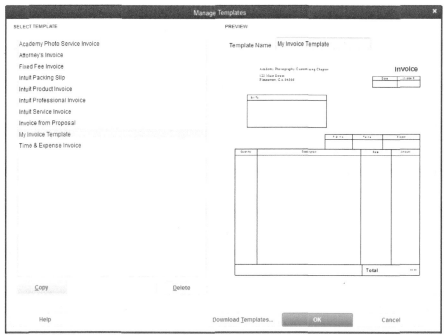

Figure 7-41 Manage Templates window

Step 7.	Click **OK** to accept the name change and close the *Manage Templates* window.
Step 8.	Click the **Additional Customization** button. The *Basic Customization* window changes to the *Additional Customization* window.
Step 9.	Review the fields in the *Header* tab. Do not edit any of the fields on this window (see Figure 7-42).

You would click the boxes in the *Screen* and *Print* columns to indicate which fields will show on the screen and which fields will be printed. You could also modify the titles for each field by changing the text in the *Title* fields.

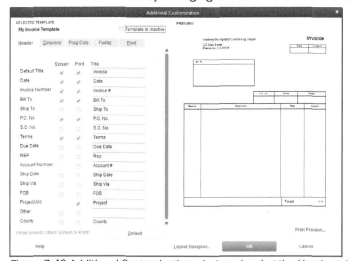

Figure 7-42 Additional Customization window showing the Header tab

Step 10.	Click the **Columns** tab to modify how the columns display on the *Invoice*. Change the order of the columns by entering the numbers in the *Order* column as shown in Figure 7-43. If necessary, scroll to see all columns. If you see the *Layout Designer* warning box, click **OK**.

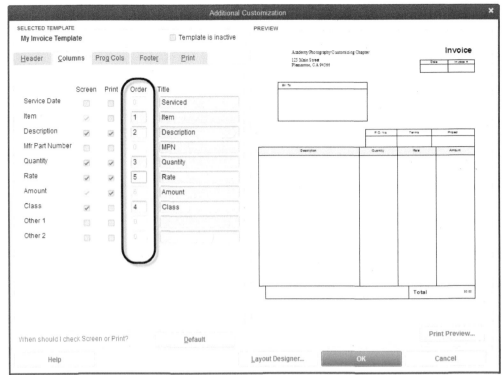

Figure 7-43 Additional Customization window showing the Columns tab

Step 11.   Click the **OK** button to return to the *Basic Customization* window.

Step 12.   Next, add a logo to the template by checking the **Use logo** checkbox (see Figure 7-44).

Adding a business logo to an *Invoice* helps customers familiarize themselves with your company. It can also help them identify your *Invoice*.

Figure 7-44 The Use logo option in the Basic Customization window

Step 13.   In the *Select Image* dialog box, navigate to your student files. Select **logo.gif** and click **Open**.

Step 14.   A dialog box warns that the logo graphic file will be copied to a subfolder of the location of your working file. Click **OK** to accept. You should see the logo in the upper left side of the preview pane of the *Basic Customization* window.

Step 15.   Click the **Select Color Scheme** drop down menu. You can choose six preset colors. Choose **Maroon** and then click the **Apply Color Scheme** button. The text and border lines on the *Invoice* change to the selected color.

Step 16.   Next, change the color of the *Invoice* title to black. Verify that **Title** is selected in the *Change Font For:* box and click the **Change Font** button.

Step 17.   The *Example* window opens (Figure 7-45). You can use this window to change font, size, style, and color of the title of the invoice. In the **Color** field, choose **Black**. When finished, click **OK**.

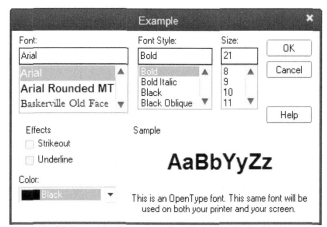

Figure 7-45 Example dialog box for changing font of labels on a template

Step 18.   Click **OK** to close the *Basic Customization* window.

Step 19.   Close the **Templates** window.

Step 20.   From the *Home Page*, click the **Create Invoices** icon.

Step 21.   To use the new template, choose **My Invoice Template** from the *Template* drop down list.

Step 22.   To view how the *Invoice* will print, click the down arrow below the **Print** button at the top of the *Create Invoices* window and select **Preview**.

Step 23.   Click **Close** to close the *Print Preview* window.

Step 24.   Close the **Create Invoices** window.

Note:
You can make further changes to the position of elements in the form by opening the *Layout Designer*. Click the **Layout Designer** button on the bottom of the *Basic Customization* window. From the *Layout Designer*, you can change the position of design elements, such as the textboxes and the logo.

Review Questions

Comprehension Questions

1. Describe the difference between User Preferences (i.e., My Preferences) and Company Preferences.

2. What commands should you put in the Favorites menu?

3. Describe the purpose of the Open Windows List.

4. How would setting a customer's default price level affect their future invoices?

5. Describe the process of adding a Custom Field to a customer record.

Multiple Choice

Select the best answer(s) for each of the following:

1. You can create Custom Fields for:
    a)   Customers.
    b)   Templates.
    c)   Vendors.
    d)   Both a and c.

2. The two types of Preferences are:
    a)   User and Company Preferences.
    b)   User and Accountant Preferences.
    c)   Favorite and General Preferences.
    d)   Income and Expense Preferences.

3. If you don't see the Favorites menu in your menu bar, you can turn it on in the:
    a)   Customize Templates window.
    b)   Customize Icon Bar window.
    c)   View menu.
    d)   Windows menu.

4. Which of the following is not an available Template type in QuickBooks?
    a)   Credit Memo.
    b)   Statement.
    c)   Check.
    d)   Sales Receipt.

5. If you pay sales tax to more than one agency, you should use which of the following Item Types?
    a)   Sales Tax Group.
    b)   Group.
    c)   Inventory Assembly.
    d)   Subtotal.

6. Which of the following can be displayed vertically on the far left side of the screen or horizontally along the top of the screen?
    a)   The Home Page
    b)   The Icon Bar
    c)   The Open Windows List
    d)   None of the above

7. You cannot customize which of the following?
    a)   The layout of Statements
    b)   The Icon Bar
    c)   The layout of the Estimate forms
    d)   The Open Windows list

8. To add an Icon to the Icon Bar, you can use:
    a)   The Add "window-name" to Icon Bar option.
    b)   The Customize Icon Bar window.
    c)   The User Preferences for Desktop View.
    d)   Either a or b.

9. Which Item Type should be selected when adding a new Item that you buy and/or sell but don't keep track of in Inventory?

    a) Service.

    b) Inventory Part.

    c) Non-inventory Part.

    d) Other Charge.

10. Use which of the following to manually design the layout of an Invoice?

    a) The Company tab of the Customize Invoice window

    b) The Format tab of the Customize Invoice window

    c) QuickBooks Company Preferences

    d) The Layout Designer

11. The two types of Price Levels are:

    a) Fixed percentage and per item.

    b) Fixed percentage and per customer.

    c) Per item and per customer.

    d) Per customer and per vendor.

12. You would like to offer a discount when some customers pay their invoice early. What List would you open to start creating this discount?

    a) Terms

    b) Item

    c) Price Levels

    d) None of the above. You can't create this type of discount in QuickBooks.

13. The simplest way to offer a regular discount to a customer is to:

    a) Set the price level on the customer's invoices.

    b) Add a Discount Item to each of the customer's invoices.

    c) Enter the discount in the Customer Discount field in the Edit Customer window.

    d) Set the default price level for that customer

14. To include shipping charges on an Invoice, it is best to use which type of Item?

    a) Inventory Part

    b) Other Charge

    c) Service

    d) Non-inventory Part

15. You can rearrange the order of columns in a template using the:

    a) Managing Templates window.

    b) Template List.

    c) Basic Customization window.

    d) Additional Customization window.

Completion Statements

1. Use a(n) _____ Item (item type) to track subcontracted labor.

2. Use the _____ _____ User Preferences to set default windows that show when you open QuickBooks and to change the color and graphics of QuickBooks toolbars and windows.

3. The _____ _____ displays common commands along with an icon representing that command along the side edge or the top of the QuickBooks window.

4. _____ _____ terms calculate based on the day of the month that an Invoice or Bill is due or a discount is earned.

5. Use a(n) _____ Item on Invoices or Sales Receipts to calculate the subtotal of the Items above that line.

Customizing Problem 1

> Restore the Customizing-18Problem1.QBM file. The password to access this file is **Sleeter18**.

1. Create the following new *Item*.

Field Name	Data
Item Type	Service
Item Name/Number	Specialist
Description	Specialist consultant on photography services
Price	125.00
Tax Code	SRV
Account	Services

Table 7-1 New Item data

2. Create a new payment term called *Net 28*. Customers who have these terms should pay within 4 weeks (28 days) and are not offered a discount for early payment.

3. Enter the following *Invoice*:

Field Name	Data
Customer	Feng, Tim
Class	San Jose
Date	2/24/2019
Invoice #	2019-106
Terms	Net 28
Tax	Santa Clara
Quantity	4
Item Code	Specialist

Table 7-2 Use this data for the Invoice

4. Print the Invoice. When prompted, save changes to Customer.

5. Print the *Item List*.

Customizing Problem 2 (Advanced)

Restore the Customizing-18Problem2.QBM file. The password to access this file is *Sleeter18*.

1. Set up the following *Terms*:

   a) 1% 7 Net 20

   b) 1% 5th Net 20th (Due next month if issued within 10 days of the due date)

   c) Net 21

   d) 3% 10th Net 30th (Due next month if issued within 10 days of the due date)

2. Create a **Terms Listing** report (Select the **Reports** menu, **Lists**, and then **Terms Listing**). Add the **Discount on Day of Month** and **Min Days to Pay** columns. Expand the columns so you can see the entire column headers. Print the report.

3. Add a *Custom Field* to your *Customers* called **How did you hear about us?**. Add these values to the *Custom Field* for the following customer records:

Customer:Job Name	How did you hear about us?
Anderson Wedding Planners: Kumar, Sati and Naveen	Web Search
Anderson Wedding Planners: Wilson, Sarah and Michael	Web Search
Anderson Wedding Planners	Web Search
Pelligrini, George	Word of Mouth
Pelligrini, George:1254 Wilkes Rd	Word of Mouth
Pelligrini, George: 4266 Lake Drive	Word of Mouth

Table 7-3 Data for custom fields

4. Create a **Customer Contact List**, modified to display only the **Customer Name** and **How did you hear about us?** columns. Print the report.

5. Create a **Sales Tax Item** for San Francisco, payable to the State Board of Equalization. The sales tax rate is 8.75%.

6. Create a duplicate *Invoice* of the Intuit Product Invoice Template. Then, make the following changes:

   a) Change the name of the template to *Academy Photo Product Invoice.*

   b) Add the **How did you hear about us?** custom field to the screen and printed Invoice using the Additional Customization Header tab.

   c) When prompted, click **Default Layout** and click **Yes** to confirm your choice.

7. Create a new *Non-inventory Part* called **Customized Package**. Set up the new *Item* using the following information:

Field Name	Data
Item Name/Number	Customized Package
Description	Customized Photography Package from Session
Price	0 (leave 0 because it's a custom package)
Tax Code	Tax
Account	Sales

Table 7-4 Item setup data

8. Create an **Invoice** for Pelligrini, George, for the 1254 Wilkes Rd job, using the *Academy Photo Product Invoice* template. Enter the following information on the header of the *Invoice*:

Field Name	Data
Class	San Jose
Date	2/28/2019
Invoice #	2019-106
Terms	3% 10th Net 30th
Tax	San Francisco

Table 7-5 Use this data for the Invoice header.

9. Enter the following information into the body of the **Invoice**:

Item	Qty	Description	Rate	Tax
Outdoor Photo Session	4	Outdoor Photo Session	95.00	SRV
Customized Package	2	Customized Photography Package from Session	750.00	Tax

Table 7-6 Item descriptions for Invoice

10. Accept the default for all other fields on the *Invoice*. Click **OK** if you get a message window regarding custom price levels. Save and print the **Invoice**.

11. Save the new changes when prompted.

Chapter 8
Inventory

Topics

In this chapter, you will learn about the following topics:

> **Restore this File:**
> This chapter uses Inventory-18.QBW. See page 9 for more information. The password to access this file is *Sleeter18*.

In this chapter, you will learn how to set up and manage your inventory in QuickBooks. QuickBooks has a number of tools for tracking goods and materials, including the *Inventory Center*.

QuickBooks Tools for Tracking Inventory

The *Vendors* section, located on the *Home* page, shows a graphical representation of the steps involved in purchasing and receiving Inventory. Figure 8-1 shows the purchasing process, beginning with creating a *Purchase Order* and ending with paying *Bills*.

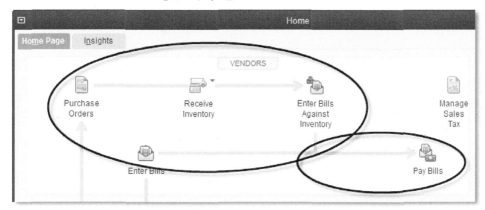

Figure 8-1 Vendors section of the Home page

Table 8-1 shows an overview of the **accounting behind the scenes** for different business transactions that involve Inventory. Familiarize yourself with this table, and refer to it when you encounter business transactions involving Inventory.

Business Transaction	QuickBooks Transaction	Accounting Entry	Comments
Purchasing Inventory with *Purchase Orders*	Purchase Orders	Non-posting entry used to record *Purchase Orders*.	You do not have to use *Purchase Orders*. If you do, QuickBooks tracks the status of your *Purchase Orders* and matches them with the *Bill* from your Vendor.
Receiving Inventory (Without Bill from Vendor)	Receive Inventory **Select Receive Inventory without Bill**	Increase (debit) **Inventory,** increase (credit) **Accounts Payable.** Increase Inventory quantities for each item received.	Use this transaction when you receive Inventory items that are not accompanied by a bill. This transaction enters an *Item Receipt* in the Accounts Payable account. Although it increases A/P, no bill shows in the *Pay Bills* window.
Receiving Inventory (With Bill from Vendor)	Receive Inventory **Select Receive Inventory with Bill**	Increase (debit) **Inventory,** increase (credit) **Accounts Payable.** Increase inventory quantities for each item received.	Use this transaction when you receive inventory accompanied by a bill from the Vendor.
Entering a Bill for Previously Received Inventory Items	Enter Bills Against Inventory	No change in debits and credits. This transaction only changes an *Item Receipt* transaction into a *Bill*.	When an *Item Receipt* is turned into a *Bill*, QuickBooks shows the *Bill* in the *Pay Bills* window.

Table 8-1 Summary of Inventory transactions

Tracking Inventory with QuickBooks

It is critical to think through your company's information needs before tackling Inventory. New users sometimes try to use Inventory parts to track products they don't really need to track in detail. You must separately enter every purchase and sale for each Inventory part. That might not seem like too much work at first, but if you have hundreds of small products with even a moderate turnover, you might overwhelm your bookkeeping system with detailed transactions.

When you use *Inventory Part Items* to track inventory, QuickBooks handles all the accounting for you automatically, depending upon how you set up *Inventory Part Items* in the *Item List*. Inventory is defined as goods that are purchased from a Vendor that will be sold at a future date. For example, a retailer has Inventory until they sell the merchandise to customers. When the Inventory is sold, it is removed from the *Inventory* Asset account and expensed through Cost of Goods Sold. This enables the sale to be properly matched to the expense in the right accounting period.

QuickBooks keeps a perpetual inventory, meaning that every purchase and every sale of Inventory immediately updates all your account balances and reports.

When QuickBooks Pro, Premier or Accountant calculates the cost of Inventory, it uses the *average cost* method, explained on page 283. These editions do not support the first-in, first-out (FIFO) or last-in, first-out (LIFO) methods. QuickBooks Enterprise Solutions does support FIFO as well as many other advanced Inventory features such as lot tracking and enhanced receiving. This chapter focuses on features available with Pro, Premier and Accountant.

> **Key Term:** *Perpetual inventory* in QuickBooks keeps a continuous record of increases, decreases, and balance on hand of Inventory items.
>
> **Key Term:** *Average Cost* method divides the cost of Inventory by the number of units in stock. It is most appropriate when prices paid for Inventory do not vary significantly over time, and when Inventory turnover is high (i.e., products sell through quickly). QuickBooks calculates the cost of Inventory using this method.

In order to keep your inventory system working smoothly, it is critical that you use *Inventory Parts* Items on all transactions involving Inventory. This means you must use the *Items* tab on every purchase transaction that involves *Inventory Part* type Items. Figure 8-2 illustrates entering a *Bill* using *Inventory Part* Items.

> **DO NOT ENTER THIS BILL NOW. IT IS FOR REFERENCE ONLY.**

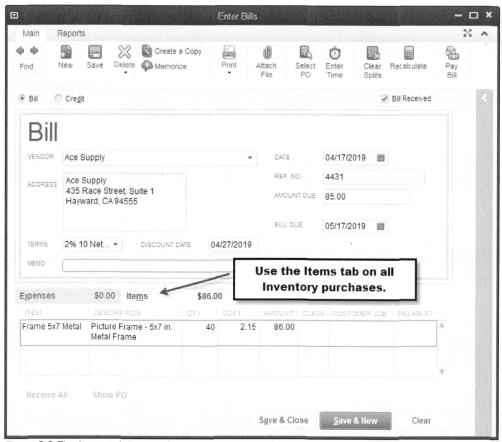

Figure 8-2 The Items tab is used for inventory transactions

Activating the Inventory Function

The first step in using QuickBooks for Inventory is to activate *Inventory* in your *Company Preferences*.

COMPUTER PRACTICE

Step 1.   Select **Preferences** from the *Edit* menu.

Step 2.   Select the **Items & Inventory** *Preference* and then select the **Company Preferences** tab.

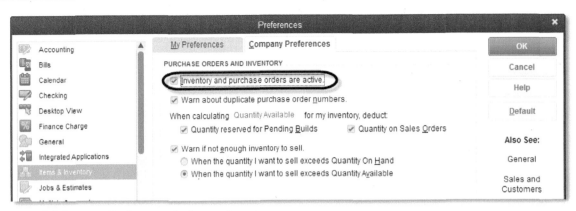

Figure 8-3 Company Preferences for Items & Inventory

Step 3.   Verify that **Inventory and purchase orders are active** is checked (see Figure 8-3).

> **Note:**
> When Inventory is activated, *Purchase Orders* are also activated. However, you are not
> required to use *Purchase Orders* when tracking Inventory.

Step 4.   Click the **OK** in the *Preferences* window.

After you activate the Inventory function, the Item List shows a new Item type called *Inventory Part* (see Figure 8-4). Only the *Inventory Part* Items are displayed in the *Inventory Center* (see Figure 8-5).

Figure 8-4 Item List window

The first time you create an *Inventory Part* Item in the Item List, QuickBooks automatically creates two accounts in your *Chart of Accounts*: An *Other Current Asset* account called Inventory Asset and a *Cost of Goods Sold* account called Cost of Goods Sold. QuickBooks uses these two important accounts to track Inventory (see Table 8-2). The *Inventory Asset* account holds the value of your Inventory until you sell it. The Cost of Goods Sold account records the cost of the Inventory *when* you sell it.

Accounts for Tracking Inventory	
Inventory Asset	A special *Other Current Asset* account that tracks the cost of each Inventory item purchased. This account increases (by the actual purchase cost) when Inventory is purchased, and decreases (by the weighted average cost) when Inventory items are sold.
Cost of Goods Sold	Cost of Goods Sold is subtracted from total Income on the *Profit & Loss Report* to show *Gross Profit*. QuickBooks automatically increases Cost of Goods Sold each time you sell an Inventory item.

Table 8-2 Two accounts that track inventory

Setting up Inventory Parts Items

To set up an inventory part in the *Item List*, follow these steps:

COMPUTER PRACTICE

Step 1.   In the *Company* section of the *Home* page, select **Inventory Activities** and choose **Inventory Center** from the menu (see Figure 8-5). Alternatively, select the **Vendors** menu and choose **Inventory Activities**, then select **Inventory Center**.

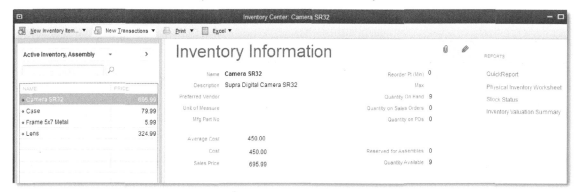

Figure 8-5 Inventory Center

Step 2.   Select the **New Inventory Item** button at the top of the *Inventory Center* and then select **New Inventory Item**. Alternatively, press **Ctrl+N**.

Step 3.   A *New Item* window opens. If needed, select **Inventory Part** from the *Type* drop-down list. Press **Tab**.

Step 4.   Enter *Frame 5x7 Wood* in the *Item Name/Number* field and press **Tab**.

You may optionally assign each item in your Inventory a part number, and then use the part numbers in the *Item Name/Number* field.

Step 5.   Skip the *Subitem of* field by pressing **Tab**.

This field allows you to create subitems of items. If you use subitems, the *Sales by Item* reports and graphs will show totals for all sales and costs of the subitems.

> **Key Term:** *Subitems* help to organize the *Item List*. Use subitems to group and subtotal information about similar products or services in sales reports and graphs.

Step 6.   Skip the *Manufacturer's Part Number* field by pressing **Tab** again.

This field allows you to enter the part number that the Vendor uses or that is listed by the manufacturer. This enables you to reference the same number on *Purchase Orders* and *Bills* to eliminate confusion.

Step 7.   If necessary, press **Tab** to skip the *Enable* button under *Unit of Measure*.

Many businesses purchase items using one unit of measure and sell the same item using a different unit of measure. For example, a retail store may purchase items by the case, but sell the items individually (or by *each*). QuickBooks Premier, Accountant, and Enterprise includes the *Unit of Measure* feature to help in these situations.

Step 8.   Enter *Picture Frame - 5x7 in. Wood Frame* in the *Description on Purchase Transactions* field and press **Tab**.

The description you enter here appears as the default description when you use this item on *Purchase Orders* and *Bills*.

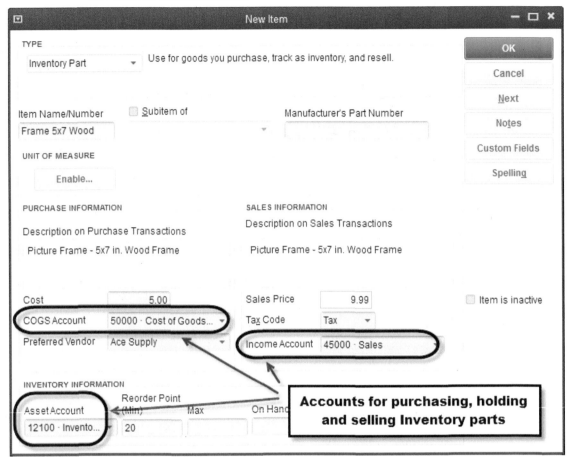

Figure 8-6 The completed New Item window

> **Note:**
> Notice that there are three account fields on the New Item window (*COGS*, *Asset*, and *Income*). In each of these fields, enter the accounts that QuickBooks should use when you purchase, hold, and sell this item. You are specifying how QuickBooks should account for the item when it is used in an Inventory transaction. Each field is covered separately in this chapter.

Step 9.   Enter **5.00** in the *Cost* field and press **Tab**.

Use this field to track the amount you pay to your Vendor (supplier) for the item. QuickBooks uses this amount as the default when you enter this item on *Purchase Orders* and *Bills*. If the cost changes, you can override the amount on the *Purchase Order* or *Bill*, or you can come back and edit the amount here.

Step 10.   In the *COGS Account* field, *Cost of Goods Sold* is already selected. Press **Tab**.

QuickBooks uses the *Cost of Goods Sold* account to record the average cost of this item when you sell it. For more information on average cost, see page 283.

Step 11.   Select **Ace Supply** from the *Preferred Vendor* drop-down list and press **Tab**.

The *Preferred Vendor* field is used to associate the item with the Vendor from whom you normally purchase this part. It is an optional field that you can leave blank without compromising the integrity of the system.

Step 12.   Press **Tab** to leave the *Description on Sales Transactions* field unchanged. The text in this field defaults to whatever you entered in the *Description on Purchase Transactions* field.

QuickBooks allows you to have two descriptions for this item: one for purchase forms and one for sales forms. If you'd like, you can use your Vendor's description when purchasing the item and a more customer-oriented description on your sales forms.

Step 13.   Enter **9.99** in the *Sales Price* field. Press **Tab**. The *Sales Price* is how much you normally charge your *Customers* for the item. You can enter a default here and later override it on sales forms if you need to.

> **Note:**
> For the *Sales Price* field to automatically calculate a price based on the cost of the item, you could modify the *Default Markup Percentage* field in the *Company Preferences* tab for the *Time & Expenses Preference*.

Step 14.   The *Tax Code* is already selected. Press **Tab**.

Tax Codes determine the default taxable status of the item. Since the *Tax Code* called *Tax* is taxable, QuickBooks calculates sales tax on this item when it appears on sales forms. You can override the default *Tax Code* on each sales form. For more information on *Sales Tax Codes* see page 99.

Step 15.   Select **Sales** from the *Income Account* drop-down list. Press **Tab**.

This is the income account to which you want to post sales of this Item.

Step 16.   In the *Asset Account* field, **Inventory Asset** is already selected. Press **Tab**.

The *Inventory Asset* account is the account that tracks the cost of your inventoried products between the time you purchase them and the time you sell them.

> **The accounting behind the scenes:**
> When you purchase Inventory, QuickBooks increases (debits) the *Inventory Asset* account by the amount of the purchase price. When you sell Inventory, QuickBooks decreases (credits) the *Inventory Asset* account and increases (debits) the *Cost of Goods Sold* account for the average cost of that item at the time it is sold. For details on how QuickBooks calculates average cost, see page 283.

Step 17.   Enter **20** in the *Reorder Point (Min)* field and press **Tab** (see Figure 8-7). Press **Tab** to leave the Max field unchanged.

The QuickBooks Reminders List will remind you when it's time to reorder Inventory items based on the *Reorder Point*.

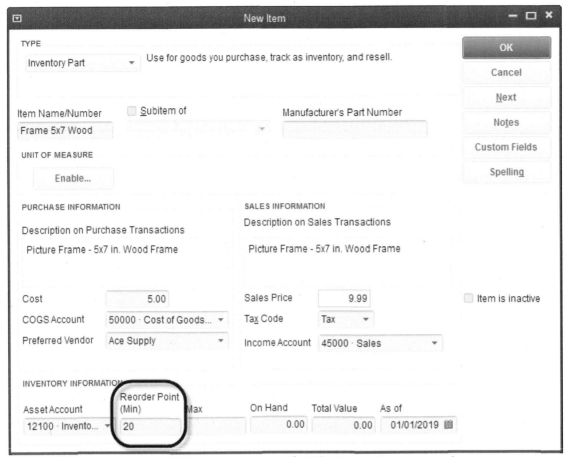

Figure 8-7 When Inventory drops below the reorder point, QuickBooks reminds you to reorder

Step 18.   Leave the *On Hand, Total Value*, and *As of* fields unchanged.

> **Note:**
> Do not enter the *On Hand, Total Value*, and *As of* fields. These fields are intended for use during the initial setup of the data file.
>
> **The accounting behind the scenes:**
> If you enter a quantity and value in this window, QuickBooks increases (debits) *Inventory Asset* for the total value, and increases (credits) *Opening Bal Equity*.
>
> However, even if you are setting up the data file it is better to leave the *On Hand* and *Total Value* fields set to zero when you set up the item. Then, as you will see later, use a single inventory adjustment transaction to set up the quantity and value on hand for *all* of the inventory items.

Step 19.   Click **OK** to save the new *Item*.

> **Tip:**
> Before setting up Inventory, think about what products you will track as *Inventory Parts*. It may not be necessary to separately track *every* product you sell as an *Inventory Part*. If you do not need detailed reports and Inventory status information about certain products you sell, consider using *Non-Inventory Part* Items to track those products. In general, use *Inventory Part* Items only when you really need to track the stock status of a product.

Calculating Average Cost of Inventory

When you enter an Inventory item on a purchase form (e.g., a *Bill*), QuickBooks increases (debits) the *Inventory Asset* account for the *actual* cost of the Inventory purchase. At the same time, QuickBooks Pro, Premier and Accountant recalculate the *average cost* of all items in Inventory.

When you enter an Inventory item on a sales form (e.g., an *Invoice*), in addition to recording income and accounts receivable, QuickBooks increases (debits) Cost of Goods Sold and decreases (credits) the Inventory Asset account for the average cost of the items.

Table 8-3 shows how QuickBooks Pro, Premier and Accountant calculate the average cost of Inventory items.

Situation/Transaction	Calculation
You have ten wood 5x7 picture frames in stock. Each originally costs $5.00.	10 units X $5.00 per unit = $50.00 total cost
You buy ten new wood 5x7 picture frames at $6.00 each.	10 units X $6.00 per unit = $60.00 total cost
The combined cost in inventory.	$50.00 + $60.00 = $110.00
The average cost per unit is equal to the total cost of Inventory divided by the total units in Inventory.	total cost/total units = average cost/unit $110.00 / 20 = $5.50 avg. cost/unit

Table 8-3 QuickBooks calculates the average cost of inventory items.

Each time you sell Inventory items, the average cost per unit is multiplied by the number of units sold. Then this amount is deducted from the Inventory Asset account and added to the *Cost of Goods Sold* account.

QuickBooks Pro, Premier and Accountant only use the average cost method for calculating Inventory value. QuickBooks Enterprise Solutions can use the First In, First Out (FIFO) method for calculating Inventory value. If you need the FIFO method for calculating Inventory, consider upgrading to QuickBooks Enterprise Solutions.

Invoicing for Inventory Items

Selling Inventory Items Using an Invoice Form

When you sell Inventory, always use an *Invoice* or a *Sales Receipt* to record the sale. This ensures that QuickBooks updates your Inventory records and your financial reports at the same time.

COMPUTER PRACTICE

Step 1.   Enter the **Invoice** as shown in Figure 8-8, recording a sale of two 5x7 metal frames.

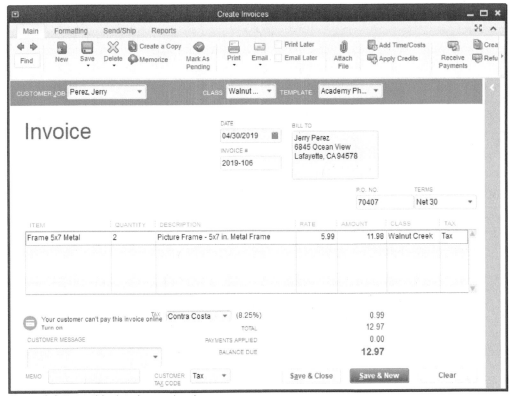

Figure 8-8 Enter this data in your Invoice.

Step 2.   Click **Save** at the top of the Create Invoices window to save the *Invoice*.

Creating a Transaction Journal Report

To see how this Invoice affects the *General Ledger*, use a *Transaction Journal Report*.

COMPUTER PRACTICE

Step 1.   If needed, display Invoice 2019-106 (shown previously in Figure 8-8).

Step 2.   Select the **Reports** tab at the top of the *Create Invoices* window and then select **Transaction Journal** (or press Ctrl+Y).

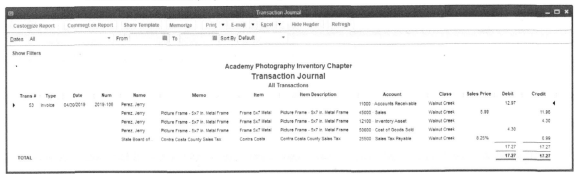

Figure 8-9 Transaction Journal Report

> **The accounting behind the scenes:**
> When you sell an *Inventory Part*, QuickBooks increases (credits) the income account defined for the item sold on the *Invoice* or *Sales Receipt* form. The *Transaction Journal Report* (Figure 8-9) shows the accounting behind the scenes of the *Invoice*. You can use the *Transaction Journal Report* to see the accounting behind *any* QuickBooks transaction.

Step 3.   Close the report by clicking the close box in the upper right corner. If the *Memorize Report* dialog box appears, check the *Do not display this message in the future* box and click **No**.

Step 4.   Close the *Invoice*.

Using Reminders for Inventory

Because you sold two Metal 5x7 Frames and Inventory fell below 20 units (its reorder point), QuickBooks reminds you that it is time to reorder.

COMPUTER PRACTICE

Step 1.   Select the *Company* menu and then select **Reminders** (see Figure 8-10).

Step 2.   Click on the *Inventory to Reorder* line. Your reminders may be different than these, depending on the system date.

Figure 8-10 Reminders list

Step 3.   Close the window by clicking the close box in the upper right corner.

Purchasing Inventory

There are several ways to record the purchases of Inventory in QuickBooks. How you record receiving Inventory depends on *when* you receive the Inventory and *how* you intend to pay for it.

You have two options for purchasing Inventory:

1.   *Pay at time of purchase/receipt of item*, for example, writing a check at the Vendor's store. These transactions are recorded with the *Write Checks* or *Enter Credit Card Charges* forms to record your receipt of Inventory. This method is not generally advised for businesses that want a complete system for tracking purchases, receipts, and payments for Inventory purchases.

2.   *Inventory ordering and receipt process*, as displayed on the *Home Page Vendors* section (Figure 8-11). If you choose this method for processing Inventory, you will issue a *Purchase Order* (PO) for each purchase and later receive part or all of the order by recording an *Item Receipt* or a *Bill*.

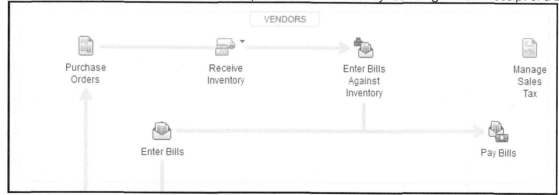

Figure 8-11 The Vendors section includes a flow chart for ordering and receiving Inventory

If the Vendor's bill does not accompany the shipment, use the *Receive Inventory without Bill* option from the *Receive Inventory* icon drop-down list (see Figure 8-12). This creates an *Item Receipt* in QuickBooks.

When the bill comes, use the *Enter Bill for Received Items* option from the *Vendor* menu. You can also click *Enter Bill Against Inventory* on the Home page. This converts the *Item Receipt* into a *Bill*.

If you receive the bill when you receive the order, use the *Receive Inventory with Bill* option from the *Receive Inventory* drop-down list (see Figure 8-12). This creates a *Bill* in QuickBooks.

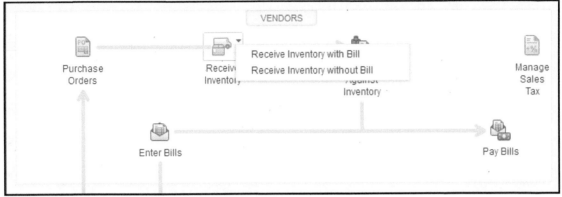

Figure 8-12 Receive Inventory drop-down list options

The *Receive Inventory* options from the *Receive Inventory* drop-down list and the *Receive Items* functions from the *Vendor* menu all record transactions that are *connected* to *Purchase Orders*. This connection is used by QuickBooks to track whether a purchase order is open or not.

Purchasing Inventory at a Retail Store with Check or Credit Card

If you buy Inventory at a retail store, use the *Write Checks* or *Enter Credit Card Charges* functions to record the purchase. Record the purchased items using the *Items* tab at the bottom of the check or credit card charge window (see Figure 8-13).

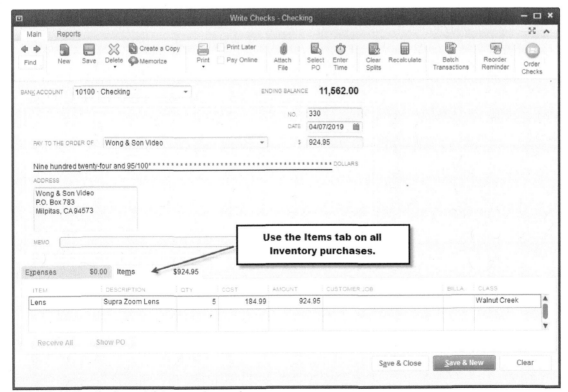

Figure 8-13 Use the Items tab to record a purchase.

Purchase Orders

Use *Purchase Orders* to track Inventory purchases, as well as to easily determine which items you have on order. If you use *Purchase Orders*, you will be able to create reports that show what is on order and when it is due to arrive from your supplier. In addition, you can create a list of open *Purchase Orders*.

Purchase Orders do not post to the *Chart of Accounts*. However, QuickBooks tracks *Purchase Orders* in a non-posting account called *Purchase Orders*. You can see this account at the bottom of your *Chart of Accounts*.

Creating a Purchase Order

Create a *Purchase Order* to reorder Inventory, filling out each item and quantity.

> **Note:**
> Since *Purchase Orders* are non-posting, QuickBooks does not include them on the *Pay Bills* windows.

COMPUTER PRACTICE

Step 1.   Select **Create Purchase Orders** from the *Vendors* menu. Alternately, click the **Purchase Orders** icon on the *Home* page. This displays the *Create Purchase Orders* window (see Figure 8-14).

Step 2.   Select **Ace Supply** from the *Vendor* drop-down list or type the name into the *Vendor* field. Press **Tab**.

Step 3.   Enter **Walnut Creek** in the *Class* field. Press **Tab**.

Step 4.   Press **Tab** twice to leave the *Drop Ship To* field blank and to accept **Custom Purchase Order** as the default form template.

Step 5.   Enter **4/7/2019** in the *Date* field (if not displayed already) and press **Tab**.

Step 6.   Enter **2019-1** in the *P.O. No.* field and press **Tab**.
            QuickBooks automatically numbers your *Purchase Orders* in the same way it numbers Invoices. It increases the number by one for each new *Purchase Order*. However, you can override this number if necessary.

Step 7.   Press **Tab** twice to accept the default *Vendor* and *Ship To* addresses.

            If you want the order shipped directly to one of your customers, select your customer from the drop-down list of the *Drop Ship To* field next to the *Class* field. By default, QuickBooks enters your company's address from the *My Company* window. To change your *Ship To* address, override it on this form here or select *My Company* from the *Company* menu. Click the *Edit* icon and then click the *Ship to Address* button to add your changes.

Step 8.   Enter the **Frame 5x7 Metal (Qty 20)** and **Frame 5x7 Wood (Qty 40)** items in the *Item* and *Qty* columns of the *Purchase Order* as shown in Figure 8-14.

            The Customer column allows you to associate your purchases with a particular *Customer* or *Job* to which you want to assign the expense for this purchase. Since you are purchasing Inventory, you do not know the customer information, so do not use this column.

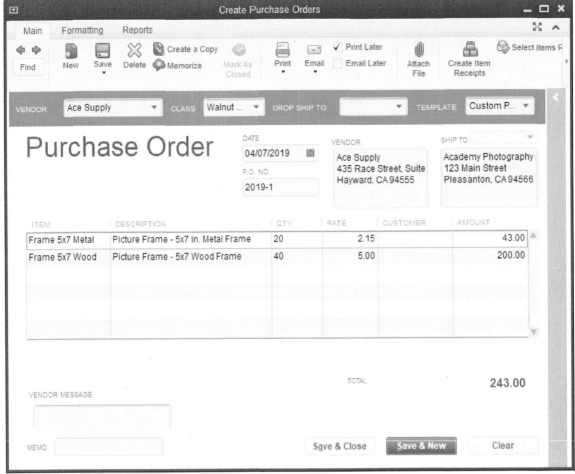

Figure 8-14 Create Purchase Orders window

Step 9.   Click **Save & Close**.

Receiving Shipments Against Purchase Orders

If you use *Purchase Orders* and you receive a shipment that is not accompanied by a bill, follow these steps:

COMPUTER PRACTICE

Step 1.   From the *Vendors* menu, select **Receive Items**. Alternatively, click **Receive Inventory** and then select **Receive Inventory without Bill** from the drop-down menu on the *Vendors* section of the *Home* page.

Step 2.   The *Create Item Receipts* window opens (see Figure 8-15). Enter **Ace Supply** in the *Vendor* field and press **Tab**.

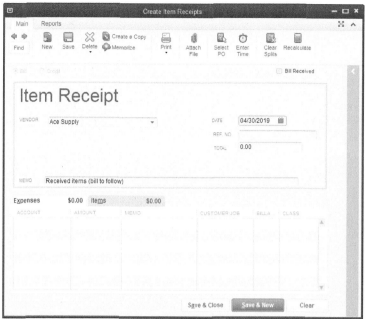

Figure 8-15 The Create Item Receipts window

Step 3.   There is an open *Purchase Order* for this Vendor, so QuickBooks displays the message in Figure 8-16. Click **Yes**.

Figure 8-16 QuickBooks displays an Open POs Exist message, if applicable

Step 4.   Check the **Purchase Order** you are receiving against from the list. (See Figure 8-17). Then click **OK**.

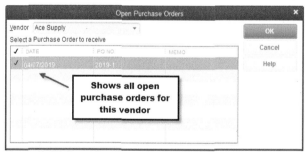

Figure 8-17 Open Purchase Orders window

Step 5.   QuickBooks fills in the *Item Receipt* with the information from the *Purchase Order*. Leave **4/7/2019** in the *Date* field. Press **Tab**.

Step 6.   Enter **4431** in the *Ref. No.* field (see Figure 8-18).

               In the *Ref. No.* field you would enter the shipper number on the packing slip that accompanies the shipment. This helps you match the receipt with the *Vendor's* bill when you receive it.

Step 7.   **Tab** to the *Qty* column. Since not all of the ordered items arrived in this shipment, change the quantity to **10** for the *Frame 5x7 Metal*, and to **20** for the *Frame 5x7 Wood*.(see Figure 8-18).

Do not worry about the Cost column. You have not received the bill yet, so QuickBooks uses the amounts you entered on the *Purchase Order*. When you get the actual bill for this shipment, you will correct or adjust the *Cost* column if necessary.

Figure 8-18 Use the shipper number in the Ref. No. field and change the Qty.

Step 8.   To save the Item Receipt, click **Save & Close**.

The accounting behind the scenes:
When you record an *Item Receipt*, QuickBooks increases (credits) *Accounts Payable* for the total amount of the *Item Receipt*. It also increases (debits) *Inventory* for the same amount.

However, since you have not received the bill, your *Pay Bills* window will not yet show the bill, even though the balance in Accounts Payable was increased by the *Item Receipt*. This may seem strange at first because you normally expect the total in *Pay Bills* to match the balance in *Accounts Payable*. However, *Item Receipts* never show in the *Pay Bills* window. This properly accrues the liability in the right period.

In fact, *Item Receipts* and *Bills* are exactly the same transaction. The only difference is that the *Bill Received* box is not checked on *Item Receipts*, and it is checked on *Bills*.

Note:
You will see that an *Item Receipt* does show up on the *Unpaid Bills Detail* and *A/P Aging* Reports. This lets you know that you have a payable to a Vendor for which you have not received a *Bill*. For cash forecasting purposes, it is important that these reports detail everything you owe, even if a *Bill* has not yet been received.

Creating Open Purchase Orders Reports

COMPUTER PRACTICE

Step 1.   Select the *Reports* menu, select **Purchases**, and then select **Open Purchase Orders**.

This report (see Figure 8-19) shows the total dollar amount for *all* open *Purchase Orders*, not just the open balance of each *Purchase Order*. To see the open balance on a specific *Purchase Order*, double click on it from this report.

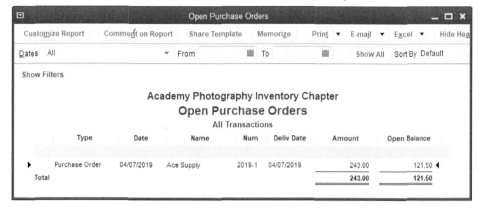

Figure 8-19 The Open Purchase Orders Report

> **Note:**
> Although you partially received Purchase Order 2019-101, it is still "open." You can double click on the Purchase Order in the Open Purchase Orders report to see more detail.

Checking Purchase Order Status

To check the status of a *Purchase Order*, to change it, or to cancel it, edit the *Purchase Order* directly.

COMPUTER PRACTICE

Step 1.   Display the **Purchase Order** by double clicking on it from the **Open Purchase Orders** report shown in Figure 8-19.

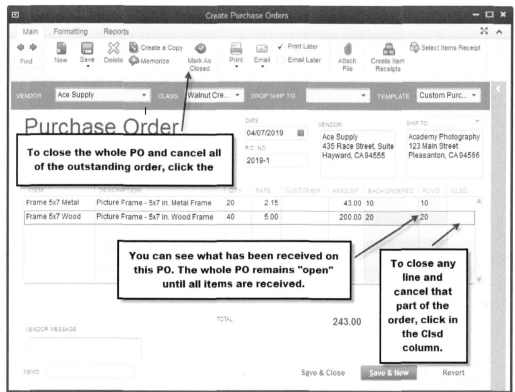

Figure 8-20 Edit the purchase order as necessary.

Step 2.   Review the quantity of each Item in the *Rcv'd* column.

Step 3.   On the *Purchase Order* in Figure 8-20, you can see that Academy Photography has received 10 *Frames 5x7 Metal* and 20 *Frames 5x7 Wood*.

                 If you know you will not receive the backordered items on a *Purchase Order*, you can close specific line items or close the whole order. To close any line of the order, click in the *Clsd* column. To close the whole order and cancel the rest of the order, click the *Mark as Closed* button at the top of the form. If you cancel an order, do not forget to notify the Vendor.

Step 4.   In this case, close the window without making any changes to the *Purchase Order*. Close the *Open Purchase Orders* report.

Entering the Final Shipment

When the final shipment of backordered items arrives, enter another *Item Receipt*.

COMPUTER PRACTICE

Step 1.   Select the *Vendors* menu and then select **Receive Items**. Alternatively, click **Receive Inventory** and then **Receive Inventory without Bill** on the *Vendor* section of the *Home* page.

Step 2.   The *Create Item Receipts* window opens. Enter **Ace Supply** in the *Vendor* field and then press **Tab**.

Step 3.   Because there is an open *Purchase Order* for this *Vendor*, QuickBooks displays the *Open POs Exist* window. Click **Yes**.

Step 4.   Select the **Purchase Order** you are receiving against from the list (see Figure 8-21) and click **OK**.

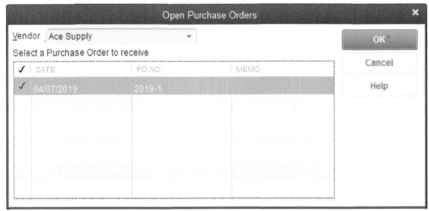

Figure 8-21 Open Purchase Orders window

Step 5.   QuickBooks automatically fills in the *Item Receipt* with the information from the *Purchase Order*.

Step 6.   Leave **4/7/2019** in the *Date* field.

Step 7.   Enter **4441** in the *Ref. No.* field (see Figure 8-22).

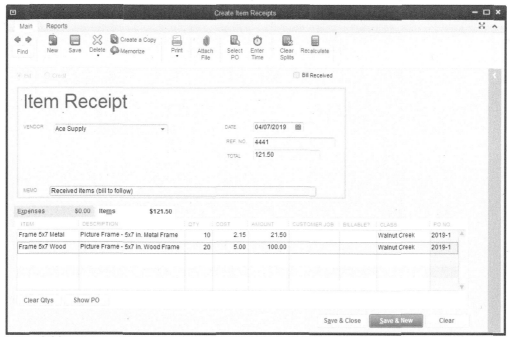

Figure 8-22 Item Receipt 4441

Step 8.   Click **Save & Close** to record the receipt.

Entering Bills for Received Inventory

Now that you have recorded *Item Receipts* for your Inventory shipments, the next step in the process is to record the bills when they arrive from the vendor.

Converting an Item Receipt into a Bill

COMPUTER PRACTICE

Step 1.   Select the *Vendors* menu and then select **Enter Bill for Received Items**. Alternatively, click **Enter Bills Against Inventory** icon in the *Vendor* section of the *Home* page.

Step 2.   Enter *Ace Supply* in the *Vendor* field and then press **Tab**.

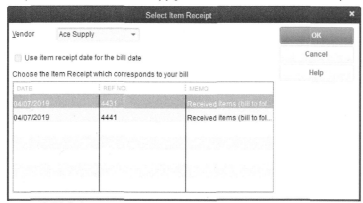

Figure 8-23 Select one shipment at a time

Step 3.   Select the first line on the window shown in Figure 8-23. Click **OK**.

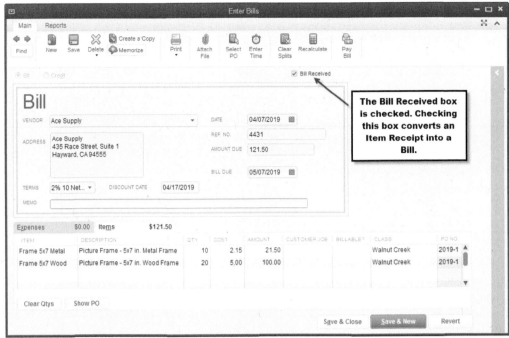

Figure 8-24 Enter Bills window

Step 4.   QuickBooks displays the *Item Receipt* and automatically checks the *Bill Received* box
               (see Figure 8-24). Checking the *Bill Received* box converts the *Item Receipt* into a *Bill*.
               Verify that the *Bill* matches your records and make changes to price, terms, due date, or
               any other field that does not match the Vendor's bill.

> **Note:**
> QuickBooks does not add a new transaction when you use the *Enter Bill for Received
> Items* function. That is because you have already recorded an *Item Receipt,* which
> increases Inventory and Accounts Payable. This function simply converts your *Item
> Receipt* into a *Bill.*

Step 5.   Click **Save & Close** to record the *Bill.*

Step 6.   Click **Yes** if the *Recording Transaction* message displays.

Step 7.   Repeat Step 1 through Step 6 to **Enter Bill for Received Items** for **Item Receipt 4441**.
               Accept the defaults for all quantities and amounts.

> **Note:**
> QuickBooks does not allow you to "group" multiple *Item Receipts* into one *Bill* if only one
> Vendor bill is received for the entire *PO*. If you receive one Vendor bill and have multiple
> *Item Receipts,* in the reference number of the *Bill* make sure to enter the same number.
> This will enable you to easily identify all the *Bills* that add up to the Vendor bill received
> when creating the Vendor's *Bill Payment* check.

Handling Overshipments

If your Vendor ships more than you ordered on a *Purchase Order,* you have three choices.

1.   You could refuse the extra shipment and send it back to the Vendor without recording anything
      in QuickBooks.

2.   You could receive the extra shipment into Inventory and keep it (and pay for it).

3. You could receive the extra shipment into Inventory, and then send it back and record a *Bill Credit* in QuickBooks.

If you keep the overshipment (and pay for it):

> **DO NOT PERFORM THESE STEPS NOW. THEY ARE FOR REFERENCE ONLY.**

1. Override the number in the *Qty* column on the *Item Receipt* so that it exceeds the quantity on your *Purchase Order*. This increases the *Inventory Asset* and *Accounts Payable* accounts for the total amount of the shipment, including the overshipment.

2. When the bill arrives from the Vendor, match it with the *Item Receipt* and pay the amount actually due. Unless you edit the *Purchase Order*, it will not match the *Item Receipt* or *Bill*. This may be important later when you look at *Purchase Orders* and actual purchase costs, so consider updating your *Purchase Order* to match the actual costs.

If you send the overshipment back after receiving it into Inventory:

> **DO NOT PERFORM THESE STEPS NOW. THEY ARE FOR REFERENCE ONLY.**

1. Override the number in the *Qty* column on the *Item Receipt* so that it exceeds the quantity on your *Purchase Order*. This increases the *Inventory Asset* and *Accounts Payable* accounts for the total amount of the shipment, including the overshipment. However, you do not plan to actually pay the Vendor for this "overshipment." Instead, you will return the extra items, and ask the Vendor to credit your account.

2. When you return the excess items, create a *Bill Credit* for the Vendor. On the *Bill Credit*, enter the quantity returned and the cost for each item. We use a *Bill Credit* here because we want to reflect the proper financial transactions between us and our Vendor.

3. At this point, the Vendor may apply your credit towards a future *Invoice* on items they send to you, or they may send you a refund if you have paid for the shipment.

4. If you receive a refund from the Vendor, record the refund directly onto your next deposit transaction. You can manually add a line to the deposit using the Vendor's name in the *Received From* column, and Accounts Payable in the *From Account* column. Then, after recording the deposit, use the *Pay Bills* screen to apply the deposit line to the *Bill Credit*.

5. To apply the *Bill Credit* to an unpaid bill for that Vendor, use the *Pay Bills* window.

Handling Vendor Overcharges

If you have a discrepancy between your *Purchase Order* and the Vendor's bill, there are several ways to handle it. If the Vendor overcharged you, the Vendor might agree to revise the bill and send you a new one. In this case, wait for the new bill before recording anything in QuickBooks. On the other hand, you might decide to pay the incorrect bill and have the Vendor adjust the next bill. In that case, use the *Expenses* tab on the *Bill* in QuickBooks to track the error. In this example, assume you were overcharged by $10.00.

COMPUTER PRACTICE

Step 1. Select the *Vendors* menu and then select **Enter Bills**. Alternatively, click **Enter Bills** on the *Vendor* section of the *Home* page.

Step 2. Click **Previous** on the *Enter Bills* window to display Bill #4441.

Step 3. Select the **Expenses** tab to record a $10.00 overcharge from the Vendor. Use the **Cost of Goods Sold** account and the **Overhead** class to track the overcharge. Alternately, you could record the overcharge to a *Current Asset* account called **Due from Vendors** so that the error does not affect the Profit & Loss statement.

Step 4.   Click **Recalculate** to update the *Amount Due* field (see Figure 8-25). (Note that if you Tab into the next line, a negative $10 will appear. You will have to clear that amount in order to properly recalculate the Amount Due.)

Step 5.   Click **Save & Close**. Click **Yes** on the *Recording Transaction* message window.

Since the *Bill* in Figure 8-25 is $10.00 too much, contact the Vendor to discuss the overage on the *Bill*. The Vendor will either issue you a credit, or if you have already paid the *Bill*, send you a refund check. The Vendor may also apply the overpayment to your account to be applied to a future bill.

Depending upon the Vendor's action, do one of the following:

- If the Vendor refunds your money, add the refund directly into your next deposit. Code the deposit to the *Cost of Goods Sold* account and the *Overhead* class (the account and class you used when you recorded the overage on the bill).

- If the Vendor sends you a credit memo, enter a **Bill Credit**. Code the *Bill Credit* to the *Cost of Goods Sold* account and the *Overhead* class (the account and class you used when you recorded the overage on the *Bill*).

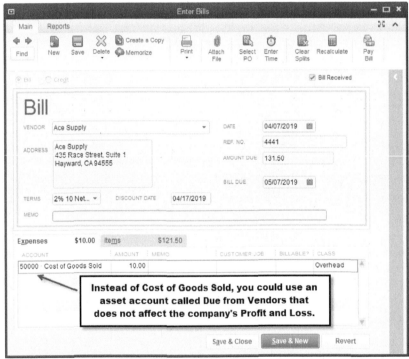

Figure 8-25 Record a Vendor overcharge in the Expenses tab

> **Note:**
> Always use the same account when you record the overcharge and the refund or credit. In the example above, the *Expenses* tab of the *Bill* for Ace Supply increases *Cost of Goods Sold* by $10.00 and the deposit or credit from the Vendor reduces **Cost of Goods Sold** by the same amount. Alternatively, you could use an *Other Current Asset* account called *Due from Vendors*, as discussed above.

Adjusting Inventory

QuickBooks automatically adjusts Inventory each time you purchase or sell *Inventory* items. However, it may be necessary to manually adjust Inventory after a physical count of your Inventory, or in case of an increase or decrease in the value of your Inventory on hand. For example, you might decrease the value of your Inventory if it has lost value due to new technology trends.

Adjusting the Quantity of Inventory on Hand

COMPUTER PRACTICE

Step 1. Select the *Vendors* menu, select **Inventory Activities**, and then select **Adjust Quantity/Value on Hand**. Alternatively, click the **Inventory Activities** icon on the *Home* page and select **Adjust Quantity/Value on Hand** from the menu. QuickBooks displays the window shown in Figure 8-26.

Step 2. If necessary, enter **Quantity** in the *Adjustment Type* field and press **Tab**.

Step 3. Enter *4/30/2019* in the *Adjustment Date* field and press **Tab**.

Step 4. Enter *Inventory Variance* in the *Adjustment Account* field and press **Tab**.

QuickBooks adjusts the account you enter into the *Adjustment Account* field to offset the change in the *Inventory Asset* account balance. In this example, we are using *Inventory Variance,* a *Cost of Goods Sold* account, but you can use whichever account is best for your records.

Step 5. The *Income or Expense expected* dialog box displays. Check the box next to *Do not display this message in the future* and click **OK**

> **Note:**
> The dialog box displays because QuickBooks is looking for an expense account to record the offsetting decrease in the Inventory asset. Although the entry can be made to an expense account (decrease in Inventory) or an income account (increase in Inventory), many people find that offsetting Inventory variances to the Cost of Goods Sold account (for either Inventory increases or decreases) more accurately reflects the recording of variances.

Step 6. Enter *2019-1* in the *Reference No.* field and press **Tab** twice to skip the *Customer: Job* field.

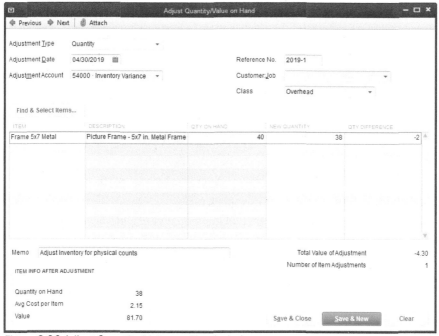

Figure 8-26 Adjust Quantity/Value on Hand window

Step 7.   Enter **Overhead** in the *Class* field and press **Tab.**

Step 8.   Enter **Frame 5x7 Metal** in the *Item* column and press **Tab.**

Step 9.   Enter **38** in the *New Quantity* column and press **Tab.**

Notice that QuickBooks calculates the quantity difference (-2) in the *Qty Difference* column. Also, notice that QuickBooks automatically calculates the *Total Value of Adjustment* in the bottom right corner. QuickBooks Pro, Premier and Accountant use the *average cost method* to calculate this value. Look at the *Inventory Valuation Detail Report* later in this chapter to see how the average cost changes each time you adjust Inventory in this way.

Step 10.   Enter **Adjust Inventory for physical counts** in the Memo field.

Step 11.   Compare your screen to Figure 8-26. To save the adjustment, click **Save & New.**

Adjusting the Value of Inventory

COMPUTER PRACTICE

With the Adjust Quantity/Value on Hand window displayed, follow these steps to record a *value* adjustment to your inventory.

Step 1.   Enter **Total Value** in the *Adjustment Type* field and press **Tab.**

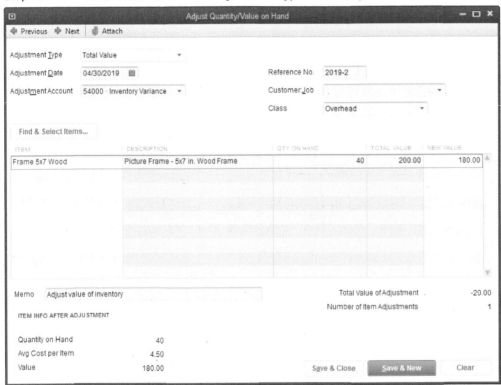

Figure 8-27 Click on the Value Adjustment box to change inventory value

Step 2.   Confirm that **4/30/2019** is already selected in the *Adjustment Date* field. Press **Tab.**

Step 3.   Confirm that **Inventory Variance** is already selected in the *Adjustment Account* field.

Step 4.   Leave **2019-2** in the Ref. No. field.

Step 5.   Leave the *Customer:Job* field blank.

Step 6.   Enter **Overhead** in the *Class* field.

Step 7.   Enter **Frame 5x7 Wood** in the *Item* column. Press **Tab.**

Step 8.   Enter *180.00* in the *New Value* column on the Frame 5x7 Wood line and press **Tab**. Notice that QuickBooks calculates the Total Value of Adjustment.

Step 9.   Compare your screen to Figure 8-27. When finished, click **Save & Close** to save the adjustment.

QuickBooks will post the amount of this adjustment ($20.00) to the *General Ledger*. Since this adjustment lowers the value of the Frame 5x7 Wood item, it reduces the average cost of each unit on hand. Therefore, the next time you sell a Frame 5x7 Wood, QuickBooks will transfer the new (lower) average cost out of *Inventory* and into *Cost of Goods Sold*.

> **Note:**
> If you need to adjust for both Quantity on Hand and the Value, select Quantity and Total Value as the *Adjustment Type*.
>
> **The accounting behind the scenes:**
> Inventory value adjustments always affect your *Inventory Asset* account. If the *Total Value of Adjustment* is a positive number, the *Inventory* account increases (debits) by that amount and the *Adjustment* account decreases (credits). If the *Total Value of Adjustment* is a negative number, the debits and the credits are reversed.

Setting up Group Items

Sometimes, you sell items in bundles. For example, Academy Photography sells three hours of services for retouching and a 5x7 Wood Frame together as a single item. Academy Photography uses *Group* Items to bundle products and/or services on sales forms. You may also purchase items in a bundle from a Vendor, so setting up a *Group* Item may make the purchasing process easier as well.

COMPUTER PRACTICE

Step 1.   Click **Items & Services** on the *Company* section of the *Home* page, or select the *Lists* menu and then select **Item List**.

Step 2.   Select the **Item** button at the bottom of the *Item List* window and select **New.** Alternatively, press **Ctrl+N**.

Step 3.   Select **Group** from the *Type* drop-down list and press **Tab**.

Step 4.   Enter *5x7 Retouching* in the *Group Name/Number* field and press **Tab** to advance to the *Description* field.

Step 5.   Enter *Retouching photograph and placing in a 5x7 Wood Frame* in the Description field and press Tab.

Step 6.   Click the *Print items in group* box (see Figure 8-28). Click this box if you want your printed *Invoices* to show the detail of each item in the group. The *Invoice screen* will always show the individual items in the group. Press **Tab**.

Step 7.   On the first line at the bottom of the window, select **Frame 5x7 Wood** from the *Item* drop-down list. Press **Tab**.

Step 8.   Enter *1* in the *Qty* column and press **Tab**. The *Qty* column indicates how many of each item is included in the *Group*.

Step 9.   On the second line at the bottom of the window, select **Retouching** from the *Item* drop-down list. Press **Tab**.

Step 10.   Enter *3* in the *Qty* column. Press **Tab**.

Step 11.   Click **OK** to save the *Group* item.

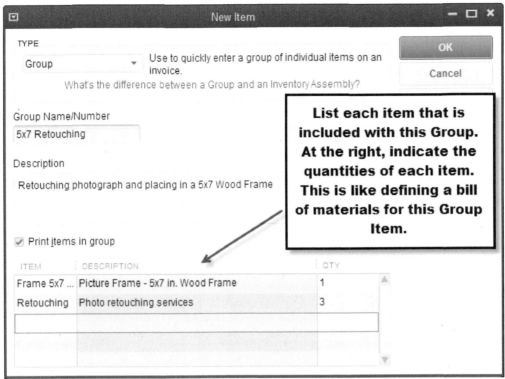

Figure 8-28 Specify Items in the group and whether to print Items on the sales form

> **Note:**
> The *New Item* window in Figure 8-28 does not include a *Sales Price* field. When you enter a *Group* Item on sales forms, QuickBooks uses the sales prices of the items within the *Group* to calculate a total price for the *Group*. You can override the price of each item within the *Group* directly on the sales form.

Inventory Reports

QuickBooks provides several reports for Inventory analysis, all of which are customizable in ways similar to other reports.

For daily management of Inventory, use the *Stock Status by Item Report*, the *Stock Status by Vendor Report*, or the *Inventory Valuation Summary Report*. These reports give a quick overview of Inventory counts, Inventory values, and pending orders.

For detailed research about transactions involving Inventory, use the *Inventory Item QuickReport* or the *Inventory Valuation Detail Report*.

> **Note:**
> In prior versions of QuickBooks, you were not able to make modifications to *Inventory Reports*, such as adding a column. QuickBooks 2018 allows more flexibility with modifying reports.

Inventory Item QuickReport

The *Inventory Item QuickReport* is useful for seeing all transactions involving an *Inventory Item*.

COMPUTER PRACTICE

Step 1.   From the *Home* page, click the **Inventory Activities** icon and choose **Inventory Center.**

Step 2.   Click on the **Frame 5x7 Metal** Item to select it in the left side of the *Inventory Center.*

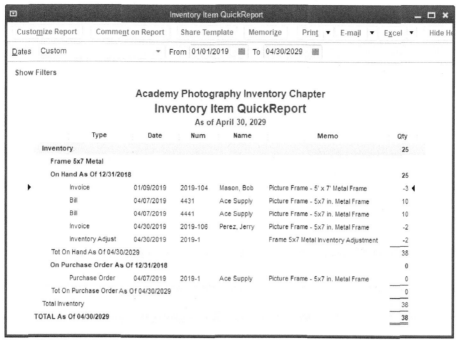

Figure 8-29 Inventory Item QuickReport

Step 3.   Click the **QuickReport** link from the right side of the *Inventory Center*.

Step 4.   Set the *From* date to **1/1/2019** and the *To* date to **4/30/2019** and press **Tab**. The *QuickReport* for the Frame 5x7 Metal displays (see Figure 8-29).

Step 5.   Close the report by clicking the close box in the upper right corner of the window. Leave the *Inventory Center* open.

Inventory Stock Status by Item Report

The *Inventory Stock Status by Item Report* is useful for getting a quick snapshot of each Inventory part, as well as the number of units on hand and on order. In addition, this report gives you information about your Inventory turnover, showing a column for sales per week.

COMPUTER PRACTICE

Step 1.   Click the **Stock Status** link on the right side of the *Inventory Center*. Alternatively, select the *Reports* menu, select **Inventory**, and then select **Inventory Stock Status by Item**.

Step 2.   Set the *From* date to **1/1/2019** and the *To* date to **4/30/2019** and press **Tab**. The Inventory Stock Status by Item report displays (see Figure 8-30).

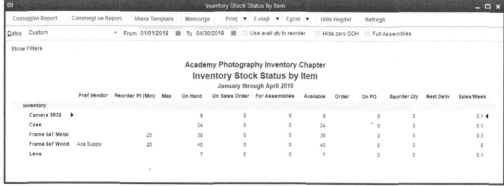

Figure 8-30 Inventory Stock Status by Item report

Step 3.   To close the report, click the close box at the top right corner of the window

Inventory Stock Status by Vendor Report

The *Inventory Stock Status by Vendor Report* gives you information about your Inventory parts, including how many are on hand, and how many are on order. This *Report* is sorted by the *Preferred Vendor* field in the item.

COMPUTER PRACTICE

Step 1.   From the *Reports* menu, select **Inventory**, and then select **Inventory Stock Status by Vendor**.

Step 2.   Set the *From* date to *1/1/2019* and the *To* date to *4/30/2019* and press **Tab**. The *Inventory Stock Status by Vendor Report* displays (see Figure 8-31).

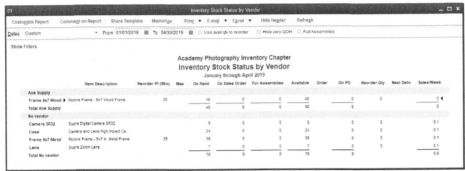

Figure 8-31 Inventory Stock Status by Vendor report

Step 3.   To close the report, click the close box at the top right corner of the window

Inventory Valuation Summary

The *Inventory Valuation Summary Report* gives you information about the value of your Inventory items on a certain date. This report shows each item in Inventory, the quantity on hand, the average cost, and the retail value of each item.

COMPUTER PRACTICE

Step 1.   Click the **Inventory Valuation Summary** link on the right side of the *Inventory Center*. Alternatively, select the **Reports** menu, select **Inventory**, and then select **Inventory Valuation Summary**.

Step 2.   Set the *Date* field to *4/30/2019* and press **Tab** (see Figure 8-32).

	On Hand	Avg Cost	Asset Value	% of Tot Asset	Sales Price	Retail Value	% of Tot Retail
Inventory							
Camera SR32	9	450.00	4,050.00	60.6%	695.99	6,263.91	56.5%
Case	24	45.00	1,080.00	16.2%	79.99	1,919.76	17.3%
Frame 5x7 Metal	38	2.15	81.70	1.2%	5.99	227.62	2.1%
Frame 5x7 Wo...	40	4.50	180.00	2.7%	9.99	399.60	3.6%
Lens	7	184.99	1,294.93	19.4%	324.99	2,274.93	20.5%
Total Inventory	118		6,686.63	100.0%		11,085.82	100.0%
TOTAL	118		6,686.63	100.0%		11,085.82	100.0%

Figure 8-32 Inventory Valuation Summary report

Step 3.　　To close the report, click the close box at the top right corner of the window. Click **No** if you are prompted to memorize the report.

Unit of Measure

Many businesses purchase items using one unit of measure and sell the same item using a different unit of measure. For example, a retail store may purchase items by the case, but sell the items individually (or by *each*). QuickBooks Premier, Accountant, and Enterprise include the *Unit of Measure* feature to help in these situations.

> **Note:**
> The Unit of Measure feature is not available in QuickBooks Pro.

The **Unit of Measure** (or U/M) feature allows you to assign units such as hours, foot, package, each, etc., to QuickBooks items. The **Single U/M Per Item** option allows you to assign a single unit of measure to each item while the **Multiple U/M Per Item** option (available only in QuickBooks Premier's Contractor and Manufacturing editions as well as Accountant and Enterprise editions) allows you to create a unit of measure set for a particular item.

Using *Single U/M Per Item* doesn't allow you to convert between units, but it does provide clarity for everyone working in the QuickBooks data file. Using *Multiple U/M Per Item* allows you to convert from one unit to another, within a defined set.

Turning on Unit of Measure – Single U/M

The following exercises will set up, assign, and utilize the *Single Unit of Measure Per Item*.

> **DO NOT PERFORM THESE STEPS. THEY ARE FOR REFERENCE ONLY.**

1. Select **Preferences** from the *Edit* menu. Select the **Items & Inventory** Preference and then select the **Company Preferences** tab.

2. Click the **Enable** button in the *Unit of Measure* section (see Figure 8-33). Note that Unit of Measure is only available in QuickBooks Premier, Accountant, and Enterprise Editions.

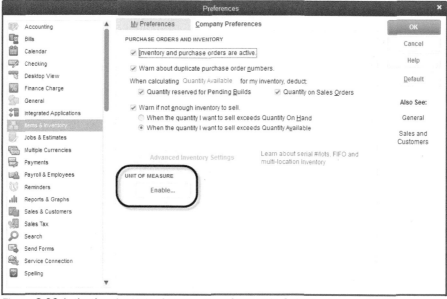

Figure 8-33 Activating the Unit of Measure preference in QuickBooks

3.   Select **Single U/M Per Item** in the *Unit of Measure* window (see Figure 8-34).

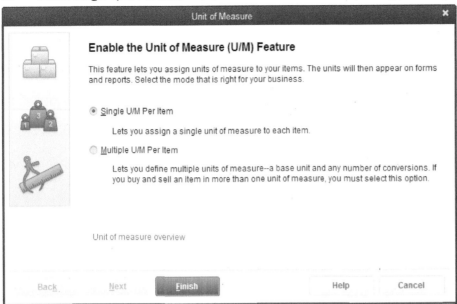

Figure 8-34 Unit of Measure window

4.   Click the **Finish** button and then click **OK** in the *Preferences* window.

5.   QuickBooks displays a *Warning* dialog box stating that all open windows must be closed in order to change the preference. Click **OK** (see Figure 8-35).

Figure 8-35 Warning dialog box that QuickBooks must close to change preferences

Applying Unit of Measure to Items

Academy Photography purchases frames by the case, but sells them individually. By setting up Single Unit of Measure, each transaction that uses this item will clearly identify the units. You should always choose the smallest unit of measure, or the *base* unit of measure, during setup. In this case, each frame is a smaller unit than a case of frames, so we will use *each*.

> **DO NOT PERFORM THESE STEPS. THEY ARE FOR REFERENCE ONLY.**

1.   Select the *Lists* menu and then select **Item List**. Alternatively, click **Items & Services** on the *Company* section of the *Home* page.

2.   Double click the **Frame 5x7 Metal** item. The *Edit Item* window opens.

3.   Enter the word *Each* in the *Unit of Measure* field and press **Tab**.

4.   QuickBooks displays the *U/M Set Not Found* dialog box. Press **Set Up** (See Figure 8-36).

Figure 8-36 U/M Set Not Found Dialog Box

5. In the *Unit of Measure window, enter **Ea*** in the *Abbreviation* field and press **Finish** (See Figure 8-37).

6. Click **OK** to save the changes to the *Item*.

Figure 8-37 Unit of Measure window

The Item List now has an additional column that lists U/M (see Figure 8-38). Once a unit of measure has been set up for an item, it can be applied to other Service, Inventory Part, Inventory Assembly, Non-inventory Part, or Group items as well.

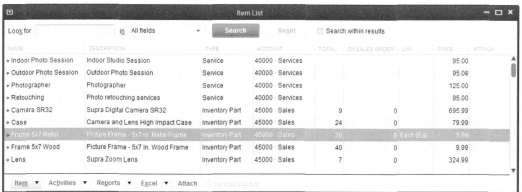

Figure 8-38 The Item list

All forms that use items, including Purchase Orders, Bills, Checks and Invoices, will now include the Unit of Measure column (see Figure 8-39).

> **Note:**
> Using the Single Unit of Measure method, when you receive a case of frames you need to enter in the total quantity of frames, not the number of cases, on all receipts.

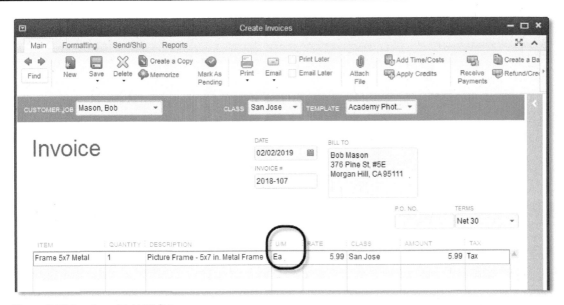

Figure 8-39 Invoice with U/M Column

Inventory Assemblies

> **Note:**
> This feature is only available in QuickBooks Premier, Accountant, and Enterprise. If you are using the Pro edition, read through this section, but do not complete the exercise.

If you build or assemble items from raw materials or assemble multiple items together, you can create an **Inventory Assembly Item** in QuickBooks to track your assembled inventory. An Inventory Assembly is defined by specifying which components (must be Inventory Part, Inventory Assembly, Non-inventory Part, Service, or Other Charge type items) are needed to produce it. Essentially, you define the *Bill of Materials* for each **Inventory Assembly Item** when you set up the item.

The feature is similar to *Groups*, but it allows you to combine several *Inventory Items* into a single *Item*. They are different from *Group Items* because the parts are removed from *Inventory* as soon as an *Inventory Assembly Item* is assembled (for more on group items see page 299).

When you "build assemblies" from individual Items into Inventory Assembly Items, QuickBooks automatically adjusts the quantities and values on hand of the inventory items (components) and the assemblies (finished goods).

When you sell the assembled inventory product (i.e., finished goods), select the Inventory Assembly Item name from the *Item* column on sales forms.

> **DO NOT PERFORM THESE STEPS. THEY ARE FOR REFERENCE ONLY.**

1.   Select the *Lists* menu and then select **Item List**. Alternatively, click **Items & Services** on the *Home* page.
2.   Select the *Item* button drop-down list at the bottom left of the Item List and select **New** (or type **CTRL+N**).
3.   Select **Inventory Assembly** from the *Type* drop-down list and press **Tab**.

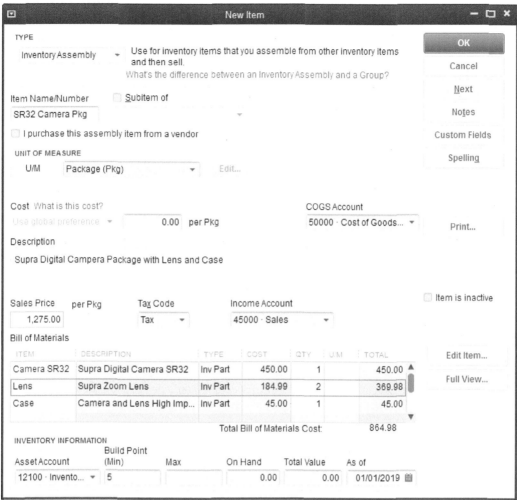

Figure 8-40 Creating an Inventory Assembly item

4. Enter **SR32 Camera Pkg** in the *Item Name/Number* field.

5. Press **Tab** two times to advance to the *Unit of Measure* field. Enter **Package** in the *Unit of Measure* field and press **Tab.** The *Unit of Measure* window opens.

6. Enter **Package** as the *Name* and **Pkg** as the *Abbreviation*. Click **Finish** to close the *Unit of Measure* window.

7. In the New Item window, press **Tab** to advance to the *COGS Account* field. **Cost of Goods Sold** is already selected from the *COGS Account* drop-down list. Press **Tab.**

   QuickBooks increases (debits) the account you enter in this field when you use this item on Invoices and Sales Receipts.

8. Enter *Supra Digital Camera Package with Lens and Case* in the *Description* field and press **Tab.**

   On sales forms, QuickBooks will enter this description by default. Unlike Group items, QuickBooks will not display the descriptions of the component items.

9. Enter *1275.00* in the *Sales Price* field and press **Tab.**

10. **Tax** in the *Tax Code* field is already selected. Press **Tab.**

11. Select **Sales** from the *Income Account* drop-down list and press **Tab.**

12. Enter the items and quantities on the *Bill of Materials* section as shown in Figure 8-40.

    List all of the items you will need to create the *SR32 Camera Pkg* Item (i.e., finished goods).

13.   Confirm that **Inventory Asset** is already selected in the *Asset Account* field. Press **Tab**.

       QuickBooks increases (debits) the account you enter in this field when you record a Build
       Assembly transaction.

14.   Enter **5** in the *Build Point (Min)* field and press **Tab**.

       QuickBooks will remind you to build more of the Assembly Item if your quantity on hand drops
       below 5. Do not enter any information into the remaining fields. These fields are designed for use
       during the initial setup of your data file.

15.   Click **OK** to save the **Assembly Item**.

On an ongoing basis, you will create *SR32 Camera Pkg* products using one Camera SR32, two Supra
Zoom Lens and one Camera and Lens High Impact Case. When you finish assembling the items, you
must record a **Build Assembly** transaction to tell QuickBooks that you have built the items.

> ## Do Not Perform These Steps. They Are For Reference Only.

1.   Select the *Vendors* menu, select **Inventory Activities,** and then select **Build Assemblies**.
       Alternatively, click **Build Assemblies** on the *Home* page.

2.   Select **SR32 Camera Pkg** from the *Assembly Item* drop-down list and press **Tab**.

3.   Enter **4/30/2019** in the *Date* field.

4.   Enter **2019-1** in the *Build Ref. No.* field. Press **Tab**.

5.   Enter **2** in the *Quantity to Build* field and press **Tab**.

6.   Enter **Build SR32 Camera Package** in the *Memo* field.

7.   Enter the information in Figure 8-41. Click **Build and Close** to record the transaction.

       After you build assemblies, QuickBooks adjusts the quantity on hand of each component as well
       as the assembly.

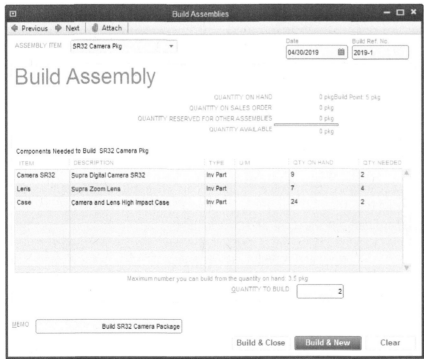

Figure 8-41 Building an Inventory Assembly

Inventory Valuation Detail Report

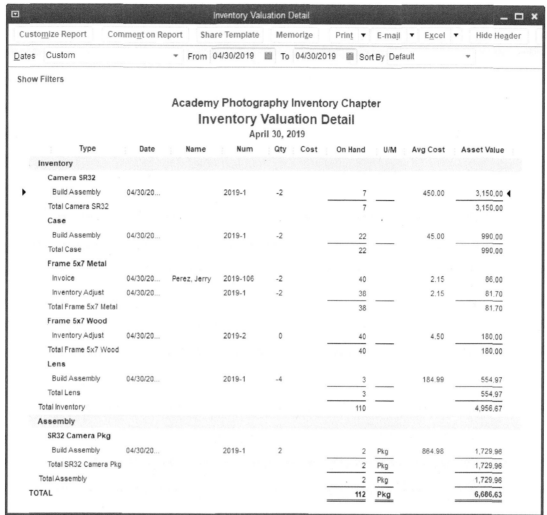

Figure 8-42 Inventory Valuation Detail report showing the building of component items into an assembly

To see the adjustment created by the Build Assembly transaction, follow these steps:

1. Select the *Reports* menu, select **Inventory,** and then select **Inventory Valuation Detail**.

2. Enter *4/30/2019* in the *From* and *To* fields as shown in Figure 8-42. The **Inventory Valuation Detail** report shows the component items being used to build the assembly items.

   As you build assemblies, the quantity of each component item decreases while the quantity of each assembly item increases.

3. Close the report by clicking the close box in the upper right corner of the window.

Review Questions

Comprehension Questions

1. Why does an item receipt add to the balance in Accounts Payable but not show up in the *Pay Bills* window?

2. What accounts will QuickBooks automatically create when you first create an Inventory Part Item in the Item list?

3. Describe the purpose of the Inventory Asset and Cost of Goods Sold accounts in QuickBooks.

4. Describe the purpose of using Purchase Orders in QuickBooks.

Multiple Choice

Select the best answer for each of the following:

1. If your Vendor ships more than you ordered on a *Purchase Order* (an overshipment), which of the following actions would not be appropriate?
    a) You could refuse the extra shipment and send it back to the Vendor without recording anything in QuickBooks.
    b) You could receive the extra shipment using an *Inventory Adjustment* transaction.
    c) You could receive the extra shipment into Inventory and keep it (and pay for it).
    d) You could receive the extra shipment into Inventory, and then send it back and record a *Bill Credit* in QuickBooks.

2. When setting up a *Group* Item, where do you enter the sales price?
    a) Enter the price in the *Sales Price* field.
    b) Enter the price in the *Item Pricing* list.
    c) The *Group* Item does not include a *Sales Price* field.
    d) Enter the price in the *Set Price* window.

3. To activate QuickBooks Inventory:
    a) Select the **File** menu and then select **Preferences.**
    b) Select Purchases - Vendors.
    c) Consult your accountant to determine the proper Inventory valuation method.
    d) Select the **Edit** menu, then select **Preferences**, then click on the **Items & Inventory** *Preference* and then click the **Company Preferences** tab.

4. The Inventory asset account:
    a) Tracks open *Purchase Orders* of Inventory items.
    b) Decreases when Inventory is purchased.
    c) Increases when Inventory is sold.
    d) Increases when Inventory is purchased.

5. In QuickBooks Pro, Premier, and Accountant, Inventory can do all of the following except:
    a) Provide reports on the status of each item in Inventory including how many are on hand and how many are on order.
    b) Use the LIFO or FIFO method of determining Inventory cost.
    c) Calculate gross profit on Inventory sold.
    d) Track the open *Purchase Orders* for every Inventory item.

6. A convenient way to track the status of orders for your inventory items is to:
    a) List the items ordered on a sheet and review it each morning.
    b) Analyze your transaction journal report monthly.
    c) Use purchase orders for all inventory purchases.
    d) Hire an outside consultant to monitor your inventory levels.

7. Which of the following statements is false regarding Purchase Orders (POs)?
    a) POs are held in a special non-posting account until you receive the item(s) ordered.
    b) POs that include inventory items are posted to the inventory account at the end of each month.
    c) You can list your open purchase orders at any time.
    d) You may close a purchase order in part or in full at any time.

8. To display the window used to record inventory adjustments in QuickBooks:
    a) Select the **Company** menu and then select **Adjust Inventory for actual counts**.
    b) No adjustments should be made. QuickBooks automatically adjusts inventory each time you purchase or sell inventory items.
    c) Select the **Vendors** menu, select **Inventory Activities**, and then select **Adjust Quantity/Value on Hand**.
    d) Perform a physical inventory count.

9. QuickBooks Pro and Premier maintain the value of inventory under which method?
    a) First in First Out, FIFO.
    b) Last in First Out, LIFO.
    c) Cost/retail method of inventory.
    d) Average Cost.

10. Which of the following is NOT a report available through QuickBooks?
    a) Goods-In-Process Inventory by Item.
    b) Inventory Stock Status by Item.
    c) Inventory Valuation Summary.
    d) Item QuickReport.

11. Which of the following statements is true regarding the recording of receipts of inventory items?
    a) How you record inventory received does not depend on how you pay for the items.
    b) Directly writing checks for inventory purchases is generally advised as a best practice.
    c) You can record a receipt against a purchase order even before you receive *all* the items ordered.
    d) You cannot enter the receipt of inventory items before entering the bill from the vendor.

12. When entering a bill for the purchase of inventory part items, what tab of the Enter Bills window should you use?
    a) Items
    b) Expenses
    c) Accounts
    d) Any of the above

13. Before setting up your inventory, it is a good idea to think about what products you will track as Inventory Parts because:

    a)   It is necessary to separately track *every* product you sell as an Inventory Part.

    b)   You could use Non-inventory Part items if you do not need detailed reports and inventory status information about certain products you sell.

    c)   It is better to use Inventory Part items rather than Non-inventory Part items when you really need to track the cost of a product.

    d)   Your accountant needs the detail information on Inventory Part numbers to be able to close your books for the year.

14. You can adjust the inventory by:

    a)   Adjusting the Accounts.

    b)   Adjusting the Item Quantity.

    c)   Adjusting the Inventory Valuation.

    d)   Both (b) and (c).

15. When processing a Vendor overcharge, what do you NOT want to do?

    a)   Wait for a new bill from the vendor before recording the bill in QuickBooks, if the vendor agrees to revise the bill and send you a new one.

    b)   Use the *Expenses* tab on the *Bill* to track the error, if you decide to pay the overcharge and have the vendor adjust the next bill.

    c)   Use two separate accounts when recording the overcharge and the refund or credit to keep the transactions from becoming confusing.

    d)   Contact the vendor to discuss the overage on the bill.

Completion Statements

1. The _____ _____ ___ _____ report is useful for getting a quick snapshot of each inventory part and the number of units on-hand and on-order. Also, this report gives you information about your inventory turnover, showing a *sales per week* column.

2. In order to track inventory purchases by item and to easily determine which items you have on order, use _____ _____ when you purchase inventory.

3. QuickBooks keeps a(n) _____ inventory, meaning that every purchase and every sale of inventory immediately updates all of your reports.

4. For detailed research about transactions involving inventory, use the _____ _____ or the _____ _____ _____ report.

5. The _____ _____ _____ report gives you information about the value of your inventory items on a certain date. This report shows all values and average cost of items as of the date of the report.

Inventory Problem 1

> Restore the Inventory-18Problem1.QBM file. The password to access this file is *Sleeter18*.

1. Create a new *Inventory Item* in the Item List with the following data.

Item Type	Inventory Part
Item Name	Frame 8x11 Bronze
Purchase Description	Picture Frame - 8x11 Bronze
Cost	$8.95
COGS Account	Cost of Goods Sold
Preferred Vendor	Leave blank
Sales Description	Picture Frame - 8x11 Bronze
Price	$15.99
Tax Code	Tax
Income Account	Sales
Asset Account	Inventory Asset
Reorder Point (Min)	25
Qty on Hand	Leave zero
Total Value	Leave zero
As of	Leave current date

Table 8-4 Data to create a new Item

2. Create *Purchase Order* 2019-1 dated 3/16/2019 to Ace Supply using the *Walnut Creek Class* for 50-Frame 8x11 Bronze. Leave the *Ship To* drop-down field at the top blank. Print the *Purchase Order* on blank paper.

3. On April 2, 2019, create an *Item Receipt* for 50-Frame 8x11 Bronze from Ace Supply against PO 2019-1. The product came without a bill, but the packing slip number was 698542. The total *Item Receipt* amount is $447.50.

4. On April 5, 2019, create *Invoice* 2019-106 to Jerry Perez for 10-Frame 8x11 Bronze (use list price). Use the *Walnut Creek* Class.

5. Create and print the following reports:

   a) Frame 8x11 Bronze **Item QuickReport** with the *Dates* field set to *All*

   b) **Inventory Stock Status by Item** for 3/1/2019 to 4/30/2019

   c) **Inventory Valuation Summary** as of 4/30/2019

Inventory Problem 2 (Advanced)

> Restore the Inventory-18Problem2.QBM file. The password to access this file is **Sleeter18**.

1. Create new *Inventory Items* in the *Item List* with the following data.

Item Type	Inventory Part
Item Name	Frame 8x11 Black
Purchase Description	Picture Frame - 8x11 Black
Cost	$9.95
COGS Account	Cost of Goods Sold
Preferred Vendor	Leave blank
Sales Description	Picture Frame - 8x11 Black
Price	$17.99
Tax Code	Tax
Income Account	Sales
Asset Account	Inventory Asset
Reorder Point (Min)	25
Qty on Hand	Leave zero
Total Value	Leave zero
As of	Leave current date

Table 8-5 Data for a new Inventory Part

Item Type	Inventory Part
Item Name	Frame 8x11 Gray
Purchase Description	Picture Frame - 8x11 Gray
Cost	$8.49
COGS Account	Cost of Goods Sold
Preferred Vendor	Leave blank
Sales Description	Picture Frame - 8x11 Gray
Price	$15.99
Tax Code	Tax
Income Account	Sales
Asset Account	Inventory Asset
Reorder Point (Min)	25
Qty on Hand	Leave zero
Total Value	Leave zero
As of	Leave current date

Table 8-6 Data to create a new Item

2. Create *Purchase Order* 2019-1 dated 4/6/2019 to Ace Supply using the *Walnut Creek Class* for 50-Frame 5x7, 50-Frame 8x11 Gray, and 100-Frame 8x11 Black. Leave the *Ship To* drop-down field at the top blank. The total *PO* amount is $1,527.00. Print the *Purchase Order* on blank paper.

3. Record the transactions below. On these transactions, unless you're told differently, keep all defaults on transactions for *Date*, prices, and *Sales Tax*.

   a) April 10, 2019 Create an *Item Receipt* for 25-Frame 5x7, 50-Frame 8x11 Gray, and 25-Frame 8x11 Black from Ace Supply against PO 2019-1. The product came without a bill, but the packing slip number was 3883. The total *Item Receipt* amount is $727.00.

   b) April 13, 2019 Create an *Item Receipt* for the remaining items from Ace Supply against PO 2019-1. The product came without a bill, but the packing slip number was 7662. The total *Item Receipt* amount is $800.00.

   c) April 17, 2019 Create *Invoice* 2019-106 to Ortega Services for 15-Frame 5x7 (use list price). Use the *Walnut Creek* Class. The total *Invoice* amount is $97.26.

   d) April 20, 2019 Received bill for *Item Receipt* 3883 from Ace Supply. Additional $7.50 delivery charges were added to the bill. Use the *Expenses* tab on the bill to record delivery charges (coded to *Postage and Delivery* expense) and allocate the cost to the *Walnut Creek Class*. The total *Bill* amount is $734.50. (*Hint:* Use the **Recalculate** button if necessary to adjust the *Amount Due*.)

   e) April 20, 2019 Received bill for *Item Receipt* 7662 from Ace Supply. The total *Bill* amount is $800.00.

   f) April 30, 2019 Enter an *Inventory Adjustment* for a broken Frame 5x7 item. Use the *Inventory Variance* account and the *Walnut Creek* class to record the adjustment. *Inventory Adjustment Reference* 2019-101. *Quantity on hand* is 56. The total *Value of Adjustment* is -$2.15.

4. Create and print the following reports:

   a) *Frame 5x7 Item QuickReport* with the *Dates* field set to All

   b) *Inventory Stock Status by Item* for 1/1/2019 through 4/30/2019

   c) *Inventory Valuation Summary* as of 4/30/2019

Chapter 9
Time and Billing

Topics

In this chapter, you will learn about the following topics:

> **Restore this File:**
> This chapter uses TimeBilling-18.QBW. See page 9 for more information. The password to access this file is *Sleeter18*.

QuickBooks helps you track billable expenses – or costs your company needs to pass on to a customer. Whether you need to pass the cost of an expense, an item, or employee time, QuickBooks helps you from when the expense occurs through billing the client.

Reimbursable (Billable) Expenses

QuickBooks allows you to pass expenses through to customers for reimbursement. Start by entering a transaction such as a *Bill*, *Check* or *Credit Card Charge* to record the original expense, and then assign the Customer or Job to which the expense applies.

On expense transactions, the *Billable?* option indicates that the expense will be passed through to the *Customer* or *Job* (see Figure 9-1). This checkbox only becomes active after you enter a name into the *Customer:Job* field in the *Expenses* (or *Items*) tab area of the expense transaction. Also, the *Billable?* option only appears if you code the transaction to one of the following account types:

*   Other Current Asset

*   Cost of Goods Sold

*   Expense

*   Other Expense

Figure 9-1 Billable Expense

> **Note:**
> The *Billable?* option will NOT appear if you code the expense transaction to an *Income* type of account.

Sometimes you want to assign expenses to *Customers* or *Jobs* so you can track all of the related costs, but you do not intend to pass them through for reimbursement. In this case, you can uncheck the *Billable?* option so that the line item is "non-billable."

If most or all of your expenses are going to be non-billable, you may wish to set the QuickBooks preference for *Time & Expenses* so that expenses appear as non-billable by default (and then you can change the option to "billable" on individual transactions as required). To change this preference, select the **Edit** menu and then select **Preferences**. Choose **Time & Expenses** and then select **Company Preferences**. Remove the checkmark from the box next to **Mark all expenses as billable** and then select **OK**.

COMPUTER PRACTICE

For simplicity, in this example, we'll use an expense account called *Reimbursable Expenses* to hold the expenses until they are reimbursed. However, you may want to use an *Other Current Asset* type account to hold all of your reimbursable expenses. If you're unsure about which account type to use for your reimbursable expenses, consult with your accountant.

Step 1.   Select the **Write Checks** icon on the *Banking* section of the *Home* page.

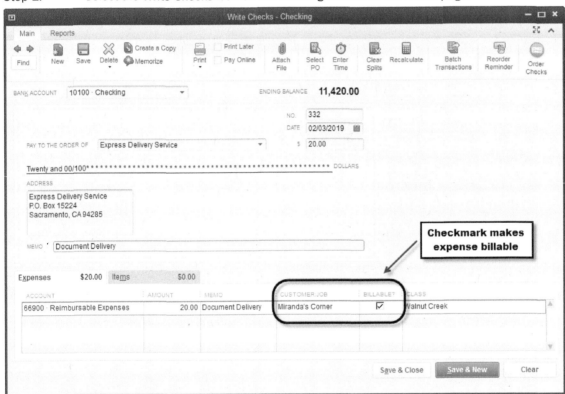

Figure 9-2 Record a reimbursable expense

Step 2.   From the *Write Checks* window, enter the *Check* shown in Figure 9-2. When you select Miranda's Corner in the *Customer:Job* column of the *Expenses* tab, the *Billable?* option appears with the checkmark already selected.

Step 3.   Click **Save & Close** to record the Check.

The next time you create an *Invoice* for the customer, you can pass the cost through to the *Invoice* by following the next steps.

Step 1.   Select the **Create Invoices** icon on the *Customers* section of the **Home** page.

Step 2.   Enter **Miranda's Corner** for the *Customer:Job* field. Once the name is entered, the message in Figure 9-3 appears to prompt you to select the expenses that you designated as billable.

Figure 9-3 Billable Time/Costs option window

Step 3.   Click **OK**.

Step 4.   The *Choose Billable Time and Costs* window opens for *Miranda's Corner* (see Figure 9-4).

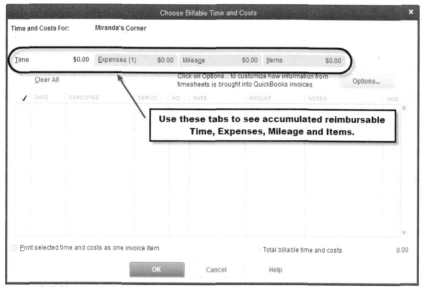

Figure 9-4 Choose Billable Time and Costs window

Step 5.   The top section of the *Choose Billable Time and Costs* screen shows four tabs where you can view pass-through expenses. The *Expenses* tab will show the billable expenses (such as the check you just wrote) that were recorded using the *Expenses* tab on checks, bills, and credit card charges.

Step 6.   Click the **Expenses** tab (see Figure 9-5).

Step 7.   Verify that **20%** is entered in the *Markup Amount or %* field.

                 The *Markup* will increase the amount due by the *Customer* to cover the costs of processing this expense. You can either enter a static dollar amount or a percentage that will change depending on the amount. *Default Markup* can be set in the *Time & Expense Company Preference*.

Step 8.   Enter **Expense Markup** in the Markup Account field.

Step 9.   In the middle section of the *Expenses* tab, click a checkmark in the far left column on the line for **Express Delivery Service** to pass the expense, with the 20% markup, to the Miranda's Corner *Invoice*.

Step 10.   Select the **Print selected time and costs as one invoice item** option. Then click **OK**.

                 When you select this option, QuickBooks prints all reimbursable expenses on a single line in the body of the *Invoice* rather than listing each expense separately. You'll always see the *details* of the reimbursable expenses, including the markup, on the screen even if you chose *Print selected costs as one invoice Item*.

If an expense appears that you don't need to bill to the customer, check the Hide column to change the billable status on the original check, bill or credit card entry. This does not delete the original expense but simply unchecks the Billable? column.

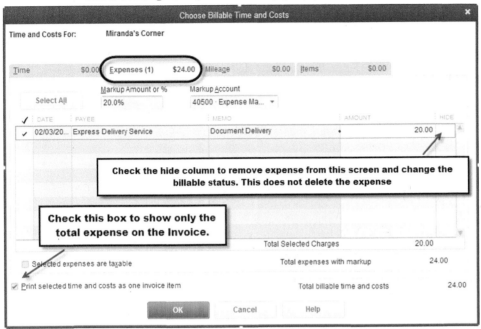

Figure 9-5 Expenses tab of the Choose Billable Time and Costs window

Step 11.   Once you are returned to the *Invoice*, enter the **Template** and **Class** and verify the *Date*, and *Invoice #* as shown in Figure 9-6. The *Invoice* now includes the reimbursable expense.

Step 12.   To see what the *Invoice* will look like when you print it, click **Print,** and then click **Preview** (see Figure 9-7).

Step 13.   When you are finished reviewing, click **Close** in the *Print Preview* window, and click **Save & Close** to record the *Invoice*.

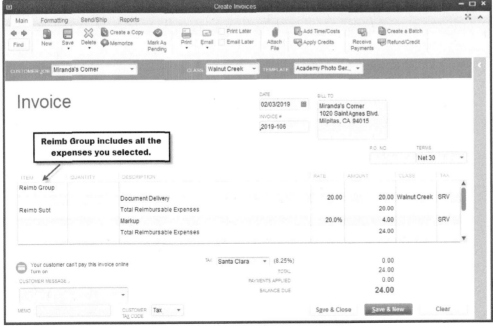

Figure 9-6 Reimbursable expenses shown on an Invoice

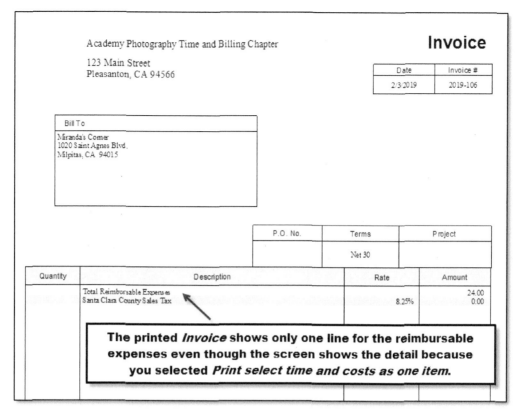

Figure 9-7 Print Preview of invoiced billable expenses

The completed example of pass-through expenses shows on your Profit & Loss statement with the date range set from 2/3/2019 to 2/3/2019, so as to include only the transaction entered earlier in this chapter as shown in Figure 9-8. Notice the markup amount appears in the Expense Markup account. The Reimbursable Expenses account shows zero here. During the pass-through process, QuickBooks increased and decreased the same expense account.

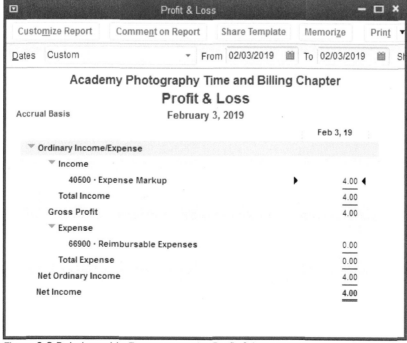

Figure 9-8 Reimbursable Expenses on the Profit & Loss report

> **The Accounting Behind the Scenes:**
> The *Reimbursable Expenses* account has a zero balance because QuickBooks increased (debited) the balance when you recorded the *Check* shown in Figure 9-2 and then decreased (credited) the account when you recorded the *Invoice* shown in Figure 9-6.

Sometimes it is more appropriate to track reimbursable expenses in one account and the reimbursements in another account. For example, you could record all reimbursable expenses in the expense account called "Reimbursable Expenses," and you could track the reimbursements in an income account called "Expenses Reimbursed." For QuickBooks to handle reimbursements in this way, you will need to make changes to your *Time & Expenses Company Preferences*.

> **Note:**
> Ask your accountant if you should treat reimbursements as income before making these changes to your company's QuickBooks file.

COMPUTER PRACTICE

Step 1.   Select the **Edit** menu and choose **Preferences**.

Step 2.   Select **Time & Expenses** on the left icon bar (you may have to scroll down on the left side of the *Preferences* window to access this selection).

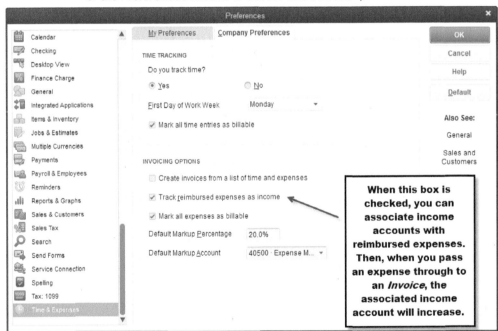

Figure 9-9 Time & Expenses Company Preferences

Step 3.   Select the **Company Preferences** tab.

Step 4.   Notice that the box next to *Track reimbursed expenses as income* is checked.

Step 5.   Notice the 20% in the *Default Markup Percentage* field is preselected. This field sets the default markup percentage for pass-through expenses.

Step 6.   Notice that Expense Markup is selected as the *Default Markup Account*

Step 7.   Click **OK** to close the window.

Now you need to associate each reimbursable expense account with an appropriate income account. You should note that for each reimbursable expense account you create, you will need to create a separate income account. You cannot have multiple reimbursable expense accounts that tie to only one income account.

Step 1.   Display the *Chart of Accounts* list and select the **Reimbursable Expenses** account.

Step 2.   Select the **Edit** menu and then select **Edit Account.** Alternatively, select the **Account** button at the bottom of the *Chart of Accounts* window and choose **Edit Account**, or press **Ctrl+E.**

Step 3.   The *Edit Account* window opens (see Figure 9-10). Click **Track reimbursed expenses in Income Acct.** and then select the **Expenses Reimbursed** income account from the *Income Account* field drop-down menu.

Step 4.   Click **Save & Close** to save your changes. Close the Chart of Accounts.

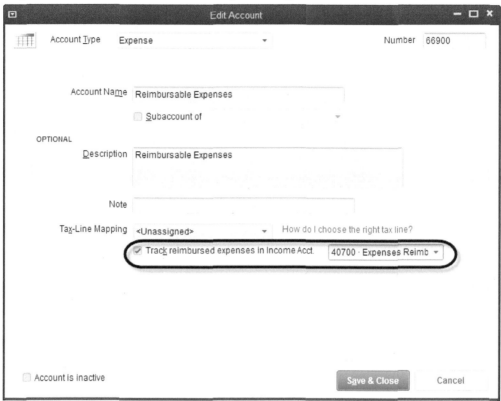

Figure 9-10 Edit the Reimbursable Expenses account

> **The Accounting Behind the Scenes:**
> Now, when you post an expense to *Reimbursable Expenses* and pass the expense through on an *Invoice*, QuickBooks will increase the *Expenses Reimbursed* income account. From our previous example, the results would be as seen in Figure 9-11. Notice the Net Income is the same in both examples but the Income and Expense accounts are tracked differently.
>
> **Important accounting consideration:**
> If you used an existing expense account in a closed accounting period (a period for which you have filed tax returns or prepared financial statements), do not select the **Track Reimbursed Expenses in Income Acct.** option on that account. Doing so will cause discrepancies between your QuickBooks reports and the company's tax returns and/or financial statements. Instead, create a new account for tracking reimbursable expenses and make the change to that account.

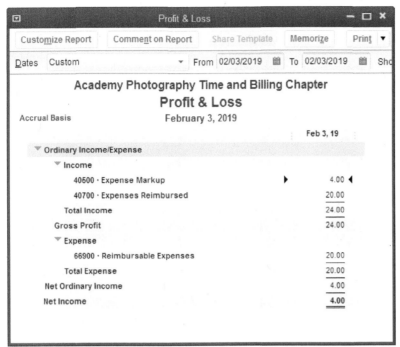

Figure 9-11 Profit & Loss report with separate income and expenses for reimbursable expenses

Using Two-Sided Items

QuickBooks allows you to use the same *Item* on expense forms (e.g., *Checks* and *Bills*) and sales forms (e.g., *Invoices* and *Sales Receipts*). When you use *Items* to track both expenses and revenue, you can generate reports showing the profitability of each Item.

> **Note:**
> **Two Sided Item** is an *Item* used on both types of forms (expenses and sales) and is commonly called a "Two-Sided Item" because the *Item* setup screen includes purchase information on the left side (expense account field) and sales information on the right (income account field).

Possible uses of Two-Sided Items include:

- **Reimbursable Expenses:** If you have numerous reimbursable expenses and you need detailed reports (such as one showing which expenses have not been reimbursed), or if you want the ability to summarize Billable costs on *Invoices* by category, you may want to create a two-sided reimbursable expense. To summarize by category, you can create two-sided *Other Charge Items* to designate categories of expenses (e.g., transportation, clerical, or material expenses). Use these *Items* on both expense transactions and sales forms as described in the *Reimbursable (Billable) Expenses* section beginning on page 317.

- **Custom Ordered Parts:** If you sell custom-ordered parts, you might want to create two-sided *Non-Inventory Part Items* to track both the purchase and the sale of each part. Doing so will show you which of the sales were profitable, and by how much.

- **Subcontracted Labor:** If you hire subcontractors, you probably want to use two-sided *Service Items* to track both the expense and the revenue for the work they perform. Then, you can find out which subcontracted services are profitable, and by how much.

Our first example of the use of two-sided Items is for tracking custom orders.

Tracking Custom Orders

If you sell products that you don't hold in inventory, you can use QuickBooks "two-sided Items" function to track the revenue and costs automatically for each *Item*.

COMPUTER PRACTICE

Step 1. Open the *Item List* and select **New** from the *Item* menu (or use **Ctrl+N** to access the *New Item* window).

Step 2. Choose **Non-inventory Part** and enter the *Custom Camera* Item as displayed in Figure 9-12. Make sure you select the checkbox next to *This item is used in assemblies or is purchased for a specific customer:job*.

When you select this option, QuickBooks provides the following additional fields: *Description on Purchase Transactions, Cost, Expense Account* and *Preferred Vendor*.

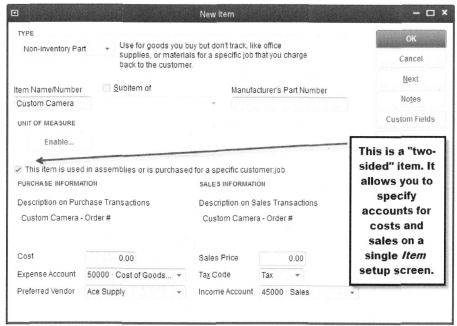

Figure 9-12 A "two-sided" Non-inventory Part Item

The Accounting Behind the Scenes:
When you use a two-sided Item on expense forms, QuickBooks increases (debits) the Expense account you enter in the *Expense Account* field. When you use a two-sided Item on sales forms, QuickBooks increases (credits) the Income account you enter in the *Income Account* field.

Step 3. Notice that the *Cost* and *Sales Price* for this *Item* are both **0.00**.

Custom-ordered parts will have a different cost and sales price every time you sell them. If you enter cost and sales price amounts in the original item, you'll need to override the numbers for each individual purchase or sale. For this reason, it's best to just leave them zero.

Step 4. Complete the fields as shown in Figure 9-12, and click **OK** to close this window.

Tip:
Once you set up the *Custom Camera* Item, you can use the *Item* for all special orders of cameras, regardless of the make or model. You can override the description of the *Item* to each time you use it on a transaction.

After creating the two-sided *Non-Inventory Part*, you are now ready to use the *Item* on expense forms.

Step 1.   Select the **Purchase Orders** icon on the *Vendors* section of the *Home* page, or choose **Create Purchase Orders** from the *Vendors* drop-down menu.

Step 2.   Prepare a **Purchase Order** as shown in Figure 9-13.

Notice that QuickBooks uses the default description you entered when setting up the *Item*. Add the number shown in the *P.O. No.* field *2019-101* to the end of this description. Enter *Custom Camera – Order #2019-101* in the *Memo* field. Choose **No** when asked whether you want to update the *Custom Camera Item* with a new cost.

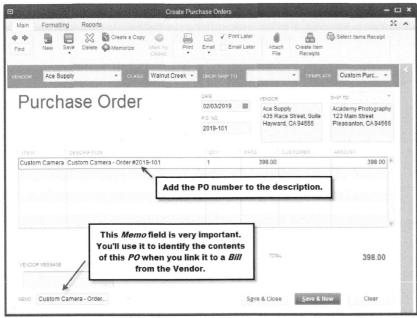

Figure 9-13 A Purchase Order for a two-sided Non-inventory Part

> **Tip:**
> Make sure you enter the description in the *Memo* field so that you'll be able to identify the *Purchase Order* in the list of *Open Purchase Orders* when you receive the *Bill*.
> **Tip:**
> Use the Windows copy and paste commands to duplicate the description to the Memo field at the bottom of the *Purchase Order* and other forms. To do so, highlight the completed description on the *PO* form and press **Ctrl+C**. Then click in the *Memo* field and press **Ctrl+V**.

Step 3.   Click **Save & Close** to record the *Purchase Order*.

When you receive a bill from the Vendor, record it as follows:

Step 1.   Choose the **Enter Bills** icon on the *Vendor* section of the *Home* page, or choose **Enter Bills** from the *Vendors* drop-down menu.

Step 2.   On the *Bill*, enter **Ace Supply** in the *Vendor* field. Then press **Tab**.

Step 3.   Because there are open *Purchase Orders* for Ace Supply, QuickBooks displays the message shown in Figure 9-14. Click **Yes**.

Figure 9-14 Open POs Exist message

Step 4.   Select *PO 2019-101* by placing a checkmark in the column to the left of the date and click **OK**.

If you had several open *Purchase Orders* for this Vendor, each would appear in the list shown in Figure 9-15.

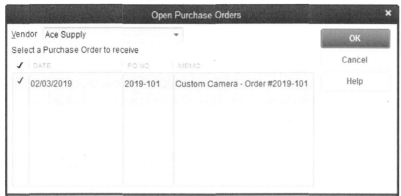

Figure 9-15 Select open Purchase Order from the list

Step 5.   QuickBooks automatically fills out the *Bill* with the data from your *PO*. Continue filling out the rest of the fields on the *Bill* as shown in Figure 9-16.

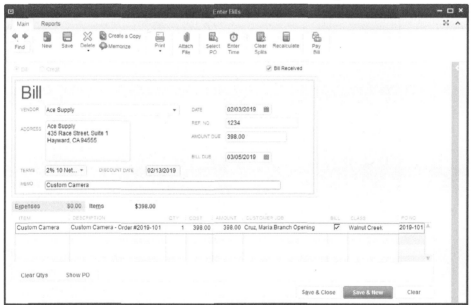

Figure 9-16 QuickBooks automatically fills in the details of the Bill.

Step 6.   Verify that *Cruz, Maria:Branch Opening* is in the *Customer:Job* column of the *Items* tab.

Step 7.   Click **Save & Close** to record the *Bill*.

> **The Accounting Behind the Scenes**
> This *Bill* increases (credits) Accounts Payable and increases (debits) Cost of Goods Sold. Cost of Goods Sold is the account in the *Expense Account* field of the *Custom Camera* Item.

When you create an *Invoice* for this job, you can pass the cost of the *Custom Camera* Item through to the customer's *Invoice* and mark it up.

Step 1.   Select the **Create Invoices** icon on the *Customer* section of the *Home* page. Use the **Academy Photo Service Invoice** template.

Step 2.   Enter **Cruz, Maria:Branch Opening** for the *Customer:Job* field.

Step 3.   Click **OK** on the *Billable Time/Costs* reminder message.

Step 4.   The *Choose Billable Time and Costs* screen opens for Maria Cruz's Branch Opening job. Select the **Items** tab.

Step 5.   Click the far left column on the first line to select the **Custom Camera** Item (see Figure 9-17). Then click **OK**.

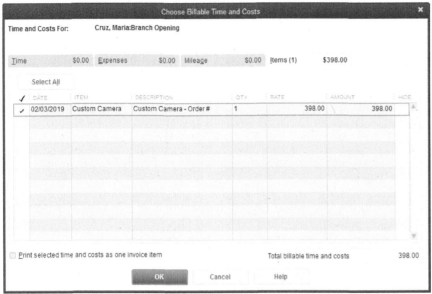

Figure 9-17 Select the Custom Camera Item.

Step 6.   When you click OK, QuickBooks adds the *Custom Camera* Item to the customer's *Invoice*. Enter the *Invoice* information as shown in Figure 9-18.

Step 7.   Complete the description so it reads **Custom Camera Order #2019-101** and copy this information to the *Memo* field.

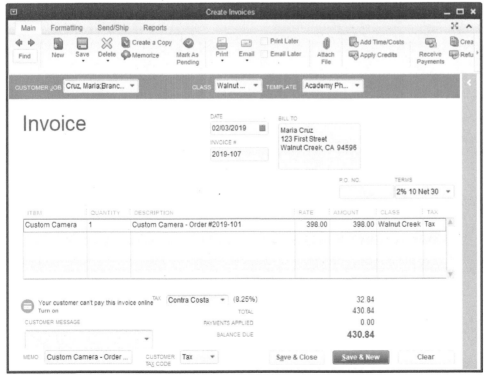

Figure 9-18 The Custom Camera Item now shows in the Customer's Invoice.

Since the *Custom Camera* Item shown in Figure 9-12 doesn't include an amount in the *Cost* field, the *Item* passes through at the cost amount recorded on the *Bill* shown in Figure 9-16, in this case $398.00.

To record the markup you'll need to adjust the price that shows on the *Invoice* manually. You can use the *QuickMath* function that allows you to do calculations without using your calculator. In this example, the *Custom Camera* cost was $398. Using *QuickMath*, we'll mark this *Item* up by 20%.

Step 8.   Place the cursor in the *Rate* column on the *Invoice* (anywhere in this field).

Step 9.   Press the ***** (asterisk) key on the keyboard to access the *QuickMath* multiplication function. Since your cursor was in the *Rate* field when you pressed the asterisk, QuickBooks copies the first number ($398.00) onto the adding machine tape (see Figure 9-19).

Step 10.   Enter *1.2* (multiply by 120%) and press **Tab** to insert the adjusted (calculated) amount into the *Rate* column.

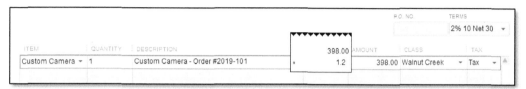

Figure 9-19 The QuickMath adding machine tape

> **Note:**
> The asterisk (*) opens the QuickMath feature because QuickBooks recognizes the asterisk as a multiplication key. You can also access QuickMath by typing a plus (+), minus (-), or back slash (/) to add, subtract or divide by any number, respectively.

Step 11.   The *Invoice* now includes the adjusted amount of **$477.60** (see Figure 9-20). Press **Tab** again to refresh the *Amount* and *Balance Due* fields. You may receive a *Did you know...* window, which you can read and then click **OK**.

Step 12.   Click **Save & Close** to save the *Invoice*.

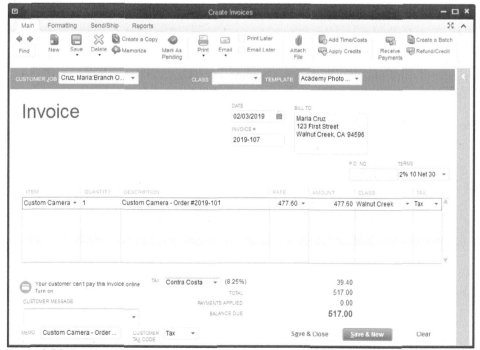

Figure 9-20 Final Invoice including the markup on the Custom Camera Item

Using Service Items to Track Subcontracted Labor

If you hire subcontractors, you may want to create a two-sided *Service Item* for each subcontracted service. This will allow you to pass subcontractor costs through to *Invoices* and it will allow you to create reports showing the profitability of your subcontracted services.

COMPUTER PRACTICE

In this example, we'll use a two-sided *Service Item* for photographer services that are subcontracted to East Bay Photographers. The *Item* is already set up.

Step 1.   Open the *Item List* and double click the **Photographer** Item. This will open the *Edit Item* screen for this Item (see Figure 9-21).

Figure 9-21 A two-sided Service Item for tracking subcontracted labor

Step 2.   Notice that the box entitled *This service is used in assemblies or is performed by a subcontractor or partner* is selected.

Just as in the last example, when this box is clicked, QuickBooks opens the *Purchase* side of the *Item*, revealing fields for entering the *Description on Purchase (and Sales) Transactions, Cost, Expense Account, Preferred Vendor, Sales Price, Tax Code,* and *Income Account.*

Step 3.   Click **OK** to close the *Photographer* Item.

When you enter a bill, write a check, or enter credit charges for a subcontractor, use the *Photographer* Item to record the expense.

Step 4.   Select the **Enter Bills** icon on the *Vendors* section of the *Home* page.

Step 5.   Enter a *Bill* for **East Bay Photographers** as shown in Figure 9-22.

Select the *Items* tab to complete the form. The checkmark in the *Billable?* column to the right of the *Customer:Job* column indicates that each line of the *Bill* is billable (i.e., available for pass-through).

Step 6.   Click **Save & Close** to record the *Bill*.

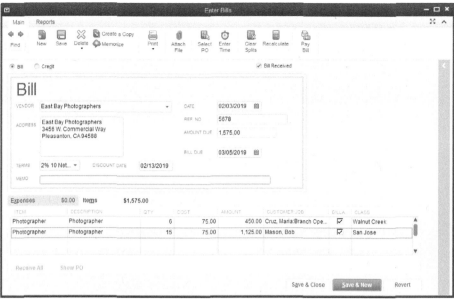

Figure 9-22 Enter a Bill for subcontracted services.

The next time you create an *Invoice* for Bob Mason or Maria Cruz's Branch Opening Job, the *Photographer* Service Item will show on the *Choose Billable Time and Costs* screen.

Step 1. Select the **Create Invoices** icon on the *Customers* section of the *Home* page.

Step 2. Enter **Cruz, Maria:Branch Opening** in the *Customer:Job* field.

Step 3. Click **OK** on the *Billable Time/Costs* reminder message. The *Choose Billable Time and Costs* screen opens.

Step 4. Click the **Items** tab. Figure 9-23 shows the *Photographer* Service Item you recorded on the bill shown in Figure 9-22. Notice that the *Rate* column shows $125.00/hour, not the purchase price of $75.00/hour. The $125.00 amount comes from the *Sales Price* field on the *Item* setup screen (see Figure 9-21).

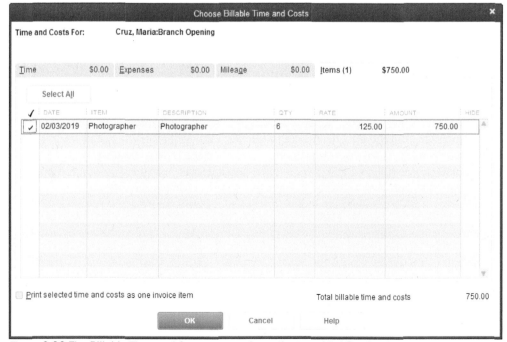

Figure 9-23 The Billable Time and Costs screen shows the two-sided Service Item.

Step 5.   Click the far left column on the first line to select the *Photographer* Item (see Figure 9-23). Then click **OK**.

               QuickBooks adds the Photographer Item in the body of the *Invoice* as shown in Figure 9-24.

Step 6.   Once you are returned to the *Invoice*, enter the information so that your Invoice matches Figure 9-24.

Step 7.   Click **Save & Close** to record the *Invoice*.

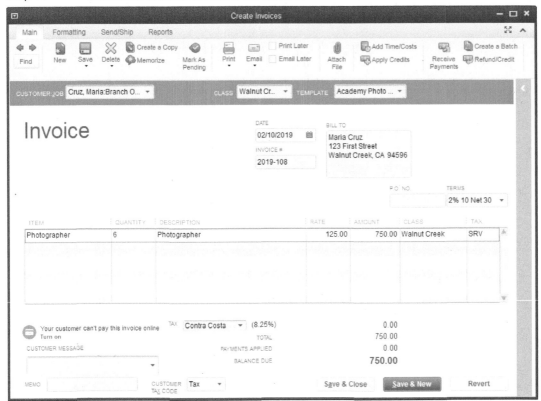

Figure 9-24 The Invoice with the subcontracted service passed-through.

> **Another Way:**
> If you want to track subcontractors' time, you can record timesheets for each subcontractor (being sure to mark the transactions as *Billable*) just as you do with your employees. You can then pass the time information through to the *Invoice* instead of passing the expense from the *Bill*. In this case, when you later enter the Vendor name in the *Bill* or *Check* window, QuickBooks will prompt you to use the time you entered in the timesheet. If you choose to do so, the *Item* field will populate with the *Item* you entered from the timesheets. This time will come through with a non-billable status which is correct.

Unbilled Costs by Job Report

Create an *Unbilled Costs by Job* report to view all of the billable expenses and *Items* that you haven't passed through to *Invoices*.

COMPUTER PRACTICE

Step 1.   Select the **Reports** menu, choose *Jobs, Time & Mileage*, and then choose *Unbilled Costs by Job*. Review this report.

Step 2.   Close the report.

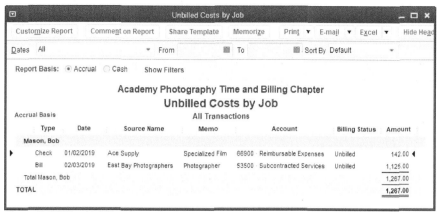

Figure 9-25 The Unbilled Costs by Job report

Billable Time

If you enter timesheet information into QuickBooks that includes a *Customer* or *Job* name, you can pass the time through to the Customer's *Invoice*. This example shows how to pass billable hours on timesheets through to *Invoices*.

The time tracking feature in QuickBooks is quite simple on the surface, but very powerful for streamlining businesses that pay hourly employees through QuickBooks Payroll, or for businesses that provide time-based services to customers.

The time tracking feature allows you to track how much time each employee, owner, partner, or subcontractor spends working on each *Job*. In addition, you can track which service the person performs and to which *Job* and/or *Class* the time should apply. Then, once you record timesheet information, you can use it to calculate paychecks and create *Invoices* for the billable time.

Activating Time Tracking in QuickBooks

Before you can use the Time Tracking feature, you must activate Time Tracking in the *Company* tab of the *Time & Expense Preferences* window.

COMPUTER PRACTICE

To activate the Time Tracking feature, follow these steps:

Step 1.   Select the **Edit** menu and then select **Preferences.** Select the **Time & Expenses** item on the left and click the **Company Preferences** tab (see Figure 9-26).

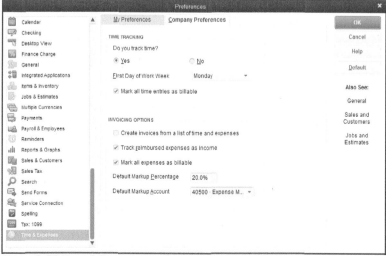

Figure 9-26 Time & Expenses preferences

Step 2.   Confirm that **Yes** is already selected under *Do you track time?*

When working with your company's data file you will need to turn on Time Tracking by clicking Yes either on the window shown in Figure 9-26 or during the file setup.

Step 3.   Confirm that **Monday** is selected in the *First Day of Work Week* field. Monday is the first day that QuickBooks will display on the *Weekly Timesheet.*

Step 4.   Click **OK** to close Preferences.

Entering Time on Timesheets

To track your employees' time, you'll enter activities on timesheets. An activity is the time spent by a single person performing a single service on a single date. For example, an attorney might enter an activity on the timesheet to record a phone conversation that she will bill to one of her clients. When an hourly employee performs a service for a customer you should include the *Customer* or *Job* name in the time activity. Each activity is recorded on a separate line of the timesheet, and you can mark each time activity as *Billable* if you wish to pass that activity through to a customer's *Invoice.*

A *Weekly Timesheet* is a record of several activities performed during a one-week period by a single employee, owner, or subcontractor. Enter *Weekly Timesheet* information using the *Weekly Timesheet* window.

Timesheets are non-posting and do not affect the Balance Sheet.

COMPUTER PRACTICE

To enter time activities, follow these steps:

Step 1.   Select the **Employees** menu, select **Enter Time**, and then select **Use Weekly Timesheet**.

Alternatively, you can click the **Enter Time** icon in the *Employee Center.*

Step 2.   Enter **Mike Mazuki** in the *Name* field.

> **Note:**
> If you need to enter the same activities for multiple employees, you can select *Multiple Names* from the *Name* field. This will open the *Select Employee, Vendor or Other Name* window, where you can check multiple names. Any activities listed in the *Weekly Timesheet*, including billable activities, will apply to each *Employee* or other *Name* you selected.

Step 3.   Click the **Calendar** icon and choose *January 7, 2019*.

Step 4.   Enter each activity on a separate line in the timesheet as shown in Figure 9-27. Be sure to select the *Kumar* job for Anderson Wedding Planners and the *Branch Opening* job for Maria Cruz in the *Customer:Job* column.

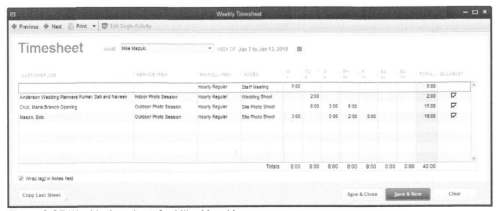

Figure 9-27 Weekly timesheet for Mike Mazuki

Step 5.   Click **Save & Close** to record the timesheet activity.

> **Note:**
> If you plan to use timesheets to create paychecks, you should record all of the time for each employee, including non-billable time (e.g., sick, vacation, and administrative time).

Printing Timesheets

In some companies, you may need to print several copies of your employees' timesheets for review by owners or managers.

COMPUTER PRACTICE

To print timesheets, follow these steps:

Step 1.   From the *File* menu, select **Print Forms** and then select **Timesheets**.

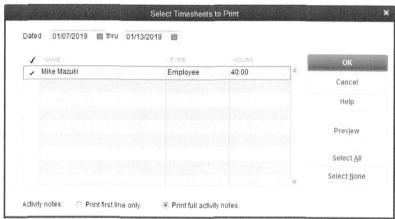

Figure 9-28 Select Timesheets to Print window

Step 2.   Set the dates to *1/7/2019* through *1/13/2019* (see Figure 9-28).

Step 3.   Select **Print full activity notes** at the bottom of the window and then click **OK** (see Figure 9-28).

Step 4.   Click **Print** on the *Print Timesheets* window (see Figure 9-29).

Timesheet

Printed on:

Name: Mike Mazuki   Jan 7 to Jan 13, 2019

Customer:Job	Service Item	Payroll Item	Notes	M	Tu	W	Th	F	Sa	Su	Total	Bill*
		Hourly Regular	Staff Meeting	5:00							5:00	N
Anderson Wedding Planner:Kumar, Sati and Naveen	Indoor Photo Session	Hourly Regular	Wedding Shoot		2:00						2:00	B
Cruz, Maria:Branch Opening	Outdoor Photo Session	Hourly Regular	Site Photo Shoot		6:00	3:00	6:00				15:00	B
Mason, Bob	Outdoor Photo Session	Hourly Regular	Site Photo Shoot	3:00		5:00	2:00	8:00			18:00	B
			Totals	8:00	8:00	8:00	8:00	8:00	0:00	0:00	40:00	

Signature _____

Figure 9-29 Printed timesheet for Mike Mazuki

Invoicing Customers for Time

You can also pass timesheet information through to *Invoices*. When you mark time activities as *Billable*, QuickBooks allows you to transfer the time information onto the next *Invoice* for that *Customer*.

COMPUTER PRACTICE

To create an *Invoice* to a *Customer*, and pass the timesheet data onto the *Invoice*, follow these steps:

Step 1.   From the *Customers* menu, select **Create Invoices** or click **Create Invoices** on the *Customers* section of the *Home* page.

Step 2.   In the *Customer:Job* section select **Cruz, Maria:Branch Opening**.

Step 3.   QuickBooks displays the *Billable Time/Costs* window. Click **OK** to continue.

Step 4.   If it is not already selected, click the **Time** tab in the *Choose Billable Time and Costs* window (Figure 9-30).

Step 5.   Click **Select All** to use all of the time activity for this Customer.

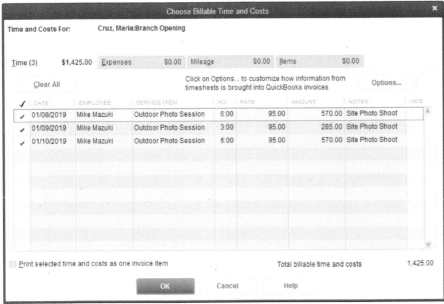

Figure 9-30 Billable time for Maria Cruz's Branch Opening job

Step 6.   Click **Options** to modify the way time activities are passed through to *Invoices*.

This window allows you to change the way time is transferred onto *Invoices*. The default setting is shown below, and you'll probably want to leave the setting alone. However, you can modify it to use either the information from the *Notes* field on the employee's timesheet or the information from the *Description* field of the *Service Items*. This information will show in the *Description* column of the completed *Invoice*. If you click *Combine activities with the same Service Item and rate*, your *Invoices* will not show any *Notes* from individual time records.

Figure 9-31 Options for Transferring Billable Time window

Step 7.   Keep the existing radio buttons (*Enter a separate line on the invoice for each activity* and *Transfer activity notes*) selected. Click **OK** to close the *Options for Transferring Billable Time* window. Click **OK** to close the *Choose Billable Time and Costs* window to transfer the time to the *Invoice*.

Step 8.   The *Invoice* now shows the time activity from Mike Mazuki's timesheets. Enter **Walnut Creek** in the *Class* field and **2/10/2019** for the date so your *Invoice* matches Figure 9-32.

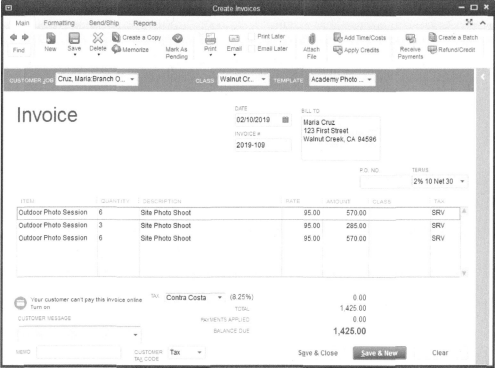

Figure 9-32 Invoice with billable time passed through

> **Note:**
> After you post timesheet information to paychecks and *Invoices*, the timesheet will affect income (because of the *Invoice*), expenses (because of the paycheck), and job cost reports (because of the job information on both the paycheck and the *Invoice*).

Step 9.   Click **Save & Close** to record the *Invoice*.

Making Activities Billable Again

After you pass *Time, Expenses,* or *Items* through to an *Invoice*, QuickBooks removes the checkmark in the *Billable* column of the original *Timesheet, Bill, Check* or *Credit Card Charge* entry and replaces it with a small gray *Invoice* icon. If you void or delete an *Invoice* that contains billable time or items, you'll need to go back to the original time activity or purchase transaction and click the gray icon in the *Billable* column to change the time activity or expenses to billable again.

> **Note:**
> When you transfer time activities onto an *Invoice*, QuickBooks changes the billable status of the time activities to "billed." However, if you void or delete the *Invoice*, QuickBooks **does not automatically** change the status backed to "unbilled."

> **Tip:**
> If you have billable time, cost, or item activity that you wish to clear from your unbilled reports (e.g., Unbilled Costs by Job), you can pass the time through to an *Invoice*, save the *Invoice*, and then delete the *Invoice*. This method is much faster than editing each billable item, cost, or time activity individually.

COMPUTER PRACTICE

To make time activities billable again, edit each time activity as described in the following steps. Note that usually the *Invoice* would first be cancelled, but we will not do that for this example.

Step 1.   Select the **Employees** menu, select **Enter Time**, and then select **Use Weekly Timesheet**.

Step 2.   Enter **Mike Mazuki** in the *Name* field.

Step 3.   Click the **Calendar** icon and choose *January 7, 2019*.

Because you already passed the time for Maria Cruz's Branch Opening Job through to an *Invoice*, QuickBooks replaced the *Billable?* checkmark with an *Invoice* icon on the timesheet activity for this *Job* (see Figure 9-33).

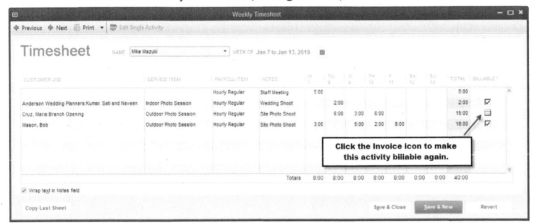

Figure 9-33 Timesheet for Mike Mazuki showing that the time for Maria Cruz's Job has been billed

Step 4.   Click the *Invoice* icon in the *Billable?* column to make the time activity for the Branch Opening *Job* billable again.

Step 5.   Click **Yes** on *Billing Status* window shown in Figure 9-34.

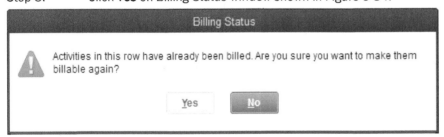

Figure 9-34 Billing Status window

Step 6.   Click **Save & Close** on the *Weekly Timesheet* window to save your changes.

Tracking an Owner's or Partner's Time

In some businesses, owners and partners do not receive paychecks, but they still need to track their time activity, record the labor costs to specific *Jobs*, and then pass the time through to their Customers' *Invoices*.

COMPUTER PRACTICE

To track an owner or partner's time for billing purposes, follow these steps:

Step 1.   Display the *Other Names* list by selecting the **Lists** menu and then selecting **Other Names List**.

Step 2.   Select **New** from the *Other Names* menu at the bottom of the *Other Names List* window.

Step 3.   Create an *Other Name* record for Vern Black, the owner of Academy Photography as shown in Figure 9-35.

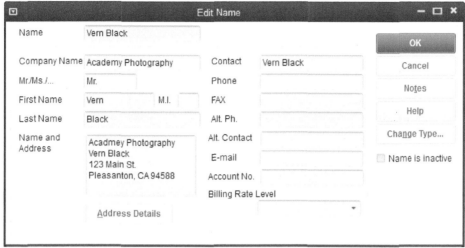

Figure 9-35 Other Name record for owner Vern Black

Step 4.   Click **OK** to save Vern Black's record, and then close the *Other Names* list.

Step 5.   Open the **Weekly Timesheet** window and enter the timesheet activity for Vern Black as shown in Figure 9-36.

Figure 9-36 Time activity for Vern Black

Step 6.   Click **Save & Close** to record the timesheet activity.

Step 7.   To pass this time through to an *Invoice* for the *Customer*, open the *Create Invoices* window and enter **Maria Cruz: Branch Opening** in the *Customer:Job* field. Click **OK** in the *Billable Time/Costs* window.

Step 8.   If needed, click the **Time** tab in the *Choose Billable Time and Costs* window (see Figure 9-37). Notice that QuickBooks shows the time for Vern Black as well as the timesheet activity for Mike Mazuki that you made billable again on the *Weekly Timesheet* window shown in Figure 9-33.

Step 9.   Click **Select All** and then click **OK** to transfer the timesheet information through to the Customer's *Invoice* (see Figure 9-37).

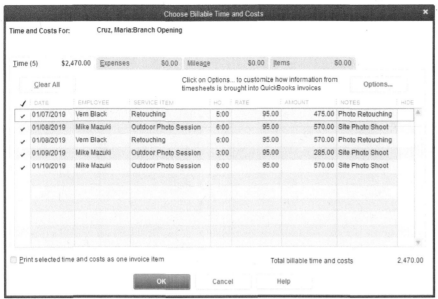

Figure 9-37 Billable Time and Costs window including owner's time

Step 10.   Enter the **Class** at the top of the *Invoice* and verify that your *Invoice* matches Figure 9-38.

Step 11.   Click **Save & Close** to record the *Invoice*.

Step 12.   The *Recording Transaction* window displays that Maria Cruz is over her credit limit. Click **Yes**.

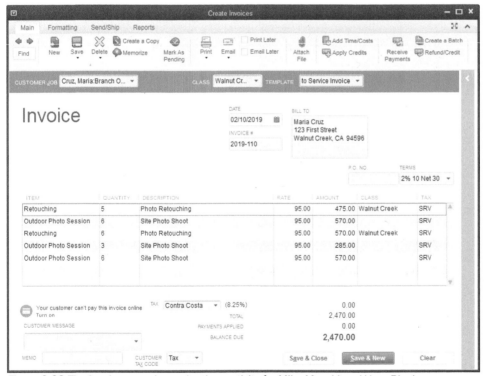

Figure 9-38 The Invoice now shows the time activity for Mike Mazuki and Vern Black.

> **Note:**
> You will not usually "pay" the owner for their time because owners generally take a "draw" (a check coded to the Owner's Drawing account) instead of getting paid through payroll. Therefore, the timesheet information for Vern Black will not get recorded as labor costs on Maria Cruz's Branch Opening *Job*.

Time Reports

There are several reports that help you summarize and track time activities.

Time by Name Report

The *Time by Name* report shows how many hours each employee, owner, or partner worked for each *Customer* or *Job*.

COMPUTER PRACTICE

To create the *Time by Name* report, follow these steps:

Step 1.   From the *Reports* menu, select **Jobs, Time & Mileage**, and then select **Time by Name**.

Step 2.   Set the date range for the report to *1/1/2019* through *1/31/2019* (see Figure 9-39). The *No job assigned* lines represent administrative (non job-specific) time. If you prefer, you can create a *Customer* record for your own company and bill your administrative time to that *Customer.* You would then have the additional option of creating *Jobs* to track various types of administrative time (e.g., marketing, travel, filing, staff meetings, etc.).

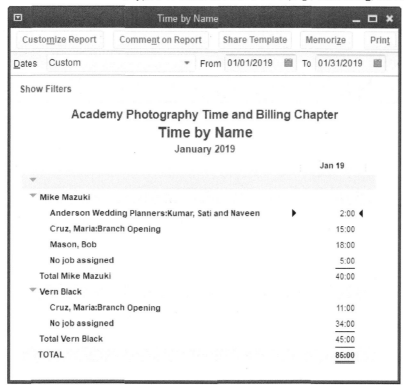

Figure 9-39 Time by Name report

Step 3.   Click the **Customize Report** button in the upper left corner of the *Time by Name* report window.

Step 4.   Click the checkbox next to the *Billed* and *Unbilled* options in the *Modify Report* window (see Figure 9-40). Click **OK**.

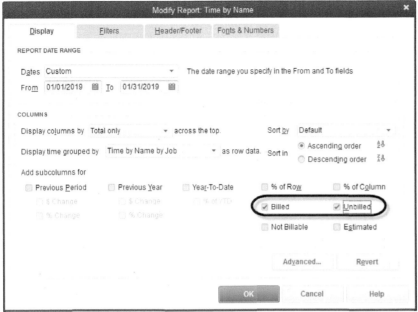

Figure 9-40 Modify the Time by Name report to include Billed and Unbilled columns.

Step 5.   The *Time by Name* report now differentiates between the *Billed* and *Unbilled* time.

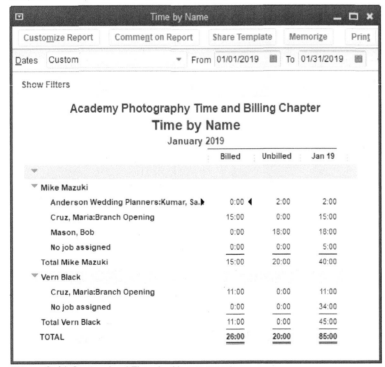

Figure 9-41 Customized Time by Name report

Step 6.   Close the report. Do not memorize it.

Time by Job Detail Report

The *Time by Job Detail* report shows the detail of each *Service Item*, totaled by Customer or Job.

COMPUTER PRACTICE

Step 1.   From the *Reports* menu, select **Jobs, Time & Mileage**, and then select **Time by Job Detail**.

Step 2.   Set the date range to *1/1/2019* through *1/31/2019*.

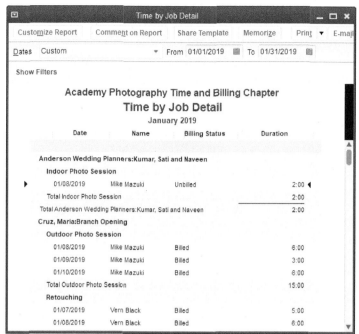

Figure 9-42 Upper portion of Time by Job Detail report

Time by Item Report

The *Time by Item* report shows the detail of each Customer, totaled by *Service Item*.

COMPUTER PRACTICE

To create a *Time by Item* report, follow these steps:

Step 1. From the *Reports* menu, select **Jobs, Time & Mileage,** and then select **Time by Item.**

Step 2. Set the date range to *1/1/2019* through *1/31/2019*.

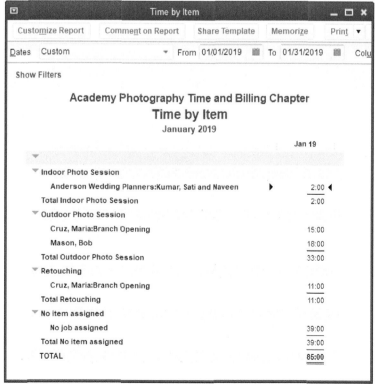

Figure 9-43 Time by Item report

Step 3.   Close all open reports and do not memorize them.

Vehicle Mileage Tracking

QuickBooks has a Vehicle Mileage Tracker that allows you to track vehicle mileage, post mileage to *Invoices*, and run reports to assist with tax preparation.

To set up mileage tracking, you'll need to create one or more *Items* and at least one Vehicle in the Vehicle list.

> **Note:** You cannot use Vehicle Mileage Tracking to reimburse your employees for mileage on their paycheck, a bill or a check.

COMPUTER PRACTICE

Step 1.   Create an *Other Charge Item* called **Mileage** with the information shown in Figure 9-44. Set the *Expense Account* to Automobile Expense and the *Income Account* to Expenses Reimbursed. In the *Sales Price* field, enter the amount per mile you will bill your customers. Click **OK** to save the *Item*.

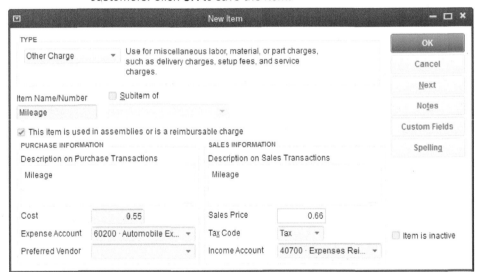

Figure 9-44 Create an Other Charge Item for passing mileage costs through to Customers

Step 2.   From the *Company* menu select **Enter Vehicle Mileage**.

Step 3.   Select **Add New** from the *Vehicle* drop-down list (see Figure 9-45).

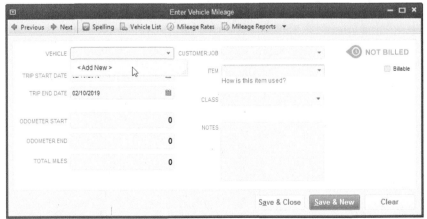

Figure 9-45 Add New Vehicle to Vehicle List

Step 4. The *New Vehicle* window opens. In the *Vehicle* and *Description* fields, enter **2015 Prius** (see Figure 9-46). Then click **OK** to save the entry.

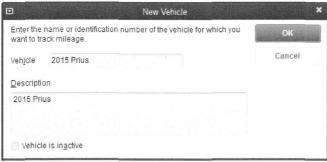

Figure 9-46 New Vehicle window

This creates a new item on the *Vehicle* list. See Figure 9-47.

You can access the *Vehicle* list by selecting the **Lists** menu, then select **Customer & Vendor Profile Lists**, and then select **Vehicle list**. Alternatively, you can click the **Vehicle List** button on the top of the *Enter Vehicle Mileage* window.

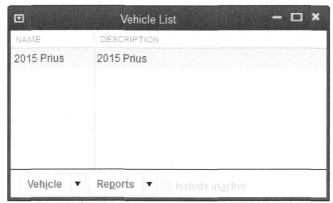

Figure 9-47 Vehicle List accessed through Enter Vehicle Mileage window

Step 5. To set up your mileage rates, click the **Mileage Rates** button on the top of the *Enter Vehicle Mileage* window (see Figure 9-48).

Figure 9-48 Mileage Rates button in Enter Vehicle Mileage window

Step 6. Enter the mileage rate designated by the IRS for the appropriate tax year on the first blank line at the bottom of the *Mileage Rates* window as shown in Figure 9-49. (Note: The actual rate for 2019 is unknown at the time of publication, so we are using $0. 55.)

Step 7. Click **Close** in the *Mileage Rates* window.

Figure 9-49 Enter Mileage Rates to calculate vehicle expenses

> **Note:**
> The rates you enter on the *Mileage Rates* window (Figure 9-49) are for reporting purposes only. These rates help you with preparing your company's income tax return. When you record mileage, you'll use the *Other Charge Item* you set up earlier (see Figure 9-44) and QuickBooks will use the rate you entered in the *Sales Price* field of the *Item* setup (Step 5 above).

Step 8.   Complete the *Enter Vehicle Mileage* window as shown in Figure 9-50. Total miles automatically calculates when you enter the start and end odometer settings.

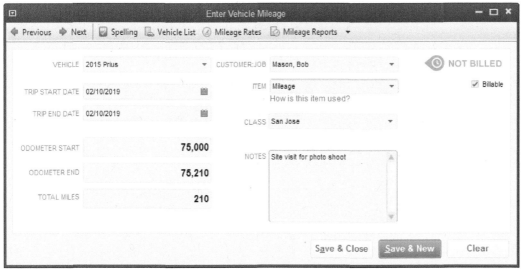

Figure 9-50 Enter Vehicle Mileage window

Step 9.   Click **Save & Close** to save your mileage entry.

To create reports about your mileage, follow these steps:

COMPUTER PRACTICE

Step 1.   Select the **Reports** menu, then select **Jobs, Time & Mileage,** and then select **Mileage by Vehicle Detail** (see Figure 9-51).

Step 2.   Set the date range to *1/1/2019* through *2/28/2019*.

QuickBooks displays the rate in the Mileage Rate column based on the year the miles occurred. It uses the *Mileage Rates* window to look up the rates.

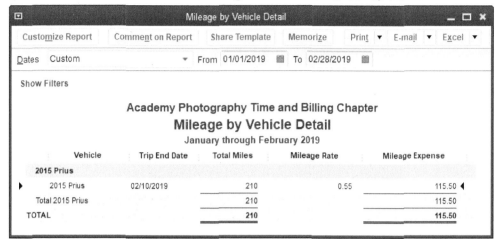

Figure 9-51 Mileage by Vehicle Detail report

Step 3.   Close the *Mileage by Vehicle Detail* report.

To see all mileage that has not yet been billed, use a mileage report such as *Mileage by Job Summary*.

Step 1.   Select the **Reports** menu, then select **Jobs, Time & Mileage,** and then select **Mileage by Job Summary**.

Step 2.   Set the date fields to *1/1/2019* through *2/28/2019*.

Step 3.   Click the **Customize Report** button to display the *Modify Report* window. Select the *Billed, Unbilled, and Not Billable* checkboxes to display the corresponding columns as shown in Figure 9-52).

Step 4.   Click **OK** to save your changes.

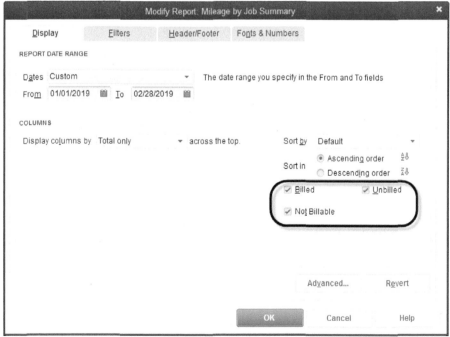

Figure 9-52 Modifying the Mileage by Job Summary report

By reviewing this report (see Figure 9-53), you can see which mileage items have not been billed. If you find a line with *No name,* double click on it to see whether the mileage should be assigned to a *Job* or not.

Not Billable Miles can also be investigated to see if some of those entries should be billable.

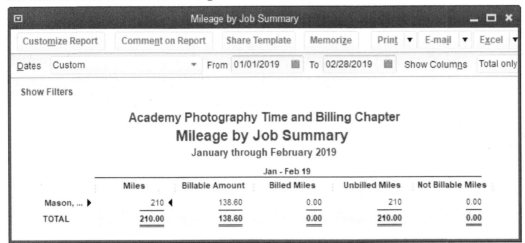

Figure 9-53 *Mileage by Job Summary report showing Bob Mason's billable mileage*

Step 5.   Close all report windows. When asked, there is no need to memorize the reports.

Multiple Pass-Throughs on One Invoice

To pass these costs through to the customer, create an *Invoice* and use the *Time/Costs* button to post the entries onto the *Invoice*.

COMPUTER PRACTICE

Step 1.   Select the **Create Invoices** icon on the *Customers* section of the *Home* page.

Step 2.   Select **Mason, Bob** from the *Customer:Job* list and click **OK** in the *Billable Time/Costs* window to open the *Choose Billable Time and Costs* window.

Step 3.   Click the **Mileage** tab (see Figure 9-54).

Step 4.   Click to place a checkmark in the left column on the *Mileage* item for 2/10/2019.

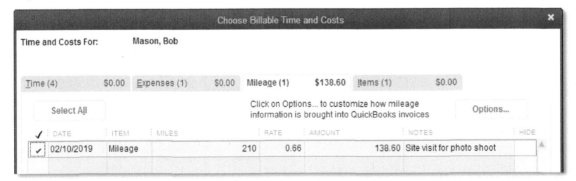

Figure 9-54 *Mileage tab of Billable Time and Costs window*

Step 5.   Next, select the *Items* tab and click to place a checkmark in the left column on the unbilled items (see Figure 9-55).

Figure 9-55 Items tab of Billable Time and Costs window

Step 6. Next, select the *Expenses* tab and click to place a checkmark in the left column on the unbilled Expenses (see Figure 9-56). Leave the *Markup Amount* **20%** and the *Markup Account* set to **Expense Markup**.

Figure 9-56 Expenses tab of Billable Time and Costs window

Step 7. Click **OK** to post all selected pass-throughs to the *Invoice*. The selected expenses, items, and mileage will display as separate line items on the *Invoice*. In the next step, we will post all the Time items to appear on the *Invoice* as one line item.

Step 8. Click the **Add Time/Costs** button to re-display the *Choose Billable Time and Costs* window (see Figure 9-57).

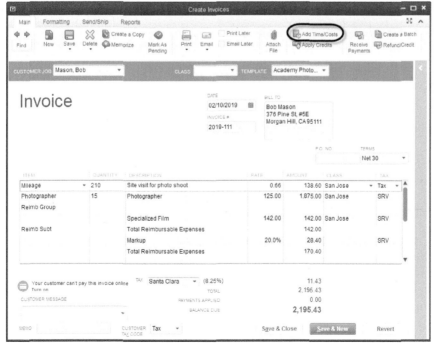

Figure 9-57 Bob Mason's invoice before adding Time

Step 9.   If necessary, click the *Time* tab and click **Select All** (see Figure 9-58).

Step 10.   Then click ***Print selected time and costs as one invoice item***. This ensures that the invoice only has one line for the billable time *when it is printed*. This summarizes billable time into one entry so the printed *Invoice* is shorter, but it might not show the customer the detail that you need. Decide what's best for you when you do your own invoices.

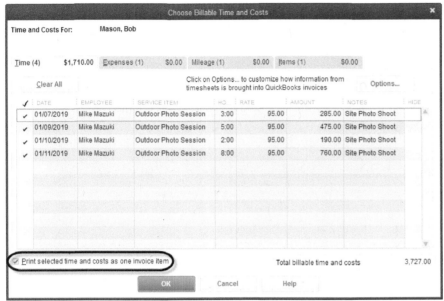

Figure 9-58 Time tab of Billable Time and Costs window

Step 11.   Click **OK** to post all of the selected pass-throughs to the *Invoice*.

Step 12.   Then scroll down to the bottom of the *Invoice* and change the *Description* from ***Total Reimbursable Expenses*** to ***Total Services***. Complete the *Invoice* as shown (see Figure 9-59).

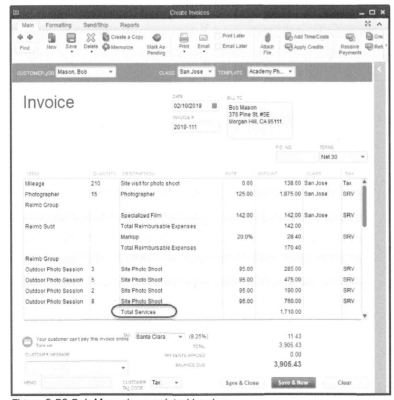

Figure 9-59 Bob Mason's completed Invoice

Step 13.   Preview the resulting invoice by choosing **Print** and **Preview**. If necessary, select **Zoom In**. (See Figure 9-60).

Step 14.   Click **Close** to close the *Print Preview* window.

Step 15.   Click **Save & Close** to close the *Invoice*.

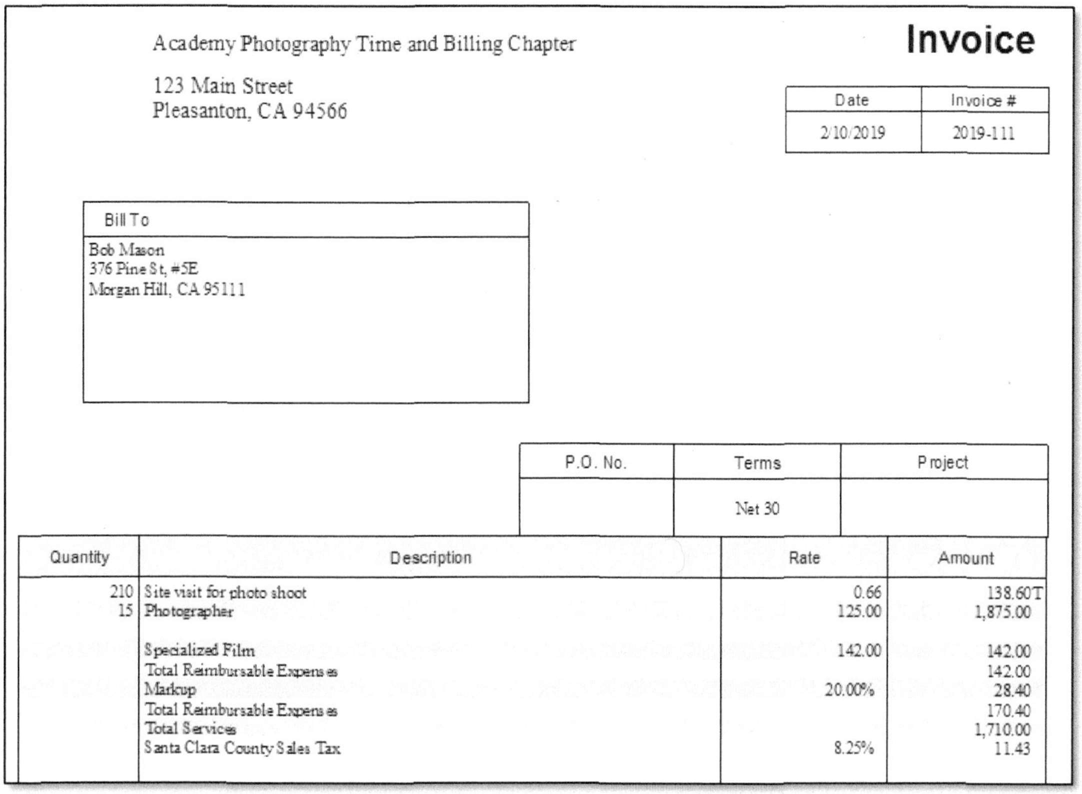

Academy Photography Time and Billing Chapter				**Invoice**

123 Main Street
Pleasanton, CA 94566

Date	Invoice #
2/10/2019	2019-111

Bill To

Bob Mason
376 Pine St, #5E
Morgan Hill, CA 95111

P.O. No.	Terms	Project
	Net 30	

Quantity	Description	Rate	Amount
210	Site visit for photo shoot	0.66	138.60T
15	Photographer	125.00	1,875.00
	Specialized Film	142.00	142.00
	Total Reimbursable Expenses		142.00
	Markup	20.00%	28.40
	Total Reimbursable Expenses		170.40
	Total Services		1,710.00
	Santa Clara County Sales Tax	8.25%	11.43

Figure 9-60 Upper portion of Print Preview of final Invoice

Review Questions

Comprehension Questions

1. Explain how to track reimbursable expenses.

2. How do you pass through billable expenses to customers?

3. What is a *two-sided Item* and under what circumstances should you use one?

4. What is the purpose of Vehicle Mileage Tracker?

5. Explain how the *Use time data to create paychecks* option can be used to streamline your payroll system.

Multiple Choice

Select the best answer(s) for each of the following:

1. In QuickBooks you are allowed to pass through billable expenses to *Customers*:
   a) Only if you paid by credit card.
   b) If you paid by check or credit card, but you don't assign the *Customer* or *Job* to the expense.
   c) If you used a *Bill, Check,* or *Credit Card Charge* and assign the *Customer* or *Job* to which the expense applies.
   d) None of the above.

2. Which account types can be used in the expense tab of a purchase transaction to make the expense *Billable?*
   a) Cost of Goods Sold
   b) Expense
   c) Other Expense
   d) All of the above

3. If you want to assign expenses to a *Customer:Job*, but do not want to pass them through for reimbursement, do the following in a purchase transaction:
   a) Do not assign the *Customer:Job*; just enter the information in the *Memo* field.
   b) Assign the *Customer:Job*, and then click the checkbox in the *Billable* column to remove the checkmark.
   c) Delete the *Invoice* icon.
   d) a or b.

4. Which of the following tabs appear in the *Choose Billable Time and Costs* window:
   a) Items.
   b) Expenses.
   c) Time.
   d) All of the above.

5. In an *Invoice*, you can automatically markup the pass-through expenses using the *Markup Account* option. It is available in the *Choose Billable Time and Costs* window on the:
    a) Items tab.
    b) Expenses tab.
    c) Time tab.
    d) All of the above.

6. To track reimbursable expenses in one expense account and the reimbursements in another income account:
    a) Select the **Track reimbursed expenses as income** option in the *Time & Expenses Company Preference*.
    b) Associate each reimbursable expense account with an appropriate income account.
    c) Both a and b.
    d) None of the above.

7. If you select **Print selected time and costs as one invoice item**, which of the following will be true?
    a) All reimbursable expenses will be printed on a single line in the body of the printed invoice.
    b) A group called *Reimb Group* will be created on the invoice displayed.
    c) *Reimb Group* will include the details of all the expenses you selected on the invoice displayed.
    d) All of the above.

8. Two-sided Items can be used for:
    a) Reimbursable expenses.
    b) Custom order parts.
    c) Subcontracted labor.
    d) All of the above.

9. For a two-sided non-inventory Item set-up without a specific cost/sales price, how would you record the markup in the sales price?
    a) Set the markup in the *Time & Expenses Company Preference*.
    b) Set the markup in the Items tab of the *Choose Billable Time and Costs* window.
    c) Manually adjust the price on the sales forms for markup.
    d) All of the above.

10. To see a detailed listing of all the billable expenses and items that you have not passed through to invoices:
    a) Create an *Unbilled Expenses* report.
    b) Create an *Unbilled Items* report.
    c) Create an *Unbilled Costs by Job* report.
    d) None of the above.

11. Vehicle Mileage Tracker allows you to:
    a) Track vehicle mileage, post mileage to invoices and run reports to assist with tax preparation.
    b) Reimburse your employees for mileage on their paycheck, a bill or a check.
    c) Track scheduled maintenance of a vehicle.
    d) All of the above.

12. Before you can use the Time Tracking feature, you must:

    a)   Enter in time activity for each employee into QuickBooks.

    b)   Go through the Payroll Setup Wizard to set up each employee.

    c)   Turn on Time Tracking in Time & Expenses *Preferences*.

    d)   Update your payroll tax tables using the *Get Payroll Updates* command.

13. If you plan to use timesheets to create paychecks, you should:

    a)   Make sure that you know which employees are hourly and which are salaried.

    b)   Record all of the time for each employee, including non-billable time (e.g., sick, vacation and administrative time), on the timesheet.

    c)   Create a Customer:Job assignment for each employee so that their time can be allocated correctly.

    d)   Purchase a time clock in order to have a backup record of your employees' time.

14. Timesheets provide the basic information for job costing, but they do not actually record job costs. To use the timesheet information to record job costs you have to pass the timesheet information onto a:

    a)   Paycheck, check, bill or credit card charge.

    b)   Invoice.

    c)   Sales receipt.

    d)   Any of the above.

15. After you post timesheet information to paychecks and invoices, the timesheet will affect:

    a)   Income.

    b)   Job Cost Reports.

    c)   Expenses.

    d)   All of the above.

Completion Statements

1. The *Choose Billable Time and Costs* window allows you to setup *Markup Amount or %* and *Markup Account* in the _____ tab.

2. An Item used on both expenses and sales forms is commonly called a(n) _____-_____ _____.

3. A(n) _____ is the time spent by a single person performing a single service on a single date.

4. A(n) _____ _____ is a record of several activities performed during a one-week period by a single employee, owner or subcontractor.

5. The _____ _____ _____ report shows the total number of hours each employee worked for each Customer or Job.

Time and Billing Problem 1

Restore the TimeBilling-18Problem1.QBM file. The password to access this file is *Sleeter18*.

1. Create the following two-sided *Non-inventory Part Item:*

Field	Data
Item Type	Non-inventory Part
Item Name	Custom Lens
Select Option	This item is used in assemblies or is purchased for a specific Customer:Job
Description on Purchase	Custom Lens Order #
Description on Sales	Custom Lens Order #
Cost	$0
Sale Price	$0
Expense Account	Cost of Goods Sold
Tax Code	Tax
Income Account	Sales

Table 9-1 Details of the Non-inventory Part Item

2. Create a *Purchase Order* by entering the following:

Field	Data
Vendor	Ace Supply
Class	Walnut Creek
Date	3/22/2019
P.O. No.	2019-101
Item	Custom Lens
Description	Custom Lens Order #2019-101
Qty	4
Rate	$235 (Do not update the item with the new cost.)
Customer	Mason, Bob
Memo	Custom Lens Order #2019-101

Table 9-2 Details of the Purchase Order

3. Enter a *Bill* (**Ref No. 99821**) on **4/1/2019** from **Ace Supply** after receiving the custom lens order. Use the *P.O. No.* **2019-101**, *Customer:Job:* **Mason, Bob**, *Class:* **Walnut Creek**, *Memo:* **Custom Lens Order #2019-101**. This *Item* is billable.

4. Create a *Sales Receipt* for **Mason, Bob** for the Custom Lens order. Use **QuickMath** to markup the *Custom Lens* Item by **20%**. Total is **$1,221.06**. *Class* is **Walnut Creek**. *Date* is **4/1/2019**. *Sale No.* is **2019-101**. *Check No.* is **11482**. *Payment Method* is **Check**.

Time and Billing Problem 2 (Advanced)

> Restore the TimeBilling-18Problem2.QBM file. The password to access this file is *Sleeter18*.

1. Create the following two-sided *Other Charge Item*:

Field	Data
Item Type	Other Charge
Item Name	Freight & Delivery
Select Option	This is used in assemblies or is a reimbursable charge
Description on Purchase	Freight and Delivery Charges
Description on Sales	Freight and Delivery Charges
Cost	$8,99
Sale Price	$12.99
Expense Account	Reimbursable Expenses
Tax Code	SRV
Income Account	Services

Table 9-3 Details of the Other Charge Item

2. Create the following two-sided *Non-inventory Part Item:*

Field	Data
Item Type	Non-inventory Part
Item Name	Custom Filter
Select Option	This item is used in assemblies or is purchased for a specific Customer:Job
Description on Purchase	Custom Filter Order #
Description on Sales	Custom Filter Order #
Cost	$0
Sale Price	$0
Expense Account	Cost of Goods Sold
Tax Code	Tax
Income Account	Sales

Table 9-4 Details of the Non-inventory Part Item

3. Create a *Purchase Order* by entering the following:

Field	Data
Vendor	Ace Supply
Class	Walnut Creek
Date	4/1/2019
P.O. No.	2019-101
Item	Custom Filter
Description	Custom Filter Order #2019-101
Qty	5
Rate	$146
Customer	Cruz, Maria: Branch Opening
Memo	Custom Filter Order #2019-101

Table 9-5 Details of the Purchase Order

4. A new partner, Alma Hernandez, has joined Academy Photography. Open the **Other Names List** and add Alma Hernandez to the list.

5. Enter a *Bill* (**Ref No. 99357**) on **4/5/2019** from **Ace Supply** after receiving the custom filter order. Use the *P.O. No.* **2019-101**, *Customer:Job:* **Cruz, Maria:Branch Opening**, *Class:* **Walnut Creek**, *Memo:* **Custom Filter Order #2019-101**. This *Item* is billable. Add a freight charge of **$8.99** using the **Freight & Delivery** Item, *Customer:Job:* **Cruz, Maria:Branch Opening** and *Class:* **Walnut Creek**. This *Item* is also billable.

6. Print **Unbilled Costs by Job report** for all transactions.

7. Using the *Academy Photo Service Invoice*, create an *Invoice* on **4/5/2019** for **Maria Cruz's Branch Opening** *Job*, *Class:* **Walnut Creek**, *Invoice #:* **2019-106**, *Description* and *Memo:* **Custom Filter Order #2019-101**. Select all the open billable Items for this *Job*. Use **QuickMath** to markup the *Custom Filter* Item by **20%**. Print the **Invoice**.

8. Use the *Weekly Timesheet* to record hours from the table below for Alma Hernandez from 4/15/2019 through 4/21/2019.

Date	Day	Hrs	Customer:Job	Service	Notes	Class	Billable
4/15/19	Mon	8.0	Anderson Wedding Planners: Wilson, Sarah and Michael	Indoor Photo Session	Photo Shoot	Walnut Creek	Yes
4/16/19	Tues	7.0	Anderson Wedding Planners: Wilson, Sarah and Michael	Indoor Photo Session	Photo Shoot	Walnut Creek	Yes
4/17/19	Wed	8.0	Perez, Jerry	Outdoor Photo Session	Photo Shoot	Walnut Creek	Yes
4/18/19	Thurs	6.0	Anderson Wedding Planners: Wilson, Sarah and Michael	Indoor Photo Session	Photo Shoot	Walnut Creek	Yes
4/19/19	Fri	7.0			Admin	San Jose	No

Figure 9-61 New owner's time log

9. Create a *Sales Receipt* for Anderson Wedding Planners' Wilson *Job*.

    a) Include all of Alma Hernandez's time, and post it to the *Sales Receipt*.

    b) *Class* is **Walnut Creek**.

    c) *Date* is **4/27/2019**.

    d) *Sale No.* is **2019-101**.

    e) *Check No.* is **10987**.

    f) *Payment Method* is **Check**.

    g) Add two (2) **Photographer** Items for **$125.00** to the *Sales Receipt*.

10. Print the *Profit and Loss by Job* report for **April, 2019**.

Chapter 10
Payroll Setup

Topics

In this chapter, you will learn about the following topics:

- Checklist for Setting Up Payroll (page 360)
- Payroll Accounts (page 360)
- Payroll Items (page 361)
- The Payroll Setup Interview (page 362)
- Setting Up Employee Defaults (page 381)
- Employee Reports (page 399)

Restore this File

This chapter uses or PRSetup-18.QBW. See page 9 for more information. The password to access this file is *Sleeter18*.

In this chapter, you will learn how to set up QuickBooks to track your Payroll. In order to use QuickBooks to track your Payroll, you must properly set up your *Payroll Accounts*, *Payroll Items*, *Employees*, and *Opening Balances*. If you plan to process payroll manually or use an outside payroll service, you will still need to set up QuickBooks to correctly record your Payroll transactions.

You have three choices for using QuickBooks to track your Payroll, Basic, Enhanced and Full Service. For detailed information on the differences between these options, go to payroll.intuit.com.

In addition, you can manually prepare your own Payroll in QuickBooks without the use of any tax tables. This option is not recommended for most users, but it is provided if you want to manually calculate your Payroll. You may also want to manually prepare Payroll if you use an outside Payroll service other than Intuit. With an outside Payroll service you would be required to re-enter Payroll details into QuickBooks. *This chapter uses Manual Payroll.*

Intuit occasionally makes changes to their Payroll options between version releases, and there may be changes since the publication of this book.

Checklist for Setting Up Payroll

Like the setup of your company file, the proper setup of your Payroll is the most important factor in getting it to work well for you. Table 10-1 provides you with a checklist for your Payroll setup. Make sure that you complete each step in the order given unless it really does not apply.

Payroll Setup Checklist

1.   Gather information about each of your employees, including the name, address, social security number, and W-4 information.

2.   Activate the Payroll function.

3.   Set up Payroll Accounts in the *Chart of Accounts*. Example accounts: Gross Wages, Payroll Tax Expense, Federal PR Tax Liabilities, and State PR Tax Liabilities.

4.   Enable your QuickBooks file for Payroll processing, either manually or by signing up for one of QuickBooks Payroll services.

5.   Using the *Payroll Setup Interview*, set up Payroll Items, Payroll Vendors, Employee defaults, Employee records, and year-to-date Payroll figures.

6.   Add additional Payroll Items directly from the Payroll Item list.

7.   Edit Payroll Items to modify the Vendor information and the way the Items affect the *Chart of Accounts*.

8.   If setting up mid-year, enter year-to-date information for additional Payroll Items on the Payroll list for each Employee, and enter year-to-date liability payments.

9.   Verify Payroll Item setup, Employee setup, and the Vendor list.

10. Proof your setup. Use the *Payroll Checkup* wizard and compare reports with your accountant's or Payroll service's reports. The *Payroll Checkup* wizard is not covered in this chapter.

Table 10-1 Payroll Setup Checklist

> **Note:**
> Form W-4 is the IRS form that each of your employees must complete when you hire them. The IRS requires employees to provide you with their name, address, social security number, and withholding information on this form. The Internal Revenue service has many payroll forms available online at **www.irs.gov**. For form W-4, enter **W4** in *Search* field.

Payroll Accounts

In your *Chart of Accounts*, confirm that you have all of the accounts you want to see on your *Balance Sheet* and *Profit and Loss Reports*. Academy Photography uses the following accounts for Payroll. These accounts are already set up in the practice file.

Example Liability Accounts for Payroll

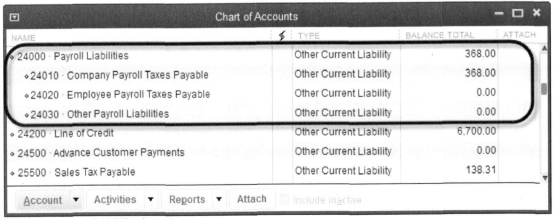

Figure 10-1 Payroll Liability Accounts

Example Expense Accounts for Payroll

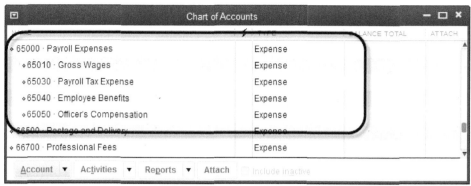

Figure 10-2 Payroll Expense Accounts

If you are not sure which accounts you should include in your *Chart of Accounts*, ask your accountant. However, you should normally have only a few subaccounts associated with the *Payroll Liabilities* account, and a few subaccounts associated with the Payroll Expenses account. Do not add unnecessary accounts and subaccounts to the *Chart of Accounts*, since the detailed tracking of Payroll comes from *Payroll Items* and not accounts.

If your *Chart of Accounts* already has too many accounts or subaccounts, you can merge some accounts until you have a manageable number of accounts.

Payroll Items

Payroll Items are used to track the compensation, additions, deductions, and other employer-paid expenses listed on the employee's paycheck. These Items include wages, commissions, tips, benefits, taxes, dues, retirement plans, and any other additions and deductions to an employee's paycheck. Like other QuickBooks Items, Payroll Items are connected to the *Chart of Accounts* so that as paychecks are created, the accounting behind the scenes is handled automatically. In addition, Payroll Items are used to accumulate Payroll Liabilities. Figure 10-3 shows the Payroll Item List after the *Payroll Setup Interview*, which is discussed beginning on page 362, has been completed.

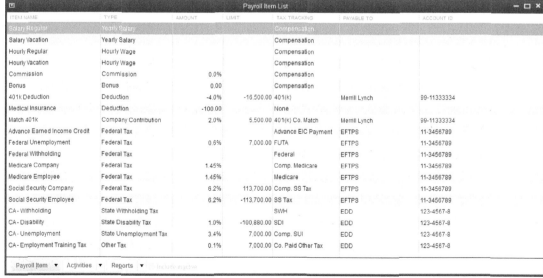

Figure 10-3 Payroll Item List

The Payroll Setup Interview

The *Payroll Setup Interview* is a set of windows that walks you through the setup of Payroll. Using this wizard is optional, but if you are starting from scratch (as shown here), you will probably find it helpful. Even if you have existing Payroll, the wizard can take the guesswork out of setting up new benefits and wages for your Employees.

COMPUTER PRACTICE

Step 1.   From the *Employees* menu, select **Payroll Setup**.

Step 2.   QuickBooks displays the *QuickBooks Payroll Setup* window shown in Figure 10-4. Click **Continue**.

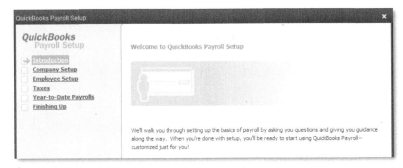

Figure 10-4 Payroll Setup Interview window

Setting Up Compensation and Benefits Payroll Items

In this section of the setup wizard, you will set up compensation Items (i.e., hourly wages, salary wages, bonuses, commissions, etc.).

COMPUTER PRACTICE

Step 1.   QuickBooks displays the Compensation and Benefits section. Click **Continue**.

Step 2.   QuickBooks displays the *Add New* window and pre-selects *Salary, Hourly wage and overtime*, and *Bonus, award, or one-time compensation* (see Figure 10-5). Select the **Commission** *Other compensation* Item and click **Next**.

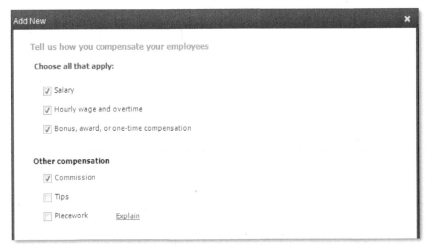

Figure 10-5 Payroll Setup Interview - Add New compensation options

Step 3.   In the next screen, QuickBooks wants to know how commissions should be calculated. Select **Percentage of sales (or other amount)** and click **Finish** (see Figure 10-6).

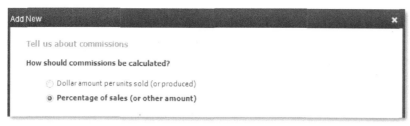

Figure 10-6 Payroll Setup Interview – commissions calculations

Step 4.   QuickBooks displays the *Compensation list* shown in Figure 10-7. At this point, we need to modify this list by editing some of the names and adding new ones.

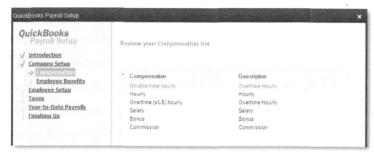

Figure 10-7 Payroll Setup Interview – Review the Compensation list

Step 5.   To change the name of the Hourly Payroll Item to *Hourly Regular*, select **Hourly** from the *Compensation list* and click **Edit**.

Step 6.   Type **Hourly Regular** in the *Show on paychecks as* field (see Figure 10-8) and select **Payroll Expenses:Gross Wages** from the *Account name* drop-down list. Then click **Finish**.

Figure 10-8 Edit Hourly Pay window

Step 7.   Edit or delete the rest of the default compensation Items, renaming and editing the accounts so that your remaining accounts match the table shown in Table 10-2. Leave all other fields set to their defaults as you edit the Items.

Default Item Name	Change to this Name	Change to this Account
Double-time hourly	Delete this Item	Delete this Item
Hourly	Hourly Regular	Payroll Expenses:Gross Wages
Overtime (x1.5) hourly	Delete this Item	Delete this Item
Salary	Salary Regular	Payroll Expenses:Gross Wages
Bonus	Bonus	Payroll Expenses:Gross Wages

Table 10-2 Compensation Item Names and Accounts

Step 8.   When you're finished editing the default Payroll Items, your list will look like the one in Figure 10-9.

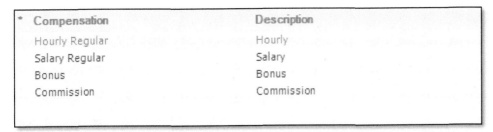

Figure 10-9 Compensation Items after renaming

Step 9.   Click **Continue** to set up Employee benefits.

Medical Insurance Deduction

Step 1.   QuickBooks displays the *Set up employee benefits* window. Click **Continue**.

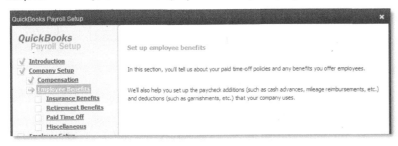

Figure 10-10 Payroll Setup Interview – Set up Employee benefits

In this section of the setup wizard, you will set up the benefits you offer (health insurance, dental insurance, retirement plans, etc.), and any other additions or deductions that affect the Employees' gross income (e.g., expense reimbursements, dues, garnishments, etc.). If your company provides benefits, there are three options for allocating the costs between the company and the Employee. First, the company could pay the entire expense; second, the company and Employee could share the expense; and third, the Employee could pay the entire expense.

If your company pays the entire expense, Payroll is usually not involved. However, there are certain circumstances when you would need to adjust the W-2s to include the benefits. Check with your tax professional.

If the costs are shared between the company and the Employees, or if the Employees pay for the entire cost via Payroll deductions, use a *Deduction Item* to track the deductions. The following method is the simplest way to handle this type of deduction in Payroll.

COMPUTER PRACTICE

Step 1.   In the *Set up insurance benefits* window (Figure 10-11), click **Health insurance** and then click **Next**.

Figure 10-11 Set up insurance benefits window

Step 2.   Select the option for **Both the employee and company pay portions**, as shown in Figure 10-12, and then click **Next**.

Even though Academy Photography pays most of the health insurance costs, this Item will be set up to deduct a portion of the expense after taxes from paychecks. We'll have to modify it later to connect the Payroll Item to the health insurance expense account. Make sure to leave the **Payment is deducted after taxes** option selected.

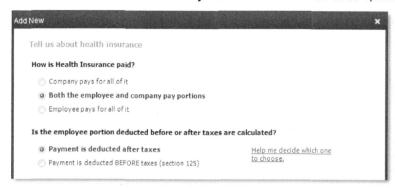

Figure 10-12 The health insurance Payroll Item setup screen

Step 3.   In Figure 10-13 the *Payroll Setup Interview* asks if you want to setup the Payee, Account #, and Payment frequency. Leave **I don't need a regular payment schedule for this item** selected and click **Finish**.

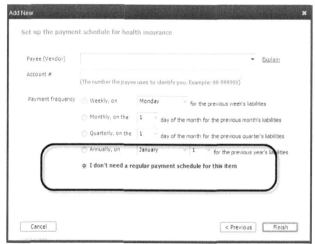

Figure 10-13 Setting up the payment schedule window

Step 4.   The *Insurance Benefits* list window displays.

Figure 10-14 Insurance Items list

Notice in Figure 10-14 that QuickBooks has added two Payroll Items. One Item, *Health Insurance (company paid)*, was added to track the accruals for the employer portion of the health insurance costs, and the other Item, *Health Insurance (taxable)*, to track the Employee deductions. However, for our example, the employer pays the health insurance bill by directly coding the bill to Health Insurance expense. Then, the employer deducts the Employees' portion of the health insurance costs from their paychecks. So we'll delete the *Health Insurance (company paid)* Item because we won't accrue the employer's portion of the health insurance costs through Payroll.

Step 5.   Select the *Health Insurance (company paid)* Item (see Figure 10-14), and then click **Delete**.

Step 6.   Click **Yes** on the *Delete Payroll Item* window.

Step 7.   Next, select the *Health Insurance (taxable)* Item and click **Edit** (see Figure 10-15). Change the name to **Medical Insurance** in the *Show on paychecks as* field and click **Next**.

Figure 10-15 Edit: After-Tax Employee-Paid Health window

Step 8.   Click **Next** to skip the option to edit the payment schedule and move to the next window.

Step 9.   In the *Edit After-Tax Employee-Paid Health* section, change the *Account type* to **Expense**. Select **Insurance Expense:Health Insurance Expense** from the *Account name* drop-down list (see Figure 10-16). Then click **Next**.

Figure 10-16 Account type and Account name window

Step 10.   Leave the defaults in the tax tracking type window and click **Next** .

Step 11.   Change the default amount to 100.00 and click **Finish** (see Figure 10-17).

Figure 10-17 Setting the default amount

Step 12.   You will return to the *Insurance Benefits list*. Click **Continue**.

401(k) Employee Deduction and Company Match Items

If you have a 401(k) plan, you can set up Payroll Items to track the employer contributions and the Employee contributions (salary deferral) to the plan.

COMPUTER PRACTICE

Step 1.   On the *Tell us about your company retirement benefits* screen (Figure 10-18), click on the **401(k)** Item and click **Next**.

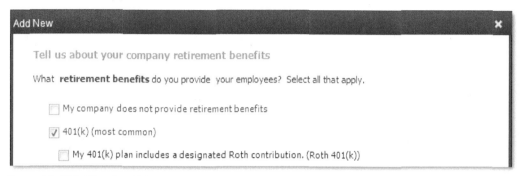

Figure 10-18 Adding the 401(k) Payroll Items

Step 2.   Click **Finish** to accept the default selection and not set up a regular payment schedule for the 401(k) at this time.

Step 3.   Next, edit each of the default Items shown in Figure 10-19. First, select the *401k Co. Match* Item and click **Edit**.

Figure 10-19 The default Item names for 401k

Step 4.   Type **Match 401k** in the *Show on paychecks as* field (see Figure 10-20). Click **Next**.

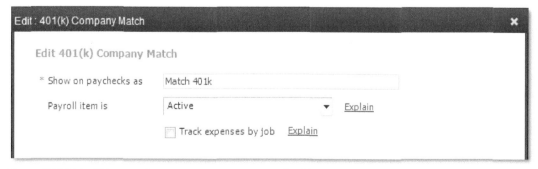

Figure 10-20 Modifying the Company Match Item name for 401k

Step 5.   Type **Merrill Lynch** in the *Payee (Vendor)* field and **99-12345678** in the *Account #* field and click **Next** (see Figure 10-21).

Figure 10-21 Modifying the Company Match Item Payee and Account # for 401(k)

Step 6.   In the *Expense account* section, select **Payroll Expenses:Employee Benefits** from the
                 drop-down list in the *Account name* field. You may need to scroll up to find this selection.
                 In the *Liability account* section, select **Payroll Liabilities:Other Payroll Liabilities** from the
                 drop-down list in the *Account name* field. (See Figure 10-22.) Click **Next**.

Figure 10-22 Modifying the Expense account and Liability account information

Step 7.   On the next window, leave **Use standard tax settings** checked and click **Next**.

Step 8.   On the *Tell us how to calculate the amount* screen, enter the information shown in Figure
                 10-23 and then click **Finish**.

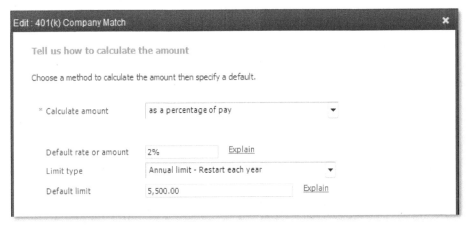

Figure 10-23 Setting the calculation method, amounts, and limit for 401(k) contribution Item

Step 9.   You will return to the *Retirement Benefit list* window. Select the **401k Emp. Item** and click **Edit**.

Step 10.   Enter the data as shown in Figure 10-24 and then click **Next**.

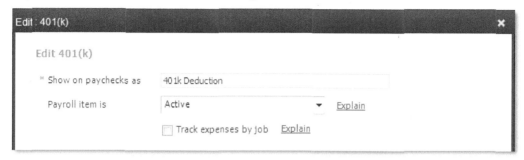

Figure 10-24 401(k) Deduction Item

Step 11.   Enter the data as shown in Figure 10-25 and then click **Next**.

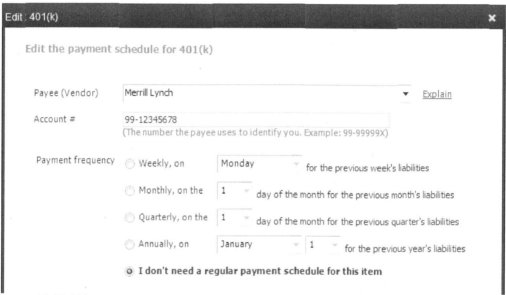

Figure 10-25 401(k) Payee and Account #

Step 12.   Enter the data as shown in Figure 10-26 and then click **Next**.

Figure 10-26 Setting the account for the 401(k) Deduction Item.

Step 13.   Leave *Use standard tax settings* checked and click **Next**.

Step 14.   Enter the data as shown in Figure 10-27 and then click **Finish**.

Figure 10-27 Setting the calculation method, amounts, and limit for 401(k) deduction Item

You're now finished with setting up the retirement benefits portion of your Payroll Item list. Your *Payroll Setup Interview* should now look like Figure 10-28.

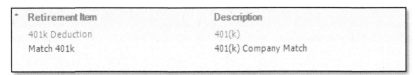

Figure 10-28 Progress in the Payroll Setup Interview.

Step 15.   Click **Continue** to proceed to the next section of the setup.

> **Note:**
> If you have 401(k) deductions for several Employees, you'll probably want to set up
> separate Deduction Items for each Employee. Enter the Employee's account number in
> the **Enter the number that identifies you to agency** field. That way, when you pay your
> liabilities, the voucher of the liability check lists deductions separately for each Employee.
> Alternatively, you could use just one Deduction Item and send a printout of your *Payroll
> Summary Report* with your payment to the 401(k) administrator. Filter that report to show
> only the *401(k) Deduction* and the *Match 401(k)* Items. You'll have to handwrite the
> account numbers for each Employee on the report.

Paid Time Off Payroll Items

If you pay Employees for time off, the *Payroll Setup Interview* will walk you through creating Items to track and pay vacation or sick pay.

COMPUTER PRACTICE

Step 1.   On the *Set up paid time off* screen (Figure 10-29), click on the **Paid vacation time off** Item and click **Finish.**

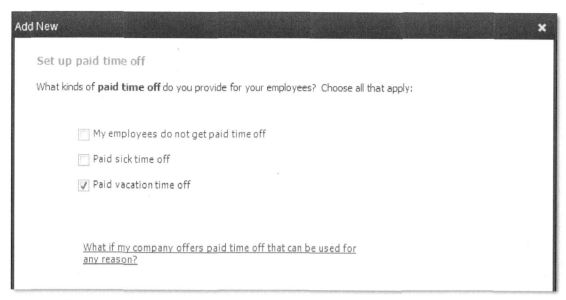

Figure 10-29 Adding Paid vacation Payroll Items

> **Note:**
> If you have a "Paid Time Off (PTO)" policy instead of separate sick and vacation time, you can use either Sick or Vacation time to keep track of how much PTO you offer your Employees. Rename it on the Payroll *Preferences* so that when it prints on your paychecks and pay stubs, it appears as Paid Time Off. Within QuickBooks, however, it continues to appear as either Sick or Vacation, depending on which one you choose.

Step 2.   Edit each of the default Items shown in Figure 10-30. First, select *Hourly Vacation* and click **Edit**.

Figure 10-30 The default Item names for vacation tracking

Step 3.   Set the expense account to **Payroll Expenses:Gross Wages** as shown in Figure 10-31. Then click **Finish**.

Figure 10-31 Modifying the Hourly Vacation Item

Step 4.   Next, edit the Salary Vacation Item to select the *Payroll Expense:Gross Wages* account. Then click **Finish**.

Step 5.   Click **Continue** to proceed to set up additions and deductions.

Step 6.   Do not check any additions or deductions. Click **Finish** .

Step 7.   Click **Continue** to advance to setting up Employees.

Setting Up Employees

You will need to enter the employee information for every person who your company will give a W-2. Enter the information for Kati Reynolds.

COMPUTER PRACTICE

After you have set up your Payroll Items, the setup wizard takes you through setting up Employees.

Step 1.   On the *Set up Employees* window, click **Continue**.

Step 2.   Enter the information shown in Figure 10-32 and then click **Next**.

Figure 10-32 Entering Kati Reynolds' address information

> **Note:**
> QuickBooks uses the Employee name fields (first name, middle initial, then last name) to distinguish between Employees. Therefore, if two Employees have the same name, you must not use their exact names in the Employee list. If necessary, add or omit a middle initial to distinguish between different Employees with the same name.

Step 3. In the *hiring information* window, enter the data as shown in Figure 10-33 and then click **Next**.

> **Note:**
> The *Gender* field has two options, *Male* and *Female*. This field can be left blank. However, some states require gender information with New Hiring Reporting. Check with your state's Employment Development Department for more details.

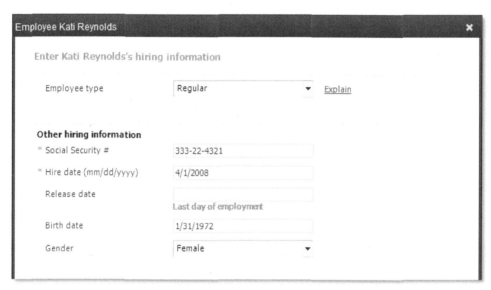

Figure 10-33 Hiring information window for Kati Reynolds

Step 4. In the *wages and compensation for Kati Reynolds* window, enter the information as shown in Figure 10-34. Then click **Next**.

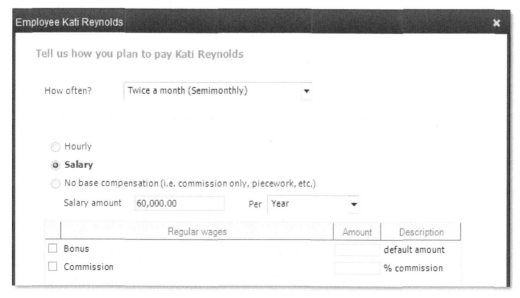

Figure 10-34 Pay frequency and compensation window for Kati Reynolds

Step 5.   Select the benefit Items as shown in Figure 10-35. Then click **Next**.

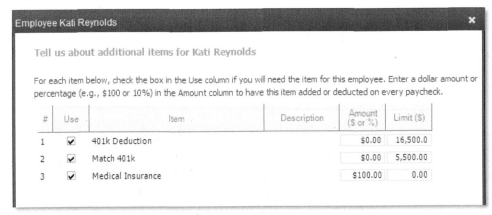

Figure 10-35 Selecting the benefit Items to add to Kati Reynolds' paychecks

Step 6.   Enter the vacation time calculation method for Kati Reynolds as shown in Figure 10-36. Leave the Current balances blank. Then click **Next**.

Figure 10-36 Vacation time calculation for Kati Reynolds

Step 7.   Click **Next** to skip the *direct deposit information* screen.

Step 8.   Enter the information shown in Figure 10-37 and then click **Next**.

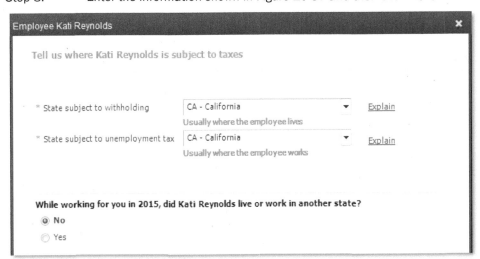

Figure 10-37 State information for Kati Reynolds – your screen may vary

Step 9.   Enter the federal tax information as shown in Figure 10-38 and then click **Next**.

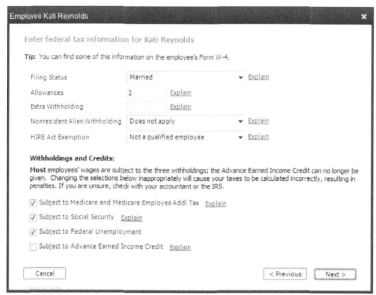

Figure 10-38 Kati Reynolds' federal tax information

Step 10.   Enter the state tax information as shown in Figure 10-39 and then click **Next**.

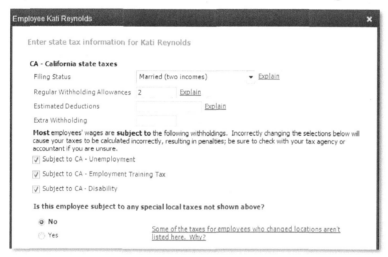

Figure 10-39 Kati Reynolds' state tax information

Step 11.   Choose S *(State Plan for Both UI and DI)* from the *Setup wage plan information for Kati Reynolds* as shown in Figure 10-40.

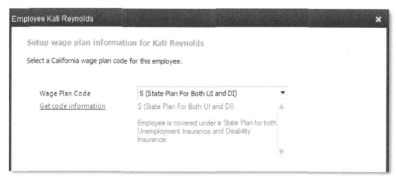

Figure 10-40 Setup wage plan information for Kati Reynolds

Step 12.   Click **Finish**.

Step 13.   You've finished setting up Kati Reynolds, your screen should look like Figure 10-41.

Step 14.   Click **Continue**.

Figure 10-41 Progress in the Payroll Setup Interview.

Payroll Tax Item Setup

COMPUTER PRACTICE

The next section of the *Payroll Setup Interview* helps you set up the Payroll tax Items. Continue on with the *Payroll Setup Interview*, following these steps:

Step 1.   The next screen is titled *Set up your payroll taxes*. Click **Continue**.

Step 2.   QuickBooks displays the federal Payroll tax Items that have been set up for you (see Figure 10-42). Click **Continue**.

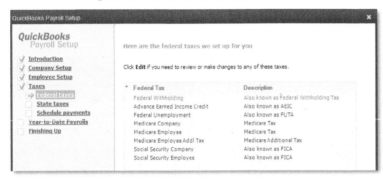

Figure 10-42 Federal Payroll tax Items

Step 3.   In the company file you are using, QuickBooks displays the *Set up state payroll taxes* window because the *Unemployment Company Rate* must be entered in manually (since we are processing Payroll manually). Enter **3.4%** in the *CA – Unemployment Company Rate* field (see Figure 10-43). Press **Tab** to accept the entry and **Finish** to move to review your state taxes.

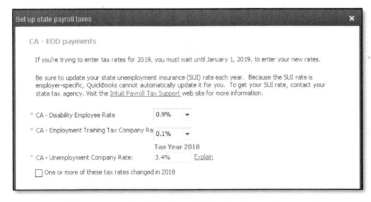

Figure 10-43 Entering in 3.4% in the California Unemployment Company Rate field – your screen may vary

Step 4.   The state tax information is displayed. Click **Continue**.

Scheduling Your Tax Payments

COMPUTER PRACTICE

The next section of the *Payroll Setup Interview* helps you to schedule your tax payments. Continue on with the *Payroll Setup Interview* following these steps:

Step 1.   The first screen in the Payroll taxes section is shown in Figure 10-44. This is where you set up the Vendor name for the payee on federal tax payments for Federal 940. The default Vendor name is United States Treasury. However, since you'll most likely make payments using the Electronic Federal Tax Payment System (EFTPS), the sample data file has already been set up with a vendor called EFTPS. Select **EFTPS** as the *Payee* (Vendor) you use to pay your liabilities for Federal taxes. In addition, select **Quarterly** from the drop down list in the *Payment Deposit Frequency* field. Click **Next**.

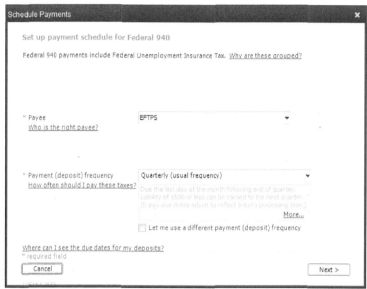

Figure 10-44 Set up payments for Federal 940

Step 2.   To set up payments for Federal 941/944, enter in the data shown in Figure 10-45 and click **Next**.

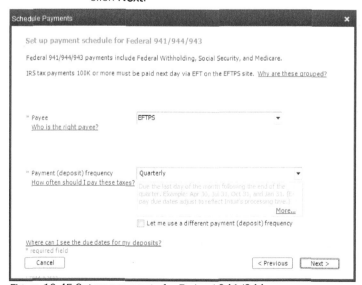

Figure 10-45 Set up payments for Federal 941/944

Step 3.   To set up payments for California Withholding and Disability Insurance, enter in the data shown in Figure 10-46 and click **Next**.

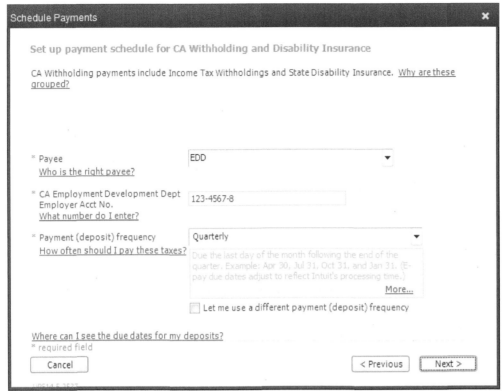

Figure 10-46 Set up payments for CA Withholding and Disability Insurance

Step 4.   To set up payments for California Unemployment Insurance (UI) and Employment Training Tax, enter the data shown in Figure 10-47 and click **Finish**.

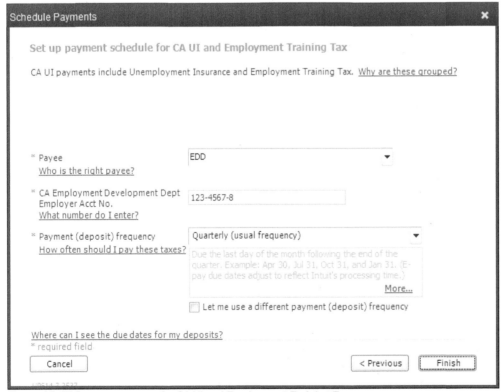

Figure 10-47 Set up payments for CA UI and Employment Training Tax

Step 5.   QuickBooks returns you to a window where you can review the list of your scheduled tax payments (see Figure 10-48). Click **Continue** to set up your year-to-date amounts.

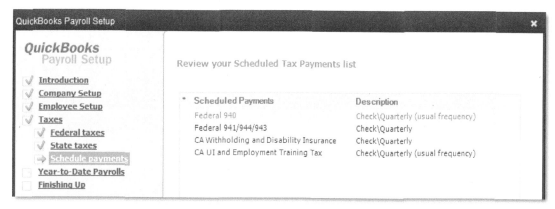

Figure 10-48 Review your Scheduled Tax Payments list

Setting Up Year-to-Date Payroll Amounts

COMPUTER PRACTICE

Step 1.   Click **Continue** on the *Enter Payroll history for the current* year window.

Step 2.   On the window shown in Figure 10-49, click **No** and then click **Continue**.

If you were setting up your own Payroll in the middle of the year, you would click **Yes** on this page and then QuickBooks would lead you down a set of screens where you would set up each Employee's Payroll history for the current year. However, this example assumes that you're setting up Payroll at the beginning of the year.

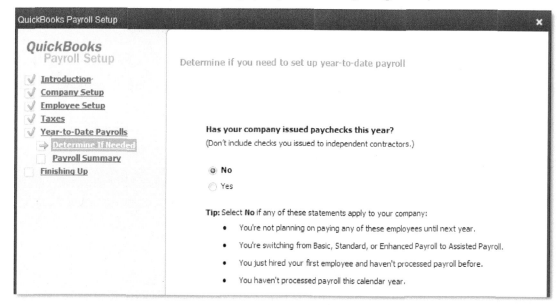

Figure 10-49 Year-to-Date Payroll Amounts

Finishing Up the Payroll Setup Interview

COMPUTER PRACTICE

Step 1.   Click **Go to Payroll Center** on the final window of Payroll Setup.

Step 2.   The *Employee Center* is shown in Figure 10-50.

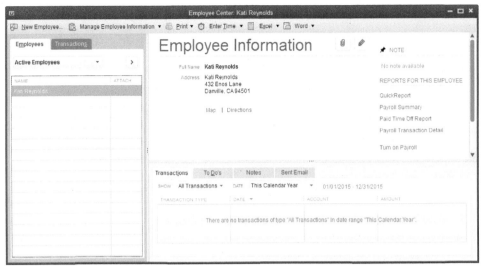

Figure 10-50 Employee Center

> **Note:**
> Because we are processing Payroll manually, the Employee Center does not display the Payroll tab. This tab displays only when Payroll is activated using a Payroll activation key.

Custom Fields for Payroll

After finishing the *Payroll Setup Interview*, you can set up custom fields and employee defaults. If you want to track more detailed information about your employees, use custom fields (see Figure 10-52). You can create up to 15 fields to be used for customers, vendors, or employees. In the practice file, several custom fields have already been added.

COMPUTER PRACTICE

Step 1.   From the **Employees** tab in the *Employee Center*, double click on Kati Reynolds and then click the *Additional Information* tab. See Figure 10-51.

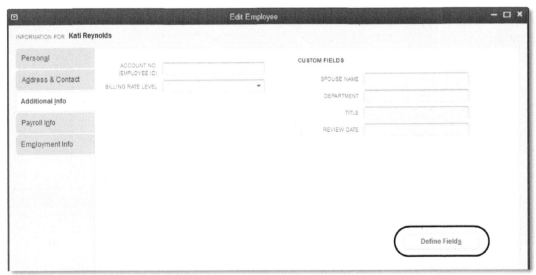

Figure 10-51 Editing an employee record

Step 2.   Click **Define Fields** on the *Additional Info* tab of the *Edit Employee* window.

Step 3.   When you're finished reviewing the field names that are already entered in your sample file, click **OK** (see Figure 10-52). Then click **Cancel** to close the *Edit Employee* window.

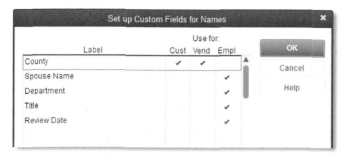

Figure 10-52 Defining custom fields

Setting Up Employee Defaults

The *Employee Defaults* feature allows you to define defaults for your Payroll records so that each time you add a new Employee, you don't have to enter the same information over and over. For example, if you pay all your Employees weekly, you can set up the defaults for weekly Payroll and that way you won't have to enter the pay period on each new Employee record. You don't have to use the *Employee Defaults*, but if you do, it will save you time and reduce the likelihood of errors.

COMPUTER PRACTICE

To set up the *Employee Defaults*, follow these steps:

Step 1.   From the *Employee Center*, select the *Manage Employee Information* drop-down and select **Change New Employee Default Settings** as shown in Figure 10-53.

> **Note:**
> Setting up *Employee Defaults* only applies to new Employees you will set up after default settings are in place.

Figure 10-53 Selecting Employee Defaults from the Employee Center

Step 2.   In the *Employee Defaults* window, Select **<Add New>** from the *Payroll Schedule* drop-down list as shown in Figure 10-54.

The *Payroll Schedule* function allows you to group together Employees with the same pay frequency (i.e., weekly, bi-weekly, monthly, etc.) in order to make processing Employees with various Payroll schedules convenient and easy.

Figure 10-54 Adding a new Payroll Schedule

Step 3.   QuickBooks displays the *New Payroll Schedule* window. Complete the schedule based upon entries in Figure 10-55. Click **OK** to continue.

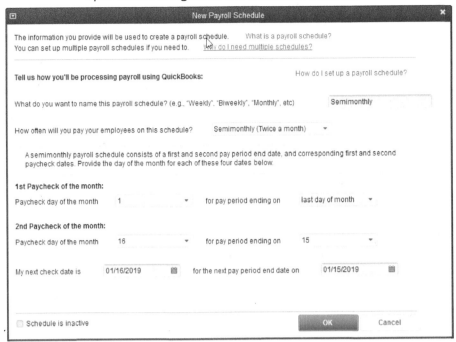

Figure 10-55 New Payroll Schedule

Step 4.   If QuickBooks displays the dialog box asking if the date is correct, click **Yes**.

Step 5.   In Figure 10-56 QuickBooks asks if you would like to assign the new schedule to all Employees with the Semimonthly pay frequency. Click **Yes**.

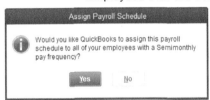

Figure 10-56 Assign Payroll Schedule dialog box

Step 6.   Figure 10-57 displays the number of Employees assigned to the new schedule. This information is helpful because it can alert you to assignment errors. Unfortunately, there is no way to undo global assignments. Click **OK**.

Figure 10-57 Number of Employees assigned a schedule dialog box

Note:
The Payroll Schedules list can be viewed in the *Payroll* tab of the Employee Center, which requires a Payroll subscription service from QuickBooks. In addition, Payroll Schedules cannot be deleted or modified without a Payroll subscription from QuickBooks.

Step 7.   Complete the remaining information as shown in Figure 10-58, by clicking the fields directly in the *Additions, Deductions and Company Contributions* section of the *Employee Defaults* window. Also make sure to check the box, **Use time data to create paychecks**, so that timesheet data can automatically transfer to the Employee's *Preview Paycheck* window.

Use the *Employee Defaults* window to set up the Payroll information that most of your Employees have in common. In the pay period, enter how often most Employees are paid. These are only defaults, so entering something here does not preclude you from overriding your choices for an individual Employee.

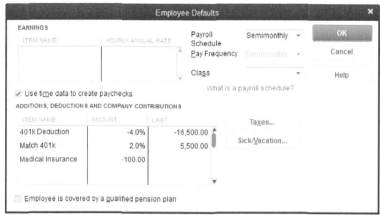

Figure 10-58 Employee Defaults window

Step 8.   Verify that your screen matches Figure 10-58, and then click **Taxes**.

Default settings for taxes

COMPUTER PRACTICE

Step 1.   In the *Taxes Defaults* window, leave the default *Federal* tax settings as shown in Figure 10-59 and click the **State** tab.

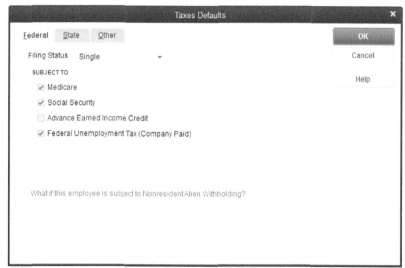

Figure 10-59 Taxes Defaults - Federal

Step 2.   On the *State* taxes default window, select **CA** from the *State* drop-down list in both the **State Worked** and **State Subject to Withholding** sections (see Figure 10-60). This window will vary depending on the states you choose. Then click the **Other** tab.

Figure 10-60 Taxes Defaults - State

Step 3.   Select **CA – Employment Training Tax** in the *Item Name* section as shown in Figure 10-61. Then click **OK**.

If your state has local taxes, the *Other* tab should include the local taxes you must withhold or accrue.

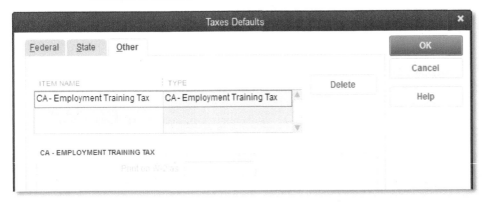

Figure 10-61 Taxes Defaults - Other

> **Note:**
> If your Employees are subject to any of the local taxes that are supported by QuickBooks, you can add those taxes here. If your local tax is not supported directly by QuickBooks, you should set up a *User Defined - Other* tax. See Payroll Taxes (Local) in the QuickBooks onscreen help for more information on these taxes.

Default Settings for Sick/Vacation Time

COMPUTER PRACTICE

Step 1.   On the *Employee Defaults* window, click **Sick/Vacation** (Figure 10-62).

This is where you choose sick and vacation time settings to match your company policies. You can choose *Beginning of year* if your policy is to give each Employee a set number of hours per year. If Employees earn sick or vacation time for each pay period, then choose *Every paycheck.* You can also choose to accrue sick and vacation time based on the number of hours worked or just once per year. Select the appropriate option from the *Accrual period* drop-down list.

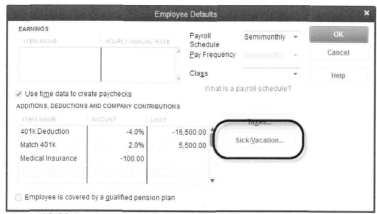

Figure 10-62 Employee Defaults window

Step 2.   Since Academy Photography only offers its Employees vacation time, we will only set up vacation defaults.

Step 3.   In the *Vacation* section, select **Every paycheck** from the *Accrual period* drop-down list to indicate how often you want vacation hours accrued.

Step 4.   Enter *3:00* in the *Hours accrued per paycheck* field and press **Tab**.

Step 5.   Enter *200:00* in the *Maximum number of hours* field.

Step 6.   Leave Reset hours each new year? unchecked.

Step 7.   Leave Sick and vacation hours paid unchecked.

Step 8.   Check Overtime hours paid.

Step 9.   Verify your results match Figure 10-63. Click **OK** to save your work on this window, then click **OK** on the *Employee Defaults* window to save your changes.

Figure 10-63 Sick and Vacation Defaults

Changing Employee Payroll Information

You can make changes to existing employees payroll information. Double click the employee's name in the Employee Center. When the Edit Employee window opens, click the Payroll Info tab (Figure 10-64). Making changes to this tab of the Edit Employees window will change the information automatically entered in future paychecks.

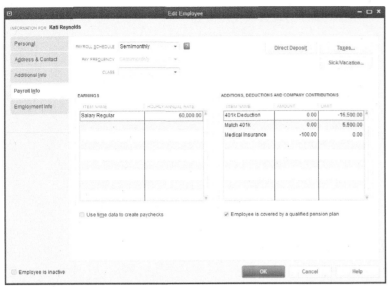

Figure 10-64 Edit Employee Payroll Info

The Accounting Behind the Scenes — Payroll Items

Now that you've finished with the *Payroll Setup Interview*, consider the accounting behind the scenes involving payroll items.

Payroll Items define the relationship between items you put on paychecks and the *Chart of Accounts*. QuickBooks uses *Payroll Items* to track each kind of compensation, withholding tax, employer tax, addition, and deduction from paychecks. Using *Payroll Items*, QuickBooks tracks the detail it needs to calculate paychecks, look up taxes in the tax table, prepare detailed reports, and prepare your payroll tax forms.

Some *Payroll Items* accumulate payroll liabilities (withholdings and company taxes) into liability accounts according to which tax vendor collects the tax. For example, the Federal Withholding Payroll Item accumulates Federal taxes withheld into the Federal PR Taxes liability account. Since the Federal Withholding Item shows *EFTPS* in the *Paid to* field, the withheld taxes are accumulated and tracked as being payable to *EFTPS*.

Payroll Items are set up so that QuickBooks automatically makes all the accounting entries when you process paychecks and payroll liability payments.

Wage Items: There are two types of **Earnings Items: Salary Wage** Items and **Hourly Wage** Items. Earnings Items track regular, over-time, sick, or vacation pay. For example, if you pay an employee for 50 regular hours and 10 hours of vacation, you'll use a regular pay Item and a vacation pay Item, with the corresponding number of hours for each.

Salary Wage Items are used to track payments of gross wages to salaried employees. Since these items represent company expenses, these items increase (debit) an expense account, usually Gross Wages or Officer's Compensation expense.

Hourly Wage Items are used to track payments to hourly employees. Just like the Yearly Salary Items, these items increase (debit) an expense account, usually Gross Wages or Officer's Compensation expense.

> **Note:**
> QuickBooks automatically accumulates sick and vacation hours, but it does not record a liability for this unpaid expense in the General Ledger. If you want to accrue expenses and liabilities for unpaid sick and vacation time, you'll need to make an adjustment using a General Journal entry.

Commission Items are used to track payments of commissions. These items can be defined as a percentage of the number that you enter when you create paychecks. Commission Items increase (debit) an expense account, usually Gross Wages expense.

Bonus Items are used to track bonuses paid to employees (e.g., performance bonuses or annual bonuses). You calculate the employee's bonus before you process payroll for the period. For example, if you give your employees a bonus based on the sales they generate for the company, you would create a Sales by Rep report and calculate the bonus based on the information in the report. Then, you would enter the calculated amount in the employee's next paycheck. Bonus Items increase (debit) an expense account, usually Gross Wages expense.

Other Payments

Addition Items are used to track amounts added to paychecks beyond gross wages. For example, you might set up an Addition Item to track Tips or employee expense reimbursements. Additions increase (debit) an expense account. Addition Items can be added before or after taxes are calculated.

Deduction Items are used to track deductions from paychecks. You can create separate deduction items for each deduction you use on paychecks. For example, if you have a retirement plan, you can create a 401(k) Deduction Item that calculates a percentage of the total gross wages to be deducted before QuickBooks calculates the federal and state income tax. Employee contributions such as the 401(k) would be excluded from taxable earning when calculating federal withholding. Since deductions are withheld from paychecks, they increase (credit) a liability account. The Item also accumulates a balance due to the vendor to whom the deductions are paid. Deduction Items can be deducted before or after taxes are calculated.

Company Contribution Items are used to track additional money that the company contributes as a result of a paycheck. A company contribution is not paid to the employee, but to a vendor on behalf of an employee. For example, if your company matches employees' 401(k) contributions, use a Company Contribution Item to track it. Since this item represents an additional company expense but is not paid directly to the employee, the item increases (debits) an expense account and increases (credits) a liability account. The item also accumulates a balance due to the vendor to whom the contribution is paid.

Federal Tax Items are used to track Federal taxes that are withheld from paychecks or are paid by the employer.

The following Federal Tax Items are employee taxes and are withheld from paychecks: **Federal Withholding, Social Security Employee,** and **Medicare Employee**. These Items are associated with a liability account and with the vendor to whom the tax is paid (usually EFTPS or your local bank).

The following Federal Tax Items are company taxes: **Federal Unemployment, Social Security Company,** and **Medicare Company**. These Items are company-paid taxes; they increase (debit) an expense account, usually **Payroll Taxes**, and increase (credit) a liability account, usually **Federal PR Taxes Payable**.

State Tax Items are used to track state taxes that are withheld from paychecks or paid by the employer. Each state has different taxes, so depending on your state, you might have a **State Withholding, State Disability,** and/or **State Unemployment Tax** Item.

State Withholding taxes are employee taxes and are withheld from paychecks. These Items are associated with a liability account and with the vendor to whom the tax is paid — usually the State Department of Revenue or Taxation.

State Disability taxes are usually employee taxes, but this varies by state.

State Unemployment taxes are usually company taxes, but this also varies by state.

Other Tax Items are used to track other state or local taxes that are withheld from paychecks or paid by the employer. Each locality has different taxes, so check in your state for which local taxes apply to payroll. If your local tax is not directly supported by QuickBooks (i.e., if you don't see the tax in the Other Tax List), you'll need to set up a *User-Defined Tax* to track it.

Calculated Items Based on Quantity

Deduction Items, Addition Items, and Company Contribution Items can be used to withhold or contribute a percentage of gross or net pay, or as a fixed amount. However, sometimes you want these Items to calculate a percentage of some other number. For example, a wage garnishment might need to be created to withhold 20% of the net paycheck. To track this, create a new deduction item with the **Based on Quantity** button checked (see Figure 10-65). Then, when the garnishment item is added to a paycheck, you'll manually enter the amount (in this example, enter net pay in the quantity field) on which the calculation should be based.

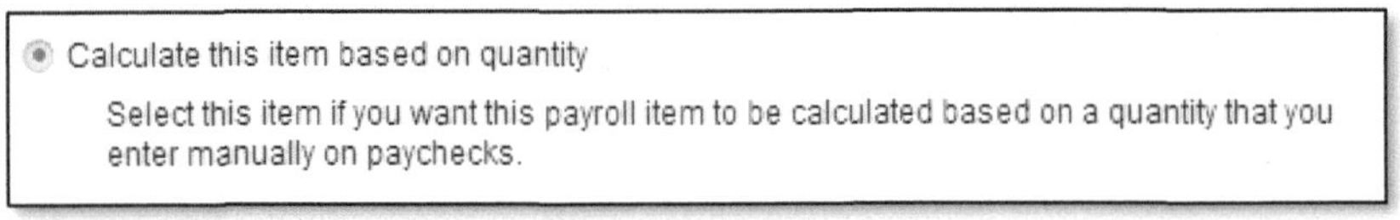

Figure 10-65 You can setup some items based on quantity.

Based on Hours

You can also use Deduction Items, Addition Items, and Company Contribution Items to withhold or contribute a fixed amount or a percentage of gross pay – based on the number of hours the employee worked. In this case, setup the payroll item with the Based on Hours radio button checked (see Figure 10-66). QuickBooks gives you the option of including or excluding sick and vacation hours when calculating the employee's deduction, addition, or company contribution.

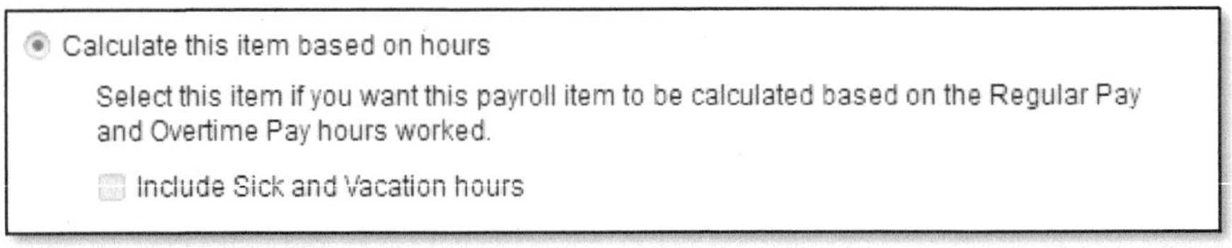

Figure 10-66 You can setup some items based on hours.

Adding Payroll Items from the Payroll Item List

The *Payroll Setup Interview* sets up most of your items, but you'll probably need to set up a few more on your own. The *Custom Payroll Item Setup* feature allows you to add or edit Payroll Items. This feature is accessible from the Payroll Item List and is described in the next section

Adding a Wage (Compensation) Item

If your company is a corporation, the IRS requires you to report compensation of officers separately from the rest of the employees. To track officers' compensation separately from the rest of your employees, you should create an additional *Compensation* Payroll Item called **Officer's Salary.** Follow these steps:

COMPUTER PRACTICE

Step 1.   Display the Payroll Items list by selecting the *Lists* menu and then selecting **Payroll Item List**.

Step 2.   The *Payroll Item List* (Figure 10-67) shows all the items that you have set up using the *Payroll Setup Interview*.

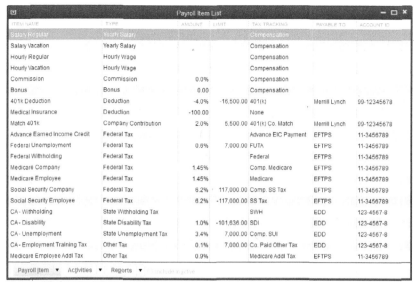

Figure 10-67 Payroll Item list – Your screen may vary

Step 3.   To add a new item, select **New** from the *Payroll Item* menu at the bottom of the *Payroll Item List*, or press **Ctrl+N**.

Step 4.   Select **Custom Setup** in the *Add new payroll item* window (see Figure 10-68). Then click **Next**.

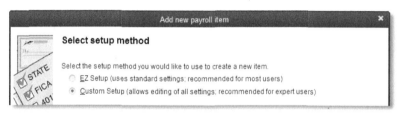

Figure 10-68 Select Custom Payroll Item setup

Step 5.   Select **Wage (Hourly Wages, Annual Salary, Commission, Bonus)** on the *Payroll item type* window and click **Next** (see Figure 10-69).

Figure 10-69 Payroll Item types

Step 6.   Select **Annual Salary** on the *Wages* window (as shown in Figure 10-70) and click **Next**.

               You can set up hourly wage items on this window too. Also, each Wage Item can be for regular pay, overtime pay, sick pay, or vacation pay. When you pay an employee for sick or vacation time, you'll use a Sick or Vacation Pay Item in addition to the regular pay item.

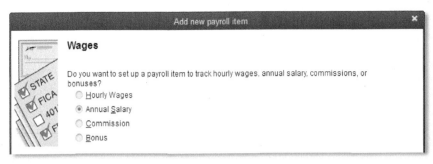

Figure 10-70 Use this window to set up salary and hourly wages.

Step 7.   Leave **Regular Pay** selected and click **Next** (see Figure 10-71).

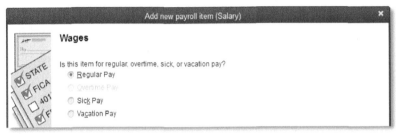

Figure 10-71 Use this window to set up regular, sick, or vacation pay.

Step 8.   Enter **Officer's Salary** in the *Enter name for salary item* field and click **Next** (see Figure 10-72).

Figure 10-72 Use this window to name the Item.

Step 9.   Select **Payroll Expenses:Officer's Compensation** on the *Expense account* window and click **Finish** (see Figure 10-73).

Figure 10-73 Expense account for payroll item

Editing Payroll Items

You will need to edit several of the items created by the *Payroll Setup Interview* so that they will affect the appropriate accounts in the Chart of Accounts. For example, the Federal withholding tax is set up to affect the *Payroll Liabilities* account instead of one of its Subaccounts (Employee Payroll Taxes Payable). You will make these changes by double clicking each Payroll item in the Payroll Item list and then making the needed changes.

Editing the Federal Withholding Payroll item

COMPUTER PRACTICE

Step 1.   Display the *Payroll Items List* by selecting the **Lists** menu, then selecting **Payroll Item List** (see Figure 10-74).

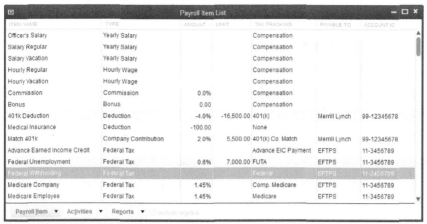

Figure 10-74 Payroll Item list

Step 2.   Double click on the **Federal Withholding** Payroll Item.

Step 3.   Click **Next** on the *Name used in paychecks and payroll reports* window.

Step 4.   On the following window (see Figure 10-75), choose which liability account you want this Item to affect. In this example, select **Payroll Liabilities:Employee Payroll Taxes Payable** from the *Liability account* drop-down list.

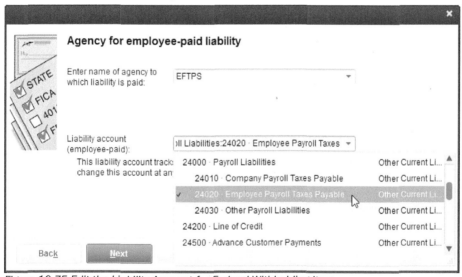

Figure 10-75 Edit the Liability Account for Federal Withholding item.

Step 5.   Click **Next** twice and then click **Finish** to save the change.

Editing the Federal Unemployment item

COMPUTER PRACTICE

Step 1.   To modify the Federal Unemployment item, double click on the **Federal Unemployment** item in the *Payroll Item List*.

Step 2.   Click **Next**.

Step 3.   On the *Agency for company-paid liability* window of the *Edit Payroll Item* wizard, change
                 the account information as shown in Figure 10-76. Choose **Company Payroll Taxes**
                 Payable for the *Liability account* and **Payroll Tax Expense** for the *Expense account*. Then
                 click **Next**.

                 The Federal Unemployment item is a company-paid item, so you need to specify the
                 expense account as well as the liability account.

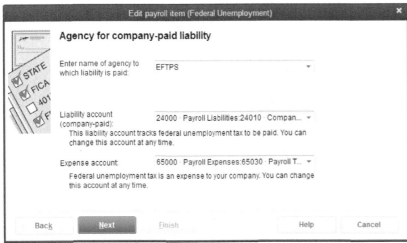

Figure 10-76 Edit the Federal Unemployment Item's accounts.

Step 4.   The tax rate of **0.6%** (as of our publication date) is already selected (Figure 10-77). Click
                 Next twice and then click **Finish**.

                 If your State has a *State Unemployment Tax* you may be eligible for a Federal
                 Unemployment or FUTA tax reduction, making your FUTA tax 0.6% instead of 6.0%. Select
                 the appropriate button on this window. If you're not sure if you're eligible for this
                 reduction, ask your accountant.

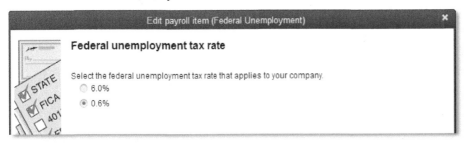

Figure 10-77 Setting the Unemployment tax rate

In the *Payroll Item List*, there are two Medicare and two Social Security Items (Figure 10-78). Although
QuickBooks has two Medicare and two Social Security items in the Payroll Items list to track employer
and employee taxes separately, the two sets of items are grouped together in QuickBooks and are
modified using a single edit window. Therefore, when you change the Medicare Company account, the
Medicare Employee account is automatically updated and vice versa. The same applies to the Social
Security accounts.

Medicare Company	Federal Tax
Medicare Employee	Federal Tax
Social Security Company	Federal Tax
Social Security Employee	Federal Tax

Figure 10-78 Medicare and Social Security tax items

Editing the Medicare and Social Security items

COMPUTER PRACTICE

Step 1.   Double click the **Medicare Company** or **Medicare Employee** payroll item in the *Payroll Item List* window. Since both items will be modified at the same time, either one can be selected.

Step 2.   QuickBooks displays the *Edit payroll item (Medicare Taxes)* window (see Figure 10-79). Click **Next**.

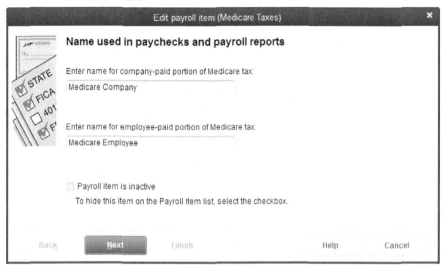

Figure 10-79 Edit Payroll Item (Medicare Taxes)

Step 3.   Select **Company Payroll Taxes Payable** from the drop-down box next to the company-paid liability account field, and **Employee Payroll Taxes Payable** from the drop-down box next to the employee-paid liability account field as shown in Figure 10-80. Click **Next**.

Figure 10-80 Editing Liability accounts for the employer and employee Medicare items

Step 4.   Select **Payroll Expenses:Payroll Tax Expense** from the drop-down list in the *Enter the account for tracking this expense* field (see Figure 10-81). Then click **Next** three times through the remaining windows and click **Finish** on the last window.

Figure 10-81 Enter the Expense account.

Step 5.   Double click the **Social Security Company** or **Social Security Employee** payroll item in the *Payroll Item List* window. Since both items will be modified at the same time, either one can be selected. Repeat steps 2 through 4 above to modify these two payroll items.

Editing the State Withholding item

COMPUTER PRACTICE

Step 1.   To modify the State Withholding Item, double click on **CA- Withholding** in the *Payroll Item List*.

Step 2.   Click **Next**.

Step 3.   On the *Agency for employee-paid liability* window, change the *Liability account (employee-paid)* by selecting **Payroll Liabilities:Employee Payroll Taxes Payable** from the drop-down list. Your screen should look like Figure 10-82.

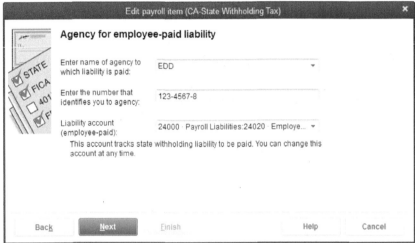

Figure 10-82 Editing the State Withholding item

Step 4.   Click **Next** twice and then click **Finish**.

Editing the State Disability item

COMPUTER PRACTICE

QuickBooks creates a State Disability Item only if your state collects disability tax. Since California collects State Disability tax, the *Payroll Setup Interview* created a State Disability Item. You'll now need to edit the item to make it affect the appropriate accounts.

Step 1.   Double click **CA – Disability** in the *Payroll Item List*, and then click **Next**.

Step 2.   Verify that *123-4567-8* is entered in the *Enter the number that identifies you to agency* box. This is your State Tax ID# that you receive from your tax agency.

Step 3.   In the *Liability account (employee-paid)* field, select **Payroll Liabilities: Employee Payroll Taxes Payable** from the drop-down list. Your screen should look like Figure 10-83.

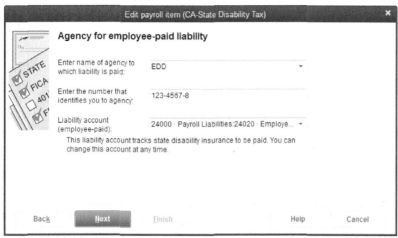

Figure 10-83 Change the liability account for the disability item.

Step 4.   Click **Next**.

Step 5.   On the *Employee tax rate* window, QuickBooks automatically fills in the rate from the tax table. Leave the default Employee rate and click **Next**.

Step 6.   On the *Taxable compensation* window, QuickBooks automatically checks all of the *Wage items* that are subject to State disability tax. Leave all of these checked. Click **Next** and then click **Finish**.

Editing the State Unemployment item

COMPUTER PRACTICE

For State Unemployment, you'll also need to edit the payroll item to make it affect the proper accounts.

Step 1.   Double click the **CA – Unemployment** item. Then click **Next**.

Step 2.   On the *Agency for company-paid liability* window, change the liability account to **Payroll Liabilities:Company Payroll Taxes Payable**. Change the expense account to **Payroll Expenses:Payroll Tax Expense**. Your screen should look like Figure 10-84.

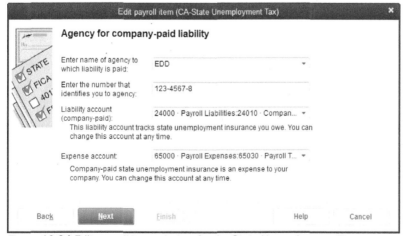

Figure 10-84 Edit payroll item window for the State Unemployment Tax

Step 3.   Click **Next**.

Step 4.   On the *Company tax rate* window (Figure 10-85), leave the tax rates as you entered them in the *Payroll Setup Interview*, or change them here if necessary. Click **Next**.

If your State unemployment tax rate changes, return to this window to update QuickBooks. The state unemployment tax rate is not supplied by the tax table because each employer has a different rate. Therefore, you must enter it here.

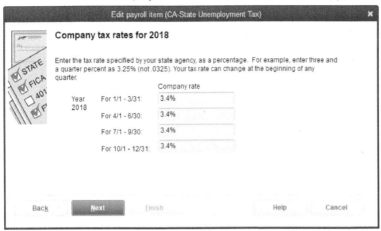

Figure 10-85 Unemployment tax rates – Your screen may vary

Step 5.   On the *Taxable compensation* window, QuickBooks automatically checks all of the *Wage Items* that are subject to state unemployment tax. Leave them all checked. Click **Next** and then click **Finish**.

Editing Other Tax items

COMPUTER PRACTICE

If you have other State-specific taxes or local taxes, set up Other Tax Items. For example, in California set up an Other Tax Item to track California Employment Training Tax (ETT).

You created the *Employment Training Tax item* in the *Payroll Setup Interview*. Now follow these steps to edit it:

Step 1.   Double click on the **CA – Employment Training Tax** item in the *Payroll Item List*. Then click **Next**.

Step 2.   On the *Agency for company-paid liability* window, change the liability account to **Payroll Liabilities:Company Payroll Taxes Payable**. Change the expense account to **Payroll Expenses:Payroll Tax Expense**. Your screen should look like Figure 10-86. Click **Next**.

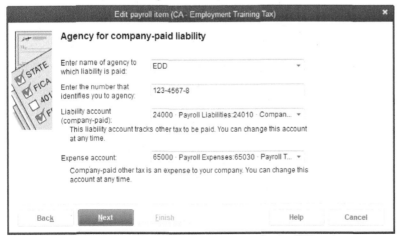

Figure 10-86 Edit the liability and expense account for the ETT tax item.

Step 3.   On the *Company tax rate* window accept the default rate of **0.1%** and click **Next**.

Step 4.   On the *Taxable compensation* window, QuickBooks automatically checks all of the Wage Items that are subject to this local tax. Leave all of these checked. Click **Next** and then click **Finish**. Then close the Payroll Item list.

Releasing Employees

When you release or terminate an employee, edit the employee record and fill in the **Released** field with the date on which the employee separated from the company (see Figure 10-87). A released employee no longer appears in the *Select Employees to Pay* window when you run your payroll, although they will still show in your *Employee Center*.

COMPUTER PRACTICE

Step 1.   Select the **Employee Center** icon on the *Icon Bar*.

Step 2.   Double click on **Kati Reynolds** from the *Name* list.

Step 3.   Select the **Employment Info** tab (see Figure 10-87).

Step 4.   Enter *2/28/2019* in the *Release Date* field (Figure 10-87) and press **Tab**.

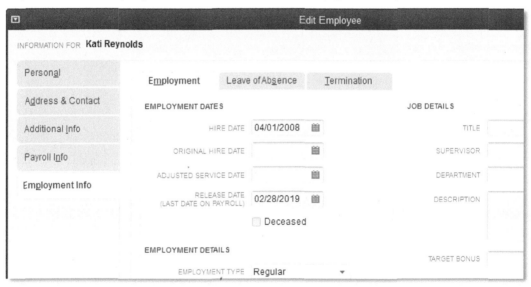

Figure 10-87 Releasing an employee

Step 5.   A warning window appears stating that the released employee will not show up on the Select Employees to Pay list after the release date. Click **OK** to close the warning window

Step 6.   Click **Cancel** to prevent this change from taking effect in your exercise file.

Deactivating and Reactivating Employees

After you've released an employee, you may wish to delete that employee from your *Employee list*. However, if an employee's name is used in any transactions (e.g., paychecks) or if the name is used in the *Rep* field on any customer record or sales transaction, QuickBooks won't allow you to delete the employee from the *Employee list*. A better option is to "deactivate" the employee so it will no longer appear in your list.

To deactivate an employee, follow these steps:

Step 1.   Right click **Kati Reynolds** in the Employee Center and select **Make Employee Inactive** (see Figure 10-88). This removes this employee from the list, but it doesn't delete the employee from your company file.

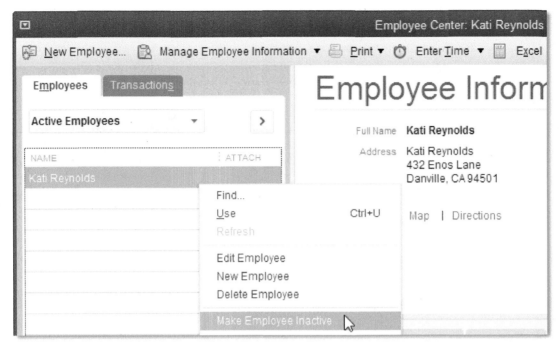

Figure 10-88 Deactivating an employee

COMPUTER PRACTICE

To reactivate an employee, first set your Employee Center to view All Employees.

Step 1.   Select **All Employees** from the **View** menu in the *Employee Center* (see Figure 10-89).

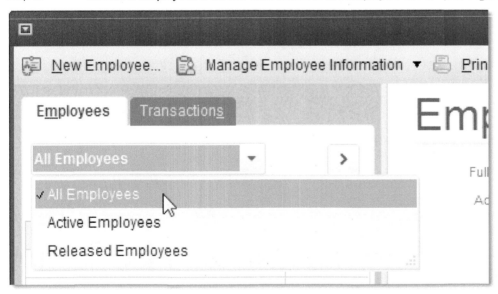

Figure 10-89 Viewing All employees including inactive ones

Step 2.   To reactivate Kati Reynolds, right click on her name and select **Make Employee Active**.
               Alternatively, click on the icon of the grey 'X' to the left of the employee name in the
               Employee List as shown in Figure 10-90 (or edit the employee record and uncheck the
               Employee is inactive box).

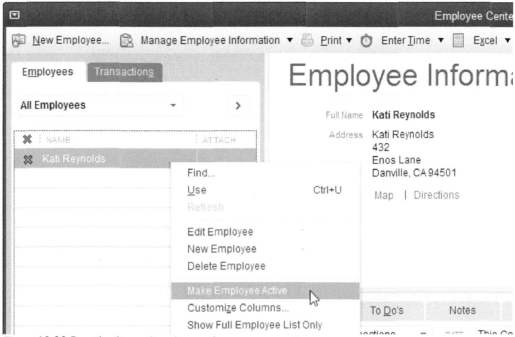

Figure 10-90 Reactivating an inactive employee

The Employee Contact List report

You can print a list of Employees by following the steps below.

COMPUTER PRACTICE

Step 1.   Select the **Reports** menu, select **List**, and then select **Employee Contact List** (see Figure 10-91).

Figure 10-91 Employee Contact List

Step 2.   Click **Print** at the top of the report and follow the prompts to print the report. Then, close the *Employee Contact List* report.

Review Questions

Comprehension Questions

1. What type of payroll item should you set up to track additional money contributed by the company as a result of a paycheck?

2. Why do you need to edit several of your payroll items (e.g., Payroll Tax Items) after you complete the *Payroll Setup Interview*?

3. Name an example of a payroll item that should be "Based on Quantity"?

Multiple Choice

Select the best answer(s) for each of the following:

1. An easy and convenient way to process Payroll in QuickBooks for Employees on different Payroll schedules would be to:
    a)   Move all Employees onto a single schedule.
    b)   Use the *Payroll Schedule* function in QuickBooks.
    c)   Outsource Payroll.
    d)   Make all Employees independent contractors.

2. Which of the following Payroll periods is not an option in QuickBooks?
    a)   Quarterly
    b)   Biweekly
    c)   Daily
    d)   Semiannually

3. Which Payroll Item cannot be created in the *Payroll Setup Interview*?
    a)   Commissions
    b)   Bonus
    c)   Medical Insurance Deduction
    d)   You can create all Items above during the *Payroll Setup Interview*

4. Which is *not* an option when setting the accrual period for sick and vacation time?
    a)   Beginning of year
    b)   Every month
    c)   Every paycheck
    d)   Every hour on paycheck

5. The *Payroll Setup Interview* will not allow you to:
    a)   Edit the default name for Payroll Items.
    b)   Associate deduction and withholding Items with Vendors.
    c)   Set the pay rate for an Employee.
    d)   Add two Employees with exactly the same name.

6. You enter the Federal ID for your company:
   a) In **Payroll Preferences** on the *Company Preferences* tab.
   b) On Step 3 of the *Payroll Setup Interview* – "Set up Company Information."
   c) In the *Company Information* window.
   d) In **General Preferences** on the *Company Preferences* tab.

7. Use a **Payroll Deduction** Item to track medical insurance costs when:
   a) The employees pay part (or all) of the cost.
   b) Costs exceed $100 per month for the employee.
   c) The employer pays the total cost.
   d) You do not track medical insurance costs as a Payroll Deduction Item.

8. Which of the following would QuickBooks exclude from taxable earnings when calculating federal withholding?
   a) Vacation salary
   b) Sick leave salary
   c) Overtime earnings
   d) Employee contributions to a 401(k)

9. Why are there two **Medicare** and two **Social Security** items in the **Payroll Items** list?
   a) Different tax rates apply to employee and employer portions.
   b) You use separate accounts because you must write separate checks for employee and employer portions.
   c) QuickBooks tracks the employee and employer portions separately.
   d) You maintain separate ledger accounts for the two portions of each tax.

10. Which of the following is *not* a feature of QuickBooks Standard Payroll Service?
    a) Tracks individual employees for hours worked and gross pay.
    b) Writes and prints paychecks on standard checks.
    c) Calculates and electronically remits federal payroll tax liabilities using EFTPS.
    d) Automatically calculates Federal, State and some local taxes using tax tables supplied through the QuickBooks Standard Payroll Service.

11. QuickBooks uses Payroll Items to:
    a) Accumulate payroll liabilities.
    b) Track each different kind of compensation.
    c) Define the relationship between items you put on paychecks and the chart of accounts.
    d) All of the above.

12. If you no longer want an employee to show in the *Select Employees to Pay* list:
    a) Stop paying the employee.
    b) Deselect the employee for payments.
    c) Enter a Release Date in the employee's record.
    d) Remove all wage items from the employee's record.

13. Which of the following payroll options does not require you to sign up for an Intuit Payroll Service?
    a) Manual
    b) Standard
    c) Assisted
    d) Complete

14. To set up local taxes for employees that are not supported by QuickBooks:
    a) Choose the *Other* tab under Tax Defaults.
    b) Set up New **Payroll Item** , and select *Other Tax*
    c) You cannot set up taxes not supported by QuickBooks tax tables.
    d) A or B.

Completion Statements

1. The ____ _____ feature allows you to define defaults for your employee records so that you do not have to enter the same information each time you add a new employee.

2. To set up custom fields for adding more detailed information about your employees, click the _____ _____ button on the *Additional Info* tab of the *New Employee* or *Edit Employee* window.

3. QuickBooks uses _____ items to track amounts withheld from gross or net pay of employees. Since these payroll items represent amounts withheld, these items usually credit a(n) _____ account.

4. When you release an employee, edit the employee record and fill in the _____ _____ field with the date on which the employee separated from the company. QuickBooks will no longer show the employee in the *Select Employees to Pay* list.

5. When you pay semi-monthly wages, you can assign employees to a(n) _____ *Schedule.* This allows you to group together all employees with semi-monthly wages.

Payroll Setup Problem 1

> Restore the PRSetup-18Problem1.QBM file. The password to access this file is **Sleeter18**.

1. Using the *Payroll Setup Interview*, add the Payroll Items shown in Table 10-3. For this setup, there are no other employee compensation items or insurance and retirement benefits.

Item Name	Setup Notes
Hourly Regular	This Item should point to Gross Wages, a subaccount of the Payroll Expenses account.
Salary Regular	This Item should point to Gross Wages, a subaccount of the Payroll Expenses account.

Table 10-3 Payroll Items

2. Using the Payroll Setup Interview, edit the Payroll Items shown in Table 10-4.

Item Name	Setup Notes
Hourly Vacation	This Item should point to Gross Wages, a subaccount of the Payroll Expenses account.
Salary Vacation	This Item should point to Gross Wages, a subaccount of the Payroll Expenses account.

Table 10-4 Payroll Items

3. Set up a new Employee with the following information:

Field	Data
First Name	Tanya
M.I.	
Last Name	Jackson
Print on check as	Tanya Jackson
Employee Status	Active
Address	2271 South Canyon Blvd. Hayward, CA 95555
Employee Tax Type	Regular
SS No.	123-45-9876
Hire Date	7/1/2017
Release Date	
Date of Birth	12/7/1980
Gender	Female
Pay Period	Weekly
Earnings	Hourly Regular – Rate $20 per hour (leave all other fields blank)
Vacation Settings	3 hours vacation time per paycheck, maximum 200 hours
Direct Deposit	No direct Deposit
Employee Works and lives	Works - CA; Lives - CA; Did not live or work in another state
Federal Filing Status	Single, 0 Allowances; Nonresident Alien Withholding: Does not apply; HIRE Act Exemption: Not a qualified employee; Subject to Medicare, Social Security, Federal Unemployment
State Filing Status	CA – Filing Status Single, 0 regular withholding allowances; subject to Unemployment, Employment Training tax, and Disability; not subject to any special local taxes
Wage Plan Code	S (State Plan For Both UI and DI)

Table 10-5 New Employee setup information

4. Other information for Payroll Setup is below.

Field	Data
State Unemployment Rate	3.4%
Federal Tax Payee	EFTPS
Payment frequency (all payroll taxes)	Quarterly
State Tax Payee	EDD
CA EDD Employer Acct No.	123-4567-8
Year-To-Date-Payroll	None

Table 10-6 Other Information for Payroll Setup

5. Create a *Payroll Item Listing Report*. Select the **Reports** menu, then choose **List** and then choose **Payroll Item Listing**. Print the report.

6. Create an *Employee Contact List Report*. Print the report.

Payroll Setup Problem 2 (Advanced)

Restore the PRSetup-18Problem2.QBM file. The password to access this file is **Sleeter18**.

1. Using the *Payroll Setup Interview*, add the Payroll Items shown in Table 10-7.

Item Name	Setup Notes
Salary Regular	This Item should point to Gross Wages, a subaccount of the Payroll Expenses account.
Hourly Regular	This Item should point to Gross Wages, a subaccount of the Payroll Expenses account.
Hourly Double-time	This Item should point to Gross Wages, a subaccount of the Payroll Expenses account.
Hourly Time-and-a-half	This Item should point to Gross Wages, a subaccount of the Payroll Expenses account.
Commission	Add a 4% commission Item. This Item should point to Gross Wages, a subaccount of the Payroll Expenses account. Commissions are calculated based upon percentage of sales.
Health Insurance	Use Health Insurance (taxable) Item to set up this Item. Leave the payee and account number fields blank. Use "Payroll Liabilities:Other Payroll Liabilities" to track the withholding. Employee pays for all of it and it is deducted after taxes at a flat rate of $50.00. Select all other defaults.
401(k) Employee	Payee is Merrill Lynch. Account number with Merrill Lynch is "99-1123456." Liability account is "Payroll Liabilities:Other Payroll Liabilities," Tax Tracking type is "401(k)," and you should use the standard tax settings. The default rate is 4% as a percentage of pay and the default limit is $16,000.00 This is a traditional 401(k) and not a Roth 401(k).
Match 401(k)	Track this expense by Job. Payee is Merrill Lynch; Account number is "99-1123456." Expense account is "Payroll Expenses: Employee Benefits." Liability account is "Payroll Liabilities:Other Payroll Liabilities." Tax Tracking type is "None." Use standard tax settings. The default rate is 2% and the default limit is $5,500.00.
Salary Vacation	This Item should point to Gross Wages, a subaccount of the Payroll Expenses account.
Hourly Vacation	This Item should point to Gross Wages, a subaccount of the Payroll Expenses account.
Salary Sick	This Item should point to Gross Wages, a subaccount of the Payroll Expenses account.
Hourly Sick	This Item should point to Gross Wages, a subaccount of the Payroll Expenses account.

Table 10-7 Add these Payroll Items.

2. Set up a new Employee with the following information:

Field	Data
First Name	Tom
M.I.	
Last Name	Fredrick
Print on check as	Tom Fredrick
Employee Status	Active
Address	12 Blossom Lane San Francisco, CA 94555
Employee Tax Type	Regular
SS No.	123-12-3123
Hire Date	7/1/2015
Release Date	
Date of Birth	4/16/1978
Gender	Male
Pay Period	Weekly
Earnings	Hourly Regular – Rate $26 per hour (leave all other fields blank)
Additions, Deductions, and Company Contributions	401(k) Employee (4%), limit $16,000.00 Match 401(k) (2%), limit $5,500.00 Health Insurance ($50)
Sick/Vacation Settings	3 hours sick time per paycheck, maximum 80 hours 3 hours vacation time per paycheck, maximum 200 hours
Direct Deposit	No Direct Deposit
Employee Works and lives	Works - CA; Lives - CA; Did not live or work in another state
Federal Filing Status	Single, 0 Allowances; Nonresident Alien Withholding: Does not apply; HIRE Act Exemption: Not a qualified employee; Subject to Medicare, Social Security, Federal Unemployment
State Filing Status	CA – Filing Status Single, 0 regular withholding allowances; subject to Unemployment, Employment Training tax, and Disability; not subject to any special local taxes
Wage Plan Code	S (State Plan For Both UI and DI)

Table 10-8 New Employee setup information

3. Schedule payments by selecting **EFTPS** as the *Payee* (Vendor) for United States Treasury Payments. You deposit your taxes quarterly. You use this to pay your liabilities for Federal taxes.

4. State tax payee is EDD with California Tax ID 123-4567-8. State taxes are paid Quarterly. The State Unemployment rate is 3.4%.

5. Set up your *Employee Defaults* for the following:

Field Name	Setup Notes
Payroll Schedule	Weekly
Pay Period End Date	1/6/2019
Paycheck Date	1/8/2019
Additions, Deductions and Company Contributions	401(k) Employee (-4%), Maximum -16,000.00 Match 401(k) (2%), Maximum $5,500.00 Health Insurance (-$50 per paycheck)
Federal Taxes	Filing Status: Single Subject to: Social Security, FUTA, Medicare
State Taxes	Default State Worked: CA Default State Subject to Withholding: CA
Other Taxes	Medicare Employee Addl Tax, CA – Employment Training Tax
Sick Hours Accruals	Accrual Period: Beginning of Year Hours Accrued at Beginning of Year: 40 Maximum number of hours: 80 Do not reset hours each new year.
Vacation Hours Accruals	Accrual Period: Beginning of Year Hours Accrued at Beginning of Year: 80 Maximum number of hours: 200 Do not reset hours each new year.

Table 10-9 Employee default settings

6. Create a *Payroll Item Listing Report*. Select the **Reports** menu, then choose **List** and then choose **Payroll Item Listing**. Modify the *Report* to include the *Payable To* column and then print the report. Set the *Report* to print on one page wide.

7. Create an *Employee Contact List Report*. Print the report.

Chapter 11
Payroll Processing

Topics

In this chapter, you will learn about the following topics:

> **Restore this File:**
> This chapter uses PRProcessing-18.QBW. See page 9 for more information. You will not need to enter a password because this is a sample file.

In this chapter, you'll learn to process your Payroll smoothly using QuickBooks Payroll. It presents the use of *QuickBooks Basic Payroll*, which helps you create paychecks by automatically calculating the Payroll taxes on each paycheck.

The exercise file for this chapter is a sample file that will allow you to interact with the automated Payroll options without requiring a Payroll subscription. All sample files will set the current date to December 15, 2019 (Figure 11-1). You can identify sample files by a warning on the upper left corner of the Icon Bar (Figure 11-2).

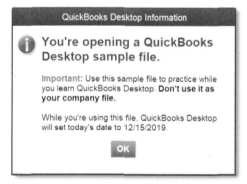

Figure 11-1 Sample File Date Warning

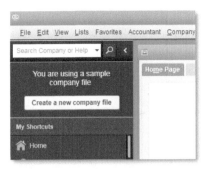

Figure 11-2 Sample File's top of Icon Bar

Payroll Processing Checklists

To keep your Payroll running smoothly and to minimize errors, you should complete the following steps at the prescribed intervals:

Every Payday

- Review the previous Payroll activity in the *Employee Center*.
- Verify that your tax tables are current and update them if necessary.
- Create, review, and correct (if necessary) paychecks.
- Print paychecks and pay stubs (if necessary).

Every Tax Deposit Due Date (monthly or semi-weekly)

- Create, review, and correct (if necessary) liability payments.
- Print liability payment checks (if necessary).

Every Quarter (after the end of the quarter)

- Verify the accuracy of all Payroll transactions for the previous quarter.
- Create Payroll reports for the previous quarter and year-to-date.
- Create Payroll tax returns (Federal Form 941 and state quarterly returns).

Every January

- Verify the accuracy of all Payroll transactions for the entire previous year.
- Create Payroll reports for the previous quarter and year-to-date.
- Create Payroll tax returns (Federal Form 941, 940, and state yearly returns).

Using the Employee Center

The *Employee Center* displays a list of all Employees and related transactions such as paychecks, liability checks, and Payroll Liability adjustments. Before processing Payroll each pay period, it is a good idea to open the *Employee Center* and review the latest Payroll activity for each Employee. Doing so will help reduce Payroll processing errors like creating duplicate checks or processing Payroll checks with incorrect data.

To open the *Employee Center*, click the **Employees** icon on the *Icon Bar*, or the **Employees** button on the *Home* page.

Payroll Center

If you have an active QuickBooks Payroll service subscription, the *Employee Center* will contain an additional *Payroll* tab called the *Payroll Center*. This *Center* has three tabs, *Pay Employees*, *Pay Liabilities*, and *File Forms*. You can use these tabs to pay Employees, pay taxes and other liabilities, and process Payroll forms (see Figure 11-3).

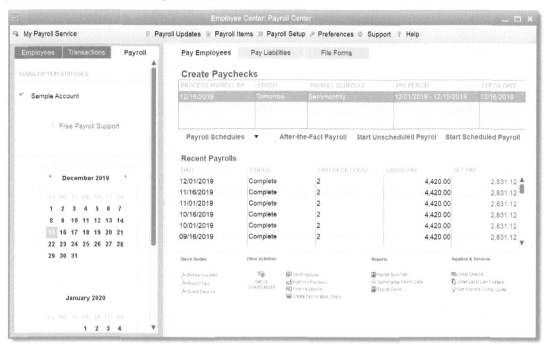

Figure 11-3 Employee Center with active subscription showing Payroll tab – Your screen may vary

Payroll Tax Tables

> **Key Term:** *Payroll Tax Tables* include the tax rates necessary to calculate an Employee's paycheck. This calculation affects the amounts of taxes that are withheld from an Employee's check (e.g., Federal and state income tax) as well as the amounts of taxes the company must pay for the Employee (e.g., Federal and state unemployment tax). The Payroll Tax Tables also include data that updates the forms that print directly from QuickBooks (i.e., 940, 941, and W-2).

In order for your paychecks to calculate automatically and your forms to print properly, you must have a current Payroll service subscription. Intuit recommends that you connect to their Web site frequently (at least every 45 days) to ensure that you're using the latest tax tables.

Paying Employees

In the previous chapter, you set up Payroll for Academy Photography. Once the Payroll setup is complete, and you have downloaded the latest tax tables (not required in the sample file for this chapter), you are ready to process Payroll.

Selecting the Employees to Pay

COMPUTER PRACTICE

Step 1.   Click **Pay Employees** on the *Home* page. The *Employee Center* opens with the *Payroll* tab selected on the left of the window and the *Pay Employees* tab selected on the right. (Figure 11-4)

Step 2.   Click the **Start Scheduled Payroll** button.

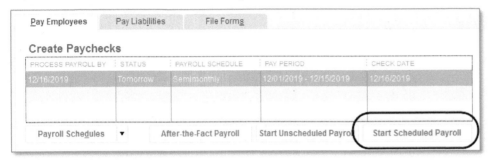

Figure 11-4 Pay Employees Section of Employee Center

Step 3.   The *Enter Payroll Information* window opens (Figure 11-5). Leave the default dates in the *Pay Period Ends* and *Check Date* fields.

The two date fields on this window are very important. The first one indicates the last day of the pay period included on the paychecks, and the second one sets the date of the actual paycheck. Make sure you always verify these dates before creating your paychecks.

> **Important:**
> The check date on paychecks determines when the Payroll expenses show on all reports. For example, if you pay Employees on the 16th of the month for wages earned during the first half of the month, the reports will show the expenses for that Payroll on the 16th.

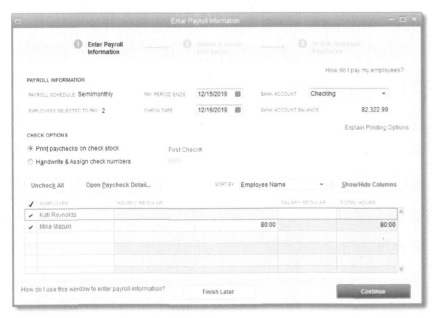

Figure 11-5 Enter Payroll Information window

Step 4. Click the **Kati Reynolds** link in the list of Employees to open the *Preview Paycheck* window (Figure 11-6). Alternatively you can select **Kati Reynolds** and click **Open Paycheck Detail** button.

The *Preview Paycheck* window displays the automatic deductions that QuickBooks has calculated for the Payroll liabilities based on the tax tables and settings entered in the previous chapter. Kati Reynolds is a salaried Employee and therefore receives *Salary Regular* earnings.

Figure 11-6 Preview Paycheck window for Kati Reynolds – your screen may vary

> **Note:**
> The tax withholdings shown in Figure 11-6 may be different than what you see on your screen. Withholdings are calculated using the tax tables loaded on your computer. Some readers with different tax tables will see differences between their exercise file and the screenshots throughout this chapter.

Step 5. In the *Earnings* section, add a second line for **Salary Vacation**. Notice that the salary defaults to automatically split evenly between the two lines.

Step 6. Enter **85** in the *Hours* column for **Salary Regular** on the first line, and **3** in the *Hours* column for **Salary Vacation** on the second line (see Figure 11-7).

With salaried Employees, QuickBooks calculates the total gross pay for the period (annual rate divided by the number of pay periods) and then divides that amount equally into each of the Earnings Items listed in the *Earnings* section. To track sick and vacation hours used, enter the number of hours for each on separate lines in the *Earnings* section. QuickBooks prorates the total salary amount to each line according to the number of hours on that line.

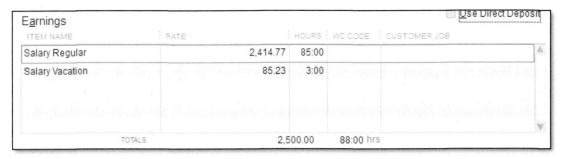

Figure 11-7 Earnings section in Preview Paycheck window

Step 7.   Confirm that **-4%** is in the *Rate* column next to *401k Deduction* and **2%** is in the *Rate* column next to *Match 401k* in the *Other Payroll Items* section of the *Preview Paychecks* window (Figure 11-8).

Other Payroll Items

ITEM NAME	RATE	QUANTITY
401k Deduction	-4.0%	
Match 401k	2.0%	
Medical Insurance	-100.00	

Figure 11-8 Other Payroll Items in Preview Paycheck window

Step 8.   Verify that your screen matches Figure 11-9 (tax items may vary). When finished click **Save & Next**.

Figure 11-9 Preview Paycheck window after data entry – tax items on your screen may vary

Step 9.   The *Preview Paycheck* window of the other Employee, Mike Mazuki, opens (Figure 11-11).

Step 10.   Notice that *Earnings* section is set to *Hourly Regular* and *80* hours. The number of hours is automatically set from the previous paycheck.

> **Note:**
> If the default setting was set up to *Use Time Data to Create Paychecks* (see page 383), QuickBooks would fill the Earnings section of the paycheck with data entered in the *Weekly Timesheet*. An example is shown in Figure 11-10. You can override any of the information that was automatically copied from the timesheet. However, any changes you make here will not change the original timesheet. If you discover errors at this point, you might want to cancel out of the *Create Paycheck* window, correct the timesheet, and then recreate the paycheck.

Earnings				
ITEM NAME	RATE	HOURS	WC CODE	CUSTOMER JOB
Hourly Regular		24.00	10:00	Garrison, John:Family Portrait 20...
Hourly Regular		24.00	16:00	Morris Consulting
Hourly Regular		24.00	36:00	Mason, Bob
Hourly Regular		24.00	18:00	Ortega Services
Totals:	1,920.00	80:00 hrs		

Figure 11-10 Example Earnings section of the Preview Paycheck window including Timesheet data

Step 11. Verify that your window matches Figure 11-11 (tax items may vary) and press the **Save & Close** button.

Figure 11-11 Preview Paycheck window – tax items on your screen may vary

Step 12. Click **Continue** in the *Enter Payroll Information* window. The *Review and Create Paychecks* window appears.

Figure 11-12 Review and Create Paychecks window

Step 13.   Click the **Print paychecks on check stock** option under *Check Options*.

Step 14.   Verify that your screen matches Figure 11-12 (taxes may vary) and click **Create Paychecks**. The *Confirmation and Next Steps* window appears. Leave this window open for the next exercise.

Printing Paychecks

When you're finished creating all of the paychecks, QuickBooks displays the *Confirmation and Next Steps* window (Figure 11-13). From this window, you can print paychecks or print pay stubs. The next exercise prints paychecks.

Figure 11-13 Confirmation and Next Steps window

COMPUTER PRACTICE

Step 1.   Click the **Print Paychecks** button on the *Confirmation and Next Steps* window.

> **Another Way:**
> If you want to print the paychecks after you have left the *Confirmation and Next Steps* window, select the **File** menu, select **Print Forms**, and then select **Paychecks**.

Step 2.   If necessary, enter **6069** in the *First Check Number* field (see Figure 11-14). Click **OK**.

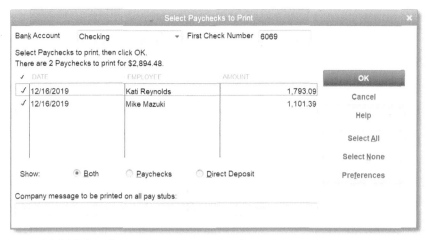

Figure 11-14 Select the paychecks to be printed – your amounts may vary

Step 3.   In the *Print Checks* window, QuickBooks lets you know that there are two checks to print and gives the total amount of those checks (see Figure 11-15).

You can also select the check style in the *Print Checks* window. Select **Voucher** as your choice of check style. When you use voucher checks, QuickBooks prints the paystub information on the voucher portion of the checks.

> **Note:**
> For this class you'll print on blank paper instead of real checks. When you're printing on real checks, make sure to load the checks into the printer before you click **Print**.
>
> **Tip:**
> It's best to use voucher checks for Payroll. Make sure your checks are oriented correctly in the printer. With some printers, you feed the top of the page in first, and for others you feed the bottom in first. With some printers, you need to insert the check face up, and with others, you insert it face down.

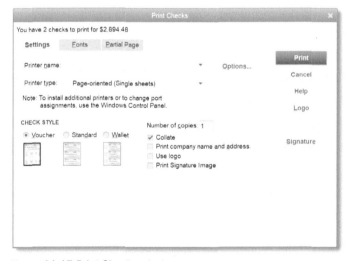

Figure 11-15 Print Checks window

The paycheck and voucher pay stubs for Kati Reynolds are shown as printed on blank paper in Figure 11-16. Note that the check number is not printed. The check number is part of the prepared check and therefore you won't see the check number when you print on blank paper.

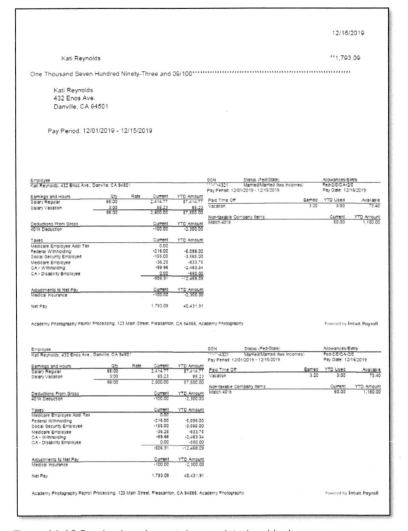

Figure 11-16 Paycheck and pay stubs as printed on blank paper

Step 4.   Verify the printer settings and then click **Print**. Click **OK** on the *Print Checks - Confirmation* message.

Step 5.   Click **Close** on the *Confirmation and Next Steps* window.

Printing Pay Stubs

If you don't print checks from QuickBooks, you can still print pay stubs for your Employees on blank paper.

> **Note:**
> You can print pay stubs at any time, even after you have printed the paychecks.

COMPUTER PRACTICE

Step 1.   Select the **File** menu, then select **Print Forms**, and then select **Pay Stubs** (see Figure 11-17).

Step 2.   Leave the default date of *12/14/2019* for the beginning date and *3/13/2020* for the thru date for the pay stubs to print. Paychecks dated in the date range you specify will show in the list.

Figure 11-17 Select Pay Stubs window

Step 3.   Click **Preview** to see what the pay stubs look like when they print (see Figure 11-18). QuickBooks prints one pay stub per page.

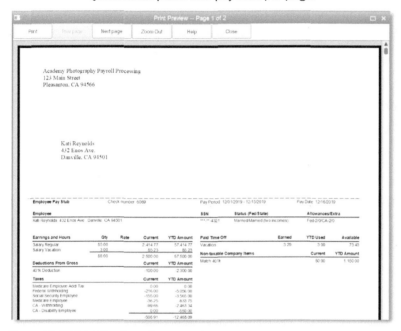

Figure 11-18 Print Preview of a pay stub

Step 4.   After previewing the pay stub, click **Close**. If you wished to print, you could print the pay stub from the preview window.

Step 5.   Close the *Select Pay Stubs* window.

Editing Paychecks

If you find errors on paychecks, you can edit, void, or delete the paychecks. However, be careful when you do any of these actions because changing transactions may adversely affect your records. When in doubt, ask your accountant.

> **Note:**
> If you edit a paycheck that you have already printed, make sure your changes don't affect
> the net pay amount. Also, if this Employee has other paychecks dated after this check,
> the changes you make may invalidate the tax calculations on the newer checks. It's best
> to avoid editing, voiding, or deleting any paycheck except the most recent paycheck for
> each Employee. If you're unsure about any adjustments you need to make, check with
> your accountant.

It's not considered good accounting practice to edit paychecks after they've been printed and sent to the
Employee. However, it is possible to edit paychecks in QuickBooks, even after they've been printed.
Editing paychecks should only be done if you haven't sent the paycheck to the employee.

COMPUTER PRACTICE

Step 1.   From the *Payroll Center*, in the lower section of the *Pay Employees* tab, select the
                 Edit/Void Paycheck link in the *Other Activities* section.

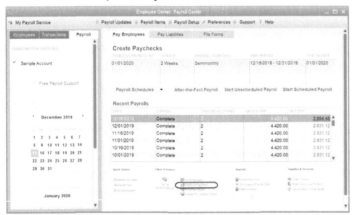

Figure 11-19 Edit Paychecks in the Payroll Center

Step 2.   The *Edit/Void Paychecks* window opens. Set the *Show paychecks dates from* to
                 12/1/2019 and the *through* date to *12/31/2019*. Then press **Tab** (see Figure 11-20).

Figure 11-20 Edit/Void Paychecks window

Step 3.   Press **Tab** to leave **Paycheck Date** in the *Sort By* field.

Step 4.   Highlight **Mike Mazuki's** paycheck dated **12/16/2019** and then click **Edit** (see Figure
                 11-20).

Figure 11-21 Click Paycheck Detail to edit the Items on the paycheck

Step 5.   To edit the Items on the paycheck, click **Paycheck Detail** (see Figure 11-21).

Figure 11-22 Any of the fields with a white background can be edited.

Step 6.   Select the *Class* field in the upper right corner to the **San Jose** class (see Figure 11-22).

Note:
You can edit only the fields without a gray background on the *Review Paycheck* window. To edit the year-to-date amounts, use the *Adjust Liabilities* window, or override the amounts on a future paycheck for this Employee.

Step 7.   Click **Cancel** and then click **Save & Close** to leave the check unchanged. Click **Done** to leave the *Edit/Void Paychecks* window.

Another Way:
You can also edit a paycheck by double clicking on the paycheck in the checking account register and then continue from Step 5 above.

Replacing Lost or Stolen Checks

DON'T PERFORM THESE STEPS NOW. THEY ARE FOR REFERENCE ONLY.

---

1.   Find the check in the *Employee Center* or the *Checking* account register, then double click to edit the paycheck, and then click the **Print Later** box at the top of the *Paycheck* window (see Figure 11-23). This clears the check number field, and replaces it with "To Print."

Figure 11-23 Payroll Check to be reprinted

2.   Click **Save & Close** and then **Yes** to save your change.

3.   Reprint the check and then give it a new check number.

4.   Enter a *new* check directly into the *Checking* account register with the same date, payee, amount, and check number as the lost check. Code it to the *Miscellaneous Expense* account.

5.   Void the new check you just created. This converts the check into a *voided* check with the same date, payee, amount and check number as the lost or stolen check.

> **Tip:**
> The reason you don't void the original transaction and create a new paycheck is a little tricky to understand. In the event that the paycheck to be replaced was not the *most recent paycheck* for that employee, QuickBooks would not be able to recreate the check exactly as the original. That's because the year-to-date information is calculated on each paycheck by taking all paychecks (regardless of their date) and adding their amounts together. The method shown here avoids this problem by simply reprinting the original paycheck using a new check number.

Voiding Paychecks

If you need to void a paycheck, make sure it's the most recent paycheck for this employee. If it's not the most recent paycheck, see the tip above.

Before you edit or void old paychecks, make a backup of your file.

> **DON'T PERFORM THESE STEPS NOW. THEY ARE FOR REFERENCE ONLY.**

1.   From the *Pay Employees* tab of the *Payroll Center*, click the **Edit/Void Paycheck** link in the **Other Activities** section.

2.   Verify that the *Show Paychecks from* date is set to your desired date range. Press **Tab**.

3.   On the list of paychecks, select the paycheck you want to void.

4.   Click **Void**. Don't actually void the check now. These are just the steps you will take when you void paychecks.

5.   Click **Done** to close the *Edit/Void Paychecks* window.

This updates the employee's year-to-date payroll information. However, if this employee has paychecks already entered and dated after this paycheck, you won't see any changes to the year-to-date amounts on those paychecks. The next paycheck you create for this employee will show the correct year-to-date amounts, as will the payroll reports and tax forms.

Deleting Paychecks

The only time you should delete a paycheck is when you created it in error and you haven't printed the check. Otherwise, you should void the paycheck so you can keep a record of it.

> **DON'T PERFORM THESE STEPS NOW. THEY ARE FOR REFERENCE ONLY.**

1. From the *Employees* menu, select **Edit/Void Paychecks**.
2. Set the *Show paychecks from* date to the desired date range. Then press **Tab**.
3. On the list of paychecks, click the paycheck you want to delete and then click **Edit**.
4. At the top of the *QuickBooks Company* window, select the **Edit** menu and then select **Delete Paycheck** (or press Ctrl+D).
5. Click **OK**.

Another Way:
You can also void (or delete) paychecks by selecting the paycheck in the *Checking* account register. Then select **Void (or Delete) Paycheck** from the **Edit** menu.

Important note:
If the paycheck you're voiding or deleting isn't the most recent paycheck, keep in mind that the year-to date information (and possibly other calculations) on all paychecks dated after a voided or deleted paycheck will be incorrect. This is because those checks were calculated using the information from this check, and now that the check is void (or deleted), those paychecks are incorrect. You need to verify that the net amount of the paychecks does not change.

To avoid this problem, delete all the paychecks for this employee dated after the paycheck. Then, after you void or delete the paycheck, recreate the paychecks that were dated after the voided (or deleted) paycheck. When you recreate those paychecks, QuickBooks recalculates all the year-to-date amounts and taxes.

If you use Assisted Payroll or Direct Deposit:
If you use the Assisted Payroll service, or if you have direct deposit service, any transactions that have been sent to the payroll service cannot be deleted. To resolve these problems, contact payroll technical support.

Paying Payroll Liabilities

Paying your Payroll liabilities correctly is a critical part of maintaining accurate Payroll information in QuickBooks. When you pay the liabilities, don't use the *Write Checks* window because doing so won't affect the *Payroll Items*. It also won't show the liability payments on tax forms 940 or 941. To correctly pay your Payroll liabilities, use the *Pay Liabilities* tab of the *Payroll Center* window.

The accounting behind the scenes:
You must use the *Pay Liabilities* feature to record liability payments. Payroll Liability payments decrease (debit) the Payroll liability accounts in addition to reducing the balance due for the Payroll Items. If you don't use the *Pay Liabilities* feature, QuickBooks won't track your payments in the liabilities reports or tax forms such as the 941.

> **Note:**
> The IRS publication, *Circular E, Employer's Tax Guide,* specifies the rules for when your Payroll taxes must be paid. Depending on the size of your Payroll, you will be either a "Monthly" depositor or a "Semi-weekly" depositor. Monthly depositors are required to pay all Payroll Liabilities by the 15th of the month following the Payroll date. Semi-weekly depositors are required to pay all Payroll Liabilities by the Wednesday after the Payroll date if the Payroll date is Wednesday, Thursday, or Friday, and are required to pay all Payroll Liabilities by the Friday after the Payroll date if the Payroll date is Saturday, Sunday, Monday, or Tuesday.

COMPUTER PRACTICE

Step 1.   Click the **Pay Liabilities** button on the *Home* page. The *Payroll Center* opens with the Pay Liabilities tab selected.

> **Note:**
> New with QuickBooks 2018, The *Home* page now includes a badge that reminds you when you have an upcoming *Payroll Liability* deadline, as shown in Figure 11-24.

Figure 11-24 Pay Payroll Liabilities Badge on Home page

Step 2.   Place checkmarks next to the two Liabilities dated *12/16/2019* (see Figure 11-25).

Figure 11-25 Payroll Center

Step 3.   Click the **View/Pay** button.

Step 4.   The first of two *Liability Payment – Checking* windows opens with the fields entered to pay the EFTPS for accumulated Payroll Liabilities (see Figure 11-26).

Step 5. Leave the date as 12/15/2019.

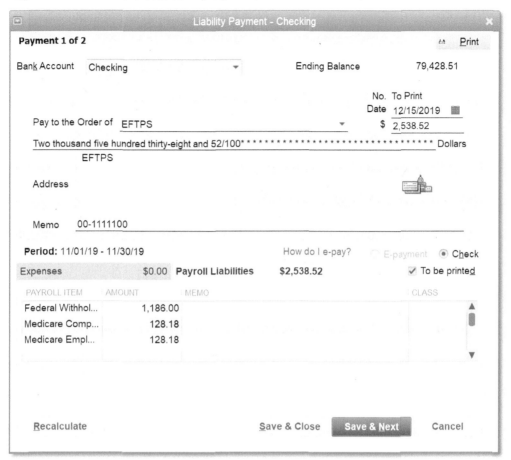

Figure 11-26 Reviewing the liability check before saving

> **Note:**
> QuickBooks allows you to modify the amounts in the *Amount* column of the *Pay Liabilities* window but you should avoid this if possible. Discrepancies here indicate incorrect Payroll calculations or misapplication of prior liability payments. These situations should be corrected at the Payroll Item or transaction level to avoid repetition of the same errors in the future. Instead, if you need to make a small change to the amount you're paying (e.g., adjust for rounding), enter an adjustment on the liability check using the **Expenses** tab. If you consistently have trouble in this area, contact your accountant or QuickBooks Pro Advisor for help.

Step 6. Click **Save & Next**. The second *Liability Payment – Checking* window opens.

Step 7. Click **Save & Close**. The *Payment Summary* window opens to show a list of Liability Payments as well as the options to Print Checks or Print Summary. Click **Print Checks.**

Step 8. Complete the printing process. Check number should start with 6071.

Step 9. Close the *Payment Summary* window.

> **Tip for correcting Payroll liabilities:**
> If you find an error in the amount that QuickBooks suggests you owe, it could be for several reasons. For example, if your state unemployment rate has changed in this period, the amount due may still be calculating at the old rate. In this case, the Payroll Item needs to be corrected and a *Liability Adjustment* could be made to correct the period in question. Another reason *Pay Liabilities* accruals may appear wrong is that prior payments were not made through *Pay Liabilities* or were dated incorrectly in the *Payment for Payroll liabilities through* field. In this case, the payments may need to be created with the improper payments voided. Finally, you could check each paycheck to see which one created the error. When you find the erroneous paycheck or paychecks, modify the Payroll Items on the paycheck. Of course, if you've already printed the paycheck, you should never make adjustments affecting net pay. Instead, use the *Adjust Liabilities* function, or make an adjustment on the next check for the affected Employees.

Step 10.   Display the **Checking** account register by double clicking it in the *Chart of Accounts* list.

                  Notice the transaction type is *LIAB CHK*, as shown in Figure 11-27 (you may have to scroll to see it). The *LIAB CHK* transaction is the only type of transaction that properly records payment of Payroll liabilities. That's because *LIAB CHK* transactions record the details of which Payroll liabilities *and* Payroll Items are paid by that check and the date they are relieved. Any other type of payment can't lower the balance due shown on the *Payroll Liabilities Report*.

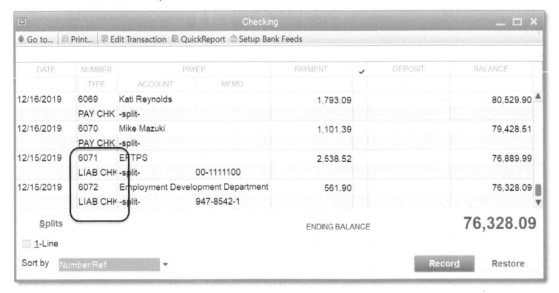

Figure 11-27 A Payroll liability payment in the Check Register

Editing a Liability Payment

If you need to edit an existing liability payment, you can edit it as shown below. However, make sure you only do this if you haven't yet submitted the payment to the tax agency. If you have submitted the payment to the tax agency, you should use the *Adjust Liabilities* window instead of editing the payment.

DON'T PERFORM THESE STEPS NOW. THEY ARE FOR REFERENCE ONLY.

1.   Double click the liability payment in the account register.
2.   The liability payment is displayed as when first created (see Figure 11-26). Edit any of the fields on the Payroll Liability Check and then click **Save & Close**.

Adjusting Payroll Liabilities

If your payroll liabilities need adjusting, you can use the *Liability Adjustment* window.

To avoid significant tax penalties, when you adjust payroll liabilities you must fully understand all the accounting and tax implications of the adjustment. Consult with your accountant or QuickBooks ProAdvisor if think your payroll liabilities need adjusting.

> **DON'T PERFORM THESE STEPS NOW. THEY ARE FOR REFERENCE ONLY.**

1. From the *Pay Liabilities* tab in the *Payroll Center*, click the **Adjust Payroll Liabilities** link in the **Other Activities** section.

2. On the *Liability Adjustment* window (see Figure 11-28), enter *12/15/2019* as the *Date* for your adjustment and *12/15/2019* as the *Effective Date* of the adjustment.

   The *Date* field is the date you actually enter the transaction. The *Effective Date* field is the date you want this adjustment to affect your liability balances on payroll reports. Use the *Memo* field to explain your adjustment.

3. Leave **Company** selected in the *Adjustment is for:* field.

4. Enter **San Jose** in the *Class* field.

   Since your adjustment will impact an expense account (Payroll Taxes), you need to allocate the expense to the appropriate class. In this case, the overstated wages were for services provided through the San Jose location. To determine the appropriate class, you will need to review the paycheck(s) on which the overstatement occurred. If you need to allocate the expense to more than one class, you will need to enter separate liability adjustments for each class.

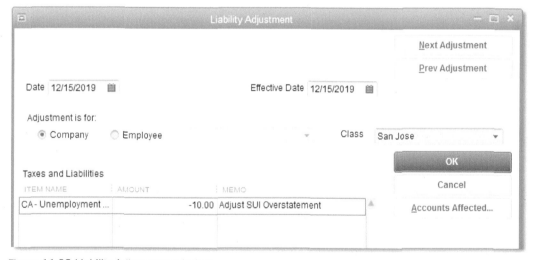

Figure 11-28 Liability Adjustment window

5. In the *Taxes and Liabilities* section, select **CA – Unemployment Company** as the *Item Name*, enter **-10.00** in the *Amount* column, and enter *Adjust SUI Overstatement* in the *Memo* column.

   Use positive numbers to increase the balance of the Payroll Item and negative numbers to reduce the balance of the Payroll Item.

6. Click **Cancel** to prevent this adjustment from being saved. **Do not save the adjustment** shown in Figure 11-28. It is for illustration only.

Creating Payroll Reports

Payroll Summary Report

There are several reports that you can use to analyze your Payroll. The *Payroll Summary* report shows the detail of each Employee's earnings, taxes, and net pay.

COMPUTER PRACTICE

Step 1.   Select the **Reports** menu, then select **Employees & Payroll**, and then select **Payroll Summary**.

Step 2.   Leave the date range From **10/1/2019** to **12/15/2019**.

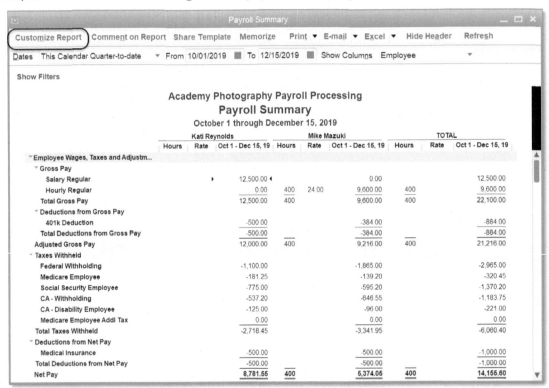

Figure 11-29 Payroll Summary report

The *Payroll Summary* report (see Figure 11-29) shows columns for each Employee, along with their hours and rates of pay. If you want to see more Employees on a page, you can customize this report not to show the *Hours* and *Rate* columns.

Step 3.   Click **Customize Report** at the top of the *Payroll Summary* report.

Step 4.   Clear the **Hours** and **Rate** boxes and then click **OK** (see Figure 11-30).

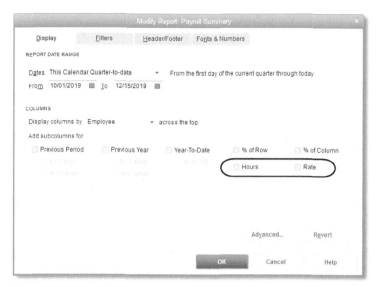

Figure 11-30 The Modify Report window

Step 5.   Your report will now look like Figure 11-31. To print the report, click **Print** (or press **Ctrl+P**).

Step 6.   Close the report.

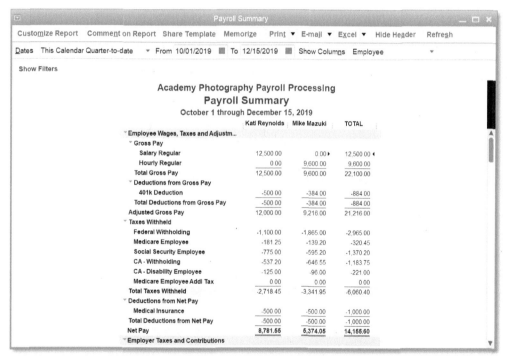

Figure 11-31 Payroll Summary report without hours and rates

Sales Rep Commissions

If you pay commissions to your Employees, you can create a *Sales by Rep Summary* or *Sales by Rep Detail* report to help calculate the commissions due. If the report basis is set to *Accrual*, it will show sales recorded on *Invoices* even if the customer has not paid the *Invoice.* If you want to show only sales for which the company has received payment, change the basis to "Cash" on this report.

COMPUTER PRACTICE

Step 1.   Select the **Reports** menu, then select **Sales,** and then select **Sales by Rep Summary** (see Figure 11-32).

Step 2.   Click the **Customize Report** button. The *Modify Report* window opens.

Step 3.   Choose **Cash** under the *Report Basis* section and then click **OK**.

Step 4.   Leave the date range From **12/1/2019** To **12/15/2019**.

Step 5.   Your report will now look like Figure 11-32. To print the report, click **Print** (or press **Ctrl+P**).

Step 6.   Close the report.

> **Important:**
> The *Sales by Rep Summary* or *Detail* report requires you to first tag each sale with the Employee who gets credit. To set this up, modify your *Invoice* and *Sales Receipts* template to include the *Rep* field. In the *Rep* field on each sales form, make sure you enter the initials of the Employee who gets credit for the sale. The *Sales by Rep* report will show the total sales for each sales rep.

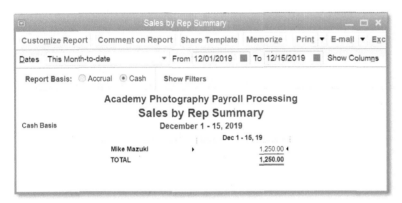

Figure 11-32 Sales by Rep Summary report

Payroll Liability Balance Report

The *Payroll Liabilities* report is used to track the status of your Payroll liabilities by Payroll Item.

COMPUTER PRACTICE

Step 1.   From the Pay Liabilities tab of the Payroll Center, click the **Payroll Liability Balances** link in the Reports section.

Step 2.   Leave the *From* date set to **1/1/2019** and the *To* date set to **11/30/2019** (see Figure 11-33).

Academy Photography Payroll Processing
Payroll Liability Balances
January through November 2019

	Jan 19	Feb 19	Mar 19	Apr 19	May 19	Jun 19	Jul 19	Aug 19	Sep 19	Oct 19	Nov 19	BALANCE
Payroll Liabilities												
Federal Withholding	0.00	0.00	0.00	0.00	0.00	0.00	0.00	0.00	0.00	0.00	0.00	0.00
Medicare Employee	0.00	0.00	0.00	0.00	0.00	0.00	0.00	0.00	0.00	0.00	0.00	0.00
Social Security Employee	0.00	0.00	0.00	0.00	0.00	0.00	0.00	0.00	0.00	0.00	0.00	0.00
Federal Unemployment	26.52	50.04	-76.56	0.00	0.00	0.00	0.00	0.00	0.00	0.00	0.00	0.00
Medicare Company	0.00	0.00	0.00	0.00	0.00	0.00	0.00	0.00	0.00	0.00	0.00	0.00
Social Security Company	0.00	0.00	0.00	0.00	0.00	0.00	0.00	0.00	0.00	0.00	0.00	0.00
CA - Withholding	0.00	0.00	0.00	0.00	0.00	0.00	0.00	0.00	0.00	0.00	0.00	0.00
CA - Disability Employee	0.00	0.00	0.00	0.00	0.00	0.00	0.00	0.00	0.00	0.00	0.00	0.00
CA - Unemployment Comp...	232.05	437.85	-669.90	0.00	0.00	0.00	0.00	0.00	0.00	0.00	0.00	0.00
Medicare Employee Addl Tax	0.00	0.00	0.00	0.00	0.00	0.00	0.00	0.00	0.00	0.00	0.00	0.00
CA - Employee Training Tax	0.00	0.00	0.00	0.00	0.00	0.00	0.00	0.00	0.00	0.00	0.00	0.00
401k Deduction	176.80	353.60	353.60	353.60	353.60	353.60	353.60	353.60	353.60	353.60	353.60	3,712.80
Match 401k	88.40	176.80	176.80	176.80	176.80	176.80	176.80	176.80	176.80	176.80	176.80	1,856.40
Total Payroll Liabilities	523.77	1,018.29	-216.06	530.40	530.40	530.40	530.40	530.40	530.40	530.40	530.40	5,569.20

Figure 11-33 Payroll Liability Balances report

> **Note:**
> The *To* date field at the top of the Payroll Liabilities report is very important. It tells QuickBooks to report on liabilities for wages paid through that date. Even if liabilities have been paid after the *To* date, the balances in the report reflect the payments. For example, even if you paid February's Federal liabilities in March, the report above would show zero balances for the Federal liabilities in the Feb 19 column (note that the number 19 refers to the year). Therefore, this report really shows your unpaid liabilities for paychecks created before the *To* date.

Step 3.   If you want to see the total unpaid balances only, select **Total only** from the *Show Columns* drop-down list (see Figure 11-34).

> **Tip:**
> If you are a semi-weekly depositor, select **Week** from the *Show Columns* drop-down list. The report will then provide a breakdown of your Payroll liabilities by week instead of by month.

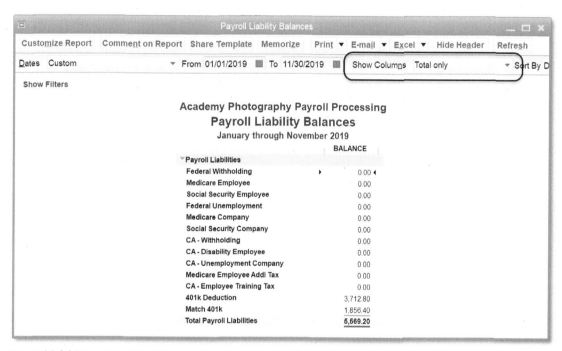

Figure 11-34 Payroll Liability Balances report showing total unpaid accruals only

COMPUTER PRACTICE

You can filter the report to show only certain liabilities. For example, if you only want to see the Federal liabilities, follow these steps:

Step 1.   Click **Customize Report** and then click the **Filters** tab.

Step 2.   Scroll down the *Filter* list on the left side of the window and then select **Payroll Item**.

Step 3.   Select **All Federal** from the *Payroll Item* drop-down list in the center of the window (see Figure 11-35).

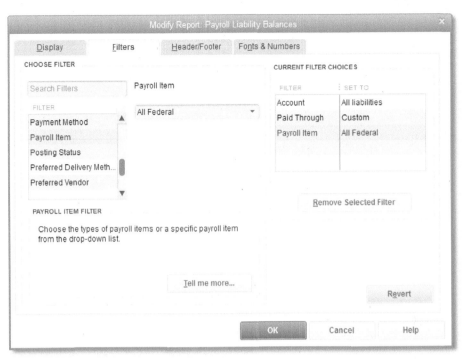

Figure 11-35 Payroll Item filter for all Federal Items

To give the report a new title to match the filtered content of the report, follow these steps:

Step 1.   Click the **Header/Footer** tab.

Step 2.   Enter *Federal Payroll Liability* in the *Report Title* field and then click **OK** (see Figure 11-36).

Step 3.   Your report will now look like Figure 11-37.

Step 4.   Close the report.

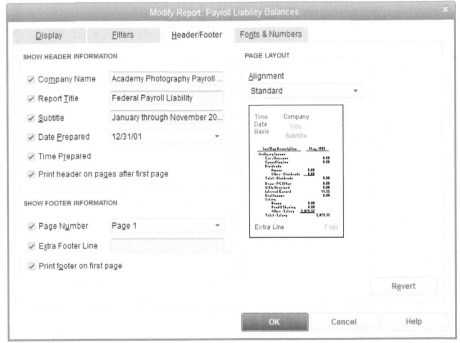

Figure 11-36 The Report Title field allows you to enter a new title

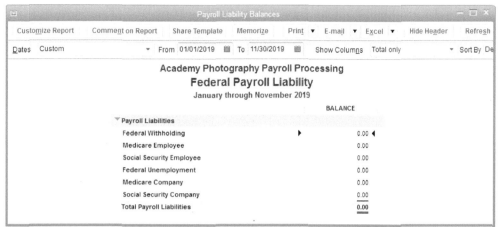

Figure 11-37 Custom Report called "Federal Payroll Liability."

Preparing Payroll Taxes

Paying Payroll taxes is an important part of Payroll processing. You can process forms such as Form 941, Form 940, and W-2s using the *File Forms* tab of the *Payroll Center* (see Figure 11-38). You will need to have an Enhanced Payroll subscription.

If you signed up for one of the QuickBooks Payroll Services, upgrade your tax tables before processing Forms 941, 940, or W-2s. Any necessary changes to the forms may be included in the most recent tax tables.

Be sure to create your tax payments in the Pay Liabilities tab prior to creating your Quarterly and Annual Payroll Forms. The 941 will use these payments for the *Deposits made* calculation. The 940 form computes your Federal Unemployment Tax based on the 940 contributions, your State Unemployment liabilities, and payments made throughout the year (if applicable). All of the Payroll tax forms calculate automatically using the information on paychecks and Payroll Liability payments.

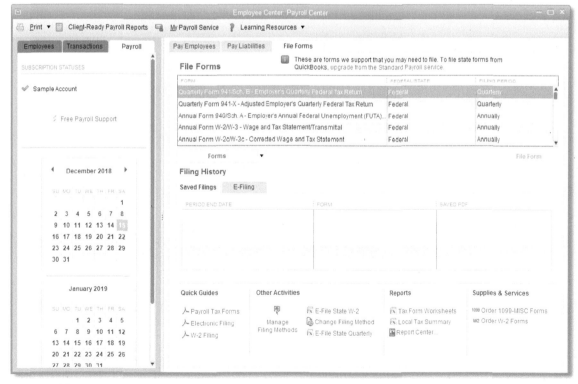

Figure 11-38 File Forms tab in the Payroll Center – your screen may vary

Review Questions

Comprehension Questions

1. When should you update your payroll tax tables?

2. How can you override the Federal income tax withholding on a paycheck?

3. What type of check (standard, voucher, or wallet) is the best choice for printing paychecks? Why?

4. Should you ever delete a paycheck that was printed and given to the employee? Why?

Multiple Choice

Select the best answer(s) for each of the following:

1. To properly affect the Payroll Items, which function (from the *Employee* section of the *Home* page) should you use to pay the Payroll taxes?
    a) Write Checks
    b) Pay Bills
    c) Pay Employees
    d) Pay Liabilities

2. Voucher style checks, when used for processing Payroll, may contain:
    a) Earnings and tax withholdings.
    b) Adjustments to net pay.
    c) Federal filing status.
    d) All of the above.

3. The *Payroll Liability Balances* report identifies:
    a) Liability payments made during the payment period.
    b) Liability amounts by Payroll Item.
    c) Liabilities for Employee deductions only.
    d) Liabilities for employer taxes only.

4. Which statement is true?
    a) You can print pay stubs at any time.
    b) Pay stubs print two per page.
    c) If you find an error in a past paycheck, you should delete and recreate the paycheck to ensure accuracy.
    d) You cannot void a paycheck.

5. To begin processing your Payroll:
    a) Select **Write Checks** from the *Home* page.
    b) Select the *Employees* menu and then select **Pay Scheduled Liabilities.**
    c) Select the *Payroll* menu and then select **Process Payroll.**
    d) Choose **Pay Employees** from the *Employees* section of the *Home* page.

6. QuickBooks automatically calculates paychecks using information from all of the following sources except:

   a)   Amounts on all previous paychecks.

   b)   The employee's current earnings shown in the earnings section of the paycheck.

   c)   The employee's tax settings in the employee record.

   d)   The employee's expense report.

7. With a Standard QuickBooks payroll subscription, which forms *cannot* be printed directly from QuickBooks?

   a)   State Payroll Tax forms from most states.

   b)   940.

   c)   W3.

   d)   All of the above can be printed if you have a Standard QuickBooks payroll subscription.

8. To correctly pay your payroll liabilities, choose one of the following options:

   a)   Write a check for the taxes and code it to payroll liabilities.

   b)   Use the *Pay Scheduled Liabilities* section of the *Payroll Center*.

   c)   Enter the tax authorities as payroll agencies.

   d)   Enter a *Bill* for all taxes due. Then use *Pay Bills*.

9. The payroll summary by employee report shows:

   a)   The detail of each employee's earnings only.

   b)   The YTD employee's earnings by job.

   c)   The detail of each employee's biographical information.

   d)   The detail of each employee's hours, earnings, taxes, and net pay.

10. If the *Pay Liabilities* window shows incorrect tax amounts due, the problem could be caused by:

    a)   Incorrect user entry of payroll item rates.

    b)   Using Write checks to pay taxes.

    c)   Users overriding calculated taxes.

    d)   Any of the above.

11. To have data from the weekly timesheet affect an employee's paychecks:

    a)   The timer must be used for all employees.

    b)   Select *Use time Data to create Paychecks* on the employee record.

    c)   Employees must enter their own time into QuickBooks.

    d)   Use job costing.

12. What is shown in the Company Summary section of the *Preview Paycheck* window?

    a)   Earnings and deductions.

    b)   Insurance withheld from employee checks.

    c)   Employer paid taxes and contributions.

    d)   All tax and liability payments due.

13. How do you pay a salaried employee for vacation time?

    a)   Vacation time is not available for salaried employees.

    b)   Use a salary vacation payroll item and enter the vacation hours in the *Hours* column.

    c)   Enter vacation time in the employee's record.

    d)   Enter vacation hours on the pay stub.

14. Every payday, you should

   a)   Create liability payments.

   b)   Process employees' W-2 forms.

   c)   Create payroll tax returns.

   d)   Verify your tax tables are current and update them if necessary.

Completion Statements

1.   To manually job-cost or classify wages, enter a separate line in the earnings section of the paycheck for each combination of Earnings Item, Rate, Hours, and ____:___.

2.   The Payroll Tab in the Employee Center is also known as the _____ _____.

3.   In order to edit the items on a paycheck, display the paycheck and click the _____ _____ button in the Paycheck window.

4.   QuickBooks prints state payroll tax forms only if you subscribe to its Enhanced Payroll service. However, if you do not subscribe to QuickBooks Enhanced payroll service, you can create reports, such as the _____ _____ _____ _____ report to help you prepare your state payroll tax returns.

Payroll Processing Problem 1

APPLYING YOUR KNOWLEDGE

> Restore the PRProcessing-18Problem1.QBM file. You will not need to enter a password because this is a sample file.

1.   Process paychecks for both Kati Reynolds and Mike Mazuki with the information shown below. Create printable paychecks, dated 1/1/2020 drawn on the Checking bank account for the Payroll period ending on 12/31/2019.

Kati Reynolds' paycheck

Field	Data
Check Date	1/1/2020
Pay Period	12/16/2019 through 12/31/2019
Earnings	Salary Regular
Other Payroll Items (Deductions)	401k Employee, -4%
	Match 401k, 2%
	Medical Insurance,-$100

Table 11-1 Kati Reynolds' paycheck

Mike Mazuki's paycheck

Field	Data
Check Date	1/1/2020
Pay Period	12/16/2019 through 12/31/2019
Earnings	80 hours – Hourly Regular
Other Payroll Items (Deductions)	401k Employee, -4% Match 401k, 2% Medical Insurance,-$100

Table 11-2 Mike Mazuki's paycheck

2. Print both paychecks on blank paper. Use voucher checks for the format of the printed checks.

3. Print a *Payroll Liability Balances* report for 9/1/2019 through 1/1/2020.

Payroll Processing Problem 2 (Advanced)

APPLYING YOUR KNOWLEDGE

Restore the PRProcessing-18Problem2.QBM file. You will not need to enter a password because this is a sample file.

1. Process paychecks for both Kati Reynolds and Mike Mazuki with the information shown below. Create printable paychecks, dated 1/1/2020 drawn on the Checking bank account for the Payroll period ending on 12/31/2019.

Kati Reynolds' paycheck

Field	Data
Check Date	1/1/2020
Pay Period	12/16/2019 through 12/31/2019
Earnings	Salary Regular, 56 hours Salary Vacation, 24 hours
Other Payroll Items (Deductions)	401k Employee, -4% Match 401k, 2% Medical Insurance,-$100

Table 11-3 Kati Reynolds' paycheck

Mike Mazuki's paycheck

Field	Data
Check Date	1/1/2020
Pay Period	12/16/2019 through 12/31/2019
Earnings	48 hours – Hourly Regular
	32 hours – Hourly Vacation
Other Payroll Items (Deductions)	401k Employee, -4%
	Match 401k, 2%
	Medical Insurance,-$100

Table 11-4 Mike Mazuki's paycheck

2. Print both paychecks on blank paper. Use voucher checks for the format of the printed checks.

3. On 1/15/2020, pay the Federal and California liabilities due on 1/15/2020. Print the Payroll liability checks on blank paper.

4. Print a *Payroll Summary* report for 10/1/2019 through 1/1/2020. Do not show the *Hours* or *Rate*.

5. Print a *Payroll Liability Balances* report for 9/1/2019 through 1/1/2020.

Chapter 12
Company File Setup

Topics

In this chapter, you will learn about the following topics:

- Choosing a Start Date – Step 1 (page 437)
- Creating the Company File – Step 2 (page 438)
- Setting Up the Chart of Accounts and Other Lists – Step 3 (page 447)
- Setting Up Opening Balances – Step 4 (page 459)
- Entering Open Items – Step 5 (page 465)
- Entering Year-to-Date Income and Expenses – Step 6 (page 468)
- Adjusting Opening Balance for Sales Tax Payable – Step 7 (page 469)
- Adjusting Inventory and Setting up Fixed Assets – Step 8 (page 470)
- Setup Payroll and YTD Payroll Information – Step 9 (page 471)
- Verifying your Trial Balance – Step 10 (page 471)
- Closing Opening Bal Equity – Step 11 (page 473)
- Setting the Closing Date - Backing up the File – Step 12 (page 474)
- Users and Passwords (page 474)

In this chapter, you will learn how to create a new QuickBooks data file, set up the Chart of Accounts, and enter opening balances. You will also learn how to set up user access rights and passwords for each person who will use QuickBooks.

Creating a new company file can be done at the inception of a new company or when an existing company decides to start using QuickBooks. It is also appropriate for a company that is already using QuickBooks to create a new company file when the existing one has many errors and fixing it is not possible.

In this section, you will learn about the 12-Step setup process for completing your QuickBooks file setup (see Table 12-1).

Choosing a Start Date – Step 1

Before you create your company file, choose a start date for your company file. Your start date is the day before you start using QuickBooks to track your daily transactions. You will need complete information for your opening balances as of this start date. Assuming you file taxes on a calendar-year basis, the best start date for most companies is December 31. If you file taxes on a fiscal year, choose the last day of your fiscal year as your start date.

Do not use January 1 (or the first day of your fiscal year) for your start date, because doing so would cause the opening balances to affect your first year's *Profit & Loss Report*. This could affect your taxes and distort the picture of the company's financial history.

The 12-Step Setup Checklist

1. Choose the Start Date (see page 437).
2. Create the QuickBooks company file (see page 438).
3. Create the Chart of Accounts and company Lists (see page 447).
4. Enter opening balances for most Balance Sheet accounts (see page 459).
5. Enter outstanding transactions as of the start date (see page 465).
6. If needed, enter your year-to-date income and expenses (see page 468).
7. Adjust Sales Tax Payable (see page 469).
8. Adjust Inventory to match physical counts and set up Fixed Assets (see page 470).
9. Set up Payroll Lists and year-to-date (YTD) payroll information (see page 471).
10. Verify that the Trial Balance report matches your previous trial balance (see page 471).
11. Close the Opening Bal Equity account into Retained Earnings (see page 473).
12. Set the Closing Date and backup your company file (see page 474).

Table 12-1 The 12-Step Setup Checklist

Keep in mind that you will need to enter all of the transactions (checks, invoices, deposits, etc.) between your start date and the day you perform the QuickBooks setup. Because of this, your start date has a big impact on how much work you will do during setup. If you do not want to go back to the end of last year, choose a more recent date, such as the end of last quarter or the end of last month.

> **Note:**
> In order for your records to be complete and accurate, you should enter every transaction (check, invoice, deposits etc.) that your company performed between the start date and the day you perform the QuickBooks setup. For example, if you are setting up the QuickBooks company file on January 5 with a start date of December 31, you will need to enter all transactions that the company performed on January 1 through January 5 for your records to be complete and accurate.

If you are starting a new business, your start date is the day you formed the company.

Creating the Company File – Step 2

There are two ways to create a file, through the *Express Start* and the *Detailed Start*. In the following section, we will show you how to create a file using both methods. *Express Start* creates a file with minimal entries and a default set of *Preferences*. Only users who are familiar with QuickBooks *Preferences* and the impact of creating a QuickBooks file without a start date should use *Express Start*. *Detailed Start* allows you to set up a number of *Preferences,* as well as set the start date for a company.

Express Start

When you first create a new file, you are given the option of choosing *Express Start* or *Detailed Start*, as well as several other options such as converting a file from another format, for example Quicken or Peachtree (see Figure 12-1).

Figure 12-1 New File window

If you choose *Express Start*, you only need to enter your Company information before creating a file. Once the file is created you can enter *Customers*, *Vendors*, *Employees*, *Items*, and *Bank Accounts*, then start using the file. QuickBooks chooses default *Accounts* and *Preferences* for you based on the *Industry* you select (see Figure 12-2).

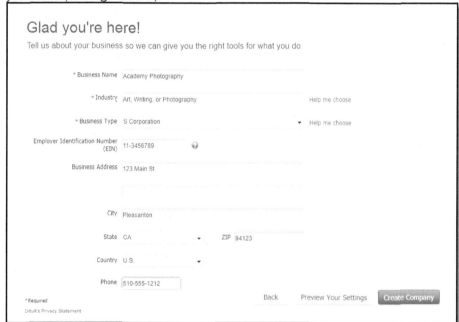

Figure 12-2 Express Start Tell us about your business screen

After completing the file setup, whether using Express Start or Advanced Setup, you can access and edit the Company Information, such as business name, address, or phone number by selecting the Company menu and selecting My Company (see Figure 12-3).

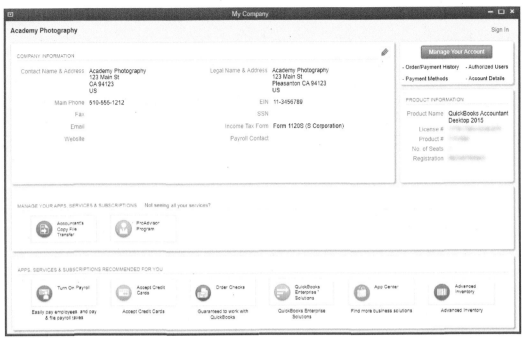

Figure 12-3 My Company window

Detailed Start

The *Detailed Start,* also called the *EasyStep Interview,* allows you to enter your Company information as in the Express Start, however, it also asks you to customize some of the most common preferences and set a start date.

COMPUTER PRACTICE

Step 1.   Select the **File** menu and then select **New Company**.

Step 2.   A new file window appears. Click **Detailed Start** to launch the *EasyStep Interview* (see Figure 12-4).

Step 3.   The *EasyStep Interview* window appears. Enter the information in the Company information screen as shown in Figure 12-4. Click **Next** when done.

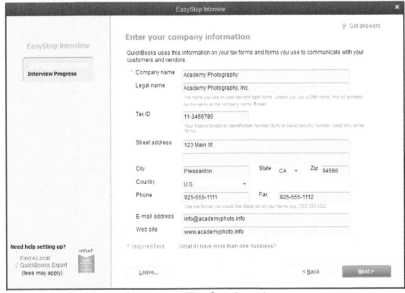

Figure 12-4 Company Information in EasyStep Interview

> **Note:**
>
> As you answer questions in the *EasyStep Interview*, QuickBooks creates your company file, *Lists*, and *Preferences*. To proceed to the next step in the process click **Next**. To go back to a previous window in the interview, click **Back**. To exit the Interview and retain all changes, click **Leave**. When you open the company file again after clicking *Leave*, you will be taken back to the EasyStep Interview.
>
> To make changes to the company information after you have completed the *EasyStep Interview*, select *My Company* from the *Company* menu.

Step 4.   Select **Art, Writing, or Photography** from the list of industry types. QuickBooks uses the industry information to suggest the appropriate income and expense accounts later in the *EasyStep Interview*. Click **Next** when finished.

Figure 12-5 Select your industry in EasyStep Interview

> **Tip:**
>
> If you are unsure how to answer the questions in the EasyStep Interview, consider contacting a QuickBooks expert. *QuickBooks ProAdvisors* are bookkeepers, accountants, software consultants, and CPAs who offer QuickBooks-related consulting services. In addition, *QuickBooks Certified ProAdvisors* are those *ProAdvisors* who have completed a comprehensive training and testing program. For more information on QuickBooks *ProAdvisors* and *Certified ProAdvisors*, refer to QuickBooks in-product Help.

Step 5.   The *How is your company organized?* window appears. Select the **S Corporation** radio button and click **Next**.

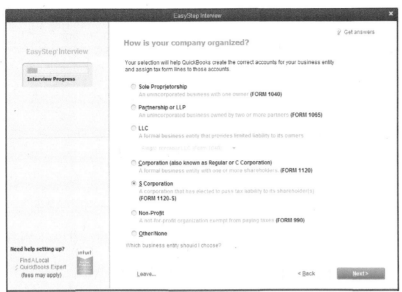

Figure 12-6 How your company is organized window in the EasyStep Interview

Step 6.   The next window prompts the user to select the first month of the company's fiscal or income tax year. Leave **January** selected and click the **Next** button.

This field indicates the beginning of the year for year-to-date reports, such as the *Profit & Loss* report.

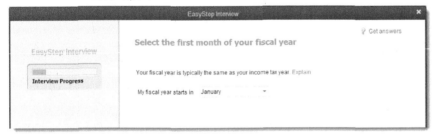

Figure 12-7 Select the first month of your fiscal year window in the EasyStep Interview

> **Note for new businesses:**
> The first month of your fiscal or income tax year is **NOT** necessarily the month you started your business. Setting the first month in your fiscal year correctly is important as it specifies the default date range for accounting reports such as the Profit & Loss and Balance Sheet. The first month in your tax year specifies the default date range for **Income Tax Summary** and **Detail** reports. If you make an error in this selection, you can correct it later by selecting *My Company* from the *Company* menu.

Step 7.   The Administrator password setup screen will appear (see Figure 12-8). Although it's optional, creating an Administrator password is highly recommended. The Administrator is the only person who has access to all functions within a company file. Establishing an Administrator password restricts other users so that they cannot execute tasks that are normally reserved for the Administrator.

However, since you are just creating a sample data file for this lesson, do not create an Administrator password at this time. Click **Next** to move to the next step.

Figure 12-8 The Administrator Password Screen in the EasyStep Interview

> **Tip:**
> If you need help during the interview, click the **Get answers** link at the top of the interview window.

Step 8.   The next window in the *EasyStep Interview* contains a message about creating your company file. Click **Next** to create the file.

Step 9.   The *Filename for New Company* window (see Figure 12-9) is where you specify the filename and location for your company file. QuickBooks automatically enters your company name and adds .QBW to the end of your filename.

In the *Save in* field, select your student data folder. Use the default file name, Academy Photography.QBW.

Figure 12-9 Filename for New Company window

Step 10.   Click **Save** to create your company file.

Step 11.   QuickBooks displays the *Customizing QuickBooks for your business* step. Click **Next** to begin the customizing process.

Step 12.   The next several screens of the *EasyStep Interview* will guide you through customizing your company file and setting up *Preferences*. Use the data in Table 12-2 to answer initial questions about your business.

Company Setup and Preferences

Question From EasyStep Interview	Response
What do you sell?	Both services and products
Do you charge sales tax?	Yes
Do you want to create estimates in QuickBooks?	Yes
Do you want to track sales orders before you invoice your customers?	Yes (Note: This option is not available in QuickBooks Pro.)
Do you want to use billing statements in QuickBooks?	Yes
Do you want to use progress invoicing?	Yes
Do you want to keep track of bills you owe?	Yes
Do you want to track inventory in QuickBooks?	Yes
Do you want to track time in QuickBooks?	Yes
Do you have employees?	Yes (check the boxes for both W-2 employees and 1099 contractors)

Table 12-2 Data for the Company Setup

Step 13.   In the next section of the interview, QuickBooks creates your Chart of Accounts. Click **Next** on the *Using accounts in QuickBooks* screen.

Step 14.   In the *Select a date to start tracking your finances* screen, select **Use today's date or the first day of the quarter or month.** Then enter *12/31/2018* in the date field. Click **Next**.

If you are setting up your file to begin at the start of the fiscal year, it is best to choose the last day of the previous fiscal year as the start date. (see page 437).

Figure 12-10 Select a date to start tracking your finances window in EasyStep Interview

Step 15.   The following screen contains a list of suggested income and expense accounts based on the industry selected earlier in the *EasyStep Interview*. These accounts can be edited after completing the *EasyStep Interview*.

Leave the default accounts checked and click **Next**.

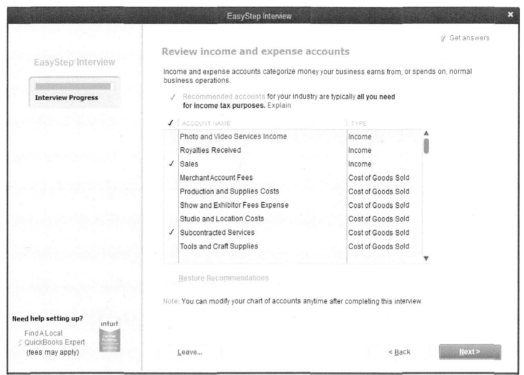

Figure 12-11 Review income and expense accounts window in the EasyStep Interview

Step 16.   Click **Go to Setup** to complete the interview.

Figure 12-12 Final screen in EasyStep interview

Step 17.   The *QuickBooks Setup Add Info* window is displayed. This window offers a quick way to enter *Customers, Vendors, Employees, Items,* and *Bank Accounts.* We will use this window to create a bank account. Click the **Add** button in the *Add your bank accounts* section in the lower part of the window.

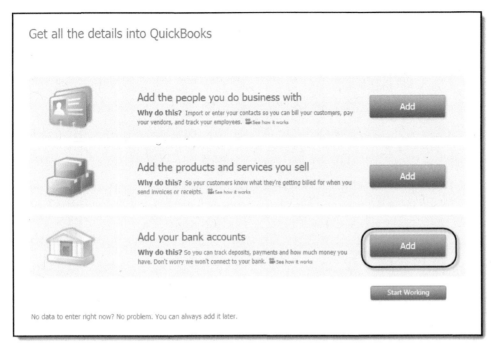

Figure 12-13 QuickBooks Setup Add Info

Step 18.   Enter the information in Figure 12-14 to setup the *Checking* account. For now, leave
                  Opening Balance blank. We will discuss setting up *Opening Balances* on page 473.

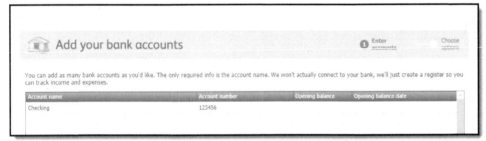

Figure 12-14 Add your bank accounts window

> Note:
> The *Account number* field in the *Add you bank accounts* window is for the account
> number assigned from your bank. This is a different number than the five digit
> QuickBooks Account Number discussed on page 447.

Step 19.   Click Continue.
Step 20.   Click **No Thanks** to the offer to order Intuit checks. If necessary, decline any additional
             offers.
Step 21.   Click Continue.
Step 22.   Click the **Start Working** link at the bottom of the window (see Figure 12-15).

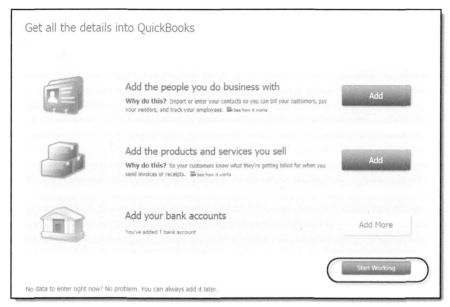

Figure 12-15 Start Working Link in QuickBooks Setup Add Info

Step 23.   QuickBooks has now created your company file with a default *Chart of Accounts* and a bank account, and has configured your *Company Preferences*.

Step 24.   If necessary, close the *Accountant Center* window.

Step 25.   Close the company file by selecting **Close Company** from the *File* menu.

Setting Up the Chart of Accounts and Other Lists – Step 3

Restore the Setup-18.QBM file. See page 9 for instructions on restoring files.

Setting Up the Chart of Accounts

The *Chart of Accounts* is one of the most important lists in QuickBooks. It is a list of all the accounts in the General Ledger. If you are not sure how to design your *Chart of Accounts*, ask your accountant or QuickBooks ProAdvisor for help.

Account Types

There are five basic account types in accounting: assets, liabilities, equity, income, and expenses.

QuickBooks breaks these basic account types into subtypes. For example, QuickBooks uses five types of asset accounts: *Bank, Accounts Receivable, Other Current Asset, Fixed Asset,* and *Other Asset.* QuickBooks offers four types of liability accounts: *Accounts Payable, Credit Card, Other Current Liability,* and *Long Term Liability.* Income accounts can be divided into *Income* or *Other Income* types. Expenses can be classified as *Expense, Other Expense,* or *Cost of Goods Sold. Equity* doesn't have subtypes.

Activating Account Numbers

QuickBooks does not require account numbers. If you prefer, you can use just the account *name* to differentiate between accounts. However, if you prefer to have account numbers, you can activate them in the *Accounting Company Preferences.*

For this section, you will turn on the account numbers, but at the end of *Setting up the Chart of Accounts* section, you will turn them off again.

COMPUTER PRACTICE

Step 1.   Select the **Edit** menu and then select **Preferences**.

Step 2.   On the *Preferences* window, click on the **Accounting** option and select the **Company Preferences** tab.

Step 3.   Check the **Use account numbers** box and click **OK**.

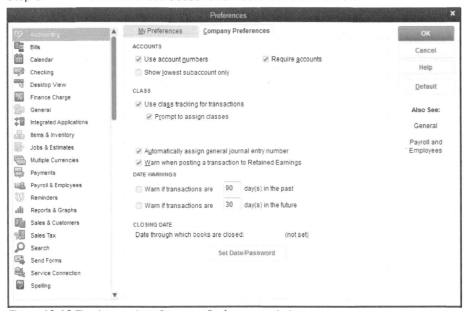

Figure 12-16 The Accounting—Company Preferences window

Did You Know?

All of the *Preferences* in Figure 12-16 are used to configure the way QuickBooks operates. For more information on these and other *Preferences*, see page 243.

Adding Accounts

COMPUTER PRACTICE

Step 1.   Select the **Chart of Accounts** icon on the *Company* section of the *Home page*.

The *Chart of Accounts* list from your sample file is displayed, showing account numbers as well as account names (see Figure 12-17).

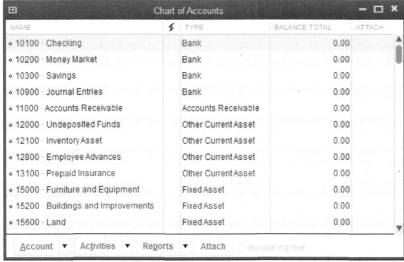

Figure 12-17 Chart of Accounts with account numbers

> **Another way:**
> To open the *Chart of Accounts*, you may also select **Chart of Accounts** from the *List* menu, or press **Ctrl+A**.

Step 2.   Select the **Account** drop-down list button at the bottom of the *Chart of Accounts* window and select **New**. Another way to add a new account is to press **Ctrl+N**.

Step 3.   Select **Expense** from the choice of account types in the *Add New Account: Choose Account Type* window (see Figure 12-18). Click Continue.

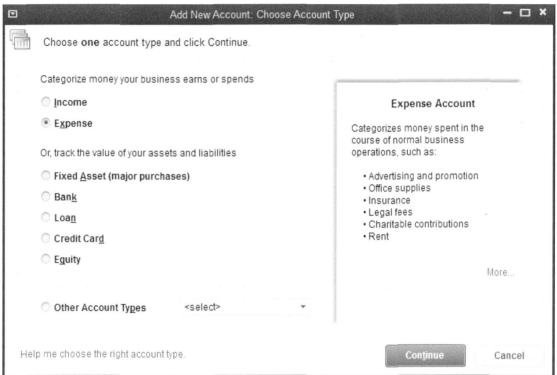

Figure 12-18 Add New Account: Choose Account Type Window

Step 4.   Enter *62600* in the *Number* field and then press **Tab**.

Step 5.   Enter *Entertainment* in the *Account Name* field and then press **Tab** twice.

Step 6.   Enter *Entertainment Expenses* in the *Description* field and then press **Tab** twice. The *Description* field is optional.

Step 7.   Select **Deductions: Other miscellaneous taxes** from the *Tax-Line Mapping* drop-down list.

If you or your accountant uses TurboTax, ProSeries, Lacerte, or other QuickBooks-compatible tax software to prepare your tax return, specify the line on your tax return that this account will feed. This allows the tax software to fill out your tax return automatically, based on the data in QuickBooks. If you do not use one of the supported tax programs to prepare your taxes, or if you do not wish to otherwise take advantage of any of the income tax reports in QuickBooks, you can leave this field blank.

Step 8.   Your screen should look like Figure 12-19. Click **Save & Close** at the bottom of the window to save the account.

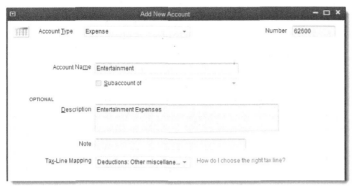

Figure 12-19 Add New Account window

Adding Subaccounts

If you want more detail in your *Chart of Accounts*, you can add *Subaccounts*. Account types for the main account and its subaccounts *must* be same. You can add up to five levels of subaccounts.

> **Did You Know?**
> Clicking the **Collapse** button on *Reports* that include Subaccounts (e.g., *Balance Sheet* and *Profit & Loss Reports*) removes the Subaccount detail from the report. The balance of each primary account on the collapsed report is the total of its subaccount balances.

COMPUTER PRACTICE

Step 1.   Display the **Chart of Accounts** using any method shown previously, if it is not already displayed.

Step 2.   Select the **Account** drop-down list button at the bottom of the *Chart of Accounts* window and select **New**.

Step 3.   Select the **Expense** option from *the Add New Account: Choose Account Type* window. Click **Continue**.

Step 4.   Fill out the **Add New Account** window as shown in Figure 12-20. Notice that the *Subaccount of* field is checked and the main account is selected in its field.

Step 5.   Click **Save & Close** to save the record.

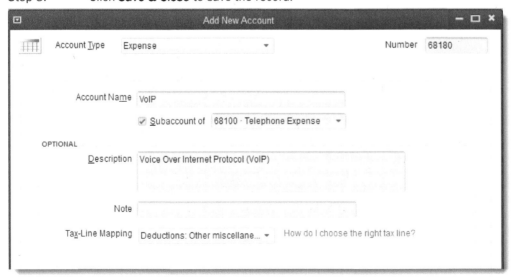

Figure 12-20 Add a Subaccount for more detail in the Chart of Accounts.

Step 6.   Now the *Chart of Accounts* shows your new subaccount slightly indented under its master account (see Figure 12-21).

> **Tip**
> Once subaccounts are set up under a main account, you should only use subaccounts and not the main account in transactions. Using the main account defeats the purpose of getting more detail.
>
> **Note:**
> In reports, whenever you see an account name with the string "-Other," it means that you used a main account instead of a subaccount. To avoid this problem, you might choose to show only subaccounts and not the main accounts in the drop-down list by selecting the **Show lowest subaccount only** checkbox in *Accounting Company Preference* (see Figure 12-22).

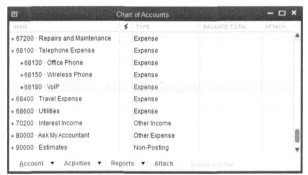

Figure 12-21 Subaccounts appearance in the Chart of Accounts

Figure 12-22 Account Numbers Preferences

Removing Accounts from the Chart of Accounts

When you no longer need an account, it is best to remove the account from the *Chart of Accounts* List. Removing unnecessary accounts helps avoid data entry errors by ensuring that no transactions are accidentally posted to these accounts. There are three ways to remove an account from the *Chart of Accounts* List: deleting the account, deactivating the account, or merging the account with another account.

Deleting Accounts – Option 1

To delete an account, follow these steps:

> **DO NOT PERFORM THESE STEPS NOW. THEY ARE FOR REFERENCE ONLY.**

1.   Select the account in the **Chart of Accounts** List.
2.   Select the **Account** menu at the bottom of the *Chart of Accounts* window and select **Delete** or press **Ctrl+D**.

QuickBooks list entries cannot be deleted if they are in use. This is true for Accounts, Items, Customers, Vendors, Employees, Payroll Items or any other list entry. An account can be in use in many different ways, such as in an Item, in a transaction, or in a Preference. In cases where you are not able to delete an account or other list item, use either Option 2 or Option 3 below.

Deactivating Accounts – Option 2

If you cannot delete an account but you still want to remove it from your list, you can deactivate it. Deactivating an account causes it to be hidden in the *Chart of Accounts* List. Deactivating an old account reduces the clutter in your Lists while preserving your ability to see the account in historical transactions and reports.

> **Note:**
> Even if an Account (or Item or Name) is inactive, all transactions using that account (or Item or Name) will show on reports.

To make an account inactive, follow these steps:

> **DO NOT PERFORM THESE STEPS NOW. THEY ARE FOR REFERENCE ONLY.**

1. Select the account in the **Chart of Accounts** list.
2. Select the **Account** button and then select **Make Account Inactive** from the menu (see Figure 12-23).

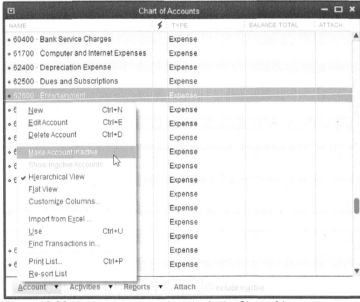

Figure 12-23 Making an account inactive in the Chart of Accounts

To view all accounts in the *Chart of Accounts*, including the inactive accounts, click **Include inactive** at the bottom of the *Chart of Accounts* window (see Figure 12-24). The icon in the far left column indicates that an account is inactive. To reactivate the account, click on the large X icon next to the inactive account.

> **Note:**
> You can make entries in most lists inactive through this same process, including *Customers*, *Vendors* and *Items*.

Figure 12-24 When Include inactive is checked, all accounts appear in the list.

> **Did You Know?**
> You can also deactivate *Customers, Vendors, Employees,* or *Items* using this same method. Click in the Inaction column (indicated by a large X) to make lines on any list active or inactive.

Merging Accounts – Option 3

When you merge two accounts, QuickBooks edits each transaction from the merging account so that it posts to the merged (combined) account. For example, if you merge the *Entertainment* account into the *Meals and Entertainment* account, QuickBooks will edit each transaction that had been posted to *Entertainment*, making it post to *Meals and Entertainment* instead. Then QuickBooks will remove the *Entertainment* account from the *Chart of Accounts* List.

You can only merge accounts of the same type. In this example, both accounts are Expense accounts.

> **Important:**
> Merging cannot be undone. Once you merge accounts together, there is no way to find out which account the old transactions used (except by reviewing a backup file). In this example, all transactions that were originally coded to *Entertainment* will post to *Meals and Entertainment*.

COMPUTER PRACTICE

Step 1.   Display the **Chart of Accounts** List.

Step 2.   Select the account whose name you <u>do not</u> want to keep. Here you will merge the *Entertainment* account into *Meals and Entertainment*, so select **62600 Entertainment**.

Step 3.   Right click on **62600 Entertainment** and then select **Edit Account**. Alternatively, press **Ctrl+E**.

Step 4.   Enter ***Meals and Entertainment*** in the *Account Name* field (see Figure 12-25) and then click **Save & Close**. You must enter the account name <u>exactly</u> as it appears in the *Chart of Accounts*. One way of ensuring this is to copy and paste the account name from the merged account to the merging account.

Figure 12-25 Change the name of the account to exactly match the name of another account.

Step 5.   Now that this account has the same name as the other account, QuickBooks asks if you want to merge the two accounts (see Figure 12-26). Click **Yes**.

Figure 12-26 Click Yes to merge the accounts.

> **Did You Know?**
> If account numbers are in use, another way to merge accounts is to change the account number of one account to match the account number of another. This has the same effect as replacing the account name of the merging account with the account name of the merged account.
>
> **Note:**
> The merge feature is not limited to just the *Chart of Accounts* List; it can be used on most Lists within QuickBooks, including *Customers* and *Vendors*.

Reordering the Account List

There are several ways to reorder the *Chart of Accounts* list. By default, the Chart of Accounts list sorts first by account type and then alphabetically by account name within the account type if account numbers are not in use or numerically by account number within the account type if account numbers are in use. For example, all of the bank accounts come first, followed by Accounts Receivable, Other Current Assets, and so on. The account types are arranged in the order in which they appear on financial statements.

> **DO NOT PERFORM THESE STEPS NOW. THEY ARE FOR REFERENCE ONLY.**

1.   Display the **Chart of Accounts** (see Figure 12-27).
2.   Click the **Name** column heading to sort the list.

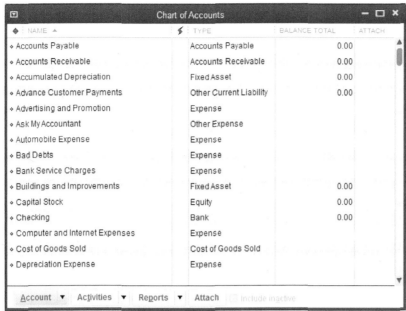

Figure 12-27 Chart of Accounts sorted by name

Note:
When account numbers are inactive and you click the *Name* header, QuickBooks sorts the account list alphabetically by account name.

However, when account numbers are active and you click the *Name* header, QuickBooks sorts the list by account number. Click the other headers to sort by ![lightning] *(Online status)*, *Type*, or *Balance*.

Tip:
When you assign account numbers, set numbering breaks that correspond to the account types. For example, number all of your asset accounts 10000-19999 and all of your liability accounts 20000-29999, and so forth. When you click the Name header to sort the *Chart of Accounts*, QuickBooks does not also sort the list by account type. Therefore, if you assign an account number of 70000 to a Bank account, QuickBooks will place that account near the bottom of the *Chart of Accounts*, regardless of its type. If you do not use account numbers, it is best not to use the Name header to sort the *Chart of Accounts*. Instead, select the **Account** menu and choose **Re-sort List**. This will sort the list by Account name (or number) while respecting the account types.

You can also use the mouse to drag the accounts up or down within the same account type. Within each account type, the order of the accounts in the Chart of Accounts determines the order of the accounts in financial statements and other reports.

Tip:
Once you have manually reordered the *Chart of Accounts*, all new accounts will automatically be added to the top of the list within its type, rather than in alphabetical order.

To reorder the *Chart of Accounts* List using the mouse, follow these steps:

DO NOT PERFORM THESE STEPS NOW. THEY ARE FOR REFERENCE ONLY.

1.   If you have sorted the list by *Name, Online Status, Type,* or *Balance* by clicking on the column headers, click on the diamond to the left of the **Name** column header. This will remove the sorting (see Figure 12-28).

Figure 12-28 Chart of Accounts, sorted by account name

2.   Hold down the mouse button on the small diamond to the left of each Account name. Drag the account up or down (see Figure 12-29).

> **Note:**
> You can reorder other lists and centers as well by dragging the diamond next to the name.

Figure 12-29 Reorder the list by moving an account with the mouse.

> **Tip:**
> To preserve proper financial statement presentation, you can only rearrange accounts within their account type. In addition, QuickBooks treats accounts with subaccounts as a group, so if you want to move your account above or beneath an account with subaccounts, you'll need to drag it above or below the group.
>
> **Tip:**
> If you use account numbers, it may be best to edit the numbers to move accounts up or down in the list. For example, if you want account #10400 to be above account #10300, you can edit its account number so that it is #10200. Then, you may need to select the **Account** menu and then select **Re-sort List**.

Turning Off Account Numbers

For the rest of this chapter, we'll turn off the display of account numbers in the Chart of Accounts.

COMPUTER PRACTICE

Step 1.   Select the **Edit** menu and then select **Preferences**.

Step 2.   In the *Preferences* window, click on the **Accounting** option and then select the **Company Preferences** tab.

Step 3.   Deselect the *Use account numbers* box and then click **OK**.

Step 4.   Close any open windows.

Setting Up Other Lists

At this point in the 12-Step process, you would enter additional information in lists, such as *Customers* and *Vendors*. You can use the *QuickBooks Setup Add Info* (see page 438) to import *Customers*, *Vendors*, and *Employees* from contact lists in other formats, such as your Outlook contact list. For this exercise, the Setup-18.QBM file you restored earlier already has this data entered. Refer to page 34 and 112 for more information on adding *Customers* and *Vendors*.

Add/Edit Multiple List Entries

You can add multiple list entries, such as *Customers, Vendors* or *Inventory Items* using a feature called *Add/Edit Multiple List Entries*. This is particularly useful when you already have a list of these entities, such as in a database or in an Excel spreadsheet. Using the *Add/Edit Multiple List Entries*, columns of data can be copied from your original file and pasted into the QuickBooks file. This can also be used to enter data into many list entries at one time.

> ### DO NOT PERFORM THESE STEPS. THEY ARE FOR REFERENCE ONLY.

1. Select **Add/Edit Multiple Entries** from the *List* menu. The *Add/Edit Multiple List Entries* window opens.

2. Select **Customers** from the *List* field. You also have the option to choose *Vendors, Service Items, Inventory Parts, Non-Inventory Parts* or *Inventory Assemblies* (see Figure 12-30).

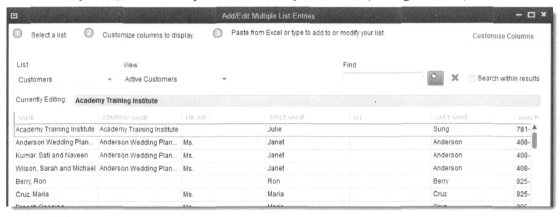

Figure 12-30 – Add/Edit Multiple Customer Items

3. Click on the **Customize Columns** button on the right. The *Customize Columns* window opens.

4. Select the fields you want to import and click the **Add** button. This copies the columns from the *Available Columns* list on the left of the window to the *Chosen Columns* on the right of the window. Select *Credit Limit* and click **Add**. Then, click the **Move Up** button so that *Credit Limit* is below *Last Name* in the *Chosen Column* field. Click **OK**.

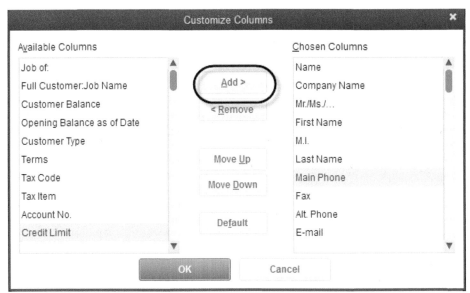

Figure 12-31 - Select Fields to Add

5. Enter **5,000** in the *Academy Training Institute* row under the *Credit Limit* column. Then right click the **5,000** entry and choose **Copy Down**. All Customers now have a $5,000 *Credit Limit*.

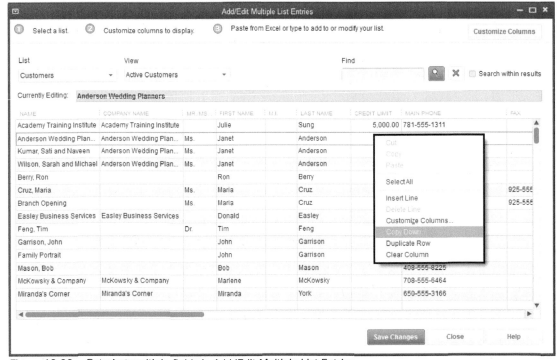

Figure 12-32 – Entering multiple fields in Add/Edit Multiple List Entries

> **Note:**
> You can also use the *Add/Edit Multiple List Entries* to enter multiple new list items by pasting in columns from a spreadsheet that contains the new data.

6. When all the information is complete, click on **Save Changes**.

Setting Up Opening Balances – Step 4

Gathering Your Information

After you've set up your *Chart of Accounts*, you're ready to enter your opening balances. To set up your opening balances, you will need to gather several documents prepared as of your start date. The following is a list of items needed to complete your setup:

Trial Balance: Ask your accountant to provide you with a trial balance for your start date. If your start date is the end of your fiscal year, ask your accountant for an "after-closing" trial balance. The term "after-closing" means "after all of the income and expenses have been closed into Retained Earnings."

If a trial balance is not available, use an after-closing Balance Sheet and a year-to-date Income Statement as of your start date. Table 12-3 shows a sample after-closing trial balance for Academy Photography on the start date of 12/31/2018.

Academy Photography		
Trial Balance		
December 31, 2018		
	Debit	Credit
Checking	$17,959.60	
Money Market	14,100.00	
Savings	500.00	
Accounts Receivable	1,253.41	
Inventory	7,158.67	
Furniture and Equipment	13,250.00	
Fixed Assets:Accumulated Depreciation		$1,500.00
Accounts Payable		142.00
National Bank VISA Gold		3,450.00
Payroll Liabilities:Company PR Taxes		368.00
Sales Tax Payable		141.79
Line of Credit		6,700.00
Truck Loan		12,000.00
Common Stock		10,000.00
Retained Earnings		19,919.89
TOTAL	$54,221.68	$54,221.68

Table 12-3 Trial Balance on Academy Photography's start date

Bank Statement *(for all bank accounts):* You will need the most recent bank statement prior to your start date. For example, if your start date is 12/31/2018 you will need the 12/31/2018 bank statements for all of your accounts.

```
                              Business Checking Account

Statement Date:                 December 31, 2018                        Page 1 of 1

Summary:

Previous Balance as of 11/30/18:          $        12,155.10
Total Deposits and Credits: 2          +  $        10,157.28
Total Checks and Debits: 9             -  $         7,027.40
Total Interest Earned                  +  $             8.62
Total Service Charge:1                 -  $            10.00
Statement Balance as of 12/31/18:      =  $        15,283.60

Deposits and Other Credits:
```

DEPOSITS				INTEREST			
Date	Description		Amount	Date	Description		Amount
8-Dec	Customer Deposit	$	6,150.00	31-Dec	Interest Earned	$	8.62
20-Dec	Customer Deposit	$	4,007.28		Interest:	$	8.62
	Deposits: $		10,157.28				

Checks and Other Withdrawals:

CHECKS PAID:				SERVICE CHARGES			
Check No.	Date Paid		Amount	Date	Description		Amount
316	2-Dec	$	324.00	31-Dec	Service Charge	$	10.00
317	3-Dec	$	128.60		1 Service Charge:	$	10.00
318	5-Dec	$	83.00				
319	8-Dec	$	285.00				
320	10-Dec	$	1,528.00				
321	12-Dec	$	3,000.00				
322	13-Dec	$	276.52				
323	15-Dec	$	142.00				
324	28-Dec	$	1,260.28				
	Checks Paid: $		7,027.40				

Figure 12-33 Bank Statement for Academy Photography on 12/31/2018

> **Tip:**
> If your bank statements are not dated on the end of each month, ask your bank to change your statement date to the end of the month. You may also be able to run a statement on your bank's Web site that ends on the date you choose.

Unpaid Bills: List each vendor bill by date of the bill, amount due, and what items or expenses you purchased on the bill (see Table 12-4).

Bill Number	Bill Date	Vendor	Amt. Due	Account/Item	Job	Class	Terms
2342	12/21/18	Wong & Son Video	$142.00	Subcontractors Expense	Mason, Bob (Not Billable)	San Jose	Net 30

Table 12-4 Unpaid bills on Academy Photography's start date

Outstanding Checks and Deposits: You'll need a list of all of your checks and deposits that have not cleared the bank as of the bank statement dated on or prior to your start date.

OUTSTANDING DEPOSTIS AT 12/31/2018		
Date	Description	Amount
12/30/2018	Customer Deposit	$3,000.00
OUTSTANDING CHECKS AT 12/31/2018		
Check No.	Date Paid	Payee	Amount
324	12/26/2018	National Bank	$324.00

Table 12-5 Outstanding deposits and checks on Academy Photography's start date

Open Invoices: List each customer invoice including the date of the invoice, amount due, and the items sold on the invoice (see Table 12-6).

Inv #	Invoice Date	Customer:Job	Class	Terms	Item	Qty	Amt Due
3947	12/18/18	Mason, Bob	San Jose	Net 30	Camera Santa Clara Tax Total	1	$695.99 8.25% $753.41
4003	12/21/18	Cruz, Maria: Branch Opening	San Jose	2% 10 Net 30	Photographer $125/hr Total	4	$500.00 $500.00

Table 12-6 Open Invoices on Academy Photography's start date

Employee list and W-4 information for each employee: Gather complete name, address, social security number, and withholding information for each employee.

> **Note:**
> The next three payroll-related lists are necessary only if your start date is in the middle of a calendar year and you want to track payroll details with QuickBooks. If your start date is 12/31, skip these lists and enter the opening balances for payroll liabilities in the liability accounts as shown later in this section.
>
> If your start date is 12/31, you need to enter the detail from these lists only if you want to use QuickBooks to create payroll reports, Form 940, Form 941, or W-2s for the previous year.
>
> All payroll setup instructions are covered in the "Payroll Setup" chapter beginning on page 359.

Payroll Liabilities by Item: List the amount due for each of your payroll liabilities as of your start date. For example, list the amounts due for federal withholding tax, social security (employer), social security (employee), and any other payroll liabilities.

Year-to-Date Payroll Detail by Employee: If your start date is not 12/31 and you want QuickBooks to track your payroll, you will need gross earnings, withholdings, employer taxes, and any other deductions for each employee so far this year. For the most detail, this list should include each employee's earnings *for each month* this year.

Year-to-Date Payroll Tax Deposits: If your start date is not 12/31, list each payroll tax deposit during the year by *Payroll Item*.

Physical Inventory by Inventory Part: List the quantity and cost for each product in inventory (see Table 12-7).

> **Tip:**
> If you don't have actual counts and costs for your inventory, you'll need to estimate. However, the accuracy of your reports will be compromised if you don't have accurate setup numbers. If possible, we strongly recommend conducting a physical inventory as of your QuickBooks start date.

Physical Inventory at 12/31/2018		
Item	Qty. on Hand	Value
Camera	10	$4,500.00
Case	25	1,125.00
Frame	25	53.75
Lenses	8	1,479.92

Table 12-7 Physical inventory on Academy Photography's start date

Opening Balances for Accounts

To enter opening balances, you can either edit the account in the *New Account* or *Edit Account* window, or create a *General Journal Entry*. Entering the *Opening Balance* in the *New Account* or *Edit Account* window is a good method for setting up a single account. General Journal Entries allow you to set up the Opening Balances for several accounts at once.

When entering opening balances for bank accounts and credit cards, it is very important to use the ending balance from the bank statement dated on (or just prior to) your start date.

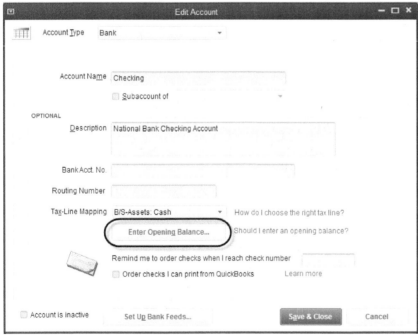

Figure 12-34 Enter an opening balance in the Edit Account window.

Directly Editing the Account

To enter the opening balances, repeat the following steps for each of your Balance Sheet accounts:

COMPUTER PRACTICE

Step 1.   Display the Chart of Accounts.

Step 2.   Select the **Checking** bank account by clicking on the account name one time.

Step 3.   Select the **Account** button at the bottom of the window and then select **Edit Account**.

Step 4.   Click on the **Enter Opening Balance** Button (see Figure 12-34).

Step 5.   In the *Enter Opening Balance: Bank Account* window (see Figure 12-35), enter
               15,283.60 in the *Statement Ending Balance* field. This amount is the ending balance on
               the bank statement.

Step 6.   Enter **12/31/2018** in the *Statement Ending Date* field.

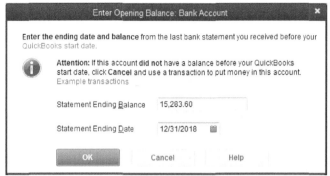

Figure 12-35 Enter Opening Balance for a Bank Account window

Step 7.   Click **OK** to finalize the *Enter Opening Balance: Bank Account* window. Then, click **Save &**
               Close on the *Edit Account Window*. Repeat Steps 2 through 7 for the *Money Market*
               account. Enter an opening balance of *$14,100.00* as of *12/31/2018* (see Figure 12-36).

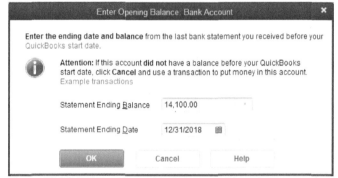

Figure 12-36 Edit the Money Market account to enter an opening balance

You can also enter bank account balances as part of a *General Journal Entry*. We will use this method to
enter the opening balance for the *Savings* bank account balance. However with this method, the starting
balance on your first *Bank Reconciliation* will be zero. If you want your starting balance to equal your
Opening Balance, enter the bank account's *Opening Balance* in the *Edit Account* window.

> **Accounting Behind the Scenes:**
> When you enter an opening balance in an account, a transaction posts to the account
> and to *Opening Balance Equity*. Also, the opening balance in a bank type account
> becomes the *Beginning Balance* for the first bank reconciliation.
>
> **Note:**
> QuickBooks does not allow you to directly enter the opening balance for *Accounts*
> *Receivable, Undeposited Funds, Accounts Payable, Sales Tax Payable*, or *Opening*
> *Balance Equity*. To enter opening balances for these accounts, see later in this chapter.

Recording Opening Balances Using a General Journal Entry

General Journal Entries allow you to record debits and credits to specific accounts. Other forms in
QuickBooks, such as *Invoices* or *Bills*, take care of the credits and debits for you behind the scenes (See

page 2). *General Journal Entries* record transactions that cannot otherwise be recorded using QuickBooks forms.

Because total debits always equal total credits, the total of the debit column and the total of the credit column must be equal or you will not be able to save the *General Journal Entry*. QuickBooks automatically calculates the amount required to make these entries balance as you create each new line in the *General Journal Entry*. Even though QuickBooks automatically enters this amount, it is only correct when you reach the last entry line. To change the amount, simply enter the correct number over the automatic number. For the final line of this *General Journal Entry*, code the amount QuickBooks calculates to the *Opening Bal Equity* account. This amount may be a debit or a credit, depending on the other figures in the entry.

Although the *Trial Balance* doesn't show any balance in Opening Bal Equity, you use this account during setup to keep everything in balance. At the end of the setup process, you'll transfer the balance from this account into Retained Earnings, as shown later in the setup steps.

You can use a *General Journal Entry* to record some, but not all, of your opening balances. Do not include the following accounts in the *General Journal Entry*: Accounts Receivable, Accounts Payable, Inventory, Sales Tax Payable, and Retained Earnings. You will enter the opening balance for these accounts later in the 12-Step setup. For example, you'll exclude Accounts Receivable and Accounts Payable because you will create *Invoices* and *Bills* to enter these accounts, respectively. See *Entering Open Bills (Accounts Payable)* on page 466.

COMPUTER PRACTICE

Use the information from the Trial Balance on page **459** to complete the following steps:

Step 1.   Select the **Company** menu and then select **Make General Journal Entries**. If necessary, click **OK** in the *Assign Numbers to Journal Entries* dialog box. If you are not using QuickBooks Accountant, your *Make General Journal Entries* window will appear differently.

Step 2.   Fill in the **Make General Journal Entries** window as shown in Figure 12-37. Make sure to uncheck *Adjusting Entry*.

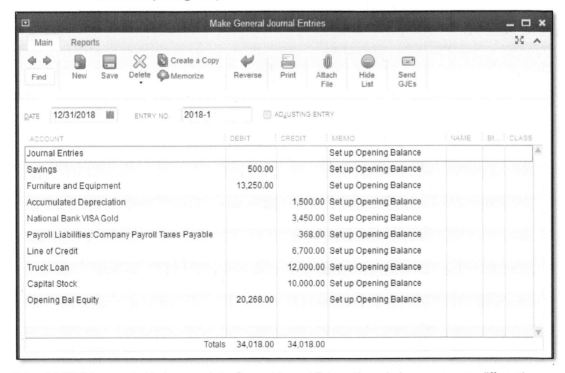

Figure 12-37 Enter opening balances using a General Journal Entry – Your window may appear differently

> **Note:**
> It is a best practice to use an account called Journal Entries on the top line of each General Journal Entry, as shown in Figure 12-37. Use the *Bank* account type when setting up this account in your *Chart of Accounts*. The *Journal Entries* account will never have a balance, so it will never show on financial statements, but it will have a register where you'll be able to look at all of your *General Journal Entries*.

Step 3.   Click **Save & Close** to save the entry.

Step 4.   QuickBooks will warn you that you can set up Fixed Asset Items from the *Fixed Asset Item List*. Click **OK**. If you see the *Items not assigned classes* dialog box, click the **Save Anyway** button.

> **Important Note:**
> In this example, you're setting up the opening balances for Payroll Liabilities directly in the accounts instead of first setting up the Payroll function. This way, you can finalize your opening balances before worrying about the Payroll setup, and you can separate the tasks of Company setup and Payroll setup.
>
> Remember though, because we've set up the liabilities outside of the Payroll system, your first Payroll Liability payment (for last year's liability), must be entered using the *Write Checks* window instead of the *Pay Liabilities* window. Alternatively, you could set up the Payroll Liability Balances using the *Adjust Liabilities* window with the *Do not Affect Accounts* setting. Then, you would use the *Pay Liabilities* window to pay your opening Payroll Liability balances.

Understanding Opening Bal Equity

As you enter the opening balances for your assets and liabilities, QuickBooks automatically adds offsetting amounts in the *Opening Bal Equity* account. This account, which is created automatically by QuickBooks, is very useful if used properly. As you'll see later in this section, each of the opening balance transactions you enter into QuickBooks will affect this account. Then, after you have entered all of the opening balances, you'll "close" *Opening Bal Equity* into *Retained Earnings* (or *Owner's Equity*). After the set up process is complete, the Opening Balance Equity account must always maintain a zero balance.

> **Tip:**
> By using the *Opening Bal Equity* account during setup, you will be able to quickly access the detail of your setup transactions by looking at the *Opening Bal Equity* register.

Entering Open Items – Step 5

Entering Outstanding Checks and Deposits

To help with the first bank reconciliations, you want all of the outstanding checks and deposits to show in QuickBooks so that you can match them with your first bank statement after the start date. If you don't enter the individual transactions, you won't see them in the QuickBooks reconciliation window. In addition, if a transaction never clears the bank, you won't know which transaction it was without going back to your old records.

COMPUTER PRACTICE

For each of your bank accounts and credit cards, enter all outstanding checks (or charges) and deposits (or payments) as additional transactions in the account register. Enter each outstanding check and deposit with the date the check was written or the deposit made, and post each transaction to *Opening Bal Equity*.

Step 1.   With the **Chart of Accounts** open, double click on the **Checking** account to display its register.

Step 2.   Enter new transactions directly in the register for each outstanding check and deposit (see Figure 12-38). See the list of outstanding checks and deposits in Table 12-5 on page 461.

               By default, the outstanding checks and deposits will sort into date order in the register, before the Opening Balance transaction. The balance including the outstanding checks and deposits must match your accountant's trial balance.

Step 3.   Notice that the ending balance in the account now matches the balance on the 12/31/2018 Trial Balance.

Step 4.   Close all open windows.

Figure 12-38 Checking account register with outstanding checks and deposits

Entering Open Bills (Accounts Payable)

COMPUTER PRACTICE

Enter your **Unpaid Bills** and **Vendor Credits** as of the start date. Use the original date of the bill (or credit) along with all of the details (terms, vendor, etc.) of the bill. By entering the individual bills, you can preserve detailed job costing and class tracking data if needed.

Step 1.   Click **Enter Bills** on the *Home page*, or select **Enter Bills** from the *Vendors* menu.

Step 2.   Enter the **Bill** as shown in Figure 12-39.

Step 3.   Click **Save & Close** to save the transaction.

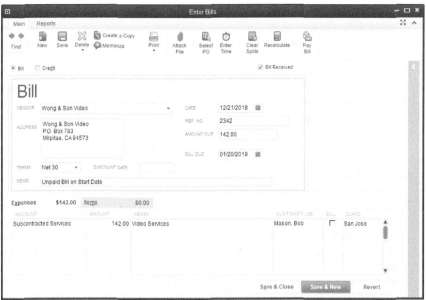

Figure 12-39 Enter the open Bill with the actual Bill date and the Bill due date.

Entering Open Invoices (Accounts Receivable)

Enter each *Invoice* or *Credit Memo* as of the Start Date. Enter each *Invoice* with its original date along with all of the details (terms, customer, etc.) of the original *Invoice*.

COMPUTER PRACTICE

Step 1.   From the *Home page* click **Create Invoices** or select **Create Invoices** from the *Customers* menu. If you see the *Professional Services Form* dialog box, click **OK**.

Step 2.   Enter the **Invoice** as shown in Figure 12-40. If you receive a warning in the *Not Enough Quantity* and/or *the Tracking Customer Orders* windows, click **OK**. Make sure the **Academy Photo Service Invoice** is selected in the *Template* field.

Step 3.   Click **Save & New** to save the transaction and display a new *Invoice*.

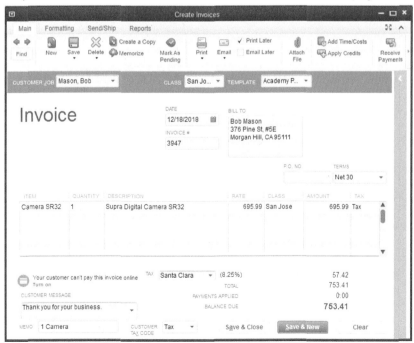

Figure 12-40 Enter the open Invoice with the original Invoice date.

Step 4.   Enter another Invoice as shown in Figure 12-41. The *Customer:Job* is **Cruz, Maria: Branch Opening**. Click **Save & Close** to save the *Invoice*.

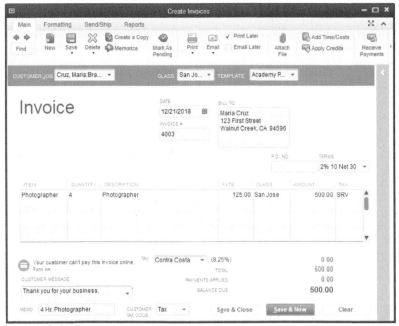

Figure 12-41 Enter this open Invoice.

> **Note:**
> When you set up your company file, it is important that you enter all *Invoices*, *Credit Memos*, *Bills*, and *Bill Credits* separately. QuickBooks needs the details of the transactions, such as the date, terms, and Customer or Vendor information, to prepare accurate aging reports (e.g., *Unpaid Bills Detail* and *A/R Aging Summary*).
>
> In addition, when you receive money against one of your prior year *Invoices* or pay a prior year *Bill*, you will need individual *Invoices* and *Bills* against which to match the receipts and payments.

Entering Open Purchase Orders

If you have open *Purchase Orders*, enter them individually, just as you did with *Bills*, *Bill Credits*, *Invoices*, and *Credit Memos*. Enter each *Purchase Order* with its original date and all of its details. If you have partially received items on the *Purchase Order*, enter only the quantities yet to be received from the Vendor.

Entering Open Estimates and Sales Orders

If you have open *Estimates* and/or *Sales Orders* (not available in QuickBooks Pro), enter them individually, just as you did with *Bills*, *Bill Credits*, *Invoices*, and *Credit Memos*. Enter each *Estimate* and/or *Sales Order* with its original date and all of its details. If you have already progress-billed a portion of the *Estimate* or delivered part of the *Sales Order*, enter only the remaining amount to be invoiced.

Entering Year-to-Date Income and Expenses – Step 6

Earlier you learned that Income and Expense accounts are totaled at the end of the fiscal year as the Net Profit (or Loss) and are combined with Retained Earnings (see page 2). In this chapter's exercise the start date is the end of the fiscal year. Later in the 12-Step process you will see the Income and Expense accounts zeroed out and their balances combined with Retained Earnings on the first day of the year (1/1/2019). However, when your company file has a start date that is *not* the end of the fiscal year, the year-to-date amounts for the Income and Expense accounts will need to be entered as a *General Journal Entry* (see Figure 12-42).

All the income amounts should be entered into the Credit column. All the expense amounts should be entered into the Debit column. Use your Opening Balance Equity account to record your net income (or loss) to date.

THE *GENERAL JOURNAL ENTRY* SHOWN IN FIGURE **12-42** IS FOR REFERENCE ONLY. IT SHOWS A MID-YEAR SETUP ENTRY. DO NOT ENTER IT NOW.

Figure 12-42 The General Journal Entry for a start date after the beginning of the year

Adjusting Opening Balance for Sales Tax Payable – Step 7

To enter the opening balance for *Sales Tax Payable*, begin by opening the *Sales Tax Payable* register to view the activity in the account. Notice that there are entries for each of the open *Invoices* you just entered. This is your *uncollected* tax. Since the total Sales Tax Liability is a combination of the *collected* tax and the *uncollected* tax, you will need to subtract the current balance in the account (the *uncollected* tax) from the amount shown on the trial balance from your accountant (or your 12/31/2018 sales tax return) to arrive at the unpaid *collected* tax.

$$TotalTaxDue = CollectedTax + UncollectedTax$$
$$CollectedTax = AmountsAlreadyCollectedButNotPaid$$
$$UncollectedTax = TaxOnOpenInvoices$$
$$...therefore$$
$$AdjustmentAmount = CollectedTax = TotalTaxDue - UncollectedTax$$

Equation 12-1 Calculating the amount of your sales tax adjustment

For example, you know from the trial balance that Academy Photography's Total Tax Due is $141.79. The Uncollected Tax has already been entered with *Invoice* #3947. The sales tax on this *Invoice* was $57.42. By subtracting the Uncollected Sales Tax ($57.42) from the Total Tax Due ($141.79), you can calculate the Collected Tax, $84.37.

You must create a *Sales Tax Adjustment* for the collected tax amount.

COMPUTER PRACTICE

Step 1.   Select the **Vendors** menu, then select **Sales Tax**, and then select **Adjust Sales Tax Due**.

Step 2.   Complete the *Sales Tax Adjustment* window as shown in Figure 12-43 and then click **OK**. If you see the *Items not assigned classes* dialog box, click the **Save Anyway** button.

If you pay sales tax to more than one sales tax agency, you will need to enter a separate adjustment for each agency.

Figure 12-43 The Sales Tax Adjustment window

Did You Know?
The *Sales Tax Adjustment* window creates a *General Journal Entry* transaction in QuickBooks. Therefore, the Entry No. field will display the next *General Journal Entry* number in sequence. If you prefer, you could instead enter this adjustment using a *General Journal Entry*.

Adjusting Inventory and Setting up Fixed Assets – Step 8

If you have inventory, you will need to create an inventory adjustment to enter the actual quantity and value on hand as of your start date. This is done *after* you enter your outstanding *Bills* and *Invoices*, so that the actual inventory counts and costs will be accurate even if some of the *Bills* and/or *Invoices* include *Inventory Items*.

As with the adjustment to Sales Tax Payable, begin by opening the *Inventory* register to view the activity and the current balance. Also, open the *Item List* to view the current stock status of each Inventory Item. Then adjust the quantity on hand and value of each item so that Inventory will agree with the physical inventory counts and the company's trial balance as of your start date.

Adjusting Inventory for Actual Counts

COMPUTER PRACTICE

Step 1.   Select the Vendors menu, then select Inventory Activities, and then select Adjust Quantity/Value on Hand.

Step 2.   Choose **Quantity and Total Value** from the *Adjustment Type* field (see Figure 12-44).

Step 3.   Enter *12/31/2018* in the *Adjustment Date* field. Press **Tab**.

Step 4.   Select **Opening Bal Equity** in the *Adjustment Account* field.

Step 5.   Click **OK** on the *Income or Expense expected* warning window.

Step 6.   Enter *2018-3* in the *Ref. No.* field. Press **Tab**.

Step 7.   Leave both the *Customer:Job* and *Class* fields blank.

Step 8.   Enter the information in Figure 12-44.

If your *Qty on Hand* column does not match, check the *Adjustment Date* to make sure it says *12/31/2018* as this column is calculated as of the adjustment date. If your date is correct and you still don't match, then make sure you entered Invoice 3947 correctly earlier in this chapter.

Step 9.   Click **Save & Close** to record the transaction. If you see the *Items not assigned classes* dialog box, click the **Save Anyway** button.

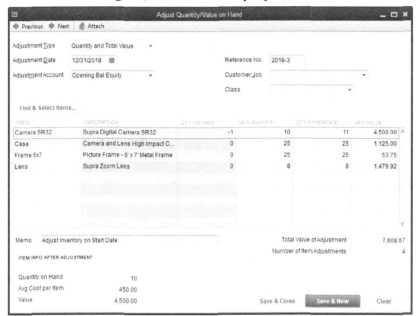

Figure 12-44 Adjust inventory as of the start date

Setting up Fixed Assets

You can track detailed information about your company's Fixed Assets. You can set up detailed information about each asset using the *Fixed Asset Item* List. Then, if you use QuickBooks Accountant, your accountant can use the *Fixed Asset Manager* to individually calculate and track depreciation on each asset.

Setting up Loans

You can track detailed information about your loans. You can individually track and amortize each of your loans so that QuickBooks will automatically allocate the principal and interest on each payment.

Setup Payroll and YTD Payroll Information – Step 9

Setting up Payroll in QuickBooks is a lengthy and involved process. Refer to the "Payroll Setup" chapter beginning on page 359 for more information about setting up the Payroll feature.

Verifying your Trial Balance – Step 10

Before you complete the set up process by transferring the balance of *Opening Bal Equity* into *Retained Earnings*, make sure the account balances in QuickBooks match your accountant's trial balance.

COMPUTER PRACTICE

Step 1.   Select the **Reports** menu, then select **Accountant & Taxes**, and then select **Trial Balance**.

Step 2.   Set the *From* and *To* date field to your start date as shown in Figure 12-45.

Step 3.   After reviewing the *Trial Balance*, write down the balance of the *Opening Bal Equity* account, and close the window. Click **No** if you are given the option to memorize the report.

Notice that the *Trial Balance* in Figure 12-45 looks slightly different from your accountant's report (in Table 12-3). For example, there are balances in several income and expense accounts as well as in *Opening Bal Equity*. Do not worry about this difference at this point as you are not finished with the setup yet. The income and expense accounts have balances because you just entered *Invoices* and *Bills* for the open invoices and unpaid bills. Those *Invoices* and *Bills* were dated during the prior year, so those transactions add to income and expenses for that year. QuickBooks will automatically close the balances in the income and expense accounts to Retained Earnings at the start of the next year on 1/1/2019.

Your *Trial Balance* could also differ from your accountant's report if the reporting basis on the two reports is not the same. For example, if you create an accrual basis *Trial Balance* and your accountant's *Trial Balance* is cash basis, the balances in the income and expense accounts may be different. Regardless of which method of accounting you use, the income and expense accounts will automatically be closed to Retained Earnings. Therefore, at this point in your setup, you should create an accrual basis *Trial Balance*, regardless of which basis you will ultimately use on reports. Just verify that all of the *Balance Sheet* account balances are accurate with the exception of Retained Earnings.

> **Note:**
> To learn more about the cash or accrual basis of accounting see the section beginning on page 198.

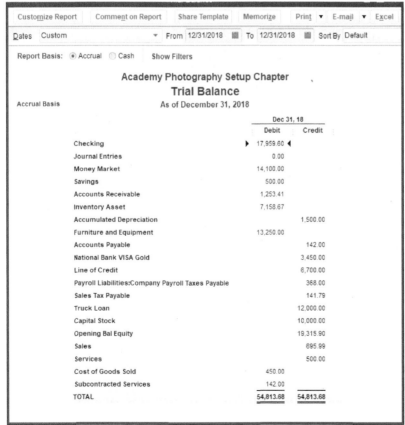

Figure 12-45 Trial Balance for Academy Photography as of the start date

Closing Opening Bal Equity – Step 11

Once you have compared your *Trial Balance* report to your accountant's report, use a *General Journal Entry* to transfer (close) the balance in *Opening Bal Equity* into *Retained Earnings*.

> **Note:**
> If your company is a sole proprietorship, use this same process, but instead of *Retained Earnings*, the account should be called *Owner's Equity*. If your company is a partnership, split the balance of *Opening Bal Equity* between each of the partners' profit accounts.

COMPUTER PRACTICE

Step 1.   Select the **Company** menu and then select **Make General Journal Entries**. If necessary, click **OK** in the *Assign Numbers to Journal Entries* dialog box. The screenshot below is from QuickBooks Accountant. If you are using a different edition of QuickBooks, your window may appear differently.

Step 2.   Set the **Date** field to your start date.

Step 3.   Enter the **General Journal Entry** as shown in Figure 12-46 and then click **Save & Close**.

Figure 12-46 General Journal Entry to close Opening Bal Equity into Retained Earnings – Your screen may vary

Step 4.   If the *Retained Earnings* window appears, click **OK**. If you see the *Items not assigned classes* dialog box, click the **Save Anyway** button.

When you are finished entering all of the opening balances and you have closed the *Opening Bal Equity* account into *Retained Earnings*, verify your *Balance Sheet*. Create a *Balance Sheet* for *the day after* your start date and verify that the numbers match your accountant's trial balance.

COMPUTER PRACTICE

Step 1.   Select the **Reports** menu, then select **Company & Financial**, and then select **Balance Sheet Standard**.

Step 2.   Set the *As of* field to *1/1/2019*, the day after your start date (see Figure 12-47).

Step 3.   Print the report and then close the window.

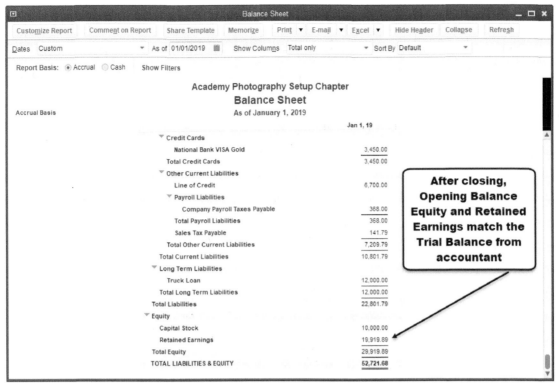

Figure 12-47 Academy Photography Balance Sheet

Setting the Closing Date - Backing up the File – Step 12

Now that you have entered all of your opening balances in the file, create a backup of the file. It is a good idea to keep this backup in a secure location so that you always have a clean record of your setup transactions. This is in addition to your regular backup process.

Setting the Closing Date to Protect your Setup Balances

For details on setting the *Closing Date* and the *Closing Date password*, see page 533.

Congratulations! You have finished the setup of your company file and are ready to begin entering transactions. First you need to set up users of the file so you can control which areas of QuickBooks can be accessed by individuals.

Users and Passwords

QuickBooks provides a feature for defining "users" of the file. This feature allows the "administrator" (the owner of the file) to set privileges for each user of the file. This provides security and user tracking when several people have access to the same data file.

Setting Up Users in the Company File

Each user should have a separate user name and password. Once users have been setup, QuickBooks will require a user name and password when a company file is opened. The privileges granted to that user by the administrator determine what functions of QuickBooks they can access. For example, a user might have access to Accounts Receivable, Accounts Payable, and Banking functions, but not Payroll or "sensitive activities" like online banking. For a complete description of each privilege, click the **Help** button on the *User Setup* windows.

COMPUTER PRACTICE

Step 1.   First you will setup the Administrator's password. Select the **Company** menu, select **Set Up Users and Passwords**, and then select **Change Your Password**. The *Change QuickBooks Password* window will appear (Figure 12-48).

Figure 12-48 Change Administrator's Password

Step 2.   Leave **Admin** in the *User Name* field and then press **Tab** (see Figure 12-48).

You could, of course, change the administrator's *User Name*, but even if you do, you'll always be able to log in (or open the file) as the administrator if you enter **Admin** in the user name field and if you enter the administrator's correct password.

Step 3.   Enter **Sleeter18** in the *Current Password* field. Press **Tab**.

Step 4.   Enter **Abc1234** in the *New Password* and *Confirm New Password* fields. Once you enter this password, you will need to remember this password to open this exercise file in the future.

Several privileges are reserved exclusively for the administrator of the file. For example, the administrator is the only one who can view or change the company information (name, address, etc.). Also, the administrator is the only one who can make any changes to the *Company Preferences* tabs in the *Preferences* section. For more information about the file administrator, see QuickBooks online Help.

> **Note:**
> To protect and secure your QuickBooks data file, always use a complex password. Complex passwords use at least seven characters, including capital and lowercase letters, numbers, and special characters. At least one of the characters should be a number and another should be an uppercase letter. It is a good practice to use passwords that could also not be easily guessed. We strongly recommend that you not use Sleeter18, Abc1234, or any other password used in your class with your company's QuickBooks file, as it could be guessed by others familiar with your course material.

Step 5.   In the *Challenge Question* field, select **Name of oldest nephew**.

Step 6.   Enter **Bill** in the *Answer* field. Click **OK**. After reading the password reminder window, click **OK** again.

Step 7.   Now you will set up the user's privileges for an individual. Select **Set Up Users** from the *Set Up Users and Passwords* submenu of the *Company* menu. The *QuickBooks Login* window displays (see Figure 12-49).

Step 8.   Type *Abc1234* in the *Password* field and click **OK**.

Figure 12-49 QuickBooks Login window

Step 9.   The window in Figure 12-50 shows the *User list* for this company file. To create an additional user, click **Add User**.

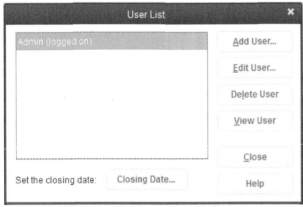

Figure 12-50 The User List for a company file

Step 10.   When you click **Add User**, QuickBooks walks you through a series of windows (a Wizard) where you set privileges for each user (see Figure 12-51). Make your selections as appropriate.

Step 11.   On the *User Name and Password* window, enter *Kathy* in the *User Name* field, and enter *Abc4321* in the *Password* and *Confirm Password* fields. Click **Next**.

Figure 12-51 The User Name and Password window

Step 12.   On the *Access for user: Kathy* window, select **Selected areas of QuickBooks** (see Figure 12-52). Click **Next**.

As the Administrator, you can give users access to all areas of QuickBooks or you can restrict access to selected areas of the program.

Figure 12-52 You can restrict a user's access

Did you know?
By selecting *Access to All areas of QuickBooks*, you give a user permission to change transactions in closed periods. Even if you want a user to have access to all areas, it's better to choose *Selected areas of QuickBooks* for all users. Then select *Full Access* in all areas but say *No* on the allow users to change or delete transactions that were recorded before the closing date. This protects your prior period accounting data without limiting the users' access to any other transactions or reporting.

Step 13.   On the *Sales and Accounts Receivable* window, select **Full Access** and click **Next** (see Figure 12-53).

Figure 12-53 The Sales and Accounts Receivable window

Step 14.   Click **Next** on each of the following windows to view the default settings.

When setting up your own file, set access rights for each new user as appropriate. If you are not sure what to select, click **Help**. Online Help will fully explain each privilege.

Each user should be restricted from *Changing or Deleting Transactions recorded before the closing date* (see Figure 12-54). This setting creates additional protection for your accounting data once you have closed the books for a period.

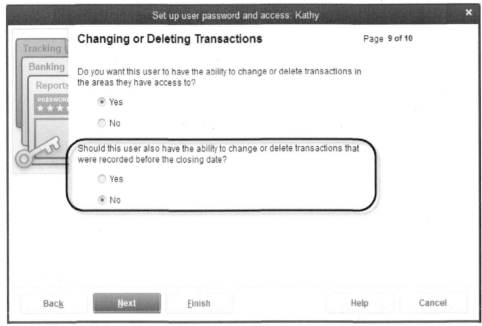

Figure 12-54 Changing or Deleting Transactions window

Step 15.   On the final window, review the privileges that you have set for this user (see Figure 12-55). If you want to make any changes, click **Back** until you see the window you want to change. To save your new user settings, click **Finish**. If you receive an Intuit Sync Manager warning, click **OK**.

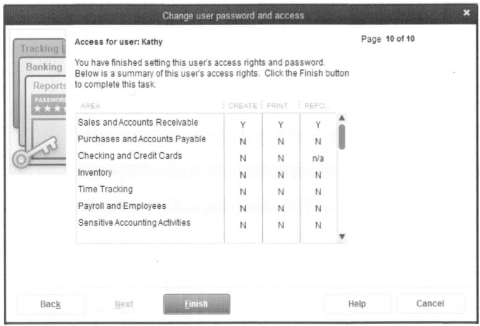

Figure 12-55 The Summary window

Step 16.   Click **Close** on the *User List* window.

Multi-User and Single-User Modes

QuickBooks is often run in a networked environment, where multiple users access the file at the same time. In such an environment, you will need to have QuickBooks open in *multi-user* mode to allow these users to access the file. However, there are a few changes that cannot be made to a file while QuickBooks is in *multi-user* mode and require you to switch to *single-user* mode. When QuickBooks is in *single-user* mode, only one person can access the file at a time. Any user, not just those with *Administrator* privileges can use QuickBooks in *single-user* mode. Some of the changes that may require *single-user* mode include making backups, exporting data, or deleting a list item.

> **Note:**
> Each user must have the same version of QuickBooks on their computer system to access the same company file. All versions of QuickBooks, including Pro, Premier, Accountant and Enterprise, support multiple users.

To switch to *single-user* mode, first contact the others in your company who are using your file and ask them to exit out of the QuickBooks file. Once they have exited the file, go to the *File* menu and select *Switch To Single-User Mode*. When you are done in *single-user* mode, you can switch back to *multi-user* from the same location on the *File* menu.

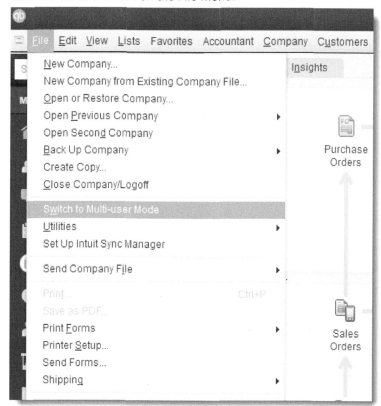

Figure 12-56 Switch to Multi-user Mode on File menu

Review Questions

Comprehension Questions

1. Explain how the Opening Balance Equity account is used when you set up a new bank account in the Chart of Accounts.

2. Explain how you would adjust your sales tax to agree with the Trial Balance from the accountant.

3. If you have been separately tracking your entertainment and meal expenses, what action would you take if you wanted to track them as one account?

4. Explain the importance of entering your outstanding checks as of the Start Date into the *Checking* account.

5. What information should you gather before setting up a QuickBooks file?

Multiple Choice

Select the best answer(s) for each of the following:

1. Your company has decided to begin using QuickBooks at the beginning of the 2019 calendar year, which is also the fiscal year. The best start date for your company file setup is:
    a) January 1, 2019.
    b) The date when you first decide to use QuickBooks.
    c) December 31, 2018.
    d) There is no best start date, you can use whatever date is convenient.

2. This chapter suggests that the best way to set up A/R and A/P balances in QuickBooks is to:
    a) Enter the total amount of A/R and A/P on a *General Journal Entry* dated on your start date.
    b) Enter the balance of each account by editing the accounts in the *Chart of Accounts*.
    c) Use a special account called A/R Setup (or A/P Setup) to record the opening balances.
    d) Enter a separate *Invoice* for each open invoice and enter a separate *Bill* for each unpaid bill.

3. Setting up a company file does not include:
    a) Obtaining a business license.
    b) Selecting the appropriate chart of accounts for your type of business.
    c) Adding accounts to the chart of accounts.
    d) Entering *Invoices*.

4. A good example of a liability account is:
    a) Inventory.
    b) Accounts Receivable.
    c) Advertising.
    d) Accounts Payable.

5. To ensure the accuracy of the information entered during setup, it is important to:
    a) Know your Retained Earnings.
    b) Verify that your *Trial Balance* matches the one provided by your accountant.
    c) Start at the beginning of the fiscal period.
    d) Know everything there is to know about accounting.

6. Close Opening Bal Equity into Retained Earnings by:
    a) Starting to enter new daily transactions.
    b) Creating a General Journal Entry.
    c) Setting the Closing Date. QuickBooks will then make the entry for you.
    d) Selecting **Close Opening Balance** on the **Activities** menu.

7. If you no longer need an account in the Chart of Accounts, you can delete it. However, if it has transactions posted to it, you cannot delete it. Instead:
    a) You should ignore it.
    b) You should rename it.
    c) You can merge it with another account, or you can deactivate it.
    d) You can move it to the bottom of the chart of accounts, which will cause it to no longer appear on reports.

8. Which of the following is NOT a way to deactivate an account?
    a) Right click on the account and select **Make Inactive**.
    b) Select **Make Account Inactive** from the **Account** menu at the bottom of the Chart of Accounts.
    c) Edit the account and click **Account is Inactive**.
    d) Select the account and check the **Include Inactive** checkbox at the bottom of the Chart of Accounts.

9. When account numbers are inactive and you click the *Name* header:
    a) QuickBooks sorts the account list alphabetically by account name.
    b) You can rename the selected account.
    c) You will see all account names.
    d) You can rename the Chart of Accounts list.

10. As the administrator, you can set up new users of the file and restrict access to several areas in the program. Which is something you CANNOT restrict?
    a) Access to all bank accounts.
    b) Access to A/P transactions.
    c) Access to Payroll.
    d) Access to one bank account, but no access to another bank account.

11. When verifying your setup, create a Balance Sheet and verify that Retained Earnings matches the Trial Balance from the accountant. If your start date is 12/31, what date should you use on this Balance Sheet?
    a) Always use the Start Date.
    b) December 31.
    c) January 1.
    d) December 30.

12. To set up the opening balance in your *Sales Tax Payable* account, wait until after you've entered your open invoices. Then adjust the *Sales Tax Payable* account for the additional sales tax due. Why is this adjustment necessary?

    a)   Because Opening Bal Equity is not involved.

    b)   Because the total amount in Sales Tax Payable is the sum of the *uncollected* sales tax (from the open invoices) plus the *collected* sales tax. Since you already entered the open invoices, the Sales Tax Payable account only has the *uncollected* sales tax and you have to add in the *collected* sales tax by adjusting the account balance.

    c)   Because there is no other way to set up the opening balance in Sales Tax Payable.

    d)   All of the above.

13. Where does QuickBooks place new accounts in the Chart of Accounts after it has been manually reordered?

    a)   Alphabetically within its account type.

    b)   Alphabetically in the list, regardless of account type.

    c)   At the top of the list, within its account type.

    d)   At the bottom of the Chart of Accounts.

14. If you have an open Invoice for an inventory item on your start date, to properly set up your Inventory balances (Quantity and Value):

    a)   Use a Journal Entry to debit Inventory for the total value of the inventory and then select **Setup Inventory Quantities** from the **Inventory** menu.

    b)   Use an Inventory Adjustment transaction *after* you enter in your opening Invoices and Bills.

    c)   Use an Inventory Adjustment transaction *before* you enter in your opening Invoices and Bills.

    d)   Use the *Opening Balance* field in the *Edit Account* window.

15. Which of the following do you set up using the *EasyStep Interview*?

    a)   Default Accounts.

    b)   Outstanding Checks and Deposits.

    c)   Inventory.

    d)   Sales Tax.

Completion Statements

1. There are five basic account types in accounting: _____, _____, _____, _____, and _____.

2. It is impossible to _____ a QuickBooks account if you have used it in transactions.

3. At the end of your setup, close the _____ _____ _____ account into Retained Earnings.

4. You can use a(n) _____ _____ _____ to record multiple accounts' opening balances at one time.

5. The account balances on your _____ _____ from your previous books and your QuickBooks file should match at the end of your file setup.

Setup Problem 1

1. Create a *new* QuickBooks company file for Academy Photography. Use Express Start and the information from the following tables and figures to completely set up the file using 12/31/2018 as your start date. Call your file Setup-18Problem1.QBW.

Company Info	
Company name	Academy Photography
Industry	Art, Writing or Photography
Company Type	S Corporation
Tax ID	11-1111111
Do you have Employees?	Yes
Legal name	Academy Photography, Inc.
Address	123 Main Street Pleasanton, CA 94588
Country	U.S.
Phone	925-555-1111
E-mail Address	info@academyphoto.biz
Web site	http://www.academyphoto.biz
Company Filename	Setup-Problem1.QBW Change the save location to your student data files folder.

Table 12-8 Express Start Setup Information

2. Add a bank account called Checking. Opening Balance is $0.00. Account Number is 12123456. Opening Balance date is 12/31/2018.

3. When finished, create an *Account Listing* report. (The *Account Listing* Report is in the *Reports* menu, under the *List* submenu).

Setup Problem 2 (Advanced)

APPLYING YOUR KNOWLEDGE

Create a *new* QuickBooks company file for Academy Photography. Use the information from the following tables and figures to completely set up the file using 12/31/2018 as your start date. Use the 12-Step setup process discussed in this chapter. Call your file Setup-18Problem2.QBW.

Company Info	
Company name	Academy Photography
Legal name	Academy Photography, Inc.
Tax ID	11-1111111
Address	123 Main Street Pleasanton, CA 94588
Country	U.S.
Phone	925-555-1111
Fax	925-555-1112
E-mail Address	info@academyphoto.biz
Web site	http://www.academyphoto.biz
Industry	Art, Writing or Photography
Income tax form	S Corporation
First month of fiscal year	January
Administrator password	*Leave blank*
Company Filename	Setup-Problem2.QBW Change the save location to your student data files folder.

Table 12-9 Company Information

Detailed Start Settings	
Products and services	Academy Photography sells both products and services, although they do not sell products online.
Sales	Academy Photography charges sales tax and creates estimates. They want to track sales orders (not available in Pro), and use billing statements and progress invoicing.
Purchases & vendors	Academy Photography will need to track bills, inventory and time.
Employees	Academy Photography has both W-2 employees and 1099 contractors. They will want to track time.
Start Date	Use 12/31/2018

Table 12-10 EasyStep Interview settings

Accounts – In the EasyStep Interview, accept the default chart of accounts suggested for your industry. After completing the Interview, add the accounts listed in Table 12-11. Since QuickBooks automatically created a Sales Income Account, you will only need to change the account number for this account. It is not necessary to enter descriptions, bank account numbers, or assign tax line items to any of these accounts for this problem. You will also create subaccounts where names are separated from the main account by a colon (:). For example, Company Payroll Taxes Payable is a subaccount of Payroll Liabilities. For a full recommended *Chart of Accounts*, see Setup Problem 3.

Additional Accounts for the Chart of Accounts		
Acct #	Account Name	Account Type
10100	Checking	Bank
10200	Money Market	Bank
10900	Journal Entries	Bank
22000	National Bank VISA Gold	Credit Card
24010	Payroll Liabilities:Company Payroll Taxes Payable	Other Current Liability
24020	Payroll Liabilities:Employee Payroll Taxes Payable	Other Current Liability
24030	Payroll Liabilities:Other Payroll Liabilities	Other Current Liability
27000	Truck Loan	Long Term Liability
40000	Services	Income
45000	Sales (*note: change number of existing account*)	Income

Table 12-11 Additional Accounts for the Chart of Accounts

Items – Table 12-12 is the *Item List* that will be used to track products and services sold by Academy Photography. Leave any other fields blank or accept the defaults if not shown in the table.

You can add the Service, Inventory Part and Non-Inventory Part during the EasyStep Interview or wait and add all items using the Item List after the interview. Sales Tax Items must be added using the Item List.

Type	Item	Description	Tax Code	Account	Cost	Price
Service	Indoor Photo Session	Indoor Studio Session	Non	Services		$95.00
Service	Retouching	Photo retouching services	Non	Services		$95.00
Inventory Part	Camera SR32	Supra Digital Camera SR32	Tax	Sales	$450.00	$695.99
Inventory Part	Case	Camera and Lens High Impact Case	Tax	Sales	$45.00	$79.99
Non-Inventory Part	Standard Photo Package	Standard Package of Photography from Session	Tax	Sales		$55.00
Sales Tax Item	Contra Costa	Contra Costa Sales Tax Vendor: State Board of Equalization (Quick Add)		Sales Tax Payable		8.25%
Sales Tax Item	Out of State (Automatically Created)	Out of State Sales Tax - exempt from sales tax		Sales Tax Payable		0%
Sales Tax Item	Santa Clara	Santa Clara Sales Tax Vendor: State Board of Equalization (Quick Add)		Sales Tax Payable		8.25%

Table 12-12 Item List

Classes – Academy Photography uses *Classes* to separately track revenues and expenses from each of their locations. You will need to turn on class tracking in the *Accounting Company Preferences*.

Class Names	San Jose	Walnut Creek	Overhead

Table 12-13 Class Tracking

Terms – Verify the following terms in the **Terms List**.

Terms	Net 30	Net 15	2% 10, Net 30	Due on Receipt

Table 12-14 Terms List

Bank Statements – Figure 12-57 shows the Checking account bank statement for Academy Photography on their Start Date of 12/31/2018. There is no bank statement available for the money market and savings accounts, but you've been told that there are no outstanding deposits or checks in those accounts. Enter the **Bank Ending Balance** as the opening balance for the Checking account.

Business Checking Account		
Statement Date:	December 31, 2018	*Page 1 of 1*

Summary:

Previous Balance as of 11/30/18	$	32,624.52
Total Deposits and Credits: 2	+ $	10,157.28
Total Checks and Debits: 9	- $	7,027.40
Total Interest Earned: 1	+ $	8.62
Total Service Charge: 1	- $	10.00
Statement Balance as of 12/31/18:	= $	35,753.02

Deposits and Other Credits:

DEPOSITS

Date	Description		Amount
8-Dec	Customer Deposit	$	6,150.00
20-Dec	Customer Deposit	$	4,007.28
	Deposits:	$	10,157.28

INTEREST

Date	Description		Amount
31-Dec	Interest Earned	$	8.62
	Interest:	$	8.62

Checks and Other Withdrawals:

CHECKS PAID:

Check No.	Date Paid		Amount
3466	2-Dec	$	324.00
3467	3-Dec	$	128.60
3468	5-Dec	$	83.00
3469	8-Dec	$	285.00
3470	10-Dec	$	1,528.00
3471	12-Dec	$	3,000.00
3472	13-Dec	$	276.52
3473	15-Dec	$	142.00
3474	28-Dec	$	1,260.28
	Checks Paid:	$	7,027.40

SERVICE CHARGES

Date	Description		Amount
31-Dec	Service Charge	$	10.00
	Service Charge:	$	10.00

Figure 12-57 Bank statement for checking account on 12/31/2018

Outstanding Checks and Deposits – Table 12-15 and Table 12-16 show a list of outstanding checks and deposits in the Checking account on 12/31/2018. Enter the outstanding check and deposit in the checking account register using the original date and Opening Balance Equity as the offsetting account. "Quick Add" each of the vendor names when prompted.

Outstanding Deposits at 12/31/2018	
Date	**Amount**
12/30/2018	$1,500.00

Table 12-15 Outstanding deposits

Outstanding Checks at 12/31/2018			
Date	**Check #**	**Payee**	**Amount**
12/26/2018	3475	Wong & Son Video	4,229.69

Table 12-16 Outstanding checks

Open Invoices - Table 12-17 shows a list of all open invoices for Academy Photography on 12/31/2018. Enter open **Invoices** using the original information and Intuit Product Invoice template. "QuickAdd" each of the customer names when prompted. Save the class, terms and tax information to be used again.

Inv #	Invoice Date	Customer:Job	Class	Terms	Item/Qty/Amt Due
2018-905	12/18/2018	Doughboy Donuts	San Jose	Net 30	Indoor Photo Session 2 Hours, $190.00 Retouching 1 Hour , $95.00 Out of State Sales Tax Total: $285.00
2018-942	12/21/2018	Scotts Shoes	San Jose	Net 30	Camera $695.99 Santa Clara Sales Tax Total $753.41

Table 12-17 Open Invoices

Unpaid Bills - Academy Photography had one unpaid bill at 12/31/2018. Enter the **Bill** with original information. "Quick Add" each of the vendor names when prompted. Save the terms information to be used again.

Bill #	Bill Date	Terms	Vendor	Amt Due	Account/Item	Job	Class
52773	12/21/18	Net 15	Boswell Consulting	$352.50	Subcontracted Services	Scotts Shoes	San Jose

Table 12-18 Unpaid bills

Physical Inventory– Below are the physical inventory counts and values at 12/31/2018. Enter the Ref. No. as 2018-1 and Opening Balance Equity as Adjusting account. If necessary, select **Save Anyway** option if a dialog box appears asking for class information.

Physical Inventory at 12/31/2018		
Item	Quantity on Hand	Value
Camera	20	$9,000.00
Case	20	900.00

Table 12-19 Physical Inventory by Inventory Part

Trial Balance – Table 12-20 shows the ending trial balance for Academy Photography on 12/31/2018. Enter opening balances as *General Journal Entries* for any remaining Asset, Liabilities (excluding Sales Tax Payable), and Equity accounts (excluding Retained Earnings) to match the trial balance amounts.

Adjust Sales Tax Payable to match trial balance amount, using *Vendor:* State Board of Equalization.

Close the Opening Balance Equity account to Retained Earnings. Verify the Opening Balance Equity account has a zero balance.

You will notice that the Trial Balance does not exactly match the one in Table 12-20. The income and expenses from the open *Invoices* and unpaid *Bills* shows in the income and expense accounts. This is CORRECT! When QuickBooks "closes" the year, those numbers will be posted into Retained Earnings. To see it work, change the date on the *Trial Balance* to 1/1/2019.

Academy Photography		
Trial Balance		
December 31, 2018		
	Debit	Credit
Checking	$33,023.33	
Money Market	$68,100.00	
Accounts Receivable	$1,038.41	
Inventory	$9,900.00	
Furniture and Equipment	$80,365.00	
Accumulated Depreciation		$45,550.00
Accounts Payable		$352.50
National Bank VISA Gold		$2,152.00
Payroll Liabilities: Company Payroll Taxes Payable		$83.00
Payroll Liabilities: Employee Payroll Taxes Payable		$285.00
Sales Tax Payable		$327.03
Truck Loan		$31,625.00
Capital Stock		$10,000.00
Retained Earnings		$102,052.21
TOTAL	$192,426.74	$192,426.74

Table 12-20 Trial balance on 12/31/2018

After completing the setup, print the following reports:

1. Account Listing

2. Item Listing

3. Open Invoices Report at 12/31/2018

4. Unpaid Bills Detail Report at 12/31/2018

5. Inventory Valuation Summary Report at 12/31/2018

6. Trial Balance as of 12/31/2018

7. Trial Balance as of 1/1/2019

8. Balance Sheet Standard on 1/1/2019

Notice that Retained Earnings on the 1/1/2019 Balance Sheet has been adjusted for the income and expenses from last year. This shows how QuickBooks automatically calculates Retained Earnings. If you change the date on the Balance Sheet to 12/31/2018, you'll see Net Income on the Balance Sheet and the Retained Earnings number will change back to the "before closing" amounts. Try it.

Chapter 13
Estimates

Topics

After completing this chapter, you should be able to:

- Prepare Estimates (page 489)
- Prepare Invoices from Estimates (page 490)
- Use the Progress Invoicing feature (page 493)
- Create Purchase Orders from Estimates (page 496)
- Create reports about Estimates (page 500)

> **Restore this File**
>
> This chapter uses Estimates-18.QBW. See page 9 for more information. The password to access this file is *Sleeter18*.

Estimates allow you to track "bids" for your sales or projects. *Estimates* do not post to the general ledger since the bid may not be accepted by the customer. They do record the bid information that has been given to the customer. In fact, you can prepare more than one estimate for the same job if a customer is not sure exactly what they want to order. Then when a bid is accepted and you perform the work, you can transfer the information from the *Estimates* onto *Invoices*.

Sometimes you can invoice for an entire estimate all at one time, but QuickBooks also provides a *Progress Invoicing* feature that allows you to prepare several invoices for a job as each stage of the job is completed. To reduce errors and provide fast data entry, QuickBooks automates the process of copying portions of an *Estimate* onto each progress invoice.

Sales Orders are very similar to *Estimates* except *Estimates* may or may not become *Invoices* while *Sales Orders* have been agreed upon and will always end up as *Invoices*. Both are used to track orders from customers while you are processing the order, or otherwise waiting to fulfill the order. Some businesses (e.g., contractors) prefer to use *Estimates* while others (e.g., retailers) prefer to use *Sales Orders*. These two features allow you to accomplish essentially the same function of tracking proposed versus actual revenues and expenses, as well as active (or open) and inactive (or closed) bids.

In this chapter, you'll learn how these features help you track the various stages of sales transactions.

Creating *Estimates* and *Progress Invoicing* can be done using QuickBooks Pro or higher editions. However, *Sales Orders* require QuickBooks Premier or higher editions, and cannot be created using QuickBooks Pro.

Creating Estimates

Entering an **Estimate** in QuickBooks is similar to entering an Invoice because you fill out all of the Customer and Item information the same way. The big difference is that Estimates do not post to the general ledger, and therefore they do not affect any of your financial reports. They do help you track your *future sales* and they do help you track how your actual revenues and costs *compare* with what was estimated, but **Estimates** do not record any financial information themselves. Additionally, you can create and print **Estimates** for your proposals and then use QuickBooks reports to help you follow up with each prospect during the sales process.

COMPUTER PRACTICE

To create an Estimate, follow these steps:

Step 1.   Select the **Customers** menu and then select **Create Estimates**. Alternatively, click the **Estimates** icon on the *Home* page.

Step 2.   Enter **Garrison, John: Family Portrait** in the *Customer:Job* field and press **Tab**.

Step 3.   Enter the remaining information shown in Figure 13-1 on the **Create Estimates** form. Make sure to enter the % symbol in the markup column.

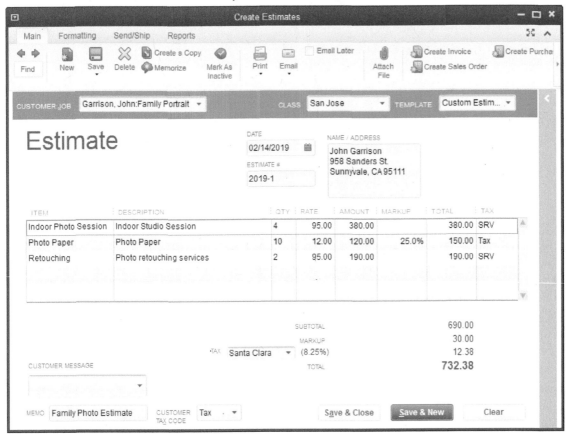

Figure 13-1 Create Estimates window

Step 4.   Click **Save & Close** to record the Estimate.

> **Note:**
> You can customize your Estimates by creating or editing templates in the same way you customize your Invoices as illustrated on page 265.

Creating Invoices from Estimates

When an Estimate is approved or accepted by a customer, you can convert the information from the Estimate into an Invoice. Doing so eliminates the need to manually enter the detail on the Invoice.

COMPUTER PRACTICE

To create an Invoice from an Estimate, follow these steps:

Step 1.   From the **Customers** menu, select **Create Invoices**.

Step 2.   Enter **Garrison, John: Family Portrait** in the *Customer:Job* field and press **Tab**.

QuickBooks displays the *Available Estimates* window (see Figure 13-2).

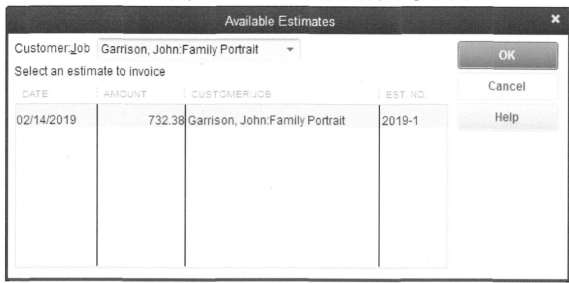

Figure 13-2 Available Estimates window

> **Note:**
> When you work with a prospect, you may need to create several Estimates (i.e., bids) showing different alternatives for the job. If you do, QuickBooks will show each of the open, active Estimates in the *Available Estimates* window.

Step 3.   Select Estimate #2019-1 on the *Available Estimates* window and click **OK**.

QuickBooks transfers the information from the Estimate onto the Invoice. If necessary, you can make changes to the Invoice before saving it.

Step 4.   Change the Quantity column for the Retouching Item on the Invoice from 2 to 1 (see Figure 13-3) and then press **Tab**.

The Estimate was for 2 hours of retouching, but Academy Photo actually completed the work in 1 hour, so you're making this change to reflect the actual charge. You will be able to compare the actual revenues with the estimated revenues on your reports later in this chapter.

Step 5.   Edit the *Memo* field so that the memo reads *Family Photo*.

Step 6.   Click **Save & Close** to record the Invoice.

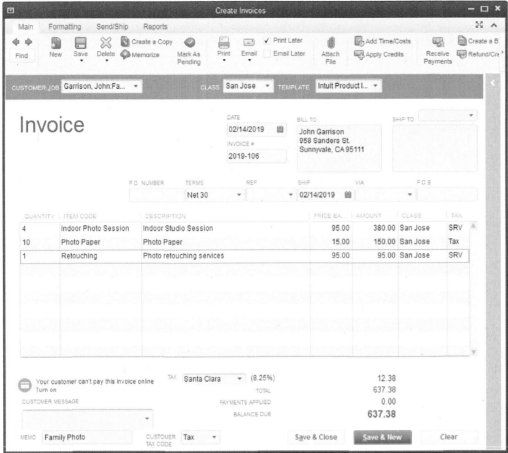

Figure 13-3 Modify the Invoice as Necessary to Reflect the Actual Charges.

Invoices can also be created directly from the *Create Estimates* window. To convert an Estimate into an Invoice using this method, click the **Create Invoice** icon in the *Create Estimates* window (as shown in Figure 13-4). This will transfer all of the line item information from the Estimate to an Invoice.

Figure 13-4 Creating an Invoice from the Create Estimates Window

If you choose to create an Invoice directly from an Estimate, QuickBooks will display the window shown in Figure 13-5, advising that the entire Estimate has been copied to an Invoice.

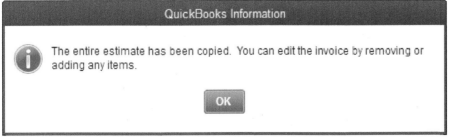

Figure 13-5 Converting Estimate into an Invoice information window

Progress Invoicing

Progress Invoicing allows you to charge your customers a portion of the total Estimate for each stage of a project. QuickBooks tracks how much of the Estimate has been invoiced, and how much remains to be invoiced.

COMPUTER PRACTICE

To create a progress invoice from an estimate, first modify your preferences. Follow these steps:

Step 1.   Select the **Edit** menu and then select **Preferences**.

Step 2.   Select **Jobs & Estimates** and click the **Company Preferences** tab (see Figure 13-6).

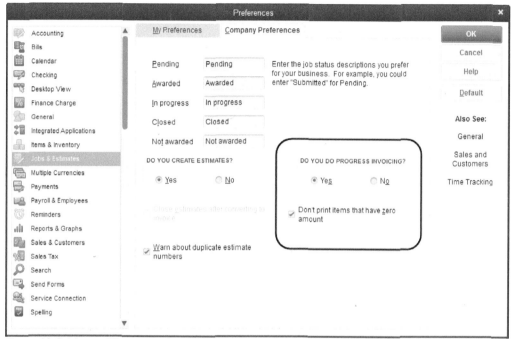

Figure 13-6 Jobs and Estimates Company Preferences

Step 3.   Click **Yes** in the *Do You Do Progress Invoicing?* Section as shown in Figure 13-6.

Step 4.   Leave *Don't print items that have zero amount* checked. Checking this box will only print items currently being invoiced.

Step 5.   Click **OK** to save your changes.

Step 6.   QuickBooks displays the window in Figure 13-7 warning that all windows will be closed to change the preference. Click **OK**.

Figure 13-7 Closing all windows warning

Step 7.   Click the *Home* icon on the *My Shortcuts* list on the *Icon* bar to display the *Home* page.

Step 8.   Click the **Estimates** icon on the *Home* page.

Step 9.   Create an *Estimate* for **Anderson Wedding Planners: Wilson, Sarah and Michael** job with the data shown in Figure 13-8.Enter **Outdoor Session Estimate** in the *Memo* field.

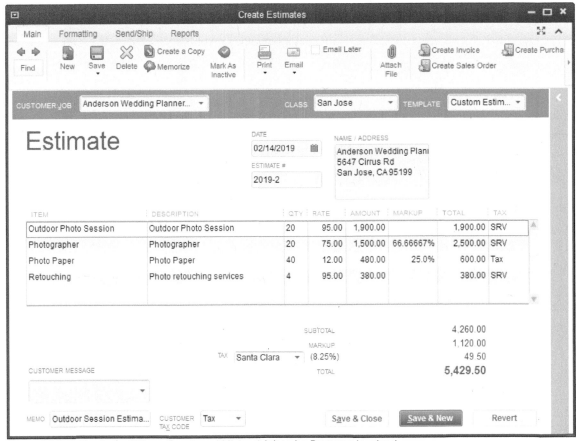

Figure 13-8 Estimate for Wilson, Sarah and Michael Job to be Progress Invoiced

Step 10.   Click **Save & Close** to record the Estimate.

Step 11.   If necessary, click **Yes** on the credit limit warning.

Step 12.   To create a Progress Invoice, select the **Customers** menu and then select **Create Invoices**.

Step 13.   Select the **Anderson Wedding Planners: Wilson, Sarah and Michael** job from the *Customer:Job* drop-down menu and press **Tab**.

Step 14.   QuickBooks displays the *Available Estimates* window. Select Estimate **2019-2** and click **OK** (see Figure 13-9).

Figure 13-9 Select the Estimate on the Available Estimates Window.

Step 15.   QuickBooks displays the *Create Progress Invoice Based on Estimate* window. Select **Create invoice for a percentage of the entire estimate** and enter **25.0%** in the *% of estimate* field as shown in Figure 13-10.

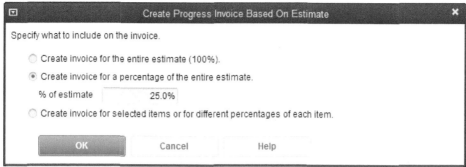

Figure 13-10 Create Progress Invoice Based on Estimate window

> **Note**
> As you can see in Figure 13-10, you can also create an Invoice for the entire Estimate
> (i.e., no Progress Invoicing) or different percentages or quantities of each item. Select the
> option that applies to your situation.

Step 16.   Click **OK**.

Step 17.   QuickBooks displays the *Create Invoices* window (see Figure 13-11) and automatically
             reduces the quantities for products and services to 25% of the estimated amount.

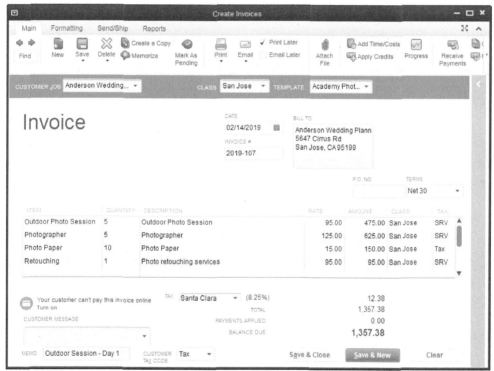

Figure 13-11 Progress Billed Invoice for Anderson Wedding Planners: Wilson, Sarah and Michael Job

Step 18.   Edit the *Memo* as shown in Figure 13-11 and then click **Save & Close** to save the
             Progress Invoice.

Progress Invoices can be adjusted directly from the Invoice window. Click the **Progress** icon in the *Create
Invoices* window as shown in Figure 13-12. This will open the *Specify Invoice Amounts for Items on
Estimate* window shown in Figure 13-13, where you can make corrections or adjustments to the
progress invoice quantity or percentage.

Figure 13-12 Progress icon in Create Invoices window

Specify Invoice Amounts for Items on Estimate   ✕

Progress Invoice for: Anderson Wedding Planners:Wilson, Sarah and Mich... | **OK** |

For each item below, specify the quantity, rate, amount or % of the estimate amount to
have on the invoice.   Cancel

☐ Show Quantity and Rate   ☑ Show Percentage   Help

ITEM	EST AMT	PRIOR AMT	PRIOR %	AMOUNT	CURR %	TOT %	TAX
Outdoor Photo Session	1,900.00		0.0%	475.00	25.0%	25.0%	SRV
Photographer	2,500.00		0.0%	625.00	25.0%	25.0%	SRV
Photo Paper	600.00		0.0%	150.00	25.0%	25.0%	Tax
Retouching	380.00		0.0%	95.00	25.0%	25.0%	SRV

Total (w/ taxes)   1,357.38

Note: All items will transfer to the invoice. The quantities and amount will be as you indicated. Although items with a zero amount display on
screen, they can be set not to print from the Jobs and Estimates Preferences.

Figure 13-13 Specify Invoice Amounts for Items on Estimate window (showing percentage)

Creating Purchase Orders from Estimates

Occasionally Academy Photography sells items like custom photo frames to their customers. When they do, they create an Estimate, and then when the customer approves the Estimate they order the frames to complete the job. In cases like this, QuickBooks Premier and above allow you to create a Purchase Order using all or part of the information on the Estimate for the job.

> QuickBooks Pro does not have the ability to create Purchase Orders directly from Estimates. The following Computer Practice will only work with QuickBooks Premier or QuickBooks Enterprise. **Readers using QuickBooks Pro should read through, but not complete, the following exercise.**

COMPUTER PRACTICE

To create a Purchase Order from an Estimate, first create the Estimate and then create a Purchase Order based on the Estimate. Follow these steps:

Step 1.   Click the **Estimates** icon on the *Home* page.

Step 2.   Enter **Cruz, Maria: Branch Opening** in the *Customer:Job* field and press **Tab**.

Step 3.   Enter the remaining information as shown in Figure 13-14.

Step 4.   Click the **Save** Icon in the top bar to save the Estimate and remain in the same window.

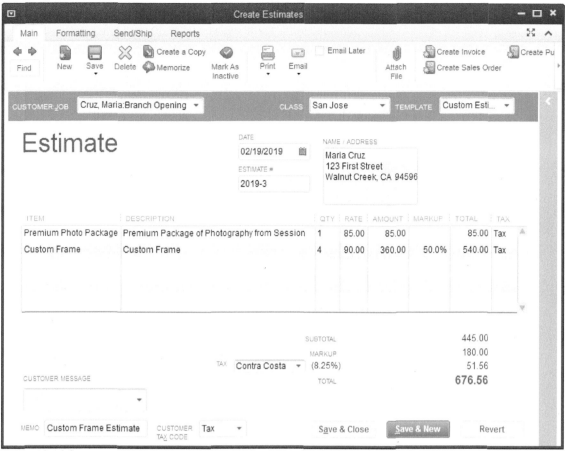

Figure 13-14 Create Estimates window

Step 5.   Select the **Create Purchase Order** icon as shown in Figure 13-15.

Figure 13-15 Select Create Purchase Order in the Create Estimates window

Step 6.   QuickBooks displays the *Create Purchase Order Based on the Sales Transaction* window. Select **Create purchase order for selected items** as shown in Figure 13-16. Then, click **OK**.

Figure 13-16 Create a Purchase Order Based on the Sales Transaction

> **Note**
> You should only select **Create purchase order for all allowed items** if you want QuickBooks to include all Service, Non-inventory Part and Inventory Part Items on the Purchase Order *and* if you purchase all of the Items from the same vendor. Since that situation will probably be rare, you'll usually select **Create purchase order for selected items** as shown in Figure 13-16. Selecting this option will allow you to control which items post to the Purchase Order and to create multiple Purchase Orders from this Estimate, if necessary.

Step 7.   QuickBooks displays the *Specify Purchase Order Quantities for Items on the Sales Transaction* window. Select the **Custom Frame** line as shown in Figure 13-17. Then, click **OK**.

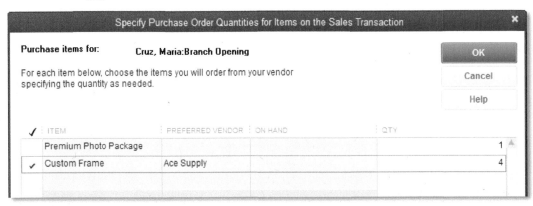

Figure 13-17 Select the Specific Items to Include on the Purchase Order

> **Note:**
> If the items on the Estimate are *Inventory Parts*, QuickBooks will show the stock status for the part in the **On Hand** column. If necessary, you can override the amount in the **Qty** column.

Step 8.   QuickBooks creates a Purchase Order for 4 custom frames as shown in Figure 13-18. If necessary, modify the P.O. # and change the Description to include the Order # from the vendor, in this case Order #271.

QuickBooks automatically adds the *Estimate Number* to the *Memo*. When you create Purchase Order reports, refer to the memo column so you can easily reference the Estimate and Job.

> **Note:**
> If a Preferred Vendor is set up on the item(s) selected, the Purchase Order will be made out to that Vendor. If not, type in the correct Vendor.

Step 9.   Click **Save & Close** to save the Purchase Order.
Step 10.   Click **Save & Close** on the *Create Estimates* window.

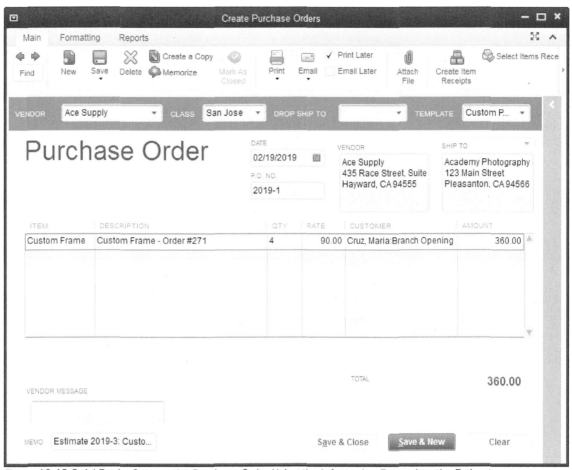

Figure 13-18 QuickBooks Creates the Purchase Order Using the Information Entered on the Estimate

Viewing and Tracking Estimates

QuickBooks provides tools that enable you to quickly view the details of an existing Estimate or to re-print an Estimate. QuickBooks also provides reports that help you manage your proposals and determine the accuracy of your estimating.

Viewing Estimates

In the **Customer Center**, you can see each Customer or Job that has an outstanding Estimate. If you need to see the details of the Estimate, you can do so directly from this list.

COMPUTER PRACTICE

To view an Estimate from the Customer Center, follow these steps:

Step 1.   Open the *Customer Center*, click on the *Transactions* tab, and click **Estimates** to open the window shown in Figure 13-19.

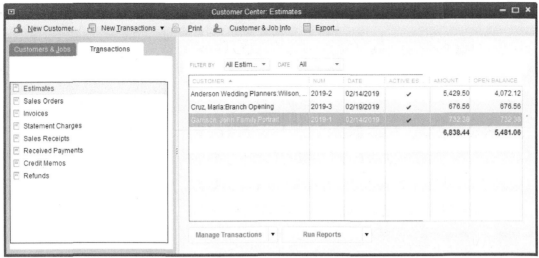

Figure 13-19 Viewing all Estimates from the Customer Center – Your screen may vary

Step 2.   Double click on **John Garrison's Family Portrait** Job and the *Create Estimates* form for that job is opened (see Figure 13-20).

Step 3.   Close the *Create Estimates* and *Customer Center* windows.

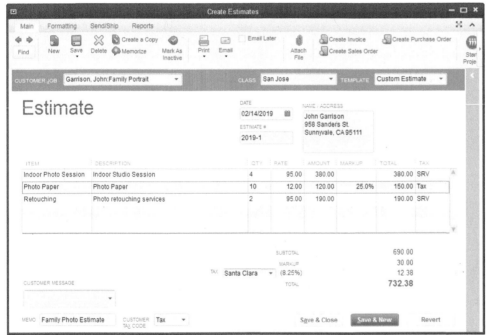

Figure 13-20 Estimate for John Garrison: Family Portrait Job

Tracking Estimates

There are several reports that help you track Estimates and analyze the accuracy of your estimating.

Estimates by Job Report

If you want to see a list of Estimates for all your Jobs, create the *Estimates by Job* report.

COMPUTER PRACTICE

To create the *Estimates by Job* report, follow these steps:

Step 1.   Select the **Reports** menu, select **Jobs, Time & Mileage**, and then select **Estimates by Job**.

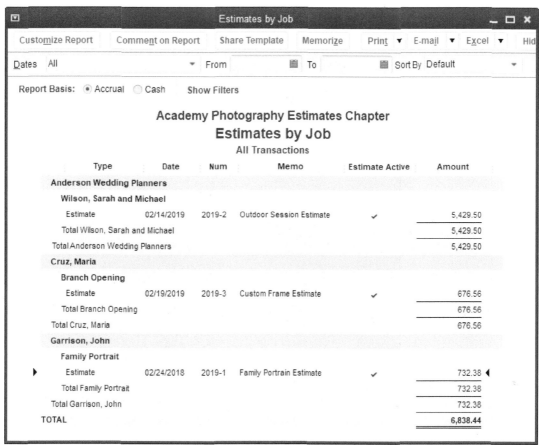

Figure 13-21 Estimates by Job report - All Customers and Jobs - Your screen may vary

The Job Estimates vs. Actuals Summary Report

Use the *Job Estimates vs. Actuals Summary* report to see the total estimated amount compared with the actual charges for Jobs.

COMPUTER PRACTICE

To create the *Job Estimates vs. Actuals Summary* report, follow these steps:

Step 1.   Select the **Reports** menu, select **Jobs, Time & Mileage**, and then select **Job Estimates vs. Actuals Summary**.

Step 2.   Click the **Collapse** button to display the report in Figure 13-22. This button changes to display the word *Expand* once the report has been collapsed.

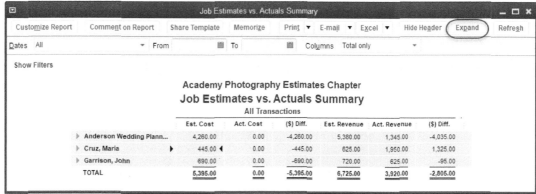

Figure 13-22 The Job Estimates vs. Actuals Summary report - Your screen may vary

Job Progress Invoices vs. Estimates Report

If you Progress Invoice customers, you can use the *Job Progress Invoices vs. Estimates* report to track your progress billing. The report shows the amount of the original Estimates, the total of the progress Invoices and the percentage of the Estimate you have currently billed the customer.

COMPUTER PRACTICE

To create the Job Progress Invoices vs. Estimates report, follow these steps:

Step 1.   Select the **Reports** menu, select **Jobs, Time & Mileage**, and then select **Job Progress Invoices vs. Estimates**. This report shows the percentage of the Estimate you have billed to the customer.

Step 2.   Select **All** in the *Dates* box and press **Tab**.

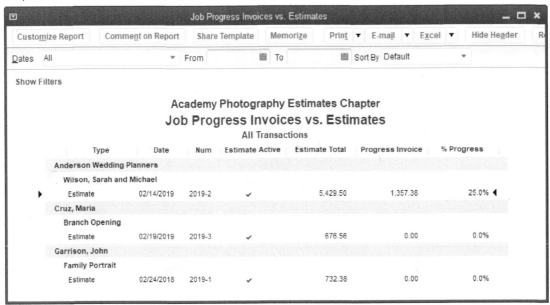

Figure 13-23 Job Progress Invoices vs. Estimates report - Your screen may vary

> **Note:**
> The *Job Progress Invoices vs. Estimates* report only shows active Estimates. After you bill 100% of an Estimate, or if you manually "close" an Estimate, QuickBooks no longer displays the estimate on this report. To track open and closed estimates as they relate to billings, use the *Job Estimates vs. Actuals Summary* report shown in Figure 13-22. To manually close an *Estimate* that a customer will not be accepting, open the *Estimate* and click the **Mark As Inactive** button.

Step 3.   Close all open reports.

Sales Orders

Sales Orders, like *Estimates*, are used to track orders from customers while you are processing or fulfilling the order. However, unlike *Estimates*, *Sales Orders* have been agreed upon and will always end up as Invoices. As with Estimates, Sales Orders do not post to the General Ledger and therefore they do not affect any of your financial reports.

You can print *Sales Orders* for use as pick lists. Pick lists are often used in warehouses or other distribution-type businesses. Warehouse staff can use these lists to "pick" items from the warehouse shelves and package them into a single shipment. *Sales Orders* can be customized in the same way as other sales forms. Once the order is ready to ship, the *Sales Order* is used to create an Invoice for the order. You can also use QuickBooks reports to keep track of open sales orders and back-ordered items.

Review Questions

Comprehension Questions

1. Explain the primary difference between an *Estimate* and an *Invoice* and describe what *Estimates* help you do.

2. Explain what *Progress Invoicing* allows you to do in QuickBooks.

3. Explain the similarities between *Sales Orders* and *Estimates* and describe what *Sales Orders* allow you to do.

Multiple Choice

Select the best answer(s) for each of the following:

1. Estimates help you to:
    a) Track your future sales.
    b) Track how your actual revenues and costs compare with what was estimated.
    c) Track and record financial information.
    d) Both a and b.

2. Creating an *Invoice* from an *Estimate*:
    a) Has little or no effect on the financial statements since *Estimates* do not post to the General Ledger.
    b) Eliminates the need to manually enter *Estimate* details on the *Invoice*.
    c) Can affect the P&L because creating an *Estimate* itself affects the P&L.
    d) Can take up to several hours because it may be difficult to locate the *Create Invoice* button on the *Estimate* form.

3. Which statement is false?
    a) Progress invoicing allows you to charge your customers a portion of the total Estimate for each stage of the Job.
    b) QuickBooks can track how much of the *Estimate* has been invoiced, and how much remains to be invoiced.
    c) Progress Invoicing can create an *Invoice* for the entire *Estimate* (i.e., no Progress Invoicing), but only after the *Estimate* is closed.
    d) Progress Invoicing allows you to create an *Invoice* for some *Estimate* items.

4. After the customer approves the *Estimate* you can create the following form(s) using QuickBooks Premier, Accountant or Enterprise:
    a) *Purchase Order*.
    b) *Sales Order*.
    c) Both a and b.
    d) Neither a nor b.

5. You should usually use the *Create purchase order for selected items* button when creating *Purchase Orders* from *Estimates* because:

   a) Selecting this option bypasses the *Specify Purchase Order Quantities for Items on the Sales Transaction* window.

   b) Selecting this option records your *Items* and directly opens up the *Purchase Order* form.

   c) Inventory and non-inventory parts will display on the *Purchase Order* number.

   d) It is rare that you will include all *Service Items* on the *Purchase Order* or acquire all *Items* from the same vendor.

6. You can view *Estimates*:

   a) In the *Customer Center*.

   b) On the *Estimates by Job* report.

   c) On the *Job Estimates vs. Actuals Summary* report.

   d) All of the above.

7. If you want to see a list of *Estimates* for all your Jobs, create:

   a) The *Estimate* form.

   b) The *Estimates by Job* report.

   c) The *Job Progress Invoices vs. Estimates* reports.

   d) All of the above.

8. Which statement is true?

   a) To track open and closed estimates as they relate to billings, use the *Job Estimates vs. Actuals Summary* report.

   b) You have to manually "close" an Estimate in order for QuickBooks to display the estimate. on the *Job Progress Invoices vs. Estimates* report.

   c) The *Job Progress Invoices vs. Estimates* report shows all Estimates.

   d) None of the above.

9. For general ledger activity, Sales Orders closely resemble which other form in QuickBooks?

   a) Bills.

   b) Estimates.

   c) Invoices.

   d) Sales Receipts.

10. If you do not have enough stock on hand to fill orders, you can:

    a) Create a *Purchase Order* from a *Sales Order* using QuickBooks Premier, Accountant or Enterprise.

    b) Send the Customer an order delay receipt from QuickBooks.

    c) Replace the order with another item the customer did not ask for.

    d) Both b and c.

11. If you wish to create multiple Purchase Orders from a single Estimate:

    a) Select various Vendors from the *Purchase Order* form.

    b) Make copies of the *Purchase Order*.

    c) Select the **Create purchase order for all allowed items** button in the *Create Purchase Order Based on the Sales Transaction* window.

    d) Select the **Create purchase order for selected items** button in the *Create Purchase Order Based on the Sales Transaction* window.

Completion Statements

1. When you work with a prospective customer, you may need to create several Estimates showing different alternatives for the job. If you do, QuickBooks will show each of the open, active Estimates in the _____ _____ window.

2. When creating Purchase Orders from an Estimate, if the Items on the Estimate are inventory parts, QuickBooks will show the stock status for the part in the _____ _____ column. If necessary, you can override the amount in the _____ column.

3. Sales Orders are not available in QuickBooks _____ Edition.

4. In QuickBooks Premier, you can create _____ Invoices from *Estimates*.

5. To view *Estimates* in the *Customer Center*, click the _____ tab and select *Estimates*.

Estimates-Problem 1

> Restore the Estimates-18Problem1.QBM file and store it on your hard disk according to your instructor's directions. The password to access this file is *Sleeter18*.

1. Anderson Wedding Planners are planning a wedding for Sati and Naveen Kumar. They have requested an Estimate for the event. Use the information in Table 13-1 to create an Estimate for Anderson Wedding Planners.

Information	Data
Customer	Anderson Wedding Planners: Kumar, Sati and Naveen
Class	San Jose
Date	5/1/2019
Estimate #	2019-1
Photographer	15 @ $90.00

Table 13-1 Anderson Wedding Planner's Estimate information

2. Create an *Estimates by Job* report. Set the date range to *All.*

3. Three hours of the photographer's time were used creating wedding dress photos at a local garden. Use the *Estimate* to create a *Progress Invoice* for 25% of the total. If needed, turn on the Progress Invoicing Preference. Date the invoice 5/10/2019 and number it 2019-106.

4. Create a *Job Progress Invoices vs. Estimates* report from **1/1/2019** to **5/31/2019**.

Estimates-Problem 2

> Restore the Estimates-18Problem2.QBM file and store it on your hard disk according to your instructor's directions. The password to access this file is **Sleeter18**.

1. Jerry Perez is looking to buy some photo equipment and service. He wants you to submit an Estimate for the job. Use the information in Table 13-2 to create an Estimate for Jerry Perez.

Information	Data
Customer	Jerry Perez
Class	Walnut Creek
Date	5/10/2019
Estimate #	2019-1
Camera SR32	10 @ $450.00 each with a 25% markup
Lens	10 @ $184.99 each with a $500 total markup
Retouching services	12 hours @ $95 per hour, No markup

Table 13-2 Jerry Perez's Estimate information

2. Create an *Estimates by Job* report. Set the date range to *All.*

3. To complete Estimate 2019-1, you will need to order additional inventory. From the Estimate, create a Purchase Order to Ace Supply on 5/10/2019 for the 1 Camera and 3 Lenses that Academy Photo does not have in stock. Change the order quantity of each. Customer is Jerry Perez. Use purchase order number 2019-1.

4. Jerry Perez requested that 50% of the job be completed on the date the project is started. If needed, turn on the Progress Invoicing Preference. Use the Estimate to create a Progress Invoice for 50% of the total Estimate. Date the invoice 5/13/2019 and number it 2019-106. If prompted, ignore the warning that you don't have enough inventory to sell to Jerry Perez.

5. Create a *Job Progress Invoices vs. Estimates* report from **1/1/2019** to **5/31/2019.**

Chapter 14
Adjustments and Year-End Procedures

Topics

In this chapter, you will learn about the following topics:

- General Journal Entries (page 507)
- Editing, Voiding, and Deleting Transactions (page 510)
- Memorized Transactions (page 514)
- Tracking Fixed Assets (page 518)
- Processing 1099s (page 523)
- Closing the Year (page 527)
- Setting the Closing Date to "Lock" Transactions (page 533)

> **Restore this File:**
> This chapter uses Adjustments-18.QBW. See page 9 for more information. The password to access this file is *Sleeter18*.

This chapter covers various ways to make adjustments as well as process end of year tasks. Topics include how to edit and void transactions in current and closed periods, and how to use journal entries and zero-dollar checks to adjust balances and close the year. You will also learn how to memorize transactions and use the closing date in QuickBooks.

General Journal Entries

General Journal Entries are transactions that adjust the balance of two or more accounts.

> **Note:**
> Good accounting practice suggests that you keep a separate record of each *General Journal Entry* you make in QuickBooks. This record will be very helpful if you are ever audited or if you have to research the reasons for the adjustment.

Here are a few examples of adjusting entries in QuickBooks:

- Recategorize a transaction from one Class to another.
- Recategorize a transaction from one account to another.
- Allocate prepaid expenses to each month throughout the year.
- Record non-cash expenses, such as depreciation.
- Close the Owner's Draw account into the Owner's Equity account.

In most cases, you will use a *General Journal Entry* to record adjustments.

Creating a General Journal Entry

> **Note:**
> Depending on your QuickBooks user settings, you may need permission from the
> QuickBooks administrator to create *General Journal Entries*.

COMPUTER PRACTICE

Step 1.   Select the **Company** menu and then select **Make General Journal Entries**. Those using QuickBooks Accountant can also select the *Accountant* menu and select *Make General Journal Entries*.

Step 2.   If the *Assigning Numbers to Journal Entries* window opens, check the **Do not display this message in the future** box and click **OK**.

Step 3.   Enter *1/31/2019* in the **Date** field and then press **Tab** (see Figure 14-1). If you are using QuickBooks Pro or Premier, your window may look different than Figure 14-1.

Step 4.   Enter **2019-1** in the *Entry No.* field. Press **Tab**.

The very first time you enter a *General Journal Entry*, enter whatever number you want in the *Entry No.* field. Then, when you create your next General Journal Entry, QuickBooks will increment the entry number.

Step 5.   If applicable, uncheck the *Adjusting Entry* checkbox.

Step 6.   On the top line of the *Make General Journal Entries* window, enter **Journal Entries** in the *Account* column. Press **Tab** three times to leave the *Debit* and *Credit* columns blank for this line.

> **Expert Tip:**
> In these examples, we use a bank account called *Journal Entries* on the top line of each *Journal Entry*. If you create the *Journal Entries* bank account and then enter it on the top line of each *General Journal Entry*, QuickBooks tracks all the *General Journal Entries* in a separate register on the *Chart of Accounts*. This register allows you to quickly look up and view all of your *General Journal Entries*. Though you use this account in every *General Journal Entry*, you will never debit or credit the account and therefore it will never have a balance.

Step 7.   Enter **Recategorize Expense** in the *Memo* column. Press **Tab** three times to leave the *Name* and *Class* columns blank for this line.

Step 8.   Enter the information on the next two lines as shown in Figure 14-1.

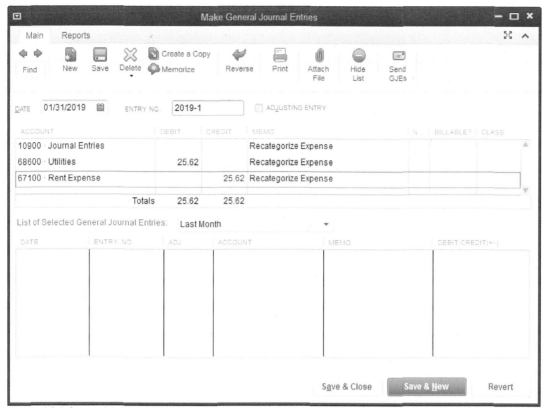

Figure 14-1 General Journal Entry window – Your screen may vary

> **Note:**
> General Journal Entries must balance. The total of the Debit column must match the total of the Credit column.

Step 9.   Click **Save & Close** to save the transaction.

Adjusting Expense Accounts Associated with Items (Zero-Dollar Checks)

If you use Items to track the details of your expenses, you may need to enter adjustments to the Items as well as the accounts to which the Items are assigned. However, the Journal Entry window in QuickBooks has no provision for entering Items as part of the Journal Entry.

To solve the problem, use a transaction (such as a Check) that allows you to use Items. The Check will be a "Zero-Dollar Check" in that it will have an equal amount of debits and credits. You can use the Journal Entries bank account so you don't clutter the normal bank account with zero-dollar checks.

> **DO NOT PERFORM THESE STEPS NOW. THEY ARE FOR REFERENCE ONLY.**

Follow these steps to use zero-dollar Checks as Journal Entries:

1.   Create a Check using the Journal Entries bank account.

2.   Enter the debits as Items with positive amounts and the credits as Items with negative amounts as shown in Figure 14-2 below. The total Check amount should net to zero.

Figure 14-2 Using the Write Checks window to create a Journal Entry affecting job cost.

3. To review the adjustment made to the *General Ledger*, save the zero-dollar *Check*, select the **Reports** tab and then select **Transaction Journal**. QuickBooks displays the report shown in Figure 14-3 below.

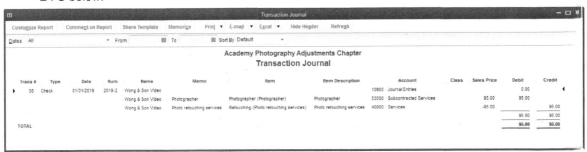

Figure 14-3 Transaction Journal from the Zero Dollar Check

In addition to the example above, zero-dollar *Checks* are very useful for adjustments involving *any combination* of *Items* and expenses. Similarly, you can use zero-dollar *Sales Receipts* to adjust items that affect income accounts.

Editing, Voiding, and Deleting Transactions

Unlike many other accounting programs, QuickBooks allows you to change any transaction at any time as long as you have sufficient privileges. However, you should almost never change transactions dated in closed accounting periods, or transactions that have been reconciled with a bank statement.

> **Key Term:**
> For the purposes of this discussion, a *Closed Accounting Period* is a period for which you've already issued financial statements and/or filed tax returns.

When you change or delete a transaction, QuickBooks updates the *General Ledger* with your change, as of the date of the modified or deleted transaction. Therefore, if you modify or delete transactions in a closed accounting period, your QuickBooks financial statements will change for that period, causing discrepancies between your QuickBooks reports and your tax return.

In QuickBooks, the *Closing Date* field is used to "lock" your data file to prevent users from making changes on or before a specified date. See page 533 for information about setting the *Closing Date* in QuickBooks.

> **Tip:**
> Using the *Closing Date*, a period can be "closed" even if there is no tax return for the period. For example, you can close the books through January 31, 2019, even though your last tax return was dated December 31, 2018. If management makes decisions based on *printed* financial information dated January 31, 2019, any changes to QuickBooks information dated before January 31, 2019 will cause the reports in QuickBooks to disagree with the printed reports. Also, many companies submit financial information to third parties (e.g., banks) during their tax year on a monthly or quarterly basis.

Some companies close their books monthly, but other companies only close their books quarterly or annually. Make sure you know how often your company closes periods before you make changes to transactions that might affect closed periods.

> **Tip:**
> At the very least, you should lock the file at the end of each fiscal and/or calendar year. You may also choose to lock the file monthly, after you perform bank reconciliations and adjusting entries for the month.

Editing Transactions

From time to time, you may need to modify transactions to correct posting errors. To edit (or modify) a transaction in QuickBooks, change the data directly on the form. For example, if you forgot to add a charge for an Outdoor Photo Shoot to Invoice 2019-106 and *you have not already sent the invoice to your customer or client*, you will need to add a line for the photo session on the previously created invoice.

COMPUTER PRACTICE

To edit an existing transaction, follow these steps:

Step 1. From the *Customers* menu, select **Create Invoices.**

Step 2. Click **Previous** to display Invoice 2019-106 dated 2/28/2019.

Step 3. Click on the second line in the main body of the *Invoice* and enter **Outdoor Photo Session** in the *Item* column. Press **Tab**.

Step 4. Enter **3** in the *Quantity* column and then press **Tab** (see Figure 14-4).

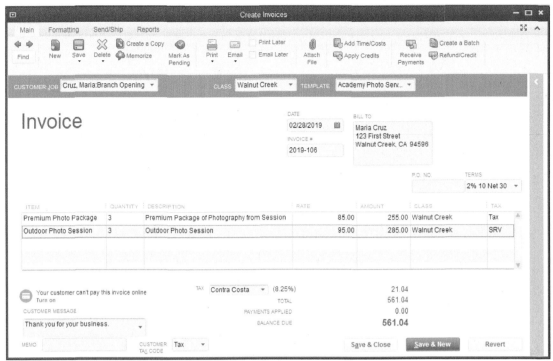

Figure 14-4 Add the Item to the Invoice.

Step 5.   Click **Save & Close** to save the *Invoice*.

Step 6.   On the *Recording Transaction* window, click **Yes**. This message confirms that you really
                want to change the transaction (see Figure 14-5).

Figure 14-5 Recording Transaction window

> **Note:**
> Do not use this method of changing transactions if you have already sent the *Invoice* to
> the customer. In that case, you would need to create a new *Invoice* with the separate
> charge. Also, you should never change transactions dated in a closed accounting period.

Voiding and Deleting Transactions

Voiding and deleting transactions both have the same effect on the *General Ledger* – the effect is to
zero out the debits and the credits specified by the transaction.

There is one significant difference between voiding and deleting. When you void a transaction,
QuickBooks keeps a record of the date, number, and detail of the transaction. When you delete a
transaction, QuickBooks removes it completely from your file. For this reason, voiding is preferable to
deleting transactions.

The *Audit Trail* feature of QuickBooks tracks changes and deletions of transactions. The *Audit Trail
Report* lists each accounting transaction and every addition, deletion, or modification that affects that
transaction. For more information about the *Audit Trail*, see the QuickBooks Onscreen Help.

In addition to the *Audit Trail*, QuickBooks has a *Voided/Deleted Transactions Report* that lists all voided
and deleted transactions. This report is very useful when you have a number of users in a file and

transactions seem to "disappear," since the report shows the time, date, and user name of the changes or deletions.

To **delete** a transaction:

1.   Select the transaction you wish to delete; it may be displayed in a register or form.

2.   Select the **Edit** menu and then select **Delete** (or press **Ctrl+D**).

3.   On the *Delete Transaction* window, click **OK.**

To **void** a transaction:

1.   Select the transaction in a register or display it in the form.

2.   Select the **Edit** menu and then select **Void** (or right click on the transaction and select **Void** from the shortcut menu).

3.   Click the **Record** button at the bottom of the window or **Save & Close** at the bottom of the form.

4.   QuickBooks will display a window asking if you want to create an Adjusting Journal Entry (see Figure 14-6). Click **Yes.**

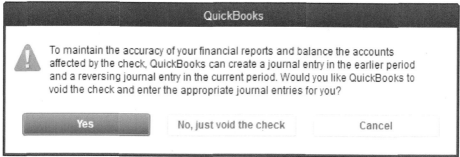

Figure 14-6 Window displays after voiding check

5.   Two adjusting *General Journal Entries* are created. One has the same date as the transaction, recording the same account entries as the voided transaction. The other has the current system date and reverses the account entries of the other Journal Entry. That way the company reports will stay the same during prior periods.

Note:
Proper accounting procedures do not allow you to simply delete transactions at will. However, in some cases it is perfectly fine to use the **Delete** command. For example, it is acceptable to delete a check that you have not printed. On the other hand, if you have already printed the check, you should **Void** it instead of deleting it so that you will have a record of the voided check and the numbering sequence remains intact in the register.

Deleting All Transactions

Occasionally, you may wish to delete all transactions from a file, while leaving the *Customers, Vendors, Employees* and other *List* information as well as the *Preferences* in the file. You may make these changes using the QuickBooks *Condense Data Utility*. You have the option to either delete all transactions, or delete all transactions except for transactions within a specific date range.

You can access the *Condense Data* command from the *Utilities* submenu under the *File* menu. QuickBooks prompts you to select a specific date to delete transactions before, or to delete all transactions. Do not do this now with your exercise file.

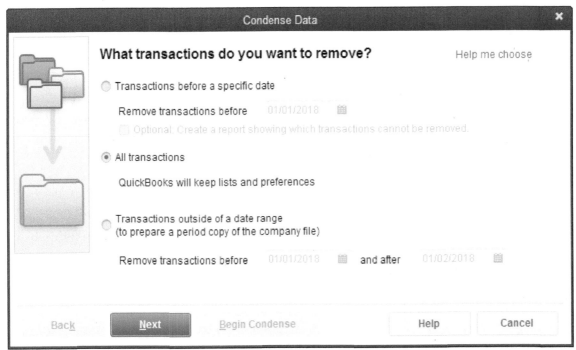

Figure 14-7 Condense Data Utility

Memorized Transactions

If you frequently enter the same transaction (or similar ones), you can memorize and schedule the entry of the transaction. For example, if you want QuickBooks to automatically enter the bill for your insurance payment each month, you can memorize the transaction and then schedule it to be automatically entered.

> **Note:**
> You can memorize *Journal Entries*, *Invoices*, *Sales Receipts*, *Bills* and other transactions, however, there are some transactions that cannot be memorized, such as *Bill Payments*, *Paychecks*, and *Receive Payments*.

Memorizing a Transaction

COMPUTER PRACTICE

To memorize a transaction, follow these steps:

Step 1.   Create a *Bill* with the data from Figure 14-8

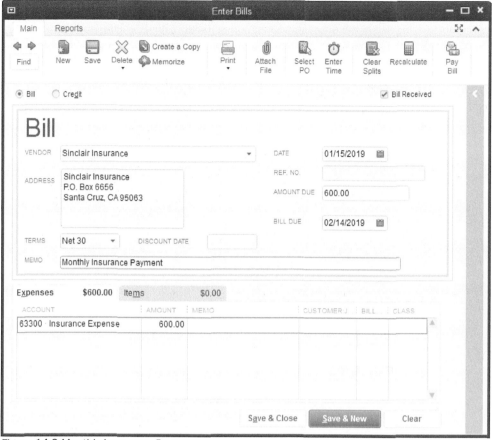

Figure 14-8 Monthly Insurance Payment

Step 2.	Before saving the *Bill*, select **Memorize Bill** from the *Edit* menu (or press **Ctrl+M**).
Step 3.	Enter *Insurance Payment* in the *Name* field.
	Use names that you will recognize so that you can easily find this transaction in the *Memorized Transaction* list.
Step 4.	Set the fields as shown in Figure 14-9 to indicate when and how often you want the transaction entered and then click **OK**.

Figure 14-9 Insurance Payment memorized information

Step 5.	Select **Save & Close** to record the *Bill*.
Step 6.	If necessary, close all your open windows by clicking the close box in the upper right corner.

> **Did You Know?**
> You can memorize *most* transactions in QuickBooks. Just display the transaction, then
> select **Memorize [Transaction Name]** from the *Edit* menu, or right click on the transaction
> and select **Memorize [Transaction Name]**. You can also press **Ctrl+M**. The *Memorized*
> *Transaction List* contains all the transactions that you have memorized. To display this
> list, select **Memorized Transaction List** from the *Lists* menu.

Now, every time you launch QuickBooks, it checks your *Memorized Transaction* list for transactions that
need to be entered automatically. If the system date is on or after the date in the *Next Date* field (minus
the number in the *Days In Advance To Enter* field), QuickBooks will ask you if you want to enter the
memorized transaction.

Deleting, Rescheduling, and Editing Memorized Transactions

Rescheduling or Renaming Memorized Transactions

COMPUTER PRACTICE

To edit the schedule or name of a memorized transaction, follow these steps:

Step 1.   Select the **Memorized Transaction List** from the *Lists* menu, or press **Ctrl+T**.

Figure 14-10 Memorized Transaction List

Step 2.   Select the Insurance Payment transaction in the *Memorized Transaction List*. Select **Edit**
               Memorized Transaction from the *Memorized Transaction* drop-down list or press **Ctrl+E**
               (see Figure 14-10).

Step 3.   The *Schedule Memorized Transaction* window displays (see Figure 14-11). This window
               allows you to reschedule or rename the transaction, but it does not allow you to edit the
               actual transaction. Click **Cancel** and close all open windows.

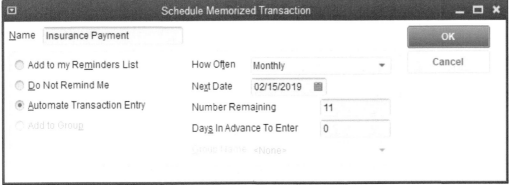

Figure 14-11 Schedule Memorized Transaction window

Editing Memorized Transactions

In addition to editing the schedule or other attributes of a memorized transaction, sometimes it is necessary to edit the actual contents of the transaction such as the *Items*, prices, or coding.

COMPUTER PRACTICE

To edit the contents of a memorized transaction, follow these steps:

Step 1.   Select the **Memorized Transaction List** from the *Lists* menu, or press **Ctrl+T**.

Step 2.   To edit the memorized transaction, double click **Insurance Payment** in the *Memorized Transaction List*.

This displays a new transaction (see Figure 14-12) with the contents of the memorized transaction. You can change anything on the transaction and then rememorize it. In this case, we will add the **San Jose** *Class*.

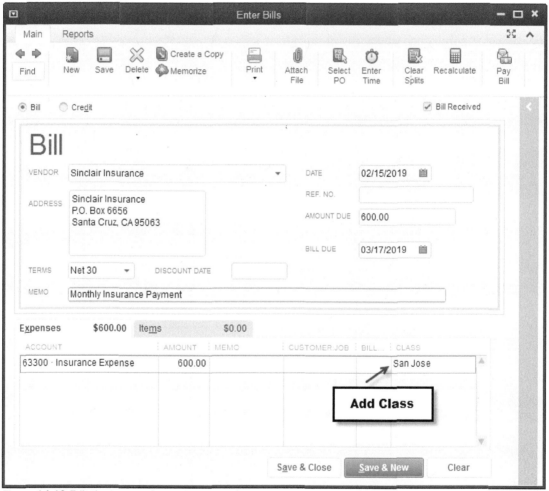

Figure 14-12 Edit the transaction and rememorize

Step 3.   To rememorize the transaction, press the **Memorize** button at the top of the form, select **Memorize Bill** from the *Edit* menu, or press **Ctrl+M**.

Step 4.   To save your edited transaction in the *Memorized Transaction* list click **Replace** (see Figure 14-13).

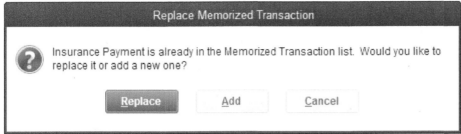

Figure 14-13 Replace Memorized Transaction message

Step 5.   Click **Clear** to erase the contents of the *Bill*. **Close** the *Bill* window. This will save the changes to the memorized transaction without entering a new transaction.

Deleting Memorized Transactions

COMPUTER PRACTICE

To delete a memorized transaction, follow these steps:

Step 1.   Select the **Memorized Transaction List** from the *Lists* menu, or press **Ctrl+T**.

Step 2.   The **Insurance Payment** is already selected because it is the first and only memorized transaction on the list.

Step 3.   Select **Delete Memorized Transaction** from the *Memorized Transaction* drop-down list or press **Ctrl+D** (see Figure 14-14).

Figure 14-14 Delete Memorized Transaction option

Step 4.   For now, click **Cancel** on the *Delete Memorized Transaction* dialog box so the memorized transaction will not be deleted (see Figure 14-15).

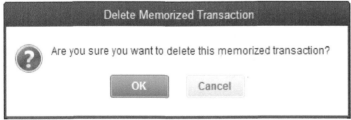

Figure 14-15 Delete Memorized Transaction

Step 5.   Close all open windows.

Tracking Fixed Assets

When you purchase office equipment, buildings, computers, vehicles, or other assets that have useful lives of more than one year, you'll want to add them to your Balance Sheet and record the depreciation of the assets periodically. Check with your accountant if you need help deciding which purchases should be added to a fixed asset account.

To track your asset values, create a separate fixed asset account for each grouping of assets you want to track on the Balance Sheet. Several accounts, such as *Furniture and Equipment, Vehicles, and Accumulated Depreciation* are created with the default Chart of Accounts.

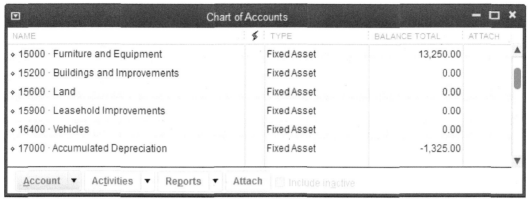

NAME	$	TYPE	BALANCE TOTAL	ATTACH
◇ 15000 · Furniture and Equipment		Fixed Asset	13,250.00	
◇ 15200 · Buildings and Improvements		Fixed Asset	0.00	
◇ 15600 · Land		Fixed Asset	0.00	
◇ 15900 · Leasehold Improvements		Fixed Asset	0.00	
◇ 16400 · Vehicles		Fixed Asset	0.00	
◇ 17000 · Accumulated Depreciation		Fixed Asset	-1,325.00	

Figure 14-16 Fixed Assets and Accumulated Depreciation Accounts

---

The accounting behind the scenes

As you purchase fixed assets, code the purchases to the appropriate Fixed Asset account. This increases (debits) the fixed asset account and decreases (credits) the checking account (assuming you paid with a check).

When you record depreciation, the entry will increase (debit) the *Depreciation Expense* account and increase (credit) the *Accumulated Depreciation* account. The *Accumulated Depreciation* account is known as a "contra" account because it normally carries a credit balance (i.e., a negative balance) given that asset accounts typically have debit balances.

Key Term:

A **Contra Account** is an account that carries a balance that is opposite from the normal balance for that account type. For example, an asset that carries a credit balance is a contra asset account since assets normally carry a debit balance. Also, an income account that carries a debit balance (e.g., Sales Discounts) is a contra income account since income accounts normally carry a credit balance.

To see the Net Book Value of Fixed Assets for *Furniture and Equipment* on the Balance Sheet, select **Company & Financial** from the *Reports* menu and then select **Balance Sheet Standard**. Enter the date *1/31/2019* in the *As of* field and press **Tab**. You will now be able to view the *Cost, Accumulated Depreciation*, and *Net Book Value* (NBV) of the Company's Furniture and Equipment Fixed Assets (see Figure 14-17).

Key Term:

Net Book Value (NBV) is the book value of your Fixed Asset at any point in time. Calculate NBV by subtracting the amount of use of the asset (accumulated depreciation) from the original purchase price to determine the value of the remaining useful life. As you can see in Figure 14-17, the original cost of Furniture and Equipment is $13,250. The accumulated depreciation to date is $1,325. Therefore, the Net Book Value of *Furniture and Equipment* is $11,925.

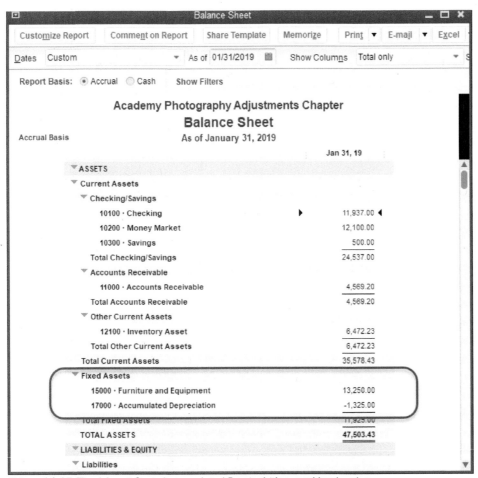

Figure 14-17 Fixed Asset Cost, Accumulated Depreciation, and book value

Another way to track your asset values would be to create three accounts for each group of assets: a control (or master) account and two subaccounts.

See Figure 14-18 for an example of how this could look in your *Chart of Accounts*.

The control account must be a Fixed Asset type of account in the *Chart of Accounts*. Each control account will have two subaccounts: a *Cost* account and an *Accumulated Depreciation* account.

NAME		TYPE	BALANCE TOTAL	ATTACH
◇ 15000 · Furniture and Equipment		Fixed Asset	0.00	
◇ Cost		Fixed Asset	0.00	
◇ Accumulated Depreciation		Fixed Asset	0.00	
◇ 15200 · Buildings and Improvements		Fixed Asset	0.00	
◇ Cost		Fixed Asset	0.00	
◇ Accumulated Depreciation		Fixed Asset	0.00	
◇ 16400 · Vehicles		Fixed Asset	11,800.00	
◇ Cost		Fixed Asset	13,250.00	
◇ Accumulated Depreciation		Fixed Asset	-1,450.00	

Figure 14-18 Alternative Setup of Fixed Assets in the Chart of Accounts

> **Note:**
> Alphabetically, the subaccount *Accumulated Depreciation* precedes the subaccount *Cost*. Therefore, QuickBooks automatically places *Accumulated Depreciation* above *Cost* when you create the accounts. However, the preferred format for financial statements lists *Accumulated Depreciation* (the contra account) below *Cost* (the asset account). To reorder the accounts to match the preferred format, open the Chart of Accounts list. Then, click the diamond next to the *Accumulated Depreciation* subaccount and drag it below the *Cost* subaccount.

Using the Fixed Asset List

You can track detailed information about your company's Fixed Assets by setting up each asset using the Fixed Asset Item List. In QuickBooks Accountant, you or your accountant can use the Fixed Asset Manager to individually calculate and track depreciation on each asset.

> **Accounting Tip:**
> Conduct a physical inventory of fixed assets annually to assure proper tracking and reporting. Your accountant may currently maintain this list for your company. QuickBooks can track the original cost for each Fixed Asset and the related depreciation for each asset of the company.

COMPUTER PRACTICE

To set up your assets in the *Fixed Asset Item List*, follow these steps:

Step 1.   Select the **Lists** menu and then select **Fixed Asset Item List**.

Step 2.   Select the **Item** menu at the bottom of the *Fixed Asset Item List* window and then select **New** (or press CTRL+N).

Step 3.   From the detail provided in Table 14-1, complete the information for the delivery vehicle. When completed, your record should match Figure 14-19.

Fixed Asset Item Detail	
Asset Name/Number	2015 Ford Escape
Item is	Used
Purchase Description	2015 Utility Vehicle
Date	12/15/2017
Cost	$20,000.00
Vendor Payee	National Bank
Asset Account	16400 · Vehicles
Asset Description	2015 Utility Vehicle
Location	San Jose
Serial Number	1FT00110011001

Table 14-1 Fixed Asset Item Detail

Figure 14-19 New Fixed Asset Item Entry

Step 4.   Press **OK** to save the fixed asset record.

> **Important:**
> There is no accounting entry made when you set up a fixed asset in the *Fixed Asset Item List*. This is why you must enter the opening balances for your fixed asset accounts in addition to setting them up in the *Fixed Asset Item List*.

Calculating and Recording Depreciation

There are different ways to calculate and enter depreciation. The Fixed Asset Manager in QuickBooks Accountant calculates and enters depreciation. Otherwise, to record depreciation each month using the straight-line method, determine the total annual depreciation, divide that amount by 12, and then record the depreciation expense each month using a journal entry (see Figure 14-20).

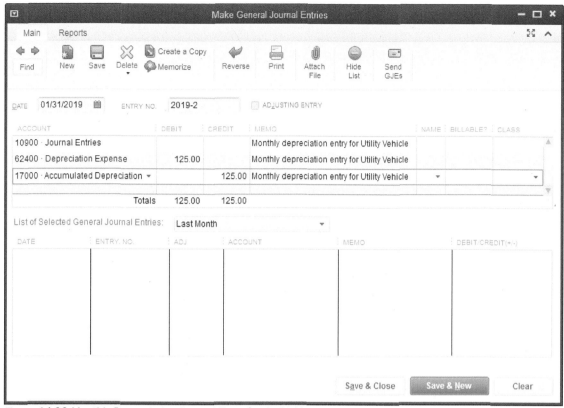

Figure 14-20 Monthly Depreciation Journal Entry for the Vehicle

Processing 1099s

At the end of each year, you must prepare and send an IRS Form 1099 to each of your eligible vendors and to the IRS. Form 1099 must be sent to your vendors by the last day of January following the applicable year.

Form 1099-MISC is used to report payments made to vendors who performed business-related services for your company. Typically, the term "services" includes work by independent contractors, professional services, rent payments, commissions, and so on. Before preparing 1099-forms, you should have a clear understanding of which vendors should receive them, as well as what types of payments are eligible for reporting on Form 1099. For IRS instructions on this topic, you may visit the IRS forms and publication site and search for 1099 instructions at http://www.irs.gov/formspubs/index.html.

> **Note:**
> QuickBooks is only capable of preparing 1099-MISC. If you need to prepare other types of 1099s (e.g., 1099-INT, 1099-DIV), you will need to do so outside of QuickBooks.
>
> IRS regulations require that if you file 250 or more 1099 forms of any type, you must submit them electronically or magnetically.

When set up properly, QuickBooks automatically tracks the details of your payments to 1099 vendors. Each time you make a payment to a 1099 vendor and use an account designated as a 1099-related expense, QuickBooks automatically adds the payment to the vendor's 1099.

At the end of the year, you can view your 1099-related payments by creating a **1099 Detail** report. After verifying that the report includes the right vendors and covers the right accounts, you can print 1099s directly onto preprinted 1099 forms.

The 1099 Wizard

QuickBooks uses the **1099 Wizard** to help create accurate 1099 and 1096 forms. Once activated, the wizard will allow users to go through four steps to process these forms:

1. Review and edit 1099 vendors.
2. Setup account mapping preferences for 1099s.
3. Run a summary report to review 1099 data.
4. Print 1099 and 1096 forms.

The option to file 1099-MISC forms will need to be turned on in the Tax: 1099 Company Preferences (see Figure 14-21).

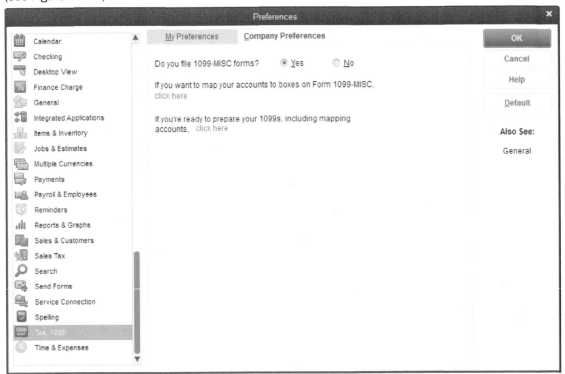

Figure 14-21 Turn on 1099 Preferences

COMPUTER PRACTICE

To activate the QuickBooks *1099 Wizard*, follow these steps:

Step 1.   From the *Vendors* menu, in the *Print/E-file 1099s* submenu, choose **1099 Wizard**.

Step 2.   QuickBooks displays the **1099 Wizard** window (see Figure 14-22). We will use the 4-Step process above to create and print 1099 and 1096 forms. Click on **Get Started**.

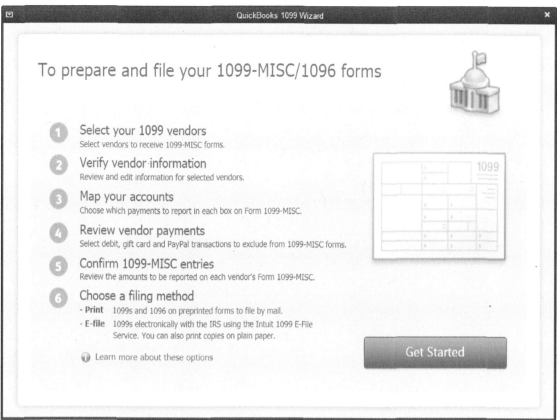

Figure 14-22 QuickBooks 1099 and 1096 Wizard

Editing 1099 Information in Vendor Records

In this first step, verify your 1099 Vendors. You can edit each 1099 vendor to confirm or update that you have their complete name, address, and identification number (e.g., social security number or federal employer identification number). Vendors are required by law to provide you with this information and it is best to collect this data when you first engage the vendor. Require the vendor to complete a W-9 Form before they begin services so that their information is on file. You can download W-9 forms in a PDF version from the IRS at http://www.irs.gov/formspubs/index.html. The IRS may reject 1099s that you submit if the taxpayer ID is incorrect.

COMPUTER PRACTICE

To review and edit the 1099 vendors, follow these steps:

Step 1. QuickBooks will display the *Select your 1099 vendors* window showing the selected 1099 vendors (see Figure 14-23). Review the *Create Form 1099-MISC* column to verify that all vendors eligible for 1099s are checked. Click **Continue**.

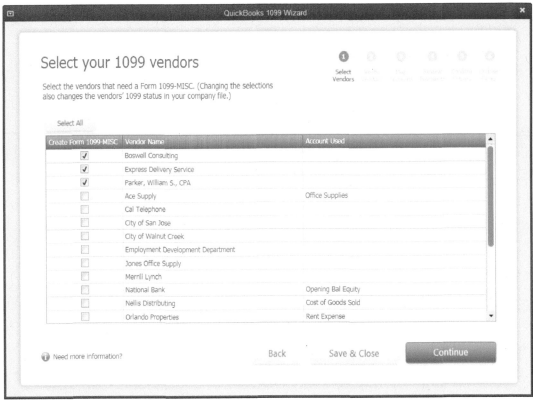

Figure 14-23 Select your 1099 vendors

Step 2.   The Verify your 1099 vendors' information window appears. You can edit any vendor
            information. (see Figure 14-24). Double click on the address information to see multiple
            lines. The address information is particularly important if the forms are mailed, however,
            the correct address is also required for e-filing. Click **Continue**.

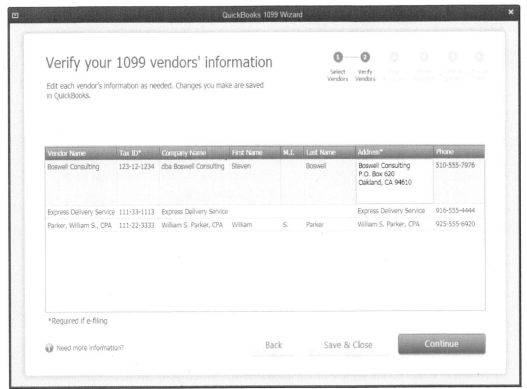

Figure 14-24 Verify your 1099 vendors' information window

Step 3.   The *Map vendor payment accounts* window appears. Check **Report all payments in Box 7** (see Figure 14-25).

Account mapping allows you to select the QuickBooks accounts you use to track 1099 vendor payments and the threshold amount you will report to the IRS. Since this is a company-wide preference, only the Administrator can modify the 1099 mapping preferences.

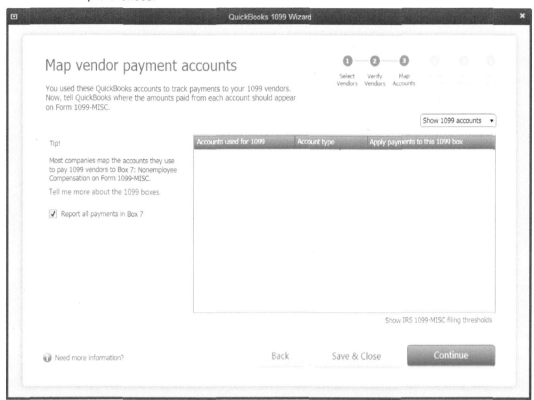

Figure 14-25 The Map vendor payment accounts window – your screen may vary

> **Note:**
> If you're uncertain which box to map an account to, talk with your accountant or QuickBooks Pro Advisor.
>
> Also, when Items are used to track purchases, these Items correspond to an account in the Chart of Accounts list. Therefore, when you use Items to track payments to 1099 vendors, make sure the proper 1099 accounts are used when creating new Items.

Step 4.   Click **Continue** on the remainder of the *QuickBooks 1099 Wizard* windows after reviewing the options and confirming the information. Click **Save & Close** on the final window without filing.

Closing the Year

At the end of each year, accounting principles dictate that you must enter an adjusting entry to transfer net income or loss into the Retained Earnings (or Owner's Equity) account. This entry is known as the *closing entry*.

However, in QuickBooks **you do not need to make this closing entry**. QuickBooks does it for you, automatically. When you create a *Balance Sheet*, QuickBooks calculates the balance in Retained

Earnings by adding together the total net income for all prior years. At the end of your company's fiscal year, QuickBooks automatically transfers the net income into Retained Earnings.

On the left side of the example in Table 14-2, notice that the *Balance Sheet* for 12/31/2018 shows net income for the year is $100,000.00. The right side shows the same *Balance Sheet*, but for the next day (January 1, 2019). Since January is in a new year, last year's net income has been automatically transferred to the Retained Earnings account.

Equity on Dec 31, 2018		Equity on Jan 1, 2019	
Opening Bal Equity	0.00	Opening Bal Equity	0.00
Preferred Stock	50,000.00	Preferred Stock	50,000.00
Common Stock	75,000.00	Common Stock	75,000.00
Retained Earnings	100,000.00	Retained Earnings	200,000.00
Net Income	100,000.00	Net Income	0.00
Total Equity	325,000.00	Total Equity	325,000.00

Table 14-2 Example of QuickBooks closing entry

There are two advantages to QuickBooks automatically closing the year for you. First, you do not have to create the year-end entry, which can be time-consuming. Second, the details of your income and expenses are not erased each year, as some programs require.

Closing the Accounting Period

The following is a list of actions you should take at the end of each accounting period. Perform these steps as often as you close your company's books. Many companies close monthly or quarterly, while some close yearly. No matter when you close, these steps are to help you create proper reports that incorporate year-end transactions. These entries may be non-cash entries such as depreciation, prepaid expense allocations, and adjustments to equity to properly reflect the closing of the year.

At the end of the year (or period), consider doing some or all of the following:

1. Enter depreciation entries.
2. Reconcile cash, credit card, and loan accounts with the period-end statements.
3. If your business has inventory, perform a physical inventory on the last day of the year. Following the inventory count, enter an Inventory Adjustment transaction in QuickBooks if necessary. See the "Inventory" chapter for more information about adjusting inventory.
4. If you are on the accrual basis of accounting, prepare *General Journal Entries* to accrue expenses and revenues. Ask your accountant for help with these entries.
5. If your business is a partnership, enter a *General Journal Entry* to distribute net income for the year to each of the partner's capital accounts. If your business is a sole proprietorship, enter a *General Journal Entry* closing Owner's Draw into Owner's Equity. See the section below for more information.
6. Run reports for the year and verify their accuracy. Enter adjusting entries as necessary and rerun the reports.
7. Print or create a PDF and file the following reports as of your closing date: *General Ledger, Balance Sheet Standard, Statement of Cash Flows, Trial Balance, Inventory Valuation Summary,* and *Profit & Loss Standard* for the year.
8. Back up your data file. The year-end backup should be permanent and stored in a safe place.
9. Set the closing date to the last day of the period and set a closing date password to prevent transactions in the closed period from being changed. See page 533 for details on setting the closing date.
10. Consider using the *Clean up Data File* utility. This will "condense" (reduce) the size of your data file, but will probably not be necessary every year. Data file cleanup is an involved process that should be done by your accountant or QuickBooks consultant.

Recording Closing Entries for Sole Proprietorships and Partnerships

> **Note:**
> **Do not enter the transactions in this section.** However, do familiarize yourself with these issues so that you can properly close the year in a sole proprietorship or partnership company.

Sole proprietorships have the following accounts in the Equity section of the *Chart of Accounts* (see Figure 14-26).

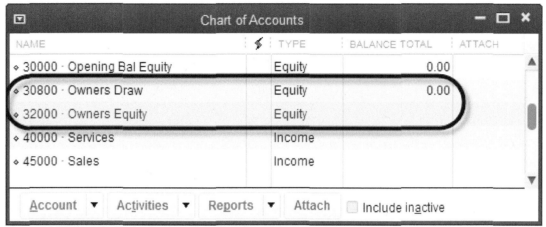

Figure 14-26 Sample Equity Section - Sole Proprietorships

Partnerships have the following accounts (or similar accounts) in the Equity section of the *Chart of Accounts* (see Figure 14-27). Although this list of accounts has a *Retained Earnings* account, it will be cleared out at the end of each year to keep it from accumulating a balance.

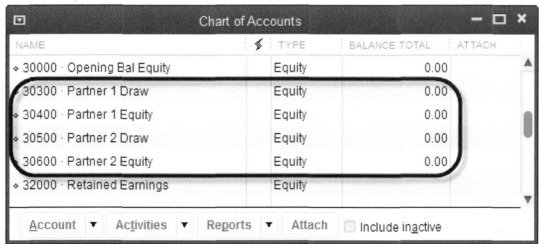

Figure 14-27 Sample Equity section - Partnerships

Throughout the year, as owners put money into and take money out of the business, you will add transactions that increase and decrease the appropriate equity accounts. In a sole proprietorship, you will use the Owner's Equity and Owner's Draw accounts. In a partnership, you will use the Equity and Draw accounts for each partner.

To record owners' investments in the company, enter a deposit transaction in your *Checking* account (or the account to which you make deposits), and enter *Owners Equity* in the *From Account* field (see Figure 14-28).

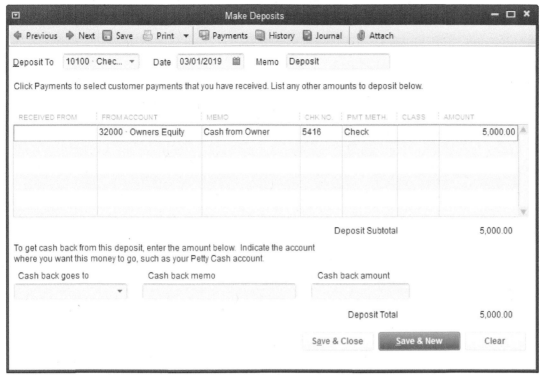

Figure 14-28 Record owner's investments in the Make Deposits window

To record owner's withdrawals from the company, enter a check transaction in the Checking account (or the account from which the owner draws money), and enter **Owners Draw** in the *Account* field (see Figure 14-29).

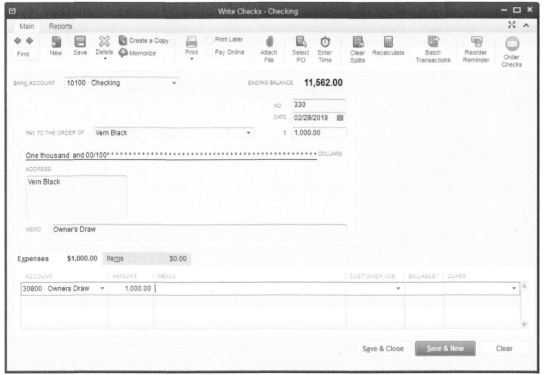

Figure 14-29 Record owner's withdrawals as a check transaction

Closing Sole Proprietorship Draw Accounts

At the end of each year, you will create a *General Journal Entry* to zero out the Owner's Draw account and close it into Owner's Equity (see Figure 14-30).

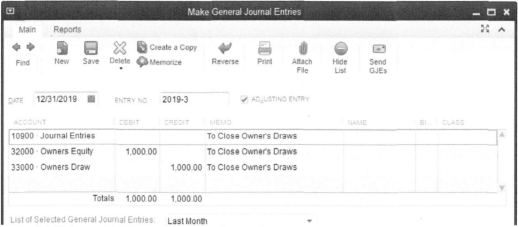

Figure 14-30 General Journal Entry to close Owners Draw

To find the amounts for this *Journal Entry*, create a **Trial Balance Report** for the end of the year. Use the balance in the Owner's Draw account for a *General Journal Entry* to close the account. For example, if your *Trial Balance* shows a *debit* balance of $1,000.00 in Owner's Draw, enter $*1,000.00* in the *credit* column on the Owner's Draw line of this *General Journal Entry*. Then enter a debit to the Owner's Equity account to make the entry balance.

Closing Partnership Draws Accounts

To close the Partners' Draw accounts into each Partner's Equity account, use a *General Journal Entry* like the one shown in Figure 14-31. Use the same process explained above to get the numbers from the year-end *Trial Balance*.

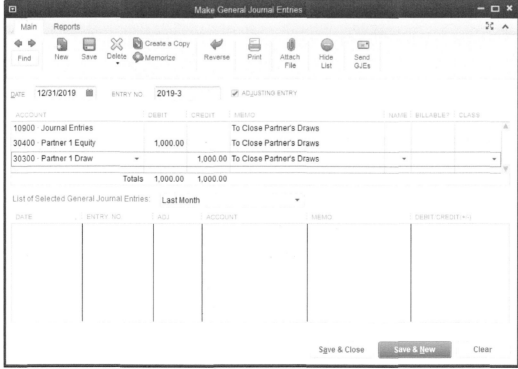

Figure 14-31 General Journal Entry to close partners' draw accounts

Distributing Net Income to Partners

With partnerships, you need to use a *General Journal Entry* to distribute the profits of the company into each of the partner's profit accounts. After making all adjusting entries, create a *Profit & Loss Report* for the year. Use the *Net Income* figure at the bottom of the *Profit & Loss Report* to create the *General Journal Entry*, in Figure 14-32. In this example, assume net income for the year is $50,000 and that there are two equal partners in the business.

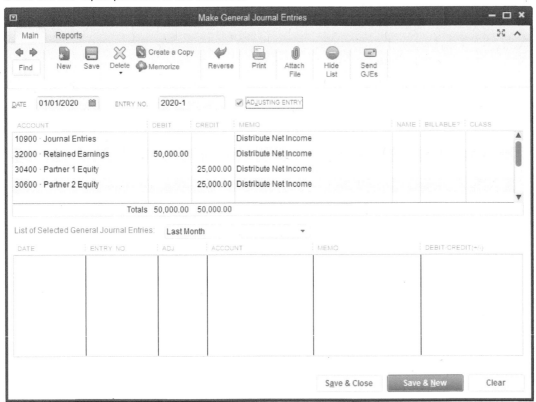

Figure 14-32 Use a General Journal entry to distribute partners' profits

Note that the *General Journal Entry* in Figure 14-32 debits *Retained Earnings*. That is because QuickBooks automatically closes net income into Retained Earnings each year. This is the entry you'll make each year to zero out the balance in *Retained Earnings* and distribute the net income to the partners.

Also, note that the *General Journal Entry* is dated January 1. This is because there is no "after-closing" *Balance Sheet* in QuickBooks. The December 31 *Balance Sheet* should show "undistributed" net income for the year. If the *General Journal Entry* were made on December 31, you would never be able to see a proper (before closing) December 31 *Balance Sheet*. Therefore, to preserve the December 31 before-closing *Balance Sheet*, use January 1 for this closing entry. If you want to see an after-closing *Balance Sheet*, use January 1 for that *Balance Sheet*.

> **Tip:**
> To preserve the after-closing date *Balance Sheet*, it is best to change the date on all normal business transactions that occur on January 1 to January 2. Use January 1 exclusively for the previous year's "closing" entries.

Setting the Closing Date to "Lock" Transactions

QuickBooks allows the administrator to set a closing date that effectively locks the file so that no one can make changes to transactions dated on or before a specified date.

Note:
Several privileges are reserved for the administrator of the file. For example, the administrator is the only one who can view or change the *My Company* information (name, address, etc.) for the file. Also, the administrator is the only one who can make any changes to the *Company Preferences* tabs in the *Preferences* section. For more information about the file administrator, see the QuickBooks onscreen Help.

COMPUTER PRACTICE

To set or modify the closing date and closing date password, follow these steps:

Step 1.   Select **Preferences** from the *Edit* menu and then select the **Company Preferences** tab for the *Accounting* preference.

Step 2.   Click the **Set Date/Password** button at the bottom of the window.

Step 3.   The *Set Closing Date and Password* window opens (see Figure 14-33). Enter *12/31/2019* in the *Closing Date* field.

The date you enter specifies that all transactions dated on or before that date are "locked." Depending on each user's access privileges, QuickBooks either prohibits additions, changes, or deletions to any transactions with a date on or before this date; or, warns users before they make additions, changes, or deletions. To further protect transactions in closed periods you can also require all users, including the administrator, to enter a password before they can add, change, or delete transactions dated on or before the closing date.

Tip:
The user's setup affects the ability to add, change, or delete locked ("closed") transactions. When setting up new users, always choose the setting that prevents them from making additions, changes, or deletions to transactions recorded on or before the closing date. Unless the Closing Date Password is set, the administrator of the file can always bypass the closing date by simply ignoring a warning window. To better protect the closing date in your QuickBooks file, require all users, including the administrator, to enter a Closing Date Password.

Step 4.   Enter **Abc1234** in the *Closing Date Password* and *Confirm Password* fields and click **Cancel** (see Figure 14-33). For this exercise, you won't save the changes. Outside of an educational environment, you will want to create a strong password.

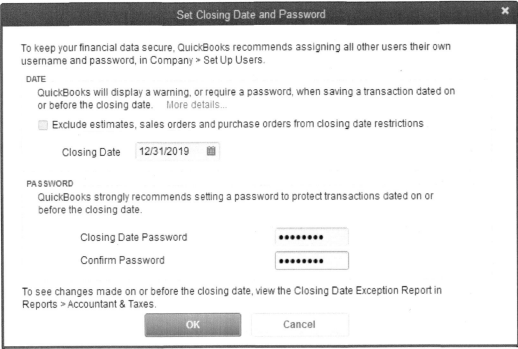

Figure 14-33 Set Closing Date and Password window

Step 5.   Click **OK** on the *Preferences* window.

                 QuickBooks will now require all users to enter this password when attempting to add,
                 change, or delete transactions dated on or before the Closing Date.

> **Note:**
> Your accountant will probably recommend that you set the Closing Date at the end of
> each year (if not more frequently) to prevent users from accidentally changing
> transactions after your company has filed its tax return.

Review Questions

Comprehension Questions

1. Discuss the difference between deleting and voiding a transaction in QuickBooks.

2. Why would you not want to make changes to transactions in QuickBooks that are dated in a closed accounting period?

3. How would you set up QuickBooks to automatically enter a depreciation journal entry each month?

4. Explain how QuickBooks automatically closes the year. What effect does it have on your income and expense accounts?

Multiple Choice

Select the best answer for each of the following:

1. Which of the following tasks does QuickBooks perform automatically at year-end?
   a) Creates adjusting journal entries to the income and expense accounts that can be viewed in the *General Ledger* report
   b) Identifies expenses that are too high in comparison with prior years
   c) Adjusts the balance in the *Retained Earnings* account to reflect the net income or loss for the year
   d) Automatically backs up the data file

2. Entering a date in the *Closing Date* field accomplishes which of the following:
   a) Determines which date QuickBooks will use to automatically close the year
   b) Determines which date QuickBooks closes your file
   c) Locks the data file so that no unauthorized users can add, change, or delete transactions dated on or before the *Closing Date*
   d) Prepares a closing entry on that date

3. Voiding and Deleting transactions both do the following:
   a) Keep a record of the date, number, and detail of the transaction
   b) Completely remove all details of the transaction
   c) Zero out the debits and credits specified by the transaction
   d) Both b and c

4. To make an adjustment to *Items* as well as their associated accounts, create a:
   a) General Journal Entry
   b) Fixed Asset
   c) Zero-Dollar Check
   d) Memorized Transaction

5. At the end of the year, you should perform the following:

   a) Enter depreciation entries

   b) Perform a physical inventory

   c) If your business is a partnership, enter a *General Journal Entry* to distribute net income for the year to each of the partner's capital accounts. If your business is a sole proprietorship, enter a *General Journal Entry* closing Owner's Draw and Owner's Investments into Owner's Equity

   d) All of the above

6. To track payments to a 1099 vendor and print Form 1099 accurately, you must complete all of the following, EXCEPT:

   a) Set your preferences to track accounts linked to 1099-related services.

   b) Enter the vendor's account number on the *Address Info* tab.

   c) Select that the *vendor is eligible for a 1099* on the *Additional Info* tab.

   d) Enter the 1099 vendor's name on the *Address Info* tab.

7. The IRS may reject the 1099s you submit if:

   a) The phone number for the 1099 vendor is incorrect.

   b) The email address for the 1099 vendor is incorrect.

   c) The taxpayer ID is incorrect.

   d) The vendor did not fill out a W-4 Form.

8. By creating a special bank account called Journal Entries:

   a) You can see all journal entries in an account register, provided you enter "Journal Entries" on the top line of each journal entry.

   b) You can create a Balance Sheet.

   c) Journal Entries are easier to read.

   d) Journal Entries automatically copy the memo field to each line.

9. When you purchase a Fixed Asset, you should code the purchase to:

   a) A Fixed Asset type account.

   b) An Other Expense type account.

   c) An Expense type account.

   d) A Liability type account.

10. Which of the following is true?

   a) You don't need to send a W-9 to any vendor in your *Vendor List* that provides professional services to your company.

   b) The IRS may reject your 1099s if you do not include the vendors' Tax ID and address.

   c) The 1099 Wizard helps you prepare 1099-MISC, 1099-INT, and 1099-DIV forms.

   d) You can only map 1099 categories to a single expense account.

11. Which of the following is an example of a fixed asset?

   a) A $5000 High-Speed Copier.

   b) Toner.

   c) A box of paper.

   d) All of the above.

12. Which of the following is false?

    a)   General Journal Entries do not allow you to reallocate transactions from one class to another.

    b)   You can use General Journal Entries to recategorize transactions to a different account.

    c)   General Journal Entries are used to reassociate funds from one item to another item.

    d)   When creating a General Journal Entry, the debits and credits are not required to balance.

Completion Statements

1. If you use the _____ basis of accounting, the goal is to properly match income and expenses to the period in which the income and expenses occur.

2. Use Form 1099-Misc to report payments made to vendors who performed business-related _____ for your company.

3. At the end of the fiscal year, QuickBooks automatically calculates the balance of _____ _____ by adding together the total net income for all prior years.

4. QuickBooks allows you to set a(n) _____ _____ that effectively locks the file so that no changes can be made to the file on or before a certain date.

5. If a bill payment has not yet been printed and you want to remove it, you can _____ it. On the other hand, if you have already printed the bill payment, you should _____ it.

Adjustments Problem 1

> Restore the Adjustments-18Problem1.QBM file. The password to access this file is **Sleeter18**.

1. Create *General Journal Entry* No. *2019-1* on *1/31/2019* to recategorize $*455.00* from **Professional Fees** Expense to **Repairs and Maintenance** Expense (*Hint*: Debit **Repairs and Maintenance**, credit **Professional Fees**). Use the **Journal Entries** account on the top line of the *General Journal Entry* as discussed in the chapter. Enter a descriptive memo *Recategorize Professional Fees* on the top line of the entry. *Class:* **Walnut Creek**.

2. Void check number *328*. Create an adjusting journal entry.

3. Create and print a **Journal Report.** (The *Journal Report* is in the *Accountant & Taxes* section of the *Reports* menu.) Set the *Date* field to **All**. Filter the report to only show *Journal* transactions.

Adjustments Problem 2 (Advanced)

Restore the Adjustments-18Problem2.QBM file. The password to access this file is *Sleeter18*.

1. Create *General Journal Entry* No. *2019-1* on *1/31/2019* to recategorize $58.00 from **Office Supplies** Expense to **Postage and Delivery** Expense (*Hint*: Debit **Postage and Delivery**, credit **Office Supplies**). Use the **Journal Entries** account on the top line of the *General Journal Entry* as discussed in the chapter. Enter a descriptive memo **Recategorize Postage** on the top line of the entry. Use *Class:* **San Jose.**

2. Create a *General Journal Entry* on *1/31/2019*, Entry No. *2019-2*, recording $150.00 in Depreciation for *Fixed Assets* (*Hint*: Debit **Depreciation Expense**, credit **Accumulated Depreciation**). Use the **Journal Entries** account on the top line of the *General Journal Entry* and enter a descriptive memo **Monthly Depreciation for Fixed Assets** on the top line of the entry. Use *Class:* **San Jose.**

3. Memorize the depreciation *Journal Entry* from the previous step and schedule it to be automatically entered every month starting on *2/28/2019* through December (*11* remaining entries). Name the transaction **Monthly Depreciation**. If you see the *Start up* message regarding automatically entering the memorized transactions, select **Later** and *do not* enter the transactions.

4. Create and print a **Balance Sheet Standard** as of *1/31/2019*.

5. Create and print a **Journal Report** for *1/1/2019* through *1/31/2019* (The *Journal Report* is in the *Accountant & Taxes* section of the *Reports* menu.) Filter the report to only show *Journal* transactions.

Chapter 15
Walker Graphic Design
Business Scenario

Description of Company

Sarah Walker has decided to follow her dream and start her own business. She developed a well thought out business plan for a graphic design business with an online store. She took her accumulated savings and started Walker Graphic Design.

Sarah lives in a metropolitan city with a growing economy and many potential clients. She decided to offer web and print graphics services, including ad layout, logo creation, and website design. She will also offer consulting services to help clients focus their design towards target markets.

In addition to working with clients, she will have an online store selling gift items printed with her designs. To do this, she utilizes an online service that handles the production, inventory, shipping, and sales tax.

To help her new start-up, she selected QuickBooks software to help manage the business. To start with she will have no employees and has organized her company as a sole proprietorship. She has leased 600 square feet of office space.

Goals

Using QuickBooks and the sample file (Walker-18.QBW), you will perform the following:
- Record initial start-up costs.
- Record a month of business transactions, including purchases, sales, deposits, Accounts Receivable and Accounts Payable.
- Reconcile bank accounts.
- Answer several questions about the finances for Walker Graphic Design (WGD).

Revenue and expense transactions will be recorded into one of the three classes that WGD uses to track performance. At the end of the month, you will reconcile the bank statement and then produce financial statements and sales analysis reports, including a report of business performance by class.

Company Set Up

> **Restore this File**
> This chapter uses Walker-18.QBW. The password to access this file is *Sleeter18*.

The company file for this exercise is mostly set up for you. Begin by familiarizing yourself with the setup of the file so you can correctly record the transactions and complete the exercises as instructed below.

Instructions

1. Restore the Walker-18.QBM file to Walker-18.QBW file.

2. Enter the transactions for May 2019 beginning on page 540.

3. Reconcile the bank account for May from the statement shown on page 545.

4. Prepare the following reports and graphs:

    a) Reconciliation Summary Report for 5/31/2019
    b) Balance Sheet Standard as of 5/31/2019
    c) Profit and Loss Standard for May 2019
    d) Profit and Loss by Class for May 2019
    e) Statement of Cash Flows for May 2019
    f) Sales by Item Summary for May 2019
    g) Graph – Sales by Month by Customer for May 2019

5. Complete the analysis questions on page 546.

Business Transactions

May 2019

May	Business Transaction	Transaction Details
1	Deposited owner investment from Sarah Walker to provide cash for operations.	Transaction type: **Deposit** Deposit to: **America's Bank Checking** Date: **5/1/2019** Memo: *Deposit Owner's Investment* Received From: **Walker, Sarah** From Account: **Investments** (Equity Account) Check #: **401** Class: **Admin/Other** Amount: **$85,000.00**
1	Paid rent plus refundable deposit to Commerce Realty.	Transaction type: **Check** Date: **5/1/2019** Pay to the Order of: **Commerce Realty** Check#: **1001** Memo: *May Rent plus $1250 Deposit* Account: **Rent Expense - $1250.00** Account: **Refundable Deposit - $1250.00** Total Check: **$2,500.00** Class: **Admin/Other**
2	Received bill from Apex Online for setup of store.	Transaction type: **Bill** Vendor: **Apex Online - V** Date: **5/2/2019** Bill Due: **6/1/2019** Account: **Computer and Internet Expenses** Amount: **$925.00** Terms: **Net 30** Ref No: **65189** Memo: *Store Setup Fees* Class: **Online Sales**

May	Business Transaction	Transaction Details
2	Received bill from Staples.	Transaction type: **Bill** Vendor: **Staples** Date: **5/2/2019** Bill Due: **6/1/2019** Account: **Furniture and Equipment** Amount: **$1,825.00** Terms: **Net 30** Ref No: **68-20** Memo: *Office Equipment* Class: **Admin/Other**
3	Received bill from Legacy Office Supply.	Transaction type: **Bill** Vendor: **Legacy Office Supply** Date: **5/3/2019** Bill Due: **6/2/2019** Account: **Office Supplies** Amount: **$632.00** Terms: **Net 30** Ref No: **6433** Memo: *Office Supplies* Class: **Admin/Other**
3	Issued check to Office Furniture Rentals for rental of office furniture for May.	Transaction type: **Check** Date: **5/3/2019** Pay to the Order of: **Office Furniture Rentals** Check#: **1002** Memo: *Furniture Rental* Account: **Equipment Rental** Amount: **$899.00** Class: **Admin/Other**
4	Issued check to Delmore Insurance for liability insurance premium for May.	Transaction type: **Check** Date: **5/4/2019** Pay to the Order of: **Delmore Insurance** Check#: **1003** Memo: *May General Liability Insurance* Account: **Insurance Expense** Class: **Admin/Other** Total: **$729.00**
8	Prepared invoice for consulting with Maple Lane Salon.	Transaction type: **Invoice** Customer: **Maple Lane Salon** Class: **Design/Consulting** Template: **Intuit Service Invoice** Date: **5/8/2019** Invoice #: **2019-101** Terms: **2% 10 Net 30** Items: **Consultation (6 @ $60.00/Hour)** Total: $360.00 Memo: *Marketing Consultation*
14	Prepared invoice for consulting and design work for Bridge Boutique.	Transaction type: **Invoice** Customer: **Bridge Boutique** Class: **Design/Consulting** Template: **Intuit Service Invoice** Date: **5/14/2019** Invoice #: **2019-102** Terms: **Net 30** Items: **Consultation (3 @ $60.00/Hour)** Items: **Design (6 @ $50.00/Hour)** Total: $480.00 Memo: *3 Consulting, 6 Design*

May	Business Transaction	Transaction Details
15	Received payment from Maple Lane Salon. Maple Lane Salon paid within 10 days and took the discount for early payment.	Transaction type: **Payment** Customer: **Maple Lane Salon** Date: **5/15/2019** Amount: **$352.80** Check No: **9864** Payment Method: **Check** Memo: *Payment Received – Inv. #2019-101* Discount Account: **Sales Discounts** Discount Class: **Design/Consulting** Apply to: **Invoice #2019-101**
16	Recorded receipt for first two weeks of sales from online store.	Transaction type: **Sales Receipt** Customer: **Apex Online – C** Class: **Online Sales** Sales No.: **2019-101** Date: **5/16/2019** Check No: **26967** Items: T-Shirts – Qty 15 Caps – Qty 13 Mugs – Qty 12 Clocks – Qty 1 Sales Tax: **Out of State** Total: **$336.00** Memo: *Biweekly Store Revenue*
17	Received bill from Image Contacts, Inc. for printing of flyers.	Transaction type: **Bill** Vendor: **Image Contacts, Inc.** Date: **5/17/2019** Bill Due: **6/16/2019** Amount: **$1,320.00** Terms: **Net 30** Ref No: **2856** Memo: *Flyer Printing* Account: **Printing and Reproduction** Class: **Design/Consulting**
22	Received bill from Zenith Productions.	Transaction type: **Bill** Vendor: **Zenith Productions** Date: **5/22/2019** Bill Due: **6/21/2019** Amount: **$2,430.00** Terms: **Net 30** Ref No: **8248** Memo: *Fees for Product Designs* Account: **Professional Fees** Class: **Design/Consulting**
24	Prepared Invoice for Lilly's Clothing Design for design services.	Transaction type: **Invoice** Customer: **Lilly's Clothing Design** Class: **Design/Consulting** Template: **Intuit Service Invoice** Date: **5/24/2019** Invoice #: **2019-103** Terms: **Net 30** Items: **Design (145 @ $50/Hour)** Total: **$7,250.00** Memo: *Magazine Campaign*

May	Business Transaction	Transaction Details
26	Received check from Lilly's Clothing Design	Transaction type: **Payment** Customer: **Lilly's Clothing Design** Date: **5/26/2019** Amount: **$7,250.00** Check No: **1079** Payment Method: **Check** Memo: *Payment Received – Inv. #2019-103* Apply to: **Invoice #2019-103**
28	Received check from Bridge Boutique.	Transaction type: **Payment** Customer: **Bridge Boutique** Date: **5/28/2019** Amount: **$480.00** Check No: **3065** Payment Method: **Check** Memo: *Payment Received – Inv. #2019-102* Apply to: **Invoice #2019-102**
29	Prepared Invoice for Western Energy Corporation.	Transaction type: **Invoice** Customer: **Western Energy Corporation** Class: **Design/Consulting** Template: **Intuit Service Invoice** Date: **5/29/2019** Invoice #: **2019-104** Terms: **Net 30** Items: **Design (75 @ $50.00/Hour)** Total: **$3,750.00** Memo: *Brochure and Ad*
29	Received bill from Cal Light & Power for utilities.	Transaction type: **Bill** Vendor: **Cal Light & Power** Date: **5/29/2019** Bill Due: **6/28/2019** Amount: **$501.00** Terms: **Net 30** Ref No: **7599** Memo: *Utility Bill* Account: **Utilities** Class: **Admin/Other**
29	Received bill from Western Bell for telephone.	Transaction type: **Bill** Vendor: **Western Bell** Date: **5/29/2019** Bill Due: **6/28/2019** Amount: **$288.00** Terms: **Net 30** Ref No: **2332** Memo: *Telephone Bill* Account: **Telephone Expense** Class: **Admin/Other**

May	Business Transaction	Transaction Details

30	Recorded receipt for two weeks of sales from online store.	Transaction type: **Sales Receipt**
		Customer: **Apex Online – C**
		Class: **Online Sales**
		Sale No.: **2019-102**
		Date: **5/30/2019**
		Check No: **27345**
		Items:
		      T-Shirts – Qty 35
		      Caps – Qty 32
		      Mugs – Qty 28
		      Clocks – Qty 9
		      Tote Bags – Qty 3
		Sales Tax: **Out of State**
		Total: **$900.00**
		Memo: *Biweekly Store Revenue*

31	Received check from Western Energy Corporation.	Transaction type: **Payment** Customer: **Western Energy Corporation** Date: **5/31/2019** Amount: **$3,750.00** Check No: **2021** Payment Method: **Check** Memo: *Payment Received – Inv. #2019-104* Apply to: **Invoice #2019-104**
31	Deposited all funds held in Undeposited Funds account to America's Bank.	Transaction type: **Deposit** Deposit to: **America's Bank Checking** Memo: **Deposit** Date: **5/31/2019** Total Deposit Amount: **$13,068.80**
31	Paid all bills in a batch sorted by Vendor.	Select **Pay Bills**, and then pay the following bills: Apex Online Cal Light & Power Image Contacts, Inc. Legacy Office Supply Staples Western Bell Zenith Productions, Inc. Total payments: **$7,921.00** Bill Payment Date: **5/31/2019**
31	Printed all checks (Chk#1004-1010).	#1004 – Apex Online #1005 – Cal Light & Power #1006 – Image Contacts, Inc. #1007 – Legacy Office Supply #1008 – Staples #1009 – Western Bell #1010 – Zenith Production
31	Issued check to Green Door Computing for computer repairs.	Transaction type: **Check** Date: **5/31/2019** Pay to the Order of: **Green Door Computing** Check#: **1011** Memo: *Computer Repairs* Account: **Repairs and Maintenance** Class: **Admin/Other** Total: **$147.00**

Business Checking Account

Statement Date:	May 31, 2019	Page 1 of 1

Summary:		Walker Graphic Design

Previous Balance as of 4/30/19	$	-
Total Deposits and Credits	+ $	98,068.80
Total Checks and Debits	- $	12,059.00
Statement Balance as of 5/31/19:	= $	86,009.80

Deposits and Other Credits:

DEPOSITS

Date	Description	Amount
1-May	Customer Deposit	$ 85,000.00
31-May	Customer Deposit	$ 13,068.80
	Deposits:	$ 98,068.80

INTEREST

Date	Description	Amount
	Interest:	$ -

Checks and Other Withdrawals:

CHECKS PAID:

Check No.	Date Paid	Amount
1001	1-May	$ 2,500.00
1002	3-May	$ 899.00
1003	4-May	$ 729.00
1004	31-May	$ 925.00
1005	31-May	$ 501.00
1006	31-May	$ 1,320.00
1007	31-May	$ 632.00
1008	31-May	$ 1,825.00
1009	31-May	$ 288.00
1010	31-May	$ 2,430.00
	Checks Paid:	$ 12,049.00

OTHER WITHDRAWALS/PAYMENTS

Date	Description	Amount
	Other Withdrawals/Payments:	$ -

SERVICE CHARGES

Date	Description	Amount
31-May	Service Charge	$ 10.00
	1 Service Charge:	$ 10.00

Figure 15-1 Bank Statement

Analysis Questions

Use the completed reports from step 4 of the instructions and your QB company file to answer the following questions. Write your answer in the space to the left of each question.

1._____   What is the net income or net loss for May?

2._____   What is the total Expenses for May?

3._____   What is the amount of Total Product Sales for May?

4._____   What is the amount of rent paid for May?

5._____   What is the net cash increase for May?

6._____   What percentage of total sales were T-Shirts in May?

7._____   What percentage of total sales was to Bridge Boutique ?

8._____   How much does Walker Graphic Design have in total assets on May 31?

9._____   What was the net income for the Online Sales Class?

10. _____   What was the amount of Total Uncleared Transactions from the May bank reconciliation?

Chapter 16
Horizon Financial Planning
Business Scenario

Description of Company

After many years with his company, William Barrett was caught by the entrepreneurial spirit. After carefully saving up enough seed capital and convincing a recently unemployed colleague to join him, he developed a well thought-out business plan and started Horizon Financial Planning (HFP).

William saw great opportunities. He lives in a large metropolitan city in Texas, close to several regional colleges and large universities, as well as hundreds of medium to large corporations. He plans to offer financial planning, investment and estate planning seminars, plus related consulting services to individual, corporate and institutional clients. Furthermore, his business plan includes the purchase and promotion of planning kits, along with several popular books and instructional DVDs related to achieving financial stability and success, which he will sell at corporate and collegiate brown-bag lunch seminars. Several times a year he conducts large seminars on financial planning and building wealth. He also offers companion seminars on estate planning and minimizing taxes.

To control his new start-up, he selected QuickBooks software to help manage the business operations while fulfilling fiduciary responsibilities from an accounting, tax and record-keeping perspective. To launch the company, he hired his former colleague, Shelly James, as a full time employee. He also was pleased to hire his daughter, Atasha, as a part-time hourly employee. He has leased 1,200 square feet of downtown office space.

Using QuickBooks and the sample file (Horizon-18.QBW), you will record initial start-up costs, complete one month of business transactions, including purchases, sales, deposits, accounts receivable, accounts payable, payroll and taxes as well as track inventory and reconcile a bank account. In the end, you will answer several questions about the finances for Horizon Financial Planning.

Company Set Up

> **Restore this File:**
> This chapter uses Horizon-18.QBW. You will not need to enter a password because this is a sample file.

The company file for this exercise is mostly set up for you, including Accounts, Customers, Vendors, Employees, Payroll, Classes, Items and Fixed Asset Items.

Instructions

1. Restore the Horizon-18.QBM file to Horizon-18.QBW.

2. Enter the transactions for October 2019 beginning on page 548.

3. Reconcile the bank statement for October for the statement shown on page 561.

4. Prepare the following reports and graphs:
    a) Standard Balance Sheet as of 10/31/2019
    b) Standard Profit and Loss for October 2019
    c) Profit and Loss by Class for October 2019
    d) Statement of Cash Flows for October 2019
    e) Sales by Item Summary for October 2019
    f) Graph – Sales by Month by Customer for October 2019
    g) Inventory Valuation Summary as of 10/31/2019

5. Create a portable file from your data file with the filename Horizon-October.QBM, and then continue entering the remaining transactions for November 2019 beginning on page 554.

6. Reconcile the bank statement for November for the statement shown on page 547

7. Prepare the following reports and graphs:
    a) Standard Balance Sheet as of 11/30/2019
    b) Standard Profit and Loss for November 2019
    c) Profit and Loss by Class for November 2019
    d) Statement of Cash Flows for November 2019
    e) Sales by Item Summary for November 2019
    f) Graph – Sales by Month by Customer for November 2019
    g) Inventory Valuation Summary as of 11/30/2019

8. Create a portable file from your data file with the filename Horizon-18Final.QBM.

9. Complete the analysis questions on page 560.

Business Transactions

October 2019

Oct	Business Transaction	Transaction Details
1	Deposited owner investment from William Barrett to provide cash for operations.	Transaction type: Deposit Deposit to: Checking-Texas National Bank Date: 10/1/2019 Memo: Deposit Owner's Investment From Account: Investments (Equity Account) Check #401 Class: Admin/Other Amount: $72,000.00
1	Issued Purchase Order to Northern Lights Media & Publications to order Books and DVDs.	Transaction type: Purchase Order Vendor: Northern Lights Media & Publications Class: Product Sales Date: 10/1/2019 PO#: 2019–101 Items: Books (130 @ $25.00) DVDs (85 @ $17.00) Memo: Order Books and DVDs
1	Paid rent plus refundable deposit to Williams Investments.	Transaction type: Check Pay to the Order of: Williams Investments Check#: 1001 Date: 10/1/2019 Memo: October Rent plus $1,000 Deposit Expense: Rent - $2,500.00 Expense: Refundable Deposits (Other Current Asset) - $1,000.00 Total Check: $3,500.00 Class: Admin/Other

Oct	Business Transaction	Transaction Details
1	Issued Purchase Order to Office Supply Depot for laptop.	Transaction type: Purchase Order Vendor: Office Supply Depot Class: Admin/Other Date: 10/1/2019 PO#: 2019–102 Items: Laptop PC $2,500.00 Memo: Purchase laptop Total purchase order is $2,500.00 Note: The item has already been added to the Fixed Asset Item list.
1	Issued Purchase Order to Lone Star Office Supply for office supplies.	Transaction type: Purchase Order Vendor: Lone Star Office Supply Class: Admin/Other Date: 10/1/2019 PO#: 2019–103 Item: Office Supplies ($750.00) Memo: Purchase office supplies Total purchase order is $750.00
4	Received bill from Office Supply Depot.	Transaction type: Receive Items & Enter Bill Vendor: Office Supply Depot PO #: 2019-102 ⇨ Items and Class auto fill from PO. Date: 10/4/2019 Bill Due: 11/3/2019 Amount: $2,500.00 Terms: Net 30 Ref No: 68-20 Memo: Laptop
4	Received bill from Lone Star Office Supply for supply items.	Transaction type: Receive Items & Enter Bill Vendor: Lone Star Office Supply PO #: 2019-103 ⇨ Items and Class auto fill from PO. Date: 10/4/2019 Bill Due: 11/3/2019 Amount: $750.00 Terms: Net 30 Ref No: 6433 Memo: Office Supplies
4	Issued check to Office Furniture Rentals for rental of office furniture for October.	Transaction type: Check Pay to the Order of: Office Furniture Rentals Check#: 1002 Date: 10/4/2019 Memo: Furniture Rental Expense: Equipment Rental ($445.00) Class: Admin/Other Memorize the check, using *Do Not Remind Me* option.
4	Received bill from Northern Lights Media & Publications.	Transaction type: Receive Items & Enter Bill Vendor: Northern Lights Media & Publications PO #: 2019-101 ⇨ Items and Class auto fill from PO. Date: 10/4/2019 Bill Due: 11/3/2019 Amount: $4,695.00 Terms: Net 30 Ref No: 8736 Memo: Books and DVDs

Oct	Business Transaction	Transaction Details
5	Entered a Weekly timesheet for Atasha Barrett's hours.	Transaction type: Weekly timesheet Name: Atasha Barrett Week of: Sept 30 to Oct 6, 2019 Payroll Item: Hourly Regular WC Code: Leave Blank Mon: 0 hours Tues: 4 hours Wed: 8 hours Thurs: 4 hours Fri: 4 hours Sat, Sun: 0 hours Billable?: Not Billable
10	Received bill from Northern Lights Media & Publications. These non-inventory products were ordered by telephone without issuing a PO.	Transaction type: Bill Vendor: Northern Lights Media & Publications Date: 10/10/2019 Bill Due: 11/9/2019 Amount: $1,320.00 Terms: Net 30 Ref No: 8100 Memo: Planning Kits Item: Planning Kits – 60 Units @ $22 Class: Product Sales
12	Entered a Weekly timesheet for Atasha Barrett's hours.	Transaction type: Weekly timesheet Name: Atasha Barrett Week of: October 7 to 13, 2019 Payroll Item: Hourly Regular WC Code: Leave Blank Mon: 8 hours Tues: 4 hours Wed: 8 hours Thurs: 4 hours Fri, Sat, Sun: 0 hours Billable?: Not Billable
15	Entered a Weekly timesheet for Atasha Barrett's hours. (Time entered early due to pay cycle.)	Transaction type: Weekly timesheet Name: Atasha Barrett Week of: October 14 to 20, 2019 Payroll Item: Hourly Regular WC Code: Leave Blank Mon: 8 hours Tues: 8 hours Wed: 4 hours Thurs: 4 hours Fri, Sat, Sun: 0 hours Billable?: Not Billable

Oct	Business Transaction	Transaction Details
16	Paid employees for payroll period 10/1/2019 – 10/15/2019.	Pay Period Ends: 10/15/2019 Paycheck Date: 10/16/2019 Bank Account: Checking – Texas National Bank Atasha Barrett: 60 hours Shelly James: Salary Starting Check Number: 1003
18	Received bill from Image Contacts, Inc. for printing and mailing of flyers.	Transaction type: Bill Vendor: Image Contacts, Inc. Date: 10/18/2019 Bill Due: 11/17/2019 Amount: $1,690.00 Terms: Net 30 Ref No: 8869 Memo: Printing and Mailing Flyers Expense: Advertising and Promotion Class: Consulting/Seminars
21	Received bill from Rash Productions, Inc. for consulting fees for an upcoming seminar to be conducted.	Transaction type: Bill Vendor: Rash Productions, Inc. Date: 10/21/2019 Bill Due: 11/20/2019 Amount: $1,711.00 Terms: Net 30 Ref No: 8248 Memo: Consulting Fees Expense: Professional Fees Class: Consulting/Seminars
24	Conducted an on-site brown-bag lunch seminar at Designer Glass USA.	Transaction type: Sales Receipt Template: Sales Receipt Retail Customer: Seminar Sales Summary Class: Product Sales Date: 10/24/2019 Sale No: 2019-101 Check No: Leave Blank Payment Method: Check Items: Books (25 @ $50.00) DVDs (20 @ $40.00) Planning Kits (26 @ $100.00) Texas sales tax applies. Total: $5,033.63 Memo: Designer Glass USA Seminar Sales
24	Prepared Invoice to Designer Glass USA for on-site seminar conducted on this date.	Transaction type: Invoice Customer: Designer Glass USA Class: Consulting/Seminars Template: Intuit Service Invoice Date: 10/24/2019 Invoice #: 2019-101 Terms: Due on Receipt Items: Seminar (1 @ $6,000.00) Total: $6,000.00 Memo: Designer Glass USA Onsite Seminar

Oct	Business Transaction	Transaction Details
27	Received check from Designer Glass USA.	Transaction type: Payment Customer: Designer Glass USA Date: 10/27/2019 Amount: $6,000.00 Check No: 1069 Payment Method: Check Memo: Payment Received – Inv. #2019-101 Apply to: Invoice #2019-101
27	Issued check to Education & Medical Fund for contributions.	Transaction type: Check Check#: 1005 Date: 10/27/2019 Pay to the Order of: Education & Medical Fund Amount: $200.00 Memo: Charitable Contribution Expense: Charitable Contributions Class: Consulting/Seminars

28	Entered a Sales Receipt to record the product sales at the seminar given at Energy Corporation of Texas	Transaction type: Sales Receipt
		Customer: Seminar Sales Summary
		Class: Product Sales
		Date: 10/28/2019
		Sale No: 2019-102
		Check No: Leave Blank
		Payment Method: Check
		Items: Books (82 @ $50.00)
		    DVDs (60 @ $40.00)
		    Planning Kits (40 @ $100.00)
		Texas sales tax applies.
		Total: $11,366.25
		Memo: Energy Corp. of Texas Seminar Sales

28	Prepared Invoice for Energy Corporation of Texas for on-site seminar conducted on this date.	Transaction type: Invoice Customer: Energy Corporation of Texas Class: Consulting/Seminars Date: 10/28/2019 Invoice #: 2019-102 Terms: Due on Receipt Items: Seminar (1 @ $6,000.00) Total: $6,000.00 Memo: Energy Corp. of Texas Onsite Seminar
28	Received bill from Texas Light & Power.	Transaction type: Bill Vendor: Texas Light & Power Date: 10/28/2019 Bill Due: 11/27/2019 Amount: $169.00 Terms: Net 30 Ref No: 925586 Memo: Utility Bill Expense: Utilities Class: Admin/Other

Oct	Business Transaction	Transaction Details
28	Received bill from South Texas Bell for telephone.	Transaction type: Bill Vendor: South Texas Bell Date: 10/28/2019 Bill Due: 11/27/2019 Amount: $91.00 Terms: Net 30 Ref No: 987546 Memo: Telephone Bill Expense: Telephone Expense:Office Phone Class: Admin/Other
29	Entered a Weekly timesheet for Atasha Barrett's hours.	Transaction type: Weekly timesheet Name: Atasha Barrett Week of: October 21 to 27, 2019 Payroll Item: Hourly Regular WC Code: Leave Blank Mon: 8 hours Tues: 4 hours Wed: 8 hours Thurs: 4 hours Fri, Sat, Sun: 0 hours Billable?: Not Billable
31	Received check from Energy Corporation of Texas.	Transaction type: Payment Customer: Energy Corporation of Texas Date: 10/31/2019 Amount: $6,000.00 Check No: 2021 Payment Method: Check Memo: Payment Received – Inv. #2019-102 Apply to: Invoice #2019-102
31	Entered a Weekly timesheet for Atasha Barrett's hours. (Time entered early due to pay cycle.)	Transaction type: Weekly timesheet Name: Atasha Barrett Week of: Oct 28 to Nov 3, 2019 Payroll Item: Hourly Regular WC Code: Leave Blank Mon: 8 hours Tues: 4 hours Wed: 8 hours Thurs: 4 hours Fri, Sat, Sun: 0 hours Billable?: Not Billable
31	Paid employees for time worked during payroll period 10/16/2019 through 10/31/2019.	Pay Period Ends: 10/31/2019 Paycheck Date: 10/31/2019 Bank Account: Checking – Texas National Bank Atasha Barrett: 56 hours Shelly James: Salary Starting Check Number: 1006
31	Deposited funds held in Undeposited Funds account to Texas National Bank.	Transaction type: Deposit Deposit to: Checking-Texas National Bank Memo: Deposit Date: 10/31/2019 Total Deposit Amount: $28,399.88

Oct	Business Transaction	Transaction Details
31	Paid all bills in a batch sorted by Vendor. Pay from the Checking-Texas National Bank account, and create *To be Printed* checks.	Select Pay Bills, and then pay the following bills: Office Supply Depot Lone Star Office Supply Northern Lights Media & Publications Northern Lights Media & Publications Image Contacts, Inc., Rash Productions, Inc. Texas Light & Power South Texas Bell Total payments: $12,926.00 Bill Payment Date: 10/31/2019
31	Printed all checks (Chk#1008-1014).	#1008 – Image Contacts, Inc. #1009 – Lone Star Office Supply #1010 – Northern Lights Media & Publications #1011 – Office Supply Depot #1012 – Rash Productions, Inc. #1013 – South Texas Bell #1014 – Texas Light & Power
31	Issued check to Clover Computing for computer repairs.	Transaction type: Check Pay to the Order of: Clover Computing Check#: 1015 Date: 10/31/2019 Memo: Computer Repairs Expense: Computer & Internet Expenses Class: Admin/Other Total: $658.00

November 2019

Nov	Business Transaction	Transaction Details
1	Issued PO for books from Northern Lights Media & Publications.	Transaction type: Purchase Order Vendor: Northern Lights Media & Publications Class: Product Sales Date: 11/1/2019 PO#: 2019–104 Items: Books (125 @ $25.00) DVDs (125 @ $17.00) Memo: Reorder Books
1	Issued check to Williams Investments for rent.	Transaction type: Check Vendor: Williams Investments Check#: 1016 Date: 11/1/2019 Memo: November Rent Expense: Rent - $2,500.00 Total Check: $2,500.00 Class: Admin/Other
4	Paid October sales tax.	Transaction type: Sales Tax Payment Check Date: 11/4/2019 Account: Checking – Texas National Bank Show Sales tax due through: 10/31/2019 Vendor: Texas State Comptroller Check#: 1017 Total Check: $1,249.88

Nov	Business Transaction	Transaction Details
4	Received bill from Northern Lights Media & Publications.	Transaction type: Receive Items & Enter Bill Vendor: Northern Lights Media & Publications PO #: 2019-104 ⇨ Items and Class from PO Date: 11/4/2019 Bill Due: 12/4/2019 Amount: $5,250.00 Terms: Net 30 Ref No: 9092 Memo: Books and DVDs
4	Received bill from Northern Lights Media & Publications. These non-inventory products were ordered by telephone without issuing a PO.	Transaction type: Bill Vendor: Northern Lights Media & Publications Date: 11/4/2019 Bill Due: 12/4/2019 Amount: $1,650.00 Terms: Net 30 Ref No: 8957 Memo: Planning Kits Item: Planning Kits – 75 Units @ $22 Class: Product Sales
9	Entered a Weekly timesheet for Atasha Barrett's hours.	Transaction type: Weekly timesheet Name: Atasha Barrett Week of: November 4 to 10, 2019 Payroll Item: Hourly Regular WC Code: Leave Blank Mon: 8 hours Tues: 4 hours Wed: 8 hours Thurs: 4 hours Fri, Sat, Sun: 0 hours Billable?: Not Billable
11	Conducted an on-site seminar at Georgia Tech.	Transaction type: Sales Receipt Customer: Seminar Sales Summary Class: Product Sales Date: 11/11/2019 Sale No: 2019-103 Check No: Leave Blank Payment Method: Check Items: Books (85 @ $50.00) 　　　DVDs (45 @ $40.00) 　　　Planning Kits (35 @ $100.00) Texas sales tax applies. Total: $10,337.88 Memo: Georgia Tech Seminar Sales
11	Prepare Invoice to Georgia Tech for on-site seminar conducted on this date.	Transaction type: Invoice Customer: Georgia Tech Class: Consulting/Seminars Date: 11/11/2019 Invoice #: 2019-103 Terms: Net 30 Items: Seminar (1 @ $6,000.00) Total: $6,000.00 Memo: Georgia Tech Onsite Seminar

Nov	Business Transaction	Transaction Details
14	Received check from Georgia Tech.	Transaction type: Payment Customer: Georgia Tech Date: 11/14/2019 Amount: $6,000.00 Check No: 5091 Payment Method: Check Memo: Payment Received – Inv. #2019-103 Apply to: Invoice #2019-103
15	Pay the Payroll Liabilities that are due 11/15/2019	Transaction type: Liability Payment Bank Account: Checking – Texas National Bank Due Date: 11/15/2019 Check No: 1018 Date: 11/15/2019 Pay to the Order of: EFTPS Amount: $1,542.22 Memo: 11-7654321
15	Entered a Weekly timesheet for Atasha Barrett's hours.	Transaction type: Weekly timesheet Name: Atasha Barrett Week of: November 11 to 17, 2019 Payroll Item: Hourly Regular WC Code: Leave Blank Mon: 8 hours Tues: 4 hours Wed: 8 hours Thurs: 4 hours Fri, Sat, Sun: 0 hours Billable?: Not Billable
16	Paid employees for time worked during payroll period 11/1/2019 through 11/15/2019.	Pay Period Ends: 11/15/2019 Paycheck Date: 11/16/2019 Bank Account: Checking – Texas National Bank Atasha Barrett: 48 hours Shelly James: Salary Starting Check No: 1019
18	Prepared an Invoice to Energy Alternatives and Operations, Inc. for a consultation.	Transaction type: Invoice Customer: Energy Alternatives and Operations, Inc. Class: Consulting/Seminars Date: 11/18/2019 Invoice #: 2019-104 Terms: Net 30 Items: Consultation (35 @ $250.00) Total: $8,750.00 Memo: Energy Alternatives Consulting Hrs
18	Received bill from Longhorn American Insurance.	Transaction type: Bill Vendor: Longhorn American Insurance Date: 11/18/2019 Bill Due: 12/18/2019 Amount: $700 Terms: Net 30 Ref No: 365250 Memo: Health Insurance Payment Expense: Insurance Expense Class: Admin/Other

Nov	Business Transaction	Transaction Details
18	Issued PO for books and DVDs from Northern Lights Media & Publications.	Transaction type: Purchase Order Vendor: Northern Lights Media & Publications Class: Product Sales Date: 11/18/2019 PO#: 2019–105 Items: Books (150 @ $25.00) DVDs (150 @ $17.00) Memo: Reorder Books and DVDs
19	Received check from Energy Alternatives and Operations, Inc.	Transaction type: Payment Customer: Energy Alternatives and Operations, Inc. Date: 11/19/2019 Amount: $8,750.00 Check No: 1055 Payment Method: Check Memo: Payment Received – Inv. #2019-104 Apply to: Invoice #2019-104
19	Received bill from Northern Lights Media & Publications	Transaction type: Receive Items & Enter Bill Vendor: Northern Lights Media & Publications PO #: 2019-105 ⇨ Items and Class auto fill from PO. Date: 11/19/2019 Bill Due: 12/19/2019 Amount: $6,300.00 Terms: Net 30 Ref No: 9144 Memo: Reorder Books and DVDs
20	Deposited funds held in Undeposited Funds account to Texas National Bank.	Transaction type: Deposit Deposit to: Checking-Texas National Bank Memo: Deposit Date: 11/20/2019

21	Conducted an on-site seminar at Central Texas University.	Transaction type: Sales Receipt
		Customer: Seminar Sales Summary
		Class: Product Sales
		Date: 11/21/2019
		Sale No: 2019-104
		Check No: Leave Blank
		Payment Method: Check
		Items: Books (50 @ $50.00)
		      DVDs (75 @ $40.00)
		      Planning Kits (30 @ $100.00)
		Texas sales tax applies.
		Total: $9,201.25
		Memo: Central Texas University Seminar Sales

21	Prepared Invoice for Central Texas University for on-site seminar conducted on this date.	Transaction type: Invoice Customer: Central Texas University Class: Consulting/Seminars Date: 11/21/2019 Invoice #: 2019-105 Terms: Net 30 Items: Seminar (1 @ $6,000.00) Total: $6,000.00 Memo: Central Texas University Onsite Seminar

Nov	Business Transaction	Transaction Details
21	Entered a Weekly timesheet for Atasha Barrett's hours.	Transaction type: Weekly timesheet Name: Atasha Barrett Week of: November 18 to 24, 2019 Payroll Item: Hourly Regular WC Code: Leave Blank Mon: 8 hours Tues: 4 hours Wed: 4 hours Thurs: 4 hours Fri, Sat, Sun: 0 hours Billable?: Not Billable
26	Received check from Central Texas University.	Transaction type: Payment Customer: Central Texas University Date: 11/26/2019 Amount: $6,000.00 Check No: 4551 Payment Method: Check Memo: Payment Received – Inv. #2019-105 Apply to: Invoice #2019-105
27	Entered Bill–Credit from Northern Lights Media & Publications for DVDs returned due to damage in shipment.	Transaction type: Bill Credit Vendor: Northern Lights Media & Publications Date: 11/27/2019 Credit Amount: $68.00 Ref No: 9144-C Memo: Credit for Damaged DVDs Item: DVDs (4 @ $17.00) Class: Product Sales
27	Issued Credit Memo to customer John R. Clark, who returned a book purchased at the seminar at Texas Central University on 11/21/2019.	Transaction type: Credit Memo Customer: John R. Clark Class: Product Sales Date: 11/27/2019 Credit No: 2019-106 Items: Books (1 @ $50.00 taxable) Total Credit Amount: $54.13 Memo: Returned Book (Refund check is issued in next step)
27	Issued refund check to John R. Clark. Applied this refund to the Credit Memo.	Transaction type: Check (created from Credit Memo using "Use credit to give refund" option button) Refund Amount: $54.13 Check Number: 1021 Date: 11/27/2019 Class: Product Sales Memo: Refund
27	Received bill from Texas Light & Power.	Transaction type: Bill Vendor: Texas Light & Power Date: 11/27/2019 Bill Due: 12/27/2019 Amount: $174.00 Terms: Net 30 Ref No: 978411 Memo: Utility Bill Expense: Utilities Class: Admin/Other

Nov	Business Transaction	Transaction Details
29	Received bill from South Texas Bell for telephone expenses.	Transaction type: Bill Vendor: South Texas Bell Date: 11/29/2019 Bill Due: 12/29/2019 Amount: $163.00 Terms: Net 30 Ref No: 1000293 Memo: Telephone Bill Expense: Telephone Expense:Office Phone Class: Admin/Other
29	A physical count verified books on hand but identified a loss of DVDs. Therefore, the Quantity On Hand for DVDs was adjusted down to match the physical count.	Transaction type: Inventory Adjustment for Quantity and Total Value Date: 11/29/2019 Ref No: 2019-1 Account: Inventory Variance Class: Product Sales New Quantity for DVDs Item: 154 Quantity Difference: -2 Memo: Adjust for Actual Quantity on Hand
29	Entered a Weekly timesheet for Atasha Barrett's hours.	Transaction type: Weekly timesheet Name: Atasha Barrett Week of: November 25 to December 1, 2019 Payroll Item: Hourly Regular WC Code: Leave Blank Mon: 8 hours Tues: 8 hours Wed: 8 hours Thurs: 0 hours Fri, Sat, Sun: 0 hours Billable?: Not Billable
29	Deposited funds held in Undeposited Funds account to Texas National Bank.	Transaction type: Deposit Deposit to: Checking-Texas National Bank Date: 11/29/2019 Memo: Deposit
29	Paid all bills in a batch sorted by Vendor. Pay from the Checking-Texas National Bank account, and create "To be Printed" checks.	Select Pay Bills and pay all existing bills. Bill Payment Date: 11/29/2019 Remember to use any existing vendor credits.
29	Printed all checks (Chk#1024-1027).	#1024 – Longhorn American Insurance #1025 – Northern Lights Media & Publications #1026 – South Texas Bell #1027 – Texas Light and Power
30	Paid employees for time worked during payroll period 11/15/2019 through 11/30/2019.	Pay Period Ends: 11/30/2019 Paycheck Date: 11/30/2019 Bank Account: Checking – Texas National Bank Atasha Barrett: 44 hours Shelly James: Salary Starting Check: 1022

Analysis Questions

Use the completed reports and template file to answer the following questions. Write your answer in the space to the left of each question.

1. _____   What is the net income or net loss for October?

2. _____   What is the total Cost of Goods Sold for October?

3. _____   What is the total amount of payroll expenses (gross wages and payroll taxes) for October?

4. _____   What is the gross profit for October?

5. _____   What is the total Product Revenue for October?

6. _____   What is the amount of rent paid for October?

7. _____   What is the Net Income for the Consulting/Seminars Class for October?

8. _____   What is the amount of Fixed Assets on October 31?

9. _____   What is the amount of Total Liabilities on October 31?

10. _____   What is the net cash increase for October?

11. _____   What percentage of October total sales was the Seminar Item?

12. _____   What percentage of October total sales was sold to Energy Corporation of Texas in October?

13. _____   How much does Horizon Financial Planning have in total assets on November 30?

14. _____   How many books does Horizon Financial Planning have on hand as of November 30?

15. _____   What is the total Product Revenue for November?

16. _____   What is the total expenses for November?

17. _____   What is the cash balance at the end of November?

Business Checking Account			
Statement Date:	October 31, 2019		Page 1 of 1
Summary:			Horizon Financial Planning

Previous Balance as of 9/30/19		$	-
Total Deposits and Credits	+	$	100,399.88
Total Checks and Debits	-	$	17,071.00
Total Interest Earned	+	$	-
Total Service Charge:1	-	$	10.00
Statement Balance as of 10/31/19:	=	$	**83,318.88**

Deposits and Other Credits:

DEPOSITS

Date	Description		Amount
1-Oct	Customer Deposit	$	72,000.00
31-Oct	Customer Deposit	$	28,399.88
	Deposits:	**$**	**100,399.88**

INTEREST

Date	Description		Amount
	Interest:	**$**	**-**

Checks and Other Withdrawals:

CHECKS PAID:

Check No.	Date Paid		Amount
1001	1-Oct	$	3,500.00
1002	5-Oct	$	445.00
1005	28-Oct	$	200.00
1008	31-Oct	$	1,690.00
1009	31-Oct	$	750.00
1010	31-Oct	$	6,015.00
1011	31-Oct	$	2,500.00
1012	31-Oct	$	1,711.00
1013	31-Oct	$	91.00
1014	31-Oct	$	169.00
	Checks Paid:	**$**	**17,071.00**

OTHER WITHDRAWALS/PAYMENTS

Date	Description		Amount
0 Other Withdrawals/Payments:		**$**	**-**

SERVICE CHARGES

Date	Description		Amount
31-Oct	Service Charge	$	10.00
	Service Charge:	**$**	**10.00**

Figure 16-1 October Bank Statement

Note:
Paychecks are calculated using the tax tables loaded on your computer. In this scenario, we have intentionally not included the paychecks in these bank statements to make the reconciliation consistent for readers using different tax tables.

Business Checking Account			
Statement Date:	**November 30, 2019**		*Page 1 of 1*

Summary:				Horizon Financial Planning

Previous Balance as of 10/31/19		$	83,318.88
Total Deposits and Credits	+	$	40,289.13
Total Checks and Debits	-	$	18,631.01
Total Interest Earned	+	$	-
Total Service Charge:1	-	$	10.00
Statement Balance as of 11/30/19:	=	$	104,967.00

Deposits and Other Credits:

DEPOSITS

Date	Description		Amount
20-Nov	Customer Deposit	$	25,087.88
29-Nov	Customer Deposit	$	15,201.25
	Deposits:	$	40,289.13

INTEREST

Date	Description		Amount
	Interest: $		-

Checks and Other Withdrawals:

CHECKS PAID:

Check No.	Date Paid		Amount
1015	1-Nov	$	658.00
1016	4-Nov	$	2,500.00
1017	8-Nov	$	1,249.88
1021	29-Nov	$	54.13
1024	29-Nov	$	700.00
1025	29-Nov	$	13,132.00
1026	29-Nov	$	163.00
1027	29-Nov	$	174.00
	Checks Paid:	$	18,631.01

OTHER WITHDRAWALS/PAYMENTS

Date	Description		Amount
	Other Withdrawals/Payments: $		-

SERVICE CHARGES

Date	Description		Amount
30-Nov	Service Charge	$	10.00
	Service Charge:	$	10.00

Figure 16-2 November Bank Statement

Appendix

Keyboard Shortcuts

Date Shortcuts

When cursor is in a date field, this key	Causes the date to become...
y	First day of displayed calendar year
r	Last day of displayed calendar year
m	First day of displayed month
h	Last day of displayed month
t	Today
w	First day of displayed week
k	Last day of displayed week
+	Next day
-	Previous day

Cut, Copy & Paste

When text is selected in any field	Causes...
Ctrl + x	Cut the text to the Clipboard
Ctrl + c	Copy the text to the Clipboard
Ctrl + v	Paste the text to the Clipboard
Ctrl + z	Undo last change
Ctrl + d	Delete selected transaction or list Item
Ctrl+Alt+y	Copy a row of data in a form
Ctrl+Alt+v	Paste a row of data in a form

Making Changes

When editing a transaction, this key	Causes ...
Tab	Move the cursor to the next field.
Shift + Tab	Move the cursor to the previous editable field
Return (or Enter)	Record the transaction (when black border is highlighting OK, Next, or Previous button)
Esc	Cancel editing and close the current window
Ctrl + h	Get the history (A/R or A/P) for the currently selected transaction
Ctrl + g	Go to the other account register affected by this transaction
Ctrl + y	Display transaction journal
Ctrl + n	New transaction (Bill, Check, Deposit, List Item, Invoice)
Ctrl + r	Go to the register associated with the current transaction.
Page Up	Scroll register view or reports 1 page up
Page Down	Scroll register view or reports 1 page down
Home, Home, Home	Go to the top of a register (first transaction)
End, End, End	Go to the bottom of a register (last transaction)
Ctrl + 1	Display information about QuickBooks and your company file details
Ctrl + e	Edit transaction or list item
Space	To check or uncheck checkbox when selected

Answer Key for End of Chapter Questions

This section shows the answers to the questions at the end of each chapter.

Introducing QuickBooks

Comprehension Questions:

1. QuickBooks has three primary files: Working Data files, Backup files, and Portable Company files. Data files are used when QuickBooks is open and transactions are being recorded. Portable files are compressed and are useful for moving data from one computer to another. Backup files are used to safeguard the company data.

2. Portable files are used for transporting QuickBooks data from one computer to another. They are compact and can be used to send QuickBooks data. Portable files should not be used as backups.

3. The *Home* page is an easily accessible window that displays the most common QuickBooks tasks. It is divided into regions with flowcharts that make the sequence of workflow easier to understand. The flow charts are comprised of icons for different tasks. The *Home* page is automatically displayed when a file is opened and can be accessed by clicking the **Home** button on the *Icon Bar*.

4. Transactions are created by filling out familiar-looking forms such as invoices, bills, and checks. As you fill out forms, you choose from lists such as the customer center, the item list, and the account list. When you finish filling out a form, QuickBooks automatically records the accounting entries behind the scenes. For example, using the Write Checks window provides options not available in the checking account register like an items tab and access to customer/class columns without having to click **Split**. The check printing process (to be printed or individual check printing) is also much easier when working with the form. By using sales forms (e.g. Invoices, Sales Receipts and Credit Memos) QuickBooks populates sales reports and provides additional fields that are not available in the Accounts Receivable register

5. Accounting's primary concern is the accurate recording and categorizing of transactions so that you can produce reports that accurately portray the financial health of your organization. Put another way, accounting's focus is on whether your organization is succeeding and how well it is succeeding. The purpose of accounting is to serve management, investors, creditors, and government agencies. Accounting reports allow any of these groups to assess the financial position of the organization relative to its debts (liabilities), its capabilities to satisfy those debts and continue operations (assets), and the difference between them (net worth or equity).

Multiple Choice:

1. c
2. c
3. b
4. d
5. d

Completion Statements:

1. forms, accounting
2. back up
3. Home page
4. Items
5. Chart of Accounts

The Sales Process

Comprehension Questions:

1. When customers pay at the time of the sale either by check or by credit card, create a Sales Receipt transaction.

2. Setting the *Payments* Company Preference option to "Use Undeposited Funds as a default deposit to account" causes the funds from your sale to increase the balance in the *Undeposited Funds* account. Later, when you "Make Deposits," you'll group all of the funds from several sales into one deposit in the bank. This will decrease your *Undeposited Funds* account. It is best to use *Undeposited Funds* when recording receipts because you can then group the receipts together when you record the deposit, by payment method. If you post each Sales Receipt and Payment directly to a bank account, QuickBooks will record a separate increase in cash for each customer receipt/payment. As a result, bank reconciliatons will be more difficult since QuickBooks deposits won't match with the bank statement.

3. When you enter a payment amount, QuickBooks looks at all of the open Invoices for that customer. If it finds an amount due on an open Invoice that is the exact amount of the payment, it matches the payment with that Invoice. If there is no such match, it applies the payment to the *oldest* Invoice first and continues applying to the next oldest until the payment is completely applied. If this auto application of payments results in a partially paid Invoice, QuickBooks holds the balance on that Invoice open for the unpaid amount.

4. When this preference is on, you can select an invoice in the table of the *Receive Payments* form before entering an Amount Received, QuickBooks prefills the amount of that selected invoice into the *Amount Received* field. QuickBooks continues to automatically calculate the Amount Received based on the invoices you select or deselect for that payment. When this preference is off, QuickBooks does not automatically calculate payments. You need to click **Auto Apply** to see the results of your payment on the amounts for selected invoices.
Where to find this preference: From the *Edit* menu, choose **Preferences**, and then select the **Payments** icon. Click the **Company Preferences** tab.

Multiple Choice:

1. d
2. a
3. b
4. d
5. d
6. c
7. d
8. a
9. a
10. d
11. c
12. c
13. b
14. b

15. c

Completion Statements:

1. Quick Add
2. bank, Undeposited Funds
3. calculating
4. Accounts Receivable
5. QuickMath

Additional Customer Transactions

Comprehension Questions:

1. Refunds are given to customers who return merchandise or who have unused services after these items have been paid for. Refunds should be given in the same type as the payment. If a customer paid with a check, he or she should be issued a refund check. If a customer paid by credit card, the refund should be issued to the same credit card type.

2. Credit memos can be used four different ways. One way is to record an order cancellation when the order has already been invoiced. The second time you would want to use a credit memo is to record a return from a customer. The third circumstance is to record a credit-on-account for a customer. And finally, credit memos are the first step when making a refund to a customer.

Multiple Choice:

1. a
2. d
3. b
4. d
5. d
6. d
7. b
8. a
9. c
10. a
11. c
12. d
13. a
14. c
15. c

Completion Statements:

1. cash, check, credit card

2. Credit Memos

3. write-off

4. Finance Charges

5. Statement

Managing Expenses

Comprehension Questions:

1. In QuickBooks, classes give you a way to *classify* your transactions. You can use QuickBooks classes to separate your income and expenses by line of business, department, location, profit centers, or any other meaningful breakdown of your business.
For example, a dentist might classify all income and expenses as relating to either the dentistry or hygiene department. A law firm formed as a partnership might classify all income and expenses according to which partner generated the business. If you use classes, you'll be able to create separate reports for each class of the business. Therefore, the dentist could create separate Profit & Loss reports for the dentistry and hygiene departments, and the law firm could create separate reports for each partner.

2. If you want to track the expenses for each customer or job (i.e., track job costs), you'll need to link each expense with the customer or job to which it applies. When you record an expense transaction, use the **Customer:Job** column to link each expense account or Item with the customer or job to which it applies.

3. The steps in tracking A/P in QuickBooks are:
   a) When you receive a bill from a vendor, enter it into QuickBooks using the *Enter Bills* window. Recording a bill allows QuickBooks to track the amount you owe to the vendor along with the detail of what you purchased.
   b) Pay the bill using the *Pay Bills* window.
   c) If you want to make a partial payment on a bill, enter only the amount you want to pay in the *Amt. To Pay* column. If you pay less than the full amount due, QuickBooks will track the remaining amount due for that bill in Accounts Payable. The next time you go to the *Pay Bills* window, the partially paid bills will show with the remaining amount due.
   d) When a vendor credits your account, record that transaction in the *Enter Bills* window as a Credit and apply it to one of your unpaid bills.
   e) When you select a Bill in the *Pay Bills* window from a vendor for whom one or more unapplied credits exist, QuickBooks displays the total amount of all credits for the vendor in the *Total Credits Available* field. Click **Set Credits** to apply the credit.
   f) To record a discount on a bill, select the bill and look for the discount terms in the *Discount & Credit Information for Highlighted Bill* section. If a discount is available on the bill, use the **Set Discount** button to record the discount.

4. In many cases, it's better to use a bill credit instead of recording a discount. For example, when you want to associate the discount with a job, or if you want to track discount items, use Bill Credits instead of using discounts in the *Pay Bills* process.

5. To track your charges and payments on your company credit card, set up a separate credit card liability account in the Chart of Accounts for each card. Use the *Credit Card* type when creating each account. Then enter each charge individually using the *Enter Credit Card Charges* window. To pay the credit card bill, use *Write Checks* and code the check to the appropriate credit card liability account.

Multiple Choice:

1. d

2.   d

3.   d

4.   a

5.   b

6.   d

7.   c

8.   c

9.   b

10.   c

11.   a

12.   b

13.   a

14.   d

15.   b

Completion Statements:

1.   Home Page

2.   10, 2%

3.   Class

4.   customer, job

5.   Pay Bills

Bank Reconciliation

Comprehension Questions:

1.   QuickBooks calculates the *Beginning Balance* field by adding and subtracting all previously cleared transactions. The resulting calculation is shown on the *Begin Reconciliation* window. The amount in the *Beginning Balance* field will differ from your bank statement if the user(s) delete or change one or more reconciled transactions. The balance will also differ if the user(s) remove the checkmark from one or more reconciled transactions (using the bank account register). Users can also adjust the *Beginning Balance* field by clicking **Undo Last Reconciliation** in the *Locate Discrepancies* window, and then re-doing the prior reconciliation, until prior reconciliation's ending balance matches the current month's beginning balance.

2.   You don't want to change transactions dated in a closed accounting period because doing so would change financial information in a period for which you have already issued financial statements and/or filed tax returns.

3.   The credit card reconciliation process is very similar to the bank account reconciliation, except that when you finish reconciling a credit card account, QuickBooks asks you if you want to pay the credit card immediately, or if you want to enter a bill for pay the credit card, or if you want to make payment later. Additionally, you enter Finance Charges, rather than Bank Charges and Interest Income, in the *Begin Reconciliation* window.

Multiple Choice:

1. c
2. a
3. d
4. c
5. b
6. b
7. d
8. a
9. d
10. d
11. b
12. c
13. c
14. d
15. a

Completion Statements:

1. reconciled
2. Beginning Balance
3. reconciliation
4. closed, audited
5. NSF (non-sufficient funds)

Reports and Graphs

Comprehension Questions:

1. QuickBooks provides a convenient feature called *QuickZoom*, which allows you to see the detail behind numbers on reports. As your cursor moves over numbers on a report, it will turn into a magnifying glass with a "z" in the middle. The magnifying icon indicates that you can double click to see the details behind the number on the report. After you double click the number, *QuickZoom* displays a **Transaction Detail by Account** report that shows the details of each transaction in the account that you zoomed in on.

2. The Check Detail report is very useful if you use Accounts Payable or Payroll. It is frequently necessary to see what expense account(s) are associated with a Bill Payment. However, most transaction reports don't give the detailed information on what expenses are associated with the Bill Payment. They only show that Bill Payments are associated with Accounts Payable. That's because a Bill Payment only involves the Checking account and Accounts Payable. Similarly, Paychecks only show in the register report as "Split" transactions because several

accounts are associated with each paycheck. The Check Detail report shows the detailed expense account information about these types of transactions.

3. To hide subaccounts on the Profit & Loss report (or any summary report), click **Collapse** at the top of the report or the collapse arrow next to individual accounts.

4. Use the **Filters** tab on the *Modify Report* window to narrow the contents of reports so that you can analyze specific areas of your business. On the **Filters** tab, you can filter for (select) specific accounts, dates, names, or items to include in the report.

5. After modifying a report, you can *memorize* it so you won't have to go through all of the modification steps the next time you want to view the report.

Multiple Choice:

1. c
2. a
3. d
4. a
5. b
6. c
7. b
8. d
9. b
10. c
11. d
12. a
13. c
14. b
15. c

Completion Statements:

1. Vendor Contact List
2. filter
3. QuickZoom
4. Search
5. Balance Sheet

Customizing QuickBooks

Comprehension Questions:

1. *Company Preferences* are used to make global changes to the features and functionality of the data file. Only the Administrator of the data file can make changes to *Company Preferences*.

User Preferences will not affect other users of the data file. Each user can make changes to his or her own *User Preferences*.

2. Any command that you use frequently can be put in the Favorites menu. You can also put items that are usually only accessible through submenus so that the options are more easily accessible.

3. The *Open Windows List* shows a brief description of each open window. You can click on the description to move between windows. The *Open Windows List* is most helpful when you have a large number of open windows, or when you select the *One Window Desktop View* User Preference. With this preference selected, the *Open Windows List* is the most convenient way to move between open windows.

4. Price levels allow you to customize different pricing for your customers. For example, some high volume customers may have negotiated discount pricing for all of their purchases. By setting the customer's default pricing level to a *Fixed Percentage Price Level*, every invoice and sales receipt will automatically use this discount pricing. A different type of price level is *Per Item.* With this type of *Price Level,* adjusted default prices can be set on some items and not others. Setting this type of level on a customer means that customer will by default receive the adjusted rate on the items specified in the *Price Level.*

To add *Price Level* defaults to customer records, create the **Price Level** in the *Price Level List.* Then, in the *Edit Customer* window, choose the **Additional Info** tab and set the **Price Level** field to the appropriate price level for the customer.

5. To add a **Custom Field** to a customer's record, open the customer's record, click the **Additional Information** tab and then click **Define Fields.** QuickBooks displays the *Define Fields* window where you can create a Custom Field. After you create the Custom Field, click the corresponding checkbox in the *Customers:Jobs* column.

Multiple Choice:

1. d
2. a
3. c
4. c
5. a
6. b
7. d
8. d
9. d
10. d
11. a
12. a
13. d
14. b
15. d

Completion Statements:

1. Service

2. Desktop View

3. Icon Bar

4. Date-driven

5. Subtotal

Inventory

Comprehension Questions

1. When you record an Item Receipt, QuickBooks increases (credits) **Accounts Payable** for the total amount of the **Item Receipt**. It also increases (debits) **Inventory** for the same amount. However, since you haven't received the bill, your *Pay Bills* window will not yet show the bill, even though the balance in Accounts Payable increases as a result of the **Item Receipt**. This may seem strange at first because you normally expect the total in **Pay Bills** to match the balance in **Accounts Payable**. However, Item Receipts never show in the *Pay Bills* window. It turns out that **Item Receipts** and **Bills** are exactly the *same transaction*. The only difference is that the *Bill Received* field is not checked on **Item Receipts**, and it is checked on **Bills**.

2. The first time you create an Inventory Part Item in the Item list, QuickBooks automatically creates two accounts in your **Chart of Accounts**: An *Other Current Asset* account called **Inventory Asset** and a *Cost of Goods Sold* account called **Cost of Goods Sold**.

3. QuickBooks uses these two important accounts to track inventory. The **Inventory Asset** account holds the value of your inventory until you sell it. The **Cost of Goods Sold** account records the cost of the inventory *when* you sell it.

4. If you use Purchase Orders, you'll be able to create reports that show what is on order and when it is due to arrive from your supplier. In addition, you can create a list of open purchase orders. Purchase Orders do not post to the **Chart of Accounts**. However, QuickBooks tracks **Purchase Orders** in a non-posting account called *Purchase Orders*. You can see this account at the bottom of your **Chart of Accounts**.

Multiple Choice

1. b

2. c

3. d

4. d

5. b

6. c

7. b

8. c

9. d

10. a

11. c

12. a

13. b

14. d

15. c

Completion Statements

1. Stock Status by Item

2. purchase orders

3. perpetual

4. Item QuickReport, Inventory Valuation Detail

5. Inventory Valuation Summary

Time and Billing

Comprehension Questions

1. To track a reimbursable cost, you'll first need to record the expense. Enter a transaction such as a *Bill, Check,* or *Credit Card Charge* to record the original expense, and then assign the customer or job to which the expense applies. Then create an invoice or sales receipt for that customer or job and select the expense from the *Expense* tab in the *Choose Billable Time and Costs* window.

2. When you create an invoice for the customer, you can pass through the billable cost to the invoice in the *Choose Billable Time and Costs* window. The top section of the *Choose Billable Time and Costs* window shows four tabs (Items, Expenses, Time and Mileage) where you can view pass-through expenses. Select the appropriate charges to be included in the invoice. Select the **Print selected costs as one invoice item** option to print all reimbursable expenses on a single line in the body of the Invoice rather than listing each expense separately. You'll always see the details of the reimbursable expenses, including the markup, on the screen, even if you chose **Print selected costs as one invoice item**.

3. QuickBooks Pro and above allow you to use the same Item on expense forms (e.g., checks and bills) and sales forms (e.g., invoices and sales receipts). When you use Items to track both expenses and revenue, you can generate reports showing the profitability of each Item. An Item used on both types of forms (expenses and sales) is commonly called a "two-sided Item" because the Item setup screen includes purchase information on the left side (*Expense Account* field) and sales information on the right (*Income Account* field). Possible uses of two-sided Items include: Reimbursable Expenses, Custom Ordered Parts, Subcontracted Labor and Cost of Goods Sold postings.

4. QuickBooks Pro and above have a Vehicle Mileage Tracker that allows you to track vehicle mileage, post mileage to invoices and run reports to assist with tax preparation. Although you cannot use vehicle mileage tracking to reimburse your employees on their paycheck, nor on a bill or check, you can pass through the mileage costs to your customers.

5. If you use QuickBooks to calculate your payroll, you can use timesheet information to calculate paychecks. This not only saves you the time of manually entering the hours, it will also allocate the payroll expenses (e.g., wages and payroll taxes) to each Job on which the employee worked.

Multiple Choice

1.   c
2.   d
3.   b
4.   d
5.   b
6.   c
7.   d
8.   d
9.   c
10. c
11. a
12. c
13. b
14. a
15. d

Completion Statements

1.   Expenses
2.   Two-Sided Item
3.   activity
4.   weekly timesheet
5.   Time by Name

Payroll Setup

Comprehension Questions

1.   Company Contribution Item.

2.   You will need to edit several of the items created by the *Payroll Setup Interview* so that they will affect the proper accounts in the Chart of Accounts. For example, the wage items are set up by QuickBooks to use the Payroll Expenses account. But if you use a subaccount of Payroll Expenses called Gross Wages (as we recommend), you'll need to edit the Wage Items to use this expense account.

3.   Any addition, deduction or company contribution item that QuickBooks calculates based on a number other than gross or net pay.

Multiple Choice

1.   b
2.   d

3. d

4. b

5. d

6. c

7. a

8. d

9. c

10. c

11. d

12. c

13. a

14. d

Completion Statements

1. Employee Defaults

2. Define Fields

3. deduction, liability

4. Release Date

5. Payroll

Payroll Processing

Comprehension Questions

1. You should verify that your payroll tax tables are current before each time you process payroll or pay payroll liabilities. You should update you payroll tax tables whenever they are out of date.

2. Change the amount in the *Employee Summary* section of the *Preview Paycheck* window.

3. *Voucher* checks are the best choice because QuickBooks prints the paystub information on the voucher portion of the checks. The paystub will include the current period information as well as year-to-date information for the employee. Other types can be used, but Paystubs would need to be printed separately.

4. No. The only time you should delete a paycheck is when you created it in error, and you haven't printed the check. Otherwise, you should void the paycheck so you can keep a record of it.

Multiple Choice

1. d

2. d

3. b

4. a

5. d

6.   d

7.   a

8.   b

9.   d

10.   d

11.   b

12.   c

13.   b

14.   d

Completion Statements

1.   Customer:Job

2.   Payroll Center

3.   Paycheck Detail

4.   Employee State Taxes Detail

Company File Setup and Maintenance

Comprehension Questions:

1.   As you enter opening balances in your QuickBooks accounts, an offsetting transaction is entered into an automatically created account calling *Opening Balance Equity*.

     This transaction is recorded differently depending on which method you use for the opening balance. If you enter the opening balance by writing a value in the *Opening Balance* field in the *New Account* window, the amount is automatically added to *Opening Bal Equity* as well as the new account. If you enter the opening balance in the new account's register, the transaction should be coded to *Opening Bal Equity*.

     Opening Bal Equity is closed into *Retained Earnings* or *Owner's Equity* at the end of setting up the company file.

2.   To adjust Sales Tax to agree with the Trial Balance from the accountant, you would first view the *Sales Tax Payable* register to view and activity in the account, then subtract the current balance in the account from the amount shown on the trial balance from your accountant and create a *Sales Tax Adjustment.*

3.   Rename the Entertainment account to "Meals." Doing so will prompt QuickBooks to merge the Entertainment and Meals accounts. When you merge accounts these two accounts in this way, QuickBooks changes each transaction that posts to Entertainment, making it post to Meals instead. Then QuickBooks will remove the Entertainment account from the Chart of Accounts list.

4.   It is important to enter all outstanding checks and deposits as of your start date so that your first bank reconciliation goes smoothly. In order for the reconciliation to go smoothly, you want all of the checks and deposits to show in QuickBooks so that you can match them with your first bank statement after the start date. If you don't enter the individual transactions, you won't see

them in the QuickBooks reconciliation window. Also, if a transaction never clears the bank, you won't know which transaction it was without going to your old records.

5.   You should have each of the following before setting up a QuickBooks file:
   a)   Trial Balance
   b)   Bank Statement for all bank accounts
   c)   Outstanding Checks and Deposits
   d)   Open Invoices
   e)   Unpaid Bills
   f)   Employee List and W-4 information for each employee
   g)   Payroll Liabilities by Item
   h)   Year-to-Date Payroll Detail for Employee
   i)   Year-to-Date Payroll Tax Deposits
   j)   Physical Inventory by Inventory Part

Multiple Choice:

1.   c

2.   d

3.   a

4.   d

5.   b

6.   b

7.   c

8.   d

9.   a

10.   d

11.   c

12.   b

13.   c

14.   b

15.   a

Completion Statements:

1.   Assets, Liabilities, Equity, Income, Expense

2.   delete

3.   Opening Balance Equity

4.   General Journal Entry

5.   Trial Balance

Estimates

Comprehension Questions

1. The big difference is that Estimates do not post to the general ledger, and therefore they do not affect any of your financial reports. They do help you track your future sales and they do help you track how your actual revenues and costs compare with what was estimated, but Estimates do not record any financial information themselves.

2. Progress Invoicing allows you to charge your Customers a portion of the total Estimate for each stage of the Job. QuickBooks can track how much of the Estimate has been invoiced, and how much remains to be invoiced.

3. Sales Orders are very similar to Estimates, but unlike Estimates, Sales Orders will always be converted into Invoices You use them to track orders from Customers while you are processing their order or otherwise waiting to fulfill the order. You can print Sales Orders for use as pick lists from your inventory and you can customize them much the same as other sales forms. You can also use QuickBooks reports to keep track of open Sales Orders and back-ordered items.

Multiple Choice

1. d
2. b
3. c
4. c
5. d
6. d
7. b
8. a
9. b
10. a
11. d

Completion Statements

1. Available Estimates
2. On Hand, Qty
3. Pro
4. Progress
5. Transactions

Adjustments and Year-End Procedures

Comprehension Questions

1. There is one significant difference between voiding and deleting transactions. When you void a transaction, QuickBooks keeps a record of the date, number, and detail of the transaction. When you delete a transaction, QuickBooks removes it completely from your file.

2. When you change or delete a transaction, QuickBooks immediately updates the General Ledger with your change, regardless of the date of the transaction. Therefore, if you make changes to transactions in a closed accounting period, your QuickBooks financial statements will change for that period, causing discrepancies between your QuickBooks reports and your tax return.

3. If you want QuickBooks to automatically enter the depreciation journal entry each month, create a journal entry to record one month of depreciation, and then memorize it and schedule it to automatically enter each month.

4. At the end of each year, QuickBooks automatically enters an adjusting entry to your income and expense accounts, posting the net income into Retained Earnings (or Owner's Equity). This entry is known as the *closing entry*. Actually, QuickBooks never *really* creates a transaction for the closing entry, but when you create a Balance Sheet, QuickBooks calculates the balance in Retained Earnings by adding together the total net income for all prior years. At the end of your company's fiscal year, QuickBooks automatically transfers the net income into Retained Earnings.

Multiple Choice

1. c
2. c
3. c
4. c
5. d
6. b
7. c
8. a
9. a
10. b
11. a
12. c

Completion Statements

1. accrual
2. services
3. Retained Earnings
4. closing date
5. delete, void

Walker and Horizon Business Scenarios

Answers to the questions at the end of the Horizon problem are available in the Instructor's Manual for this book.

Index